PUBLICATIONS OF THE
MINNESOTA HISTORICAL SOCIETY

EDITED BY

SOLON J. BUCK
SUPERINTENDENT OF THE SOCIETY

A HISTORY OF MINNESOTA
VOLUME III

THE FALLS OF ST. ANTHONY, 1869

THE FALLS OF ST. ANTHONY, 1926

[From photographs in the museum of the Minnesota Historical Society.]

A HISTORY OF MINNESOTA

BY

WILLIAM WATTS FOLWELL

PRESIDENT OF THE MINNESOTA HISTORICAL SOCIETY AND PRESIDENT EMERITUS
OF THE UNIVERSITY OF MINNESOTA

IN FOUR VOLUMES

VOLUME III

PUBLISHED BY THE
MINNESOTA HISTORICAL SOCIETY
SAINT PAUL, 1926

... *for it is the true office of history to represent the events themselves together with the counsels, and to leave the observations and conclusions thereupon to the liberty and faculty of every man's judgment.* —*Bacon*, Advancement of Learning, *book* 2.

EDITOR'S INTRODUCTION

THE sixty years that have elapsed since the close of the Civil War have seen the transformation of Minnesota from a frontier community with a white population of two hundred and fifty thousand to a modern commonwealth of about two and a half million people. This volume presents the history of the state during those sixty years, mainly from the political and administrative points of view, though with recognition of the economic and social forces in the background. The arrangement is in the main chronological and for the period from 1876 to 1909 the author has found it convenient to group his materials by gubernatorial administrations, with the exception of a chapter on "Minnesota in the Wars with Spain and the Philippines." The period since 1909 receives more summary treatment. The desirability of preserving the continuity and balance of the main narrative has necessitated the relegation of nineteen special studies to the appendix, but the reader will find in them some of the most interesting and valuable material in the volume. Although this volume carries the chronological narrative to the present time, it does not complete the work. A fourth and final volume, which will probably be published in about two years, will contain topical studies of various phases of the state's history.

As with the previous volumes the author has made extensive use of the state archives in the custody of the Minnesota Historical Society and of its newspaper files and collections of personal papers. Unfortunately the papers of some important men of the period are no longer in existence and those of others, for example, of Cushman K. Davis and Bishop Henry B. Whipple, were not available for consultation. Much information was also obtained by correspondence and interviews with persons who had first-hand knowledge of the subjects dealt with. The correspondence is to be found in the Folwell Papers in the possession of the Minnesota Historical Society and the interviews are as a rule recorded in the author's notebooks, which, it is expected, will later be turned over to the society. Bibliographical information about books and pamphlets is given in connection with the first citation of each work.

Because of the absence of the editor from Minnesota during the latter stages of the work on the volume, considerable responsibility, especially in connection with the selection of illustrations, has devolved upon Dr. Theodore C. Blegen, acting superintendent of the society. The detailed work of getting the manuscript ready for the printer and seeing it through the press has been done by Miss Mary E. Wheelhouse and assistants working under her direction. The maps were drawn by Dr. Warren Upham and the index is the work of Miss Livia Appel.

SOLON J. BUCK

NEW YORK CITY
June, 1926

CONTENTS

CONTENTS

Minneapolis and St. Paul, 1890 — (13) The Nelson-Washburn Senatorial Contest of 1895 — (14) Pine Timber Investigations — (15) Home Rule Charters — (16) The Mutiny in the Fifteenth Minnesota — (17) The 151st Field Artillery — (18) The Nonpartisan League and the Farmer-Labor Party — (19) The Minnesota Commission of Public Safety

ILLUSTRATIONS

MAPS

A HISTORY OF MINNESOTA

VOLUME III

I. AFTER THE WAR, 1865–69

NINE years of territorial life and three of statehood, full of promise, had passed when the war of the slaveholders' rebellion, soon followed by the Indian war on her own border, checked, but did not block, the progress of Minnesota. Notwithstanding the drain of her best blood to the armies, the privation of families in the absence of their protectors, and heavy taxes, there were gains from year to year in population, industry, wealth, and general comfort. The state census of 1865, as already noted, showed a total population of 250,099, a gain of about forty-five per cent since 1860. Abundant crops, high prices for agricultural staples, and the depreciation of the currency enabled the farmers to clear their mortgages and other debts. The large expenditures of government funds for the Indian war stimulated business in the cities. The muster-out of the regiments and battalions and the return of the soldiers to their homes after the wars opened a new campaign of peaceful and beneficent industry. Everywhere there were signs of hope and enterprise.

The rapid increase in population, which the Civil and Indian wars had not checked, went on at a still higher ratio during the period now under consideration. This was due partly to the stimulation of immigration by the state. A board consisting of the governor, the secretary of state, and a third member to be appointed was intrusted with the expenditure of money to promote immigration from foreign countries. Many thousands of pamphlets were printed and distributed both at home and abroad and numerous agents were employed to turn the tide toward Minnesota. Colonel Hans Mattson was sent to invite the Scandinavian emigrants to a region and climate believed to be especially suitable to

them.[1] Such an augmentation of population was naturally
accompanied by an increase of cultivated farms, of crops,
of lumber cut and manufactured, and of resulting trade.
But the market for produce was local and business was cor-
respondingly restricted. Minnesota had very little produce
which could stand distant transportation by existing facilities. Some wheat was sent down the Mississippi in barges
and some logs and lumber were sent down in rafts. Passenger travel by steamboat or stagecoach was costly and
wearisome. The need of railroads, keenly felt in early
territorial days, was now more deeply appreciated, especially the need for a road which might open the markets of
the East. The start had been hard and slow and progress
for some years was still to be disappointingly gradual.[2]

In 1866 but 105 miles of railroad were built, by five different companies, not over 26 miles by any. In the year
following 114 miles were built by four companies, 63 miles
by one of them. The Milwaukee and St. Paul interest,
which for ten years had desired to extend its lines into Minnesota, now bought the railroad property — not the land
grant — of the Minnesota Central, successor to the Minneapolis and Cedar Valley, and built northward from
McGregor, Iowa, opposite Prairie du Chien, Wisconsin, to
connect with track already laid. A pontoon bridge across
the Mississippi connected those towns. St. Paul was now
but thirty hours from Chicago; and Minnesota, no longer a
far-off hyperborean province, came into the great world.
The extensions of 1868 and 1869, aggregating 131 and 206
miles respectively, were piecemeal additions to nine different
lines terminating, with the one obvious exception, casually
in the timber or on the prairie. The operation of 750 miles
of railroad within the state had its effect in extending set-

1 Minnesota, *General Laws*, 1867, p. 52; annual messages of Governor Marshall, in Minnesota, *Executive Documents*, 1866, p. 20; 1867, p. 21; 1868, p. 16;
1869, p. 25; *St. Paul Pioneer*, March 14, 1867, p. 1; Hans Mattson, *Reminiscences: The Story of an Emigrant*, 97 (St. Paul, 1891).
2 On the struggle for railroads see *ante*, 1: 327–350; 2: 37–58.

tlement beyond previous limits, but the great body of the
people still had their homes in twenty southeastern counties.
In 1868 sixty-two per cent of the cultivated land was devoted
to wheat, almost the only product which would stand transportation.[3]

The ratification of the thirteenth amendment, proclaimed
by the secretary of state on December 18, 1865, worked the
legal destruction of African slavery, but it did not endow
the freedmen with knowledge of civil duties nor with habits
of self-directed industry. Many of them were homeless
wanderers; all needed guidance and protection even from
their own improvidences. The legislatures of some southern
states, probably relying upon presidential leniency, undertook by the enactment of stringent laws against vagrancy
the experiment of treating the negro, no longer the slave of
individual masters, as the bondman of society. Magistrates
were authorized to impose fines on idle negroes and to order
them assigned to the highest bidder to work out the fines.
There were other disabilities in regard to labor contracts,
carrying arms, and giving testimony in courts. These " black
codes " were at once fiercely denounced by the radical
Republican press and were condemned by Republicans generally. The Minnesota legislature in 1866 adopted a series
of resolutions expressing the belief that southern traitors,
though vanquished in arms, were still hostile; demanding
that freedom and civil rights should be guaranteed to all,
irrespective of color; and declaring that Minnesota would
look to Congress for the true policy of reconstruction.[4]

[3] Edward D. Neill, *History of Minnesota: From the Earliest French Explo-
rations to the Present Time*, insert opposite p. 786 (fourth edition, Minneapolis,
1882) ; Minnesota, Commissioner of Statistics, *Reports*, 1869, pp. 7, 105; Minnesota, Railroad Commissioner, *Reports*, 1871, appendix, 54, 64; Edward V.
Robinson, *Early Economic Conditions and the Development of Agriculture in
Minnesota*, 38 (University of Minnesota, *Studies in the Social Sciences*, no. 3 —
Minneapolis, 1915). For excellent graphic illustrations of the distribution of
the population and the amount of land devoted to the production of wheat, see
pages 61, 63, and 65 of the last-mentioned work.
[4] William A. Dunning, *Reconstruction, Political and Economic, 1865–1877*,
11, 53–57 *(The American Nation: A History*, vol. 22 — New York, 1907);

The fourteenth amendment to the national Constitution was proposed by Congress to the legislatures of the states on June 16, 1866. There is no occasion for describing here the irreconcilable reconstruction policies of President Johnson and the Congress nor for discussing their respective merits. The essence of the prevailing congressional policy was embodied in the four diverse articles of the amendment, which are too familiar or too easily accessible to need repetition. Commended to the favorable consideration of the Minnesota legislature by Governor Marshall, they were ratified in both houses by strict party votes, except that one Democrat in the House voted with the Republicans. On February 4, 1867, the governor gave the joint resolution his unnecessary approval.[5]

The legislature of 1867 and the Republicans of the state were much concerned about the behavior of the junior United States senator, Daniel S. Norton, elected to that office, as already stated, by a Republican legislature as a Republican. The first session of the Thirty-ninth Congress was passing with notable but not alarming departures on his part from the line of Republican policy. On February 2, 1866, he voted "no" on the civil rights bill and on the twentieth his vote was recorded against the passage of the supplementary Freedmen's Bureau bill. These votes apparently would have passed unnoticed, had not attention been called to them by William Pitt Murray, a Democratic member of the Minnesota Senate. At the last moment before the close of the session on March 2 Murray moved the adoption of a resolution of thanks to Senator Norton for his states-

Minnesota, *House Journal*, 1866, pp. 295–297; *Senate Journal*, 242. On the ratification of the thirteenth amendment by the Minnesota legislature, see *ante*, 2: 342.

[5] Josephus N. Larned, *History for Ready Reference*, 5: 3565 (Springfield, Massachusetts, 1895); Marshall's message of January 10, 1867, in *Executive Documents*, 1866, p. 25; *House Journal*, 1867, pp. 25, 95; *Senate Journal*, 23. The vote in the House was 40 to 5; that in the Senate was 16 to 5. For the literature of reconstruction, see Dunning, "Critical Essay on Authorities," in his *Reconstruction*, 342–357.

manlike views and votes upon the great questions which were agitating the country; " which," reads the journal, " was adopted." It may be guessed that the mover of the resolution had been favored with information in regard to the views of Norton and the votes he would be likely to cast, information which had not been imparted to the Republican members, who accordingly saw no reason for opposing adoption. On that same day, March 2, Senator Norton was voting " no " on the bill to exclude southern senators and representatives until Congress should have found the states or any of them entitled to representation. Norton had now parted company with Senator Ramsey. On April 6 he voted " no " on the passage of the civil rights bill over the veto and on June 8 he voted against the joint resolution to submit the fourteenth amendment to the Constitution to the legislatures of the states.

When the Minnesota legislature of 1867 assembled there was no doubt about the views and votes of Norton and the session was hardly begun before resolutions of censure were introduced. On January 19 the House committee to which they had been referred reported a substitute preamble, declaring that Senator Norton had " wickedly betrayed and renounced fidelity to his former expressed principles," together with a resolution that he be instructed to resign his office as senator from Minnesota. An effort to substitute a complimentary resolution received but three votes. The report was agreed to by a vote of 32 to 4. The Senate put the preamble and resolution into a less spiteful and more decorous form and agreed to them by a vote of 17 to 3. Whether Norton had already decided to break from the Republican ranks or whether he considered himself read out of the party by the Minnesota legislature are questions of minor importance. He thereafter ceased to be counted as a Republican and voted steadily with the Democratic minority of the Senate. He offered neither apology nor explanation, trusting, it may be believed, that when the reconstruction quarrel was over and passion had spent itself a sobered public would vindicate him.[6]

Senator Norton, of course, opposed the Tenure of Office Act passed to take from the president the power to remove from office civil appointees without the consent of the Senate — particularly members of his cabinet and, more particularly, one of its members, Edwin M. Stanton, secretary of war. The absurd, if not unconstitutional, measure, humiliating to all concerned in its passage, was virtually repealed one month after Grant's inauguration in 1869 by a disguised amending act.[7] The joint resolution of March 6, 1868, of the Minnesota legislature giving hearty approval to the impeachment of President Andrew Johnson, which had been formally presented on February 25, was an impertinent mandate to the senators about to become judges in the impending trial. If influenced at all by it, Norton was only the more resolved to vote according to the evidence which might be adduced. His expected verdict of " not guilty " at the close of the trial, blocking a two-thirds vote, saved the country from the disgrace of having its chief magistrate, impeached for one set of misdemeanors and tried on another set, convicted by a prejudiced jury of senators. But the acquittal left the accused to answer at the bar of history for blunders, extravagances, and misuse of his prerogatives against the counsel of his true friends.[8]

[6] 39 Congress, 1 session, *Senate Journal*, 132, 179, 199, 317, 505 (serial 1236) ; Minnesota, *Senate Journal*, 1867, pp. 34, 69; *House Journal*, 18, 22, 40, 85, 89; *Saint Paul Daily Press*, 1867: January 15, p. 1; February 2, p. 2; *St. Paul Pioneer*, 1867: January 15, p. 4; February 2, p. 2. The Murray resolution is given in *Senate Journal*, 1866, p. 262. For Norton's defeat of Senator Wilkinson and his career in the Senate, see Harlan P. Hall, *Observations: Being More or Less a History of Political Contests in Minnesota*, 64–68 (St. Paul, 1904). See also *ante*, 2: 340–342.

[7] 39 Congress, 2 session, *Senate Journal*, 419 (serial 1275) ; James G. Blaine, *Twenty Years of Congress: From Lincoln to Garfield*, 2: 274 (Norwich, Connecticut, 1886) ; David M. DeWitt, *The Impeachment and Trial of Andrew Johnson*, 609–611 (New York, 1903) ; United States, *Statutes at Large*, 16: 6.

[8] Minnesota, *General Laws*, 1868, p. 195; 40 Congress, 2 session, *Senate Journal*, 217 (serial 1315) ; United States Senate, *Trial of Andrew Johnson, President of the United States, before the Senate of the United States, on*

Norton was not to serve out his term in the Senate. Pulmonary disease of long standing became acute and on July 13, 1870, ended his life. The *Saint Paul Press* in an obituary editorial charitably mentioned him as a kindly, warmhearted gentleman, faithful to his friends. The *Pioneer* went further and praised him as a man of courage and candor, clear-headed, big-hearted, free from cant — no demagogue. Neither his city nor his state has yet raised over his grave an appropriate monument. The legislature of 1871, however, after a delay suggesting reluctance, passed by unanimous votes a joint resolution of regret at the loss of " an able and incorruptible Senator, an estimable and honest citizen, and a true friend." [9]

Of public affairs in which there was no personal partisan concern the question of negro suffrage was uppermost in the years following the close of the wars. The extension of the elective franchise to the emancipated negro seemed to Republicans, or to many of them, a logical step. The Minnesota legislature of 1865 submitted to the electors an amendment to the state constitution expunging the word " white " from article 7. At the polls in the following November the proposition was defeated by a margin of 2,513 votes out of a total of 26,789. Governor Miller in reporting the result in his message recommended the extension of the suffrage to males of Indian, African, or mixed blood twenty-one

---

Impeachment by the House of Representatives for High Crimes and Misdemeanors, 2: 487, 496 (Washington, 1868); Blaine, *Twenty Years of Congress*, 376, 378. For a statesmanlike speech of Senator Norton, see the *Saint Paul Pioneer*, October 7, 1868. A speech of Norton in personal vindication is given in the issue of the same paper for February 19, 1869, p. 2.

[9] *Saint Paul Press*, July 14, 1870; *Saint Paul Pioneer*, July 15, 1870; *House Journal*, 1871, pp. 37, 65, 87, 128; *Senate Journal*, 27, 46, 66, 103. In the *Winona Daily Republican*, August 30, 1889, p. 4, is a discriminating yet forceful eulogy by the Honorable William Mitchell, associate justice of the supreme court of Minnesota. By a second joint resolution the legislature ordered printed five hundred copies of a memorial pamphlet which was to contain the remarks of Sibley and others. No copy of the pamphlet has been found; but the *Pioneer* for February 4, 1871, p. 2, gives a full account of the proceedings in the houses, with the speeches of Senators Buck, Waite, and Yale and Representatives Jones, Sibley, and Cool, all of them highly eulogistic and eloquent.

years old and upwards who could read and write and added
the strange proposal to require of all electors a property
qualification of three hundred dollars.   Marshall in his
inaugural address ventured only to question whether the
time was ripe for resubmission of a suffrage amendment.
The legislature of 1866 took no action.   In his first annual
message Governor Marshall urged the legislature of 1867
to give " impartial suffrage " another trial because it was
" just and right."   The legislature was like-minded, but the
" people " as represented at the polls in the following
autumn were not quite of the same mind.   The amendment
was lost by a margin of 1,315 votes out of a total of over
56,000 on the question.   The high-hearted governor, believing that another trial would result in the success of the good
cause, besought the legislature of 1868 in an impassioned
strain to offer it again; and he quoted Byron's lines:

> For freedom's battle once begun
> . . . .
> Though baffled oft, is ever won.

His expectation was realized at the November election by a
majority of 9,372 of a total vote of 69,614; and the governor
congratulated the legislature on the final triumph of " EQUAL
MANHOOD SUFFRAGE " in the " free young State of Minnesota
— now altogether free." [10]

The act of Congress of February 26, 1857, authorizing a
state government for Minnesota offered the gift of ten sections of land — 6,400 acres — for the completion or erection
of public buildings at the seat of government.   The location
of the capital in 1849 on the eastern verge of the immense
area of the territory was acquiesced in as a temporary one,
with the assumption on the part of many that later a more
central site would be chosen.   The heavy majorities of the

[10] Return I. Holcombe, in *Minnesota in Three Centuries*, 3: 455 (New York,
1908) ; *General Laws*, 1865, p. 118; 1867, p. 43; 1868, p. 149; *Executive Documents*, 1865, pp. 21, 35; 1866, p. 25; 1867, p. 28; report of the secretary of
state, in *Executive Documents*, 1865, p. 453.

legislature of 1857 for the removal of the capital to St. Peter, thwarted by a disreputable if not criminal suppression of the bill, came in part from a desire for a more central location. The state constitution, ratified in October, 1857, confirmed the existing locations of the university and the state prison, but, while naming St. Paul as the seat of government, provided that the legislature might submit the question of a change to a vote of the people or might, without referendum, locate it upon the land granted to the state by Congress for a seat of government.[11] The ten sections of land were located in Kandiyohi County and it was to be expected that at some time the legislature would be asked to exercise its prerogative and place the capital on the land thus donated and selected for it. The legislature of 1861 was asked; and a bill for removal was passed by the House but was defeated by the Senate. In 1869 a bill for removal introduced in the House was passed with a degree of alacrity which suggests a previous understanding and count of noses. The vote was 39 to 7. In the Senate a lively opposition made a futile attempt to delay action but the bill passed, under operation of the previous question, by a vote of 12 to 10. On March 4 Governor Marshall promptly sent a suave message to the House, in which he suggested that the proposed site was but twenty miles nearer the geographical center of the state than St. Paul; that there was no reason for precipitous action of the legislature without opportunity for reversal by the people; and that in a period of depreciated currency it was no time to spend a million dollars on buildings. The scheme to raise money by land sales was a risky one and the legislature would do well to remember the five million loan fiasco and look before it leaped. The governor's sane counsel had its intended effect and the vote in the House to pass over the

[11] Enabling act, section 5, part 3; Minnesota, Constitution, article 8, section 4; article 15, sections 1, 5. Both of these documents may be found in any issue of the Minnesota *Legislative Manual*. On the project to remove the capital, see *ante*, 1: 382–387.

veto was: yes, 24; no, 21 — not two-thirds. A similar bill was submitted to the legislature of 1872, but was not seriously entertained.[12]

As already understood the Republican party was triumphant in Minnesota from Lincoln's first election in 1860 to the close of the Civil War. The Democrats, to their credit be it said, maintained, however, a strong organization and performed the duties of an opposition, always wholesome in a republic. William R. Marshall's judicious administration earned for him, though not easily, a renomination in 1867. At the November election he won from his popular opponent, Charles E. Flandrau, by only 5,372 votes out of a total of 64,376. Grant's Republican majority over Seymour in 1868, when the total presidential vote of the state was 71,818, lacked but 490 votes of being three times that of Marshall the year before. In the same year, 1868, Morton S. Wilkinson obtained in the first congressional district a majority over a Democratic opponent of 9,118 out of a total of 38,410 votes.[13]

While the Republicans retained their superiority in numbers during the period, there was no little discord in the household. The dissensions of factions are always more bitter and venomous than the contests of the great parties. A large part of the responsibility for the wrangling which

[12] *House Journal*, 1861, pp. 229, 240, 273, 274, 279, 289; 1869, pp. 195, 377–379; *Senate Journal*, 1861, pp. 270, 333; 1869, pp. 238–242. The bill was House file 134. By reference to the *Minneapolis Daily Tribune*, February 25–March 14, 1869, the reader may find that the project for the removal of the capital from St. Paul to Kandiyohi County was not a trivial matter. In the issue of March 9, p. 1, the *Tribune* stigmatized Governor Marshall as governor of St. Paul. See also the *Saint Paul Pioneer* for the same dates. The country press was much divided on the question. When the legislature provided for the erection of a new capitol, the question of the site of the capital was again renewed by a suit to restrain the commissioners from expending the money. See *General Laws*, 1893, pp. 6–15. In the case of Fleckton and others *v.* Lamberton and others, the supreme court held that St. Paul was the proper legal site until the capital should be removed in accordance with article 15 of the constitution. 69 *Minnesota Reports*, 187–192.

[13] *Legislative Manual*, 1869, p. 92; 1925, pp. 113, 115. The *Saint Paul Press* of September 12, 1867, referring to Governor Marshall's renomination, speaks of his "remarkable success, in spite of a fierce and unrelenting opposition."

was to disturb the Republican peace of mind must be laid at the door of Ignatius Donnelly. Some repetition of the early career of this personage may be pardoned. Donnelly, who was of distinguished Irish ancestry, was reared and schooled in Philadelphia and came to Minnesota in 1856 at the age of twenty-four. He established himself in a spacious mansion at Nininger, near Hastings, with a farm in the neighborhood, and there he kept his home for nearly half a century. He had been attached to Democracy, but along with thousands of others of that faith he broke over into the Republican fold when that party was fully organized. He entered the political arena at once, only to be beaten in 1857 as candidate for the state senatorship from Dakota County. In the following year he repeated the venture and lost the election by six votes. In 1859 the state Republican convention gave him the nomination for lieutenant governor, probably because of the speaking ability he had already displayed. He was elected and two years later was reëlected. In the fall of 1862, while still in office as lieutenant governor, Donnelly obtained the nomination for representative in Congress from the second district and was elected. Two reëlections followed, so that he served through the Thirty-eighth, Thirty-ninth, and Fortieth Congresses, from 1863 to 1869. His renomination in 1864 by the Republican convention of his district was unanimous and that of 1866 was accorded by a satisfactory majority.[14]

Throughout his service Donnelly was diligent in introducing petitions, memorials, and land grant and other bills on behalf of constituents and the state and in running the errands which were, as they still are, among the important

[14] Everett W. Fish, *Donnelliana: An Appendix to " Cæsar's Column,"* part 1, pp. 7–13, 21, 27–29, 31, 40 (Chicago, 1892); James H. Baker. *Lives of the Governors of Minnesota,* 339–342 *(Minnesota Historical Collections,* vol. 13 — St. Paul, 1908): *Saint Paul Press,* 1864: August 3. p. 1: 1866: September 11, p. 1; 21, p. 4; Franklin F. Holbrook. " The Early Political Career of Ignatius Donnelly, 1857–1863 " (University of Minnesota, 1916). The last work is a manuscript thesis, copies of which are in the libraries of the university and the Minnesota Historical Society. For citations to seventeen bibliographical

duties of a representative in Congress. He was sufficiently modest for the youngest member of the House and for one serving a first term, but he did not neglect to display his oratorical gifts. On February 27, 1864, speaking on a bill he had introduced to establish a bureau of immigration, he expressed his wish to see a bridge of gold over the Atlantic by which the chosen races of mankind might cross to the chosen lands of the world. On May 2 of the same year he made a long and, for Donnelly, turgid speech in behalf of the " Congressional plan " for reconstruction in the Confederate states. To Donnelly belongs the credit of originating, by the introduction of a resolution on December 14, 1865, a movement in Congress which resulted in the creation of the national bureau of education. Half a year later, on June 5, 1866, Garfield introduced a bill to establish such a bureau and allowed Donnelly to make the opening address. It was one worthy of the cedar. His conception of a great national mouthpiece and rallying point for universal education has not yet been appreciated and may never be. He would have Bacon's dream of a " university with unlimited power to do good, and with the whole world paying tribute to it " realized. France, Germany, and even Russia had taken the education of their peoples under the care of the state. In France such great philosophers and scholars as Cousin and Guizot had been superintendents of schools. His most earnest appeal was for a rallying ground for North and South, so lately engaged in a desolating war, and he could not resist the temptation to throw into his peroration a dash of sentiment. " As war dies," he said, " let peace arise from its ashes, white-winged, white-robed, and luminous with the light of a new morning — a morning never to pass away while the world shall stand."

dictionaries and other works which give information concerning Donnelly, see Warren Upham and Rose B. Dunlap, *Minnesota Biographies, 1655–1912*, 182 (*Minnesota Historical Collections*, vol. 14 — St. Paul, 1912). See also *ante*, 1:60 and citations. Probably no citizen of Minnesota has attained a wider notoriety.

The same confidence in the efficacy of education as a civilizer and peacemaker was shown by Donnelly in a previous speech on February 1, 1866, in advocacy of an amendment to authorize the commissioner of the Freedmen's Bureau to provide a common school education for all refugees and freedmen who should apply for it. The South could not be trusted to undertake this duty; the nation must discharge it. He denounced in terms of great asperity the black codes of some of the southern states. This speech, abounding in statistics, must have been studied with time and care. On March 13, 1867, there was a debate in the House over a proposition to spend a million dollars in relief of many thousands of people, white and black, in southern districts where the crops of the previous season had failed. Against an opposition by Butler and others, which now seems incredible, Donnelly pleaded fervently for a generous policy which should prove to the South that the North was her friend and to the world that a new standard of beneficence had been set up by us.

In the lively debate which took place on July 1, 1868, on the question of appropriating the money to fulfill the treaty negotiated by Seward for the purchase of Alaska, Donnelly took the affirmative, although he thought the action premature. He would vote the money because the annexation would involve the acquisition of western British America. British dominion over that desirable area would " disappear between the upper and the nether mill-stones " of American sovereignty. And his imagination carried him forward to behold our nationality covering the whole domain of the continent. Nothing less than a continent could suffice " as the . . . foundation for that nation in whose destiny is involved the destiny of mankind. Let . . . those foundations . . . abut only on the everlasting seas."[15]

[15] *Congressional Globe*, 38 Congress, 1 session, 196, 856–858, 2036–2039; 39 Congress, 1 session. 60, 585–590, 2966–2967; 40 Congress, 1 session, 84, 86, 91; 40 Congress, 2 session, 3660.

The high tide of Donnelly's peculiar gift as a speaker was reached in the spring of 1868 in the course of an unhappy controversy which, temporarily composed, had its effect upon the political fortunes of both parties. In a letter to a constituent Donnelly gave as a reason for his delay in introducing a land grant bill the objection of Elihu B. Washburne, a member of the House from Illinois, and remarked that he had previously encountered that gentleman's opposition. No offensive language was used, the matter was of slight importance, and it might have been passed over without notice; but the Illinois member was excited to a high degree of exasperation, real or feigned, and in a letter dated April 10, 1868, and published in the *Saint Paul Press* on the nineteenth he charged Donnelly with participation in " every corrupt, extravagant, and profligate measure . . . before the House " and with schemes of plunder and aggrandizement, citing two or three instances not commensurate with accusations so grave. He then assailed Donnelly's private character with a violence ill justified by the few particular instances adduced. On May 2 Donnelly rose in the House to a question of privilege, had the two letters read by the clerk of the House, and broke forth in defense. He had plausible explanations for the particular instances of corrupt behavior cited. When he came to reflections on his private character he did not long remain on the defensive, but carried the war into Africa. He made no charges of misconduct against Washburne, but with a pitiless storm of raillery and invective exposed certain weaknesses and gave out what he believed to be, and what probably was, the ultimate object of Washburne's attack. The publication of Washburne's letter in the leading Republican newspaper in Minnesota was expected to destroy Donnelly's reputation as a man, to discredit him as a representative, and to get him out of the daylight of Washburne's brother, who had long been waiting for that event. Washburne made a very brief reply in the subjunctive mood. He had never made a personal explanation during his long period of service in the House, but *if* he ever should make one, it would not be in reply to a man who had been a criminal and whose record was covered with venality and corruption.

The subsequent apologies to the House and the futile report of a select committee of investigation need no further mention in this place. We are more concerned with the effect of the congressional bullfight on the politics of the second district of Minnesota. At the close of the session Donnelly came home in triumph to be received at a great mass meeting in St. Paul, which he entertained and delighted as only Donnelly could. When he went to his rest that night he doubtless felt as sure of a Republican renomination to Congress as of next morning's sunrise and he may have dreamed of higher honors to follow. But he did not appreciate the power of the Ramsey dynasty, its alarm at having so dangerous a political maverick running loose on the range, and its resolution to give him opportunity to rest from his labors at Washington.[16]

If Donnelly was not beaten for reëlection to the House, his prestige might land him in the Senate the following year. A split into Ramsey and Donnelly factions then occurred in the Republican ranks. Each held a series of caucuses and conventions and nominated its candidates. Donnelly was, of course, the candidate of his wing for representative. The Ramsey men, having an advantage in point of regularity, had expected to make William D. Washburn of Hennepin County, brother of the Illinois representative who had disturbed Donnelly's peace of mind, their nominee; but when their convention assembled and a first ballot was taken, Washburn, not desirous of making a hazardous race, retired in favor of General Lucius F. Hubbard, late colonel of the Fifth Minnesota. This gallant officer and stanch Republican

[16] For further discussion of the Donnelly-Washburne controversy, see the Appendix, no. 1, *post*.

had also the same indisposition and presently declined to run. Major General Christopher C. Andrews, late colonel of the Third, after receiving assurances of substantial support in his campaign, was persuaded to carry the party standard. This division in the Republican ranks gave the Democrats an opportunity which they did not fail to improve by nominating a man of high character, of winning manners, and of marked ability as a lawyer, Eugene M. Wilson of Minneapolis. He was elected and served with much credit in the Forty-first Congress.[17]

The legislature of 1869 had before it as its most absorbing task the election of a United States senator to succeed Ramsey, whose term was expiring. Here again we have an example of the fierce contentions which raged in the Republican camp. Ramsey's friends had given ample notice of their intention to support him. Donnelly, released from any allegiance he might have thought due to that veteran leader of his party, now openly sought the Republican nomination. Morton S. Wilkinson, who had succeeded General Shields in the Senate in 1859, was desirous of further experience in that body. As the time for the caucus, January 14, drew near, the whippers-in of the aspirants applied themselves by all the devices known to their craft not only to secure adherents, but also to obtain irrevocable pledges of their votes. On the eve of the caucus Donnelly, unable to count as secure more than twenty-six out of twenty-eight votes necessary to nominate, withdrew from the contest and advised his friends to support Wilkinson. Failing of his first desire, the nomination, he thus hoped to gratify a wish hardly less ardent, that of retiring Ramsey to private life. In this expectation he was disappointed, for on the first balloting in caucus Ramsey received the exact number of votes necessary to a

17 *Saint Paul Press*, 1868: September 4, p. 1; 29, p. 1; October 2, p. 1; *Saint Paul Pioneer*, 1868: September 4, p. 1; 10, p. 4; October 9, p. 4; Hall, *Observations*, 76–90; *Legislative Manual*, 1869, p. 93. Wilson received 13,506 votes; Donnelly, 11,265; and Andrews, 8,598.

choice. His manager had had the shrewdness to secure the previous adoption of a resolution that there should be no informal balloting.[18]

The Ramsey wing, however, was generous and perhaps deemed it good policy not to punish Donnelly too bitterly. He might after this discipline be serviceable. In the fall of the same year, 1869, its principal organ proposed that the Republican convention called for September 9 should name Donnelly for the governorship. The inconsiderable vote cast for him in the convention showed, however, that the party, for the time being at least, was through with Donnelly. Still he did not renounce allegiance to the party nor disown the name of Republican, for in the next year, 1870, he came out as an independent Republican candidate for representative in Congress. With an eye to business, he early declared himself to be in favor of a tariff for revenue only. As expected, the Democrats of the state gave him their support, but when the votes were counted he lacked some twenty-six hundred votes of a majority in a total vote of thirty-two thousand, in round numbers. The Republican platform had taken the wind from his mainsail by declaring that the tariff ought to be reduced " to the imperative revenue necessities of the government." General John T. Averill, the straight Republican candidate, was elected and two years later was accorded a reëlection.[19]

The Republican convention of 1869, which declined to make Donnelly its candidate for governor, conferred that distinction upon a man who had not been prominent in state politics — Horace Austin. Austin was a native of Connecti-

[18] Hall, *Observations*, 78, 101–107; *Saint Paul Press*, January 15, 20, 1869; *Saint Paul Pioneer*, January 15, 16, 1869; *House Journal*, 1869, p. 34; *Senate Journal*, 29.

[19] *Legislative Manual*, 1871, p. 137. For the support of Donnelly by the *Saint Paul Press*, see the issues for September 8, 9, 1869; for Donnelly's defeat for the governorship see the *Press* for September 10, p. 4. His announcement as an independent candidate for Congress is printed in the issue of August 21, 1870, p. 4. The *Press* of September 1, p. 1, gives his platform in a petition to Donnelly from voters of his district asking him to become a candidate. The petition, says the *Press*, was written by Donnelly himself. For his indorse-

cut who had resided and married in Maine, had moved to Minnesota in 1856 at the age of twenty-five, and had settled in St. Peter to practice law about the time when that village was aspiring to become the capital city of Minnesota. Some years passed in the quiet practice of his profession, during which he gained friends and the confidence of his neighbors by the independence and sincerity with which he held his opinions rather than by any of the arts of conciliation practiced by demagogues. When the Indian war broke out he raised a company of mounted rangers and gained no little reputation by his conduct in the campaign with Sibley in 1863. As a district judge he showed the qualities just mentioned in a degree which convinced people of the district that he was such a man as the state ought to have in the executive office. So ardent and united was their support in the convention that his nomination was secured on the first ballot. The party, however, had been so rent by the late convulsions that it gave him at the polls only a little less than two thousand majority over the able and popular Democratic candidate, George L. Otis. As Austin was not securely attached to the Ramsey following, that body did not sorrow over the meager majority accorded him.[20]

The legislature of 1860 provided by law for the appointment of a commissioner of statistics to hold office for five years without salary, but to own the copyright of his reports. One hundred dollars were appropriated for stationery, postage, and circulars. State and county officers were required

ment by the Democratic convention, see the *Press* for September 16, pp. 1, 4. The attitude of the *Press*, a Republican organ, is apparent in the issues of September 1, 14, 15, 18, 20, 21, 1870. An account of the Republican convention is given in the *Press* for September 2, p. 4.

[20] *Saint Paul Press*, September 10, 1869, pp. 1, 4; Baker, *Governors of Minnesota*, 169–172, 181; Upham and Dunlap, *Minnesota Biographies*, 24; *Legislative Manual*, 1870, p. 130. Austin received 27,348 votes; Otis, 25,401; and Daniel Cobb, 1,764. For side lights on the Republican politics of 1869, see letters to Donnelly from H. P. Hall, June 3, September 26; from Averill, June 4; from W. L. Wilson, June 4; from John McKusick, August 30; from H. T. Johns, November 4; and from D. Bassett, November 16, 1869, in the Donnelly Papers.

to furnish information from their records for a small fee, but were under penalty of a fine of fifty dollars for neglect or refusal. Governor Ramsey at once appointed Joseph A. Wheelock commissioner. On July 1 Wheelock transmitted to the governor a work entitled *Minnesota: Its Place Among the States; Being the First Annual Report of the Commissioner of Statistics for the Year Ending January 1st, 1860.* It was a pamphlet of 176 octavo pages and was printed in Hartford, Connecticut. It would appear that the work had been prepared in part, if not wholly, before the author's appointment. The legislature of 1861 amended the act of the previous year by providing for the publication of the reports at state expense and according the commissioner a salary of one thousand dollars a year. The act provided also for the printing of five thousand copies, the greater number of which were to be distributed in a manner to stimulate immigration, and appropriated the sum of fifteen hundred dollars for that and for the printing. In pursuance of this act there appeared a pamphlet of 171 pages entitled *Minnesota: Its Progress and Capabilities; Being the Second Annual Report of the Commissioner of Statistics, for the Years 1860 and 1861.* It was transmitted in December, 1861. The legislature of 1862 made an appropriation of one thousand dollars for the expenses of the commissioner. On January 19, 1863, Governor Ramsey informed the legislature by a special message of Commissioner Wheelock's resignation on the first of that month, to take effect as soon as his report for 1862, which was partly in type but which had been delayed for returns from some disorganized western counties, should be completed, or as soon as a successor should be appointed. Wheelock would be willing to complete the report without pay and to make future annual reports gratuitously, provided suitable appropriations should be made for hiring clerks and for printing and postage. The legislature, constrained doubtless by the need of economy in the midst of an Indian war, decided that the statistical service was one that could be dispensed with and, instead of accepting Wheelock's offer of gratuitous service, abolished his office and ordered him to turn over its files to the secretary of state. The two reports published were excellent compilations, well worth all they had cost. It is a matter of regret that the series of reports was so abruptly ended.[21]

In his message of 1867 Governor Marshall, anticipating the relief of the secretary of state from the superintendence of schools, suggested that a bureau of statistics might be established in the secretary's office. It was not until 1869 that this counsel prevailed and the legislature on March 5 established the bureau. The duties fell upon Pennock Pusey, who for seven years had been assistant secretary of state and for part of that time deputy superintendent of schools. No one in the state was better fitted for the business than this old resident, skilled in accounting and generally informed and cultured. His reports for 1869 and 1870 formed the models for a long series, rudely terminated without good reason in 1900. There was frequent criticism of the reports and it is true that, aside from census and other official reports, there was a wide range of footings resting only upon rather rough estimates. But in regard to these it should be remembered that the inaccuracies and deficiencies were themselves tolerably stable from year to year, so that they served fairly well as a basis for comparison and as indications of progress. Had the appropriations been

---

21 *General Laws*, 1860, pp. 107–110; 1861, p. 168; 1862, pp. 155, 157; 1863, p. 104; Ramsey's message of January 9, 1862, in *Executive Documents*, 1861, p. 18; *House Journal*, 1863, p. 53. The general statutes of 1866 contained a provision not found in previous session laws, requiring county auditors to furnish blanks to the assessors for taking the acreage and produce of eleven field crops, the returns to be made to the county auditors' offices and forwarded to the auditor of the state. As assessors were not required by law to collect the figures, the state auditor advised the legislature of 1867 that the returns were valueless. The experiment was abandoned. *General Statutes of Minnesota*, 1866, p. 173 (St. Paul, 1867); report of the auditor, in *Executive Documents*, 1867, p. 451. See Fish, *Donnelliana*, part 1, p. 42, for a spiteful story of the way in which Wheelock came to be appointed commissioner of statistics.

more liberal the primary figures would have been much more exact and reliable. But for this series of reports the very able work of Professor Edward Van Dyke Robinson, *Early Economic Conditions and the Development of Agriculture in Minnesota,* could not have been written.[22]

In his message to the legislature of 1868, Governor Marshall called attention to defects in the election laws and recommended the passage of a law which would disfranchise any persons found guilty of illegal voting or of making false election returns. In his judgment there was no crime, unless it was treason, which was more heinous than " to violate the sanctity of the ballot box." The last election had developed defects in the registration and election laws. He doubtless had in mind the extraordinary results of the election of 1867 in Wabasha County, where the question of moving the county seat from Wabasha to Lake City was involved. The returns showed a total vote of 7,960 for governor. The population of the county, according to the state census in 1865, was 11,363 and, at the same rate of increase as that for 1860–65, would have been about 13,500 in 1867. The number of legal electors, according to the ordinary ratio, should have been about 2,635. The remarkable access of 5,325 votes naturally aroused the suspicions and the indignation of Governor Marshall.[23]

[22] *Executive Documents,* 1866, p. 21. Brief biographical sketches of Pusey may be found in the *St. Paul Dispatch,* 1903: February 16, p. 7; March 28, p. 13. The reports of Pusey as commissioner of statistics for 1869 and 1870 were printed as separates and may also be found in *Executive Documents,* 1869, pp. 781–932; 1870, vol. 2, pp. 893–1079. For further bibliographical data on Robinson's book, see *ante,* p. 3, n. 3. The work appeared in an inconvenient form — 10½ by 14 inches — and was printed without an index in the absence of the author in Europe.

[23] *Executive Documents,* 1867, p. 28; report of the secretary of state, in *Executive Documents,* 1865, p. 446. The vote in Wabasha County in 1867 was as follows: for Marshall, 4,045; for Flandrau, 3,915; total, 7,960. The total presidential vote in 1864 was 2,026; the total vote for governor in 1865 was 1,120; the total presidential vote in 1868 was 2,974. See the *Legislative Manual,* 1869, p. 90. For incidents of the county seat contest and mutual charges of rascality, see the *Lake City Leader,* October 11–November 15, and the *Wabasha Weekly Herald,* October 17–November 14, 1867. The *Leader* of November 14 charged that at Wabasha a mob extorted the ballot box from the canvassers and filled it up with ballots enough, as estimated, to secure their

The Sioux and the Winnebago were banished from Minnesota by the act of Congress of February 16, 1863, but the Indian question survived. There remained in the northern forests of the state some six thousands of Chippewa located on reservations, large and small. There was still work for the devoted missionary, the hopeful teacher, and the trader willing to endure exile from civilization for adequate returns upon his capital, his risks, and his labors. There were to be opportunities for treaties, with their traditional emoluments. One of these took place within a few days after Congress voted to banish the Sioux from Minnesota and to confiscate their lands. Although it is doubtful if any individuals or bands of Chippewa seriously thought of joining with the Sioux in their outbreak in August, 1862, many white people believed that they did. There were intelligent Indians who deplored the temptations and influences to which their people were subjected on the border and desired to have them removed from it. The government had long adhered to a policy of concentrating Indian tribes. All these considerations concurred in a project for eliminating six reservations of the Chippewa of the Mississippi and establishing their bands on an enlarged area northeast of Leech Lake, already partly occupied by the Pillager and Winnebagoshish bands. Arrangements were made for a treaty to be negotiated at Washington on March 11, 1863. The government was represented by the commissioner of Indian affairs, William P. Dole, and Clark W. Thompson, superintendent of the northern Indian superintendency; the Indians were represented by Henry M. Rice as their commissioner, the expiration of whose term as United States senator on March 3 had left him free for other engagements. The

desired majority. See also the *Saint Paul Pioneer*, November 8, 9, 13, 17, and the *Saint Paul Press*, November 8, 9, 13, 16, 17, 21, 1867. A *Press* editorial of November 16 denounced " The Wabashaw Outrage " and the villains who committed it, but declared that the Lake City gang was equally culpable. The early dispatches vary widely as to the number of " bogus votes." The *Press* of November 21, p. 1, estimated the number at five thousand.

proposed treaty contained some civilization articles, among
them one for the appointment of a board of visitors to over-
see the conduct of employees about the agencies and the
distribution of annuity goods. The articles of moment for
the present object were: (1) The Indians ceded to the
United States the Gull Lake, Mille Lacs, Sandy Lake, Rabbit
Lake, Rice Lake, and Pokegama Lake reservations in
exchange for a large tract about Leech Lake. (2) Three
hundred acres of land in lots proportioned to the strength
of the several bands were to be cleared and plowed by the
government. (3) The government was to move a sawmill
from Gull Lake to Leech Lake and was to build a road from
Leech Lake to the mouth of Leech Lake River.

It appears from the record that the Senate ratified the
treaty with unusual promptness on March 13, but only after
amendment. A clause providing the sum of $30,000 to
enable the Indians to fulfill "their present just engagements" — the old familiar phrase for traders' claims —
was stricken out. An absurdly small limit of $3,600 was
fixed for plowing the three hundred acres and building
chiefs' houses and the meager sum of $3,000 was allowed
for the sawmill and the road. These amendments were
explained to Rice and the twenty-five Chippewa chiefs and
headmen present, who on the fourteenth agreed to them all.
In regard to possible inducements which may have been
held out to secure this alacrity no information has been
found. The secretary of the interior on April 26, 1864, sent
to the committee of ways and means of the House of Representatives an estimate of amounts required to carry out the
provisions of the treaty. For the clearing and plowing of
the three hundred acres, $15,000 were asked; for the saw-
mill, $6,000; and for the road, $15,000. There followed
estimates for outlays implied, which, though not explicitly
named in the treaty, were such as experienced persons
would understand must be expected, if the Senate did not:
for removing the agency, $25,000; for the transportation of

two thousand Indians, $20,000; and for the subsistence of the same number for six months, $54,000.[24]

Ignatius Donnelly, representative from the second Minnesota district, was not pleased to learn by accident of so large a proposed expenditure of money in his district and was doubtless glad of an opportunity to gain popular applause by exposing an inordinate requisition. On May 2 he sent to Thaddeus Stevens, chairman of the House committee of ways and means, a letter protesting against some of the estimates as ridiculously excessive. For half of the $15,000 asked for clearing and plowing three hundred acres of land, he said, farm lands fenced, broken, and provided with buildings could be bought in the most densely settled parts of Minnesota; the sum of $25,000 would rather build a palace than an Indian agency; the Indians could transport themselves, so that there was no need of paying $20,000 to men who might superintend the movement; the $54,000 asked for six months' subsistence was more than enough by half. A similar letter sent to the secretary of the interior moved him to recall the estimates and to write Donnelly a letter of thanks for exposing an intended fraud.[25]

This act Donnelly believed had more to do with his future career than any other. He was praised by many individuals and by some of the Republican newspapers of the state, but the *Saint Paul Press* had no word of approval. On the contrary, to borrow a clause from the *Pioneer*, the *Press* held him " guilty of a species of treason which makes him worse than a copperhead." To the attacks of the *Press* he replied in a letter of May 30, 1864, defending his course and promising, if God should spare his life, to persevere in it and " rip open this whole Indian system." In the campaign

[24] *Statutes at Large*, 12: 1249–1255; Charles J. Kappler, ed., *Indian Affairs, Laws and Treaties*, 2: 839–842 (Washington, 1904) ; *Senate Executive Proceedings*, 13: 304; *Estimates for Chippewa Treaty, 1863* (38 Congress, 1 session, *House Executive Documents*, no. 76 — serial 1195). On the act of February 16, 1863, see *ante*, 2: 246.

[25] Fish, *Donnelliana*, part 1, p. 47; Donnelly Papers, May 25–June 18, 1864.

which followed in the summer of 1864 for the selection of a
candidate for representative in Congress Donnelly was at
once announced as an aspirant for renomination. Other
aspirants were as good Republicans as he and had good
right to seek the position. He therefore called for support
not only upon his record, but in particular because of his
bold and fearless denunciation of the " Indian swindle."
He charged that friends of his principal competitor, William D. Washburn, had not only connived at the fraudulent
estimates for the fulfillment of the Chippewa treaty, but
were probably expecting to profit by it. His letter to Stevens was published in the newspapers and widely disseminated about the state. It may be allowed that some small
number of Washburn's supporters might have been concerned in Chippewa affairs with the profits in mind, but it is
not credible that Washburn or any of his " friends " were
engaged in any such disreputable commerce. Donnelly's
crusade proved to be good politics, however, for when the
district convention met in St. Paul on August 2 he was
renominated by acclamation. In his speech of acceptance
he took care to express his regret for harsh or unkind words
which might have escaped his lips in the heat of the canvass
and explicitly withdrew them. In a letter to the *Press,* dated
August 5, he further gave utterance to the hope that an honest difference of opinion about certain matters which had
been the subject of discussion should not divide the Republican ranks. These soft words must have had their effect,
for at the election in November his vote was 10,874 against
8,211 for John M. Gilman; but they did not make a bosom
friend of Washburn.[26]

As will have been surmised, the Congress of 1863 made
no appropriation for fulfilling the Chippewa treaty of that
year. The Indians were not satisfied with the treaty. Hole-

[26] Fish, *Donnelliana,* part 1, pp. 48–51; *Saint Paul Press,* May 22, June 1, 5,
7, 17, July 20, August 3, 6, November 27, 1864; *Saint Paul Pioneer,* May 15,
20, June 9, July 13, 17, 20, August 3, 7, 1864.

in-the-Day on June 7, 1863, addressed a letter to the president in which he declared that the proposed Leech Lake reservation was mostly swamp and marsh, with but little land fit for farming. It was too near white settlements, especially to those on Lake Superior. Fish and wild rice were too scarce. As a more suitable home for the consolidated bands he proposed a tract on the Wild Rice River, east of the Red, between the forty-seventh and forty-eighth parallels of north latitude. To conciliate this reluctance William P. Dole, commissioner of Indian affairs, and Clark W. Thompson, superintendent, on May 7, 1864, negotiated a new treaty with Hole-in-the-Day and Misquadace, who had been brought to Washington for the occasion. In general it resembled the treaty of March 11, 1863. The same old reserves were ceded and practically the same new one was accepted in exchange; but Hole-in-the-Day and Misquadace were allowed to retain each a section of land about his old home. The same concession was made to the chief of the Mille Lacs band. A half section at Gull Lake with the Breck mission buildings was given to John Johnson Enmegahbowh. Hole-in-the-Day was allowed $5,000 for the destruction of his house and goods by lawless white men in 1862. These concessions undoubtedly lubricated the negotiation. The sum of $7,500 was allowed for clearing and plowing three hundred acres of land and $5,000 were allowed for six chiefs' houses. For new agency buildings at Leech Lake $25,000 were granted and $7,500 were allowed for roads and bridges. It was agreed that the old annuities should be paid in cash and not half in goods, as was provided in the treaty of 1863, a provision which had displeased the Chippewa. Another agreeable concession was that the bands need not move to the new reserve until after the United States had cleared and plowed the land and had built the road and the bridges. The Mille Lacs band might remain in its old home during good behavior and the band at Sandy Lake until directed to move by the president. For carrying

out the provisions of this treaty the Thirty-eighth Congress
in its second session, on March 3, 1865, made liberal appropriations, equal to or in excess of some of the items
denounced as outrageous by Donnelly the year before.[27]

The debates do not show that the Minnesota representative was active in opposing these appropriations. But he
was not forgetful of the welfare of the Indian whose cause
he had taken up and he presently worked out a plan for a
new and improved Indian system which he embodied in a
speech before the House on February 7, 1865, hoping doubtless that it might uproot and disintegrate the old Indian ring
to whose destruction he had so passionately devoted himself. His denunciation of the iniquities of that system, as
might be expected, was worthy of such a master of invective.
Out of men of at least ordinary virtue the system had made
Indian agents wolves when they ought to have been shep-
herds of the Indian flocks. He believed the Indian capable
of civilization and devoted a large part of the conclusion of
his speech to the Mexicans as an example. For the establishment of a new system Donnelly gave a number of
proposals. First of all, he would have the practice of treaty-
making with Indians wholly abandoned. Then, the whole
body of Indians should be transferred to some region outside any organized state; an area of two or three counties
would suffice for the three hundred thousand Indians. There
should be a military post in the neighborhood. Each Indian
family should have one or two hundred acres of land secured
to it by irrevocable patent and should be provided with animals and implements of farming. The Indians should not,
however, live on the isolated farms, but in villages, according to their ancient custom. A log house should be built
for each family and there should be a garden plot of five or

---

[27] *Statutes at Large*, 13: 560–562, 693–697. Hole-in-the-Day's letter, which
was probably written by Judge David Cooper, is in Indian Office, *Reports*, 1862,
pp. 328–331 (reprinted in 37 Congress, 2 session, *House Executive Documents*,
vol. 2 — serial 1157). On this series of reports, see *ante*, 2: 111, n. 3.

ten acres adjacent to it. The children should be required to attend schools in which the English language should be used. There was a vague suggestion of the use of Christian influence to train in habits of right conduct. As a check on the agents, all distributions of money or goods should be made by a military officer at the neighboring post. It was the expectation of the impractical enthusiast that about the time when the Indians had become fully civilized white settlements would have multiplied about their reservation. Their isolation would then cease and the Indians, admitted to citizenship, would be merged into the general community. There would be no Indian system, no Indian problem.

Donnelly sent a copy of his speech to Joseph R. Brown with a request for his criticism. He got it in a letter of about twenty-eight hundred words written at Fort Wadsworth on March 12, 1865. The veteran Indian trader, agent, and friend of the Indian praised the young congressman for taking the lead in a much-needed reform. His speech, wrote Brown, "breathes the true spirit of Indian improvement." He apparently agreed with Donnelly's plan of isolating the Indians, establishing them on inalienable land, and allowing them to perpetuate their village life. He, too, would abolish Indian treaties, but would modify rather than recast the Indian system. The Indian agent should hold office during good behavior and thus should become a father to the tribe. No traders should be allowed in the neighborhood of an Indian settlement, for they encouraged hunting and discouraged agriculture. No money should be paid or given to Indians and no supplies should be furnished them except for labor performed and duly certified. The Indian should build his own house. He opposed compulsory school attendance, it being in human nature to resist culture and salvation the more they are forced on men. Under no circumstances would he tolerate the interference of military officers with the agent's administration. He would not object to a military man being agent provided he should be detailed to the duty for life. As for their character, Brown considered Indian agents to be about on a par with other officeholders — generally square, with occasional exceptions of dishonesty. He advised Donnelly to make his Indian code simple. It need not be more complicated than a charter of a university or a railroad company.[28]

Either Donnelly had become fatigued with the burden of Indian reform and drafted no code or, having drafted one, found no hospitality for his project. The Indian policy, evolved in the course of two centuries and a half, was not to be suddenly supplanted by an ideal philanthropic scheme such as that contemplated by Donnelly or modified in details, as Brown recommended. It was to run on in the old rut, so that in 1869 Bishop Whipple in a communication to the *Saint Paul Pioneer* was constrained to repeat his seven-year-old arraignment.[29]

The reader will have observed that the concentration of the Chippewa of the Mississippi was not intended to be effected hastily and two bands, those of Mille Lacs and Sandy Lake, were virtually excepted from removal. The liberal appropriations by Congress in the spring of 1865 for carrying out the provisions of the treaties of 1863 and 1864 were no doubt expended, but no large proportion of the Indians could have been transferred to Leech Lake in that year. In 1866 a few stragglers may have left their old reservations for the new one, but the bands did not migrate. The dissatisfaction that Hole-in-the-Day had voiced with the swamps and marshes around Leech Lake must have been shared by the Indians generally. His suggestion that a better home might be found in the Red River Valley seems to have met with the approval of the Indian officials in Washington and there need be no doubt that the white people

[28] *Congressional Globe*, 38 Congress, 2 session, appendix, 61–65; Brown to Donnelly, March 12, 1865, Donnelly Papers.

[29] Letter from Bishop Whipple, January 9, 1869, in the *Saint Paul Pioneer*, January 12, 1869, p. 2. See also *ante*, 2:208, and note.

on the upper Mississippi, especially any who were interested
in lumbering, were willing to have the pine lands about
Leech Lake left unencumbered by the departure of the
Chippewa to a region then distant. Agitation of the matter
led to the negotiation of a new treaty at Washington on
March 19, 1867. It was therein agreed that those Indians
who so desired might cede their proportion of the lands
assigned to them at Leech Lake in the previous treaty and
receive in exchange thirty-six townships in a square form
about White Earth and Rice Lakes.[30]

There was no need of a prophet to foretell the establishment of great industries at the Falls of St. Anthony. Franklin Steele and Robert Smith understood perfectly the value
of their preëmptions. The manufacture of lumber was, of
course, the primary industry, but in the fifties and early
sixties five flour mills of trifling capacity were erected on
the margins of the east channel of the Mississippi. Developments on the west side of the main channel awaited the
patenting to preëmptors of the reduced Fort Snelling reserve
in 1855, the incorporation of the St. Anthony Falls Water
Power Company and the Minneapolis Mill Company in the
year following, and the completion of the first section of the
canal on the west side in 1857. A few small mills were at
once erected, but during the Civil War only meager additions were made. In 1865 the canal was greatly extended
and on it in the course of a decade sprang up the great
cluster of flour mills which long ago gave Minneapolis its
distinctive character. Ancillary industries, such as cooper
shops, foundries, machine shops, planing mills, and sash
and door factories, multiplied. In the very midst of this
development came an alarm which thrilled the whole population of the city and evoked commiseration from St. Paul.
In October, 1869, a portion of the Mississippi began to flow

---

[30] *Statutes at Large*, 16: 719–723; Kappler, *Indian Affairs*, 2: 974–976. This
treaty was the beginning of a long sequel of fortunes, happy and other, for
those Chippewa, an account of which will be found in the next volume.

under the limestone rock which formed the crest of the falls, instead of over it. The cry was heard, " The falls are going out! " And they would have gone out and left a stretch of furious rapids, had not that flow been stopped. It took seven years and nearly a million dollars contributed by citizens, by the two water power companies, and by the government to establish a complete and probably permanent stoppage of the flow of water under the limestone.[31]

The " extrication " of the University of Minnesota from a burden of debt by the sacrifice of nearly one-third of the original territorial land grant for its endowment, the opening of a preparatory department in October, 1867, the organization of the first faculty for college work in September, 1869, and the progress of that institution and of the state normal school at Winona will be dealt with in a later volume, where the matters may be considered in their relation to general accounts of the institutions.[32]

[31] George E. Warner and Charles M. Foote, eds., *History of Hennepin County and the City of Minneapolis*, 174, 389-391, 404-413 (Minneapolis, 1881); Henry T. Welles. *Autobiography and Reminiscences*, 2: 152-187 (Minneapolis, 1899); *Saint Paul Press*, October 6, 1869, p. 4. The vast importance of this salvage not only to Minneapolis but to the whole state may justify its fuller treatment in the Appendix, no. 2, *post*.

[32] See *post*, vol. 4.

II. RAILROAD REGULATION AND THE GRANGERS, 1870–76

THE lively extension of railroads in the five years following the close of the war, 1865–69, wrought great advantages to Minnesota. The remotest villages were now in the great world, with the daily mail coming to most of the homes. The roads were operated, however, in a manner which caused great dissatisfaction. When the companies were chartered railroads were so ardently longed for that their attorneys were allowed to frame the statutes in a form to secure to them the right to fix and determine fares for passengers and rates for freight. Charges were necessarily high, in some cases equalling the cost of wagon transportation, but they were commonly believed to be excessively high. It was seen that at " competitive points " they were lowered, while at intermediate stations they were maintained at the high levels. This meant prosperity to the favored towns and poverty to others. The belief was general that corporations which had been so liberally endowed with public lands and with municipal contributions should be able to afford their services at moderate charges instead of exacting " all that the traffic would bear," as was the fashion of the day.[1]

Governor Austin in his inaugural address on January 7, 1870, stated the popular complaints against the railroad companies and the averments of the companies in extenuation. His counsel was to secure an impartial investigation of alleged abuses, point out proper remedies if needed, and

---

[1] *General Laws*, 1858, p. 170; Railroad Commissioner, *Reports*, 1871, pp. 12, 17–20; Commissioner of Statistics, *Reports*, 1871, p. 193. According to the latter report, on December 31, 1871, there were inuring to fifteen railroads belonging to nine companies 10,757,803 acres, of which 3,171,327 had been patented. The railroad commissioner, however, gives 12,222,780 as the number of acres inuring to the roads.

thus "put the question forever at rest." A bill to create a commission to inquire into alleged railroad abuses was passed by the Senate but was lost in the House.[2] Throughout that year agitation was lively and continuous. The Republican district convention held at Owatonna on July 6 denounced the consolidation of parallel railroads, extortionate freight rates, and the operation of the corporations in the interests of jobbers, speculators, and monopolies. The Democrats at Owatonna on September 15 side-stepped the issue. In the conventions of the two parties in the second district held in St. Paul, the Republican convention on September 1 and the Democratic on September 15, but slight references were made to railroad abuses.[3] The party leaders were not yet ready to take the offensive against the companies, which were very liberal with passes; but the people in large numbers were becoming impatient. An antimonopoly mass meeting held at Rochester on December 1, after denouncing the Winona and St. Peter Railroad Company in particular, passed resolutions calling for laws to compel railroads to carry passengers and freight at fair and reasonable charges, to make discriminations under any form a criminal offense, and to forbid the companies to own elevators or to buy grain.[4]

[2] *Executive Documents*, 1869, pp. 6–14; *Senate Journal*, 1870, p. 288; *House Journal*, 380, 481.

[3] *Minneapolis Tribune*, 1870: July 7, p. 1; September 2, p. 1; *Saint Paul Pioneer*, 1870: September 16, pp. 1, 4; 17, p. 1.

[4] *Federal Union* (Rochester), December 3, 1870, p. 1. Alpheus B. Stickney, in his *Railway Problem*, 73–75 (St. Paul, 1891), says: "At first they [*railway passes*] were given sparingly to the more important personages in the communities, who had little occasion to travel, and as a compliment, something like Christmas cards; then to a larger circle in payment of trifling services . . . then to that very numerous class known as 'political workers'; and finally to every person supposed to be able to do something to aid a railway company in case of political or judicial emergency . . . But it was not long before the recipients came to regard the passes they were accustomed to receive as a right, and then began to ask as a favor that the members of their families and their friends might also ride free. . . . Thus the masses reasoned that charging five cents per mile to one half the travel, and carrying the other half free, was equivalent to carrying all for two and one half cents, and therefore they were paying the expenses of carriage of their more prosperous neighbors, and were being charged twice as much as they ought to pay. . . . Thus . . . the pass system . . . has been, possibly, a more active influence than the

The railroad companies were not much disturbed by the storm of indignation ever increasing in violence about them and they felt so secure in their position that they not only adhered to their high charges and inequalities of service, but they also prepared to descend upon the legislature for additional state aid in their enterprises. A digression is here in order for an account of the audacious " land-grab " scheme of 1871, which did not mitigate the popular wrath.

In Governor Marshall's time a discovery was made by Elias F. Drake, then president of two Minnesota railroad companies, of a forgotten act of Congress dated September 4, 1841, granting to certain existing states and to each new state thereafter admitted 500,000 acres of public lands for internal improvements. The department of the interior recognized the belated claim of Minnesota and authorized the selection of the lands, which was presently made. Aware of various projects for the use and disposition of these lands, in particular of the expectation of certain railroad corporations to divide them as their spoil, Governor Austin in his inaugural address on January 7, 1870, recommended that a constitutional amendment be submitted to the people providing that these 500,000 acres should not be disposed of for any purpose until after a referendum ratified by a majority of electors.[5] Instead of taking the action thus recommended the legislature of that winter entertained a proposition to parcel out the grant to the railroad companies, but took no action. On the assemblage of the legislature of 1871 it was believed by railroad functionaries that a very large majority of the members of both houses had come up to the Capitol pledged, or relied upon, to consummate that scheme. A month and more passed before the conflicting interests could agree upon the details of the proposed division and then

---

more important matters pertaining to the evil effects of discrimination." Stickney was president of the Chicago Great Western Railroad for many years.

[5] Marshall's message of January 10, 1867, in *Executive Documents*, 1866, p. 18; Austin's message, in *Executive Documents*, 1869, p. 5. In the *Saint Paul Press*, February 5, 1875, p. 2, is Senator Drake's account of his discovery.

the exclusion of a number of aspirants alienated so many votes that the bill was imperiled. A careful canvass of the houses, however, emboldened the "land-grabbers" to go ahead. On February 16 a Senate bill to divide the 500,000 acres among the several counties came back from the committee on public lands without recommendation, had its second reading, and went on "general orders." In committee of the whole the bill of the conspirators was substituted for the original bill and was reported favorably. A motion that the new bill be read was voted down. After a long session of fruitless filibustering, it was ordered to a third reading and on February 17 was passed by a vote of 12 to 8. On the twenty-eighth the House by the close vote of 26 to 21 consummated the "divide" so far as legislative action was concerned.

On March 2 Governor Austin sent to the Senate a veto message which ought to have made the ears of the majority tingle for a year and a day. It is a fine piece of work from any point of view. He told them that they had been either cajoled or bullied into the support of a measure which their judgments could not approve; that they had voted to divert the grant from the purpose stipulated in the statute; that they had no power to divide the lands, but only the proceeds of sales; that they had cut off the north half of the state without an acre and had concentrated their benefactions chiefly in the southeast quarter of the state, in some cases favoring districts already well supplied with railroads; that they had divided the grant into so many parcels that they would be insufficient to insure completion of roads; that they had voted to invest the lands, the only remaining assets of the state, in a venture of uncertain promise, instead of reserving them to pay the existing state debt; and, finally, that they had refused to submit the question to popular vote, not daring to take their chances at the polls. The bill proposed a division of the whole grant of half a million acres worth, according to Governor Austin, $3,500,000, into eleven parcels among

seven different companies, but two great "interests," the
Southern Minnesota and the ancient Minnesota and Northwestern, were to absorb 265,500 acres. The two political
parties were represented on the two sides of the question in
such equal proportions that neither could consistently lay
claim to superior virtue. From the date of the veto a reëlection for Governor Austin was a foregone conclusion.[6]

The same legislature, that of 1871, which was so willing to
bestow 500,000 acres of land on the railroad companies as
a gift and was prevented from doing it only by the veto of
Governor Austin, nevertheless saw new light and before its
session was over took action of a drastic character for the
regulation of railroads. A joint committee was appointed to
make an investigation over a field absurdly extensive for
the allotted time. The report submitted to the Senate on
February 15, consisting mainly of testimony taken without
findings, was disappointing. It was not known at the time
that the report had been written by an attorney paid by the
railroad companies. A leading newspaper declared that it
was not worth the paper on which it was written, and so it
turned out.[7] But the legislature was prepared for vigorous
action. Another digression is here necessary to explain its
ambiguous conduct.

In the year of the organization of Minnesota Territory,
1849, a young man from Boston, Massachusetts, arrived and
took up a claim in what became the town of Elk River in
Sherburne County, near the forgotten village of Itasca. On

[6] *House Journal*, 1871, pp. 250–255, 276; *Senate Journal*, 124–130, 138, 319–324; *St. Paul Dispatch*, March 14, 1871, p. 1; *Saint Paul Pioneer*, March 3, 1871, p. 1; *Executive Documents*, 1870, vol. 1, p. 38. For a list of the rail-road companies expecting to share in the "divvy," see Hall, *Observations*, 98, and the *Saint Paul Press*, 1871: February 16, p. 1; 17, p. 1. The text of the bill as passed by the Senate is given in the *Saint Paul Pioneer*, February 18, 1871, p. 2. Austin's increased popularity as a result of the veto is indicated in quotations from newspapers from all over the state in the *St. Paul Dispatch*, March 7–13, 1871.

[7] *Senate Journal*, 1871, pp. 10, 21, 27, 114; *House Journal*, 29, 34, 166; W. P. Clough to Donnelly, July 29, 1873, Donnelly Papers; *Minneapolis Tribune*, February 17, 1871, p. 1. The *Saint Paul Press*, February 16, 1871, p. 2, and the *Minneapolis Tribune*, February 17, 1871, p. 2, give the report.

his claim Oliver Hudson Kelley remained in obscurity for fifteen years, but his brain was not idle. In 1864 Senator Ramsey obtained for him a clerkship in the department of agriculture in Washington. In January, 1866, he was sent by the department on a tour of the southern states to study their agricultural resources. Among other things he observed that there was need of coöperative action among farmers through associations more efficient than existing farmers' clubs and societies, which should broaden out to state boundaries and at length become national in scope. A member of the Masonic order, he easily conceived the idea of a secret organization on the model of that great fraternity. On this he meditated during the summer of 1866 while at work on his farm. In the following year, while holding a clerkship in the post-office department, he persuaded a small group of men, most of them government clerks, to entertain his project of a secret order of men and women engaged in agriculture. In December, 1867, with six others he organized in Washington the " National Grange of the Patrons of Husbandry." Kelley took the position of executive secretary. A local grange corresponding to the lodge of Masonry was at once established, in which the ritual of the order was rehearsed.[8]

After futile attempts to organize granges in a few other states, Kelley decided to return to his own state and try his fortune among his fellow farmers. In St. Paul in August,

[8] Oliver H. Kelley, *Origin and Progress of the Order of the Patrons of Husbandry in the United States; a History from 1866 to 1873*, ch. 1 (Philadelphia, 1875) ; Solon J. Buck, *The Agrarian Crusade; a Chronicle of the Farmer in Politics*, 1–5 (*The Chronicles of America Series*, vol. 45 — New Haven, 1921). The latter is an admirable essay without citation of sources. An account of the extinct village of Itasca is given in Warren Upham, *Minnesota Geographic Names*, 24 (*Minnesota Historical Collections*, vol. 17 — St. Paul, 1920). D. Appleton, ed., *American Annual Cyclopædia and Register of Important Events*, 1873, pp. 622–625 (New York, 1874), gives much credit to William Saunders, superintendent of the gardens and propagating houses of the United States Department of Agriculture, for working out the plan and drafting the original constitution, which is there given in full. The declaration of the aims and purposes of the order adopted by the National Grange at St. Louis, February 4–14. 1874, is given in the same volume, page 626.

1868, he made the acquaintance of Colonel Daniel A. Robertson, widely known as the former editor of the *Minnesota Democrat* and otherwise in public life, who some time before had retired to a farm on land which has long since been covered by the expanding city. On September 2 the North Star Grange was organized, the first permanent grange in the state. Colonel Robertson then recast the prospectus of the order, which had laid emphasis on the social and educational advantages, so as to announce a far more ambitious program than had been contemplated by the founders. The revised circular set out as the grand objects of the order the promotion of education, the dignifying of the farmer's profession, the collection of statistics of crops and markets and the diffusion of the resulting information among farmers, the establishment of depots for the sale of farm produce in the cities, the exchange of seeds and stock, the testing of new farm implements, and the protection of farmers against fraud in general and against the machinations of corporations in particular. " It was on this circular," says Kelley, " we based the real foundation of the Order, and on North Star Grange as the leader in a forlorn hope. . . . When we seek for founders of this Order, Col. Robertson must be COUNTED IN." Even with this alluring program the start of the order in Minnesota was slow, doubtless in part because of ancient prejudice against secret societies. There were eleven local granges to unite in the formation of a Minnesota State Grange, the first in the United States, on February 23, 1869. By the close of that year Minnesota had forty local granges out of forty-nine in the whole country and toward the end of 1870 she had some fifty active granges. The growth of the order was less rapid in 1871, but Minnesota gained forty-six new granges in 1872. In January, 1873, the National Grange, having been incorporated by act of Congress, revised the constitution in a manner to increase the number of persons eligible to membership. A new article provided that " any person interested in agricultural

GRANGE ROOM SHOWING OFFICERS IN POSITION
[From an engraving in Wells, *The Grange Illustrated*.]

pursuits " might become a member. Under this liberal provision the number of Minnesota granges rose to 362 by October 18 of that year and was swelled to 538 on September 1, 1874.⁹

The leaders of the movement had not contemplated an assault upon railroad abuses, but it was soon thought of. On May 20, 1870, W. W. Corbett, the editor of the *Prairie Farmer* of Chicago, wrote a letter to Kelley in which he declared it to be his conviction that the Patrons of Husbandry ought to take sides with the people in the opening campaign against those merciless monopolies — railroad, insurance, warehouse, and telegraph companies. Opposition to monopolies he thought consistent with the design of the order. It could not, according to its constitution, be political in the ordinary sense of the term, but it could by influence control politicians and officeholders and oblige them to take sides with the people. This letter was read at a meeting of the Minnesota State Grange on June 23 and the members were so well satisfied with it that they ordered it to be printed for circulation. The granges, however, responded but tardily to the proposition and at a nonpartisan mass convention held at St. Paul on January 4, 1871, for the purpose of discussing the railroad monopoly evil, the Patrons were not largely represented. They suspected that certain disappointed politicians were desirous to rally them around the standard of a new party.¹⁰

Governor Austin in his inaugural address delivered on January 7, 1870, had briefly referred to complaints of railroad abuses and had advised the appointment of a commit-

⁹ Kelley, *Patrons of Husbandry*, 123–130, 165, 216, 219, 294–296, 422; *Minnesota Monthly*, 1: 97, 98 (March, 1869) ; Solon J. Buck, *The Granger Movement; a Study of Agricultural Organization and Its Political, Economic and Social Manifestations, 1870–1880*, 50, 54, 57, chart following 58 (*Harvard Historical Studies*, vol. 19 — Cambridge, 1913). Kelley states that up to April, 1875, upwards of twenty-three thousand dispensations for granges had been issued in the country.

¹⁰ Kelley, *Patrons of Husbandry*, 256–259; *St. Paul Dispatch*, 1871: January 5, p. 1; 6, p. 4. Donnelly made the principal speech.

tee to make an impartial investigation. In his first annual message, addressed to the legislature of 1871, he took a long step in advance, to which doubtless he had been moved by the popular agitation of the year which had passed. He was now ready with definite recommendations, which may be briefed as follows: (1) All special railroad charters should be void if the roads should not be in operation within a time named. (2) Every company doing business in the state should maintain an office in the state. (3) There should be no consolidation of parallel or competing railroad lines. (4) All railroads should be declared public highways open to all at reasonable charges fixed by the legislature. (5) No securities should be issued but for money, labor, or property used for the purposes of the corporation. (6) The right of eminent domain should apply to corporation property. (7) Adequate penalties, extending, if necessary, to forfeiture of franchises, should be fixed for unjust discrimination and extortion. A similarity of phrasing indicates that the new constitution of Illinois, which had been adopted within a year, had been studied.[11]

It will now be easily understood why the legislature of 1871 saw that it would be bad politics to ignore the railroad question and, although somewhat tardily, got to work upon it with ostentatious industry. Two bills were passed near the close of the session, one of which the most radical of reformers could hardly have expected. Chapter 24 of the *General Laws* of Minnesota, approved on March 6, 1871, was the first of the so-called " Granger acts." It declared all railroads in the state to be public highways and prescribed reasonable maximum fares and rates. Passenger fare was limited to five cents per mile. Freight rates were to vary according to mileage of haul and the character of

11 *Executive Documents*, 1870, vol. 1, pp. 53–55; Francis N. Thorpe, ed., *The Federal and State Constitutions, Colonial Charters, and Other Organic Laws of the States, Territories, and Colonies,* 2: 1042 (Washington, 1909); Rasmus S. Saby, " Railroad Legislation in Minnesota, 1849–1875," in *Minnesota Historical Collections,* 15: 97.

the loads, which were classified under five heads: (1) farm produce; (2) lumber, coal, and salt; (3) merchandise; (4) fourth-class freight, including sugar in barrels; and (5) wood. The maximum rate on farm produce was fixed at six cents per ton per mile up to twenty miles, five cents from twenty to fifty miles, four cents from fifty to one hundred miles, and three and one-half cents for distances over one hundred miles. For less than carload lots the rate was twenty per cent higher. The merchandise rate was twenty-five per cent above that on farm produce. The act required the companies to grant equal facilities to all shippers, to receive all kinds of freight without additional charges for handling, and to transport it in the order received in a reasonable time. It further provided that, in case of neglect by a company to comply with the provisions of the act, an aggrieved party might recover in a civil action the sum of one thousand dollars with costs. Still more stringent was the paragraph which declared any demand by a company for rates or fares higher than those prescribed to be a misuse of its powers and required the attorney-general, upon receiving proper proofs, to prosecute for the forfeiture of its franchise or for a fine of one thousand dollars for each and every offense at the discretion of the court.[12]

Some administrative mechanism was, of course, necessary for the operation of this law. Accordingly a companion act, on the model of similar ones already in effect in eastern states, was passed creating the office of railroad commissioner to be filled by an appointee of the governor, the Senate consenting, for a two-year term. He was empowered to examine into the physical and financial condition of the roads and their management, to watch for violations of law, and to report thereon for the information of the legislature. This act contained some stringent provisions. The accept-

---

[12] *General Laws*, 1871, pp. 61–66. Stickney, in his *Railway Problem*, 89–97, gives an imaginative debate between the railroads and the people on the pending bill, presenting the opinions current at that time.

ance by the commissioner of any compensation other than his salary of three thousand dollars and his necessary expenses was declared a felony punishable by a fine of ten thousand dollars or ten years' imprisonment or both. Neglect by railroad directors and officials to make sworn returns was made a felony and the making of false returns, perjury. The neglect of the legislature to make an appropriation of money for the commissioner's salary was an oversight which was remedied at the next session. The first appointee was Alonzo J. Edgerton, a former captain in the Tenth Minnesota, colonel of the Sixty-fifth United States Colored Infantry, and brevet brigadier general, an experienced attorney, and a man of high character.[13]

The first annual report of Commissioner Edgerton to the legislature of 1872 was full of interesting information, but the predominating item was that the land grant companies, without exception, had refused to obey the regulatory act of 1871 on the ground that their charters were contracts of the kind which the state under the national Constitution, as interpreted by the Supreme Court, had no power to impair. Those charters, it was claimed, conferred upon the several corporations the privilege of fixing their charges for service according to their own judgment of what would be reasonable.[14] The question of the constitutionality of the act of 1871 was presently taken into court. John D. Blake and Company brought suit in the district court in Olmsted County against the Winona and St. Peter Railroad Company for the recovery of two bales of cotton cloth detained by that company for nonpayment of transportation from Winona to Rochester. Blake and Company were willing to pay and offered to pay the legal charge of fifty-seven cents, but the railroad company demanded one dollar and held the goods.

[13] *General Laws,* 1871, pp. 56–59; 1872, p. 183. Holmes, in *Minnesota in Three Centuries,* 4: 104, gives a brief biographical sketch of Edgerton.
[14] Railroad Commissioner, *Reports,* 1871, pp. 10, 32–39, appendix, 16, 32, 43, 56, 79.

The district court found for the defending company, taking
the view that the state had no right to fix charges for service
on that road. The case was appealed by the plaintiffs to
the state supreme court and the issue was simplified by a
stipulation between the parties that, should the court find
the regulating act valid, judgment should be for the plaintiffs. The attorney-general of Minnesota, as authorized and
virtually directed by the legislature, brought suit in the
state supreme court to vacate the charter of the company for
violation of the said act. The two cases were heard together
at the October, 1872, term of the court and were decided on
May 27, 1873, in favor of the plaintiffs. The court held
that, while the company's charter invested it with a contrac-
tual right to collect *some* tolls, the state had not parted with
its sovereign power to regulate and limit them. The railroad
company appealed the suit to the national Supreme Court,
which, after three years' continuance decided it as one of a
batch of Granger cases. The decision, which was in favor
of Blake, upheld the validity of the regulating act of 1871.[15]

The power of the legislature thus questioned and the
Blake case continued without date, general legislation in
Minnesota for railroad regulation was obviously superfluous and none was attempted in 1872 and 1873. Some
special railroad acts were passed in the former year per-
mitting companies to build branch lines, most of them specifically reserving to the state the right to regulate charges
for service and some of them, the right to punish for unjust
discrimination.[16] An act of the same year is notable as

[15] Reports of the attorney-general, in *Executive Documents*, 1871, vol. 1, p.
74; 1872, vol. 1, p. 541; 1873, vol. 2, pp. 832–835; Railroad Commissioner,
Reports, 1871, p. 11; 1873, pp. 241–247; Buck, *Granger Movement*, 161; John
D. Blake *et al. v.* Winona and St. Peter Railroad Company, 19 *Minnesota*, 418.
[16] Minnesota, *Special Laws*, 1872, pp. 480–491. The attorney-general in his
report for 1873 remarked that, whatever might be the result in the cases
appealed to the United States Supreme Court, it was a matter of little practical
importance to the state, so far as its policy toward railroads operated within
the state was concerned, since the legislature was competent to modify or
amend the charter of any company seeking aid from the state in return for
such aid. *Executive Documents*, 1873, vol. 2, p. 835.

showing that railroads, with all their shortcomings and abuses, were still much desired in parts of the state not yet supplied. To put an end to excessive grants of bonds voted by municipalities for railroad facilities, a constitutional amendment was proposed to limit grants to ten per cent of the assessed value of the property to be taxed. The amendment was ratified at the fall election of the same year.[17]

In his message to the legislature of 1873 Governor Austin renewed his recommendation for a committee to investigate railroad affairs and proposed that a law be passed making conspiracy in restraint of trade indictable and providing that if railroad directors or officials should be convicted the companies concerned should forfeit their franchises. The legislature did not respond, however, and it was equally indifferent to the recommendations of the railroad commissioner, excepting that it gave to the state treasurer the duty of collecting railroad taxes. While the legislatures of these years were thus quiescent the people were not dormant on the railroad question. Extortions and discrimination continued and railroad directors and their attorneys became ever more insolent. The companies steadily refused obedience to the act of 1871, some of them endeavored to evade their taxes, and some were dilatory in paying them. Some sold land under contracts intended to continue their exemption from taxation after sale to private purchasers. One company, the Minnesota Central, successor to the Minneapolis and Cedar Valley, in 1867 sold its road and equipment to the McGregor Western, which a few weeks later sold out to the Milwaukee and St. Paul, but the Minnesota Central held its government lands, retaining its franchise as a railroad company to protect the lands from taxation.[18]

The people of Minnesota had welcomed the extension of railroads, especially when they were built in advance of set-

17 Railroad Commissioner, *Reports*, 1872, p. 39; *General Laws*, 1872, p. 60.
18 *Executive Documents*, 1872, vol. 1, p. 8; *General Laws*, 1873, p. 225; Railroad Commissioner, *Reports*, 1872, pp. 31, 39; 1873, pp. vi-xv, xxvi, 1.

tlement, but their joy had been changed into wrath. Three
considerations continually rose in their minds: (1) The
constitution of the state provided that common carriers
enjoying rights of way for public use should transport the
mineral, agricultural, and manufactured productions of the
state on equal and reasonable terms. (2) Railroads were
in their nature public highways and not mere private investments. (3) The companies had been richly endowed by
the general government and by the state and her municipalities. In his report for 1873 the railroad commissioner
estimated that, with 11,250,000 acres of land from Congress, 1,950,000 acres from the state, $1,561,500 worth of
municipal bonds, and 240 miles of graded track, the grants
must be worth not less than $51,000,000. That sum, if in
hand, would have built all the railroads in the state. Five
cents per mile for passenger fare, and freight rates running
up as high as $.64 per ton per mile for short distances did
not seem reasonable terms to travelers and shippers. As
elsewhere and later, however, there was less grumbling
over fares and rates than over the discriminations between
stations on the lines. That the Winona and St. Peter, for
instance, should haul wheat from Owatonna to Winona at
$.026 per ton per mile and exact $.06 from Rochester, 40
miles nearer Winona, did not seem " equal." It was also
difficult to understand why freight from New York via
Duluth over 156 miles of rail to St. Paul at $.35 per hun-
dred pounds could not be hauled to Faribault, only fifty-six
miles farther, for less than $.39 per hundredweight addi-
tional. There were other conundrums such as these: the
rate on a carload of lumber from Minneapolis to Faribault,
56 miles, was from $28.00 to $29.50, to Owatonna, 15 miles
farther, $18.00, and to Mason City, Iowa, 247 miles distant,
$25.00; Faribault millers were paying $.20 more per barrel
on flour to Milwaukee than were the Minneapolis millers;
and Faribault merchants were paying $1.10 on merchandise
from Chicago, while those of St. Paul were paying $.80.

Such discriminations were so general and, under the circumstances, apparently so unreasonable, that exasperation was widespread. Politicians of all stripes vied with one another in reviling the rapacious corporations. The governor of the state, in a public address, declared that " it was time to take these robber corporations by the scruff of the neck and shake them over hell." [19]

The legislature of 1873, like that of the previous year, had found no remedy for the continued extortions and discriminations of the railroad companies, controlled by absentee stockholders. It may be suggested that a certain exasperating insolence exhibited by them toward the public was founded on the ruling of the Supreme Court of the United States in what have long been known as the " Slaughterhouse Cases," which greatly enlarged the scope of the fourteenth amendment of the national Constitution. That amendment provided that no state shall " deprive any person of life, liberty, or property, without due process of law," the intention being to protect human beings in the enjoyment of certain inalienable rights with which the Creator had endowed them antecedent to government. The extension of the term " person " to include artificial quasi personalities created by law, as if also endowed with rights before law, gave to men who held the control of corporations a sense of independence and immunity. Against the resulting " public-be-damned " insolence there arose a wave of indignation.[20]

There were two developments which concurred to revive and redouble the agitation for railroad reforms — the rapid organizing of the farmers and the founding of a new political party. The Patrons of Husbandry, which at the

---

[19] Railroad Commissioner. *Reports.* 1871, p. 17; appendix, 40; 1873, pp. l-lii, lxiii, 73, 74. The author heard Governor Austin make the statement in a speech at the Dakota County fair at Farmington.
[20] 16 *Wallace*, 36–130 (83 *United States*); Max West, " The Fourteenth Amendment and the Race Question," in *The American Journal of Sociology*. 6: 248–254 (September. 1900).

close of 1870 numbered about fifty local granges in Minnesota, could count in May, 1873, more than two hundred. The constitution of the order forbade political discussions in the grange meetings; but no written constitution could prevent the kind of men and women who entered the order from thinking about public affairs and in particular about a matter so closely related to their home interests.[21] The local granges did technically conform to the constitution and refrain from action which could be stigmatized as political, but the constitution could not and did not forbid members from attending as citizens certain nonpartisan gatherings which took the name of " county councils." In many instances these meetings were made up almost wholly of Grangers, who thus avoided the constitutional prohibition. In the spring and summer of 1873 Ignatius Donnelly lectured before many granges, mostly in the first and second congressional districts, on a variety of subjects, such as tariff, paper money, and patent laws, not forgetting to touch upon railroad abuses. He tickled the Grangers by praising them for the influence they had exerted toward bringing railroads under the control of the state, but more by suggesting that they were to become the great party of the people, which would name the next president. A pamphlet made up of extracts from these addresses was given a wide circulation.[22]

At a county convention held in Brownsdale, Mower County, on July 26, which was addressed by Donnelly, a bold departure was taken. A resolution expressing lack of confidence in both political parties was adopted and two calls were issued — one for a county convention to nominate candidates for the coming election and the other for a state " mass convention." In response to the latter call a state

[21] Buck, *Granger Movement*, table following p. 58. The constitution is given in John G. Wells, *The Grange Illustrated; or, Patron's Hand-book, in the Interests of the Order of Patrons of Husbandry*, 75 (New York, 1874).
[22] Ignatius Donnelly, *Facts for the Granges* (n.p., n.d.).

convention assembled at Owatonna on September 2. The long series of resolutions which were adopted doubtless underwent the scrutiny of Donnelly and it would not be a wild guess that they were the product of his facile pen. It was resolved that no government *could* alienate its sovereign powers and that no candidate should receive support who would tolerate the so-called " vested right " of corporations against the public welfare. A high protective tariff, high official salaries, and back pay for members of Congress were denounced. Farmers and laborers were advised to select their own candidates for office, independent of the old parties. A full state ticket was nominated. The attendance at this Anti-Monopoly convention did not meet the hopes and expectations of those who called it.[23]

A third contributory factor, which intensified the exasperation of the people of Minnesota, ought perhaps to have notice. When the Lake Superior and Mississippi Railroad was opened for traffic in August, 1870, that road began carrying large amounts of wheat to be shipped by steamers to eastern markets. Much of this was brought into St. Paul by roads centering there from distant western and southwestern counties of Minnesota. The management of the Milwaukee and St. Paul Railroad did not relish this competition and resolved to curtail, if not to annihilate it. At some time in 1872 the "man of iron nerve" who dominated its directorate ordered that its rate sheets be so arranged that every one of its stations should be financially as near to Chicago as to Duluth. The arrangement brought St. Paul within 156 miles of Chicago instead of over 400 miles. More effectually to prevent the shipment of wheat to Duluth the Milwaukee management placed buyers at all the stations of independent lines centering in St. Paul, with orders to buy

[23] *Saint Paul Pioneer*, 1873: July 27, p. 1; September 3, p. 1; F. A. Elder to Donnelly, June 12, 19, July 16, August 22, 1873, Donnelly Papers. Donnelly's speech is given in *Facts for the Granges*. The platform is in Edward W. Martin, *History of the Grange Movement; or the Farmer's War Against Monopolies*, 510–513 (Philadelphia, [1873]).

all wheat offered without regard to price. The Lake Superior and Mississippi retorted by shipping millions of bushels to its lake terminus without a cent of revenue, a policy which ended in a receivership. This war was still raging in the fall of 1873; but, after the close of navigation on the lakes, an increase of three cents per bushel on wheat to Chicago added to the exasperation of the farmers.[24]

As the months wore away the party leaders, who had been taking notice of the political air currents, trimmed their sails accordingly. At the Republican state convention held in St. Paul on July 16, 1873, the platform adopted was sympathetic with Granger demands. The Democratic and Liberal-Republican rump in convention at St. Paul on September 24 went even farther and appropriated the candidates of the Anti-Monopoly convention at Owatonna. At the November elections the usual Republican majority for the head of the ticket was greatly reduced and two of the fusion candidates for state offices were elected.[25] It is now obvious that the legislature of 1874 was expected to deal with the railroad problem. The Republicans were in sufficient numbers to control the organization of the two houses, after an ineffectual effort of Anti-Monopolists to rally enough votes in caucus to nominate the speaker of the House, though they lacked but three votes. A majority of the Republican members of the House were Grangers and they were strongly represented in the Senate. The Republicans understood what was expected of them and what was good politics.[26]

Governor Austin in his final message, delivered on January 9, 1874, less confident than in previous years about railroad policy, contented himself with recommending that

[24] Stickney, *Railway Problem*, 40–42, 98; *Saint Paul Press*, 1873: September 14, p. 2; September 16, p. 1; Railroad Commissioner, *Reports*, 1871, p. 31; appendix, 39.
[25] *Saint Paul Press*, July 17, 1873, pp. 1, 4; *Saint Paul Pioneer*, 1873: July 17, pp. 1, 4; September 25, pp. 2, 4. See also the references in Buck, *Granger Movement*, 91, n. 3. On the election of 1873, see *post*, pp. 81–85.
[26] *Saint Paul Pioneer*, 1874: January 6, pp. 2, 4; January 7, p. 2; March 5, p. 2; *Saint Paul Press*, January 8, 1874, p. 1; *House Journal*, 1874, p. 4.

the attorney-general or the railroad commissioner be required to prosecute cases similar to the Blake case at state expense, although he regarded the Granger law of 1871 as arbitrary and inelastic. He also recommended that a board composed of the railroad commissioner and other capable men be appointed to investigate complaints against the railroad companies and suggested that an approximation to the French scheme of railroad supervision and regulation would be more practicable than any other scheme. Governor Davis, equally modest, made but two suggestions in his inaugural address. One of them was that the principle of eminent domain be applied to railroad property so that the state, by paying proper compensations, might recover from the land grant companies their " vested rights " to make rates and fares according to their own discretion. The other recommendation was that the state constitution be so amended as to provide that whenever the state granted any charter or concession to a company it should be a necessary implication that the company should be subject to such duties and control by the state as the constitutional amendment should impose. Commissioner Edgerton reported to the legislature that for lack of power he had done little but collect and digest statistics. The railroad companies persisted in refusing to obey the act of 1871 and it was his opinion that their contumacy would only heap up wrath against a day of wrath. Some of the companies had not paid their taxes and he had no power to enforce collection. His only recommendation of importance was that the legislature declare by law what rates and fares were reasonable and force the companies to rebut in court. This suggestion was entertained by the legislature.[27]

It is not important that the various bills and resolutions, including one for an amendment of the state constitution,

[27] Austin's message, in *Executive Documents*, 1873, vol. 1, pp. 16, 18, 19; Davis' message, in the same volume, p. 13; Railroad Commissioner, *Reports*, 1873, pp. vi, xxvi, xlv.

be described or even enumerated. On February 19, 1874, the railroad committee of the Senate introduced a comprehensive bill which was made a substitute for all others then pending and was passed on February 24 by a vote of 29 to 7. The House railroad committee reported a more stringent bill as a substitute for the Senate bill, which was recommitted. After further consideration of the matter, the committee reported back the Senate bill with an amendment. It took the work of two conference committees to adjust the disagreements, but the bill was finally put in a form so acceptable that it passed the House by a vote of 83 to 3 and the Senate by one of 34 to 2, the nays being those of Senators Drake and Donnelly.[28]

The essential element of the Granger law of 1874 was the creation of a board of commissioners with power to establish a schedule of fares and rates for each and every railroad company doing business in the state, taking into consideration their several conditions and circumstances. The published schedules were to be *prima facie* evidence of maximum reasonable legal charges, subject to revision at the discretion of the board. Charges for service were to be proportioned to mileage of haul and unjust discriminations of every kind were forbidden. Severe penalties were pronounced against violations of the law, whether by the corporations or by their agents and employees willfully conniving with them. Should a company refuse to pay a fine finally adjudged against it, the board was required to bring suit for vacation of its franchises and, if refusal to pay was persisted in while the suit was pending, the court might appoint a receiver for the company.[29]

The passage of the act was good politics for the Republican majority. It had thrown a welcome sop to the Grang-

[28] *Senate Journal*, 1874, pp. 291, 344, 431, 440, 474, 481; *House Journal*, 407, 424, 452, 463, 497, 549, 563; *Saint Paul Press*, 1874: February 25, p. 2; March 4, pp. 1, 4.
[29] *General Laws*, 1874, pp. 140–150.

ers, while such lawyers as Austin and Davis knew that until
the Supreme Court of the United States had decided the
Blake case against the railroads and in favor of the state,
the companies, intrenched behind the Dartmouth College
decision, would cling doggedly to their vested rights. The
leading newspapers were divided in their opinions of the
efficacy of the act. The people generally were content with
another experiment which might give relief in the way of
lessening discriminations, if it did not much reduce railroad
tariffs.[30]

Governor Davis appointed as commissioners Alonzo J.
Edgerton, William R. Marshall, and John J. Randall, each to
serve for two years at a salary of three thousand dollars.
When they assembled for business they found that a change
had taken place in the general situation. The Minnesota
railroads had been hard hit by the panic of 1873. All the
land grant roads had been building in advance of settlement
on a scale too great for the times. Their land sales on long-
time credits had fallen off. Indeed, the companies were not
desirous to sell extensively, preferring to hold their acres for
the better prices which would follow the completion of the

[30] *Saint Paul Press*, March 6, 1874, p. 1; *St. Paul Dispatch*, March 6, 1874,
p. 4; *Minneapolis Tribune*, March 7, 1874, p. 2; Trustees of Dartmouth College
v. Woodward, 4 *Wheaton*, 518-715 (47 *United States*). In 1769 the royal
governor of New Hampshire granted a charter establishing Dartmouth College.
In 1816 the legislature of the state created Dartmouth University. The trustees
of the university installed a new faculty in the buildings and obtained possession of the original charter, the records, and the seal, valued at fifty thousand
dollars. The college trustees brought suit for their recovery. The Superior
Court of Appeals of New Hampshire decided against them and an appeal was
taken to the Supreme Court of the United States, Daniel Webster being the
principal counsel for the appellants. On February 2, 1819, the court considered " that this [charter] is a contract, the obligation of which cannot be
impaired, without violating the constitution of the United States." An
account of this case is given in Albert J. Beveridge, *The Life of John Marshall*,
4: 224, 230-236, 261, 272 (Boston and New York, 1916-19). The classical
story of the case is John M. Shirley, *The Dartmouth College Causes and the
Supreme Court of the United States* (St. Louis, 1879). For the operation of
the decision see Thomas M. Cooley, *A Treatise on the Constitutional Limitations Which Rest upon the Legislative Power of the States of the American
Union*, 175, 268, 316, 343, 360, 388, 392, 403, 502, 836 (Boston, 1903). The
effect has been much diminished by constitutional and legislative reservations
of power to limit and regulate corporate franchises.

roads and the flow of population thereupon. The old fashion of building railroads from paid-in stock, never extensive, already had practically disappeared. The only remaining source of ready money was the funds of adventitious capitalists willing to gamble on the future of the Northwest. They did not make their game on any narrow discounts. In some instances not over forty per cent of the face of the bonds sold was applied to construction. By midsummer of 1873 there was a bonded debt of $54,500,000 and $20,000,000 worth of stock liabilities raised the " capitalization " to $74,500,000 — about $48,000 per mile. The business of the roads had not met expectations. The promoters forgot that Minnesota railroads could carry, besides local traffic, only passengers and goods arriving in and departing from the state. There was as yet no farther West to pour its grain, lumber, and live stock across the state. High rates discouraged travel and shipments. On the other hand, operating expenses were heavier than estimated. The roads had been hastily built, with sharp curves and heavy grades. The rails were mostly fifty pounds to the yard and had been bought at ninety dollars per ton. Operating expenses in 1873 rose to eighty per cent of gross earnings. The balance was but $1,400,000. The reader can easily figure out how far that sum would go toward paying interest and dividends on the capitalization mentioned. In the collapse of 1873–74 the Minnesota railroads went down to disaster.[31]

The commissioners read the signs of the times and, aware that their authority to enforce rates and fares unacceptable to the companies was doubtful, were not inclined to drastic procedure. The companies, under the circumstances, wanted no trouble with the commissioners, who might annoy if they could not compel. The result was a truce. The schedules

[31] Davis' message, January 8, 1875, in *Executive Documents*, 1874, vol. I, p. 30; Railroad Commissioner, *Reports*, 1872, p. 194; 1873, pp. xx, xxiii, xxiv, lvi–lxxi; 1875, p. 4.

of reasonable maximum charges published on July 24 made
no sweeping changes in tariffs for the several roads. Before
many weeks of the remaining five months of the year had
passed it became evident that the new law had not met public expectations. The reduction of rates at some stations
was too slight materially to advance the price of wheat in
the respective neighborhoods and the increase of rates at a
few places had only increased dissatisfaction. The changes
made had not put an end to discriminations, more offensive
than mere excessive rates.[32] The attitude of the public was
represented by the action of the Patrons of Husbandry. The
order had increased its Minnesota granges in number
between August 2, 1873, and September 1, 1874, from 327
to 538 and its membership to some twenty thousand. The
state grange held its annual meeting at Mankato on December 15. In his annual address the master stated that the law
of 1874, instead of affording relief to the farmers, had been
turned against them and made an agent of greater oppression. One of the resolutions adopted by the grange declared
the law to be useless to the people and vexatious to the railroads and, in the name of twenty thousand voters, demanded
the passage of a law which should guarantee cheap transportation for wheat. Another resolution declared that,
while the order could not discuss politics or religion, each
grange had the right to discuss " all the great economic
questions of taxation " and that the members of the order
would exercise that right regardless of effects upon political
parties. In their first and only report to the legislature of
1875, the commissioners announced a general and willing
compliance with the law on the part of the companies. In
extenuation of their resolution not to order sweeping reductions of tariffs, they informed the legislature that two companies were in the hands of receivers, three had defaulted
in their interest, two had funded it for a term, and others had

---

[32] Railroad Commissioners, *Reports*, 1874, pp. 5–7; *St. Paul Dispatch*, July
25, 1874, p. 4; Buck, *Granger Movement*, 162–164.

assessed their stockholders in one way or another. New building had almost ceased. As all the roads were doing business at a loss, it was found impossible to adjust rates to income. As there were many who suspected, if they did not believe, that the commissioners had been in cahoots with the railroad magnates, the fate of the Granger law of 1874, which was costing the people more than ten thousand dollars a year in salaries and expenses, was easily foreseen.[33]

The Grangers of Minnesota reached their extreme expansion in September, 1874, when there began a decline in numbers which in two years left them with a little more than half their greatest number of local granges. By the time the legislature of 1875 met thirty-two granges had been lost, but as they were still strongly represented, it was necessary for the Republican majority to heed the late demands of the state grange for a new law. A change of heart on the part of the public as well as on that of the railroad companies soon became evident. The Blake case was still hung up in the Supreme Court of the United States. The act of 1871 for imposing legal charges had been a complete failure and that of 1874 had not bettered the situation. The report of the three commissioners had dispelled much hostility against, and had even aroused sympathy for, the bankrupt companies; and they, hard pressed to save their franchises, were in no mood to revive their former insolence toward the public. The result was a bill introduced into the House on February 18, 1875, in which no provisions were made for compulsory fares and rates and none to require the attorney-general to prosecute offenders. Citizens aggrieved were left to their common law remedies for extortions and discriminations, with the chances of paying costs. It is probable that the published experience of the Massachusetts railroad commission had brought to some minds the conviction that rail-

[33] Buck, *Granger Movement*, table following p. 58; *Anti-Monopolist* (St. Paul), December 24, 1874, p. 3; Railroad Commissioner, *Reports*, 1874, pp. 5-7, 11, 16; *General Laws*, 1874, p. 140.

road companies should be allowed to conduct their affairs
free from technical legal restraints and curbed only by the
moral force of public opinion, to which in the long run they
must yield. The new bill passed the House on February 27,
with but slight opposition, by a vote of 67 to 28. It met with
lively resistance in the Senate from Amos Coggswell and
others, who believed that the law of 1874 had not injured
the railroads. But the vote on passage stood 28 to 13. Governor Davis, who had mildly favored the old law, nevertheless gave the new one his approval. It was the last of the
Granger acts, if it may be rightly so considered.[34]

The new act provided for a single commissioner to be
elected for a two-year term. It was his duty to inspect the
physical condition of the roads, to investigate their finances,
and to " enquire into " any alleged violations of law by the
companies and their employees. He was given the same
power that judges had to issue subpoenas, to examine railroad officials and employees under oath, and to scrutinize
their books and papers. There were the usual articles forbidding extortionate charges for service and discriminations
as they might be judicially determined. If the act had been
framed by the attorneys of the companies it could hardly
have been more satisfactory to them. The commissioner
had power to hold down a swivel chair and transmit the
required annual reports of the railroad presidents or managers.[35]

Although the Blake case thus became a matter of indifference for the time being, the decision of the Supreme Court
of the United States in October, 1876, was of far-reaching
importance in connection with later findings of the court.
Whether by chance or purposely, the court delayed its action

[34] Buck, *Granger Movement*, 58 (table), 161, 163–165, 199; *House Journal*,
1876, pp. 288, 411, 505, 507; *Senate Journal*, 337, 338, 407–410; Davis' messages, January 8, 1875, January 7, 1876, in *Executive Documents*, 1874, vol. 1,
pp. 29–31; 1875, vol. 1, p. 7; *Saint Paul Pioneer*, 1875: March 3, pp. 1, 2; 4,
p. 2; *Saint Paul Press*, 1875: March 3, pp. 1, 2; 4, pp. 1, 4.
[35] *General Laws*, 1875, pp. 135–138.

in this case until it had disposed of one arising in Illinois involving the question at issue. A citizen named Munn questioned the right of the legislature to fix charges for the use of warehouse facilities. It was the judgment of the court that when an owner devotes his property to a public use, he thereby submits to be controlled by the public, that a state may regulate such use, and that the legislature is the sole judge of the propriety and extent of such regulation.[36]

[36] Munn v. Illinois, 4 *Otto*, 113–154 (94 *United States*); Winona and St. Peter Railroad Company v. Blake, 4 *Otto*, 180 (94 *United States*); Buck, *Granger Movement*, 206–214.

III. PROGRESS AND POLITICS, 1870–76

THE year 1870, which was marked by the opening of a new state administration, was not signalized by any crisis but, as the ninth decennial census was taken in that year and the state bureau of statistics was in operation, it is convenient to take a brief inventory of Minnesota. It is a frequent and just complaint that older historians filled their pages with accounts of great military campaigns, of battles and sieges, and of the politics of sovereigns and courtiers, as if the mass of the people had no history. A better fashion has arrived. It is proposed in the following paragraphs to indicate who the Minnesota people were, how they were employed, and something of their general culture at a time when they had just emerged from pioneer conditions and the effects of the Civil and Indian wars.

The total population was 439,706 — an increase of 267,683 since 1860 — constituting 82,471 families housed in 81,140 dwellings. From a place at the bottom of the list of states in point of population Minnesota had risen in twenty years to number twenty-eight in a list of thirty-seven. Of 305,568 persons over ten years of age, 132,657 were engaged in gainful occupations — 75,157 in agriculture, 28,330 in professions and personal services, 10,582 in trade and transportation, and 18,588 in manufactures. The dwellers in cities and villages were 112,008, leaving a rural population of 327,698. There were 96,793 children in schools and but 12,747 adults who could not read and 24,413 who could not write. For 877 churches there were 582 edifices with seats for 158,266; but many religious meetings were held in schoolhouses and dwellings. Ninety-five newspapers were distributing 9,543,656 copies annually. There were 1,412 libraries with 360,810 volumes. Of the total population —

439,706 — 279,009 were native born, 160,697 were foreign born, and 285,516 had one or both parents of foreign nationality.[1] Of the foreign-born, 46,606 were from British countries, including 21,303 Irish. The Scandinavian immigrants numbered 59,390 and the German, 48,457. The commissioner of statistics congratulated the state on these accessions of " the best blood of Europe ": the Scandinavians, honest and laborious, with sympathy for popular institutions; the Germans, " with an intellectual organism in which the massive properties and the tough Saxon fibre needed for laborious research are mingled with the finer qualities of the musician and the prophetic spirit of the poet "; and the Irish, with their " muscular power and gifts of a warm and impassioned nature." [2] Of the 279,000 native-born people, 126,000, in round numbers, had been born in the state; 81,000 had come from the North Atlantic states — 39,500 from New York alone; the North Central region had sent 64,500 — 24,000 of them from Wisconsin.[3] An American commonwealth truly, with an infusion to the amount of thirty-seven per cent of the most virile, industrious, ambitious, and moral of foreigners, who had come from far-off countries to a free land to make homes and raise families. Such a people, native and foreign born, needed no missionaries to convert them to a true faith or to teach them how to plant and organize the institutions of civilization. Indeed, they had only to build on foundations already laid. There was, however, no little competition between emissaries of the different churches to obtain the first footholds in the settlements, in some cases carried to an excess. But that was better than the absence of rivalry.

The area of settlement had not greatly extended since the census of 1860. The main body of the population still

---

[1] *United States Census*, 1870, *Population*, 3, 176–182, 299, 394, 396, 474, 482, 506, 595, 670; Robinson, *Agriculture in Minnesota*, 254.
[2] Commissioner of Statistics, *Reports*, 1870, pp. 125–127.
[3] *United States Census*, 1870, *Population*, 313, 328–335.

resided east of the fourth principal meridian and south of
the sixth standard parallel — roughly, east of New Ulm and
south of St. Cloud. There were eleven cities and villages of
2,500 or more — none north of Stillwater except Duluth
and none west of Mankato. About twenty-six million acres,
half of the area of the state in round numbers, had been
surveyed, fifteen million had been granted to railroads,
half a million to the state, and twelve and one-half million
had gone into private hands. Of the 6,483,828 acres constituting 46,500 farms, 2,322,102 were improved and about
1,725,111 were under cultivation. Sixty per cent of this
cultivated area was devoted to wheat. The total yield for
1870 was 18,866,073 bushels.[4]

The lumber manufacture was still in the lead. The census report gives the number of mills as 207, employing
2,952 persons and a capital of $3,311,140, paying wages
amounting to $880,028, using material valued at $2,193,965,
and issuing a product worth $4,299,162. The flour manufac-
ture came next in importance, with a capital of $2,900,915,
216 mills, 790 employees, materials valued at $6,090,006,
and an output worth $1,289,665. The estimated total wealth
of the state was $228,909,590, but the valuation of all the
real and personal property for taxation was but $84,135,332.[5]

To one looking back, as can the writer, on the events of
the six-year period beginning with 1870, none are more
conspicuous than the rapid extension of railroads in the
first three years and the economic and social consequences,
direct and indirect, thereof. The completion of the road
from St. Paul to Duluth in 1870 brought the former city
almost as near to the Atlantic seaboard as Chicago and gave
to Minnesota grain and lumber and to eastern coal and merchandise a continuous waterway between " The Head of the

[4] Robinson, *Agriculture in Minnesota*, 47, 63, 75, 102, 250–254; *United States Census*, 1870, *Population*, 176–182; *Wealth and Industry*, 180; Commissioner of Statistics, *Reports*, 1870, pp. 149–151; 1871, pp. 12, 30.
[5] *United States Census*, 1870, *Wealth and Industry*, 10, 598, 612.

Lake " and New York City.[6] The location of the Lake
Superior terminus of this road was a question of importance.
The natural site was on the south side of the mouth of the
St. Louis River, where an unlimited extent of level land
offers an ideal terrain. But the Minnesota interest was
strong enough to lead the track along the left bank of the
St. Louis River to the rocky hillsides of the north shore of
the bay. On these the city of Duluth was laid out and settlement was invited. As if by magic the new city sprang into
life. Wealth and population have ever since continued to
flood in and doubtless one of the great inland cities of the
continent will be built at " The Head of the Lake."

In the following year, 1871, the main line of the St. Paul
and Pacific, now the Great Northern, was pushed to Breckenridge on the Red River of the North and the " River Division " of the Milwaukee and St. Paul, following the west
bank of the Mississippi except between St. Paul and Hastings, was built to Winona, whence a prolongation financed
by the same company and completed in 1872 extended
farther down the river to La Crescent. At Hastings the first
iron railroad bridge in Minnesota, completed in 1871, carried the track across the Mississippi. In the same year the
Northern Pacific, which had been surveyed the previous
summer, was built from Duluth to Moorhead on the Red
River of the North. Meanwhile the Southern Minnesota
was extended to the Blue Earth, at Winnebago, and the
Winona and St. Peter was prolonged to the Minnesota River
and, the following year, on to the Dakota line. At the close
of the season of 1872 Minnesota had 1,906 miles of completed railroads, of which seventy per cent had been built
in four years.[7]

As the railroad lines extended, the prairie schooner, the
stagecoach, and the steamboat lost importance. The steam

[6] Railroad Commissioner, *Reports*, 1871, p. 39.
[7] Railroad Commissioner, *Reports*, 1871, p. 75; 1872, pp. 8–14, 19, 42; Commissioner of Statistics, *Reports*, 1872, p. 103.

cars ran every day and their arrivals and deliveries were punctual. Journeys of days were shortened to hours. Grain and dairy products, which previously could stand but fifty or sixty miles of transportation to primary markets, could now be hauled hundreds of miles, and heavy commodities like coal and lumber could be shipped out in return. The movement of merchandise and mails was greatly expedited. The opening of new areas of free land to homesteaders had much to do with raising the average yearly increment of population from about 27,000 in the decade 1860–70 to more than 32,000 a year between 1870 and 1875, which brought the total population to 597,407 in 1875. The effect upon the distribution of the population was quite as notable. The old river counties and those next behind them received goodly additions and population now flowed past them into the " back counties." The cultivated area of the state, which was not much over 600,000 acres in 1865, was trebled in the next five years and was enlarged to 2,816,413 acres in 1875. While the multiplication of farms was thus rapid, equally so was the planting of villages along the railroad lines.[8]

Before the extension of railroads beyond the Big Woods settlers were reluctant to move out on the prairie and preferred the long and costly task of converting forested sections into farms. They feared the fierce winds and the terrible prairie fires. There was no timber for fuel or building except in the slight fringes along the watercourses. In some districts very deep wells had to be dug or bored or driven. Because the prairie was bare of trees, many believed that the soil was so poor that trees could not grow; they did not conceive that a soil which could yield such good grass and so splendid a show of wild flowers was not barren. But the lure of free or cheap land soon gave opportunity for learning the attractions and advantages of the prairie. Settlers who arrived at their claims early in

[8] Commissioner of Statistics, Reports, 1869, p. 5; 1870, p. 12; 1875, pp. 14, 118, 119, 130–132.

DULUTH IN 1872

[From a photograph in the museum of the Minnesota Historical Society.]

the season often planted a crop of sod corn and potatoes by dropping the seed into clefts made with an ax. Of self-sown pasturage there was no lack and there was plenty of good forage for animals in the tall grasses of the bottoms or in the shorter growths of the uplands to be had for the cutting. Before the snows should fly the farmer had good time to run up a " shack " or, what was far more comfortable, a sod house and a similar shelter for his animals. Happy months and sometimes years even were passed in those primitive dwellings, in which one might have seen the latest magazines, good books, and violins and pianos. In from three to five years the settler would have his farm as completely subdued and improved as that of the farmer in the timber after twenty years of exhausting labor. Prairie farming began as early as possible in the season with breaking the tough sod with stout plows, drawn by teams of six or eight oxen, which turned over a broad but shallow furrow. This " breaking " was commonly done for an agreed price per acre by persons owning the equipment. In the fall back-furrowing followed, which added to the rotten sod a scale of subsoil. In the following spring regular cultivation began.

It was not necessary for the thrifty prairie farmer to live long in his shack or sod house. The managers of sash and blind factories in the principal river towns early developed a plan for furnishing all the timber, boards, shingles, and finishings for houses, as well as the doors and windows and their frames, and shipping them out in carload lots. On a ready foundation the balloon frame of light timbers, nailed together without mortise or tenon, was soon run up, and the roof boards and shingles were nailed on. The rough sheathing of the walls next went on, often reënforced by a layer of heavy tarred paper. Outside of these was put the siding, which had been planed smooth at the factory. The frames for doors and windows were next put into their places and the moldings were run around the openings. When the floors were laid, the stairs built, and the doors and windows adjusted, the house was habitable for summer weather. Plastering followed at convenience or, if materials were not at hand, linings of building paper were used instead. With air-tight wood stoves or base-burning coal stoves the family was comfortable even when the fiercest of cold waves swept over the prairie.

There was abundance of staple provender for man and beast in the youthful state, but the shortage of fruit was much felt by immigrants from the older states. Apples were more missed than any other. The primitive crab apple, educated into the pretty transcendent and the duchess, served for jellies, preserves, and pies, but the Rhode Island greening, the Spitzenberg, the northern spy, and the winesap had to be imported. The native wild plums, generally astringent and puckery, were no substitute for the green gage. The peach could not stand the extremes of temperature of the high latitude. The immigration agents did not emphasize these drawbacks in their illustrated pamphlets. It ought, however, to be added that the abundance of native berries went far to mitigate the shortage of fruit. Wild cranberries were plentiful in some districts, but the supplementary sugar had to be brought from the far south, except in the hardwood region, where the hard maple supplied it. More widely available were the wild strawberry, the high bush cranberry, the elderberry, the raspberries, black and red, the huckleberry, and the blueberry, all delicious in their seasons. The immigration agents did not forget to mention these.[9] The Minnesota bill of fare was enriched by a profusion of vegetables, suitable to a temperate climate, which grew in great luxuriance in the "black dirt" on alluvial areas or, as in the case of the Irish potato, on sandy soils. The young state was

[9] Frequent interviews of the author with early settlers, in particular with Morris B. Foster, a graduate of the University of Michigan who took up a homestead in Renville County, on which he still resides. He once walked twenty-one miles to get the share of his breaking plow sharpened. For an account of the wealthy apple, discovered among many seedlings by Peter M.

A TYPICAL PIONEER SOD HOUSE

A TYPICAL PIONEER FRAME HOUSE

[From photographs in the museum of the Minnesota Historical Society.]

rich in soil and forests and waters and her climate was favorable to health and activity. Her people, released from the strain and burden of war, not unduly burdened with taxes, and busied with their industries, looked forward with hope and confidence to continued prosperity.

Physiographers have not yet agreed as to what causes either prevented the growth or led to the denudation of forests over many millions of acres of land in the North Central States. Throughout whole counties and groups of counties in Minnesota away from watercourses there stood not a tree nor a stump to divert the plow from a continuous furrow from section to section. Recognizing the facts that prairie lands were cheap, that they did not need to be cleared before cultivation, and that they were generally sufficiently undulating to allow easy run-off of surface waters, enterprising citizens entered upon a new kind of farming, which was soon called " bonanza farming " from a word descriptive of rich western mines. This plan implied the acquisition or control by purchase or rent of thousands of acres of prairie land, chiefly railroad sections, the breaking of it as rapidly as possible, and its cultivation by gangs of hired men and machinery. The foreman of the bonanza farm was, as a rule, a man of energy and of first-rate business talent. It chanced that in these years the gang plow, the twelve-foot seeder, the harvester and self-binding reaper, and the giant threshing machine driven by steam were evolved out of earlier types adapted to the uses of the little eastern farm. With such apparatus, the bonanza farm was operated with great efficiency. At plowing time forty or more teams following a leader might turn over as many furrows so long that it would be " nooning " when the plows came back. In harvest time as many reaping machines might be seen deployed en échelon, like the batteries of an army corps, moving away until lost

Gideon on Lake Minnetonka, see Gideon to John H. Stevens, June 16, 1873, in the *Farmers' Union* (Minneapolis), June 28, 1873, p. 1. The only poor quality that the apple has is that it does not keep long.

from sight. The giant threshing machines made short work of separating the grain from the straw, after which the farm gang dispersed, with the exception of a few men who remained to care for the animals during the winter months.[10]

The principal crop of Minnesota from the beginning of cultivation had been spring wheat, which experiment had proved to be adapted to the soil and climate. In 1860 the crop was reported to be five million bushels and in 1865, nine and a half million bushels, at twenty-three bushels to the acre. Five years later it stood at nearly fifteen and a half millions, which figure was doubled in 1875.[11] The problem of storing so much wheat was solved in a way unknown to eastern farmers. The small cultivator could not afford to build a granary sufficient to hold his crop; the bonanza farmer might, but generally he preferred to market his crop as soon as it was gathered. The grain elevator came in to accommodate both. This tall, ungainly structure soon appeared at every railroad station in the wheat belts. Above a main quadrilateral structure, built without frame, of planks piled up flat and spiked together, towered a cupola story much narrower. In flour mills there had been in use since the time of Oliver Evans an apparatus for elevating meal from the grinding floor to the bolting floor. It consisted of an endless belt of leather armed with metallic cups inclosed in a tight casing, either vertical or inclined, moving over pulleys at top and bottom. The apparatus was easily adapted to the grain storehouses and, perhaps because of the novelty of the device, they came to be called " elevators." The grain dumped into the boot was carried up into the cupola and thence spouted to the storage bins. A steam

10 Personal inquiry and observation of the author. For an account of the Dalrymple farm near St. Paul, see Pennock Pusey, " Farming That Pays," in the *Minnesota Monthly*, 1: 218 (July, 1869). Accounts of the Grandin farm and others in the Red River Valley in North Dakota are given in George N. Lamphere, " History of Wheat Raising in the Red River Valley," in *Minnesota Historical Collections*, 10: 21–23 (part 1), and in Commissioner of Statistics, *Reports*, 1877, pp. 17, 160.

11 Commissioner of Statistics, *Reports*, 1871, p. 16; 1876, p. 22.

engine, or in some cases a horse, operated the simple machinery. On one side of the building was a platform provided with scales for weighing, onto which the farmer drove his load of wheat unsacked; on the other side was a railroad " siding," on which stood the railroad car while being filled for shipment out. But for the elevator it would have been impossible to handle the Minnesota wheat crops.

The sites for the elevators were fixed by the active railroad officials, who, along with friends whom they pleased to " let in on the ground floor," made comfortable little fortunes by operating in the town lots. The rapidity with which some of these station villages grew was often marvelous and always very agreeable to lucky proprietors. The order in which there rose about the railroad " depot " the elevator, the store, the blacksmith shop, the saloon, the school, the church, and the post office became almost stereotyped. In a single season all these would sometimes appear. The development of these railroad towns was disastrous to many older villages, planted at what seemed before the railroad surveys to be points of vantage. In some cases, when these were not too far from new towns at the railroad stations, they were literally put on wheels and moved thither. Some well-built towns farther away, such as Garden City and Mantorville, were gradually deserted and their buildings afterwards actually rotted down. About these railroad villages the lands were rapidly taken up and put under cultivation. The prices paid, varying according to distances out, well exemplified the doctrine of economic rent in one of its phases.

Grain delivered to the station elevators directly from the threshing machine frequently contained dirt, seeds of cockle or other weeds, and a mixture of grains. If it was perfectly clean it might be deficient in weight or color. Buyers accordingly " docked " for estimated screenings, light weight, and dull color. As buyers generally enjoyed a monopoly advantage at the station, it was easy to suspect them of excessive dockages and presently loud complaints were made for public regulation. The legislature of Minnesota in 1885 provided for a system of public grading, which, with necessary modifications, is still in operation. Beginning with perfectly clean grain, sound and of full weight and bright color, as number 1, inferior grades are distinguished according to their departure from the standard.[12]

The evolution of the railroad station elevator was presently followed by that of the " terminal elevator " at points of concentration for export, of which those of Duluth and Minneapolis were on the greatest scale. Built to house a million or more bushels of grain, they had their cupolas raised to three stories. The top story contained cleaning machines which took out dirt and screenings. Below them were hoppers resting on the levers of weigh scales and still below them was a story devoted to conveyors and spouting for the distribution of the grain to the various bins of the main building. The primitive screw conveyor, adapted from the flour mill long ago, gave place to the belt conveyor without raised edges, which, moved at a high speed, carries its load hundreds of feet. It was at the terminal elevators that dirt and screenings were cleaned out and inferior grades were advanced with considerable profit to the operators. In some of them apparatus was installed for drying grain which had come in damp.

There remains to be mentioned a circumstance which had much to do with expanding the area of wheat culture in Minnesota. Spring wheat had long been grown in the older states but its flour, although equally nutritious, was inferior in color and clearness to that of winter wheat and therefore was in light demand in the great markets. That relation was reversed in the early seventies by the adoption of a manufacturing device. In the primitive process of milling the meal delivered by the ingenious furrows of the millstone was carried to an upper " bolting floor," so-called, by means of an elevator such as gave name to the storage and handling estab-

[12] *General Laws*, 1885, pp. 136–148. See also *post*, p. 208.

lishment already described. On the bolting floor a proper number of sieves, called "bolts," with polygonal sections separated the meal into flour, bran, and a large residuum called "middlings." These middlings, by an improvement on this process, were put between another set of mill-stones and a quantity of inferior flour was separated from the resulting meal. In the case of spring wheat it had been discovered that the middlings, although inferior in appearance, contained the most nutritious elements of the grain.[13] French millers were already in possession of a rude apparatus for treating middlings so as to recover these elements. In 1870 Edmund N. La Croix, a French immigrant by way of Canada, constructed one in a Minneapolis mill operated by George H. Christian, who had for some time been studying the "middlings purifier." The machine was rapidly improved upon, chiefly through the ingenuity and persistence of Christian. The middlings purifier came into general use and revolutionized spring-wheat milling. Spring wheat was now "king" in the Northwest and the Minnesota "patent flours" took the highest place in eastern and, eventually, in foreign markets. An enterprising employee of Christian's, George A. Smith, obtained a patent for an ancillary attachment consisting of a set of traveling brushes to keep the bolting cloth of the machine from clogging with dust. It was the last increment needed to perfect the apparatus. For a time there was an advance of from one to three dollars a barrel in the selling price of spring-wheat flour and a premium of one dollar a barrel over winter-wheat flour. The millers were somewhat tardily compelled to hand on to the farmers a part of their profits and spring wheat between 1870 and 1880 gained a permanent advance of twenty per cent. Minnesota farmers now had a market for a grain suited to the climate and soil of the state, which, but for this revolution in milling, if produced at all, must have been marketed at inferior prices.

[13] From the personal experience of the author in a milling business.

About 1874 Christian, alert for possible improvements in flour manufacture, learned of the use in Germany of metallic rollers running in pairs for crushing or cracking the wheat berry before the finer grinding by the immemorial millstones. He installed one or more pairs, manufactured of chilled iron at Ansonia, Connecticut, to his order, and obtained promising results. Improved apparatus for cleaning wheat was introduced about this time and there was a general perfection of machinery in great mills, especially adapting them to the milling of the hard red wheat of Minnesota and the Dakotas. The activity of men of great energy and foresight soon placed the city of Minneapolis in the forefront of flour manufacture, a prominence she has ever since maintained. The most prominent of these men, without question, was General Cadwallader C. Washburn, a resident of Madison, Wisconsin, who built the great Washburn flour mills at the Falls of St. Anthony. Most fortunately the lake and rail transportation route via Duluth and Buffalo for Minnesota's flour and wheat prevented the railroad companies from absorbing the profits of her farming and milling. Later the completion of Canadian railroads secured to them rates more favorable than those enjoyed by some neighboring states.[14]

14 *Northwestern Miller*, 1877: February 16, p. 1; August 24, p. 7; 1879: February 21, pp. 118–122; 28, p. 133; March 21, p. 174; August 22, pp. 122, 124; September 5, pp. 153, 156; 1880: December 31, p. 436; 1882: October 6, p. 260; 1889: December 20, p. 705; George H. Christian, "Early Roller Mills and Their Treatment by the Railroads," in Return I. Holcombe and William H. Bingham, eds., *Compendium of History and Biography of Minneapolis and Hennepin County*, 160–162 (Chicago, 1914); Charles A. Pillsbury, "American Flour," in Chauncey M. Depew, ed., *One Hundred Years of American Commerce*, 1: 266–273 (New York, 1895); George D. Rogers, "History of Flour Manufacture in Minnesota," in *Minnesota Historical Collections*, 10: 47–49 (part 1); William C. Edgar, *The Story of a Grain of Wheat*, 149–172 (New York, 1903); Peter T. Dondlinger, *The Book of Wheat; an Economic History and Practical Manual of the Wheat Industry*, 267–271 (New York, 1908); Robinson, *Agriculture in Minnesota*, 77; George H. Christian to the author, June 4, 1906; interviews with Christian, recorded in the author's notebooks, 3: 41; William R. Fieldhouse, "History of the Flour Milling Industry of Minneapolis," 12, 20, 23, 27 (University of Minnesota, 1916); Charles B. Kuhlmann, "The Development of Flour Milling in Minneapolis," 30, 40–49 (University of Minnesota, 1920). The last two works are manuscript theses, copies of which are in the libraries of the university and the Minnesota His-

The year 1873 was marked by certain disastrous visitations and by a turn in the tide of abundant prosperity which had been enjoyed since the close of the war. On January 7, a snowstorm struck the western border of Minnesota and swept over the southern half of the state in the course of the following night. This was a true "blizzard," a word connoting a heavy fall of dry snow minutely granular — "as fine as flour" — driven by a furious wind and filling the whole atmosphere so completely as to cause absolute darkness. The cold was not excessive, the temperature at St. Paul being but fourteen degrees below the Fahrenheit zero. It was twenty degrees below at Chicago. The weather of the morning had been so fine that many people had ventured far from home to trade in the towns, to haul wood, to go to mill, or to pay

torical Society. Perhaps the best source of all is the article by Legrand G. Powers, "Inventions in Flour Making Machinery and the Prices of Wheat, Flour, etc.," in Minnesota, Bureau of Labor Statistics, *Reports*, 1891–92, pp. 156–222. Powers was commissioner of the bureau. Note especially the tables showing the increase in prices of spring wheat and flour due to the new processes. See also the article by Christian in the *Pioneer Press* (St. Paul and Minneapolis), April 14, 1877, p. 6. An unpublished "Early History of Washburn-Crosby Company, 1866–90," which the author was permitted to read, gives due credit to the La Croix brothers and to Christian for the new process grinding and for the first experiment in rollers. The prominent part taken by General C. C. Washburn in the adoption of the roller gradual-reduction process is emphasized and credit is given to William de la Barre, who, after a visit to Hungary, where he worked in a roller mill, made all the plans and specifications for the Washburn A mill as rebuilt. The name of the author of the work is not given, but it is known to be Lucille Brown, an employee of the company. The narrative is founded on printed material, which is not cited, and information furnished by the personnel, proprietary and other, of the company. A copy of an autobiographical sketch by Christian, in the possession of Mrs. George Chase Christian of Minneapolis, is in the Folwell Papers.

Smith organized a company for the manufacture of the purifier and demanded of all millers using the process a royalty of $250 a run of stones. He brought suit against one company and notified others that they would be prosecuted unless they paid the sum demanded. Meanwhile another patentee of a purifier, W. F. Cochrane, appeared and demanded of the millers $2,000 a run of stones. He brought suit against Christian and Company, whose cause members of the state association of millers took up. The patent was declared invalid by the United States circuit court. Smith, who had let his claims rest pending the outcome of Cochrane's suit against Christian and Company, now combined his company with that of Cochrane and formed the Consolidated Middlings Purifier Company, which prosecuted Smith's claims. In the end the Consolidated company reduced the royalty demanded from $250 to $25 a run of stones and the millers agreed to pay it to avoid further litigation.

visits. On their return they were overtaken. In the darkness they wandered from the roads and, ignorant of the devices of protection known to *voyageurs,* many perished in the fierce blasts which swept the prairie. According to early rumors eight hundred so lost their lives, but when the state statistician came to sift the testimony he could not find that more than seventy had perished. Many more, of course, were frostbitten and maimed. The legislature of 1873 at the instance of Governor Austin made an appropriation of five thousand dollars for relief of the sufferers. The sum of $3,385 was distributed to ninety-four persons in thirty-four counties, an average of $36 per person.[15] About the middle of June came the first of the grasshopper invasions, which are discussed in the following chapter, and finally, on September 18, 1873, the collapse of the banking house of Jay Cooke and Company, of national reputation and affiliations, precipitated a financial stricture and panic throughout the whole country. The depression resulting from the panic was less ruinous to the people of Minnesota, busy with opening new farms and gathering harvests, than to those of older states. Still, prices for their produce were low in the sluggish markets and the costs of handling and transportation were high, so that they felt themselves poorer than they really were. Railroad building in the state had ceased and several years passed before it was resumed and industry was revived to its usual proportions.[16]

[15] *Saint Paul Pioneer,* January 9-15, 1873, *passim; Mankato Weekly Review,* February 4, 1873, p. 1; *Saint Peter Tribune,* 1873: January 15, p. 3; 22, p. 3; 29, p. 2; *American Annual Cyclopædia,* 1873, p. 509; Commissioner of Statistics, *Reports,* 1873, p. 298; Austin's messages of January 15 and March 6, in *Senate Journal,* 1873, pp. 378–381; *House Journal,* 515–517; Austin's message of January 9, 1874, in *Executive Documents,* 1873, p. 26; *General Laws,* 1873, p. 254. There is a graphic account of the blizzard by W. A. Peterson in John A. Brown, ed., *History of Cottonwood and Watonwan Counties,* 1: 305–310 (Indianapolis, 1916). See also Alexander Berghold, *Prairie-Rosen,* 313, 337 (New Ulm, 1880), and Victor E. Lawson and Martin E. Tew, eds., *History of Kandiyohi County,* 46 (St. Paul, 1905). Richard Pfefferle gave his recollections of the blizzard of 1873 and that of February, 1866, in which a company of United States cavalry was overtaken and Captain Fields and four men perished, in a letter to the author, July 19, 1920.

[16] An account of the panic of 1873 and its effects upon the country at large is given in Dunning, *Reconstruction,* 235–237.

In pursuance of constitutional authority, the legislature of 1875 provided for an enumeration of the inhabitants of the state in that year to be made by the assessors of towns, villages, and cities. The results appear in the seventh annual report of the commissioner of statistics. The total number of inhabitants was 597,407, with a remarkable division of sexes — 315,976 males and 281,286 females, with 145 unknown. The native-born population was 376,000, of whom 205,949 had been born in Minnesota. The New England states sent 29,657, New York 41,344, Wisconsin 30,834, Ohio 13,320, Illinois 12,574, and Pennsylvania 12,044. The foreign-born numbered 217,429. The Scandinavians stood first with a total of 88,325, Germany and Austria next with 67,030, then the English-speaking countries with 52,932. A remainder of 9,142 came from other countries.[17]

The vacancy caused by the death of United States Senator Daniel S. Norton on July 14, 1870, was not filled until January 17, 1871, when the legislature elected Ozora P. Stearns for the term expiring on March 3 following and William Windom for the usual term of six years as his successor. The election of Judge Stearns was merely a compliment to a worthy public man and a prominent Republican. As to Windom, there was nothing to do but to record the undisputed preference of Republicans throughout the state. He had come to Minnesota from his native state of Ohio at the age of twenty-eight and had settled in Winona in 1855. He had taught school, studied law, and had a little legal practice under an able preceptor. Having been brought up under the discipline of the Society of Friends, William Windom possessed in an eminent degree the simple, courteous, unaffected manner of that people. Without practicing any of the arts of the sycophant or the demagogue, he presently won a strong

[17] Constitution, article 4, section 23; *General Laws*, 1875, pp. 161–164; Commissioner of Statistics, *Reports*, 1875, pp. 110–135; 1876, pp. 293–304. The distribution of the population in 1875 is shown on the map opposite p. 74, *post*.

body of clients and supporters. His district, the first, sent him to Congress in 1858 and gave him four successive reëlections, so that he had a service of ten consecutive years.[18] The same qualities which gained him the support of his neighbors won for him the good will and respect of colleagues in Congress. His discretion, fair-mindedness, and practical sense secured all reasonable demands of his constituents. With Ramsey reseated in the Senate and Donnelly utterly discredited by his dalliance with the Democracy, there was none other than Windom among the Republican leaders thought of for the vacancy. No second balloting was necessary in the caucus, which gave him a virtually unanimous nomination. His long acquaintance in the capital city and among public men and his ripened experience in legislation gave him immediate prestige in the Senate. In the national Congress, as well as in many state legislatures, the " burning question " of the early seventies was how to regulate railroads. To this Windom presently addressed himself. His preliminary studies convinced him that the tyranny of " railroad combines " must be mitigated, if not destroyed, by waterway competition. On December 17, 1872, he was elected chairman of the select committee of the Senate on transportation routes to the seaboard and he devoted to the problem before the committee for many months his extraordinary intelligence and power of analysis. The report submitted by him in April, 1874, filling two octavos, was the first great and thorough discussion of the subject. One colleague, Senator Hoar, did not hesitate to praise it as " the most valuable state paper of modern times." Disposed by nature and training to attend to matters of present and practical importance, in this discussion he was carried by irresistible logic to announce conclusions and projects whose consummation lay in the future. It took Congress thirteen years to come up to his high ground and establish an

---

[18] *House Journal*, 1871, pp. 38, 46; *Senate Journal*, 29; *Memorial Tributes to the Character and Public Services of William Windom, together with His Last Address*, 1–5 (Cambridge, 1891) ; *Legislative Manual*, 1925, p. 116.

MINNESOTA IN 1875

Showing county lines, railroads, and the distribution of population by minor civil divisions according to the state census. Each dot represents 100 people or major fraction thereof. Solid black areas represent cities or villages of over 350 population.

0   20   40   60
SCALE OF MILES

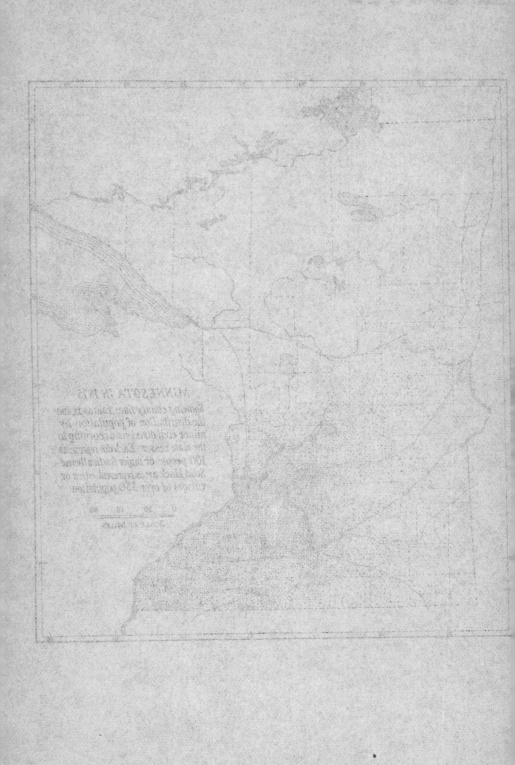

interstate commerce commission as the executive bureau of commerce which Senator Windom recommended.[19]

During the six-year period now under consideration the Republican party held its accustomed majority in Minnesota, but not without question and anxiety. Dissatisfaction with the reconstruction policy continued through Grant's first administration and charges of fraud and corruption tolerated by party chiefs impelled many Republicans to oppose the president's reëlection and to seek for a successor who would restore local government in the South and invite the southern people to reunion by peaceful and amicable conciliation. A convention of these dissentients, including a volunteer delegation from Minnesota, held in Cincinnati on May 1, 1872, proclaimed the organization of a separate party called the " Liberal Republican " and put in nomination for the presidency Horace Greeley, long and widely known for his extreme leniency toward the South. It was hoped that the Democrats would make no nomination or, if they did, that great numbers of them would vote for Greeley in expectation of some share in the spoils of political warfare. The Liberal Republican movement spread to Minnesota, where it found no more ardent advocate than Ignatius Donnelly. But the Republicans of Minnesota were not yet ready for a sugarplum policy toward the South and they had little confidence that the probable cabinet and other appointees of Greeley would give the country a more honest administration than that of Grant. The November elections in Minnesota gave

[19] Hall, *Observations*, 72; *Memorial Tributes to Windom*, 7; 42 Congress, 3 session, *Senate Journal*, 75 (serial 1544); *Transportation-Routes to the Seaboard* (43 Congress, 1 session, *Senate Reports*, no. 307, part 1 — serial 1588). The salient features of the report are: (1) an argument for the expansion of the power of Congress " to regulate commerce among the several states " (pages 79–99); power to regulate implies power to facilitate the construction of means of transportation; (2) an assertion of the power of Congress to fix rates for services (pages 122–140); (3) a consideration of a proposal for government ownership of one or more railways from the Mississippi to the Atlantic (pages 140–161); (4) advocacy of the construction and improvement of waterways, with a proposition for four routes to be called " the Mississippi," " the Northern," " the Central," and " the Southern " (pages 161–234). A summary is given on pages 240–254. See also map 4.

55,708 votes to Grant and 35,211 to Greeley, indicating but few defections from the old Republican ranks and a large Democratic vote for Greeley.[20]

In the first year of Governor Austin's term occurred an event little marked by the large number of younger citizens of the state or by recent immigrants; but it touched the hearts of the smaller number of early pioneers. That was the sudden death in New York City, on November 9, 1870, of Joseph Renshaw Brown. At the Masonic burial at Henderson, Minnesota, on the seventeenth General Henry H. Sibley, his ancient friend and comrade, delivered the funeral address. So closed the career on earth, at the age of sixty-five, of one of the most notable characters in Minnesota history.[21]

The period of Governor Austin's administration was unhappily diversified by the impeachment of the state treasurer, William Seeger, for corrupt conduct in the handling of funds. After appearing for trial Seeger resigned his office to the governor, saying in his letter that the state had not lost a dollar by any act or omission of his (which was true) nor had he converted a farthing to his own use. He had been confident of a speedy trial and an honorable acquittal; but he was now assured that the trial might continue for some weeks and, as he had no five or six thousand dollars to pay the expenses, he preferred to quit the office. As it was the right of Seeger to resign his office, the governor felt obliged

---

[20] American Annual Cyclopædia, 1872, p. 777; Legislative Manual, 1873, pp. 120–122; 1925, p. 115; Eugene V. Smalley, The Republican Manual; History, Principles, Early Leaders, Achievements, of the Republican Party, 64–67 (New York, 1880); Buck, Agrarian Crusade, 11, 12, 14–17. For an inside view of the Cincinnati convention of 1872, see Henry Watterson, "Marse Henry"; an Autobiography, 1: 236–267 (New York, [1919]).

[21] Saint Paul Pioneer, 1870: November 12, p. 1; 13, p. 1; 15, p. 1; 17, p. 1. The Pioneer reports Sibley as speaking extemporaneously and gives no abstract of his address. Nathaniel West, in his Ancestry, Life, and Times of Hon. Henry Hastings Sibley, LL. D., 405 (St. Paul, 1889), quotes a portion of the address as an example of Sibley's " gift and aptitude of expression," which, " in thought and feeling, never desert him." He spoke, says West, " eloquently, simply, and tenderly . . . beside the coffin of the brave soldier he loves so well, the man whose virtues he delighted to extol, his life-long friend." Some biographical incidents of Joseph R. Brown are given in the Appendix, no. 3, post.

to accept the resignation. The Senate court, however, ignored
it and proceeded with the trial at an adjourned session,
when Seeger pleaded guilty and was sentenced to disqualification for office. The horse having been stolen, the legislature — that of 1873 — proceeded to lock the stable door
by raising the salary of the state treasurer from the absurd
figure of $1,000 to $3,500 and by passing a rigid act for the
better administration of the department. The legislature also
submitted to the electors an amendment to section 12, article
9, of the state constitution forbidding any custodian of state
funds to deposit the funds in banks or elsewhere in his own
name or in any name but that of the State of Minnesota. At
the election on November 4, 1873, it was adopted by a vote
of 27,143 to 5,438. Why there should have been negative
votes is an enigma.[22]

Governor Austin's activities in the last year of his service
were varied by an effort to secure the release of four fellow
citizens from confinement in prison at Winnipeg, still called
Fort Garry. In the fall of 1871 an Englishman came to Minnesota representing himself as Lord Gordon Gordon, a nobleman highly connected and wealthy. The principal object of
his visit, it was announced, was to select a body of Minnesota land on which to plant a colony of Scotch. His bearing
and manners were such as to inspire confidence and the land
commissioner of the Northern Pacific Railroad Company
thought it worth while to take him out to see some of the
desirable lands which he had for sale. Some time was spent
in Otter Tail County, where the stranger marked on a map
numerous sections to be reserved for the colonists who would
be arriving the next season.

His lordship passed the winter of 1872 in New York City,
living in great style at the Metropolitan Hotel. Some stock-
jobbing operations of an extraordinary character led to his
arrest on a charge of swindling. After being liberated on

---

[22] *General Laws*, 1873, p. 95; 1874, p. 15. The Seeger impeachment is
treated more fully in the Appendix, no. 4, *post*.

bail to the amount of thirty-seven thousand dollars he fled to Canada, leaving his bondsmen in the lurch. It was ascertained in the early summer of 1873 that the fugitive was living in clover at or near Fort Garry, Manitoba. One of the bondsmen came to Minneapolis as a convenient point from which to carry out a scheme of seizing his person, which was believed, on legal advice, to be justifiable. The mayor of Minneapolis gave leave of absence to two members of his police force, who traveled to Winnipeg, seized the person of the noble lord, and with a swift team drove toward the international boundary. This outrage on a personage of importance, whose real character was as yet unknown at Fort Garry, aroused immediate and intense excitement. The customs officer at Pembina, who was also a justice of the peace, was apprised by telegraph and arrested the two policemen with their prisoner. He liberated the prisoner and sent the policemen back to be clapped into Fort Garry. Two Minnesota citizens, the Honorable Loren Fletcher, a member of the state legislature, who chanced to be in Winnipeg on private business, and George N. Merriam, were arrested and likewise incarcerated on a charge of aiding in an unlawful attempt to abduct a British citizen. The magistrate before whom the four were examined refused bail to all except Merriam.

Appeals were at once made to Governor Austin, who was the more willing to interfere because one of the two fellow travelers, Fletcher, was an old friend and former townsman. With his attorney-general he hastened to Washington and with the aid of Senator Ramsey stirred up the state department. The secretary interviewed the British ambassador, only to be politely informed that as a diplomatic official he could not interfere in a matter purely judicial. An appeal to the Canadian premier in Ottawa met with no better success. Meantime the three Minnesotans, indicted for a serious felony and denied bail and American counsel, were languishing in close jail confinement. In the middle of September, 1873, the cases came up for trial in the provincial court. By this time the true character of the noble lord had become known and the court probably was advised that leniency would be in order. The policemen pleaded " guilty " and were sentenced to twenty-four hours' imprisonment in jail. Fletcher pleaded " not guilty " and was freed on four thousand dollars' bail.[23]

In the summer of 1872 the general quiet of the times was disturbed by a riotous affair at Brainerd, a village then two years old situated on the upper Mississippi at the crossing of the Northern Pacific Railroad.[24] On April 28 Helen McArthur disappeared from her home near Crow Wing and no trace of her was then or has since been found. Early in July two Chippewa half-breeds were reported to have boasted at Leech Lake that they had murdered the white woman and had sunk her body in a slough. The sheriff of Crow Wing County was informed of the report and had the men arrested and lodged in jail at Brainerd. When they were brought up for examination they asked for time to get witnesses in their behalf. The case was continued to July 25. The local populace was much displeased at this delay of punishment of bad men whom they in their private capacities had found guilty and deserving of death. Citizens or sojourners, estimated at three or four hundred in number, assembled in a mob late on the twenty-third, broke open the jail, brought out the untried prisoners, and summarily hanged them in front of the Last Turn Saloon. The next morning an alarm spread that one or two hundred Indians were before the town arrayed in war paint and feathers, keen for vengeance. A runner was said to have brought in word that the Pillagers and Mille Lacs Chippewa were gathering. Sheriff John Gurrell telegraphed to Governor Austin: " Brainerd, July 24, 1872. . . . Please send troops *immediately;* town full of Indians, and have been ordered to leave . . . but do not. Three (3) white families have left to-day. Two Indians hung last night

[23] For a fuller discussion of this episode, with references, see the Appendix, no. 5, *post.*
[24] Upham, *Minnesota Geographic Names,* 156.

by a mob by breaking jail and taking them out." Under the governor's authority Adjutant General Mark D. Flower assembled and dispatched by rail three companies of the First National Guard, four officers and sixty-six men. The adjutant general accompanied the expedition. Governor Austin at once communicated with Major General W. S. Hancock, commanding the department of Dakota, requesting him to order out a squad of soldiers to prevent undue excitement and stampede, though he believed that there was no probability of fighting. An order was accordingly issued on July 25 to the commanding officer of Fort Ripley to march with his whole garrison, with rations for thirty days, to White Earth to give such protection to settlers as might be needed and to encourage them to remain at their homes.

The state troops arrived at the seat of war at seven-thirty in the evening of July 25. General Flower and Captain Bunker, commander of the troops, made a tour of the place and found peace and quiet reigning. The next day two companies were sent home and on Saturday, the twenty-seventh, the third company, less a captain and ten men, left. At two o'clock in the morning of the twenty-eighth the sheriff demanded a parade of the guard to quell a disturbance which was going on at a Swedish boarding house. Three men had been wounded, one of them, it was thought, mortally. A number of arrests were made and the prisoners were disarmed and held in durance. In the afternoon of the same day it was reported that the wounded man would die and that the railroad men would lynch the prisoners. Fortunately the wounded man decided to live and no lynching took place. On July 29 the rear guard of the detachment left for St. Paul. The casualties mentioned were all that occurred in what the newspapers derisively called the "Blueberry War."[25]

In anticipation of the state election of 1873 a lively correspondence took place between the Democratic and the Liberal

[25] *Brainerd Tribune,* 1872: May 18, p. 1; July 13, p. 1; 20, p. 1; 27, p. 1; August 3, p. 1; *St. Paul Dispatch,* 1872: July 25, p. 1; 26, p. 1; *Weekly*

Republican leaders, which resulted in a "Liberal Democratic" state convention in St. Paul on September 24, where it was agreed to make no separate nominations but to indorse and support the nominees of the late Owatonna convention. A separate platform was adopted, but it did not differ in principle from that adopted at Owatonna.[26]

The grand encounters between the political parties, great and small, were momentous, but far more intense and interesting to the individuals concerned were the controversies, not to say squabbles, of aspirants for office, notably those of the Republican persuasion. As already shown, Alexander Ramsey had steadily held his leadership against powerful opposition and had secured reëlections by narrow margins. In the course of Austin's administration this opposition was reenforced by a new contingent of young Republicans, many of whom had seen service in the Civil and Indian wars and were seeking political reward as their due for patriotic labors and sacrifices. "The Ramsey dynasty has ruled long enough," was their talk. The old clique of state and federal officers had fed quite long enough at the public crib. It was time for the young Republicans to have a hand and a share. A willing and capable leader was needed, and he appeared. At the close of the war there settled in St. Paul a young lawyer named Cushman Kellogg Davis. He was born in Jefferson County, New York, in 1838, was graduated from the University of Michigan, and served with credit in the line of a Wisconsin regiment and on the staff of General Gorman. He was well-enough learned in the law, possessed the power of ready and acute analysis, and was a master of clear and eloquent

---

Record (Detroit), 1872: July 20, p. 4; 27, p. 1; Saint Paul Pioneer, 1872: July 25, p. 1; 26, p. 1; 27, p. 1; Saint Paul Press, July 26, 1872, p. 1; Adjutant General, Reports, 1872, pp. 21, 23–25. In volume E, pages 61–70, of the Records in the Governor's Archives, in the custody of the Minnesota Historical Society, may be found many letters and telegrams, mostly of minor importance, exchanged in the course of the "war."

[26] Saint Paul Pioneer, September 25, 1873, p. 2; St. Paul Dispatch, September 25, 1873, p. 2; numerous letters in the Donnelly Papers, August and September, 1873. On the Owatonna convention, see ante, p. 48.

statement. He rapidly built up a remunerative law practice and interested himself the while in public affairs. He served as a member of the Minnesota House of Representatives in 1867 and, by the grace of Senator Ramsey, became United States district attorney for the state in the year following. Intent on higher things, he did not work for state or local office, but practiced law, enlarged his acquaintance, and watched the signs of the times. In 1870 he wrote and delivered before the literary societies of the state university and elsewhere an address entitled " Modern Feudalism," a searching, profound, and almost prophetic arraignment of corporation evils and dangers. It gained for its author a reputation more than local for discernment and courage.[27] In fact, this address made so favorable an impression on the Grangers that their leaders debated among themselves the proposition to nominate Davis for governor at the Owatonna convention. After some dalliance with them, he decided to stay in the old Republican ship.[28]

The candidature of Davis for the Republican nomination came from an unexpected source. Harlan Page Hall, who was born and educated for the bar in Ohio, came to St. Paul in 1862 at the age of twenty-four. As a temporary employment he became night editor of the *St. Paul Press* and, two years later, he was a part owner of the paper for a short time. On February 29, 1868, the first issue of the *St. Paul Daily Dispatch* appeared under his editorship as an independent Republican organ. Ignatius Donnelly held a financial interest in it and became a frequent contributor. In 1870 Hall was appointed pension agent for Minnesota and received his commission. As he afterwards learned, influential relatives in Ohio had secured the appointment, which was worth some six thousand dollars a year, from Grant through James

[27] Baker, *Governors of Minnesota,* 191–194; Upham and Dunlap, *Minnesota Biographies,* 165. Davis' views and suggestions on corporations may be found in a letter from him to W. W. Williams, in the *St. Paul Dispatch,* July 30, 1873, p. 2.
[28] Donnelly Papers, July 17–August 24, 1873.

A. Garfield. This invasion of his sphere of influence was not pleasing to Senator Ramsey. Hall went to Washington, saw the senator, and promised that if his appointment should be confirmed by the Senate he would publish a good straight Republican newspaper. Senator Ramsey knew his local politics and his obligations to the *St. Paul Press* too well to grant the best place in his gift to an ambitious parvenu, however " good " his promises might be; and it may be true, as Hall later boasted, that " he wrote his political death warrant by turning me down." [29]

On April 19, 1873, the *St. Paul Dispatch* published a leading editorial article under the heading " Another Richmond," in which it announced that the young Republicans of Minnesota would present, at the proper time, the name of Cushman K. Davis for governor of Minnesota. The suggestion, coming from a political outlaw and mischief-maker, was not at first taken seriously by Davis himself or by anybody; but as the proposition was favored by county newspapers and in letters to him, he decided to try his fortune against the dynasty. On May 9 the *Winona Republican* announced that it had learned " in a very direct manner " that Davis would be an aspirant for the governorship. A small body of friends in St. Paul now obtained his consent to an open candidature upon the understanding that Governor Austin would not enter the field. The *St. Paul Press* of June 15, 1873, printed two letters — one, an inquiry as to his intentions and the other, his reply that he would be a candidate and would be grateful for Republican support. A campaign was opened but, with little money for expenses, no state-wide organization was effected. Marshall and Hubbard, veterans in state politics as they were, lent their influence to the young Republican aspirant, and there was some hope, but little expectation, of his nomina-

---

[29] Henry A. Castle, in a memorial address in honor of Hall, in *Minnesota Historical Collections*, 12: 735–738, 744; Hall, *Observations*, 113–117. Hall says that he had long since come to the conclusion that Senator Ramsey did exactly what he ought to have done and adds that he (Hall) was ashamed that he had been ready to sell his soul for a mess of pottage.

tion. The dynasty looked forward with confidence to the success of its logical candidate, William Drew Washburn.[30] Washburn was the youngest of a large family of brothers from Maine, four of whom became members of Congress from as many different states. He had come to Minnesota in 1857 with a college diploma and an attorney's certificate. An appointment as agent of the Minneapolis Mill Company, owner of the vast water power on the west side of the river, diverted him from law practice. In 1861 he accepted the office of surveyor-general of Minnesota, which took him to St. Paul for four years and turned his attention to lumbering. Later he became interested in flour milling and railroad building. Along with engrossing business engagements he found time to give his share of attention to state and municipal affairs, but for some years he accepted no office except a year's service in the legislature of 1871.[31] Always an ardent Republican, he was at length singled out by the old dynasty as the best man to make the race for the governorship in 1873. The old Republicans went into convention at St. Paul on July 16 fully confident that their prestige and organization would prevail over a suddenly recruited faction. The informal ballot indicated danger, but not disaster, and on the first formal ballot Davis had but 78 votes. He made large gains on the second and third ballots and on the fourth received 155 votes out of the 307 cast and was nominated.[32]

The old guard ate its crow with the best grace it could, but did not turn out in great numbers at the polls. Davis' slender

[30] Hall, *Observations*, 124–129; Henry A. Castle, "Reminiscences of Minnesota Politics," in *Minnesota Historical Collections*, 15: 560–563. The two writers ignore each other but both doubtless state facts. See also Hall to Donnelly, April 27, May 11, 1870, in the Donnelly Papers.

[31] Warner and Foote, *Hennepin County*, 654; Alonzo Phelps, *Biographical History of the Northwest*, 39–47 (*American Biography of Representative Men*, vol. 4 — Boston, 1890).

[32] For accounts of the somewhat riotous convention, see the *St. Paul Press* and the *St. Paul Dispatch* of July 17, 1873, p. 2. On a previous ballot 308 votes ballots, and that it was not counted. Had it been counted, however, the result would have been the same. Castle, in *Minnesota Historical Collections*, had been cast. Hall, in his *Observations*, 133, states that Major Camp found a Washburn ballot in the lining of his hat, which had been used to receive the

majority was but 4,460 out of a total of 77,022 votes.[33] It may now be observed that the nomination went to him with the expectation that his sympathy with the demands of the Grangers for reform of railroad abuses would keep some Republicans who had joined the order from renouncing their old party loyalty to vote for the Anti-Monopolist–Democratic nominee. The stout plank in the Republican platform denouncing railroad extortions and discriminations had the same purpose. A less emphatic declaration and a nominee not known to be sympathetic with the Grangers would have lost the election. In the campaign Davis' adherents made no secret of their intention to place him in the governorship that he might be in training for the senatorship upon the expiration of Ramsey's second term. Nothing occurred in the course of his term to disappoint this expectation. Davis' messages repeated the sentiments of his lecture on " Modern Feudalism," and he appealed with great earnestness to the legislatures to settle with the holders of the state railroad bonds of 1858.[34]

Senator Ramsey's second term was to expire in March, 1875. He desired to succeed himself and the support of a body of steadfast friends gave him a right to expect reëlection; but he could not have been ignorant of the ambition of the young Republican who had defeated his favorite aspirant for the governorship. The Republican caucus met on January 14 with Ramsey, Davis, Austin, and Washburn in the field. It was agreed that the voting should be by secret ballot. The number of Republicans in the legislature was eighty-three, of which forty-two is the least integral majority. Upon

15: 564, says a disputed ballot stuck in the lining of General Sanborn's hat, but that it was no doubt properly counted. After a checking of the list of accredited delegates, which was found to be 308, the vote was acquiesced in. The *St. Paul Dispatch* was jubilant over Davis' nomination.

[33] The *Legislative Manual*, 1874, p. 108, gives the detailed count of the vote. The vote in brief may be found in the *Legislative Manual*, 1925, p. 113.

[34] *Saint Paul Press*, July 17, 1873, p. 1; Castle, in *Minnesota Historical Collections*, 15: 565; Hall, *Observations*, 119. See especially Davis' message of January 8, 1875, and that of January 7, 1876, in *Executive Documents*, 1874, vol. 1, 24–26; 1875, vol. 1, 36–42.

the third ballot the veteran lacked but two votes of a nomination. The Davis men, who had lost nine votes solemnly pledged in their preceding conference, asked for a recess of ten minutes, which was agreed to. Upon their return they demanded either a roll call, which would reveal their " traitors," or an adjournment. The Ramsey adherents, perhaps none too sure of holding their solid vote, agreed to an adjournment. Upon reassemblage the following night some of the supporters of Davis were absent and some refused to vote. On the last of two ballotings fifty-four votes were cast, forty-two for Ramsey; but the Davis men chose to regard it as a rump caucus and bolted the nomination. Opinions differ as to whether this action was or was not dishonorable; but it was certainly bad politics on the part of Davis' friends.[35]

On the evening of January 18 the Democrats and the Anti-Monopolists held their joint caucus with fifty-one in attendance. The nomination went to Ignatius Donnelly, an event not relished by old-line Democrats.[36] On January 19 the two houses, as required by law, balloted separately. The combined result was: Ramsey, 60; Davis, 24; Donnelly, 53. Balloting now went on for some days in joint convention of the houses without result. On January 27 Donnelly released his supporters and they transferred their votes to William Lochren, a veteran of the First Minnesota, whose place at the Minnesota bar was hardly second to another. But Republicans, divided as they were among themselves, had no desire to

---

[35] St. Paul Dispatch, 1875: January 15, p. 4; 16, p. 1; Castle, in Minnesota Historical Collections, 15: 568; Saint Paul Press, January 15, 16, 1875; Hall, Observations, 135–142. Hall states that he had two reporters hidden above the ceiling whose notes, mostly verbatim, were swelled into the long accounts in the Dispatch. William P. Murray told the author that he persuaded the St. Paul chief of police, a Democrat like himself, to fill the galleries with young St. Paul men to cheer for Davis. This interview is recorded in the author's notebooks, 3: 88.

[36] Saint Paul Pioneer, January 19, 1875, p. 1. In 1874 Donnelly, who had professed himself a Liberal Republican, with a small but zealous following, began the publication of the Anti-Monopolist at St. Paul as the organ of the Anti-Monopoly party. The editor's talent for sarcasm and vituperation was abundantly employed in its columns. The party did not multiply in numbers or in influence and the paper ceased its existence in 1878. Fish, Donnelliana, part 1, pp. 83–85.

bestow the toga on any Democrat, however distinguished he might be for ability and character.

On February 13 Ramsey, whose highest figure had been sixty-one, and Davis, who had gained but few votes, agreed to withdraw from the contest. Why no caucus was called for a new party nomination is not known. For four days the Republicans scattered their votes among various prominent statesmen. On February 17 the Honorable Samuel J. R. McMillan, chief justice of Minnesota, whose name had been proposed early in the contest, received two votes. On the following day he had fifty-seven and on the nineteenth the requisite number of eighty-two votes gave him the election.[37] The *St. Paul Press* of February 19, 1875, declared the Republican party in Minnesota dead and suggested that Chief Justice McMillan would be as good a man as any " to bury the corpse and administer the estate." This pleasantry cost the editor of that journal, Joseph A. Wheelock, his office of postmaster of St. Paul, which went to the senator's brother-in-law. The Republican party survived and Senator McMillan's service in the national Senate was so satisfactory and his standing at home was so firm that he was easily elected for a second term. Davis returned to his law practice and his literary work. Twelve years later the senatorship came to him as if by common consent, so strong was the hold he had by that time obtained on the Republicans of the state. The state lost the services of Alexander Ramsey, her wise and experienced Nestor, but the nation did not. President Hayes placed him on his cabinet as secretary of war in 1879. Modern democracies, like one of old, tire of hearing Aristides called just.[38]

[37] *Senate Journal*, 1875, p. 44; *House Journal*, 52, 216–220, 230–233, 252–255, 273, 287, 301; C. H. Graves to the author, February 28, 1923. The ballotings are summarized in Hall, *Observations*, 145–152. William Pitt Murray told the author that at a night caucus it was agreed to cast the Democratic votes for Wilkinson, if he could rally enough Republican votes to elect him. The secret got out and at an early morning caucus the Republicans suddenly resolved to concentrate upon Judge McMillan. This interview is recorded in the author's notebooks, 3: 49.

[38] *St. Paul Dispatch*, February 19, 1875, p. 1; Hall, *Observations*, 153; Castle, in *Minnesota Historical Collections*, 15: 569; *Pioneer Press*, January

A disagreeable task fell to Governor Davis in his second and last year in office. In his message to the legislature of 1875 he was obliged to inform that body that a Senate committee appointed in the previous session had submitted a report in which it was charged that Charles McIlrath, who had been state auditor and land commissioner from 1861 to 1873 with an unblemished reputation, had received on account of sales of timber from state lands $77,041.13 more than he had paid to the state treasurer; also, that through his mismanagement the state had suffered loss amounting to $12,518.04. By Governor Davis' advice the attorney-general had brought suit against McIlrath in the district court of Ramsey County to recover $94,641.69. The legislature was asked for an appropriation to meet the expenses of the suit.[39]

As the case was one in which many witnesses would have to be summoned, some from distant places, and a long time would have to be taken up in examining them and thereafter in adjusting an account of moneys received and paid or not paid, running through many years, Judge Westcott Wilkin on April 17, 1875, according to stipulation by counsel, appointed as referee to take testimony, hear arguments, and suggest a conclusion, Greenleaf Clark, already eminent at the bar and later to become a justice of the Minnesota supreme court. The attorney-general employed William Lochren, the distinguished lawyer above mentioned, later to be a judge of the United States district court, to assist in the prosecution. The taking of testimony occupied seven months and nearly three months more passed before the case was argued and left in the hands of the referee for his disposition. Another six months ran by before his report advising judgment for the defendant was filed. The finding was that McIlrath had paid into the treasury $250,663.65, all the moneys he

14, 1881, p. 4; Upham and Dunlap, *Minnesota Biographies*, 624. On Davis' election to the Senate in 1887, see *post*, p. 174.

[39] Davis' message, January 8, 1875, in *Executive Documents*, 1874, vol. 1, p. 8; report of the attorney-general, in the same volume, 8; *Senate Journal*, 1874, pp. 155, 198–204, 222. For McIlrath's statement to the Senate committee see the *Saint Paul Press*, February 17, 1874, p. 4.

had received for stumpage, except some eight thousand dollars which he had lawfully expended in paying explorers, fees of surveyors-general, and other small expense items; hence Clark's brief finding, " Defendant is entitled to judgment." The decision was the more grateful to McIlrath and his friends because it was rendered by a stanch Democrat before whom the case for the state had been conducted, and it had been argued by another. Judge Lochren told the author that the decision was a just one, although he lost the case. There was no room for a charge that McIlrath, a Republican office-holder, had been whitewashed by a partisan tribunal.[40]

McIlrath's vindication in a civil proceeding was complete. He was equally fortunate in the result of a criminal prosecution. On October 6, 1874, the Ramsey County grand jury filed twenty-six indictments against him. Two of them charged him with having assumed the duties of his office without having filed bonds of twenty thousand dollars on resuming office after reëlections. The court threw these out on the ground that they did not constitute a public offense. The remaining twenty-four indictments, nearly identical in form and substance, charged irregular and unlawful sales and grants to cut timber from school lands to as many different parties. But one of the number was brought to trial, the one doubtless which the prosecution selected as most likely to be successful. The jury promptly found McIlrath not guilty. The cases still remaining were thereupon dismissed.[41] Gov-

---

[40] Judgment roll of case 8581, State v. McIlrath, on file in the office of the clerk of the district court of Ramsey County. The record of testimony is missing. See also reports of the attorney-general, in *Executive Documents*, 1875, vol. 1, p. 10; 1876, vol. 1, p. 578. The suit was brought on April 17, 1875, and the testimony closed on November 22, 1875. The case was submitted to the referee for consideration on February 2, 1876, and the referee's report was filed on August 14, 1876.

[41] Criminal register of the court of common pleas of Ramsey County, on file in the office of the clerk of the district court of Ramsey County, 133–159. The indictment was filed on October 6, 1874. See the *Saint Paul Press*, October 8, 1874, p. 2, for an editorial characterizing all the indictments as "extremely frivolous." See also the *Saint Paul Pioneer*, October 7, 1874, p. 2. The single verdict of " not guilty " was returned on October 12, 1875, and the nolle prosequi was entered the same day. See the Appendix, no. 14, *post*.

ernor Pillsbury in his message to the legislature of 1877 had the pleasure of remarking that this " honorable acquittal, should receive fitting recognition." [42]

Ignatius Donnelly was easily the most brilliant planet in the political galaxy of Minnesota in the decade following the close of the Civil War, but there were other lustrous wandering stars, few of which, if any among them, were more brilliant than William Smith King. He was born on December 16, 1828, in Malone, Franklin County, New York. His father, a Methodist Episcopal minister, settled on a farm in the same town when the boy was eight years old. Four years later the family was broken up by the death of the mother. For six years thereafter King was a farm hand in summer and in winter worked for his board and went to district school. At eighteen he engaged in a fire insurance agency which occupied him until he reached the age of thirty, when, in 1858, he came to Minnesota. In 1852, at the age of twenty-four, he had entered politics as a Free-soiler and editor of a small campaign newspaper; in 1853 he had organized the Young Men's Republican Club of Cherry Valley, New York. This he always claimed was the first actual formal organization of that party. In the year following his arrival in Minneapolis he began the publication of the weekly *State Atlas,* which in 1867 was merged into the *Minneapolis Tribune.* His firm opposition to the use of the state railroad bonds of 1858 for banking purposes brought his paper and himself into state-wide notice. Next to the Republican party in his interest, if it was not first, was the growth and prosperity of the city of his choice. While Minneapolis was but an unknown village with a town government and St. Paul a smart young

[42] *Executive Documents,* 1876, vol. 1, p. 16. If Governor Pillsbury's compliment was intended as a suggestion toward an appropriation to reimburse McIlrath for the expense he had incurred to establish his innocence, there was a disappointment. McIlrath presented a petition to the Senate and a bill was introduced for such an appropriation. It was recommended for passage in committee of the whole but was defeated by a vote of 24 to 4. The Senate evidently thought that McIlrath did not need the money. *Senate Journal,* 1877, pp. 275, 386, 424.

city known throughout the country, King believed that the
city at the Falls of St. Anthony must become the manufacturing and commercial metropolis of Minnesota. So long as the
rivalry of the two cities lasted Colonel King was the foremost
champion of Minneapolis. For years it would be hard to find
any issue of a St. Paul newspaper which had no fling at
" Bill King," and his papers returned full measure.

Although he frequently coöperated with Ramsey and his
" dynasty," King had no real love for either, but sympathized
with the sentiments of William Windom. Doubtless by the
aid of political friends and admirers in New York, King was
elected postmaster of the national House of Representatives
for the Thirty-seventh Congress, 1861–63. He seemed to like
the position and to give satisfactory service, for he held it
for twelve years, which would have been consecutive but that
he was not in office during the Thirty-ninth Congress, 1865–
67. During the sessions of Congress he was, of course, in
Washington and the Washington correspondence of the *Atlas*
and the *Tribune* was of a lively strain and is still very good
reading. His somewhat bluff but ever hearty and engaging
manner gained him a very large acquaintance and a strong
body of friends at home and elsewhere. Availing himself of
opportunities for investments which naturally came to his
knowledge, King accumulated wealth enough by 1868 to buy
a farm, lying then far outside the limits of Minneapolis, on
which he built an ample farmhouse and outbuildings. He
added to the area of the farm until it embraced some fourteen hundred acres, east of Lakes Harriet and Calhoun. Here
he indulged a fancy for the breeding of blooded stock, in
particular of shorthorn cattle, of which he soon owned the
finest herd in the country — according to some people, the
finest in the world. This baronial recreation he continued for
some years, until financial embarrassments and a tedious
litigation, though resulting in his favor, obliged him to relinquish it. At the fall election of 1874 Colonel King was
elected as a representative in Congress from the third Min-

nesota district and he served through the Forty-fourth Congress, from 1875 to 1877. At the close of his term in Congress Colonel King returned to his private affairs at home and to the end of his life in 1900 he was foremost in every movement to enrich and glorify his beloved city, which gave him ample assurances of appreciation.[43]

[43] Phelps, *History of the Northwest*, 189–191; Warner and Foote, *Hennepin County*, 345; Daniel S. B. Johnston, "Minnesota Journalism from 1858 to 1865," in *Minnesota Historical Collections*, 12: 198–200; *Minneapolis Journal*, February 24, 1900, p. 7; *Pioneer Press*, February 24, 1900, p. 4; *Minneapolis Sunday Tribune*, February 25, 1900, p. 7; Isaac Atwater, ed., *History of the City of Minneapolis*, 1: 379–386, 410 (New York, 1893). For a decision of great importance in favor of King, see Caroline M. King and William S. King v. Philo Remington and others, 36 *Minnesota*, 15–38. There is an article about the Lyndale farm in the *Saint Paul Pioneer*, May 7, 1872, p. 3.

IV. THE GRASSHOPPER INVASION, 1873-77

IN 1873 and the four years following large areas of Minnesota were infested with the Rocky Mountain locust, at first by invading swarms only but later by those and others hatched within the state. Because of its general resemblance to the familiar grasshopper, the strange insect was naturally called " grasshopper " and the name soon came into common use in talk and print. It was used in newspapers, in governors' messages and proclamations, in legislative journals, and in state laws. But to entomologists the creature is not specifically a grasshopper, but a locust. The name " Rocky Mountain locust " proposed by Riley for common parlance has also been widely used and is preferable.[1]

[1] Charles V. Riley, *The Locust Plague in the United States; Being More Particularly a Treatise on the Rocky Mountain Locust,* 18–21, 69–72, 78, 82, 207 (Chicago, 1877) ; *The Grasshopper, or Rocky Mountain Locust, and Its Ravages in Minnesota,* 3, 15, 27. On the latter work, see *post,* n. 14. See also United States Entomological Commission, *Reports,* 1877, pp. 42, 52, 220–225, 260, 280; 1880–81, p. 37. The report of 1877 was issued as a publication of the United States Geological Survey under the department of the interior. That for 1878–79 was issued by the department of the interior, the report being made direct to the secretary. The report for 1880–81 was made to the commissioner of agriculture and was issued as 47 Congress, 2 session, *House Miscellaneous Documents,* no. 44 (serial 2154).

The individual locust, about an inch and a quarter long, slender, its body some shade of brown, its wings pale, is not formidable in appearance. Its mouth is provided with a pair of broad, short, and solid jaws with cutting and grinding edges. The true wings are broad, thin, and membranous and when at rest fold under smaller forward ones which are mere wing covers. They are thus kept safe from injury when not needed for flight. There are six legs, the hindmost pair being very large and strong, adapted to hopping. Breathing takes place through a system of air tubes ramifying throughout the body.

The life history of an individual locust is about as follows: When warm spring weather comes, from a tiny kidney-shaped egg, which has lain buried in the ground all winter, is born an infant locust which, after three times shedding its skin, enters its second stage with rudimentary wings. After two more molts, in six or eight weeks from the time of hatching, appears the perfect insect with fully developed wings. The full-grown locust has now a short period, varying from two to four weeks, to expatiate and enjoy life and then comes the serious business of procreating a new generation. After coition with the male, the female devotes herself to egg-laying. After selecting a spot of dry ground, compact rather than loose, she bores with the armed cylinder made up of her hinder segments a hole perhaps an inch in depth and

The permanent home of this formidable insect is, or was, in the foothills of the Rocky Mountains and bordering plains from the middle of Colorado northward to fifty-three degrees north latitude, the timber line of British America. The whole area, embracing about four hundred thousand square miles, is elevated and free from timber; its rainfall is insufficient for agriculture, but there is a general covering of bunch grass. The actual breeding grounds are not on the plains and slopes, but in river valleys and sunny uplands, whence the young spread in quest of food.[2] The life of the locust swarm is full of mystery. Even in the infant stage the individual reaches out for everything succulent within its feeble range of locomotion. In the second stage, the hopping stage, it begins to associate and to travel in masses in quest of food. Moving as if in battle formation, the host devours everything green on the ground, mounts into shrubbery, and even climbs trees to reach their foliage. In the final stage, when the wings are full grown, a new impulse observed by science but not explained, an instinct for emigration in masses, sets in. After trying their wings for three days, more or less, hordes of the insects rise together in the air, circle around as if to obtain an orientation, and then fly away toward new feeding grounds scores or hundreds of miles away. It is held by some, however, that they merely fly with the wind, but even in that case they appear to know how to choose favorable breezes and to wait for them. These flights radiate from the mountain home, but, especially on the eastern slopes of the Rockies, there is a trend of the main flights toward warmer latitudes, resulting in southeastward movements. As a general fact the swarms alight at nightfall, to rise in the morning

a scant quarter of an inch in diameter, oblique to the surface. Into this she projects her eggs along with a cementing fluid, disposing them generally in four rows of seven each. Here they rest, if not disturbed or hatched by some untimely warm weather, until the following spring. The last deposit made, the female soon gives up her life. The male, who seems to have no reason for existence but his part in procreation, will have faded away, and thus the billions of locusts which have lived in the season perish from the earth.

[2] Entomological Commission, *Reports*, 1877, pp. 131–136, map facing title-page; 1880–81, pp. 24, 276.

after the dew has gone and move on, feeding as they go. Later swarms following the same route are obliged to continue their flights overhead and have been known to extend them two or three hundred miles without alighting. In such long flights they remain at a high altitude, probably to keep in the dry and rarified air to which they have been accustomed.[3]

The numbers composing a swarm are literally " greater than any assignable quantity," to borrow an algebraic definition of infinity. " Their flight," says one observer, " may be likened to an immense snow-storm, extending from the ground to a height at which our visual organs perceive them only as minute, darting scintillations. . . . It is a vast cloud of animated specks, glittering against the sun. On the horizon they often appear as a dust tornado, riding upon the wind like an ominous hail storm." Another, writing of the numbers as they alight, says: " They circle in myriads about you . . . driving into open doors and windows; heaping about your feet and around your buildings," literally covering the ground two or three inches deep. The noise made by the swarms when engaged in feeding has been likened to the roar of a prairie fire. Southey compares it to the roar of a wild ocean in a storm. The prophet Joel writes, " Like the noise of chariots on the tops of mountains shall they leap, like the noise of a flame of fire that devoureth the stubble." [4]

The flight of the swarm from its ancient nesting place at length comes to an end at some point where vegetation is abundant. After a few days' feeding the urge for procreation appears and when that is over the life of the swarm is over along with the lives of the individuals which composed it; but it has left behind the innumerable eggs from which a new generation is to emerge. Normally the hatching waits

[3] Entomological Commission, *Reports*, 1877, pp. 143, 145, 215, 233, 234; *The Grasshopper and Its Ravages in Minnesota*, 20; Riley, *Locust Plague*, 57, 83, 217.
[4] Entomological Commission, *Reports*, 1877, pp. 213–215; Robert Southey, "Thalaba, the Destroyer," book 3, stanza 30; Joel, 2: 5. In verse 3 the prophet says: "The land is as the garden of Eden before them, and behind them a desolate wilderness."

until the following spring, the time varying with latitude and temperature. The newly fledged swarms repeat the advances and ravages of their predecessors, but not indefinitely. Degeneration due to unaccustomed heat and moisture sets in, parasites attack, flocks of birds prey on the hatching grounds, toads, frogs, snakes, mice, and such small deer make boot of the eggs, and, in cultivated areas, human agencies unite with those of nature to check breeding. In a few years the visitation is over and in some cases it ends as suddenly as it came.[5]

It is now to be understood that these swarm emigrations do not come with annual regularity. Some years may be skipped altogether, or small colonies may leave for neighboring regions. The greatest migrations are at long intervals and the fanciful suggestion of eleven-year periods, coinciding with times of maximum sun spots, has been broached. It is generally agreed by entomologists who have studied the subject that the migrating instincts of the locust result in great part from the physical effects of a dry and thin atmosphere modified by conditions of moisture and temperature.[6]

Jonathan Carver, who explored in Minnesota in 1767, recorded in his *Travels:* " I must not omit that the LOCUST is a septennial insect, as they are only seen . . . every seven years, when they infest these parts . . . in large swarms, and do a great deal of mischief. The years when they thus arrive are denominated the locust years." From that time on there are occasional records and numerous traditional accounts of locust visitations between the Mississippi and the Pacific from the Gulf of Mexico far into British America. Some of them reached the area of Minnesota, but as there were but few white people to suffer from their mischief, no account of them need be taken here. The greatest migration known, that of the period from 1873 to 1877, ex-

[5] Entomological Commission, *Reports,* 1877, pp. 231, 238–249; 1880–81, pp. 18, 40, 43; *The Grasshopper and Its Ravages in Minnesota,* 35–39.
[6] Entomological Commission, *Reports,* 1877, pp. 181–184, 201; 1878–79, pp. 73–82; 1880–81, pp. 65–85.

tending southward through Iowa, Missouri, and Arkansas to Texas and southwestward over Dakota, Kansas, Nebraska, and Colorado, brought ruin and sorrow to a large portion of Minnesota.[7]

About the twelfth of June, 1873, on a fresh breeze from the southwest, swarms of Rocky Mountain locusts came across the Dakota border into Minnesota and spread themselves over some thirteen southwestern counties, which form an area roughly quadrilateral. The distribution was not uniform, but detached bodies alighted apart from one another, leaving islands of farms unmolested. Even whole towns escaped. Succulent vegetation was at once consumed and the growing crops were greatly damaged when not ruined. The heaviest losses occurred in Cottonwood, Martin, Watonwan, Brown, and Jackson counties; lighter injuries fell upon eight adjoining counties. This migration was part of an immense movement which covered large parts of southwestern Dakota and northwestern Iowa. In the townships from which reports were received concerning grasshopper damages the estimated yield of wheat was reduced below six bushels to the acre. The devastations brought hardship and even impoverishment to settlers raising their first or second crops, but generous aid by neighbors saved them and their animals from immediate starvation. Supplies of food and clothing were soon sent on by volunteer committees in the larger cities. General Sibley as chairman of the relief committee of the St. Paul Chamber of Commerce became informed of the devastation and found that at least six hundred families in Cottonwood, Jackson, Nobles, Watonwan, and Rock counties would have to be fed and clothed during the coming winter and would need seed grain in the spring. Seventy-nine families in Murray County were in absolute want. On January 23, 1874, he wrote to Governor Davis describing the situation and advising him

[7] Jonathan Carver, *Travels through the Interior Parts of North-America, in the Years 1766, 1767, and 1768*, 493 (London, 1778); Entomological Commission, *Reports*, 1877, pp. 53–57; *The Grasshopper and Its Ravages in Minnesota*, 5–13; report of Allen Whitman, in University of Minnesota, Geological and Natural History Survey of Minnesota, *Reports*, 1876, p. 95.

that, as private gifts had almost ceased, legislative action was necessary. The letter was laid before the Senate and the subject was promptly taken up. As the locust visitation was confined to so small a portion of the settled area of the state and was commonly believed to have ended with the season, the legislature of 1874 set aside only five thousand dollars for the supply of food and clothing, but it made a liberal appropriation of twenty-five thousand dollars for seed grain, both amounts to be distributed under the supervision of the governor.[8]

The visitation did not terminate with the close of the season. With the advent of warm weather in 1874 the eggs laid in the previous season hatched out and the young in infinite numbers began a new devastation. By July they got their wings and great swarms flew into Blue Earth, Sibley, and McLeod counties and farther into Renville and Faribault. Smaller new invading swarms from the northwest strung themselves from the north side of the quadrilateral of 1873 along or near the western line of the state as far as Polk County. Twenty-eight counties were infested and there were sudden unimportant raids into others.[9] The devastation wrought by these swarms brought to Governor Davis alarming accounts and piteous appeals for help. Perhaps none moved him more than a report by Bishop Whipple of the ravages in a portion of the district he had visited. Instead of calling a special session of the legislature, which would have cost perhaps twenty thousand dollars, the governor adopted the plan of calling on county commissioners to furnish relief for the stricken communities. In his letter he said that the new locust progeny had laid the region almost bare. During repeated visitations the people had expended all their

[8] *St. Paul Press*, 1873: June 13, p. 4; 14, p. 4; 29, pp. 2, 4; *The Grasshopper and Its Ravages in Minnesota*, 11; Whitman's report, in Geological and Natural History Survey, *Reports*, 1876, p. 96, map facing p. 91; Commissioner of Statistics, *Reports*, 1874, pp. 9–41; Entomological Commission, *Reports*, 1877, pp. 78, 89; *Senate Journal*, 1874, p. 81; *General Laws*, 1874, pp. 251, 253.

[9] Commissioner of Statistics, *Reports*, 1875, p. 19; *The Grasshopper and Its Ravages in Minnesota*, 12.

accumulations. Generous neighbors had divided their substance with the less fortunate until whole communities had been reduced to a common destitution. Merchants and men of means had given and lent until they would be ruined unless they could be sustained. The governor was hopeful of an early termination of the mischief. Such visitations were not unknown in the state; they had come once in about twenty years, never infesting the country for more than two seasons in succession. He therefore requested the county boards to make appropriations according to the tax valuations of their counties and the example set by Ramsey County, which had appropriated five thousand dollars.[10]

In response to Governor Davis' request, General Sibley undertook to be his commissary for the receipt and distribution of the moneys. But ten county boards, including that of Ramsey, adopted Governor Davis' plan. Goodhue gave $2,000, Winona and Wabasha each $1,000, and six other counties, exclusive of Ramsey, $1,800. The Hennepin County board declined to appropriate public funds and it may be presumed that the boards of other counties also doubted the legality of such action. The commissioners of Houston County appropriated $1,000 and those of Mower, $500 and sent the money direct to the places they preferred to aid. Citizens of Minneapolis subscribed and paid in $4,891.40 and there were other private gifts amounting to $3,159.12. The sum of $316.80 was contributed by twenty-eight granges, in addition to money sent by the National Grange to aid suffering Patrons. The fund handled by General Sibley amounted to $18,959.12, for which he duly accounted without thought of compensation. In his report he remarked that a more equitable apportionment of the

[10] *Senate Journal*, 1875, p. 99. On July 14, 1874, Bishop Whipple issued a pastoral letter to be read in all the churches of the diocese of Minnesota. " The scourge is an awful one," he wrote. " It may be for our sins. It may be to try our faith in God." He added a form of prayer in which his people would ask God to " overrule this calamity to Thy glory and the good of Thy people." *Saint Paul Pioneer*, July 18, 1874, p. 2. See also Cushman K. Davis to Eugene M. Wilson, July 21, 1874, in the possession of the Minnesota Historical Society.

money might have been made had it been disbursed by reliable and active men in important localities acting as general relief committees with subcommittees in the townships. County commissioners lived too far apart from one another to act efficiently. In closing his report, which was submitted on January 2, 1875, General Sibley reminded Governor Davis that from twelve hundred to fifteen hundred farmers were utterly impoverished and he made the sinister suggestion that if they were not relieved by the state " they will, from necessity, seek some other homes." It was his judgment that one hundred thousand dollars were " imperatively demanded " to carry the suffering families over to another harvest and half as much more was needed to furnish seed for the next spring's planting. The legislature of 1875, before which General Sibley's report was laid, perhaps better informed by members from the devastated districts, appropriated but twenty thousand dollars to buy food and clothing for the impoverished people, but raised the appropriation for seed to seventy-five thousand dollars.[11] The state statistician recorded the total number of acres under cultivation in the twenty-eight infested counties in the season of 1874 as 641,209 and the total number of damaged acres, according to assessors' returns of farmers' estimates, as 351,218. The acres of wheat damaged were 240,417, with a loss of 2,646,802 bushels worth about half as many dollars on the farm.[12]

The locust swarms hatched out in the season of 1875 did not extend their depredations far. For some unexplained reason those in the outer counties, leaving some remnants behind, flew backward into the districts visited in the previous years, where they added to the ravages going on and then

[11] Senate Journal, 1875, pp. 97–106; General Laws, 1875, pp. 182, 183; Buck, Granger Movement, 283. A letter of Mayor Eugene M. Wilson to Governor Davis, July 22, 1874, gives notice of the advance of five thousand dollars by citizens of Minneapolis through John S. Pillsbury. See Minneapolis Tribune, July 24, 1874, p. 4. In the Governor's Archives are numerous letters containing accounts of misfortunes and destitution in the grasshopper localities, pleas for help, and records of the distributions of the relief fund.

[12] Commissioner of Statistics, Reports, 1875, pp. 19, 57.

deposited eggs. But nineteen counties, including practically all in the quadrilateral of 1873, reported " grasshopper damages," and the vermin seem to have been somewhat less voracious than in previous years. There were 263,063 acres, planted to eight crops, damaged to the amount of 4,141,230 bushels. The wheat acreage was 167,872 and the loss was 2,024,972 bushels. More than half of the damage to wheat took place in Blue Earth, Brown, and Nicollet counties — 1,157,787 bushels on 93,488 acres. The destruction of oats, corn, and barley in those counties was likewise immense, but Cottonwood, Sibley, and Watonwan also suffered heavily in corn and barley.[13]

These losses, added to the privation and distress in families already impoverished, increased their discouragement. Governor Davis, whose hopes of an early termination of locust ravages had been disappointed, now thought it was time to obtain some exact knowledge of the species and appointed a commission of three men to make a " grasshopper investigation " and report its findings under eleven heads, as to behavior of the insects, their incursions into Minnesota, their ravages, and, " specifically," the places where they had laid their eggs in 1875. The commissioners, after visiting the ravaged districts and sending circulars to town and county officers, in 1876 published a report containing valuable information under the heads prescribed by the governor and particularly stressing means for the destruction of the pests.[14]

---

[13] Commissioner of Statistics, *Reports,* 1876, pp. 106–109; *The Grasshopper and Its Ravages in Minnesota,* 13.

[14] Davis' message, in *Executive Documents,* 1875, vol. 1, p. 33. The report was published under the title, *The Grasshopper, or Rocky Mountain Locust, and Its Ravages in Minnesota* (St. Paul, 1876). The eleven heads were: (1) history of the grasshopper incursions into Minnesota; (2) origin of the grasshoppers; (3) the times of their arrival and departure; (4) the time when they deposit eggs; (5) manner of deposit; (6) the character of land where eggs are deposited; (7) the best practicable means for their destruction; (8) what, if any, grains or vegetables are exempt from their ravages; (9) acreage ravaged by them in 1875 and the amount of damage done; (10) to what extent and, specifically, where, they have deposited eggs this year; (11) such other useful information as may be brought to the knowledge of the commission. The members of the commission were John C. Wise, Warren Smith, and Allen Whitman. The last-named was a native of Massachusetts, a graduate

In May and June of 1876 the hatching of locust eggs began in the counties where eggs had been laid in the fall of 1875, chiefly in Murray, Cottonwood, Watonwan, and Brown and large fractions of Lyon, Jackson, Redwood, and Martin. There appears to have been a considerable area of hatching grounds in the Red River Valley. The young larvæ of 1876 began at once to devour the vegetation about them and, as their powers of locomotion and consumption increased, the crawling vermin spread on diverging lines into thirteen counties, most numerously into Renville, Douglas, and Otter Tail. But the area of devastation was immensely extended by new invading swarms. There were two principal movements, called by an authority " raids." The first was that of July, made by swarms apparently from breeding grounds in British America. They appeared at Pembina as early as July 8, at Grand Forks on the ninth, the next day at Crookston, and later at Breckenridge. The right wing of this host struck east and south in enormous masses, passed gradually over the counties which had been ravaged during the spring by " our own stock," and reached the southern border of the state at the end of the month, many passing on into Iowa. Eggs were laid only in the southern tier of Minnesota counties. The left or eastern flank of this body reached a line traced through Todd, Stearns, Meeker, McLeod, and Sibley counties. The other great raid, that of August, was begun by swarms collected in Otter Tail, Grant, Stevens, and Big Stone counties and swelled by additions from eastern Dakota. Favorable winds carried a large detachment over a great portion of the western part of the state and remains of it into Iowa. The main host, however, spread south and southeast, its front reaching a line running east of the Mississippi

of Harvard College, who came to Minnesota in 1872. He was the only member who had expert knowledge of insects. What his education in entomology had been is not known, but his work was treated with respect by the United States entomological commission, to which he made reports. The scientific paragraphs of the report were probably written by him. Entomological Commission, *Reports*, 1877, appendix 1; Upham and Dunlap, *Minnesota Biographies*, 850.

through the western parts of Benton and Sherburne counties, then crossing the Mississippi and extending on in a zigzag fashion in a general southerly course through Hennepin, Scott, Rice, Steele, and Mower counties. A sporadic swarm was seen near Hastings. Eggs were deposited in all the counties named, in the central counties in vast numbers.[15]

Appeals from many quarters for counsel and relief reached the ears of Governor Pillsbury. Although the season was far advanced, he issued on August 30, 1876, a proclamation designed to encourage active and coöperative defense against the scourge. He urged the farmers to employ unitedly all the means of checking ravages which the experience of three years had disclosed: plowing the infested fields and harrowing thoroughly, crushing the larvæ by means of rollers, catching and destroying the young before their wings developed, firing piles of straw near hatching grounds, burning prairie grass in windrows on township lines, and, most effective of all, digging deep and narrow ditches with deep holes at intervals; and " finally," as a last desperate recourse to be taken when the vermin were ready to fly, scaring them to death or to flight by dragging ropes over the fields of grain and annoying them with smudges and with " loud and discordant noises made by striking tin vessels, and by shrieking and yelling with the voice." [16]

Accounts of privations in the sorely stricken counties in the southwest accumulated to such an extent that Governor Pillsbury left his secretary to run his office and went down to see with his own eyes the ruin which was going on. The noble patience of the settlers whom he saw around their hay fires, scantily clothed, excited both his admiration and his sympathy. He witnessed also painful instances of man's inhumanity to man. In his annual message for the year the governor expressed his righteous indignation against two

---

[15] Whitman's report, in Geological and Natural History Survey, *Reports,* 1876, pp. 90, 105–111, 114, map facing p. 115; Entomological Commission, *Reports,* 1877, appendix 1.

[16] Governor's Archives, Records, E: 528–530.

classes of offenders. Of chattel mortgage sharks, he said,
" In some of the towns . . . not only is the farm of nearly
every resident incumbered, but scarcely a cow, horse, team,
or farming implement is uncovered by a chattel mortgage,
and the summary remedies . . . often strip a helpless family
of its last defense against impending starvation." Agents
for the sale of agricultural machinery, sold to farmers with
verbal promises of liberal treatment in case of misfortune,
he found remorselessly enforcing " their inexorable for-
feitures." Upon his return he made an appeal through the
press and through circulars to churches to the humanity of
the people of the state at large. The response was gratifying to him and much suffering was relieved and averted.
The recording angel alone knows the amount of the governor's own contributions. Assisted by his wife, he attended
personally to the distribution of relief.[17]

It now occurred to Governor Pillsbury that as so many
states had been invaded and devastated by the locust hordes
coöperation might be invoked in a general defense. Accordingly, on August 1, 1876, he invited the governors of those
states to a personal conference at Omaha on October 25,
1876. It was attended by the executives of Iowa, Kansas,
Minnesota, Missouri, Nebraska, and Dakota Territory. The
state entomologists of Illinois and Missouri, Cyrus Thomas
and Charles V. Riley, were present and Governor Pillsbury
had with him his secretary, Pennock Pusey, and Allen Whitman, a member of Governor Davis' grasshopper commission.
The proceedings and discussions, which were published in
pamphlet form and quoted by the newspapers, probably did
not add greatly to existing knowledge, but they disseminated
information and inspired courage for future activity.[18]

[17] Pillsbury's message, January 4, 1877, in *Executive Documents*, 1876, vol.
I, p. 39; Phelps, *Biographical History*, 17.
[18] *The Rocky Mountain Locust, or Grasshopper; Being the Report of Proceedings of a Conference of the Governors of Several Western States To Consider the Locust Problem* (St. Louis, 1876). The pamphlet was probably
edited by Charles V. Riley. Pages 1–32 record the proceedings. On pages
2–4 may be found Governor Pillsbury's opening address as chairman, which

When the legislature of 1877 convened on January 2, a dark cloud of gloom hung over the state and the capital. While the damage by locusts of the previous year had been less severe in the old counties where the people had fought for their crops, a 'much larger area had been infested and "peppered" with eggs. About forty counties had been visited, some but slightly, and some five hundred thousand acres of crops had been damaged. The gloom was deepened by the fact that the average yield of wheat throughout the state had been less than ten bushels to the acre — hardly half a crop. " Twenty millions of bushels of wheat is a grievous loss," said the state statistician. Minnesota felt poor.[19]

Governor Pillsbury's message presented the " grasshopper question " as one of state-wide and even national importance and outlined an aggressive grasshopper policy. The first action of the legislature thus aroused was the appointment on January 10 of a joint committee, with Ignatius Donnelly at its head, to investigate the grasshopper question and report its findings. This was followed by the adoption of a joint resolution on January 17, 1877, calling on Congress to devote the proceeds of the sales of public lands in the grasshopper states to destroying grasshopper eggs. The pests, the memorial read, had already invaded nine states and four territories and there was danger that they would spread over the whole country. It was the duty of the general government to assist in opposing this enemy, as the governments of

was made the basis of discussion. Pillsbury's proclamation of August 30, 1876, is given on pages 11–13. The resolutions adopted are printed on pages 20–23. On pages 26–31 may be found Pillsbury's historical paper, probably prepared by Allen Whitman. Page 33 gives a memorial to Congress invoking national interposition and an appropriation. On page 35 is a letter to the president asking him to recommend action by Congress. Pages 37–58 contain practical suggestions for repression of the locust plague, summarized on page 57. On page 54 is a strong recommendation of state bounties for the destruction of eggs and young. See also Whitman's report, in Geological and Natural History Survey, Reports, 1876, p. 121.

[19] Commissioner of Statistics, Reports, 1877, pp. 9, 19, 24; Whitman's reports, in Geological and Natural History Survey, Reports, 1876, pp. 122–127; 1877. p. 134.

Russia, Turkey, France, Spain, and China did. A second memorial of January 23 declared the Rocky Mountain locust to be a national scourge and requested the Minnesota delegation in Congress to secure an appropriation for liberal bounties for the destruction of eggs and grasshoppers. In a later period Congress might have paid more attention to such appeals, instead of regarding the matter as one for state action.[20]

Having appealed to Jupiter to no evident purpose, the legislators resolved to put their shoulders to the wheel and set to work on a bill for making war on Minnesota grasshoppers. They appear to have been influenced by the results of experiments with bounties for the destruction of eggs and young in certain counties in the season of 1876 and by the advice of the Omaha conference. The bill became a law on March 1, 1877. The earlier sections provided for a system of bounties beginning with one dollar a bushel for grasshoppers caught up to May 25 and dropping down to twenty cents for those caught after July 1, with intermediate proportionate sums. Fifty cents per gallon were offered for eggs at any time. It was made the duty of the governor to appoint a state measurer in each infested township to serve for such compensation as the county commissioners might determine, to be paid out of county revenue. The measurer was to make a report to the county auditor of eggs and hoppers delivered by individuals. The county auditor would then draw an order on the state auditor, who in turn would issue a warrant on the state treasurer. Neglect or malfeasance on the part of a measurer made him liable to fine or imprisonment as for a misdemeanor. The later sections of the act

[20] *Executive Documents*, 1876, vol. i, pp. 36–38; *Senate Journal*, 1877, pp. 7, 25; *House Journal*, 32; *General Laws*, 280–282. For the elaborate report of the joint committee, signed by Ignatius Donnelly and William Crooks, see *House Journal*, 1877, pp. 515–518. This report was not submitted to the House until March 1, 1877. The investigation was extensive and laborious. Four hundred letters were received from thirty-eight counties. Appropriations for seed grain and bounties were recommended. On January 5 Donnelly proposed that the salaries of all county officers be reduced to a figure not exceeding the average income of taxpayers. *Senate Journal*, 1877, p. 14.

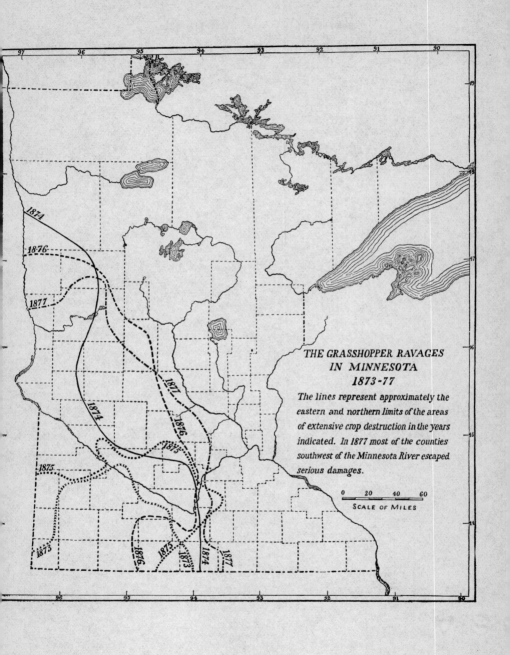

THE GRASSHOPPER RAVAGES
IN MINNESOTA
1873-77

The lines represent approximately the
eastern and northern limits of the areas
of extensive crop destruction in the years
indicated. In 1877 most of the counties
southwest of the Minnesota River escaped
serious damages.

SCALE OF MILES

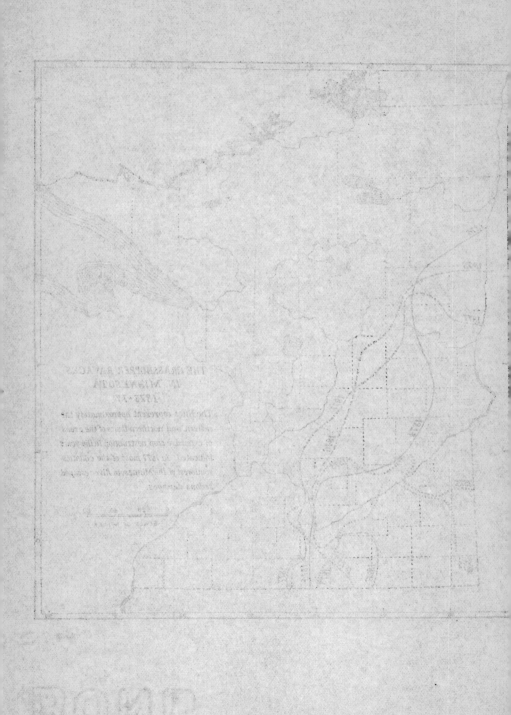

required every male inhabitant of the infested districts over twenty-one years old and under sixty, excepting paupers, idiots, and lunatics, to devote one day a week for five weeks to killing grasshopper eggs or young, but any might commute by paying one dollar a day. A final provision of the act authorized county boards to employ competent men with the best known contrivances to destroy the vermin, and to pay them according to measure or time employed. By a separate bill the governor, the state auditor, and the state treasurer were authorized to borrow $100,000 to carry out the act. The absurd bounty and poll-tax scheme of the legislature was printed with the other session laws. It got no further. Governor Pillsbury declined the task of appointing several hundred township measurers, when it became apparent that the appropriation would be altogether inadequate.[21]

Other grasshopper laws were enacted by this alarmed legislature. One appropriated five thousand dollars for immediate relief. A second authorized the state auditor to abate all penalties for defaulted payments for school, agricultural college, and internal improvement lands in 1877 upon verified petition by settlers whose crops had been damaged. Another appropriated seventy-five thousand dollars to be lent to farmers whose crops had been destroyed in 1876 for the purchase of seed grain. Still another authorized city and municipal councils to levy a special tax for grasshopper destruction after a referendum to the electors. It was the opinion of Governor Pillsbury that the effect of all these measures was to add a million dollars to the value of the crop of 1877 and that the policy of lending instead of giving had preserved the respect of the beneficiaries.[22]

The legislature of 1877 did everything it knew how to do for the relief of the grasshopper sufferers. Either the people of the infested districts put little confidence in the

[21] *General Laws*, 1877, pp. 171–175; Pillsbury's message, January 11, 1878, in *Executive Documents*, 1877, vol. 1, p. 43.
[22] *General Laws*, 1877, pp. 205, 207, 243, 246–248; Pillsbury's message, January 11, 1878, in *Executive Documents*, 1877, vol. 1, p. 44.

laws it had passed or conceived that they would be more efficacious if especially seconded by Divine Providence. Many of them called on Governor Pillsbury personally and by letter to appoint a day of prayer for deliverance from the affliction. The Omaha conference had already recommended the observance of such a day. On April 9, 1877, in a proclamation sounding in appeals for divine mercy for sins, for the intervention of the only hand which could stay the pestilence, and for united action in relief of the sorrowful, he accordingly named April 26 for the purpose. The appointed day of fasting, humiliation, and prayer was kept with varying fidelity. In the infested districts the observance was general by union meetings in churches. In other portions of the state the day was one of sobriety and thoughtfulness. Expectations varied according to people's views as to the place of prayer in an ordered universe. No miracle was wrought, but the subjective effect of the day's observance was wholesome.[23]

The grasshopper program opened as usual in 1877. By the middle of April hatching had begun in the southern counties. It went on through the remainder of that month, through May, and through the first half of June — an unusually long period of hatching. A snowfall at the end of April and many days of heavy rainfall in the first half

---

[23] Governor's Archives, Records, F: 18; Phelps, *Biographical History*, 18. See the *Pioneer Press* (St. Paul and Minneapolis), 1877: April 10, p. 4; 26, p. 3; 27, p. 6, for accounts of the observation of the day in Minneapolis. The statement was made that the treatment of the Sioux Indians by the white people of Minnesota was a sufficient cause for the sore scourge and that the first petition for a day of prayer came from Christian Sioux. The flour mills of Minneapolis continued in operation, except those in which Governor Pillsbury was interested.

In the *Minneapolis Times*, August 6, 1899, part 1, p. 10, is a poem with the title "How Prayer Stopped the Grasshopper," signed "J. N. C.," and Governor Pillsbury's story, told after he had perused the poem. Pillsbury is recorded as saying: "And the very next night it turned cold and froze every grasshopper in the state stiff; froze 'em right up solid, sir. . . . Well sir, that was over twenty years ago and grasshoppers don't appear to have been bothering us very much since." From an intimacy of thirty-five years, the author does not believe that Governor Pillsbury ever talked in that style.

In his *Lights and Shadows of a Long Episcopate*, 323 (New York, 1900), Bishop Henry B. Whipple says that on April 26, 1877, "before the sun went

of June had the double effect of retarding hatching and stimulating the growth of wheat, oats, and wild hay. It was soon seen that the weakened larvæ were doing little damage where wheat was thick and strong, which gave the farmers courage to renew the fight by all known means of attack. The *Pioneer Press* on May 19 published a letter written by the Honorable Andrew B. Robbins, state senator from Kandiyohi County, urging the more general use of an improved apparatus which, not so well constructed, had already been in use to some extent. The apparatus consisted of a strip of sheet iron two feet wide and from ten to sixteen feet long turned up to form back and ends. The front side was also slightly turned up and the inside of the pan so formed was smeared with coal tar. The improvement was the substitution of sheet iron for cotton cloth. By means of ropes attached to rings near the ends the " tar-pan " was slowly drawn over the growing grain to dislodge and catch the young locusts. At convenient intervals the loads were scraped out. Governor Pillsbury was so much impressed with reports of the successful operation of the device that he telegraphed to county authorities that he would supply the materials if they would promise to pay for them out of county funds. Twenty-nine counties responded. The governor bought, partly out of a balance of the five-thousand-dollar relief fund and partly on his personal credit, fifty-six thousand pounds of sheet iron and three thousand barrels of coal tar. The railroad companies carried them to their destinations without charge for freight. Upon the governor's recommendation

down, a violent storm of sleet and snow came and every locust was destroyed." The *Tribune* (Minneapolis), May 1, 1877, p. 3, says: " Special dispatches . . . from a number of prominent points in the grasshopper districts show that the heavy storm of snow and rain has not done much damage to the hoppers, but on the contrary they seem as lively as ever." The *Faribault Republican*, May 9, 1877, p. 2, states that reports from the grasshopper districts conflicted. " In some sections it is reported that all the young hoppers have been frozen to death and the eggs are rotten, while in others it is said that the storm did not destroy any of the hoppers, or at best, but very few." According to the newspapers of the time, the storm was on April 27 and 28. *Tribune* (Minneapolis), April 30, 1877, p. 1.

the legislature of the following winter made an appropriation of state funds to cover this expense in part. The effects
of the tar-pan, of ditching, and of other devices were the more
noticeable in this season because of the condition of the
locusts, weakened by unfavorable weather and probably by
parasites, a " silky mite " being observed especially.

Still the program of the four previous years went on with
some variation until near the first of July, when the full
development of wings was due. Then took place a change
which no one anticipated and which has not been explained.
In the previous years the winged locusts, after devouring the
vegetation near their hatching places, would fly into the next
county, there to devour and perhaps fly again. After one or
more flights they would proceed to egg-laying. Not so in
1877. This year the flights were migrations, not mere
changes of base. In some cases the swarms rose at once
high in the air and flew out of the state. Those which temporarily alighted did little damage and made no preparations for egg-laying. The varying directions of the flights
were a puzzle to observers. Some of the earlier ones were
toward the northwest, but the conjecture that they were
return migrations to the original home of the locust in the
Rockies has not been verified. By the middle of August
Minnesota was free from the grasshopper scourge.[24]

Another marvel followed the departure of the locust
swarms of 1877, as welcome as if it had been miraculous.
Notwithstanding grasshopper damages, the crop of the year
was abundant beyond parallel. The yield of wheat from
1,829,167 acres was 30,693,969 bushels and it weighed
sixty-three pounds to the bushel. Governor Pillsbury made

[24] Whitman's report, in Geological and Natural History Survey, *Reports*,
1877, pp. 139, 142–145; Entomological Commission, *Reports*, 1877, appendix 1,
pp. 6–11; *Pioneer Press*, May 19, 1877, p. 5; Pillsbury's message, January 11,
1878, in *Executive Documents*, 1877, vol. 1, p. 45; Judson W. Bishop, " History
of the St. Paul & Sioux City Railroad, 1864–1881," in *Minnesota Historical
Collections*, 10: 407–411 (part 1) ; *General Laws*, 1878, p. 177. The legislature
appropriated $4,213.32 to reimburse the governor. See also Entomological
Commission, *Reports*, 1878–79, map facing p. 160.

no allusion to the grasshopper question in his message to the legislature of 1879.[25]

In the same year which witnessed the departure of the locusts another insect pest, the chinch bug, appeared in some southern counties in numbers which caused alarm, but the damage at harvest proved to be slight. Three years later there was another visitation in the same region which aided in reducing the yield of wheat below the average.[26]

In 1887 a small swarm of locusts appeared in Otter Tail County and deposited eggs. When in the following spring the young began to hatch out over an area of a hundred square miles, the farmers, not liking to have their county advertised as a " grasshopper county," attacked them so vigorously that the mischief was reduced to a comparatively small amount. Thirty-five thousand bushels of eggs and young were captured and destroyed and but few eggs were left for another season.[27]

[25] Commissioner of Statistics, *Reports*, 1878, pp. 10, 15.

[26] Commissioner of Statistics, *Reports*, 1877, p. 18. On page 94 is a letter from the auditor of Houston County estimating the damage to wheat in that county at two-thirds of the crop. For the history and habits of the chinch bug, see Commissioner of Statistics, *Reports*, 1880, pp. 22, 72–74. The name in science is *blissus leucopterus*.

[27] McGill's message, in *Executive Documents*, 1888–89, vol. 1, pp. 15–17. For a learned discussion of the probability of further locust visitations to Minnesota, see an undated communication of Cyrus Thomas to Governor Pillsbury, in Entomological Commission, *Reports*, 1878–79, pp. 303–307. The counsel of this expert was to clothe the Coteau des Prairies with timber, to plant trees everywhere, and to preserve all the lakes, ponds, and even the marshes of the state. The legislature of 1878 passed acts for supplying seed grain. See *General Laws*, 1878, pp. 157–161, 174; 1879, p. 71. See United States, *Statutes at Large*, 19: 54, 55; 20: 114; 21: 11, for extensions of terms to tree-growers, homesteaders, and preëmptioners suffering from grasshopper ravages. A résumé of state legislation in regard to grasshoppers is in Minnesota, *General Statutes*, 1878, pp. 1024–1030.

V. THE PILLSBURY REGIME, 1876–81

CUSHMAN K. DAVIS had desired the governorship only as a stepping-stone to a higher office. That not being accorded, he did not seek a reëlection, as precedent would have justified. When the Republican state convention assembled on July 28, 1875, it ratified by a single ballot the already well-known choice of the party, voiced through the press and by local conventions, of John Sargent Pillsbury for governor.[1] Pillsbury had been a resident of Minnesota since 1855. He was born in the town of Sutton, New Hampshire, on July 29, 1827, of parents of Puritan stock. His education consisted of attendance in the common school, learning the painter's trade, and clerking in a country store during the last five years of his minority. After four years devoted to merchandising in Concord, New Hampshire, he decided to try his fortune in the West and selected the village of St. Anthony Falls as the most promising point. Here he engaged in a hardware business in 1855. Two years later, 1857 — the panic year — a fire destroyed his whole stock in trade. The Boston firm to which he was chiefly indebted refused to allow him to assign, but urged him to continue in business and proposed to supply him with goods on his personal credit. It is related that the head of the firm told him he might hold his notes and whenever he had redeemed one by remittance he might tear it up. In five years he had cleared off all his obligations and had firmly established a business which was to last many years. Pillsbury had good right to aspire to the governorship. He had battled in the front rank of the Republican party from the time of its organization in Minnesota the year he came to the state and had served for six terms in the state Senate.

[1] *Pioneer-Press* (St. Paul and Minneapolis), July 29, 1875, p. 2.

With the rift in the Republican ranks now closed, his election followed as a matter of course.[2]

Governor Pillsbury brought to the office a ripe and successful business experience, large knowledge of state and national politics, an extraordinary capacity for judging men, and an art in proposing practicable measures at right times rarely equaled. Such was the influence these qualities enabled him to exert that during his administration legislatures willingly enacted measures commended by predecessors with arguments they did not pretend to refute but which did not move them to action. So active, so forceful, so practical was Governor Pillsbury throughout his long period in office that his biography for the period might almost serve as the history of the state. He was ready in his inaugural address of January 7, 1876, with suggestions for the improvement of administration with reduced expenses, for the redemption of the repudiated bonds of 1858, and for wise and generous treatment of railroads, about to be declared by the United States Supreme Court subject to the control of the sovereign power of the state, a conclusion with which he was more than content.[3]

The first year of Governor Pillsbury's service was marked by the perpetration of a crime as yet without parallel in our state annals. Robbery is too frequent a crime even in the most civilized states, particularly since the multiplication of automobiles in America, and its details are ordinarily of too trifling interest, except to the persons visited, to deserve mention on the page of history. But there took place in Minnesota in the early fall of 1876 an instance so far out of the ordinary that neglect to remark upon it would be a fault. A band of desperadoes from a distant state attempted to rob the First National Bank of Northfield, Rice County. A street fight ensued, in which two of the gang

[2] Baker, *Governors of Minnesota*, 227–230, 232; Phelps, *Biographical History*, 4: 11–14; Upham and Dunlap, *Minnesota Biographies*, 603, and citations.
[3] Pillsbury's inaugural message, in *Executive Documents*, 1875, pp. 6–11, 17–24: Stickney, *Railway Problem*, 120.

were shot dead, two others were wounded, and one citizen was mortally wounded. Three of the wretches entered the bank, shot dead the cashier, Joseph Lee Heywood, after he had refused to open the safe, and wounded the bank teller, Alonzo E. Bunker. The survivors were forced to mount their horses and ride away without having taken a single dollar. A pursuit lasting a fortnight resulted in the capture of three men, Thomas Coleman Younger and his brothers, James and Robert, and the killing of a fourth. On November 16 the three were arraigned for murder in the first degree in the district court of Rice County, to which charge they pleaded guilty. As the law of Minnesota then stood it was made the duty of a trial jury to decide whether a person convicted of murder in the first degree should suffer death or be imprisoned for life. In these cases there was no jury and the court refused to impanel a jury to pass on the nature of the punishment. It therefore sentenced the convicts to life imprisonment. The behavior of the men in prison was so orderly and their demeanor was so courteous that the officials and later many citizens became their friends. The youngest of the brothers died in prison in 1889. Modifications of the law relating to paroles and pardons permitted the parole of the two survivors in 1901 after twenty-five years of confinement. One of them committed suicide in 1902 and the other received a pardon in 1903, on condition that he would leave the state and never return. Two members of the gang separated from the other four a week before the capture of the Younger brothers and escaped on stolen horses into South Dakota and from there into Missouri.[4]

4 Thomas C. Younger, The Story of Cole Younger, 79–105 (Chicago, 1903); George Huntington, Robber and Hero, 10–38, 47–71, 75, 78 (Northfield, 1895); John J. Lemon, The Northfield Tragedy; or the Raid of the Younger–James Bros., 6–12, 25–76 (St. Paul, 1881); James W. Buell, The Border Outlaws, 206–222 (St. Louis, Missouri, 1881); W. C. Bronaugh, The Youngers' Fight for Freedom, 238–261 (Columbia, Missouri, 1906); Faribault Republican, September 13, November 15, 22, 1876; General Laws, 1868, p. 130; 1901, p. 321.

The main stream of Minnesota politics during the period now in view, 1876–81, except for certain minor disturbances, flowed on in quiet. The Republican party, strengthened by the return to the fold of stray sheep from the Liberal wilderness, held secure control of all offices and emoluments. Still, it should not be forgotten that there remained a strong and compact opposition party composed of old-line Jeffersonian Democrats with a few recruits from Liberal ranks. The relative strength of the two great parties in the state as shown by the votes cast for Hayes and Tilden in November, 1876, was almost exactly the same as that in the Grant-Greeley contest in 1872. In 1877 Governor Pillsbury, endeared to many by his generous behavior toward the grasshopper sufferers, was renominated by acclamation and was elected by an increased majority. Again in 1879, after two years more of efficient service and devotion to the rescue of Minnesota from the slough of dishonor in which she had been floundering since the repudiation of her bonded railroad debt of 1858, he received the extraordinary compliment of a second renomination. An opposition somewhat threatening was made by some voters who disapproved of a third term on general principles and by some who believed that the old railroad bonds should not have been redeemed; but at the polls Pillsbury's majority was not only maintained but increased.[5]

William Windom had made so considerable a figure in the United States Senate and had so strong a body of friends that no Republican seriously disputed his claim to the reëlection which the legislature accorded him in the winter of 1877. President Garfield upon his accession to office on March 4, 1881, called Senator Windom into his cabinet as secretary of the treasury and Governor Pillsbury appointed

[5] *Pioneer Press*, September 28, 1877; September 3, 1879. The vote for president in 1872 was: Grant, 55,708; Greeley, 35,211. In 1876 the vote was: Hayes, 72,955; Tilden, 48,787. These figures, as well as the results of the gubernatorial elections of 1877 and 1879, may be found in the *Legislative Manual*, 1925, pp. 113, 115. See also Eugene V. Smalley, ed., *History of the Republican Party*, 205–209 (St. Paul, 1896), and Hall, *Observations*, 232–238.

Alonzo J. Edgerton to fill his vacancy. On July 2 President Garfield was shot by the insane assassin, Guiteau; and on September 19 he died and the vice president, Chester A. Arthur, succeeded to the office. Windom, of course, resigned and retired to private life, but for no long time. The extra session of the Minnesota legislature, which had been called for another purpose, took up the duty of electing a United States senator. General Edgerton decided not to aspire to an election and, there being no other Republican candidate, Windom was reëlected for the remainder of his second term, which expired on March 3, 1883. Edgerton served from March 14 until October 26, 1881. In the last year of the period, 1881, Senator McMillan received a renomination with but slight opposition from friends of Ramsey and Davis and was, of course, reëlected.[6]

The disturbances in the main stream of Minnesota politics hinted at were caused by the antics of a third political party, under different titles, dominated by the irrepressible Donnelly. On March 29, 1876, the Anti-Monopoly party, as if intending to take time by the forelock, held a state convention in Owatonna. The party was given the name " Independent " and a platform was adopted consisting of a series of " demands," of which the essential ones were: (1) that greenbacks be made legal tender for all debts except such as had been declared by law payable in coin; (2) that all money be created by the nation; (3) that national bank notes be retired and greenbacks be issued in their place; (4) that the act of January 14, 1875, providing for the resumption of specie payment on January 1, 1879, be repealed; and (5) that greenbacks be made interchangeable

---

[6] Appleton, *Annual Cyclopædia*, 1881, pp. 846–848; *House Journal*, 1877, p. 53; 1881, p. 48; 1881, extra session, 64; *Senate Journal*, 1877, p. 39; 1881, p. 331; 1881, extra session, p. 39; Castle, in *Minnesota Historical Collections*, 15: 576; Holmes, in *Minnesota in Three Centuries*, 4: 104. In November, 1881, General Edgerton was appointed chief justice of Dakota Territory, which office he held until 1885. He was appointed judge of the United States district court for South Dakota in 1889 and held the position until his death on August 9, 1896.

with government bonds bearing interest not to exceed 3.65 per cent per annum. On May 17, 1876, there assembled in Indianapolis a convention of the " Independent National " or " Greenback " party. Ignatius Donnelly was the temporary chairman and made a characteristic keynote address. A platform was adopted which embraced all the essential demands of the Independents at Owatonna with slight variations and additions. Donnelly had been elected a state senator in 1873 as an Anti-Monopolist and he was reëlected in 1875. The duties of this position did not prevent him from aspiring to higher ones. His failure to secure an election to the United States Senate in the winter of 1875 has already been mentioned. At the election of November, 1876, he appeared as a Greenback candidate for representative in Congress from the second district but was defeated.[7]

Still desiring to raise his voice under the dome of the national Capitol, Donnelly in 1878 again pulled the wires for a nomination to Congress. A convention of the Greenbackers of the third congressional district was held in Minneapolis on September 5. The now well-worn platform was adopted and Ignatius Donnelly was nominated for representative in Congress. A committee was appointed to open conference with the Democratic district convention called for the next day. The Democrats of Minnesota knew very well that, acting independently, they could not possibly secure any of the important offices. But they were not disposed to leave the arena of politics and allow their organization to weaken. They therefore decided to try the effect of coöperation with the third party. Their district convention held in St. Paul on September 6 accordingly indorsed the nomination of Donnelly. Hopeful of success with a large, if not a united, Democratic support behind him and willing

[7] Anti-Monopolist (St. Paul), 1874: November 12, p. 4; 1876: April 6, p. 4; May 25, p. 1; November 2, p. 4; 9, p. 1; 16, p. 1; Hastings Gazette, November 6, 1875; Thomas H. McKee, The National Conventions and Platforms of All Political Parties, 1789 to 1900, 173 (Baltimore, 1900) ; Fred E. Haynes, Third Party Movements since the Civil War, with Special Reference to Iowa, 91, 105–112 (Iowa City, 1916) ; Legislative Manual, 1875, p. 87.

to settle some old scores with William D. Washburn, his Republican opponent, Donnelly made a campaign of extraordinary brilliance, only to meet with a great disappointment. The old-line Democrats could not stomach the mountebank politician, as they deemed him, and either did not vote or voted for Washburn. He had some satisfaction in cutting down the Republican majority to a figure not pleasant for that party to contemplate. As the margin was so slight compared with the aggregate vote and with previous Republican majorities and, as he conceived, was obtained by the operation of an unconstitutional election law passed in the previous winter, Donnelly decided to contest the election. Complicated by an extraordinary incident, the contest went on throughout the whole of the Forty-sixth Congress and was left technically undecided. Washburn, of course, held the seat, but his influence was impaired for the time being.

According to a practice which had become customary, Washburn was accorded a renomination by the Republicans of the third district in the campaign of 1880. The Democrats, who had taken nothing by their trek into the wilderness with Donnelly, returned to their ancient domain and put up in opposition the strongest man in their ranks, Henry Hastings Sibley. His high personal standing and distinguished services for state and nation did not avail; Washburn was elected by a majority of 12,624 out of a total vote of 60,232. A second renomination, equivalent to a reëlection, as representative from the fourth congressional district followed in 1882. Washburn's service as representative through three Congresses fully justified the expectations of his friends. He trained in party ranks with reasonable regularity but, independent and fearless, diverged on some important issues.[8]

[8] *Minneapolis Tribune*, September 7, 1878, p. 2; *Pioneer Press*, September 7, 1878, p. 9; November 21, 1880, p. 4; November 28, 1882, p. 7; *Anti-Monopolist*, September 12, 1878, p. 4; *Legislative Manual*, 1881, p. 272; 1883, p. 309; Phelps, *Biographical History*, 44. For the Donnelly-Washburn contest, see the Appendix, no. 6, *post.*

In the course of Governor Pillsbury's six-year term of service, chiefly upon his recommendation, certain amendments to the state constitution were adopted and laws were enacted which, if not of capital importance, were of moment and had lasting consequences. Some of them will come into view later in this history. Among the constitutional amendments were that of 1876 authorizing the governor to veto items in appropriation bills;[9] three in 1877 — one providing for biennial sessions of the legislature,[10] a second doubling the terms of state senators and representatives,[11] and a third creating a state board of canvassers to open and canvass the election returns for all officers composing the executive department of the state government;[12] and one of importance in 1881 providing for the sale of the swamp lands granted to the state by Congress, the establishment of a separate fund from the proceeds, and the equal division of the annual income between the state school fund and the educational and charitable institutions of the state.[13] Among laws should

[9] General Laws, 1876, p. 17; 1877, p. 17; William Anderson (in collaboration with Albert J. Lobb), History of the Constitution of Minnesota with the First Verified Text, 169 (University of Minnesota, Studies in the Social Sciences, no. 15 — Minneapolis, 1921). It was ratified on November 7, 1876, by a vote of 47,302 to 4,426.

[10] General Laws, 1877, p. 19; 1878, p. 14; 1887, p. 6; 1889, p. 2; Anderson, History of the Constitution, 165. It was ratified on November 6, 1877, by a vote of 37,995 to 20,833. An amendment of 1887 limited the biennial sessions to ninety days and provided that no bills should be introduced in the last twenty days, except upon the written request of the governor. It was ratified on November 6, 1888.

[11] General Laws, 1877, p. 20; 1878, p. 14; Anderson, History of the Constitution, 165. It was ratified on November 6, 1877, by a vote of 33,072 to 25,099.

[12] General Laws, 1877, p. 20; 1878, p. 15; Anderson, History of the Constitution, 174. It was ratified on November 6, 1877, by a vote of 36,072 to 21,814. These returns had previously been canvassed by the legislature in joint session. Constitution, article 5, section 2.

[13] General Laws, 1881, p. 23; 1883, p. 3; Anderson, History of the Constitution, 181–184. It was ratified on November 8, 1881, by a vote of 51,903 to 8,440. In 1860 Congress donated to Minnesota all the land within her boundaries which should be marked as "swamp" by the government surveyors, on condition that the proceeds of sales should be devoted to the drainage of the lands so far as might be necessary. As there were millions of acres of dry land ready for clearing and cultivation, the early legislatures saw no necessity for draining swamps. There was no difficulty in getting rid of the burden of the gift. Beginning with a donation of 694,400 acres to the Lake Superior

be mentioned that of 1876 rendering effective the constitutional amendment of the previous year extending the elective franchise to women in regard to school officers and measures and authorizing women to hold school offices;[14] the act of 1877 creating a school textbook commission;[15] and that of 1878 for the encouragement of higher education by the creation of the high school board and by appropriating money to be distributed to high schools offering free preparation for admission to the university.[16]

It was a natural thing that Governor Pillsbury, who was not a lawyer, as the greater number of his predecessors had been, but an experienced and successful man of business, should be concerned about administrative affairs. It was a matter of common observation that public officials charged with the handling of public funds often proved incompetent and sometimes dishonest and that banking and other corporations too frequently became insolvent. Governor Austin in his first inaugural address had remarked on the frequency with which county treasurers retired from office with increased wealth as a notorious fact. This may have moved

and Mississippi Railroad Company in 1861, in the course of twenty years nearly two million acres were granted to railroad companies. The people at length became weary of the importunity of railroad companies and began to understand that some swamp lands when drained became the best land for some purposes. They therefore cheerfully ratified the constitutional amendment of 1881. In 1914 the state auditor stated that six forties of swamp land were on the tax rolls for twenty-eight million tons of iron ore with prospective royalties of more than ten million dollars. Reports of the state auditor, in *Executive Documents*, 1880, vol. I, p. 215; 1913-14, vol. I, p. xxxi; United States, *Statutes at Large*, 9: 519; 12: 3.

[14] *General Laws*, 1875, p. 18; 1876, p. 29; 1878, p. 13; 1897, p. 331; 1899, p. v. The amendment was ratified on November 2, 1875, by a vote of 24,340 to 19,468. An amendment ratified on November 11, 1898, extended woman suffrage to officers and measures relating to public libraries. The vote was: yes, 71,704; no, 43,660.

[15] *General Laws*, 1877, p. 156. The report of the commission forms an appendix of forty-eight pages to the *Senate Journal*, 1878. Superintendent David Burt was not in favor of the law. See his letter, dated December 12, 1877, in the *Pioneer Press*, December 13, 1877, p. 5; his pamphlet entitled *Concerning Those Books* (Winona, n. d.); and his *Report* as state superintendent of public instruction, 1877, pp. 78-93.

[16] *General Laws*, 1878, p. 154. A new act was passed in 1881, that of 1878 having become inoperative by failure of the legislature of 1879 to make the expected appropriation. *General Laws*, 1881, p. 186.

Governor Pillsbury in 1876 in his first inaugural address
to suggest the creation of a new office whose incumbent
should supervise the financial transactions of public officials.
The novel proposition met with no more hospitality than
had Governor Austin's remark; but the legislature of 1878
responded to a renewal of the recommendation and passed
a stringent act so well drawn that little room was left for
later amendments.

The act provided for the appointment by the governor,
with senatorial approval, of a skillful accountant, not a
public official nor a stockholder, officer, or employee of a
corporation, as " public examiner " for a term of three
years at a salary of $3,500. The acceptance of any other
compensation was declared a felony punishable by a fine
of $10,000 or ten years' imprisonment. Bonds were fixed
at $50,000. The duties of the public examiner, prescribed
in a series of sections, were to visit all educational, charitable, penal, and reformatory institutions, state banks, and
offices of state and county auditors and treasurers at irregular periods without notice and make exhaustive examinations
of their accounts; to investigate the standing of bondsmen
and verify all assets and securities; and to prescribe uniform
systems of bookkeeping and instruct officers therein. He
was authorized to examine under oath all officials, custodi-
ans of funds, managers, and employees. Refusal of officials
and others to make returns and exhibits was made a felony
and false returns, perjury.[17]

After taking time for consideration Governor Pillsbury
selected Henry Martyn Knox, cashier of the First National
Bank of St. Paul, as first public examiner and made no
mistake. Knox qualified for the office on May 1, 1878, and
submitted his first report on December 20, 1878. In that
and in the reports for the following two years he furnished

[17] Inaugural addresses of Austin and Pillsbury and Pillsbury's message of
January 11, 1878, in *Executive Documents*, 1869, p. 18; 1875, vol. 1, p. 16; 1877,
vol. 1, pp. 20–22; *General Laws*, 1878, pp. 129–132.

abundant reason for Governor Pillsbury's desire to have
the office created and evidence of the good sense of the legislature in responding. As to the public institutions, he had
not much to criticize except the lack of uniformity of the
bookkeeping and the diversity of prices paid for supplies.
The greater number of state banks were found individually
in good condition and doing a legitimate business. There
were cases of shortage of cash; of overdrafts, some evidently
allowed to enable favored customers to avoid penalties for
delinquent taxes; of excessive loans to individuals, including bank directors; and of loans by a bank on the security
of the shares of its own capital stock. Under the operation of a banking law pronounced worthless by Knox, " paid
in " capital was represented by a comical variety of pretended assets. He also found instances of conspiracy between banks to prevent the payment of interest on public
funds.

At the county " capitals " ample occasion was found for
examinations. Where there should have been 140 bonds of
county officers on file in the office of the secretary of state only
57 were found and of these only 32 were complete and in
proper form. As a rule there was no orderly bookkeeping by county treasurers; instead of recording transactions as they occurred from day to day, they made up their
books from time to time from memoranda on loose slips.
In utter violation of existing law there were held as cash
items stacks of orders and warrants of town and school district boards, tax receipts, due bills, memorandum receipts,
checks and drafts often of ancient dates, deposit slips of
persons and firms, wheat tickets, memoranda of advances
to towns and school districts, and town railroad bonds and
coupons. The county treasury was apparently treated as a
kind of bank. In counties where there were banks, interest
on deposits of public funds was considered the perquisite of
the treasurer; where there were no banks moneys were kept
in private safes or in the hands of merchants, or were car-

ried about in the pockets of the treasurers. Quite commonly
deposits were made in the treasurer's name and mixed with
his private funds. Most deplorable of all defects was the
general absence of any system of checks to show for what
moneys treasurers ought to be held responsible. Irregularities were found in the transactions of county commissioners:
the legal limit of their fees was commonly disregarded, their
records were written up after long intervals, and county
orders were issued in large amounts to be bought up at a discount by a favored few and held for payment when the
money had come into the treasury. The examiner thought
that the common belief in the existence of courthouse rings
involved "too indiscriminately the character of all our
public servants."

After three years of intense labor Knox was able to report
that he had made a complete visitation of all the institutions,
banks, and offices under his supervision and to make a gratifying showing of progress. The accounts of public institutions had been brought into uniformity and irregular bank
transactions had been abated. A great transformation had
been wrought in the accounting of county officers. Auditors
and treasurers were keeping cash accounts with persons as
well as with funds. There were registers of daily collections
and payments which, in large counties, were balanced daily.
A like transformation had taken place in regard to cash
items. The stacks of miscellaneous vouchers had disappeared. Orders and warrants were canceled and at once
turned over to auditors, who gave credit on their books.
Constructive fees had become disreputable. Public funds
were no longer available for the accommodation of treasurers and their friends having private notes to meet. Governor
Pillsbury was fully justified in saying to the legislature of
1881, "No single act of legislation in this State has ever
been productive of more good in purifying the public
service . . . than the creation of this office of Public
Examiner." Knox remained in office until 1888, when he

returned to his banking employment. Few citizens have rendered more valuable services to Minnesota than this modest, intelligent, indefatigable man.[18]

Any person, whether lawyer or layman, who has had occasion to resort to the volumes containing the laws of Minnesota passed from year to year, commonly called the " Session Laws," will have noted the great bulk of those segregated under the title " Special Laws." The state constitution as originally adopted had but a single inhibition of special legislation, that contained in section 2 of article 10 forbidding the legislature to create any corporations under special acts except for municipal purposes. Following territorial precedent, the state legislatures continued to enact special and private laws in number and variety too great to be scheduled. The encumbrance of the statute books was not the only evil. A greater one was the multiplication of bills of local and temporary interest on the calendars of the houses which absorbed time needed for measures of general and permanent importance. In his message to the legislature of 1881 in regular session Governor Pillsbury said that it was well known " that at least two-thirds of the time, labor and expense required of an average session are consumed in the passage and printing of acts of a purely private, special or local nature." Another vice crept in — that of allowing local bills to run through the routine stages and be passed without proper scrutiny, as a matter of courtesy to members standing as sponsors.

The demand for a restriction of such piecemeal lawmaking culminated in the submission to the electors of an amendment to the state constitution by the legislature of 1881. It was ratified at the November election and was added to article 4 of the legislative department as sections 33 and 34. The legislature was therein forbidden to enact any special

[18] Minnesota, Public Examiner, *Reports*, 1878, pp. 13–17, 20–22, 26; 1879, pp. 6–8, 16–21, 30, 34, 42; 1880, pp. 3, 8–16, 33–36, 41, 48–56; Pillsbury's message, January 6, 1881, in *Executive Documents*, 1880, vol. 1, p. 18. In 1887 the duties of the state auditor as superintendent of banks were transferred to the public examiner. *General Laws*, 1887, p. 300.

or private law in eleven specified cases. All seemed well; the legislature would enact no more special laws for the assessment or collection of taxes or for extending the time for their collection and would shut its doors to importunate petitioners for acts to permit them to lay out roads, operate ferries, and change county seats; but many a bypath was still left for the intrusion of special laws. There was no prohibition of special laws relating to cities, and their number multiplied. Nor was the amendment of existing special laws forbidden, and the files of the houses were crowded with bills to amend them.[19] Still the ancient mischief grew. The legislature of 1887 passed so many special laws that a separate volume had to be printed to contain them. The old practice increased in virulence until 1891, when the special laws occupied 1,138 pages and the general laws but 462. It may have been this extravagance which moved the legislature of that year to make another experiment for the restriction of special statutes and to submit to the electors a constitutional amendment in the shape of a recast of section 33 of article 4. The remodeled section, which was ratified on November 8, 1892, increased the number of forbidden cases to sixteen. More important, however, than any particular inhibition was the sweeping general opening clause, which reads, "In all cases when a general law can be made applicable no special law shall be enacted." Next in importance was the final paragraph: "The legislature may repeal any existing special or local law, but shall not amend, extend, or modify any of the same." The principle of the amendment of 1892 has been fairly efficient, but the legislatures have found ways to evade it when they have really wanted to. The commonest device has been that of passing a law general in terms, but which it was known and understood could apply only to a particular place or emergency.[20]

[19] *Executive Documents*, 1880, vol. 1, p. 22; *General Laws*, 1881, pp. 21–23; 1883, p. 2. The amendment was adopted by a vote of 56,491 to 8,369. On special legislation relating to cities, see the Appendix, no. 15, *post*.

[20] Anderson, *History of the Constitution*, 169; *General Laws*, 1891, pp. 19–21; 1893, p. 3. The amendment was adopted by a vote of 77,614 to 49,583.

The discovery of vast deposits of gold in Australia and California about the middle of the nineteenth century and the opening of numerous gold mines, placer and other, had the effect of enormously increasing the annual gold production of the world. In consequence silver became relatively too dear to make money of and went out of use for principal money in all civilized countries. In recognition of this fact and usage Congress on February 12, 1873, passed an act declaring the gold dollar of a certain standard weight and fineness the standard unit of value. In the financial depression of that year and the hard times which set in and persisted for a long period, mortgagees and other long-time debtors found difficulty in exchanging commodities for money to meet their money obligations. For them money was scarce, and their number was great.[21] The Greenback party from its organization had for its principal object the enlargement of the circulation, or at least the prevention of its diminution by the retirement of United States legal-tender notes, better known as "greenbacks" from the circumstance that the reverse sides of the notes were printed with green ink. Neither of the two great political parties was disposed to declare against a sentiment so general and peremptory and to adopt a policy of contraction; and Congress, by act of May 31, 1878, forbade the further retirement of greenbacks and prescribed that when received into the treasury they should be reissued and paid out and kept in circulation. This law has not been changed to this day and 346,681,016 greenback dollars are in circulation, unless in part temporarily held in the treasury.

A secondary object of the Greenback party was to secure the increase of money by remonetizing silver through the repeal of the act of 1873. This proposition was also one which neither of the great parties cared to oppose and the "silver question" did not become a national issue until a

[21] J. Laurence Laughlin, *The History of Bimetalism in the United States*, 77, 92–105, 111–115, 217, 218 (New York, 1894); *Statutes at Large*, 17: 424–435.

later time. The resumption act of Congress of January 14, 1875, gave the Greenbackers and their sympathizers occasion for loud outcry against demonetization. The act of 1873, they clamored, cut the people's money in two and robbed them of half. In response to a very general sentiment that in some way silver money should again be seen and handled, the Republican Congress of 1878 passed the so-called "Bland-Allison Act," which provided for the monthly purchase by the United States of not less than two million dollars' worth nor more than four million dollars' worth of silver bullion to be coined into dollars, the issue of "silver certificates" to owners depositing the dollars in the treasury, and the redemption of the same on demand in silver.[22]

This bill was pending in Congress when the Minnesota legislature of 1878 assembled on January 8. Early on the second day Senator Ignatius Donnelly, Greenbacker, offered a resolution to instruct the United States senators from Minnesota to support the Bland bill and to oppose any amendments which would prevent silver coin from again becoming legal tender. Senator Michael Doran, Democrat, immediately offered a resolution favoring the repeal of the resumption act of 1875 — to take effect on January 1, 1879 — to save the country from financial wreck and universal suffering. The Senate finance committee to which the resolutions and amendments were committed could come to no agreement about them and reported them back without recommendation. A motion for indefinite postponement was rejected by a two-thirds vote. Thereupon Senator Alonzo J. Edgerton, Republican, offered a substitute for the Donnelly resolution: "That our Senators in Congress be instructed, and our Representatives requested, to vote for a bill repealing the act

[22] James A. Woodburn, *Political Parties and Party Problems in the United States*, 136–144, 158 (New York, 1916); Frank W. Taussig, *The Silver Situation in the United States*, 1–10 (New York, 1893); Davis R. Dewey, *Financial History of the United States*, 377 (*American Citizen Series* — New York, 1918); *Statutes at Large*, 20: 25, 87.

of February 12th, 1873, demonetizing silver." The vote
was: ayes, 34; nays, 3; absent or not voting, 4.[23]

Although the Edgerton resolution was in form concurrent,
it does not appear to have been communicated to the House,
where on January 11 a Democratic member introduced a
resolution, needlessly verbose, to instruct the Minnesota
delegation in Congress to vote for the repeal of the specie
resumption act of 1875 and to use their influence and votes
for the remonetization of silver. Thereupon Patrick H.
Rahilly, Democrat, offered three resolutions, also needlessly verbose: one declared that there should not be two
kinds of currency, a silver currency for the poor man and
a gold currency for the rich man; a second asserted that
the United States government had practiced a fraud when
it demonetized silver after having issued bonds payable in
gold and silver coin; a third opposed the cancellation of
greenbacks, " the currency of the people," which cost nothing
but the printing. In lieu of these a single resolution was
proposed that the Minnesota legislature favor both silver
and gold as money and demand the remonetization of silver,
but that the coinage and valuation of the metals should be
so regulated that the government could keep faith with its
creditors. When the matter came up on January 18 Thomas
W. Purdie, a Republican member, moved as a substitute
" That we [the legislature] favor the repeal of the act of
Congress demonetizing silver, and are in favor of restoring
the silver dollar to its position prior to February, 1873."
Fifty-five members voted " aye," 41 " nay," and 10 were
absent or did not vote. There was no division on party lines
in either house. Behold the learning and wisdom of the
fathers of 1878! [24]

The legislature of Minnesota, in its twentieth session,
was called upon for the second time to exercise its functions
in the case of a public official impeached for corrupt con-

[23] Senate Journal, 1878, pp. 8, 22, 25.
[24] House Journal, 1878, pp. 21, 39, 43.

duct in office and for crimes and misdemeanors. On January 22, 1878, a petition, signed by citizens of Mower County, was presented to the House of Representatives accusing the Honorable Sherman Page, judge of the tenth judicial district, of misconduct in office and demanding that he be impeached therefor. The judiciary committee, to which the petition was referred, after a month's deliberation brought in a report stating that the allegations of the petitioners were in part true and recommending that Page be impeached. The House thereupon, by a vote of 71 to 30, resolved to impeach him. The House appointed a board of managers which appeared before the Senate and exhibited articles of impeachment against Page. The Senate organized as a high court of impeachment and thereupon adjourned from March 8 to May 22 to give the parties time for preparation. The trial began on May 23 and ended on June 17. A week and a day were then occupied with the arguments of the managers and of the counsel for Page. On June 28 the voting took place. Five of the ten charges were at once disposed of as frivolous, there being but one vote for conviction on four and three on a fifth. On two other articles the majority voted for acquittal. On the remaining three there was a majority for conviction, but not the necessary two-thirds. By a unanimous vote it was thereupon " considered, ordered and adjudged . . . that . . . Sherman Page . . . is hereby acquitted of each and every article and specification of impeachment." The outstanding feature of the trial was the argument of ex-Governor Cushman K. Davis in behalf of Judge Page.[25]

There has been but one later instance of impeachment in Minnesota. It took place in the last year of Governor

[25] *House Journal*, 1878, pp. 54, 246–252, 362, 551–584; *Journal of the Senate of Minnesota, Sitting as a High Court of Impeachment, for the Trial of Hon. Sherman Page*, 1: 6–21, 35, 70, 73; 2: 539; 3: 1, 146–255, 364–370 (St. Paul, [1878]); report of the state treasurer, in *General Laws*, 1879, appendix, 63. The cost of the trial to the state was $9,996.34. A more detailed account of the impeachment of Judge Page is given in the Appendix, no. 7, *post*.

Pillsbury's administration and did not result so happily as the Page case. During the extra legislative session of 1881 a petition signed by two citizens was brought before the House of Representatives asking for the impeachment of the Honorable E. St. Julien Cox, judge of the ninth judicial district. The principal charge was drunkenness while discharging judicial duties at sundry times and places, with two supplementary charges of immoral behavior, which were presently ignored. There were some preliminary sessions of the Senate court before the close of the extra session of the legislature and still others between December 13 and 16, but the trial was postponed until January 10, 1882. The remaining days of that month, all of February, and four days in March were occupied with the examination of witnesses and the incidental wrangling of the lawyers. Beginning on March 7 for two weeks the managers on the part of the House and the counsel for Cox poured out a continuous stream of oratory; and on March 22 began the voting, which was probably not materially affected by all the eloquence. In the course of the trial six of the original charges had been dismissed. On seven there was an acquittal by large majorities, but on the remaining seven the verdict was " guilty " by large majorities, except on one on which there was barely a two-thirds vote. The judgment of the court was removal from office and disqualification for all judicial offices of honor, trust, or profit for the period of three years, beginning on March 22, 1882, on which the vote stood: yeas, 25; nays, 12. Fruitless objection was made to the disqualification from office. It is a pleasure here to record that the legislature of 1891, in consideration of the fact that the conviction cast no reflection on the integrity of Judge Cox as a man nor on his incorruptibility as a judge and because the state " deigns not to tarnish its escutcheon with oppression," ordered by joint resolution that all the proceedings of the House in framing and presenting articles of impeachment and all proceedings of the Senate sitting as a high court of impeachment in the case be "vacated, canceled and expunged."[26]

The list of calamities which visited Minnesota in the period now in view was lengthened by one of much general interest, although it occurred in a single city, Minneapolis. Brief mention has been made of the great development of flour manufacture at the Falls of St. Anthony, along with bonanza farming and improved milling processes. By 1878 there were eighteen mills in operation at the falls, conspicuous among them the Washburn A mill, with a capacity of about fifteen hundred barrels of flour a day. It was owned by ex-Governor Cadwallader C. Washburn of La Crosse, Wisconsin, but was operated in the year named by John A. Christian and Company. The building was a solid construction of blue limestone from the local quarries, 138 by 100 feet on the ground and six stories in height. Five other mills were closely grouped about it so as to draw water for their wheels from the main headrace of the Minneapolis Water Power Company — the Diamond, the Humboldt, the Pettit-Robinson, the Galaxy, and the Zenith, the last three of which were not in operation at the time.

At six o'clock on May 2, 1878, the day workers of the mills — the receiving, shipping, and packing crews and the sweepers — went to their homes, leaving only the smaller force of expert millers to carry on the night's grinding. The mills were running at their usual speed with all machines and appliances apparently in order. At seven-twenty o'clock a roaring sound, like that of a tremendous thunderclap, was heard far and wide over the city. Distant buildings were shaken and glass was shattered in windows many blocks away. Persons in and near the mill district saw an immense column of black smoke, with flames darting

[26] House Journal, 1881, extra session, 23, 135, 137, 256–265; Journal of the Senate of Minnesota, Sitting as a High Court of Impeachment, for the Trial of Hon. E. St. Julien Cox, 1: 3, 13, 14, 163; 3: 2076, 2913–2958, 2989 (St. Paul, 1882); General Laws, 1891, p. 399. The impeachment of Judge Cox is more fully discussed in the Appendix, no. 8, post.

through it, rise from the Washburn A mill. They also saw the roof of the mill heaved upward and then drop, carrying the successive floors with it, and the walls crumble and fall outward. The walls of two other mills, the Diamond and the Humboldt, standing west and south, were seen to collapse and their roofs and floors fall to the ground in ruins. The three other mills named, standing across the canal a little more distant, were not exploded but were a mass of flames in the course of a few minutes and were completely consumed. Another mill, the Washburn B, with a capacity of four hundred barrels, standing forty feet away to the west and south, remained uninjured save for a hole in the roof through which the water thrown over it by firemen ran in and flooded its floors. It is difficult to account for this comparative immunity. The wheat elevator near the Washburn A mill took fire and, being wholly of wood, was almost immediately a mass of flame. The finding of a fragment of its iron roofing two miles away led to the belief by some that an explosion also wrecked this structure. This was probably erroneous, for an explosion would have wrought complete and instantaneous destruction. The amount of wheat in store was small — some ten thousand bushels. Destruction or damage was done to adjacent small buildings, to a lumber yard, and to some forty loaded cars.

The financial loss, direct and indirect, was never precisely ascertained but it exceeded a million dollars, a considerable sum for a young city of less than forty thousand people. But that loss was as nothing compared with the sacrifice of eighteen workmen's lives, fourteen of them in the Washburn A mill. Ten bodies or fragments of bodies were identified; the remaining eight had been burned beyond recognition. On June 2 a public funeral was celebrated over the unidentified dead.

The cause of all this damage to life and property was, of course, at once a matter of general curiosity. A report that a box of dynamite, for use in a neighboring rock excavation,

The Ruins after the Mill Explosion

A   Washburn A Mill
B   Washburn B Mill
C   Pettit-Robinson Mill
D   Zenith Mill
E   Galaxy Mill
F   Guilder's Shop

G   Diamond Mill
H   Butler's Shop
J   Humboldt Mill
K   Planing Mill
L   Dry Shed
M   Palisade Mill

N   Round House
O   Anchor Mill
P   Elevator
Q   North Star Woolen Mill
R   Russell-Hineline Mill
S   Empire Mill

T   Dakota Mill
U   City Water Works
V   Pillsbury Mill
W   Covered Canal
X   Morrison Mill
Y   Paper Mill

[From an engraving in Sturtevant, *The Great Mill Explosion*. The letters Q, T, and U do not appear on the engraving.]

had been stored in the A mill, was immediately silenced. Another guess was that the new middlings purifiers had generated "flour gas," which was, of course, absurd. But the explosions were more than a matter of disinterested curiosity. The policies of the many companies carrying insurance on the destroyed buildings and their contents contained this common reservation: " This company will not be liable by virtue of this policy . . . for explosions of any kind, unless fire ensues, and then for the loss . . . by fire only." The question at once arose, Is this a case of fire followed by explosion or of explosion followed by fire? There was a faint tradition of dust explosions in small mills, but nobody had anything but mere guesses to offer as to the cause of this novel and colossal disaster. Agents of twenty-five companies were presently on the ground to study this question. If it was a case of fire, their companies would be fully responsible, but if it was a case of explosion, they would not.[27]

The question came up in concrete form before the coroner's jury, which was immediately summoned and which deliberated for over a fortnight. The foreman was Joseph C. Whitney, a captain in the Sixth Minnesota in the Civil War. Doubtless at the instance of the mill owners, two men of science, Louis W. Peck, instructor of physics, and Stephen F. Peckham, professor of chemistry in the University of Minnesota, were set at work on an investigation, whose results might be laid before the jury. Their conclusions were delivered on May 20 at a session of the jury in the Agricultural College Building. Peck showed the members

[27] *Northwestern Miller*, 1878: May 3, supplement; 10, pp. 1, 3; 17, pp. 1, 2; 24, p. 1; *Pioneer Press, Tribune* (Minneapolis), May 3–21, June 3, 1878; Ernest A. Sturtevant, ed., *History of the Great Mill Explosion at Minneapolis, May 2, 1878, with a View of the Ruins after the Fire*, 5–16, 20–24, 39–43 (Minneapolis, 1878). A list of the insurance companies concerned is given on page 45 of the latter work. The state insurance commissioner, Andrew R. McGill, in his *Report*, 1878, p. xxxviii, records the damage of eight mills, one elevator, two machine shops, one planing mill, one cooper shop, three dwellings, one tenement, one storehouse, three barns, one roundhouse, one lumber yard, and freight cars.

of the jury by experiments before their eyes that nine different products and dusts of a flour mill could be laid out
in as many heaps on a piece of board and played upon by
the fierce flame of a Bunsen gas burner with no result but
a little blaze lasting from one to four seconds. He then
showed that every one of the meals and dusts, with the
exception of coarse bran, when blown in a cloud into the air
by a bellows over a flame would burn with explosive rapidity. Other demonstrations followed, one of them of especial
interest under the circumstances. An uncovered lighted
lamp was placed in a strong wooden box, over which a heavy
loose cover was placed. Two men stood on the cover. A
small charge of any one of the dusts, except coarse bran,
blown in by a bellows would take fire from the lamp,
explode, lift the cover with the two men, and spread a sheet
of flame several feet in all directions. Peck's conclusion
was that mill dusts would explode just like gunpowder,
provided there was flame or fire to touch them off.

Professor Peckham assured the jury that mill products
were not gasses. To enable them to appreciate the immense
violence of the late explosion, he informed them that from
a sack of flour weighing ninety-eight pounds and four thousand cubic feet of air force enough might be generated to
throw a weight of twenty-five hundred tons a hundred feet
high. Peckham, however, did not confine himself to the
chemistry of the explosions, but was ready with a rationale
of them deduced from Peck's experiments and from the
testimony of witnesses. There were six runs of stone on
the east side of the Washburn A mill employed at the time
in regrinding middlings, a process which generates more
heat than the original grinding of wheat. The meal from
these runs emptied into a common conveyer, which carried
it to an elevator at the outer end; this carried it to the bolting
floor in an upper story. From the outer end of the conveyer
extended horizontally a spout to carry off the dust and hot
air from the grinding, with a revolving fan to hasten its

movement to a dust house at the side of the mill. The trouble began in one of those six runs of burrs, possibly out of balance, which ran dry from a stoppage of feed, or between which some bit of metal or gravel had come in with the feed. A stream of sparks started a flame that smoldered a moment and was drawn along by the suction of the fan into the dust spout. Here a primary explosion took place in the spout and dust bin which jarred the whole building and dislodged the accumulated dust of years from ledges and level places where it had rested. The great explosion followed and spread instantaneously from story to story, tossing the roof into the air and throwing the walls outward. Flames from the A mill flashed through the windows of the Diamond mill, but twenty-five feet distant, from corner to corner and exploded its dust, already jarred loose by the shock. In the same way the flames of the Diamond were communicated to the Humboldt, twenty-five feet from the Diamond, and its destruction followed. All these explosions taking place in a few seconds seemed like one, but the overlapping of ruined walls showed that they were successive.

The verdict of the coroner's jury, delivered on May 22, recited the fact of the death of eighteen men named and expressed the unanimous belief of the jurors that the fire had its origin in the manner described by Professor Peckham, whose observations and suggestions were commended. It was a case of fire followed by explosions. The insurance companies were not in a hurry to accept the mere theory of a college professor. There was not a shred of evidence that any such series of things took place in a certain corner of the A mill. Nor was there anything to show that there could have been no other cause of the disasters. It was in evidence that there had been two recent flashes of ignited dust in the A mill, one of which ran from the grinding floor to the roof and scorched a section of it. The other came from a stream of middlings falling on an open gas burner.

Says one writer, " The 80 purifiers had small fans, but no dust collectors. The mill was full of dust, and the millers commonly wore sponges for the protection of mouth and nose." Still there stood beyond all question the demonstration of Peck that dust in heaps would not explode and that it surely would explode if suspended like a cloud in the air and touched off by fire or flame. The companies dallied but eventually all not insolvent paid without conclusive litigation, doubtless much influenced by their local agents, who naturally desired to enable their clients to repair and rebuild. The property owners still suffered many losses.[28]

There were incidental results of the great local disaster of 1878. Within a few days after its occurrence, William de la Barre, a young Austrian engineer, brought from Philadelphia a prospectus of the Behrens system of high pressure millstone ventilation which had been favorably reported on at the Centennial Exposition of 1876. The essential features

---

[28] Rogers, in *Minnesota Historical Collections*, 10: 51 (part 1); **Warner and Foote**, *Hennepin County*, 391; Jacob A. Stone, *The Flouring Mills of Minneapolis, Minn. . . . as viewed by an underwriter* (Minneapolis, 1878). Beginning on page 122 of the latter work are the reports of Peck and Peckham and the verdicts of the coroner's jury. Accounts of the experiments of Peck and Peckham before the coroner's jury and their conclusions are given in the *Pioneer Press* and the *Tribune* (Minneapolis), May 21, 1878. The verdict of the coroner's jury is in the issues of the same papers for May 23. The results of the experiments and the conclusions reached may also be found in an article by Peck, " Explosions from Combustible Dust," in the *Popular Science Monthly*, 14: 159–166 (December, 1878), and one by Peckham, " On the Explosion of the Flouring Mills at Minneapolis, Minnesota, May 2, 1878, and the Causes of the Same," in the *American Journal of Science and Arts*, third series, 116: 301–306 (October, 1878). The substance of the two was merged into one article by Professor Peckham and was published under the title, " The Dust Explosions at Minneapolis, May 2, 1878, and Other Dust Explosions," in the *Chemical Engineer*, 7: 97–105, 146–151, 194–197 (March, April, May, 1908). B. W. Dedrick and R. B. Fehr, in their *Grain-Dust Explosions; Investigation in the Experimental Attrition Mill at the Pennsylvania State College*, 49 (United States Department of Agriculture, *Bulletins*, no. 681 — Washington, May 18, 1918; also published as Pennsylvania State College, Engineering Experiment Station, *Bulletins*, no. 26), express the opinion that the explosions at Minneapolis in 1878 possibly, and even probably, originated from the open lights which were in use at the time. Experiments made at the Pennsylvania State College are described on pages 12 to 39 of this bulletin. In the bibliography given on page 53 the articles of Peck and Peckham head the list of American publications. For further information on

of the apparatus were an air-tight inclosure of each run of millstones with a single opening for the admission of air and an exhaust suction pipe to carry away the air current after the dust from grinding had been filtered out by a " long-haired flannel " cloth. De la Barre put in three units in the Washburn B mill at his own expense to convince the doubting Minneapolis millers. Governor C. C. Washburn was pleased to reimburse him for the outlay with a generous bonus. The apparatus was at once introduced into the Minneapolis mills and remained in use until millstones were supplanted. A second result was the extension of the use of rolls in place of millstones in flour manufacture and the introduction of the gradual reduction process. Some porcelain rolls were put into use in the Washburn B during the rebuilding of the A mill and a beginning of the new process was made. That process consists of passing the wheat between successive pairs of rolls with diminishing interspaces. After each " break " a bolt separates any flour which may have been broken out. In 1880 De la Barre was sent to Budapest to make a study of the Hungarian machinery and manufacture. On his advice the new A mill was fitted with chilled iron rolls arranged for the gradual reduc-

grain-dust explosions, see David J. Price and E. B. McCormick, *Dust Explosions and Fires in Grain Separators in the Pacific Northwest* (Department of Agriculture, *Bulletins*, no. 379 — Washington, August 4, 1916); R. H. Folwell, " Prevention of Grain Dust Explosions," in the *Grain Dealers' Journal*, 46: 938; *Proceedings of Conference of Men Engaged in Grain Dust Explosion and Fire Prevention Campaign Conducted by United States Grain Corporation in Cooperation with Bureau of Chemistry, United States Department of Agriculture* (New York, 1920); David J. Price, Harold H. Brown, and others, *Dust Explosions, Theory and Nature of Phenomena, Causes, and Methods of Prevention* (Boston, [1922]). The last-mentioned work exhausts existing information and ideas on the subject. Notes of interviews with William de la Barre, engineer of the Minneapolis Water Power Company since 1880, and with John Kraft, head miller of the rebuilt A mill for thirty years, are recorded in the author's notebooks, 9: 9, 10. Both of these men had on many occasions seen flashes of flame from mill stones and they believe that the explanation of the explosions stated in the verdict of the coroner's jury is the correct one. De la Barre said that it was " a very dusty mill." The author reached the scene of the explosions on horseback a few minutes after they took place. In his *Report*, 1878, p. xxxix, the state insurance commissioner gives the total estimated loss as $800,720 and the amount of insurance paid up to the time when the report was issued as $469,159.

tion process and millstones were entirely discarded. The new process soon spread through the country.[29]

Still another must be added to the list of casualties during this period. The original state Capitol, completed in 1853, had been enlarged to about four times its first capacity and virtually rebuilt, chiefly by appropriations made in 1878. The twenty-second legislature met in the new halls on January 4, 1881. The houses were in evening session on March 1. At about nine o'clock a sudden alarm of fire was heard and presently pieces of burning timbers came down through the ceilings. The whole dome and roof were on fire. The people instantly swarmed out. Some furniture and records of the state offices on the main floor were carried out. The books and collections of the Minnesota Historical Society in the basement were saved, though somewhat damaged, but the law library in the second story was nearly a total loss. The damage was estimated at two hundred thousand dollars. The origin of that fire has never been discovered.

The city of St. Paul had built and had ready for occupation a spacious market house on the corner of Seventh and Wabasha streets, two blocks distant from the Capitol. This the city authorities offered for use until the new capitol should be ready for occupancy, and at nine o'clock the next morning the state offices were open for business in hastily extemporized apartments. The legislature assembled in two large rooms before noon. For two years the St. Paul market house served as the state capitol. Governor Pillsbury, believing that the old site was ill suited both as to size and location, recommended the erection of a temporary building on the old site and the legislature appropriated seventy-five thousand dollars for the purpose. But the architect and the building committee, influenced, as some said, by St. Paul interests, provided otherwise. The legislature of 1881 in extra session found it necessary to add the

[29] De la Barre to the author, April 18, 1922; interview with De la Barre, recorded in the author's notebooks, 9: 14.

sum of one hundred thousand dollars to complete the structure.[30]

The crowning event of Governor Pillsbury's administration, in point of time and moment, was the " adjustment " of the Minnesota State Railroad Bonds of 1858, issued in due and legal form and pledging the faith and credit of the state for the payment of the principal and interest, which the state had for more than twenty years refused to acknowledge and redeem. The signing of the " Minnesota State Railroad Adjustment Bonds " occupied the last days of Pillsbury's governorship and it was a duty which he performed with greater satisfaction than any in his long period of public service.[31]

Persons who have accustomed themselves to interpret statistics and to allow their imaginations to play freely over repulsive tables, diagrams, and charts will find in the report of the tenth United States census, that of 1880, and in the annual reports of the Minnesota statistician abundant illustrations of the progress of Minnesota during the decade ending with the year 1880. The most conspicuous fact is the increase in her population of 77.6 per cent, from 439,706 to 780,773 souls. Quite as impressive is the novel fact that the rate of increase of the town population was very much greater than that of the country. The town ratio was 112 per cent, that of the country, 66 per cent. The city of St. Paul increased from 20,030 to 41,473 and Minneapolis, from 13,066 to 46,887. Settlement, which up to 1870 had clung to the edge of the hardwood timber, had spread, though sparsely, out on to the prairies of the west and southwest portions of the state and far down the Red River Valley. The great coniferous region of the north and northeast por-

---

[30] *Pioneer Press*, 1881: March 2, p. 1; 3, p. 5; *House Journal*, 1881, pp. 573–577; *General Laws*, 1881, p. 232; 1881, extra session, 89; *Legislative Manual*, 1889, p. 248. Governor Pillsbury's desire was to put a new capitol at some convenient point between St. Paul and Minneapolis. Interviews of the author with Pillsbury.

[31] The redemption of the railroad bonds is dealt with more fully in the Appendix, no. 9, *post*.

tions of the state remained an almost untrodden wilderness. The foreign-born people of Minnesota in 1880 numbered 267,676, of whom 68,182 were English-speaking, 107,768 Scandinavian, and 66,592 German. A large proportion of the immigrants of these nationalities were spreading into the west and southwest parts of the state and into the Red River Valley.

Notwithstanding the lower increment of country population, the acreage of farm lands increased 107 per cent and that of improved lands, 212 per cent between 1870 and 1880. This discrepancy may be attributed to the invention or improvement of farm machinery and to the multiplication of bonanza farms. To the increased use of farm machinery, which reduced the demand for hand labor, may doubtless be attributed the detention of immigrants in the towns, if not an actual shift of population from country to town. The efficiency of farm machinery is also shown in the increase of farm products — that of wheat being eighty-three per cent, a much higher rate than the sixty-six per cent population increase in the country. The increase in the average size of farms from 139 to 145 acres also indicated a larger employment of machines. A comparison of the values of farm products of the initial and final years of the decade yields a deduction not so cheering. While the number of farms, the acreage of cultivated lands, and the amount of farm products had been increasing as described, the value of farm products had increased but forty-eight per cent. This figure indicates overproduction, of wheat in particular, which may be attributable to the improved processes of flour manufacture. It is the opinion of a careful student of Minnesota agriculture that if Minnesota farmers were better off in 1880 than in 1870, it was due to the increased value of their lands. One-crop farming was still dominant, but there were notable beginnings of diversification before the close of the decade. It was time for a change, since the average yield of wheat to the acre had fallen from twenty-two bushels in the Civil War period to a little more than half of that figure.

Although Minnesota had been, as she still is, regarded as an agricultural community, the tenth census showed the aggregate value of her manufacturing products to be much in excess of that of farm produce. The farm products of 1879 amounted to $49,468,951 and those of manufacture, $76,065,198. It is notable that the 436 flour mills converted grains worth $37,155,429 into flour and other mill products valued at $41,519,004, fifty-five per cent of the whole output of machinery. The 234 sawmills changed $4,529,055 worth of logs into $7,366,038 worth of lumber. The remaining products of manufacture, which amounted to $27,180,156, were distributed among 2,823 establishments.[32]

As already related, railroad building came to a standstill in the fall of 1872. The great financial depression of the next year, the grasshopper scourge which broke out in 1874, the deflation of the national currency in progress, bringing hardship to people who in previous flush times had gone in debt for long terms, were good reasons for the general resulting stagnation of industry and the postponement of new enterprises. The railroad companies, naturally desirous to extend their lines and obtain possession of more public land, loaded with debt after squandering the millions they had borrowed at home and abroad, could borrow no more and were forced to wait for better times. In the four years from 1873 to 1877 but eighty-seven miles of road were built — mere fractional additions. The crop of 1877 was exceptionally bounteous and a more hopeful state of mind in the community led to a sure, although slow, revival of business. In that year 212 miles of railroad were built and yearly additions after 1877 aggregating 1,291 miles brought the total up to 3,278 at the close of the year 1881. The warfare

[32] Robinson, *Agriculture in Minnesota*, 63, 76, 83–102, 104, 106; *United States Census*, 1880, *Population*, 226, 229, 492–495; *Statistics of Manufactures*, 138.

against the unrighteous extortions and discriminations of railroad companies had been mitigated by their deference to public opinion and by the decision of the United States Supreme Court, establishing firmly and finally the right of a state legislature to regulate fares and rates. In consequence the history of the Minnesota railroads for some years was monotonous, as the meager reports of the state railroad commissioner will show.[33]

[33] Railroad Commissioner, *Reports*, 1877, pp. 3, 10; 1881, pp. 4, 15. There was one exception, however, in the case of the company which succeeded the Minnesota and Pacific, one of those created by act of Congress in 1857 and endowed with an immense land grant. The story is told in the Appendix, no. 10, *post*.

VI. HUBBARD AND HIS TIMES, 1882–87

WITH the close of Governor Pillsbury's administration in 1882 the state of Minnesota may be said to have ended her period of adolescence, although but twenty-three years had passed since her organization and admission to the Union. Many of these had been years of hardship for her people; but better days had come. Succeeding years of abundant crops had effaced the effects of the panic of 1873, of the locust plague, and of other calamities. The long-disputed claims of the holders of the state railroad bonds of 1858 had been satisfactorily adjusted. The railroad mileage had been greatly augmented during the last five years and the population had increased over seventy-five per cent in the preceding decade.[1] The subsequent history of Minnesota is happily one of general, though fluctuating progress, of the extension of settlements, of the development of natural resources, of the growth of industries, of advancement in good government and education, and of consequent prosperity, health, and happiness. To illustrate this central fact will be the purpose of the following chapters.

Governor Pillsbury's administration had given so much satisfaction that many friends and partisans desired his reëlection for a fourth term and he was not indifferent to the proposition. On September 7, 1881, the *Pioneer Press* announced him as a candidate to succeed himself. Numerous protests from the friends of other aspirants against allowing any Republican, however meritorious, to stand in their daylight were at once heard. Governor Pillsbury had never been greedy for the mere glory of office and his private affairs had suffered during his already long incum-

---

[1] *United States Census*, 1880, *Population*, 66; Commissioner of Statistics, *Reports*, 1881, p. 20; Railroad Commissioner, *Reports*, 1881, p. 15.

bency. It was therefore without reluctance that he published
a declination of the nomination a few days before the Republican convention. There were plenty of good Republicans
capable of succeeding him and willing to do so but the
informal ballot showed that General Lucius F. Hubbard,
the gallant colonel of the Fifth Minnesota in the Civil War,
was the favorite. The first formal ballot gave him the
nomination, which in those days was equivalent to election.
The Democrats gave their complimentary nomination to
Major General Richard W. Johnson, U.S.A., retired, a
graduate of West Point appointed from Kentucky. At the
outbreak of the Civil War he had refused to desert the
national flag and service. He held important commands
and was retired with the high rank of major general after
being wounded in Sherman's Atlanta campaign. He came
to Minnesota soon after the peace and remained an active,
loyal citizen to the end of his life in 1897. The vote, which
stood 65,025 for Hubbard and 37,168 for Johnson, indicated
the relative strength of the parties. General Hubbard had
been engaged chiefly in railroad enterprises after his discharge from military service, but he had served two terms
in the state Senate and had been active in party affairs. He
was reëlected in 1883, without effective opposition from the
opposing party or within his own for the constitutional two-
year term. He remained in office, however, a third year.[2]

The system of biennial legislatures, in operation since
1879, had worked so well that there was a general consent

    [2] *Pioneer Press* (St. Paul and Minneapolis), 1881: August 19, p. 4; Sep-
tember 7, p. 4; 9, p. 4; 11, p. 4; 13, p. 4; 15, p. 4; 29, p. 1; Holmes, in
Minnesota in Three Centuries, 4: 101, 131; Upham and Dunlap, *Minnesota
Biographies*, 350. Smalley, in his *Republican Party*, 211, says that Pillsbury
did not desire a fourth term, for he had spent one hundred and twenty-five thousand dollars more than the salary of his office; but his name was put before
the convention " as the most effective way of beating General Hubbard." The
informal ballot, which stood 140 for Hubbard and 57 for Pillsbury, seems to
indicate that Pillsbury was at least a receptive aspirant. For Castle's views,
see *Minnesota Historical Collections*, 15: 576. For the renomination of Hubbard and the nomination of McNair, see the *Pioneer Press*, 1883: June 28, p. 2;
August 3, p. 8. The vote for governor may be found in the *Legislative
Manual*, 1925, p. 113.

to the obvious proposition that biennial elections were equally desirable. At the instance of Governor Hubbard the legislature of 1883 proposed an amendment to article 7 of the state constitution providing for such elections, which was ratified at the state election on November 6 of the same year. The amendment provided that general elections for state and county offices, except judicial offices, should be held biennially, beginning in 1884, on the first Tuesday after the first Monday in November. As there would be no general election in 1885, it was obvious that there would be vacancies in all offices in which the terms would expire in that year. The amendment, therefore, was so drawn as to continue the incumbents in office an additional year. Governor Hubbard, accordingly, was five years in office. Additional adjustments were needed to complete the biennial system. A second amendment, to article 5, had therefore been proposed extending the term of office of the state auditor from three years to four. This amendment was also ratified at the election of 1883. A third amendment, to article 6, adopted at the same time, reduced the terms of judges of the district and supreme courts from seven years to six and extended that of the clerk of the supreme court from three years to four. Accordingly, since then all state and county officers have served for terms of two years or some multiple of two years. Elections take place in the even-numbered years and legislatures meet in the odd-numbered years. State election days coincide with those of congressional and presidential elcetions. The official year begins on the first Monday in January. The fiscal year has lately been changed to begin on July 1 and the scheme is likely to continue indefinitely.[3]

The year 1882 was an off year in Minnesota politics and the elections or reëlections of representatives in Congress

---

[3] Hubbard's message of January 4, 1883, in *Executive Documents*, 1882, vol. I, p. 33; *General Laws*, 1883, pp. 5–9; 1885, pp. 1–3; *Legislative Manual*, 1925, p. 293; Anderson, *History of the Constitution*, 225, 281.

from the four old congressional districts were not attended with notable incidents. In a new fifth district, embracing substantially all the northern half of the state, a contest took place which was especially noteworthy because it brought into wider prominence a character ιalready well known in domestic politics and about to begin a national career, which will be touched at many points in the further progress of this history. Knute Nelson was born in Voss, an inland district of Norway, on February 2, 1843. A widowed mother brought him to America in 1849 and four years later established a home in Dane County, Wisconsin. After a common school course the youth studied at Albion Academy from 1858 to 1861. At the outbreak of the Civil War, along with a group of classmates, he enlisted in the Fourth Wisconsin Infantry and he served with the command in the ranks or line of file closers until its muster out in 1864. He was severely wounded at the battle of Port Hudson on June 14, 1863, and was held captive for a month. After his return from the army he finished his course at Albion Academy. Nelson was not the unlettered person sometimes represented. He had by this time doubtless established his habit of industrious and systematic reading which made him one of the most truly learned and well-informed men of his time. He studied law with William F. Vilas and was admitted to the bar in 1867. In the fall of the same year he was elected to the lower house of the Wisconsin legislature, and he was reëlected the following year. In 1871 he migrated to Minnesota and took up a farm adjoining the village of Alexandria, which remained his home until his death in April, 1923. He was attorney of Douglas County from 1872 to 1874 and in the fall of the latter year he was elected to the state Senate to serve until the close of the session of 1878.[4]

[4] General Laws, 1881, extra session, 70; Olof N. Nelson, ed., History of the Scandinavians and Successful Scandinavians in the United States, 1: 449 (Minneapolis, 1904); Baker, Governors of Minnesota, 13: 330–351; Bjorn

When the new fifth district was created, Nelson had good right to aspire to the nomination and probable election by the Republicans as representative in Congress. Other men of ability and prominence were proposed for the position, but he was to find his most powerful rival in a citizen as yet little known in Minnesota public life, Charles F. Kindred, who had come to the state some years before as land agent of the Northern Pacific Railroad Company and had established his office and residence at Brainerd. He had acquired a large property by operations legitimate or, as alleged, illegitimate. In particular, it was believed and later charged that he had pursued a policy of selling railroad lands to ignorant buyers for cash or other full value and then turning in to the company its preferred stock, worth about fifteen cents on the dollar and convertible into lands at par. Possessed of large means, which he was willing to use in politics, and a genial personality, he had obtained a large following along the line of the Northern Pacific and resolved to run for the new seat in Congress. The story of the campaign which followed might be taken as the finest example of dirty politics known in America outside of certain great cities. It has been commonly believed that Kindred spent a hundred thousand dollars or more, a good round sum of money in that day.

The district convention met in Detroit, Minnesota on July 12, 1882. The situation and the proceedings were closely analogous to those of the Minnesota constitutional convention of 1857. There were double delegations from practically every county in the district. Two chairmen mounted the platform and called the convention to order, but nobody came to order. The Kindred faction had the advantage that

Holland, "A Sketch of the Late Senator Nelson's Boyhood Days," a typewritten manuscript in the possession of the Minnesota Historical Society. See Upham and Dunlap, *Minnesota Biographies*, 542, and numerous citations for other biographical sketches of Nelson. The new district included the counties of Big Stone, Stevens, Pope, Stearns, Benton, Aitkin, Carlton, and all counties north of them.

its chairman had the lease of the hall. It called on the sheriff of Becker County to shut out intruders. The Nelson chairman wisely yielded to the majesty of the law and led his men out to a tent on the prairie, which somebody had had the foresight to erect. There were no chairs nor benches but the proceedings were duly gone through with. Nelson was nominated by a large majority and delivered his speech of acceptance. Kindred was, of course, nominated by his following. Both conventions adopted resolutions resounding in patriotism and Republican gospel.[5]

The three months which passed before the November election were employed by both Republican factions with great industry. Kindred started three or four newspapers, at least one in the Norwegian language. In one of the offices he had printed a circular evidently intended for circulation among Scandinavian farmers. In it Nelson was charged with being an attorney of the Minneapolis Millers' Association, with having been granted large amounts of land by the St. Paul and Pacific Railroad Company for his vote in the state Senate, with being false to promises, with being an infidel and a persecutor of churches, and, worst of all, perhaps, with running as an independent candidate after the regular district convention had refused him a nomina-

---

[5] Elmer E. Adams, " The Nelson-Kindred Campaign of 1882," in the *Minnesota History Bulletin*, 5: 87–107 (May, 1923), also in the *Fergus Falls Journal*, 1923: January 17, p. 5; 20, p. 2; 25, p. 2; 30, p. 2. Few authorities are cited, but the account was written from personal knowledge and a study of documents and other sources. The resolutions adopted by the two conventions are given in the *Tribune* (Minneapolis), July 13, 1882, p. 2, and the *Pioneer Press* of the same date, p. 2. Castle, in *Minnesota Historical Collections*, 15: 579, says: " I attended this convention and witnessed its turbulent proceedings . . . its scenes of disgraceful confusion cannot be exaggerated; it was for a considerable period nothing but a howling mob, and bloodshed was narrowly escaped. . . . Impartial observation on the ground thoroughly convinced me that Mr. Nelson had a decisive majority of the bona fide delegates. . . . Governor Davis and many other friends favored Kindred." Hall, in his *Observations*, 285–295, estimates Kindred's expenditures during the campaign at $150,000. Baker, in his *Governors of Minnesota*, 337, calls it " the most bitter and heated political contest the state ever had, but out of it Knute Nelson came with increasing prestige and promise for future advancement." See also Folwell to Adams, February 24, 1923, in the Folwell Papers.

tion. A Nelson campaign pamphlet was prepared by Hanford L. Gordon, at the time prominent in politics, refuting the charges of the Kindred broadside, and touching on unconscionable manipulations of caucuses and conventions, the irregularity of Kindred's nomination at Detroit, and his alleged frauds in the sale of railroad lands. Nelson spoke in almost every county of the district, which comprised nearly forty thousand square miles. The election returns showed that there was need of such activity on the part of Nelson and his friends. They stood, in a total vote of 35,442: Nelson, 16,956; Kindred, 12,238; and Barnum, the Democratic nominee, 6,248.[6]

A political event of more than local importance occurred in the winter of 1883, when Dwight M. Sabin defeated William Windom in his candidacy for the United States senatorship. Senator Windom was about to complete his second term with his usual efficiency and it was the general expectation that the legislature of 1883 would elect him for a third term. He was himself so confident of reëlection that he remained at his post of duty in Washington until summoned to St. Paul by friends in alarm. To their surprise, the preliminary conferences indicated to the politically wise that there was an opposition, which, though not united on any other aspirant, would probably render Windom's election impossible.

Various influences converged to Windom's defeat. The circumstance that he had established himself in a fine house on Massachusetts Avenue in the capital city, thus indicating an expectation of an indefinite residence, aroused prejudice in some minds. Extravagant eulogies of admiring supporters accompanied by unnecessary disparagement of other aspirants estranged others. Some were like the Athenians

---

[6] Adams, in the *Minnesota History Bulletin*, 5: 102 (May, 1923); *Legislative Manual*, 1883, p. 310. A copy of the Gordon pamphlet, *An Address to the Voters of the Fifth Congressional District of Minnesota* (n.p., n.d.), is in the possession of the Minnesota Historical Society. The society has also a copy of the Kindred broadside.

who tired of hearing Aristides called just. The decisive
opposition, however, arose from a political disturbance in
the first congressional district, where Windom had, it was
alleged, coöperated to defeat the nomination of Mark H.
Dunnell for representative in Congress. Dunnell did not now
seriously aspire to the senatorship but his vigorous opposition
placed an effective barrier in Windom's path. The legislature
numbered 160 members, of whom 110 were Republicans.
The sixty-two of that party who voted at the caucus gave
Windom a unanimous but futile nomination. In the preliminary separate voting of the houses on January 16 he
obtained but sixty-eight supporters. In the numerous joint
ballotings, which began on the day following, sixty-five was
the highest number of votes accorded him. On the thirty-
first Dwight M. Sabin first appeared as a candidate, receiving seventeen votes. On February 1 Sabin on a sixth ballot
obtained a majority of Republican votes. Thereupon,
according to previous understanding, the whole Democratic
vote was thrown to him, insuring his election. During the
whole contest Sabin was indisposed and confined to his
rooms in the Metropolitan Hotel, but he was well enough to
hold conferences with friends. Windom believed that large
sums of money, brought in part from outside the state, had
been used to compass his defeat. Sabin was at the time
forty years old and at the head of extensive manufacturing
and commercial enterprises at Stillwater. He had been
active and successful in party affairs. He had sat in the
state Senate during three sessions and at the time of his
promotion was serving a third term in the lower house. A
reputation for extraordinary business ability and a very
agreeable personality secured him willing supporters. His
term in the national Senate was without notable incident
and at its close he returned to his private engagements.[7]

⁷ *House Journal*, 1883, pp. 39, 47, 67, 78, 132, 152–156; *Senate Journal*,
1883, pp. 29, 30; Smalley, *Republican Party*, 214–218, 323, 348; Baker,
Governors of Minnesota, 268. Castle, in *Minnesota Historical Collections*, 15:

The skill and experience of Windom, although repudiated by his state, were not lost to the nation. President Harrison appointed him his secretary of the treasury and he filled the great office in a manner consistent with its traditions during the brief remainder of his life. He was stricken with heart failure upon the conclusion of a speech at a banquet of the New York Board of Trade on January 29, 1891. The Minnesota Senate on January 30 adopted resolutions of regret and appreciation. In seconding the motion to adopt the resolutions, Ignatius Donnelly spoke as follows:

It is a fit and proper expression . . . of the profound feeling with which the people of our state have heard of Mr. Windom's unexpected death. . . . In some sense Mr. Windom's death, in the midst of that brilliant banquet scene, his lips yet warm with his own eloquence, and his ears still ringing with the plaudits of one of the greatest assemblages possible in our country, was a fitting close for the most uninterruptedly successful career ever known in the history of the United States. . . . the great political leader has departed in the midst of the very glory, beauty and triumph of life. "Like the stag sunstruck," he "tops the bounds and dies." . . . His sagacity was unerring, his practical wisdom great, his intuitions keen. In political life he advanced so smoothly that he seemed to have solved the problem of motion without friction. His nature was noble. His heart was kindly. . . . The fierceness and ferocity of party strife did not take hold upon him.

He was identified with the most important part of our national life at a time when the history of the nation transcended in importance all the previous records of civilized man. He bore himself

579–583, testifies that Sabin was not a party to any conspiracy to defeat Windom and gives grounds for his (Castle's) opposition to Windom. Thomas B. Walker, in an interview with the author, said that to his knowledge Sabin was not looking for the nomination. Senator Windom told the author after the contest was over that he knew of seventy thousand dollars in Kentucky whisky money sent into the state to compass his defeat. Notes on these interviews are recorded in the author's notebooks, 9: 39. The *Pioneer Press*, January 12, 1883, p. 5, gives an account of the caucus. It may be noted that on January 16, the day the balloting began, Senator Michael Doran, a prominent Democrat, offered a resolution, which was adopted, for the appointment of a special committee to investigate allegations that certain members of the legislature had been "improperly and corruptly influenced by promises of money, public office, or other valuable considerations [to cast their votes] for a certain candidate for United States senator." The same resolution was adopted by the House. No reports of the committees have been found. On Sabin, see Appleton's *Cyclopædia of American Biography*, 5: 363 (New York, 1887–1900).

honorably and conspicuously in this great era. His record is part of the imperishable heritage of our state.   It cannot be ignored or forgotten.
We lament his loss.   We advance and place upon his bier a wreath of remembrance wet with tears.[8]

The period of Governor Hubbard's administration will be distinguished in Minnesota history as one of abundant and beneficent legislation. In his message of 1883 Hubbard suggested that it was time for Minnesota to follow the example of other states in making efforts to improve upon her institutions for public charities and corrections.   With but slight opposition a bill was passed by the legislature of 1883 for the creation of a board of corrections and charities, to consist of six persons appointed by the governor to serve without pay for three-year terms.   The governor was to be the seventh member and the president.   This board was authorized to investigate the whole system of public charities, to examine into the condition and management of jails and prisons, and to exact from the officers in charge statistics and information on prescribed forms.   The governor was authorized to order, at his discretion, special investigation of institutions by the board or its committee.   Provision was made for a secretary with a salary of twelve hundred dollars a year.   The Reverend Malcolm McGregor Dana, D.D., the first vice president of the board, probably drew up the bill and looked after its passage.   The Reverend Hastings Hornell Hart of Worthington was appointed executive secretary of the board.   Dr. Hart gave his whole time to the work and from time to time extended the range of inquiries and visitations, the results of which were embodied in a series of valuable reports.   He won and held the confidence of heads of institutions, who found in him a friend both critical and just.   In the course of the fifteen years that

[8] Charles E. Flandrau, *Encyclopedia of Biography of Minnesota*, 1: 209–214 (Chicago, 1900) ; Smalley, *Republican Party*, 348; *Pioneer Press*, January 30, 31, 1891; *Minneapolis Tribune*, January 30, 31, 1891; *Senate Journal*, 1891, p. 119; *Memorial Tributes to Windom*, 46–52.

he remained in the service, with the support gladly given him by his board, he placed Minnesota in the front rank of states endeavoring to improve their methods of caring for the destitute, the delinquent, and the defective. Dr. Hart's later appointment to the staff of the Russell Sage Foundation of New York City was a well-deserved promotion, made good by many years of service, which, happily, are not yet ended.[9]

The legislature of 1885 created a new institution of public charity, the State Public School at Owatonna. Up to the time of its opening in December, 1886, the care of dependent and neglected children had been left to orphan asylums supported by churches or by private endowment, of which the Washburn Home at Minneapolis was and is a conspicuous example. For a state which had long pretended to furnish elementary schooling to all children and had provided it for those who could reach the schoolhouses from their homes, it was logical that it ought at length to provide instruction for those who had either no homes or unfit ones. The new law provided for a " State Public School " to which neglected and dependent children of school age might be committed through the probate courts and further provided that no such children should be maintained in the county poorhouses. The institution was to be, and has been, more than an asylum and a school; its more important function is that of an agency for placing its wards in safe and comfortable homes, either by adoption or contract, with supervision until they reach majority. It is a pleasure to record that the admirable service of the school is due in very large measure to the wise and devoted superintendency of Galen A. Merrill, who is still in office.[10]

[9] Executive Documents, 1882, vol. I, p. 20; House Journal, 1883, p. 323; Senate Journal, 427; General Laws, 1883, p. 171. Most of the reports of the board of corrections and charities may be found in the Executive Documents. They were also issued as separates. For biographical sketches of Dana and Hart, see Upham and Dunlap, Minnesota Biographies, 159, 305, and citations.

[10] General Laws, 1885, pp. 172–179; Legislative Manual, 1925, p. 275.

If Governor Hubbard was especially sympathetic with a proposition to enlarge the powers of the state board of health, it may have been due to the influence of his townsman and neighbor, Dr. Charles N. Hewitt, a Civil War veteran like himself. Dr. Hewitt had secured the creation in 1872 of a state board of health with merely advisory powers and had been its executive secretary on a nominal salary. With Governor Hubbard's encouragement he came before the legislature of 1883 with a bill to enlarge the powers of the board and to give it executive as well as advisory authority. The resulting act, amended in details, became a code of law for the preservation of the public health and established an administrative system for its purposes. Every town, village, and city was required to have a board of health, one of its members to be a physician and health officer. The health officer was required to make in the month of May of every year a thorough sanitary inspection of his district and to submit a report in writing to his board and a copy of it to the state board of health. He was required, at any time when necessary, to examine into nuisances, sources of filth, and causes of sickness and to enforce the orders of his board with regard to them. Penalties of fine and imprisonment were attached to disobedience and the health officer himself was liable for neglect of duty. In regard to infectious diseases, local boards of health were required to obey instructions of the state board, but they were also authorized and required to act instantly of their own motion and when necessary to order the cleansing or disinfection of buildings, vessels, and vehicles, or the disinfection or destruction of bedding, clothing, or other articles which had been exposed to infection. In cases of smallpox, scarlet fever, and diphtheria, they were empowered to establish quarantine and to forbid the passage of any persons except medical attendants or spiritual advisers. Children with these diseases could not be readmitted to schools until after permission had been given by the local board. One section of the act directed parents and guardians to have minors promptly, frequently, and effectively vaccinated against smallpox. Such were the leading provisions of this drastic law, which was intended to establish a separate health government, like the school government, outside politics, with the *salus populi* its justification for large encroachments on the immemorial liberty of the citizen. Most of the essential provisions of the act are still in force and there are no two opinions as to its beneficent operation.[11]

The general code of health of 1883 was followed in 1885 by other acts germane to it. The most important of them, recommended and doubtless drafted by Dr. Hewitt, was that forbidding the pollution of rivers and other sources of water supply for domestic use. The state board of health was given power to take any measures that were required for the public health and severe penalties were attached to disobedience of its directions. In another act both the state and local boards were authorized to regulate or forbid the exercise of trades and employments dangerous to public health. Still another act, whose importance was later augmented, was that for preventing the spread of contagious or infectious diseases among domestic animals. Local boards of health were authorized to isolate infected animals and to have them killed and the bodies buried. By a later statute the supervision of this branch was taken from the state board of health and was reposed in a state live stock sanitary board but the coöperation of local boards was still required.[12]

It was an ancient American assumption that every citizen had the right to decide for himself and for his dependents whether he or they were sick or well and, if any were thought to be sick, to employ as physician any person, without regard to special education for the healing art. The legislature of

[11] *General Laws*, 1872, pp. 64–66; 1883, pp. 178–186. A law was passed in 1903 to prevent the compulsory vaccination of children. *General Laws*, 1903, p. 530.

[12] *General Laws*, 1885, pp. 267–270, 292–294, 296–298; 1903, pp. 636–643.

1883 put an end to this liberty by passing an act creating a
state medical examining board and requiring all persons
desiring to practice medicine to have a certificate from this
board. It was generously provided that all graduates in
medicine then in practice should receive certificates upon
verification of their diplomas; other persons practicing medicine must undergo an examination to prove their qualifications. The penalty for practicing medicine or surgery in
Minnesota without the certificate of the examining board was
a fine of as high as five hundred dollars or imprisonment
for as long a time as 365 days, or both. The act was altogether acceptable to educated physicians and became at once
effective. The beginning thus made was followed up in
1885 by two similar acts. One of them forbade any person
other than a registered pharmacist to compound or dispense
drugs, medicines, or poisons. A state board of pharmacy
was created to examine applications and to award certificates
to those found qualified. A fine which might amount to
fifty dollars for each offense awaited all convicted violators
of this law. The other act referred to was one entitled " An
act to insure the better education of practitioners of dental
surgery." Here again a state board was established with
power to grant certificates of qualification to graduates of
reputable dental colleges on presentation of their diplomas
and to other persons who could pass the examinations.[13]

Of a piece with these regulations was an act of 1885 creating a board of inspectors of steam boilers and, incidentally,
of the hulls, machinery, and equipment of steam vessels,
with minute specifications of their duties. One section of
the law imposed a fine of two hundred dollars on any person
who should construct a faulty or imperfect steam boiler or
should even " drift any rivet hole to make it come fair."
The law did not apply to railroad locomotive engineers.[14]

[13] *General Laws*, 1883, pp. 167–169; 1885, pp. 179–184, 264–267. See
General Laws, 1887, pp. 46–49, for the later organization of the state board
of medical examiners.
[14] *General Laws*, 1885, pp. 184–189.

With these as precedents a long line of similar laws have since been passed for the protection of the unlearned public and, incidentally, for the discouragement of undesirable persons seeking admission to certain arts and professions. At the present time Minnesota has state boards appointed by the governor to examine and issue licenses to citizens aspiring to be attorneys at law, certified accountants, physicians and surgeons, osteopaths, nurses, dentists, optometrists, pharmacists, barbers, veterinarians, horseshoers, chiropodists, and electricians. Midwives obtain licenses from the state board of medical examiners and embalmers obtain their certificates from the state board of health.[15]

The evil effects of one-crop farming, which in Minnesota meant spring-wheat farming, began to show themselves in the seventies. In those years it was not necessary for Minnesota farmers to be informed by politicians and big city newspapers that diversification of crops would be beneficial. Without superior instruction they began to raise cattle and hogs and to make butter and cheese. At the state fair in October, 1876, factory butter of very high quality was shown. Two years later the Minnesota Dairyman's Association was organized for the encouragement of the dairy industry. By 1885 dairying had become a large factor in Minnesota agriculture. There were sixty-three creameries and forty-six cheese factories. Butter production had already found greater favor than that of cheese. In the early eighties an alarm was raised among Minnesota dairymen by the sudden increase in the sale of oleomargarine. It was estimated that during the season of 1884–85 as many as four million

---

[15] *General Statutes of Minnesota*, 1913, pp. 1085–1115 (St. Paul, 1913); *Laws*, 1917, pp. 541–545. The *Legislative Manual*, 1925, pp. 234–243, gives the titles of nine administrative " departments " and forty-nine boards and commissions. An example of the custom of American legislatures to descend to minute particulars is an act passed in 1901 for the regulation and supervision of barber schools and colleges. The barbers' state board of examiners is required to see that all utensils are sterilized, that all razors and scissors are kept sharp, and that every pupil shall have a clean white apron with sleeves or a white jacket each day. Penalties are fixed for neglect. *General Laws*, 1901, pp. 292–295.

pounds were shipped into the state. The organized dairymen resolved not to let the so-called fraud live and demanded the passage of a prohibitory law. The legislature of 1885 responded by passing an act imposing a penalty of from one hundred to five hundred dollars or imprisonment from six to twelve months, or both, on any person who should manufacture or sell oleomargarine or any other article designed to take the place of butter or cheese made from pure milk. By the same act the sale of impure, diluted, or adulterated dairy products was heavily penalized, as was also keeping cows in unwholesome places and feeding them unhealthful foods. To enforce these prohibitions the law made provision for a dairy commissioner with ample powers and made an appropriation for his salary and the salaries of agents and experts to be employed by him.[16]

The operation of the inspection system for dairy products presently called attention to the need of its extension to other objects. Food adulteration had no doubt been practiced occasionally from early times but it did not become intolerable until after the establishment of the modern custom of retailing tea and coffee, spices, maple sugar, honey, lard, and many other articles in sealed containers. Then the honest grocer had no protection against his fellow citizen who undersold him with adulterated goods not distinguishable in appearance from the genuine. Successive legislatures enlarged the scope of the pure food laws with provisions which, gathered up in the Code of 1905, have not been materially changed. Some possible antiquarian of a future century reading this chapter may wonder at a state of civilization in Minnesota in the time of Governor Hubbard when citizens had to be restrained by law under heavy penalties from selling pulverized cocoanut shells for pepper, inscrutable gelatin compounds for jams and jellies, maple sugar, honey, and lard artificially compounded, process and reno-

[16] Robinson, *Agriculture in Minnesota*, 80, 111–113; *General Laws*, 1885, pp. 189–192; Minnesota, Dairy Commissioner, *Reports*, 1885–86, pp. 26–30.

vated butter, and oleomargarine and butterine colored and seasoned to deceive the consumer. The principle of the pure food laws was extended to painting materials, used in immense quantities in a land of wooden buildings. Adulterations had long been practiced and detection was very difficult. It was not the policy of the pure food laws absolutely to prohibit the manufacture of substitutes and adulterants. The more effective plan was adopted of requiring all package goods to have on their containers true and easily readable statements of the proper name and quantity of each ingredient, under penalties for misbranding. Forty years have passed since the first of the laws was enacted. The effect has been altogether salutary. Consumers know what they are buying and the sale of adulterated goods in quantities has become a thing of the past.[17]

It was the judgment of Governor Hubbard that the laws of 1875 and 1878 which had created the office of railroad commissioner had but partially fulfilled expectations, although the right of the state to regulate railroads had been securely established by tardy judicial decisions. In successive messages he dwelt upon the need of enlarged powers for the commission to exact from the railroad companies the measure of service they owed the state. They had received from or through the state grants amounting in 1882 to $76,490,000, equal to $23,331 a mile. As such beneficiaries the companies were bound to render ample service without extortion or discrimination. Moved by his exhortations the legislature of 1885 produced a brief statute which formed a good foundation for later developments. The act created a board of commissioners of three electors appointed by the governor to serve for two years at salaries of three thousand dollars. It was evidently the intention of the legislature to compel the remedy of abuse by the moral effect of the " sunlight of publicity " shining freely on all the transactions

[17] Code of 1905, pp. 347–358; Supplement, 1909, pp. 473–482; *General Statutes*, 1913, pp. 854–857.

of the railroad companies. A prominent section of the act required each and every railroad company doing business in the state to submit full and true annual reports of all its affairs under forty-one headings. A penalty of from one hundred to five thousand dollars was to be imposed for every period of ten days' neglect to make a report after it should be due. The commission had the further power to make additional inquiries at its discretion and to exact answers to them. Authority was also conferred upon the commission to examine the books, records, accounts, papers, and proceedings of the companies and to take testimony under oath. The board was required to have one of its members visit once in three months every county in which there was a railroad station and inquire into the management of the railroad business. Extortion of excessive fares and rates and unjust discriminations were, of course, to be penalized according to the provisions of former statutes.

A preëxisting evil much complained of was the virtually exclusive privilege allowed to favored individuals of maintaining grain elevators at railroad stations, a privilege for which it was suspected that they shared their profits with railroad managers. The new law made it the duty of railroad companies to provide sidetrack connections for elevators built by any person or company and to furnish prompt transportation for grain received in such private elevators. A provision of no little importance was one forbidding railroad companies to limit *ex parte* their common law liability for the safe delivery of goods received for transportation. It was not until a later year that a legislature went to the length of establishing legal fares and rates.[18]

A companion bill, intended to put an end to abuses in the marketing of Minnesota's great harvests of grain, was also passed. With the great extension of merchant milling there

---

[18] *Executive Documents*, 1882, vol. 1, pp. 28–31; 1884, vol. 1, pp. 40–43; *General Laws*, 1875, pp. 135–138; 1878, p. 125; 1885, pp. 243–253; *General Statutes*, 1913, p. 947.

had grown up a reasonable custom of separating grain into grades according to purity and to such conditions as shrinkage and dampness. The grading of Minnesota grain had been controlled by boards of trade in the principal terminal markets of Minneapolis, St. Paul, and Duluth. The belief became widespread among Minnesota farmers that the inspectors thus appointed by these boards were the willing and paid tools of elevator owners and speculators. Complaints of dishonest grading, excessive storage charges, and unconscionable dockages were loud and long. The new law declared all the elevators in the cities named public elevators to be operated only under licenses obtained from the state railroad and warehouse commissioners, thus extending the title as well as the functions of the board. Warehouses were required to receive marketable grain, without discrimination, up to the limit of capacity and to issue numbered receipts for each consignment. Receipts thus given were negotiable and " went into circulation " in large amounts. In September of each year the commission was required to establish for the ensuing year " Minnesota grades " of all grains handled by public elevators. All grain going into store in such elevators was to be inspected and weighed by appointees of the commission. The commission was given power to establish rules and regulations in regard to the handling, inspection, and storage of grains. Many of these were afterwards enacted into law.[19]

Other notable acts of the busy legislature of 1885 were those revising the military and penal codes, requiring the incorporation of villages by general law, providing for the punishment of frauds in the use of trade marks, and revamping the act of 1883 for the organization of trust companies, which have become such important agencies for the custody and investment of funds.[20]

[19] *General Laws*, 1885, pp. 136–148; *General Statutes*, 1913, pp. 988–995.
[20] *General Laws*, 1883, pp. 72–96, 133–140; 1885, pp. 14–16, 148–172, 219–222, 311. The legislature of 1885 provided for the publication of the penal code in a separate volume. The law relating to the incorporation of villages was a recast of an act passed in 1883.

There was one event of Governor Hubbard's time which, though not widely nor very seriously regarded, must not be passed in silence because of the remarkable developments which have followed. When the Chippewa treaty of 1854 was made it was expected that mines of copper, and possibly of gold and silver, would be discovered in the ceded region north of Lake Superior. Eleven years later a state geologist was employed to visit the triangle and to report on whatever indications of metals he might find. In a reconnoissance made in 1865 traces of gold were found near Vermilion Lake, which gave rise to a spasmodic and presently disastrous gold craze. Incidentally, the geologist observed an outcrop of iron ore between fifty and sixty feet thick, with "quite a mural face." Little attention was given to a find so remote from civilization, more than sixty miles from the shore of Lake Superior, and nearly twenty years passed before anyone had enterprise enough to open the Minnesota Iron Mine near Tower. In 1884 more than sixty-two thousand tons of iron ore were shipped down the lake. The opening of mines on the great Mesabi Range did not take place until 1891. At the present time more than one-half of all the iron ore produced in the country comes from Minnesota mines.[21]

It was on the evening of November 7, 1834, that Henry Hastings Sibley, then a young man of twenty-three, rode into the rude hamlet of log huts at St. Peter's, later named Mendota. On the fiftieth anniversary of that event a banquet was given at the Metropolitan Hotel in St. Paul, with General Sibley as the guest of honor. The principal address was made by Cushman K. Davis, a warm personal admirer although a political opponent of Sibley. Referring to the

[21] Holmes, in *Minnesota in Three Centuries*, 4: 375–377; Newton H. Winchell, *The History of Geological Surveys in Minnesota*, 3 (Geological and Natural History Survey of Minnesota, *Bulletins*, no. 1 — St. Paul, 1889); Winchell, "The Discovery and Development of the Iron Ores of Minnesota," in *Minnesota Historical Collections*, 8: 27–29; Geological and Natural History Survey of Minnesota, *Reports*, 1884, p. 8; 1891, p. 113. A more adequate account of iron mining in Minnesota will be attempted in the next volume.

unwavering and persistent advocacy by General Sibley of the full redemption of the state railroad bonds of 1858, Davis said, " The instructive impulses of his magnificent integrity have wiped clean every stain from the escutcheon of his beloved state, befouled by the discredit of a wrecked financial policy." In illustration of Sibley's kindness of heart, Judge Flandrau related that when he received a dispatch announcing General Sibley's intention to hang several hundred Sioux prisoners in the fall of 1862 should they be convicted and sentenced to death by the military commission, he, Flandrau, turned the paper over and wrote on the back, " He says he will, but he won't do it." General Sibley's reply to these eulogies was modest and graceful. He had already retired from official life but held his regency of the state university until his death on February 18, 1891. In 1888 Princeton University conferred upon him the honorary degree of doctor of laws in consideration of " high personal character, scholarly attainments, and eminent public services, civil, military and educational." [22]

At the close of his term Governor Hubbard returned to Red Wing to care for his private interests and to aid in the improvement of that charming city. At the outbreak of the Spanish-American War in 1898 the president appointed him a brigadier general of United States volunteers, which rank he held until the muster out of the volunteer army in the following year. Soon after this Governor Hubbard took up his residence in St. Paul, and there he lived most of the time until his death on February 5, 1913. He gave freely of his time to boards and commissions of public importance and to the Minnesota Historical Society, for which he wrote a number of valuable papers. He was one of the commissioners for the publication of *Minnesota in the Civil and Indian Wars,* to which he contributed the narrative of the Fifth Regiment. A Minnesota county bears his name.

[22] West, *Sibley,* 55, 375; Upham and Dunlap, *Minnesota Biographies,* 702; *Pioneer Press,* November 8, 1884, p. 3.

"Few men," wrote General James H. Baker, "have retired from the position of governor who were held in as high regard and esteem by the people of the state as Governor Hubbard. His practical good sense, the important measures he proposed and achieved, the steadiness and cleanness of his administration, his open and manly nature, all conspire to give him an elevated place in the affections and memory of the people of Minnesota." [23]

[23] *Minneapolis Tribune,* February 6, 1913; *Pioneer Press,* same date; Baker, *Governors of Minnesota,* 13: 251–277. A list of General Hubbard's printed works is given on page 280. For a memorial by Warren Upham, see *Minnesota Historical Collections,* 15: 776. On the publication of *Minnesota in the Civil and Indian Wars, 1861–1865* (St. Paul, 1891–99), see *ante,* 2: 77, n. 34.

VII.   McGILL   AND   HIS   TIMES,   1887–89

THE tardy conclusion of his contest with William D. Washburn for a seat in Congress in the summer of 1879 left the versatile Ignatius Donnelly without hope of early public employment and with a slender bank balance. He therefore turned to the field of letters, in which as a youth he had made a trivial venture in a thin volume of poems published under the title *The Mourner's Vision*. Shut up in his great farmhouse at Nininger near Hastings, surrounded by an extensive and very miscellaneous collection of books and pamphlets, he prepared for a new adventure in authorship. In the winter of 1881 in the course of a month he wrote out on sheets of brown wrapping paper the copy of his *Atlantis*. Around a nucleus of tradition, recorded by Plato in his " Timæus," of a prehistoric continent off the northwest coast of Africa, sunk by some geologic cataclysm beneath the waves of the Atlantic Ocean, Donnelly assembled, in a style facile and brilliant, an amazing wealth of lore and ingenious conjecture which to many of his readers seemed like an " ower true tale." Gladstone, versed in classic lore, wrote him that after reading a portion of the work he was " much disposed to believe in an Atlantis." [1] The immediate and extensive sale of *Atlantis* encouraged its author to attempt another and bolder romance. Under the title *Ragnarok* he undertook to show

---

[1] Fish, *Donnelliana*, part 1, pp. 14, 106–108. *Atlantis: the Antediluvian World* was published in New York in 1882. The core of the passage from the " Timæus " is as follows: " And there was an island situated in front of the straits which you call the columns of Heracles; the island was larger than Libya and Asia put together, and was the way to other islands. . . . Now in this island of Atlantis there was a great and wonderful empire which had rule over the whole island . . . and . . . subjected the parts of Libya . . . as far as Egypt, and of Europe as far as Tyrrhenia. . . . and then, Solon, your country . . . defeated and triumphed over the invaders. . . . But afterwards there occurred violent earthquakes and floods; and in a single day and

that the drift covering a large part of the northern hemisphere of the earth is not, as geologists fancy, the result of glacial grind and transportation but is a deposit of stones, gravel, and dust from a great meteor into which the earth at some time shouldered as it traversed her orbit.[2]

But literature was not an engrossing passion with Ignatius Donnelly. He longed for further opportunities to display the talent for statesmanship with which he believed himself endowed. The compliments received for his two romances easily suggested an increase of confidence on the part of his fellow citizens in his capacity for public affairs. In the political season of 1884 he announced himself as a candidate for representative in Congress from the third Minnesota district. The Republicans renominated Horace B. Strait, a veteran officer of the Civil War and deservedly popular. The election returns showed that Donnelly was justified in

night of rain . . . the island of Atlantis . . . disappeared, and was sunk beneath the sea." Benjamin Jowett, tr., *The Dialogues of Plato*, 4: 370 (New York, n.d.).

Some of Donnelly's conclusions are: "The Antediluvian World was none other than Atlantis" (p. 74). "And this land was the garden of Eden of our race. This was the Olympus of the Greeks" (p. 322). "The story of the Deluge plainly refers to the destruction of Atlantis" (p. 369). "In Egypt we have the oldest of the Old World children of Atlantis" (p. 369). "Atlantis was the older country, the parent country [*of the Peruvians*]" (p. 395). "The population of Ireland . . . was one of the many waves of population flowing out from the Island of Atlantis" (p. 412). For the fancied connection of the "Mound Builders" of the Mississippi Valley with Atlantis, see page 385.

[2] *Ragnarok: the Age of Fire and Gravel* was published in New York in 1883. The following are some of Donnelly's conclusions: "The conclusion, therefore, is irresistible that the drift is not due to ice" (p. 42). The drift was confined to one side of the globe, the hemisphere between longitude ninety degrees east of Greenwich and ninety degrees west (frontispiece and p. 93). It is probable that one of the millions of comets, in the course of thirty, fifty, or a hundred thousand years, may have struck the earth (p. 90). The earth was struck by comets many times (p. 431). "The probability is, that . . . the comet brought down upon the earth the clay-dust and part of the gravel and bowlders; while the awful force it exerted, meeting the earth while moving at the rate of a million miles an hour, smashed the surface-rocks, tore them to pieces, ground them up and mixed the material with its own, and deposited all together on the heated surface of the earth, where the lower part was baked by the heat into 'till' or 'hardpan,' while the rushing cyclones deposited the other material in partly stratified masses or drifts above it" (p. 255). Pages 113–340 treat of legends, including the books of Genesis and Job, pointing to a great antehistoric cataclysm. The human race "survived the great cataclysm and renewed the civilization of the pre-glacial age" (p. 366).

entering the contest, but they did not show the desirable majority of votes. He was defeated by 994 votes out of a total of 32,062.[3]

With a prospect of indefinite exemption from the labors and cares of public office, Donnelly returned to his study and set to work, or perhaps resumed work, on the task of disentangling the cipher fancied by him to be involved in the plays of Shakespeare, or in some of them. He procured a facsimile copy of the great folio of 1623 and it was not long before he discovered that the pagination was in some places duplicated, in others transposed, and in still others wanting. He observed that words were bracketed, italicized, and hyphenated in a manner superfluous and capricious. In the first part of "Henry the Fourth," act 2, scene 1, he observed that the words "Bacon," "son," "Nicholas," "Bacon's," and "Francis" occurred on three consecutive pages. He counted the words in the first column of page 53 and found "Bacon" to be the three hundred and seventy-first word. The number of the italicized words on the page was seven. Seven multiplied by fifty-three is equal to three hundred and seventy-one. Here was his clue. In a somewhat similar manner he marked out the locations of the other words, but to get the word "son" it was necessary to count backward. But this experiment and its results were purely elementary. A system of "root numbers," 505, 506, 513, 516, and 523, all modifications of one number and all modified by numerous multipliers, was elaborated. Guided by these mystic numbers, Donnelly drew out by counting word after word on page after page stories hidden in the text. It was, as he says, "an incalculable labor, reaching through many weary years." *The Great Cryptogram* fills an octavo lacking but two of one thousand pages, the first half of which are devoted to arguments to prove *aliunde* the improb-

---

[3] Smalley, *Republican Party*, 219, 367; Fish, *Donnelliana*, part 1, p. 104; *Legislative Manual*, 1885, p. 329.

ability of William Shakespeare's authorship and the likelihood that Sir Francis Bacon wrote plays and poems.[4] The book was not widely circulated, but its author was made known by it to a new circle. He was called or volunteered to lecture or debate in many cities. In England he engaged in debates in both of the ancient universities. At Cambridge, where it was the custom to test the effect of such discussion by a vote of the whole audience, 120 voted that Shakespeare wrote the plays and 101, that Bacon wrote them, a larger remainder not voting. The learned world has not yet accepted the "Baconian theory" and it has been suggested that with a goodly supply of "root numbers" and "modifiers" any desired story could be worked out of the text of any book. The stories which Donnelly did work out reveal no important historical secrets and have no literary interest. He claimed, however, to have made but a bare beginning of revelations.[5]

Governor Hubbard's long term drew to its close with the year 1886. Because of a new situation the leaders of both great political parties became more than usually concerned about the choice of a candidate for the succession. The Granger movement of the previous decade had languished but a new concatenation of reformers and dissentients had

---

[4] The Great Cryptogram: Francis Bacon's Cipher in the So-called Shakespeare Plays, 551–558, 581–583, 647 (Chicago, 1888). The worked-out "Cipher Narrative" may be found on pages 619–889. See also two articles by Donnelly, "The Shakespeare Myth" and "Delia Bacon's Unhappy Story," in the North American Review, 144: 572–582 (June, 1887); 145: 57–68 (July, 1887); 148: 307–318 (March, 1889); and an article by Arthur D. Vinton, "Those Wonderful Ciphers," in the same magazine, 145: 555–562 (November, 1887). In a later work, The Cipher in the Plays, and on the Tombstone (Minneapolis, 1899), Donnelly modified some of his modifiers and ventured to unravel a narrative concealed in the strange inscription on the tombstone of Shakespeare in the church at Stratford-on-Avon. On this work, see the Representative (Minneapolis), 1899: March 29, p. 2; November 9, p. 4.

[5] Fish, Donnelliana, part 1, pp. 111–119; Donnelly, The Cipher in the Plays, 357. For an amusing burlesque of the method of the Great Cryptogram, see J. Gilpin Pyle, The Little Cryptogram: a Literal Application to the Play of Hamlet of the Cipher System of Mr. Ignatius Donnelly (St. Paul, 1888). It was originally published in the Pioneer Press, May 6, 1888, p. 4. See also William D. O'Connor, Mr. Donnelly's Reviewers (Chicago, 1889).

T̲H̲E̲ GREAT CRYPTOGRAM:
FRANCIS BACON'S CIPHER in The
SO-CALLED SHAKESPEARE PLAYS.

By IGNATIUS DONNELLY, Author
of "Atlantis: The Antediluvian World,"and
"Ragnarök: The Age of Fire and Gravel."

"And now I will vnclaspe a Secret booke
And to your quicke conceyuing Difcontents
Ile reade you Matter, deepe and dangerous,
As full of perill and aduenturous Spirit,
As to o'erwalke a Current, roaring loud,
On the vnftedfaft footing of a Speare."
Ist Henry IV., Act I, Sc. 3.

·Chicago·
·New York and London·
R. S. Peale & Company.
1888.

THE TITLE-PAGE OF THE GREAT CRYPTOGRAM

come in its place under the name of "Farmers' Alliance." Nuclei of this aggregation had existed for some years in other states but it did not show strength in Minnesota until about 1881. From that time it grew so fast in numbers and influence that it had to be reckoned with. The number of local alliances had grown by 1886 to 438.[6] On September 1 of that year a joint state convention of the Farmers' Alliance and the Knights of Labor took place in St. Paul. Here was an opportunity for Donnelly again to emerge on the field of politics, from which he had so lately retired in disgust. To lead a great aggregation of citizens fervently advocating the reforms for which he had been pleading for years was a temptation which he could not resist. He appeared in the convention, made one of his most brilliant addresses, and dictated the multifarious platform.

Conscious that it did not represent a great party with traditions of power and privilege, with a great body of members born into it as into a church, the convention refrained from nominating a state ticket, preferring to offer support to the Republican or the Democratic party, whichever should show the liveliest hospitality to the principles to be embodied in its platform. That platform consisted of two series of "demands," one for the farmers and the other for workingmen. For the farmers the platform demanded legislation to reduce railroad rates to such an extent that there should be nothing left for dividends on watered stock and to prevent the further issue of watered stock by corporations; an amendment to the state constitution limiting the exemption from taxation of railroad property to tracks, rights of way, and depot grounds; the enactment of laws declaring combi-

---

[6] Historical sketch of the Alliance, in the *Great West* (St. Paul), February 14, 1890, p. 2; John D. Hicks, "The Origin and Early History of the Farmers' Alliance in Minnesota," in the *Mississippi Valley Historical Review*, 9: 203–226 (December, 1922). The account in the text was prepared before the appearance in print of Hicks's full and well-studied paper. For a succinct account of the rise and progress of the Farmers' Alliance in the South and the Northwest, see Buck, *Agrarian Crusade*, 111–124.

nations for the control of markets criminal conspiracies; the establishment of a system of local inspection of grain and scales; legislation declaring the issue of railroad passes to federal, state, or local officials, or the acceptance of passes by such officials, to be a crime; and the reduction of interest on loans to eight per cent. For workingmen the platform demanded the enactment by Congress of an income tax law and the establishment of a state bureau of labor statistics. It declared the farming out of convict labor at forty cents a day " a great wrong." It demanded legislation to furnish school textbooks free to pupils; protection for those engaged in mining and manufacturing industries and indemnification for those injured through lack of proper safeguards; the employment of workingmen for municipal work, rather than the letting out of such work to contractors; the payment of equal wages to men and women doing the same work; the reservation of public lands for actual settlers, rather than the selling of the lands to corporations and speculators; the organization by the government of financial exchanges and facilities for small deposits in connection with the post office; the prohibition of child labor in mines, workshops, and factories; provision for arbitration in cases of disputes between workingmen and their employers; the abrogation of all laws not bearing equally upon capital and labor; the removal of unjust technicalities, delays, and discriminations in the administration of justice; the recognition by incorporation of trade unions; and legislation to compel corporations to pay their employees in lawful money and to give mechanics and laborers a first lien upon the products of their industry to the full extent of their wages. As the reader will have observed, a goodly number of the demands on the part of labor have long since been conceded.[7]

The joint convention appointed a committee of thirty with Ignatius Donnelly at its head to lay the demands before the

[7] *Pioneer Press* (St. Paul and Minneapolis), September 2, 1886, p. 8.

state conventions of the two great parties soon to assemble. The Democratic convention in session on September 14, 1886, gave the cold shoulder to the Alliance coalition. The Republican convention met in St. Paul on September 22. Donnelly and his tail of committeemen appeared and were given seats on the floor. The delegates listened to the overture and to Donnelly's delicious blarney and straightway lifted into their platform substantially all the "demands" of the Alliance and its associates. Both the old parties passed resolutions of sympathy for Ireland, suffering injustice under British rule.[8]

It was another off year in politics and neither great party could expect to carry its ticket on a wave of presidential enthusiasm. Neither could expect to hold its membership strictly in its ranks; much less could the Republicans expect a solid Alliance vote, although they had absorbed the Alliance platform. There was no strenuous competition among the leaders of either party for the precarious nomination for the governorship. The Republican nomination fell to a man of admirable qualities, though not yet very conspicuous in public affairs — Andrew Ryan McGill. He was born of Irish parents in Pennsylvania in 1840 and had come to St. Peter in 1861. He enlisted in Company D of the Ninth Minnesota Infantry and after one year's service was discharged for disability, with the rank of sergeant. He became superintendent of schools of Nicollet County, editor of the *Saint Peter Tribune*, and clerk of the district court. In 1869 he was admitted to the bar and in the following year he was selected by Governor Austin as his private secretary. Austin appointed him insurance commissioner when that office was created and for thirteen years, 1873–87, McGill held the office through successive appointments by Governors Davis,

[8] John D. Hicks, "The Political Career of Ignatius Donnelly," in the *Mississippi Valley Historical Review*, 8: 106–108 (June–September, 1921). Accounts of the conventions may be found in the *Pioneer Press*, 1886: September 15, p. 1; 23, p. 1. Donnelly's report of his experience is given in the issue of September 24, p. 5. See also Smalley, *Republican Party*, 220, 223.

Pillsbury, and Hubbard. These appointments were amply justified by his intelligent and industrious discharge of the duties.[9]

The Democrats selected for their candidate for governor Dr. Albert Alonzo Ames of Minneapolis, a man of ability and engaging manners. His parents had brought him from Illinois in 1851 at the age of ten. He attended high school in Minneapolis and the Rush Medical College of Chicago, from which he was graduated in 1862. In that year he accepted the position of assistant surgeon of the Seventh Minnesota Infantry. He was later promoted to the rank of surgeon and served with satisfaction until the muster out of the command on August 18, 1865. He was elected a representative in the state legislature in 1867. In the year following he went to California, where he engaged in editorial work; he remained there until 1874, when he returned to Minnesota. He was mayor of Minneapolis in 1876, in 1882, and again in 1886. Ames was gifted in many ways, was generous to the needy, especially to old comrades in arms, and his winning personality brought him a large following of workingmen. While personally temperate, he believed that every man should regulate his habits for himself.[10]

The campaign of 1886 was still further complicated by a liquor question. A bill for high license and local option had been defeated in the last legislature by the organized liquor interests. The Republicans in convention, moved by a " ringing speech " by the Reverend Samuel G. Smith of St. Paul and by a willingness to attract, if possible, prohibition votes, put a high license plank into their platform. As the Democrats had declared against all sumptuary legisla-

[9] Baker, *Governors of Minnesota*, 285–291; Colin F. Macdonald, " Narrative of the Ninth Regiment," in *Minnesota in the Civil and Indian Wars*, 1 : 417; Smalley, *Republican Party*, 340; Upham and Dunlap, *Minnesota Biographies*, 467.
[10] Warner and Foote, *Hennepin County*, 502; Flandrau, *Encyclopedia of Biography*, 1 : 372.

tion and as Ames was a violent opponent of such measures, the liquor interests were solidly arrayed against McGill, who was outspoken for high license.[11]

Another disturbing element of no little moment was Ignatius Donnelly. The Democratic convention had given him the cold shoulder as spokesman for the Alliance, but for reasons not easy to divine the Alliance leaders were more sympathetic toward the Democrats than toward the Republicans, who had invited them into their fold. Donnelly much preferred the Republican platform but would have accepted a Democratic nomination as representative in the state legislature had it not been refused him. He therefore cut loose, ran as an independent candidate, and was elected. The state campaign was a lively one and the contest finally centered chiefly on high license. The official canvass of the vote gave McGill the slender plurality of 2,600 votes out of a total of 220,558.[12] At the time it was believed by some that Ames would have won had not some heated partisans of his assaulted a Republican procession in the streets of Minneapolis on the night before election. The news was spread at once by telegraph to all important cities and villages and this may have turned many votes to McGill. The prophecy of a Republican leader during the balloting in convention that the nomination would defeat the party barely escaped fulfillment.[13]

Governor McGill in his message to the legislature of 1887 recommended to its attention the measures covered by the Republican platform. The speakership of the Minnesota House has always been an important position for the reason that the incumbent has been allowed to appoint the standing

[11] *Pioneer Press*, September 23, 1886, pp. 1, 2; Baker, *Governors of Minnesota*, 290.

[12] Hicks, in the *Mississippi Valley Historical Review*, 8: 107. The vote may be found in the *Legislative Manual*, 1925, p. 113. The total given includes 9,030 Prohibition votes. McGill did not receive a majority of all the votes. Baker, *Governors of Minnesota*, 291.

[13] *Minneapolis Tribune*, November 2, 1886, editorial, p. 4; Baker, *Governors of Minnesota*, 291.

committees of the House. It will be understood, of course, that election to the office was in some degree the result of combinations of influential members desiring chairmanships or appointments where they could advance bills in which they had some interest. On this occasion the speakership might have fallen to Donnelly, who, after the fall elections, had made his peace with the Alliance and its associate groups, but for unknown considerations he preferred to further the election of William R. Merriam, a new Republican member and a banker of St. Paul. Donnelly was given the chairmanship of the committee on railroads and was placed on other committees of importance. It may be that, with the strong following behind him at the opening of the session, Donnelly thought the time favorable for the passage of reform measures for which he had been laboring. He introduced no less than fifty-seven bills. But a small proportion of them became laws, and they were passed only after they had been liberally amended. Before the session was over Donnelly's incessant palaver had disgusted the whole House.[14]

The legislature of 1887 found before it the responsible duty of electing a senator in Congress in place of Senator Samuel J. R. McMillan, who was about to complete his second term. He had discharged the usual duties with diligence and intelligence, without having aspired to distinction in debate or in the introduction and advocacy of measures of capital importance. He had therefore established no claim to a third term. Ex-Governor Cushman K. Davis, whose premature aspiration to the United States Senate in 1875 had been rudely blighted, had returned to his law practice and literary avocations. His defense of Sherman Page had added to his repute as a lawyer. He had lectured on Hamlet and Madame Roland and had published his book on *The Law in Shakespeare*. He had not sought minor political

---

[14] *Executive Documents*, 1886, vol. 1, p. 43; Hicks, in the *Mississippi Valley Historical Review*, 8: 109, and citations; Hall, *Observations*, 221–224.

Union of the Diocese of St. Paul, itself a unit in a national organization.[17]

The earliest commercial use of the word " saloon " known to the writer was as the name for a small building or room in which ice cream or oysters were served for treats. Not long after the close of the Civil War the light German " lager beer " — light as compared with English beers and ales, which were little drunk in America — was introduced by German immigrants and a fashion was set for it by numerous young Americans who had studied in the German universities. It was a refreshing drink when freshly drawn from the wood and when taken in small quantities it was but slightly intoxicating. The saloon soon became a convenient place of resort for men in leisure hours, especially for workingmen who did not read nor attend lectures or concerts. A custom of drinking in social groups grew up in place of the individual " perpendicular drinking " which had long been customary in America and the American custom of treating to drinks was unfortunately perpetuated. The drinking places were made cheerful and attractive and the keepers were hospitable and, in many instances, generous and helpful to customers in need of counsel or aid. Had the saloon retained this elementary character it might have served a useful purpose and might have been considered respectable.

Not many years passed before Bishop Ireland found, as did other temperance advocates outside his communion, that he had before him something more than the mere task of reforming drunkards. He found established a powerful aggregate of interests coöperating to persuade old drunk-

[17] *Archbishop Ireland, Prelate, Patriot, Publicist, 1838–1918; a Memoir,* 6, 26 (St. Paul, n.d.); James M. Reardon, " The Catholic Total Abstinence Movement in Minnesota," in *Acta et Dicta,* 2: 44, 47, 53, 55, 83 (July, 1909); *Saint Paul Pioneer,* January 27, 1869, p. 4; *North-Western Chronicle* (St. Paul), October 16, 1875, p. 4. In the *Pioneer,* April 23, 1869, p. 4, is an account of a powerful address by Ireland on the evils of drink. See also the *Pioneer Press,* August 3, 1882, p. 5, for a summary of a speech by Archbishop Ireland before the annual convention of the Catholic Total Abstinence Union. For Father Ireland's services as chaplain of the Fifth Minnesota, see *ante,* 2: 97.

ards not to reform and to entice young men to take the downward road. He had to deal with the American saloon, diverted and expanded from its early and relatively innocent function. Bishop Ireland attacked the saloon with all his force and eloquence in a long series of addresses. A typical and, for the present purpose, a sufficient example is his address on " Intemperance and the Law," delivered in Buffalo, New York, on March 10, 1884, before the Citizens' Reform Association. The liquor traffic had by this time reached the zenith of its power. There was in Boston a licensed saloon for every 150 inhabitants, in Chicago one for every 140, and in Buffalo and Albany one for every 100. In cities there was, on an average, a saloon to every 35 persons likely to drink. In Chicago there were 2,761 shops of butchers, bakers, and grocers, and at least 5,000 saloons, licensed or unlicensed. In this address the bishop declared intemperance to be the great cause of pauperism, the parent of vice and crime, and the destroyer of life and health; he arraigned the liquor traffic as the chief cause of intemperance and denounced the saloon as the lawless agency of a great commercial and political combination. To remedy this he advocated the imposition of high license fees, which would reduce the number of saloons and would secure the coöperation of licensed dealers with the police in discovering unlicensed resorts. The influence of Bishop Ireland personally and through his clergy without doubt carried the state for high license and elected McGill in the fall of 1886.[18]

18 John Ireland, *The Church and Modern Society*, 1: 261–305 (New York and St. Paul, 1903–04). In an article entitled " The Catholic Church and the Saloon," in the same volume, p. 318, Bishop Ireland wrote, " The American saloon is responsible for the awful intemperance which desolated the land and which is the physical and moral plague of our time." On page 322 he contrasts the American saloon with the European beer garden and cafe. See page 324 for a letter in English dated March 27, 1887, from Pope Leo XIII commending the Catholic Total Abstinence Union and bestowing upon Bishop Ireland and his associates the apostolic benediction. Bishop Ireland was elevated to the archbishopric in 1888. Upham and Dunlap, *Minnesota Biographies*. 362.

It may be here remarked that the high license law of 1887 had some of its intended effects realized: the reduction of the number of saloons, the elimination of the low dive, and the enlistment of saloon-keepers on the side of the police in discovering and suppressing "blind pigs." But the law left the saloons in the control of the distillers, brewers, and wholesale liquor-dealers, who virtually owned them and maintained an army of keepers whose business it was to make drunkards and to keep them made. More than ever the saloon became the sphere of political activities and the convenient place for insnaring the venal vote. These evils grew more and more hateful and intolerable until in 1920 the people as a nation arose in majestic exasperation and declared by a constitutional amendment that the saloon and the manufacture of and traffic in liquor should be no more.

Among other memorable acts of the legislature of 1887 recommended and approved by Governor McGill may be mentioned the establishment of the Soldiers' Home on the beautiful grounds adjacent to Minnehaha Park in Minneapolis and of the State Reformatory at St. Cloud; the creation of the bureau of labor statistics; and the provision for the maintenance of state farmers' institutes. A recast of the general railroad law of the state was accompanied by a number of statutes imposing additional regulations on railroad management. The eighth section of the general act presumed to empower the state railroad and warehouse commission to prescribe freight rates which should be *ipso facto* just and reasonable. Proceeding under the statute, the commission directed the Chicago, Milwaukee, and St. Paul Railway Company to put in force certain reduced rates for the transportation of milk from certain stations in Minnesota to St. Paul and Minneapolis. The company refused obedience and appealed from the mandamus issued by the state supreme court. On March 24, 1890, the Supreme Court of the United States held that the section was unconstitutional

because it deprived the company of its right to a hearing in
court and to a judicial determination of the reasonableness
of rates. Thus one of Donnelly's cherished schemes for the
control of corporations came to naught.[19]

Governor McGill had the pleasure of announcing that the
University of Minnesota had become a real university by
reason of the opening in the fall of 1888 of the colleges of
law and medicine. The former began its career in a very
modest way. Upon the recommendation of the Honorable
Gordon E. Cole, one of their number, the regents of the university selected William S. Pattee to open the law school.
Dean Pattee was born in Maine in 1846 and, after his graduation at Bowdoin College, settled in Northfield in 1874.
There he superintended the schools and studied law. He
began the practice of law in 1878 and was a representative
in the legislature of 1885. In September, 1888, he opened
the law school in a basement room of the "Old Main"
building, with his yet small private library on a few shelves
near his desk. Dean Pattee remained at the head of his
college until his death on April 4, 1911. His industry and
learning, his sound discretion, his consideration for his colleagues, and his friendly interest in his students qualified
him for conspicuous usefulness in his day. He prepared
numerous textbooks and toward the close of his life embodied
his general views in a volume on *The Essential Nature of
Law*. The college of medicine was established when the
Minnesota Hospital College of Minneapolis, a private institution, which had already acquired a deserved reputation,
was taken over in 1888. In the same year there had been
organized in the university a "school of agriculture," below

---

[19] McGill's message, January 5, 1887, in *Executive Documents*, 1886, vol.
1, p. 43; *General Laws*, 1887, pp. 49-66, 67-76, 199-201, 249-257, 329-335,
380; Smalley, *Republican Party*, 34; Chicago, Milwaukee, and St. Paul Railway Company *v*. Minnesota, 134 *United States*, 418-466. The suit was the
well-known "Milk Suit." Three justices dissented because the holding of
the majority overruled the principle laid down in Munn *v*. Illinois, 4 *Otto*,
113 (94 *United States*), that the regulation of railroad rates is a legislative,
not a judicial, prerogative.

college grade, which was destined to work results far beyond and differing from expectation.[20]

Upon his retirement from executive duties Governor McGill for some years devoted himself to his private affairs at his old home. In 1899, having taken up his residence in St. Paul, he was elected a state senator and he served for four successive terms. His service in the Senate was conspicuously efficient. In 1900 he was appointed postmaster of St. Paul, and he was holding the two offices at the time of his sudden death on October 31, 1905. No one of Minnesota's governors has left a cleaner or a more honorable record.[21]

[20] McGill's message, in *Executive Documents*, 1888, vol. I, p. 12; E. Bird Johnson, ed., *Forty Years of the University of Minnesota*, 119, 141, 156, 391 (Minneapolis, 1910). Johnson's omission of any credit to Professor Edward D. Porter is unfortunate. He actually started the school of agriculture. The complete title of Dean Pattee's book is *The Essential Nature of Law; or the Ethical Basis of Jurisprudence* (Chicago, 1909).

[21] *Pioneer Press*, November I, 1905, p. 2.

VIII. MERRIAM AND HIS TIMES, 1889–93

E VER since the Civil War it had been a custom of the
Republican party to allow the governors and other
state officers elected by it the right to claim a renomination.
Governor Davis alone had not desired a second term, but
all others had enjoyed the benefit of the unwritten law.
Governor McGill was accordingly looking forward in his
second year to the customary renomination and probably
expected but little open opposition. He became aware,
however, that a silent opposition in the interests of other
aspirants was brooding and prepared as best he could for a
contest. That he had discharged the duties of the governorship with diligence and fidelity weighed less in the minds of
political workers than the circumstance that he had been
elected by a very small majority on the high license issue.
It was feared that a strong Democrat backed by the liquor
interest might win the governorship and the numerous
appointive offices that went with it. When the Republican state
convention met on September 5, 1888, it took but four ballots
to give the nomination to William Rush Merriam, a banker
of St. Paul. A biographer of McGill, in writing of the
action of the Republican convention, expressed his view thus:
" The convention, having thus [in its platform] cordially
endorsed Governor McGill, proceeded to stultify itself by
rejecting his unqualified right, under all party usages, and
by every sense of personal justice, to a renomination. It is
not too much to characterize the action of the convention as
the most flagrant piece of wrong ever perpetrated by a political party in the state of Minnesota. It was simply a transcendent injustice, which had its basis in the corruption of
delegates, if we credit the newspapers of the day." [1]

[1] Baker, *Governors of Minnesota*, 293–295, 310; Hall, *Observations*, 196–
201; Castle, in *Minnesota Historical Collections*, 15: 590; Smalley, *Republican*

Merriam, although he had for his Democratic opponent the Honorable Eugene M. Wilson, a former representative in Congress, an able lawyer, and a man of high social standing and personal popularity, was elected by a handsome plurality. There were insinuations, even open allegations, that large sums of money had been corruptly used to secure his nomination and election.[2] That the successful aspirant and his friends had paid, and had paid liberally, for time, traveling expenses, printing, and oratory in the campaign would probably not have been denied, but it was not necessary to deny charges that votes or delegations were purchased. The machine did not need to be bribed to work for its own perpetuation. Governor Merriam's appointments to office were not of a character to warrant the suggestion that they were made in consideration of services or contributions toward his nomination and election. Indeed, there were complaints of neglect and ingratitude.

Governor Merriam, who was at this time under forty years of age, had been in the state from childhood. Although he was the son of a wealthy father, he sought from boyhood no life of ease and idleness but one of strenuous activity in business and public affairs. After his graduation as valedictorian from Racine College in 1871, he entered upon a banking career as a clerk in the First National Bank of St. Paul. He was made cashier of the Merchants' National Bank in 1873 and vice president in 1880, and four years later he became president of the bank. In 1883 he was a member of the legislature and was one of the number who

Party, 229; *Pioneer Press* (St. Paul and Minneapolis), 1888: August 29, p. 3; September 6, 7; Hicks, in the *Mississippi Valley Historical Review,* 8: 111–113. Ignatius Donnelly had also been nominated by a conference of labor leaders and Alliance men at St. Paul on August 28, 1888. It took the name "Farm and Labor Party" and adopted a platform of multifarious reforms. Donnelly made a few speeches but, finding no substantial support, he abandoned the unpromising candidacy and came out for Merriam. No evidence has been found for a rumor that Donnelly was paid substantially for this concession.

[2] Baker, *Governors of Minnesota,* 312; Hall, *Observations,* 197. In the November election Merriam received 134,355 votes; Wilson, 110,251; and Harrison, the Prohibition candidate, 17,026.

defeated Senator Windom for reëlection to the United States Senate. After his reëlection to the legislature of 1886 he became speaker of the House, and he gave great satisfaction in that capacity, especially to the rural members. It was to their partiality, doubtless, that he owed his election to the presidency of the State Agricultural Society the next year. Together with prompt and thorough efficiency in affairs, his good nature, gracious manners, and attractive personality added to his list of friends and supporters. Into the executive office Governor Merriam carried his native talent for administration, refined by some years of experience in large concerns.[3]

The one duty of the legislature of 1889 which was looked forward to with greatest interest was the election of a senator in Congress to succeed Dwight M. Sabin. According to the unwritten law of the Republican party Sabin had a right to expect a reëlection, and the choice of a speaker of the House known to be his friend was thought to indicate a large if not a prevailing vote for him in caucus. It had long been known, however, that the friends of William D. Washburn would make a strong effort to secure the nomination for him on account of his claims upon the party and his superior qualifications. It was easy for them to argue that by supplanting Windom in 1883 Sabin had renounced the benefit of the two-term custom of the Republicans and that Windom had probably not forgotten that favor and would not strain himself to see Sabin reëlected; and he did not. The Republican caucus was held on January 17, 1889, with 122 members present. On the third formal ballot Washburn received 62 votes and became the party nominee. As required by law, the two houses voted separately on January 22. The Senate gave Washburn 24 of the 27 votes cast; since there were 47 members of the Senate, this was a majority of 1. Of the 100 votes cast in the House, Washburn received

[3] Baker, *Governors of Minnesota*, 305–310; Upham and Dunlap, *Minnesota Biographies*, 504.

80, a majority of 29. In joint convention on the twenty-third the journals of the houses were read and the presiding officer announced that William D. Washburn had received a majority of votes in the separate houses and that he was therefore elected senator of the United States for the term of six years. Under ordinary circumstances the election would have been indisputably complete; but objection was made to the election in the House because, having got into a wrangle on Tuesday, the day fixed by law for the separate voting in the houses, it had taken a recess and postponed its vote until the following day. Therefore the houses in joint convention proceeded to a viva-voce vote. Washburn received 107 votes, an unquestionable majority, and was again and finally declared elected.[4]

In the morning after the caucus a suggestion was made in the Senate of improper and excessive use of money on behalf of one or the other of the principal candidates. The House somewhat tardily entertained a similar suggestion. Committees of investigation were appointed, which submitted without recommendation the testimony taken. Neither house found occasion for definite action and the subject was dropped.[5] But there was one person who had received fifteen votes in the Republican caucus and who perhaps cherished

[4] *Pioneer Press*, 1889: January 6, p. 2; 18, p. 1; 23, p. 1; 24, p. 1; *St. Paul Daily News*, 1889: January 5, p. 1; 18, p. 1; 23, p. 1; *Minneapolis Journal*, 1889: January 5, p. 4; 18, p. 1; 22, pp. 1, 4; 23, p. 1; *House Journal*, 1889, pp. 89–94; *Senate Journal*, 70–72; Hall, *Observations*, 279–284; Smalley, *Republican Party*, 231.

[5] *Senate Journal*, 1889, pp. 40, 54, 62, 71; *House Journal*, 83, 89–91; *Report of Investigating Committees upon Charges of Bribery in the Senatorial Caucus for United States Senator for State of Minnesota* (n.p., n.d.). The report of the Senate committee was read in secret session. At the close the Senate by a rising vote expressed its confidence in the honor and integrity of Senator C. B. Buckman and declared its resentment of " all imputations growing out of the recent bribery investigations reflecting upon his good name." No other action was taken. The House committee reported that it had found no evidence implicating either Washburn or Sabin, but that there was some proof that overzealous friends had made improper offers for votes, none of which had been consummated. The House refused to have the report of its committee read. The testimony was not printed at the time, but the Senate of 1891, of which Donnelly was a member, ordered the printing of the two reports but refused, by a vote of 19 to 6, to direct its secretary to mail

a hope that, when the two principal candidates should have become stalled, he might be the lucky horse to get away with the senatorial prize. That was the irrepressible Donnelly, whose righteous soul was stirred, as his biographer says, by "a holocaust of corruption," "boundless and unfathomable," in "the worst legislature that had ever been known in the world." It seemed to him that not only was the country going straight to the "demnition bow-wows" of Dickens' Mantalini but that civilization itself was in danger of extinction. Filled with alarm, he sat down the very night

copies to members of the legislature. See *Senate Journal*, 1891, pp. 151, 186, 196, 235, 502.

The report, of which ten thousand copies were ordered printed, appears to justify the legislature of 1889 in ignoring the ill-supported charges of corruption against the two candidates. Witnesses, mostly members of the legislature, testified that they had been approached and had been told that deals were going on and that if they would talk with so and so they would be better informed. Not one of them had accepted money and but two had seen any money. It is probable, however, that, in a period when, according to many converging indications, money was pretty freely used in politics, overzealous friends of the two candidates made secret suggestions of "boodle," of which no proof will ever come to light.

One instance perhaps worthy of notice will serve for example. Representative Underwood, well known to the writer as a man of truth, testified that a member of the House, whose name he was not required to disclose, told him that there was a deal by which a syndicate intended to obtain Indian pine lands after Sabin should get a bill through Congress and that Buckman was to be appointed surveyor of logs and lumber to manipulate the survey so that the land would not cost much. The deponent could have two thousand dollars and a percentage of the profits of the deal if he would vote for Sabin and he could have the money if he would go to the house of a citizen of Minneapolis on Sunday. He entertained the matter long enough to be fully informed of the deal and then rejected the proposition. See *Report upon Charges of Bribery in the Senatorial Caucus*, 11.

The *St. Paul Daily Globe* on January 19, 1899, p. 4, prophesied that nothing would come of the investigation. "Nothing ever does come of these investigations." On January 24, 1889, p. 4, remarking on the proceedings of the investigating committees, the *Globe* called the investigations farcical. They exonerated the lady of the house, but inculpated the hired girl. They exonerated the principals, but inculpated their henchmen; but it was preposterous that the latter would spend their own money. See the *Pioneer Press*, 1889: January 14, p. 1; 15, p. 2, for correspondence of Horace G. Stone and T. B. Walker, in regard to Sabin's character and fitness. The *Globe*, March 5, 1891, p. 1, has a general write-up of the contest. Records of interviews with Harlan P. Hall, Curtis H. Pettit, William Pitt Murray, John B. Gilfillan, James T. Wyman, Simon Michelet, Thomas B. Walker, and John Day Smith, in the author's notebooks, 3: 64, 81, 89, 94–96; 6: 107, 110; 7: 37, 42, 48; 9: 23, 39, 49, 53, illustrate the variety of information and the infirmity of memory. See also Graves to the author, April 23, 1923; Hall, *Observations*, 281–284; *Minneapolis Journal*, 1889: January 18, p. 1; 21, p. 1; 22, p. 1.

of the election and wrote the first chapter of a novel to which he gave the strange title, *Cæsar's Column*. It proved to be the best seller of all Donnelly's books.[6] Whether or not the survival of some remnants of civilization may be credited to the lurid warnings of the " Sage of Nininger " the reader may consider.

So satisfactory to the Republican party was Governor Merriam's conduct of the state's business that its convention on July 24, 1890, gave him a unanimous nomination after one informal ballot. In that year of grace, however, an election after Republican nomination was not to be a matter of course as it had been two years before. Governor Merriam had to contend not only against the Democratic nominee, the Honorable Thomas Wilson, a very able lawyer with a large personal following who had been chief justice of the state supreme court and a state senator, but also against the standard bearer of a new political aggregation which was likely to draw, and did draw, largely from the Republican ranks.[7]

In 1890 the Farmers' Alliance, which in previous years had pursued the policy of throwing its compact minority vote to whichever of the two old parties would promise most toward the acceptance of its principles and the fulfillment of its demands, came into the field of politics as a third party. In December of the previous year, 1889, the National Farmers' Alliance, commonly known as the " Northwestern " Alliance, and the Farmers' and Laborers' Union of America, called the " Southern " Alliance, held conventions in St.

---

[6] Fish, *Donnelliana*, part 1, p. 119. *Cæsar's Column; a Story of the Twentieth Century* (Chicago, [1890]), was published under the pseudonym of " Edmund Boisgilbert, M.D." See the Appendix, no. 11, *post*, for a discussion of this work. Other publications of Donnelly were: *Doctor Huguet; a Novel* (Chicago, [1891]), an appeal in behalf of negroes; *The Golden Bottle, or the Story of Ephraim Benezet of Kansas* (New York and St. Paul, 1892) ; *The American People's Money* (Chicago, 1895) ; and innumerable articles, communications, and editorials.

[7] *Pioneer Press*, July 25, 1890; Baker, *Governors of Minnesota*, 312; Smalley, *Republican Party*, 232; Upham and Dunlap, *Minnesota Biographies*, 868.

Louis.   An attempt at union failed and the two organizations adopted separate platforms.   The principal demands of the Northwestern Alliance were the reservation of public lands for actual settlers only and the prevention of aliens from acquiring titles to lands; the abolition of national banks and the government issue of money " in sufficient volume for the requirements of business "; the early payment of the public debt; an income tax and a tax on real estate mortgages; economy and retrenchment in government management; revision and reduction of the tariff; " amendment " of the public school system; government ownership and management of railroads; the payment of the debt of the Union and Central Pacific railroads by foreclosure and sale; the improvement of waterways and national aid for experiments to determine the practicability of irrigation; and the Australian or some similar system of voting.   Ignatius Donnelly, as state lecturer, spread wide the principles of " the order " and, playing upon the chronic discontent of farmers and the actual low estate of agriculture at the time, tolled farmers by thousands into the local alliances.[8]

The state Farmers' Alliance of Minnesota met in convention at St. Paul on July 16, 1890.   It adopted most of the principles of the national Alliance platform as well as some additional demands, among them the election of United States senators by popular vote, the reduction of interest rates, the arbitration of disputes between labor and capital, and a new schedule of railroad rates and fares.   As Donnelly's coquetry with the Republicans had lost him the presidency of the state Alliance, so also it cost him the nomination of the Alliance for governor.   That fell to a dark horse, a sometime Democrat, Sidney M. Owen of Minneapolis.   The

[8] Haynes, *Third Party Movements*, 230–234; Frank M. Drew, " The Present Farmers' Movement," in the *Political Science Quarterly*, 6: 290–294 (June, 1891) ; Buck, *Agrarian Crusade*, 111–124; Hicks, in the *Mississippi Valley Historical Review*, 8: 113; Appleton, *Annual Cyclopædia*, 1890, pp. 299–301. On the organization, constitutions, and platforms of both the Northwestern and the Southern alliances, see N. B. Ashby, *The Riddle of the Sphinx* (Chicago, 1892).

agricultural journal, *Farm, Stock and Home,* edited by him, had attained a deservedly wide circulation. His irreproachable private character, his Civil War record, and a fine gift of public speaking had won for him a great body of friends. The choice was politically wise, for if the new party could elect anybody it would be Owen. At the election in November he received 58,514 votes, which, drawn in large proportion from the Republican ranks, left Governor Merriam with a plurality over Judge Wilson of only 2,267 votes. As 8,424 votes had been cast for a Prohibition candidate, Merriam's vote was 32,336 short of a majority.[9]

The detachment of so many votes from the Republican ranks had further effects. In three of the five congressional districts the Democrats elected their candidates for representative and in one district the Alliance nominee won; in but one district, the second, were the Republicans successful, and there by the trifling plurality of 482. The effect in the state legislature of 1891 was that the Republicans held but 27 out of 54 seats in the Senate and but 40 out of 114 in the House. A coalition of Democratic and Alliance votes put a Democrat in the speakership and took from the lieutenant governor the privilege, never before denied, of appointing the standing committees of the Senate. For the first time since 1873 the Democrats elected a state officer, Adolph Biermann, as auditor.[10]

The most conspicuous act of legislation in Governor Merriam's time, and one of the most beneficent in the history of the state, was the adoption of the Australian ballot system for general elections. The legislature of 1889 put it in operation in cities with a population of more than ten thousand — Duluth, St. Paul, Minneapolis, Winona, and Still-

[9] *Pioneer Press,* July 17, 18, 1890; Hicks, in the *Mississippi Valley Historical Review,* 8: 113–115; Smalley, *Republican Party,* 236. See Appleton, *Annual Cyclopædia,* 1890, p. 556, for the dates of all the conventions and the result of the election. The platform of the state Alliance as adopted at its annual meeting is given in the *Minneapolis Tribune,* March 7, 1890, p. 1.

[10] Smalley, *Republican Party,* 235; Appleton, *Annual Cyclopædia,* 1890, p. 557; Holmes, in *Minnesota in Three Centuries,* 4: 180, 181.

water — and that of 1891 extended it throughout the state. It obviously implied the use of ballots printed at public expense. The secretary of state was empowered to prepare and have printed on white paper the names of all candidates duly nominated for state offices; city clerks were required to have printed on red paper the names of all candidates for city offices; and county auditors were charged with the preparation and printing of the blue ballot showing the names of all other candidates, principally those for county and judicial offices. At polling places the voter, after identification, is provided with one ballot of each kind to be voted, retires to a small curtained box called a " booth," and there in secret makes an X mark against the names of the candidates of his choice. The intended and realized effect of the system is to give the elector the opportunity to cast his vote without being watched by a spy of any private or corporate employer or of a bribe-giver. It was an emancipation of great numbers of voters whose jobs hung upon their voting for or against certain candidates or propositions, but it cannot be doubted that there are still timid souls whose votes are virtually extorted by fears of danger to their bread and butter. Although a great reform, the Australian ballot is far from the ideal, which would allow the citizen to stand up in the face of his neighbors and, without fear or favor, give his voice and vote for the men and measures commended to his judgment. But this is not yet an ideal world and the secret ballot is better than a vote extorted by fear or gained by purchase.[11]

The fact that the legislature of 1889 enacted a probate code may seem, to the casual reader at least, a matter of little importance; but thoughtful and experienced persons will recognize the subject as one of the most serious which lawmakers are obliged to handle. The historian is not called upon to argue the justice or the policy of private property. It is sufficient for him to accept as defensible, or at any rate

[11] General Laws, 1889, pp. 16–22; 1891, pp. 37–39.

tolerable, that immemorial right cherished among civilized men. The rights of succession and inheritance are necessary corollaries of the right of private property. Of the law of inheritance De Tocqueville remarks: "When the legislator has once regulated the law of inheritance, he may rest from his labor. The machine once put in motion will go on for ages." In the course of each generation the great mass of private property passes from the dead to the living. The transfers have for ages been regulated by custom and supplementary laws. Some of the laws are of the character called substantive, intended to secure to decedents while living the right to designate by will the persons to whom their estates shall inure and to name their executors. Others of the same character declare to what relatives property shall descend in the cases in which decedents have left no wills, usually according to degrees of consanguinity as extended by English common law. The great mass of probate law, however, is of the adjective character, regulating the operation of the laws of descent and succession, securing the rights of creditors of decedents, and protecting beneficiaries from frauds, for which opportunities are abundant. Laws of this class require amendment as new conditions arise and the number of amending statutes becomes confusing; hence so-called "revisions" take place from time to time. The legislature of 1887, deeming a revision desirable, directed the governor to appoint from a list to be furnished by judges of the district courts a commission of three men to revise the probate law and to report to the next legislature. The commission discharged its duty, collected the probate laws standing on the statute books, arranged them in proper order, and submitted to the legislature of 1889 a new "probate code." Duly enacted and approved, this code became chapter 46 of the general laws of that session.[12]

[12] Alexis de Tocqueville, *Democracy in America*, 1 : 60 (translated by Henry Reeve — London, 1862) ; *General Laws*, 1887, p. 267; 1889, pp. 94–160. Probate practice yields to the legal profession an assured and remunerative compensation. Under the fee bill now in force in Hennepin County the charge for legal services in probating an estate, however small in value, is two

The legislature of 1889 proposed a constitutional amendment authorizing the legislature to provide by law that " The agreement of five-sixths (5/6) of a jury in any civil action . . . after not less than six (6) hours deliberation, shall be a sufficient verdict." It was adopted at the general election in November, 1890, but it was not until 1913 that it was made effective by an act of the legislature, which also extended the minimum time for deliberation to twelve hours. Up to this time but few fractional verdicts have been rendered, the great majority of cases not requiring so long deliberation.[13]

In 1890 the eleventh federal census was made under the act of Congress of March 1, 1889. The detailed figures for Minnesota need not be given here for they may be found in the census reports; but a few outstanding totals and percentages are worth while to indicate general progress and some particular developments in population and agriculture. Between 1880 and 1890 the total population increased from 780,773 to 1,301,826, or 68 per cent. The town population, including that of all places having over twenty-five hundred inhabitants, rose 153.5 per cent, while the country population increased by 30.4 per cent. There was an actual decline in the country population of thirteen southeastern counties, accompanied by a decline in the number and an increase in the size of farms. The change may be attributed to the removal of farmers into towns or into regions of virgin soils where land was still cheap. The increase in the number of farms in the state was 27 per cent and the increase in the number of acres of improved farm land was 53.6 per cent.

per cent of the value of the estate, with a minimum fee of fifty dollars. If there is no litigation, but two appearances in court are necessary. In cases of large estates lawyers' fees run up into large figures. In recent years such amounts have been charged and allowed as $13,115, $28,000, $25,000, and $50,000. Notes on an interview with the Honorable John A. Dahl, probate judge of Hennepin County, recorded in the author's notebooks, 9: 52; Dahl to the author, April 25, 1923, Folwell Papers.

13 *General Laws*, 1889, p. 3; 1913, p. 54; 1891, p. 17. The vote at the November, 1890, election was: yeas, 66,929; nays, 41,341.

That bonanza farming had not gone out of fashion is indicated by the facts that the number of farms of from five hundred to a thousand acres had increased from 741 to 1,594, or 115 per cent, and that farms of one thousand acres or more had grown in number from 145 to 282, or 94.5 per cent. The area of wheat culture increased but 11 per cent, while the output of the harvest of 1889 was 51 per cent above that of the previous census, an indication of improved farming or of occupation of virgin soils. Certain products attained an extraordinary increment. The percentage of increase was highest in factory butter; but the amount of it produced was still relatively so small that the total increase on butter was but 153 per cent. The increase in factory cheese was 682 per cent. The number of milch cows and other cattle increased 115 per cent. Flaxseed, which was to fall off in the next decade, had a great accession of 2,697.7 per cent. In the number of chickens the increase was 112 per cent. The total value of farms in Minnesota increased during the decade from $194,000,000 to $340,000,000, in round numbers, or 75.5 per cent, and the value of farm products, from $49,500,000 to $71,000,000, or 44 per cent. Decreases of from 37 to 95 per cent in the output of a few crops — tobacco, hops, broom corn, maple sugar, and sorghum — indicate that they were not found profitable in Minnesota.[14]

A notorious, not to say scandalous, feature of the population census of Minnesota was the necessity of recounting the inhabitants of St. Paul and Minneapolis on account of irregularities in the original enumeration. The result was a considerable reduction in the numbers as hopefully imagined and indicated by the first returns.[15]

[14] *Statutes at Large*, 25: 760–767; *United States Census*, 1890, *Population*, 25; Robinson, *Agriculture in Minnesota*, 113, 114, 134. Note especially in the last work the figures on pages 115, 117, and 164–168, derived from reports of the eleventh census.

[15] See the Appendix, no. 12, *post*, for an account of the census of Minneapolis and St. Paul.

Upon his retirement from office on January 4, 1893, Governor Merriam did not relinquish his lively interest in public affairs or his efforts to promote the success of the Republican party. As a delegate to the national convention of that party in 1896 he strove valiantly for the nomination of William McKinley as president and as a committeeman he coöperated in framing the sound money platform which rallied the victorious party around the gold standard. On March 7, 1899, President McKinley appointed Merriam director of the twelfth census. For this office his education, his business experience, and his practice while governor in judging men fitted him admirably. One of his first acts was to choose five chief statisticians of experience and repute and to delegate to them an ample discretion. A leading authority has declared the twelfth census to be the best ever compiled in the United States. Director Merriam performed a notable service in persuading Congress to pass the act of March 6, 1902, for the establishment of a permanent census bureau. His address, his intelligent advocacy, and his persistency moved Congress to the action which his predecessors had failed to secure. His resignation not long afterward is proof that he was not working for his own personal advantage. Since then he has continued to reside in Washington, where he has engaged in private business.[16]

[16] Baker, *Governors of Minnesota*, 316–320.

IX. NELSON AND HIS TIMES, 1893–95

AS THE time for opening the political campaign of 1892 drew near it was evident that as a minority incumbent Governor Merriam would not be wise to aspire to a third term; and it is not known that he did so aspire. It was equally evident that the Republican party would do well to select as its gubernatorial candidate the best vote-getter among its leaders. The choice had been virtually made through consultations and correspondence before the assemblage of the state convention, which on July 28 nominated Knute Nelson by acclamation without a ballot. There were plenty of good reasons for this nomination, not the least weighty of which was the necessity of recalling to Republican allegiance great numbers of electors of Scandinavian parentage who had strayed away into the wilderness of Populism and Prohibition.

Nelson's election to Congress in 1882 against an opposition fiery and malevolent has been related. His devotion to duty as a representative, his diligence in attending to the affairs of constituents at the capital, and his modest but sturdy adherence to principle soon gained him such a body of supporters that two years later and again in 1886 renominations fell easily to him. A third renomination and election might have come to him had he not let it be known that he did not desire it. He preferred to go back to his Alexandria farm and, perhaps, to care for affairs of old clients at his law office in the village. As a member of the House he generally voted with his Republican colleagues but at times he broke away from party lines. The most notable examples of this independence were his support of the Morrison tariff of 1884 and of the Mills bill in 1888. He was then and long after an advocate of " tariff revision downward." His con-

stituency, almost wholly agricultural, thought none the less
of him for this recalcitration. That this Norwegian-born,
American-educated, battle-scarred veteran soldier, already
experienced in state and national affairs, would lead his party
to victory if any man could, was a well-founded opinion of
the Republican delegates in convention, to whom it was
important that " a winner " be nominated.[1]

The Democrats put up against Nelson Daniel W. Lawler
of St. Paul, an able lawyer with oratorical gifts, sure of a
strong support from fellow Catholics, in deference to whose
prejudices the Democratic platform contained a paragraph
of protest against the interference by the state with parental
rights in the education of children.[2]   Another opposing aggregation not to be undervalued was the People's party, which,
it was declared, had swallowed the Farmers' Alliance and was
" the toy and plaything " of Ignatius Donnelly.   The state
convention of that party on July 13 was addressed by Robert
Schilling of Milwaukee, highly esteemed in socialist circles.
Donnelly was heard in one of his most brilliant and flamboyant orations.   The pending contest was but part of the
war of the sixties, he declared.   The people were fighting for
their liberties.   A horde of millionaires expected soon to become titled aristocrats and would so become if their progress
was not arrested.   An organized conspiracy of railroad men
and grain speculators had robbed the farmers of Minnesota
and the Dakotas of a billion dollars.   The platform declared
for a referendum of all bills passed by the legislature and for
the erection of state terminal elevators at Duluth, St. Paul,
and Minneapolis.   An antisaloon paragraph was laid on the
table and this Donnelly thought " a blunder."   The nomination for governor went to Donnelly by acclamation.   Had his
views prevailed and an antisaloon proposition been adopted,

---

[1] *Pioneer Press* (St. Paul), July 29, 1892, p. 1; Baker, *Governors of Minnesota*, 337; Smalley, *Republican Party*, 238, 242. For Nelson's campaign in
1882, see *ante*, pp. 147–149.

[2] *Pioneer Press*, August 4, 1892, p. 1.

the Prohibition party might have been content to indorse the
action of the People's party and to name no candidate of its
own.   The Prohibitionists, however, did nominate William
J. Dean, an excellent citizen of Minneapolis, and gave him a
vote of 12,239.   Donnelly received 39,863 votes and Lawler,
94,600.   Nelson's plurality over Lawler was 14,620, but he
lacked 37,482 to equal the total number of votes cast for his
opponents.[3]

In the fall of 1894 the political situation in Minnesota had
not materially changed.   The filling of a few federal offices
with Democrats by President Cleveland had not seriously
damaged the Republican machine.   Governor Nelson had
added to his reputation by a wise and efficient administration
and was as obviously the logical candidate as he had been
two years before.   The Republican convention, composed
of a thousand delegates, gave him a second nomination by
acclamation.   The " young Republicans " had made it desirable for the party managers to increase greatly the number
of delegates.   This procedure did not retire the " old guard "
and it gave the younger patriots a forum.   The Democrats
put forward that veteran party leader, George L. Becker, who
was the one of the three men elected to serve in Congress at
the first state election in 1857 who was eliminated by lot
when Congress refused to allow the state more than two representatives.   The Populists, not willing to experiment further
with Ignatius Donnelly, gave their nomination to that worthy
and patriotic citizen who had been the candidate of the Alliance party four years before, the Honorable Sidney M. Owen.
The Prohibitionists made their independent nominations with
no expectation, of course, that their candidates would be
elected.[4]

This being an off year in national politics, the state
conventions were free to embody in their platforms any propo-

[3] *Pioneer Press*, July 14, 1892, p. 1; *Legislative Manual*, 1925, p. 113.
[4] *Pioneer Press*, 1894: July 12, p. 1; 19, p. 2; September 6, p. 1; Smalley,
Republican Party, 243.   On Becker's election to Congress in 1857, see *ante*,
2:18.

sitions thought to be likely to invite new adherents. Apparently, the smaller and weaker the party, the more elaborate and formidable the platform. The commercial crisis of 1893, accompanied by panic and the failure of many banks and business concerns, doubtless revived the contention of the seventies that the money supply was inadequate and that the money had been kept out of circulation by unconscionable speculators. Money planks had, accordingly, prominent places in all the platforms. The Republican resolutions asserted the party's approbation of the restoration of silver as ultimate money to the currency of the world; of a tariff sufficient to equalize home and foreign wages, along with reciprocity; a free ballot and a fair count for all, white and black; the suppression of trusts; the arbitration of labor disputes; the reservation of the public domain for actual settlers; the exclusion of pauper, criminal, and other undesirable immigrants; convenient and ample elevator and warehouse accommodations and proper and speedy transportation for agricultural products at reasonable charges; the cessation of all discriminations and extortions by railroads and telegraph companies; the allotment of generous pensions to veteran soldiers and sailors; the taxation of lands granted to railroads and not used for railroad purposes; and the extension of the terms of the president and vice president to six years, with no reëlection.[5]

The Democratic convention at first adopted only resolutions indorsing the Cleveland administration and the national party platform of 1892, approving the election of United States senators by the people, counseling the investment of state funds in municipal securities, and insisting upon economy in state affairs. As this list seemed rather meager, a bunch of additional propositions was later brought in and agreed to. They embraced congratulations to workingmen upon the enactment of the Wilson tariff and favored the arbitration of

---

[5] *Pioneer Press*, July 12, 1894, p. 3.

labor disputes, generous pension laws, and the just taxation of railroad lands and mines.[6]

Far more sweeping was the platform of the Populist party. It opened with a reaffirmation of the platform of the national People's party adopted at Omaha on July 4, 1892, and a recapitulation of its principal " demands," which were: the issue by the government, direct to the people, of a national currency to an amount not less than fifty dollars per capita; the free and unlimited coinage of silver at the ratio of 16 to 1; the establishment of government savings banks; the graduated taxation of incomes and inheritances; government ownership and operation of railroads, telegraphs, and telephones; the abolition of land speculation, the reclamation by the government of all lands held by aliens and lands held by railroads and other corporations in excess of their actual needs, and the reservation of these lands for actual settlers only; and the election of the president, the vice president, and United States senators by direct popular vote. In addition to these planks of the Omaha platform, the convention declared itself in favor of the prohibition of trusts and other unlawful combinations and the enforcement of all laws relating to and governing corporations; it demanded legislation to secure to farmers an absolutely free market for their products; it declared its opposition " to the centralizing tendencies of the age, which are destroying the just powers of the several states "; it arraigned the Republican party for frauds in the management of school and other public lands, resulting in the loss of millions of dollars; it advocated economy in the administration of public affairs and legislation for the discouragement of ownership of real estate by nonresidents and aliens; it demanded that taxes be collected semiannually and that mining lands be taxed equally with other property; it de-

---

[6] *Pioneer Press*, September 6, 1894, p. 2.

clared itself in favor of the full initiative and referendum;
it demanded the removal of the sex limitation upon suffrage;
it advocated the nationalization of the liquor traffic and its
management by the state without profit; and it protested
against the use of public revenue or funds for sectarian purposes. A number of resolutions were piled on top of this
monumental aggregation. One of these called for the judicious management of native forests, the prevention of their
further monopolization, the prevention of forest fires, and
the conservation of the water system of the state; another
expressed sympathy with oppressed workers and with organized labor; a third declared the arrest of Eugene Debs
and his associates unwise, unjust, and a dangerous encroach-
ment by the judiciary upon rights and liberties. A committee
was appointed to carry to the American Railway Union, the
members of which were then striking, a resolution expressing
the sympathy of the convention.[7]

It remained for the Prohibition party convention to
assemble the most elaborate catena of propositions for the
consideration of the electors. The platform was introduced
by a reverent allusion to the Divine Being as the source of
good government, followed by a reaffirmation of allegiance to
the national Prohibition party. In a series of paragraphs
the convention marshaled its articles of faith, the first of
which included a declaration in favor of the abolition of the
liquor traffic and the prohibition of the manufacture, sale,
transportation, exportation, and importation of intoxicating
liquors for beverage purposes; a protest against the license
system, which made the state " a partner in the debauchery

---

[7] *Pioneer Press*, July 12, 1894, p. 6. Haynes, in his *Third Party Movements*,
221–281, 508–515, discusses the sources of the People's party since the Civil
War, the formation of the party in 1890, and its campaigns in 1892 and 1894,
with citations of authorities. Frank L. McVey, in his *Populist Movement*,
142 (American Economic Association, *Economic Studies*, vol. 1, no. 3 — New
York, 1896), gives a tabular synopsis of the " issues " made in the conventions
at St. Louis on December 6, 1889; at Ocala, Florida, on December 7, 1890; at
Cincinnati on May 20, 1891; at St. Louis on February 22, 1892; and at Omaha
on July 4, 1892.

of its citizens and the devastation of the home "; and a demand for the regulation of the sale of alcoholic liquor for medicinal and other legitimate purposes as the sale of " other poisons " is regulated. The platform demanded further that tariffs be levied " only as a defense against foreign governments, which levy tariff upon or bar out our products from their markets "; that a nonpartisan tariff commission of experts be appointed to revise the tariff from time to time; that all money and currency be issued directly by the government, every dollar to be legal tender for all debts and taxes; and that silver be remonetized according to the laws in operation before 1872. To these propositions was added the corollary that the turning of the nation's annual drink bill of $1,700,000,000 " into the legitimate channels of trade " would solve the money question more effectually than any other conceivable device.

The platform also demanded equal suffrage for men and women and equal wages for the same labor; legislation for the exclusion of insane, pauper, criminal, and anarchistic immigrants; the enactment and enforcement of more rigid laws for the prohibition of child labor; the arbitration of differences between labor and capital; liberal provision for public instruction in the English language; the allotment of liberal pensions to all needy veterans; legislation for the protection of all persons in their right to one day's rest in seven; and the establishment of postal savings banks. It favored greater economy in the administration of public affairs and the election of the president, the vice president, and United States senators by direct vote. It advocated that speculating in margins, cornering grain and other products, forming pools, trusts, and combinations, and watering stocks be prohibited. It declared itself in favor of government control and, as soon as practicable, government operation of all railroad, telegraph, and other public corporations. It demanded that railroads be required " to resume their common law duties as common carriers " and to provide warehouses and elevators for agricultural produce without discrimination. It declared that nonresident aliens should not be allowed to acquire land; that individual and corporate ownership of land should be limited; and that all unearned grants of land to railroad companies and other corporations should be reclaimed and held as homesteads for the people. It favored an amendment to the Australian ballot law abolishing or materially reducing the fee required of candidates for office; the adoption of the initiative and referendum; and legislation to secure to political parties proportional representation. It made a sweeping denunciation of the Republican and Democratic parties as " the agents and servile tools " of trusts and railroad corporations, of the " gold bondocracy," and of the " saloon combine."

The convention was disposed to be hospitable and tolerant but there were a number of propositions submitted from the floor which it declined to entertain. Among them were proposals for the establishment of free trade, for the adoption of the single tax on land, for the issue of notes by the national government as the only circulating medium, and for the prohibition by Congress of the movement of " industrial trains " on Sunday.[8] It is an elementary fact in political science that great parties can be held together only by a few questions of importance or sometimes by a single great issue; small parties are free to experiment with all possible overtures. Surviving members of that convention may view with some complacency the later adoption of a goodly number of its platform units by one or both of the great parties and their enactment into law and may think of themselves as having been " Progressives " before the days of Roosevelt.

The results of the campaign of 1894 were easily foreseen by those not blinded by partisan prejudice. There was but little noise and heat about it. The Republican nominees for

8 *Pioneer Press*, 1894: July 18, p. 8; 19, p. 2.

state positions were elected by large majorities. Nelson received 147,943 votes, a plurality of 60,053 over Owen, the Populist leader. The smallness of Becker's vote (53,584) was due in part to a widespread belief that he was too closely related to railroad and hard money influences.[9]

The first term of Cushman K. Davis in the United States Senate was to expire in March, 1893. He had thrown all his admirable powers unreservedly into his legislative duties, had won the respect of his colleagues, and had been accorded the highly responsible chairmanship of the committee on pensions. It was he who framed and championed the Dependent Pension Act of 1890.[10] Quite naturally this service had confirmed to him the confidence and support of the great body of Minnesota veterans, already his friends. The Republican state convention of 1892 gave Davis a hearty indorsement. Substantially all the local legislative conventions of the party instructed their nominees to favor him and there appeared to be a general understanding throughout the campaign that there would be no serious opposition to his reëlection. No other Republican was publicly named as a possible rival. The Republican legislative caucus was held on January 4, 1893, eighty-five of the ninety-six Republican senators and representatives being present. The vote for Davis was unanimous. On January 17 the houses voted separately as required by law. Davis had a clear majority of votes in the House but lacked eight votes in the Senate. This result threw the election into a joint convention of the houses, which met on the following day. By this time the votes of all the 168 members had been ascertained, with one exception. When the name of the " odd man," John A. Holler, was called and he responded " Davis," the contest was over. The completed tally gave Senator Davis a sufficient majority of one. One Alliance senator had voted for him. Eleven Republican

[9] Legislative Manual, 1925, p. 113; Holmes, in Minnesota in Three Centuries, 4: 195; Castle to the author, August 26, 1913.
[10] The Dependent Pension Act will be discussed in the next volume.

members, seven senators and four representatives, all supposedly instructed for Davis, had cast their votes for six different persons. It was claimed by friends of Senator Davis that a conspiracy had been concocted to frustrate his election on a first ballot and to bring forward at an opportune moment thereafter the name of a prominent Republican on whom it was hoped all could unite. The fact that Senator Davis afterward used his influence to prevent the appointment of ex-Governor Merriam to an ambassadorial position and to a seat in the cabinet apparently points to the conclusion that the senator believed Merriam to have been connected with the attempt to bring about his defeat. Merriam certainly did not coöperate toward Davis' reëlection. Suspicions current at the time that lavish expenditure of money against Davis accounted for much of the Republican apostasy in the legislature were never officially investigated and therefore remain unverified.[11]

A senatorial contest not less dramatic took place two years later, in January, 1895. Senator William D. Washburn had added to his excellent record in the House of Representatives a chapter of creditable achievement in the Senate. He had been loyal to his party but not servile. He had voted against the Force bill and had urged the passage of an act to abolish

[11] *Pioneer Press,* July 29, 1892, p. 2; January 5, 1893, p. 1; *Minneapolis Tribune,* January 18, 1893, p. 1; *Senate Journal,* 1893, p. 84; *House Journal,* 75, 80; Holmes, in *Minnesota in Three Centuries,* 4: 191; Baker, *Governors of Minnesota,* 317; record of an interview with Henry A. Castle, in the author's notebooks, 7: 1. In *Minnesota Historical Collections,* 15: 592, Castle says: "A secret campaign of debauchery and corruption had been inaugurated to defeat Davis, with the hope of electing an unavowed, but well recognized Republican aspirant in his stead. No more brazen, defiant, and demoralizing movement was ever inaugurated in any state. Votes were shamelessly trafficked in, and so recklessly that the price paid in many instances was well known, in advance. . . . Enough Republican votes were bought and actually paid for to prevent a majority for Davis on the first joint ballot, but several of the bribed members weakened at the last moment and Davis received precisely enough votes to elect him, not one to spare. I was cognizant of all the details of the contest." In a letter to the author, November 25, 1912, Castle makes the statement that each of twelve men, whose names he gives, with possibly two exceptions, received a cash price for voting against Senator Davis, as did three or four other men who took the money and then weakened and voted for Davis.

option trading on produce exchanges. He was credited with having secured liberal appropriations for the construction of the great system of reservoirs about the headwaters of the Mississippi River. The Republican convention gave him the usual indorsement and throughout the campaign he was uniformly declared to be the proper person to succeed himself in the Senate. His expectation was to be disappointed. On January 3, five days before the assemblage of the legislature, Governor Nelson announced himself as a candidate for the senatorship — " a sensation, but not a surprise," said the *St. Paul Globe* of January 4. The Republican caucus held on January 18 made no nomination and the houses voting separately on January 22 made no election. On the following day in joint convention Nelson received 102 out of 167 votes. He resigned the governorship on January 31 and was succeeded by Lieutenant Governor David M. Clough. The term of service begun by Knute Nelson in the United States Senate on March 4, 1895, renewed by successive reëlections, did not close until his sudden death on April 28, 1923, near Baltimore, Maryland, on a railroad car which was carrying him toward his Minnesota home.[12]

The legislative acts of the session of 1893, the only one during Governor Nelson's incumbency, were mostly of a remedial character. An excellent example was an act placing all manufacturing establishments under the supervision of the state bureau of labor and requiring safeguards for operators of dangerous machinery, with heavy penalties for employers who failed to obey the law. Another important

[12] Baker, *Governors of Minnesota*, 344–350; Smalley, *Republican Party*, 244, 247; Atwater, *History of Minneapolis*, 550; Holmes, in *Minnesota in Three Centuries*, 4: 199; *Pioneer Press*, January 19, 1895; *House Journal*, 1895, pp. 60, 65–67; *Senate Journal*, 41, 80; *Minneapolis Sunday Tribune*, April 29, 1923. The votes on Nelson's reëlections were as follows: 1901: 94 to 22 in the House, 42 to 18 in the Senate; 1907: 98 to 16 in the House, 45 to 16 in the Senate; 1912: popular referendum preceding the election by the legislature, 173,074 to 102,691; 1918: popular election, 206,684 to 137,296. See *House Journal*, 1901, p. 82; 1907, p. 93; *Senate Journal*, 1901, p. 75; 1907, p. 105; and *Legislative Manual*, 1913, p. 502; 1919, p. 670. The Nelson-Washburn contest is more fully discussed in the Appendix, no. 13, *post*. The reservoirs of the upper Mississippi will be discussed in the next volume.

act was that creating a board of commissioners to select a site for a new state capitol and to erect an appropriate building thereon.[13]

In the first year of his administration Governor Nelson was constrained by legislative pressure to direct the prosecution of a firm of lumbermen charged with having made a better bargain with the state auditor, as land commissioner, than the law allowed. The matter originated in the House of Representatives, where, on March 1, 1893, on motion of Robert C. Dunn of Mille Lacs County, a resolution was adopted for the appointment of a committee to investigate the sale of pine timber on a certain school section in that county. On April 14 the committee submitted a brief report embodying the opinion of the attorney-general, Henry W. Childs, that the auditor was within his discretion in making the sale. The House adopted the report but did not thereby conclude the matter. A minority of the committee had submitted a dissenting view accompanied by a body of testimony tending to show that in its opinion the state auditor had not conformed to law in making the sale and that the purchasers were privy to the illegal transaction. Although the minority report was rejected by the House by a formal vote, its record of testimony made a deep impression. Upon Dunn's motion the House passed a concurrent resolution authorizing the governor to take prompt action to secure a full investigation, to employ counsel for a prosecution, and to incur expenditure at his discretion. The Senate concurred unanimously. Pursuant to this instruction Governor Nelson employed an able St. Paul attorney to bring suit against the purchasers and was able to report to the legislature of 1895 that the sum of $10,302.48 had been recovered.[14]

13 *General Laws*, 1893, pp. 6–15, 96–106.

14 *House Journal*, 1893, pp. 351, 361, 368, 375, 795, 822, 829–831; *Senate Journal*, 90; *Princeton Union*, December 7, 1893, pp. 1, 8; Nelson's message, January 9, 1895, in *Executive Documents*, 1894, vol. 1, p. 25. In the *Pioneer Press*, April 12, 1893, p. 6, is an article entitled "Lumbermen's Defense." On February 25, upon Dunn's motion, a request was made to Adolph Biermann,

The activity of Representative Dunn appears to have aroused the attention of Senator Ignatius Donnelly to the invasion of a field of action peculiarly his own — the investigation and exposure of abuses. On the very same day that Dunn introduced his resolution in the House, Senator Henry Keller, doubtless at Donnelly's instance, introduced into the Senate a resolution for the appointment of three senators to investigate " generally known " fraudulent exemptions from taxation due to the corrupt and unlawful action of county officers, which was adopted. The number of senators on the committee, of which Keller was chairman and Donnelly a member, was later increased to five. On April 10 Donnelly read to the Senate the committee's report. From a catena of instances drawn from the testimony taken, it charged that the school and university funds had been robbed of large amounts of money. The report was " accepted and adopted." It is evident that Governor Nelson intended that no one should have a pretext for insinuating that he was affiliated with or was under the influence of any pine-land ring. On April 17 he sent to the Senate a request that Senator Donnelly be permitted to introduce a bill for a joint resolution for the appointment of a commission to investigate certain frauds in the sale of public lands of the state. Donnelly introduced the resolution, which was adopted without debate and with but three opposing votes. The House concurred unanimously.[15] The " Pine Land Investigating Committee," as it came to be called, was duly appointed with large powers to perform its duty during the recess of the legislature. Its report was submitted to the governor on December 21, 1894. The direct effect of the committee's labors was the recovery

the state auditor, for an account of his action in regard to the sale of timber on the school section in question. Biermann replied that he had made the sale and gave the name of the buyer, the date of the sale, and the price for which the timber was sold. The sale was made to C. A. Smith and Company of Minneapolis. Harris Richardson of St. Paul was the attorney. Record of an interview with Richardson, November 28, 1923, in the author's notebooks, 9: 82.

[15] Senate Journal, 1893, pp. 318, 748, 760, 858, 872; House Journal, 836.

of relatively small sums of money from lumber firms; the indirect effect, of greater import, was the enactment of a new law for the safeguarding of the state lands and the timber on them.[16]

On a foregoing page some account was made of the act of the legislature of 1885 declaring that all grain elevators at St. Paul, Minneapolis, and Duluth which received grain in bulk for storage and mixed that of different owners should be public terminal elevators and requiring the proprietors to obtain licenses from the state railroad and warehouse commission and to operate under the supervision of that board. The commission published its rules and regulations and its scheme of grades and appointed weighmasters and inspectors for wheat and other grains. The result was disappointing. In 1892 the commission reported to the legislature that but two terminal elevators, both in Minneapolis, were operated as public elevators under license. All others had remained or had become private warehouses. The act of 1885 gave no relief from an evil felt in every rural community. Why it should have been expected to give relief remains a matter of speculation. The bonanza farmer could ship his crop in carloads and could dicker with terminal elevator men in regard to its quality. But the ordinary quarter-section farmer was obliged to take his grain by wagonloads to the local elevator and accept the grade assigned by the manager. The manager or owner was generally himself a buyer, either

<hr />

[16] *Report of the Pine Land Investigating Committee, to the Governor of Minnesota*, 78 (St. Paul, 1895); *General Laws*, 1895, pp. 349–371. An account of the investigations and findings of the committee is given in the Appendix, no. 14, *post*. Accounts in the *Pioneer Press*, March 10, 1894, p. 6, and the *Minneapolis Tribune* of the same date, p. 4, of the purchase by a syndicate of 1,500,000,000 feet of timber in the Leech Lake and Cass Lake regions for $6,000,000 from the Walker, Akeley, and Pillsbury interests indicate the magnitude of the pine timber business in Minnesota at this time. In an article in the *Minneapolis Times*, January 1, 1895, p. 1, Thomas B. Walker says that the amount of the cut in 1894 — 491,000,000 feet — broke all records. It would be undesirable for the cut for Minneapolis to exceed 500,000,000 feet annually. At that rate the pine would last from twenty to thirty years more. The transportation of logs to the sawmills by rail which had recently been put into practice was a saving in cost.

NELSON AND HIS TIMES

NELSON AND HIS TIMES

on his own account or on that of a milling company or a speculator. For injury, real or fancied, the farmer had no redress. For years complaints were rife of injustice done by elevator men through excessive dockages for color, weight, dirt, foul seeds, and mixtures of grains. Governor Merriam in his message to the legislature of 1891 referred to the wrongs thus suffered by farmers but could suggest only some provision for appeals. Albert C. Clausen, the state inspector, expressed the opinion that there could be no satisfactory system of grain inspection at primary markets and that there was no need of any.[17]

Governor Merriam in his final message to the legislature of 1893 referred again to discriminations in the grading and docking of grain at country points as " one of the most intricate questions." Governor Nelson in his inaugural address delivered at the same time recommended vigorous action and submitted a proposition of the railroad and warehouse commission to make all elevators public and to put them under the control of the commission. The farmer, he said, " has no state umpire " and no remedy except at common law. The situation was anomalous and unjust. The legislature thus addressed was not ready for such sweeping action and contented itself with the passage, by slight majorities, of an act providing for the regulation of country elevators. The new law declared that all elevators situated on or near the right of way of any railroad should be public, should be licensed by the railroad and warehouse commission, and should be required to operate under rules and regulations established by the board.[18]

[17] *General Laws*, 1885, p. 136; message of Governor Merriam, January 14, 1891, in *Executive Documents*, 1890, vol. I, p. 38; Railroad and Warehouse Commission, *Reports*, 1890, p. 9; Railroad and Warehouse Commission, " Fourth Biennial Report to the Legislature as to Amendments and Revision of the Railroad and Warehouse Laws," in *Executive Documents*, 1892, vol. I, pp. 717, 718. On the act of 1885 see *ante*, p. 68.

[18] *Executive Documents*, 1892, vol. I, pp. 23, 43; *General Laws*, 1893, p. 131; *Senate Journal*, 1893, p. 568; *House Journal*, 734, 735. The vote in the Senate was 28 to 23 and that in the House was 58 to 43. The bill had been lost in

Governor Nelson was pleased to inform the legislature of 1895 that all country elevators had taken out licenses, that no burdens had been laid upon honest warehousemen, and that farmers had enjoyed the expected protection. The legislature of that year passed a recast of the act supplying details overlooked in the original act or suggested by experience. The essential features of the law are few: All country elevators must be licensed from year to year by the state railroad and warehouse commission. They must receive for storage and shipment all grain of suitable condition offered in the ordinary course of business up to their warehouse capacity. For each lot of grain received a warehouse receipt must be issued to the person delivering it, showing his name and residence, the kind and grade of the grain, its gross weight, and the dockage. The receipts must be numbered serially and a proper record of their issues must be kept; as they guarantee delivery to the owner or his order, they may be assigned in payment of debt or as collateral security for loans of money. Every warehouseman must render to the commission an annual report of all business transacted and, in particular, of the gross weight and dockage of all grains on hand at the end of the year, September 1. The commission may exact special reports at any time and may at pleasure, in person or by agents, inspect the property, books, accounts, and papers of any warehouseman.[19]

An early function of the commission, that of entertaining and deciding upon appeals from inspectors, by an act of 1899 devolved upon two boards of appeals — one at Minneapolis and the other at Duluth — appointed by the governor. To these boards, consolidated for the purpose, was still later transferred the duty of establishing Minnesota grades for all

the House by a vote of 46 to 51, but a motion to reconsider was passed. A draft for a bill is given in Railroad and Warehouse Commission, " Report as to Amendments and Revision of the Railroad and Warehouse Laws," in *Executive Documents*, 1892, vol. 1, pp. 726–729.

[19] *Executive Documents*, 1894, vol. 1, p. 20; *General Laws*, 1895, pp. 313–320. Numerous amendments to the act have since been made. *General Statutes*, 1913, pp. 988–1001.

grain, subject to state inspection. The grades are published annually on or before September 15. Standard samples of each Minnesota grade are prepared for distribution. The Minnesota grades were virtually annulled by the act of Congress approved on August 11, 1916, providing for federal inspection of grain and establishment of grades in interstate commerce. Since that time the Minnesota board has contented itself with adopting verbatim the published grades of the United States Interstate Commerce Commission for interstate transactions.[20]

The legislature of 1893, which passed the act for the regulation of country elevators, apparently was not satisfied that the law would abolish the great mischief at which it was aimed. A still more radical measure was therefore enacted, providing for the building and operation of a state elevator at Duluth. This act authorized the railroad and warehouse commission to buy land at Duluth and erect thereon a terminal elevator with a capacity of a million and a half bushels and to put it into operation. An appropriation of $200,000 was made. Perhaps in expectation of an opposition likely to arise, the board acted deliberately, but it proceeded to buy a tract of land for $11,000 and to entertain a bid for the erection of a building for $198,700. On August 8, 1893, Henry Rippe, a grain dealer, prayed the district court of Ramsey County for an order to restrain the commission from concluding the contract for the building. Holding that the real purpose of the act was to remedy a great wrong and that it was therefore a proper measure of public policy, the court, the Honorable John Willey Willis presiding, refused the order. An appeal was taken to the state supreme court. That court, on December 8, 1893, rendered an extensive opinion, written by Justice William Mitchell, in which it was stated that the act had no justification as a measure of public policy; it was a clear case of " internal improvement " in the

<hr>

[20] General Laws, 1899, pp. 207–209; General Statutes, 1913, p. 992; United States, Statutes at Large, 39: 482.

traditional sense of the phrase and as such it was clearly in violation of section 5 of article 9 of the Minnesota constitution, in particular of the clause reading, " The state shall never contract any debts for works of internal improvement." [21]

The second year of Governor Nelson's administration was signalized not so much by any social or political event as by the great forest fires which broke out at the end of the summer, causing the death of more than four hundred persons and losses and suffering to many more. Many counties in the timbered regions of the state were visited but the great calamity fell upon Pine County, where large portions of the splendid pine forests of the St. Croix and its tributaries still awaited the lumberman's ax. There were also great areas of " cut-over " pine, where " slashings " invited the starting and spreading of fires. The climate of Minnesota is relatively dry, but the drought that season was unparalleled. In July there fell but .13 inches of rain, though the normal amount is 3.42 inches. In August the rainfall was but .36 inches, instead of the ordinary precipitation of 2.98 inches. But 2.20 inches fell between May 16 and September 10, a period when the rainfall is normally 13.61 inches. The temperature during the same period was far above the average. Under these conditions sporadic fires broke out in the timbered regions but they were kept under control by the settlers. On September 1 occurred the great " Hinckley fire of 1894," which destroyed Hinckley and several smaller towns near it and caused lamentable losses of life and property. The catastrophe called out from far and near immediate and generous contributions of food, clothing, and money. Governor Nelson appointed a commission of high qualifications, which received and distributed donations to the amount of $165,581, and there were large contributions through other channels. In the course of a year the smitten villages,

---

[21] *General Laws*, 1893, pp. 140–143; Henry Rippe *v.* George L. Becker, *et al.*, 56 *Minnesota*, 100–118.

without exception, were provisionally rebuilt and normal conditions were reëstablished.[22]

The second year of Governor Nelson's administration was but a few days old when the last summons came to one of the earliest residents of Minnesota and one of the state's most eminent citizens, Henry Mower Rice. He died, after a long illness, on January 15, 1894, in San Antonio, Texas, at the age of seventy-eight.[23] On the day following Rice's death the editor of the St. Paul *Pioneer Press*, for a long time a political opponent of Rice, had this to say:

Henry M. Rice is dead. In a broad sense he was the founder and father of St. Paul, and the people of the city will mourn his death as the children of a household bereaved of their patriarchal head. . . . While active in business and politics Mr. Rice was perhaps the most popular man who has ever figured in public life in this state. This was due to the fascinating charm of his personality; to the warm-hearted liberality and to the generous enthusiasm which were the most prominent features of his character. He was distinguished throughout his life for his sanguine faith in St. Paul and in its future. . . . A great part of his life was spent in advancing its interests. It owes him a great debt of gratitude, which will be repaid in the only coin in which such debts can be paid, the grateful remembrance of posterity. For centuries to come the name of Henry M. Rice will figure in the history of St. Paul as one of the first and foremost among the small group of its distinguished founders.

At the funeral, which took place on January 20 in Christ Church, St. Paul, the principal address was made by the Right Reverend Mahlon N. Gilbert, who challenged any person to point out a single work of the deceased which had not been true and right. " Let this life so full of usefulness," said he, " stand up before you, young men of the present generation, as an example." [24]

[22] William Wilkinson, *Memorials of the Minnesota Forest Fires in the Year 1894 with a Chapter on the Forest Fires in Wisconsin in the Same Year*, 18–20 (Minneapolis, 1895). The *Report of the Pine Land Investigating Committee*, 56, makes the extravagant statement that the insurance companies openly charged that the timber thieves had caused the great Hinckley fire by setting fire to their cuttings to cover up their tracks. A more detailed account of the forest fires of 1894 will be given in the next volume.

[23] *Pioneer Press*, January 16, 1894, p. 4.

[24] *Pioneer Press*, January 21, 1894, p. 7.

Minnesota was tardy in availing herself of the privilege offered to each state of the Union by act of Congress of July 2, 1864, of placing statues of two of her most distinguished citizens in the National Statuary Hall in the Capitol at Washington. In 1905 the legislature designated Alexander Ramsey as one of the citizens to be so honored, but no appropriation was made for the erection of a statue.[25] More than ten years later Henry Mower Rice was also selected for that distinction. On February 8, 1916, his effigy in marble was unveiled in the Statuary Hall. The principal address was made by Knute Nelson, chairman of the commission appointed to attend to its erection. On behalf of the commission Senator Nelson presented the statue to the state of Minnesota. Senator Moses E. Clapp accepted it and presented it to the United States. Vice President Marshall welcomed to the hall the " counterfeit presentment of one who shed so much luster upon the civic virtue of the Commonwealth of Minnesota." On February 19 Senator Nelson submitted to the Senate a joint resolution to accept the statue in the name of the United States and to tender the thanks of Congress to the state of Minnesota for its contribution of the statue of Henry Mower Rice, " one of its most eminent citizens, illustrious for the purity of his life and his distinguished services to the State and Nation." Having spoken at length at the unveiling, Senator Nelson made but a brief address in support of the resolution. He was followed by Senators Underwood of Alabama, Harding of Ohio, Gallinger of New Hampshire, and Clapp of Minnesota. The Senate resolution came up in the House as a special order on March 11, 1916, with Andrew J. Volstead in the chair. There were abounding eulogies by each of the ten representatives from Minnesota, happily free from the extraordinary rhetorical embellishments so frequent on similar occasions. That departures

---

[25] *General Laws*, 1905, p. 383; Thomas B. Walker to the author, August 15, 1924, with an indorsement by Dr. Warren Upham, Folwell Papers. See *post*, p. 268.

from historical accuracy, chiefly in details, were numerous
was probably due to hasty perusal of secondary authorities
for the perfunctory duty.[26]

[26] *General Laws*, 1913, p. 882; United States, *Statutes at Large*, 13: 347;
39: 1600; United States, Sixty-fourth Congress, *Statue of Henry Mower Rice,
Erected in Statuary Hall of the United States Capitol by the State of Minnesota; Proceedings in Statuary Hall, in the Senate, and in the House of Representatives of the United States upon the Unveiling, Reception, and Acceptance
of the Statue of Henry Mower Rice from the State of Minnesota* (Washington.
1916). Congress on April 8, 1916, ordered 16,500 copies of the latter printed and
bound. The legislature of 1913 appropriated $7,500 for the statue. In a
letter to the author, March 28, 1916, in the Folwell Papers, Congressman
Clarence B. Miller said: " I don't believe there is a single member of the
Minnesota delegation who thought this honor was deserved by Henry M. Rice."
On April 12, 1899, the Minnesota legislature had adopted a joint resolution approving the erection of a statue of Rice in the Capitol at Washington, with the
condition that it should be no expense to the state. *Senate Journal*, 907, 937;
House Journal, 1087, 1126.

X. CLOUGH AND HIS TIMES, 1895–99

THE career of David Marston Clough is a capital example of usefulness and distinction attained with but little schooling. He was born in Lyme, New Hampshire, on December 27, 1846. In 1857 Clough's father brought his wife and fourteen children to Minnesota and settled on a piece of land near the nascent village of Spencer Brook, Isanti County, which was then in the remote wilderness. With the help of his boys he worked his farm in summer and engaged in logging in a small way in winter. The boy David doubtless got some desultory instruction in the common schools before and after the migration. At the age of seventeen he hired out to drive a six-ox team in the woods and in the second winter thereafter he was promoted to a six-horse team. This work he carried on for four years, varying it with driving logs in the spring and working in Minneapolis sawmills in the summer. At the end of this apprenticeship he had become expert in all the processes of lumbering, both in the woods and on the rivers, had saved something from his wages, and was ready for the next step, that of logging on his own account. For this he associated with him a brother who had had similar experience. Provided with cash and credit and equipped with teams, sleds, implements, provisions, and forage, they undertook, for an agreed price, to cut the trees belonging to owners of timber, to haul the logs to the landing places, and, at the close of the season, to drive them to the sawmills of Stillwater or Minneapolis. This was a profitable business for men who understood it and who had business capacity. Later the enterprising brothers moved to Minneapolis, where they advanced from logging to complete lumbering — buying timber, logging and driving, building a sawmill, and manufacturing boards, dimension, lath, and shingles.[1]

Although his lumbering business expanded and prospered, Clough was not so engrossed in it as to be indifferent to community and public affairs. He was disposed to be of service and might have aspired earlier to political positions, but it was not until 1883 that he became a member of the city council of Minneapolis. There he served four years, holding the presidency during his second term. At what time and how Clough became interested in agricultural affairs is not known. It may be true that, like Governor Merriam and many another public character, he was less concerned about the cultivation of farms than about the cultivation of farmers. At the annual election of the Minnesota State Agricultural Society on January 13, 1891, he was elected first vice president and in April following he was promoted to the presidency. The state fair of that year was " a success of the character of a great victory " and at the end of the year the treasury had a balance of more than ten thousand dollars. The good will of farm leaders and a state-wide acquaintance thus obtained aided, no doubt, in gaining Clough the nomination and election as lieutenant governor on the Republican ticket in 1892. As such he presided over the Senate in 1893 and, after being reëlected in 1894, was suddenly promoted to the governorship when Governor Nelson was elected to the United States Senate.[2]

The advancement of Lieutenant Governor Clough raised a question in regard to the vacancy thereby created. A section of article 5 of the Minnesota constitution provides that " Before the close of each session of the senate, they shall elect a president pro tempore, who shall be lieutenant governor in case a vacancy should occur in that office." Frank A.

[1] Clough to the author, January 10, 1924; Baker, *Governors of Minnesota*, 361–364; Upham and Dunlap, *Minnesota Biographies*, 130; " Building a Fortune in the West," in the *Mississippi Valley Lumberman*, April 4, 1902, p. 17; Smalley, *Republican Party*, 341.

[2] Smalley, *Republican Party*, 341; Darwin S. Hall and Return I. Holcombe, *History of the Minnesota State Agricultural Society*, 239–242 (St. Paul, 1910).

Day of Martin County was elected president pro tempore of the Senate on January 25, 1895. When Lieutenant Governor Clough succeeded to the governorship on January 31, Day immediately assumed the presidency of the Senate but continued throughout the session to vote as a senator. One very important bill, to be told about later, the " Anderson bill " for taxing railroad lands not used for railroad purposes, would have failed but for his affirmative vote. Since the Senate did not declare a senatorial vacancy, the governor did not issue a writ of election, as the constitution authorized him to do when a vacancy occurred in the legislature. On April 23, the last day of the session, the Senate elected George T. Barr president pro tempore, impliedly assuming that Day had become lieutenant governor.[3]

The next legislature, the thirtieth, met on January 5, 1897, and the Senate was called to order by Lieutenant Governor John L. Gibbs, who had been elected the previous fall. When the roll was called Day answered as senator from the sixth district, whereupon Howard H. Dunn stepped forward with a certificate of election from the sixth district in proper form and asked to be seated. Dunn's credentials were referred to the Senate committee on elections, which reported that the attorneys of the contesting parties were agreed on a statement of facts and advised hearings by the Senate as a committee of the whole. Two days were consumed in argument by the very able counsel. On January 23 a motion declaring the senatorship in the sixth district vacant was passed by a vote of 30 to 23 and Dunn was seated by the same vote, 30 to 23. Day claimed that his performance of certain duties of the lieutenant governor had not vacated his senatorship and that he had a right to serve out his four-year term, for which he was elected in 1894. In the campaign of 1896 his sympathies were with the silverites and it was believed that his allegiance to his old party was not maintained. Dunn was elected at

---

[3] *Senate Journal*, 1895, pp. 58, 80, 390, 838; *House Journal*, 25; Constitution, article 4, section 17. See *post*, p. 225.

the general election of 1896 as an ardent Republican. Whether or not the views of the Senate on this constitutional question would have been different had Day remained loyal must remain a matter of conjecture. Day, like others who left the Republican road by the silver bypath, later found himself at home in the Democratic party.[4]

There were worthy gentlemen willing and even desirous to wear gubernatorial honors at the close of Governor Clough's second year of service in 1896, but no one cared to contest in a serious way his renomination by the Republicans. They were content to figure as expectant aspirants biding their time and meanwhile supporting the party nominee. By an overwhelming majority of votes in the Republican convention Governor Clough was named to succeed himself.[5] It may have been that some of the aspirants were content to have another take the chances of a defeat, which, under the circumstances, was conceived to be not improbable.

For many years " the silver problem " had been festering in national politics, but the nomination of William Jennings Bryan for the presidency by the Democratic party and the adoption by that party of the doctrine of the free and unlimited coinage of silver at the ratio of 16 to 1 without awaiting international action brought that question to the front as the dominant issue of the campaign and there was dissension in the Republican household. A considerable number of electors, headed by public men of high standing and acknowledged familiarity with public questions, were affected by the clamor that Europeans, especially British financiers, were directing American finances in order to have

[4] *Senate Journal*, 1897, pp. 3, 8, 62–68, 83, 87; Holmes, in *Minnesota in Three Centuries*, 4: 232. The decision of the Senate was reversed the following year by the state supreme court in a notable lawsuit. See State *ex rel.* Marr *v.* Stearns, *72 Minnesota*, 200. A resolution was offered in the legislature of 1899 to allow Day his per diem for the session of 1897, deducting his per diem as senator from the beginning of the session to January 23, the day upon which the Senate declared his seat vacant.

[5] *Pioneer Press* (St. Paul), July 2, 1896, p. 1. Clough received 860 votes and 283 votes were cast for three other aspirants.

their debts paid in the dearer money; that silver had been
demonetized in 1873 by a stealthy and unconscionable trick;
and that holders of government bonds had an unrighteous
advantage in receiving their interest in gold. These people
could see little sense in the new Republican proposition to
postpone the remonetization of silver until an international
agreement could be made. That, they suggested, would be
a hypocritical postponement to the Greek calends.[6]

The most prominent among the Minnesota Silver Republican apostles was John Lind, whose career had been honorable to himself and satisfactory to the Republican party,
which had given him three terms — from 1887 to 1893 —
in the national House of Representatives. On July 16, 1896,
the Silver Republicans nominated Lind for governor; on August 4 the Democrats, in convention, put a free-silver plank in
their platform and ratified the Silver Republican nomination
by acclamation; and on August 26 the Populists pledged their
support. The three bodies divided the other state offices share
and share alike. This arrangement for united action was
made, doubtless after conversations among leaders, because
it was evident that none of the three organizations could elect
a candidate alone. The Democrats had not elected a governor
since Sibley's time and could not expect to do so now; much
less could the Populists or the Silver Republican rump count
on having such good fortune. The campaign which followed
was one of the most hotly contested in Minnesota history.
The best stumping talent of all parties was employed. Senator Nelson defended hard money in a singularly clear and
forcible address and Senator Davis was heard in some of his
most brilliant speeches. Lind arrayed the arguments for free
silver in a formidable series of addresses and in a style of
oratory tinged with humor and with sympathy for people

---

[6] Dewey, *Financial History*, 460–462; Alonzo B. Hepburn, *History of Coinage and Currency in the United States and the Perennial Contest for Sound
Money*, 385–388 (New York, 1903) ; Charles J. Bullock, *Essays on the Mone-
tary History of the United States*, 110–121, and citations (New York, 1900) ;
Taussig, *Silver Situation*, 97.

struggling to pay debts out of low wages and low prices which they received for their commodities. Perhaps the most illuminating contribution to the money question was an elaborate historical account of American coinage and the principles underlying it by James T. McCleary of Mankato, one of the representatives of Minnesota in Congress.[7]

In the election of 1896 Governor Clough's plurality over Lind was but 3,552; that of McKinley over Bryan on the national ticket was 62,768 — a result which indicates that, after all, local considerations rather than the great silver issue governed the voting for the state tickets. Among such considerations have been suggested Lind's deserved personal popularity and his support by electors of Scandinavian birth or parentage, elated at the prospect of seeing another of their race at the head of the state. Another complication of barely appreciable influence was the entry into the gubernatorial contest of Dr. Albert A. Ames for a second time. He received but 2,890 votes.[8] A still further explanation of

[7] *Pioneer Press*, 1896: July 17, p. 1; August 5, p. 1; 27, p. 3. The *Pioneer Press* of August 2, pp. 1–3, gives a speech made by Nelson at Alexandria, in which he reviews silver legislation, and the issue of September 15, p. 1, reviews speeches of Nelson and Davis. A speech by Davis on the evils of inflation is given in the issue of August 5, p. 1, and that of September 17, p. 1, prints a letter from Davis in reply to a charge that he had favored silver in 1890, giving the reasons for his change of views. The issue of August 27 gives Lind's speech accepting the Populist nomination. Lind said to the Populist convention: " I shall accept that nomination [*of the Democratic convention*], but not as a Democrat. I accept yours, but not as a Populist. I accept it not as a Republican, but as a citizen willing to contribute his quota to this struggle. . . . I was during all the years of my early manhood a Republican. I would be glad to support that party to-day . . . but when it turned its back on the traditions of its past . . . who can blame me or any other man for leaving it?" Lind's speech accepting the Democratic nomination, in which he advocates free silver coinage, is in the *Pioneer Press* of September 12, p. 10. In the *Representative* (Minneapolis and St. Paul), August 12, 1896, p. 3, is a letter from Lind to Dobbyn, dated August 8, in which Lind says that he would have voted for free silver in 1890, but, informed that the bill would be vetoed, he voted for the Sherman bill as the next best. The *Pioneer Press* of October 4, p. 16, prints an abstract of an address made by Lind at Stillwater and that of October 25, p. 8, gives an abstract of a speech of McCleary in favor of sound money. The national Republican plank on silver may be found in Appleton, *Annual Cyclopædia*, 1896, p. 760.

[8] *Legislative Manual*, 1925, pp. 113, 115. The announcement of Ames's candidacy is in the *Minneapolis Tribune*, August 27, 1896. O. N. Nelson, in his *History of the Scandinavians*, 433, gives as a reason for Lind's defeat in 1896 the bitter opposition of the Swedish Lutheran clergy in the state.

Clough's slender majority, as compared with that of McKinley, was found by his friends in the apathy, not to say hostility, of Republicans who had expected the reëlection of William D. Washburn to the United States Senate in January, 1895, and had laid the blame for their disappointment at Clough's door. To secure his accession to the governorship upon Nelson's promotion to the Senate he had, as they conceived, not only disappointed expectations but had broken faith. There came a time when Clough could take jubilant requital for this disservice. He had some satisfaction at the close of the polls in this election, according to Donnelly, who in his paper said, " He [*Washburn*] set out to bury Dave Clough and now Clough sits on his grave stone grinning." [9]

It was not altogether a happy season for Ignatius Donnelly. The Populist national convention had been called to sit at St. Louis on July 22. Five out of seven district Populist conventions had named Donnelly as their choice for the presidency and he journeyed to St. Louis evidently in the high hope of having his name presented for the great office by his Minnesota colleagues. At the least, he would have a place on one of the most important committees, probably that on resolutions; he had written nine-tenths of the Omaha platform. To his surprise and disgust he was treated like a stranger. His name was not even mentioned as a candidate and no committee duty was assigned him. He sat through the sessions like a spectator. A single suggestion by him was ruled superfluous by the chair. On his return to his editorial office he poured out his grief in the *Representative*. He had been humiliated by Populists of his own state before the whole world. This was his reward for twenty-five years of labor for reform and thousands of dollars spent in the cause. His very lifeblood had been wasted in gigantic efforts to build up a party in Minnesota. He had foregone literary work which would have added honor to his name and thousands of dollars to his fortune. He was done. He would support

[9] *Representative*, November 18, 1896, p. 2.

Bryan and the Populist state ticket to the end of the campaign and would then withdraw from public life forever. The sorrowing statesman found a grain of comfort in his nomination by the Populists of Dakota County as representative in the legislature and his election by a sufficient plurality over three other candidates.[10]

Donnelly's service on the floor in the session of 1897 was not conspicuous, but he participated cheerfully in an investigation of moment. The state auditor, Robert C. Dunn, in 1896 reported to the legislature that, through an error of a predecessor, the state school fund had been depleted of some twelve million dollars' worth of iron ore property. The session was but a week old when Donnelly introduced a joint resolution providing for a joint committee of investigation. The resolution passed both houses and Donnelly became chairman of the committee. After a preliminary inquiry the committee concluded that the state had been robbed by a combination of certain persons and recommended the appointment of a joint committee to take necessary proceedings to recover possession of the described iron ore lands and the profits already derived from them by illegal occupants. A bill to carry out the recommendation passed the House on April 14 by a vote of 96 to 6. The Senate returned the bill with amendments, to which the House did not agree. On April 20 a committee of conference reported a substitute providing for further proceedings by a committee to be composed of the governor, the state auditor, and the attorney-general, to which the House agreed by a vote of 84 to 0. That legislature had no desire to liberate Donnelly for another tour of investigation which would probably end nowhere and

[10] *Representative*, 1896: June 10, p. 4; July 29, pp. 2, 4. In an editorial in the *Representative* of November 4, p. 2, entitled "How It Happened," Donnelly remarks that one of the great mistakes of the People's party convention at St. Louis was the attempt "to force the Populists and Democrats into an unnatural marriage." In an editorial entitled "Burying the People's Party," in the issue of December 9, p. 2, he says, "It is no wonder the People's Party was slaughtered at St. Louis." The vote in Dakota County is given in the *Legislative Manual*, 1897, p. 495.

which would be quite likely to cast suspicion upon the conduct and motives of officials doing their best to develop the resources of the state. The committee found that the state had never had any title to the property in question and that no action, therefore, could be maintained for its recovery.[11]

The legislature of 1895 was unusually industrious in proposing amendments to the state constitution. The first in a group of six created a board of pardons to consist of the governor, the attorney-general, and the chief justice of the supreme court and transferred the pardoning power from the governor to that board. The second took the right to vote from alien declarants. The third authorized cities and villages to frame so-called " home rule " charters, subject to the laws of the state. The fourth required that just compensation be made for private property taken, destroyed, or damaged for public purposes. The fifth authorized the investment of school and university funds in the bonds of municipalities and school districts. The sixth levied a property tax upon sleeping-car, parlor- and drawing-room-car, telegraph, telephone, express, mining, boom, and shipbuilding corporations, as well as upon individual owners in such concerns, and gave the legislature power to assess an ad valorem tax or to impose a tax upon gross earnings. All these propositions were agreed to at the general election of 1896 and became parts of the state constitution.[12]

[11] Report of the state auditor, in *Executive Documents*, 1896, vol. 1, pp. 344–346; Attorney-General, *Reports*, 1897–98, p. 35; *House Journal*, 1897, pp. 35, 55, 60, 85, 987, 1018–1021, 1159, 1181, appendix 73-107; *Senate Journal*, pp. 50, 71, 904, 921. For a detailed account of " The Loss of the Mountain Iron Mine," see Matthias N. Orfield, *Federal Land Grants to the States, with Special Reference to Minnesota*, 229–234 (University of Minnesota, *Studies in the Social Sciences*, no. 2 — Minneapolis, 1915).

[12] *General Laws*, 1895, pp. 6–16; 1897, pp. iii–ix; Anderson, *History of the Constitution*, 157, 170, 175, 182, 189, 281, 282, 285. An account of the home rule charter amendment is given in the Appendix, no. 15, *post*. All these amendments would have failed of ratification if an affirmative majority of all the electors voting at the election had been required. The adoption of the suffrage amendment reduced the vote for governor from 337,229 in 1896 to 252,562 in 1898. The amendment in regard to the investment of school and university funds merely extended the operation of an amendment proposed in 1885 and adopted in 1886, authorizing the investment of school funds only in the bonds

Three other referenda were also made at the same session. The first was a recommendation by two-thirds of the legislature to the electors of the state to require the legislature at its next session to call a convention to revise the state constitution. At the election there was a majority of 25,740 in favor of a constitutional convention, but less than half of the electors voting cast their votes on the proposition. As the constitution requires an affirmative vote of a majority of all electors voting at the election to call a constitutional convention, there was no mandate for revision. The electorate was either indifferent to the matter or was unwilling to put its whole organic law in supposition.[13] Another referendum was a recommendation to merge the income from the internal improvement land fund with the road and bridge fund. This met with the same fate as the foregoing, although it was favored by a very large majority of the electors who voted on it.[14] The third of the number was a proposition for taxing railroad lands that were not being used for railroad purposes. This was a truly popular proposal at the time and it was agreed to by a large majority of all the electors voting at the election.[15]

Governor Nelson in his message to the legislature of 1895, of which he was soon to take leave, reviewed the work of

of school districts and municipalities. An amendment ratified in 1916 recast the section, number 6 of article 8, to authorize investments of school funds in first mortgage loans on improved and cultivated farms in the state.

[13] General Laws, 1895, p. 5; Anderson, History of the Constitution, 145. The total vote at the election of 1896 was 343,319; 171,660 affirmative votes were necessary for the adoption of the recommendation for a constitutional convention. The total vote cast on the proposal was 166,876; the affirmative vote, 96,308; the negative vote, 70,568.

[14] General Laws, 1895, p. 778; Anderson, History of the Constitution, 146, 219. In General Laws, 1897, p. xi, it is erroneously stated that the measure was "Declared adopted and ratified December 22nd, 1896. 152,765 votes for, and 28,991 against said proposition." Article 4, section 32b, of the constitution provides that the moneys belonging to the internal improvement land fund shall not be appropriated for any purpose without the approval of a majority of the electors voting at the next general election following the passage of the act for the appropriation.

[15] General Laws, 1895, p. 378; 1897, p. x; Anderson, History of the Constitution, 146. The vote for the measure was 235,585; against it, 29,530. This law was later declared unconstitutional.

certain departments of the state government and urged extreme economy in appropriations in consideration of existing industrial stagnation. His mind, doubtless, was occupied with other affairs, for he suggested but few matters for new legislation. That legislature, so fruitful in propositions for amending the state constitution, enacted but few statutes of first importance. It recast the banking and insurance codes and passed a general act for the incorporation, organization, and government of cities. It provided for taking the fourth decennial state census, but it did not follow the advice of Governor Nelson to extend it beyond a mere enumeration of the inhabitants and include statistics of property, manufacturing, mining, commerce, agriculture, labor, and capital. According to the published result the population of the state was 1,574,619. There were 841,755 males and 727,281 females, 1,560,125 white people and 3,878 colored persons, 1,057,084 native-born and 517,535 foreign-born, and 4,914 Indians and mixed-bloods who were not living on the reservations.[16]

Governor Clough in his message to the legislature of 1897 also emphasized the importance of economy in a continuing period of financial depression and urged the employment of business methods in public affairs. He proposed for consideration a compulsory system of free textbooks for common schools, a small bounty for beet sugar production, a county road system, a further restriction of child labor, and the encouragement of immigration. In the session of 1897 acts were passed for putting into operation the constitutional amendments ratified in the previous year creating a board of pardons and taxing certain large quasi corporations. The latter act exacted an impost on gross earnings. The military code was revised, a new legislative apportionment was made providing for sixty-three state senators and one hundred and

---

[16] *Executive Documents*, 1894, vol. I, pp. 19–38; *General Laws*, 1895, pp. 16–131, 298–311, 392–445, 465–472; Minnesota, *Fourth Decennial Census*, 276–279 (St. Paul, 1895).

nineteen representatives, and an act taxing inheritances was passed.[17]

The legislature of 1897 proposed two amendments to the state constitution, both of which were ratified at the general election of 1898. One extended the right of suffrage granted to women by the amendment adopted in 1875 and made effective by subsequent legislation, giving them the right to vote upon all matters pertaining to public libraries and for library officers, a necessary corollary.[18] The other amended section 1 of article 14 by requiring for the ratification of a constitutional amendment the affirmative votes of a majority of all the electors voting at the election. An unexpected result has been that, because of the indifference of electors or their reluctance to act upon such amendments, the required majority has been obtained on relatively few occasions, and the number of constitutional amendments has been, perhaps happily, small.[19]

A curiosity in legislation is exhibited in certain proceedings of the two houses in the sessions of 1891, 1895, and 1897. Under early English common law " special juries " might be summoned when issues came up for trial which, in the opinion of a judge, were " of too great nicety for the discussion of ordinary freeholders." The sheriff might be ordered to start proceedings to obtain such a jury " upon motion in court and a rule granted thereupon." [20] Such juries were lawful in all the American colonies which recognized

[17] *Executive Documents*, 1896, vol. 1, pp. 34, 35, 38, 40, 45, 47, 48; *General Laws*, 1897, pp. iii, viii–ix, 18–20, 204–240, 245–257, 307–313, 546–555, 572–576, 581–582.

[18] *General Laws*, 1875, p. 18; 1897, p. 331; 1899, p. iii; Anderson, *History of the Constitution*, 179. This amendment was ratified on November 8, 1898, by a vote of 71,704 to 43,660.

[19] *General Laws*, 1897, p. 345; 1899, p. iv; Anderson, *History of the Constitution*, 147, 282–285. The amendment was ratified on November 8, 1898, by a vote of 69,760 to 32,881. Anderson remarks that, had the new rule been applied at this election, the amendment would have failed by 55,866 votes. Since 1898, forty-eight amendments have been submitted and but twelve have been ratified.

[20] William Blackstone, *Commentaries on the Laws of England*, vol. 2, book 3, p. 276 (New York, 1853).

the English common law and came to be called "struck juries." Early Minnesota legislatures appear to have assumed that struck juries would need statutory authority. The Code of 1851 provided for them in courts of justices of the peace but it was not until 1864 that an act was unanimously passed authorizing struck juries in district courts. This act did not repose discretion in judges but allowed either party to a civil case to demand a struck jury as of right. Upon such demand duly filed the sheriff was required to select on an appointed day forty persons qualified for jury duty who, in his opinion, seemed "most indifferent between the parties" and best qualified to try the issue. Each party thereupon, in person or by attorney, would strike off names alternately until the number was reduced to sixteen. These sixteen would then be summoned as jurors and the first twelve who appeared, if not challenged for cause or set aside, would be impaneled. It is obvious that a sheriff might select the forty persons from a community or a class most likely to be sympathetic with the party calling for the struck jury. To prevent litigants from obtaining struck juries too easily the law provided that the demanding party must pay all the extra costs and expenses involved. It appears as fact that calls were not excessively numerous. The act of 1864 was embodied in the general statutes of 1866 and reappeared in those of 1878. What consideration influenced the legislature of 1891 to repeal the struck jury act remains to be discovered. The vote for repeal was unanimous in the Senate and 68 to 3 in the House. Equally mysterious was the reënactment of the struck jury law in 1895 by votes of 29 to 4 in the Senate and 62 to 42 in the House.[21]

An early experiment under the reënacted law was made on behalf of the state in an action to recover twenty-five thou-

[21] *The Revised Statutes of the Territory of Minnesota, Passed at the Second Session of the Legislative Assembly*, 306 (St. Paul, 1851) ; *General Laws*, 1864, pp. 79–81; 1878, p. 785; 1891, p. 157; 1895, p. 736; *Senate Journal*, 1864, p. 54; 1891, p. 508; 1895, p. 681; *House Journal*, 1864, p. 177; 1891, p. 632; 1895, p. 921.

sand dollars from a well-known lumbering firm which, it was alleged, had unlawfully cut pine timber on state land. In the suit brought in the district court of Hennepin County the state was defeated and applied for a new trial, which the sitting judge denied. The state then appealed to the supreme court and obtained a reversal of the order of the lower court denying a new trial. On the second trial, which was held before a struck jury, the defendants were ordered to pay the state $9,211.87, without exemplary damages, however, on the ground that the admitted cutting had been done under a permit which the lumber firm took over by assignment, believing in good faith that it was a legal permit, though in fact it had been originally issued illegally. The state was therefore entitled only to the proved value of the standing timber. A motion was then made by the defendants for a new trial, which the court granted; thereupon the plaintiff appealed from this order to the supreme court, which affirmed the order of the court below. The third trial, which was also held before a struck jury, resulted in a verdict for the state, with an award of $5,359.88 for damages, a considerable reduction from the amount set at the second trial. No notable advantage appears to have attended the demands of the state for the two struck juries.[22]

The constitutionality of the struck jury law was soon attacked in a case which was otherwise of small importance. In a suit brought by a citizen of Minneapolis against the Minneapolis Gaslight Company in the district court of Hennepin County the gas company demanded and obtained a struck jury. After the trial the jury brought in a verdict in

---

[22] Minnesota v. Shevlin-Carpenter Company, 62 *Minnesota*, 99–109; 66 *Minnesota*, 217–219. This was one of the prosecutions started by the Pine Land Investigating Committee of 1893. Its progress may be followed in the documents preserved in file case no. 60,995 in the office of the clerk of the district court of Hennepin County. The complaint was filed in Ramsey County on March 17, 1894. On May 16 it was removed to Hennepin County, but the trial did not begin until January 8, 1895. It was held before Judge Robert D. Russell and an ordinary jury. The second trial began on January 23, 1896, and the third, on January 15, 1897. The matter was kept alive by dilatory motions and continuances until July 11, 1898, when the judgment roll was filed.

favor of the company. An appeal was taken by the defeated plaintiff to the supreme court and issue was joined solely upon the constitutionality of the act. The firm of eminent lawyers employed by the company to contend for the constitutionality of the act made an extraordinary array of citations of adjudged cases in support of their several contentions. In an opinion of unusual length the court held that the regulation by the legislature of the manner of selecting and summoning the struck jury did not deprive the plaintiff of his right to an impartial jury and that therefore there had been no violation of the constitution. Two of the five judges rendered dissenting opinions. Their chief objection was that the act allowed a party to demand a struck jury as of right with no discretionary intervention of a judge, as required at common law. Under favoring circumstances or arrangements a party might virtually select his own jury.[23]

No evidence has been found of any general dissatisfaction with struck juries and it is probable that the general public did not much concern itself about them. There is reason to believe that litigants who had had some experience with them at heavy costs had not found them better than the ordinary jury. Lawyers generally found few or no advantages in them. A certain class of lawyers, of the species shyster, prosecuting personal injury claims against employing corporations, believing that the ordinary panel was more sympathetic with injured clients, clamored for the abolition of the struck jury. The legislature, thus influenced, repealed the struck jury act in 1897 by unanimous votes in both the Senate and the House. There has been no demand for its revival.[24]

[23] Mary Lommen v. Minneapolis Gaslight Company, 65 Minnesota, 196–228.
[24] General Laws, 1897, p. 11; Senate Journal, 1897, p. 171; House Journal, 255; letters to the author from Gilfillan, December 26, 1923; Rockwood, January 18, 1924, Folwell Papers.

XI. MINNESOTA IN THE WARS WITH SPAIN AND THE PHILIPPINES

THE period of Governor Clough's administration was diversified by three military events, of which the Spanish-American War was the one of capital importance. It is not necessary to recount here the long series of distressing events that led up to that war. They may be found admirably summarized in the message of President McKinley to Congress on April 11, 1898, in which he asked for power to secure an end to the war between Spain and her rebellious colony and the establishment of a stable and free government on the island of Cuba. On the eighteenth of the same month Congress passed a joint resolution equivalent to a declaration of war. On the twenty-third the president called for 125,000 volunteers to be apportioned among the states and territories according to their population.[1] In Minnesota the requisition had been expected and it was understood that regiments of the national guard would promptly volunteer for the service. Company commanders were directed to fill up their companies to one hundred men. On April 25, 1898, the call of the secretary of war for three regiments of infantry to serve for two years or the war was received. On the twenty-eighth the state's three infantry regiments were ordered to assemble on the next day at St. Paul with one day's cooked rations. The order was obeyed and Governor Clough led them out to Camp Ramsey on the state fair grounds. The muster-in of the regiments was completed on May 8 and they were called the Twelfth, Thirteenth, and Fourteenth regiments of Minnesota infantry volunteers. But a week was allowed to clothe, equip, and drill the troops. On the sixteenth all departed — the Twelfth and Fourteenth for

[1] Larned, *History for Ready Reference*, 6: 170–182, 583–592.

Camp Thomas at Chickamauga, Georgia, and the Thirteenth for San Francisco.[2]

The Thirteenth was the only Minnesota regiment which saw service beyond seas. It sailed from San Francisco on June 27, made a short landing at Honolulu, and arrived in Manila Bay on July 31. It was actively engaged in the battle before Manila on August 13, during which two captains were severely wounded. Presumably on account of its excellent discipline, the regiment was detailed as provost guard of the captured city. It was relieved from this service on March 19, 1899, and on March 29 it was assigned to the duty of guarding the few miles of railroad which ran north from the city, a duty which exacted great vigilance and activity by night and day. From time to time detachments were sent out to break up collections of insurgents. For about a month, beginning on April 23, two battalions were attached to Lawton's expedition into the interior of the island of Luzon. On May 8 Major Arthur M. Diggles, on duty with his battalion, received a death wound. The guarding of railroads continued until August 4, when the regiment was relieved and ordered to prepare to embark for home. It sailed on August 12, made short stops at Nagasaki and Yokohama, and arrived at San Francisco on September 7. The muster-out did not take place until October 3. Governor John Lind and his staff went on to San Francisco to welcome the regiment and citizens of Minnesota raised a fund to pay for its transportation to Minnesota. Upon its arrival in Minneapolis on October 12, 1899, the regiment passed in review before Governor Lind and President McKinley, both of whom made addresses to a large concourse of spectators. The members, having already received their honorable discharge papers, at once

[2] Governor's Archives, Records, J: 582, 583; Minnesota, Adjutant General, Reports, 1897–98, p. 15; 1899–1900, pp. 30–32; Pioneer Press (St. Paul), April 18–May 17, 1898. The numbers of the regiments were assigned in succession to those of the Minnesota volunteer regiments in the Civil War. Franklin F. Holbrook, Minnesota in the Spanish-American War and the Philippine Insurrection, 20 (St. Paul, 1923).

dispersed. The losses of the command were: killed in battle or died of disease, accident, and wounds, two officers and forty-two enlisted men; wounded, six officers and sixty-eight men. Colonel Charles McCormick Reeve, son of a general officer in the Civil War, an old West Pointer, was brevetted brigadier general for gallant and meritorious service.[3]

The Twelfth and Fourteenth regiments remained in Camp Thomas until the last week in August, undergoing drill and discipline. The Twelfth was then sent to Camp Hamilton, Kentucky, and the Fourteenth to Camp Poland, Tennessee, from which points they were ordered home about three weeks later. A few days after their arrival the members of the regiments were given thirty days' furlough. The Twelfth was mustered out at New Ulm on November 5 and the Fourteenth at St. Paul on November 18. The delay in the discharge of the Fourteenth was occasioned by its recall to the ranks by Governor Clough to assist in the suppression of the small Indian war in the Chippewa country.[4]

The president's call for seventy-five thousand additional men to serve in the war against Spain was issued on May 25, 1898. It was estimated that Minnesota's quota would be two regiments, but a war department order of May 27 requiring nine hundred and ninety additional men to fill the ranks of the three regiments already in the field made it plain that but one regiment could be organized. As there was no fourth

---

[3] Adjutant General, *Reports*, 1899–1900, pp. 43–45; Holbrook, *Minnesota in the Spanish-American War*, 46–72, 125. For proceedings in the Minnesota legislature of 1899 to secure the early return of the Thirteenth, Governor Lind's message to the houses stating that he could obtain no response to his appeal to the war department, and the final conclusion of the legislature to take no action, see *Senate Journal*, 1899, pp. 475, 486, 1062–1064, 1237, and *House Journal*, 587, 647, 1248. A series of very interesting letters containing gossip about the regiment and its experiences, written by Harry P. Ritchie, assistant surgeon, is in the *Pioneer Press*, 1898: July 20, p. 3; October 27, p. 2; November 7, p. 8; 16, p. 3; 1899: July 23, p. 17. For detailed accounts of the Thirteenth Minnesota in the Philippines, see Karl Irving Faust, *Campaigning in the Philippines* (San Francisco, 1899), and John Bowe, *With the 13th Minnesota in the Philippines* (Minneapolis, [1905]). The *Minneapolis Tribune*, October 12, 13, 1899, gives an account of the welcome given the Thirteenth upon its return home.

[4] Adjutant General, *Reports*, 1899–1900, pp. 41, 46.

national guard regiment to volunteer in a body, it was necessary to call for volunteers from the state at large and for the governor to appoint the field and staff officers. John C. Shandrew of St. Paul was appointed colonel and had charge of the organization of the new regiment, which was called the " Fifteenth Regiment of Infantry, Minnesota Volunteers." On July 29 Colonel Shandrew was suddenly stricken with paralysis resulting from cerebral hemorrhage, which caused his immediate retirement and, a year later, his death. Lieutenant Colonel Harry A. Leonhaeuser, a graduate of West Point and a captain in the Twenty-fifth United States Infantry who had been military instructor at the University of Minnesota, was promoted to the vacancy.

The month of June passed before the needed recruits for the old regiments had been enlisted. On July 5, 6, and 7 twelve companies for the new regiment reported at Camp Ramsey on the state fair grounds, three from Minneapolis and nine from as many other places. The muster-in began on July 8 and was completed ten days later. The command did not leave the country and was mustered out near Augusta, Georgia, on March 27, 1899.[5] But for two incidents of a painful character its story might be told in the statement that a fine body of young Americans ready and desirous for active service had patiently endured, for soldiers' pay, the restraints and drudgery of camp life.

The first of these incidents was an epidemic of typhoid fever, which broke out before the end of July. In August the number of cases rapidly increased until, on the twenty-first, 180 from the regiment had been sent to the hospitals of St. Paul and Minneapolis. Advised that a change of camps might be favorable, Colonel Leonhaeuser obtained leave to move the command to the Fort Snelling Reservation. On

[5] Governor's Archives, Records, J: 596, 599; Adjutant General, *Reports,* 1899–1900, p. 46; Holbrook, *Minnesota in the Spanish-American War,* 25–31, 359–433; Tell A. Turner, *Story of the Fifteenth Minnesota Volunteer Infantry,* 9–31 (Minneapolis, [1899]). Turner was chaplain of the regiment. The order to the governor for the additional regiment is dated June 18, 1898.

August 23 a new camp was made on fresh ground on the
rifle range. There was some decline in the number of cases,
but by September 3 eighty-three patients had been sent to the
post hospital. When the regiment left that camp on September 15, in pursuance of orders, 360 men were left behind,
sick or convalescent. The order to move took the Fifteenth
to Camp Meade near Harrisburg, Pennsylvania. There were
enough more cases of typhoid to raise the number over four
hundred, but under improved conditions the fever practically
disappeared.[6]

The other unfortunate incident in the career of the Fifteenth was a mutinous outbreak of a considerable body of
enlisted men at Camp Mackenzie near Augusta, Georgia, to
which the regiment had been transferred on November 17.
Late in the afternoon of February 4, 1899, a private of Company F was shot and instantly killed, after a brief altercation,
by the keeper of a saloon in a suburb of Augusta. It was
alleged, and it was probably true, that an insulting epithet
had been used by the soldier. On the following day near
noon a number of enlisted men, estimated at between one
hundred and two hundred, led by a private of Company F,
broke into a storehouse, seized a quantity of ball cartridges,
and, intent upon revenge for the murder of a comrade,
started for Augusta. A detachment of the Third United
States Cavalry sent in pursuit surrounded the gang, which
had been reduced in number by desertions to about seventy,
and marched the men back to camp. A general court-martial
convicted eight of the mutineers and sentenced them to be

[6] Turner, *Fifteenth Minnesota*, 33–49; Holbrook, *Minnesota in the Spanish-
American War*, 90–93; report of Surgeon-General George M. Sternberg, in War
Department, *Reports*, 1899, vol. 1, part 2, p. 395 (56 Congress, 1 session, *House
Documents*, vol. 3 — serial 3900). Most important is Walter Reed, Victor C.
Vaughan, and Edward O. Shakespeare, *Report on the Origin and Spread of
Typhoid Fever in U. S. Military Camps during the Spanish War of 1898*, 414–
433 (58 Congress, 2 session, *House Documents*, no. 757 — serial 4748). The
Walter Reed board visited Camp Meade on September 30, 1898. Without find-
ing the origin of the typhoid germs, the board concluded that the fever was
propagated by a tent, squad, or comrade infection through the regiment and not
by some common or general condition like polluted water or contaminated soil.

dishonorably discharged, to forfeit all pay and allowances due them, and to be imprisoned at hard labor for terms ranging from six months to six years. Early in March the main body of the mutineers was released from confinement in the guardhouse on the ground that, although they had been participants in the mutiny, they had not been promoters of it. The general officer who on March 16 confirmed the sentences of the convicted men severely censured "nearly all" the commissioned officers present for inefficiency and cowardice, going so far as to say that two of them deserved the extreme penalty of military law. Application was at once made for a court of inquiry, but the war department refused it on the ground that the regiment was so soon to be discharged. Colonel Leonhaeuser as an officer of the regular army was accorded as his right a court of inquiry, which sat at St. Paul in April, 1899. Its decision was that the censure of the corps commander did not apply to him.[7]

Minnesota's part in the war with Spain was not confined to the contribution of her four infantry regiments — three national guard regiments and one regiment of volunteers at large; she also furnished recruits to national volunteer regiments. In expectation that such troops might be much needed in operations in Cuba, Congress on May 11, 1898, gave the president power to authorize the secretary of war to organize a brigade of volunteer engineers from the nation at large. The secretary, in orders, called for three regiments — the first to be raised in New England and the Middle States, the second in the upper Mississippi Valley and Pacific states, and the third in the Southern States. The place of rendezvous for the second regiment, or rather, for the first two battalions, was fixed at Fort Sheridan, near Chicago. St. Paul was designated as a recruiting station for Company G, which, when mustered in on July 8, contained seventy-seven Minnesotans

[7] Holbrook, *Minnesota in the Spanish-American War*, 93–101; Turner, *Fifteenth Minnesota*, 87, 105–119, 140–144, 148–152. A more extended account of the mutiny is given in the Appendix, no. 16, *post*.

— seventy-four men and three officers — all of whom had been especially examined and found qualified for the service. On the same day, July 8, it departed for Fort Sheridan, where it was included in the Second Battalion. It remained there under instruction until August, when it was transferred to Montauk Point, Long Island, where for nearly two months it was employed in engineering work incident to the establishment of a great hospital for convalescents returned from Cuba and the south. On October 7 Company G, with another, was sent to Huntsville, Alabama, where a large concentration camp was under construction. On December 29 it was dispatched to Havana, Cuba, as part of a detachment of volunteer engineers. There it passed the winter, engaged in construction and sanitation operations. When the army was withdrawn after the treaty of peace was signed on April 19, 1899, the company was stationed at Camp Mackenzie. It was mustered out on May 18, 1899, after ten months of useful service, having lost but one man, who was drowned.[8]

The protocol signed at Washington on August 12, 1898, put an end to hostilities between Spain and the United States and the treaty of Paris, executed on December 10, 1898, and later duly ratified, reëstablished amity between the two nations. An unexpected component of the treaty, which met with opposition in the Senate, was the purchase by the United States of the Philippine archipelago, comprising fifty principal islands with an area of 119,542 square miles and a population estimated at eight million. Had the American commissioners at Paris, one of whom was Cushman K. Davis, known what a burden the Spaniards were unloading they would have been less eager to close the bargain, and the Senate, it may be believed, would not have ratified that treaty without having it modified.[9] For years before the Spanish

[8] *Statutes at Large*, 30: 405; report of Adjutant General H. C. Corbin, in War Department, *Reports*, 1898, vol. 1, part 2, pp. 296, 305, 313 (55 Congress, 3 session, *House Documents*, vol. 2 — serial 3744); Holbrook, *Minnesota in the Spanish-American War*, 103, 443–470.

[9] See Larned, *History for Ready Reference*, 6: 367, 369, 621–626, 634–638, for the discussion of the treaty in the Senate. The correspondence of the

War there had been insurrections in the Philippines against Spanish rule. In 1896 an uprising led by Emilio Aguinaldo was temporarily quieted by concessions and largesses. When, as it was alleged, faith was not kept and payments were defaulted, the revolt was renewed, and when Admiral Dewey arrived in Manila Bay with his fleet there was not much left of Spanish control. A Philippine army coöperated in the capture of the city of Manila on August 13. Upon the dissolution of the Spanish power in the Philippines a civil government was organized, with Aguinaldo as its dictator. A few months later he was proclaimed first president of the Philippine Republic. For some six months this was the only government which stood between order and anarchy in a region inhabited by some millions of people. On January 5, 1899, Aguinaldo issued a declaration of independence and on the twenty-seventh of the same month he demanded that the American commander recognize the Philippine Republic as a sovereign power. The absurd demand was not, of course, conceded. On the evening of February 4, after many gestures intended to exasperate the Americans into committing some hostile act, the Philippine army launched an attack upon the American camp and a battle of considerable magnitude resulted on the following day.[10]

The United States, which had sent its army and its fleet to make war against Spain, was now confronted with a war with the Philippine Republic, which had an army of twenty thousand or thirty thousand fairly well-armed men and a horde

---

American commissioners is in *Papers Relating to the Treaty with Spain* (56 Congress, 2 session, *Senate Documents*, no. 148 — serial 4039). Davis opposed the payment of the twenty millions for the Philippines. He would "quietly spread ourselves over the Philippines . . . and then annex them formally by an act of Congress." It took a hundred thousand soldiers, more or less, and four years of warfare to "spread ourselves over the Philippines." Davis to Castle, October 11, 30, November 15, 23, 1898, Castle Papers.

[10] John Foreman, *The Philippine Islands; A History of the Philippine Archipelago and Its Political Dependencies, Embracing the Whole Period of Spanish Rule*, 510–550 (London, 1899) ; Charles B. Elliott, *The Philippines to the End of the Military Régime: America Overseas*, 184, 311–313, 317, 396, 446, 449, 452, 493 (Indianapolis, [1916]) ; Larned, *History for Ready Reference*, 6: 620.

of unknown numbers of savages equipped with bolos and lances. The progress of that war, which lasted two years and which was followed by as many more years of guerrilla operations, cannot be followed here. The point of interest is that a new army was needed for that war and that Minnesota was to have a small but reputable part in it. At the close of the Spanish War the volunteers who had enlisted for it were entitled to honorable discharge. Large numbers of the regular army were also closing their terms of enlistment. On March 2, 1899, Congress provided by law for the raising of twenty-seven regiments of United States volunteer infantry. Probably in the hope that, after all, they might not be needed, the secretary of war did not issue his order for the enlistment of ten regiments until July 5, but he followed this with other orders during the next two months for fourteen more.[11] The Forty-fifth Regiment of United States Volunteer Infantry, recruited from several middle western states, was assembled, with the exception of two companies which had been recruited on the Pacific coast, at Fort Snelling in September. The whole command arrived in Manila in December and was at once put into active service against the insurgents. For more than a year it was employed in hunting down parties of marauders, with small losses but with great fatigue. When its services had become dispensable the regiment returned to San Francisco and there it was mustered out on June 3, 1901. Nine officers and 189 men were Minnesotans.[12]

To these troops organized in the state must be added to the credit of Minnesota over three thousand more of her inhabitants who took part in the war in other organizations. Nearly two thousand of them enlisted in the regular army — some six hundred of them in the Third United States Infantry,

[11] Elliott, *The Philippines*, 462; *Statutes at Large*, 30:979; report of Adjutant General H. C. Corbin, in War Department, *Reports*, 1899, vol. I, part 2, pp. 16, 43, 65, 72, 74 (serial 3900); Holbrook, *Minnesota in the Spanish-American War*, 102.

[12] War Department, *Reports*, 1899, vol. I, part 2, p. 20 (serial 3900); Holbrook, *Minnesota in the Spanish-American War*, 104–107, 462–470.

which had been stationed at Fort Snelling. The regiment went to Cuba, where it participated with gallantry in the capture of Santiago, and it returned to Fort Snelling in September, 1898. In the winter of 1899 four companies for a new battalion were recruited, chiefly in Minnesota. The regiment, which was ordered to the Philippines, arrived in time to join in the general move against the insurgent army in March, 1899. The command remained in Luzon fighting small battles and skirmishes, pursuing fugitive bands, and garrisoning captured towns until it was recalled in March, 1902. Minnesota furnished, all told, about eighty-five hundred men for the Spanish and Philippine wars.[13]

The third military event of the period, which was of minor account, was an outbreak in the fall of 1898 of a small band of Chippewa in the Leech Lake region, exasperated by a supposed indignity put upon their chief by a government official. There was no danger of molestation of the white people of the region by the Indians, but the usual alarm set in and Governor Clough was appealed to for protection. By leave of the war department he distributed the Fourteenth Minnesota Regiment, which had returned from its service in the war against Spain, in the villages supposed to be threatened and the alarm died out in a few days.[14]

---

[13] Holbrook, *Minnesota in the Spanish-American War*, 102, 107–114, 625 (tables). According to Holbrook's tables there were 5,348 men and officers in the four Minnesota regiments, 428 in United States volunteer troops from Minnesota, 133 enlisted in other state organizations, 562 in the navy and the marine corps, and 2,027 in other organizations in the regular army, making a total of 8,498. The troops are classified according to the branch of service entered first.

[14] Holmes, in *Minnesota in Three Centuries*, 4: 245–254; Louis H. Roddis, "The Last Indian Uprising in the United States," in the *Minnesota History Bulletin*, 3: 273–290 (February, 1920). A further account of this affair, which was a sequel to a long series of Chippewa exasperations, will be given in the next volume.

XII. LIND AND HIS TIMES, 1899–1901

A S THE biennial state election of 1898 drew near the same combination of opposing parties which two years before had reduced Clough's majority over Lind to less than four thousand resolved upon another trial of strength. According to concerted arrangement the Silver Republican, Democratic, and Populist parties held their conventions in Minneapolis on June 15. Seven conferees from each body made up a slate, which was accepted by the several conventions. John Lind again headed the ticket for governor and the other state officers were allotted equitably enough to the Democrats and the Populists. In the Populist body, however, there was a dissenting minority opposed to merging with the great parties. This group, which was presently dubbed "Middle-of-the-Road" Populists, after an all-day debate seceded and the following day nominated a full state ticket, indorsing Donnelly for United States senator. The debate was enlivened by a colloquy between Donnelly and Sidney M. Owen, in which such compliments as "villain" and "monster" were freely exchanged. To illustrate the sacrifices he was making in standing by the Populist cause, Donnelly said that he could get five hundred dollars a speech stumping for the Republican ticket.[1]

The nomination of Lind was good politics, not only because he was the most available candidate but also because he was well fitted for the duties of governor, as a brief sketch of his life will show. At the time of his nomination he was forty-four years old, having been born on March 25, 1854, in a country parish in southern Sweden. In 1867 he came to the

---

[1] *Minneapolis Tribune*, 1898: June 16, pp. 1, 4; 17, p. 5; *Pioneer Press* (St. Paul), 1898: June 16, p. 1; 17, p. 6; *Representative* (Minneapolis and St. Paul), 1898: June 15, pp. 1, 4; 22, pp. 1, 2; Baker, *Governors of Minnesota*, 375, 383.

United States with his parents, who made a home in Goodhue County. It may be assumed that he had been well taught in the primary branches in one of the excellent schools of Sweden. Although he had a new language to learn, after three years of schooling he was granted, in 1870, a certificate to teach in the public schools. He taught a year in a district school in Sibley County, after which he settled in New Ulm, where for three years he supported himself in various employments while he learned the German language and studied law under a preceptor. In the school year 1875–76 he studied in the preparatory classes of the state university. The next year he was admitted to the bar and began the practice of law. For two years he served as superintendent of schools of Brown County, after which, beginning in 1881, he was receiver in the United States land office at Tracy, Lyon County, for four years. During these six years he enlarged his knowledge of law, handled many important cases in court, and greatly extended his acquaintance. Widely known as a Republican leader throughout a very large district, he easily won the nomination for representative in Congress in the fall of 1886. He was elected and two years later he was re-elected by a gratifying vote; but a third election, in 1890, was won by only a slight majority against General James H. Baker, who had a very creditable war record behind him. In 1892 Lind declined a renomination and returned to his law practice, which soon became extensive.[2]

During these six years of congressional service Lind was a sturdy supporter of Republican measures generally and did not fail to gather his share of plums for his state and his district. He took an active interest in Indian affairs and in public land matters, upon which he was well informed, urged the enforcement of the interstate commerce act, favored a low

2 Baker, Governors of Minnesota, 377–380, 381; Upham and Dunlap, Minnesota Biographies, 442; C. W. G. Hyde and William Stoddard, eds., History of the Great Northwest and Its Men of Progress, 196–198 (Minneapolis, 1901); Smalley, Republican Party, 369; Nelson, History of the Scandinavians, 430–434. Nelson says that Lind is a good Icelandic scholar.

tariff on lumber, and pleaded for free sisal, the material for farmers' binding twine, and for free sugar. On the money question of the time Lind shared the opinion of a large minority — if not an actual majority — of his party that prosperity would follow a return to the use of silver as principal money. In a long address delivered on June 6, 1890, he advocated the passage of the so-called "Sherman bill" providing for the issue of treasury notes as paper money against deposits in the treasury of silver bullion. Accepting the quantity theory, he argued that the decrease in gold production, which caused falling prices, ought to be met with an increase in the use of silver to enlarge the money supply and raise prices. Bondholders in 1873 had demonetized silver by stealth. The Bland Act of 1878 had but partially remedied the mischief. The time had not come for the free and unlimited coinage of silver, but the pending bill would, if enacted, raise the price of silver and restore that metal to par at its old ratio. Speaking two years later on a bill for free coinage of silver under international agreement, Lind said that the Sherman Act had met his expectations. Although he favored free international coinage, he thought it better to let well enough alone until a Republican Congress should assemble in which the people would have confidence. Lind did not need to leave the Republican party at any time before 1896 because of his views on silver.[3]

At this point should be noted a romantic element which entered into the politics of 1898. The call came in April of that year for Minnesota troops to serve in the war against Spain. When the three national guard regiments were volunteering, John Lind asked for some duty in the Twelfth Regiment, commanded by his neighbor, Colonel Joseph Bobleter of New Ulm. He was offered by Governor Clough the position of first lieutenant and quartermaster. He accepted

---

[3] *Congressional Record*, 51 Congress, 1 session, 5692–5697; 52 Congress, 1 session, 2521; Baker, *Governors of Minnesota*, 380–382; Nelson, *History of the Scandinavians*, 432. For the Sherman Act see *Statutes at Large*, 26:289.

at once, locked his office door, and reported for duty. As might have been expected, he discharged the multifarious duties of a regimental quartermaster with efficiency. We may leave him for the moment in Camp George H. Thomas on the Chickamauga battle field in northwestern Georgia.[4]

A biographer of long personal acquaintance with Lind states that after his defeat by Clough for the governorship in 1896 he resolved never again to enter the field of politics but to stick to his law practice, which was always his strongest suit. He was in no haste, therefore, to accept the nomination of the combination at St. Paul on June 15 and he might have adhered to his resolution but for an incident which changed the whole situation. The Republicans held their state convention in St. Paul on June 30. They were well aware of the strength of the combined opposition and remembered the slight majority by which they had elected a governor two years before; but with no national ticket in the field they hoped and expected to add another to their long and unbroken series of victories. They put in nomination for the governorship William Henry Eustis of Minneapolis, an aspirant worthy of the honor. He had come to Minnesota in 1881 with a college and law-school education, an attorney's certificate, and some experience at the bar. His tastes and his sense of duty at once threw him into public life and his unusual oratorical ability gave him prominence. He was elected mayor of Minneapolis in 1892 and conducted his administration in such a manner as to win both much praise and some criticism.[5]

Governor Clough had not forgotten the activity of friends of Washburn in cutting down his vote in 1896 and, selecting Eustis — against whom he was "singularly bitter," says Baker, "in a way which was ungenerous" — as a vicarious

---

[4] Baker, *Governors of Minnesota*, 384; Holbrook, *Minnesota in the Spanish-American War*, 16, 32, 34.

[5] Baker, *Governors of Minnesota*, 384, 389; *Pioneer Press*, July 1, 1898, p. 1; Phelps, *Biographical History*, 122, and portrait of Eustis opposite; Hyde and Stoddard, *Great Northwest*, 173–175; Smalley, *Republican Party*, 395.

representative, he resolved " to get even." In Lind's nomination he found an opportunity to effect his purpose. He sent
an emissary to Camp Thomas to let Lind know that if he
should accept the nomination of the Silver Republicans and
their allies he might expect an access of votes from straight
Republicans. The cryptic message, " The business is done,
and we are all well," to a friend of Governor Clough gave
assurance that Lind would run.[6] Lind had not yet irrevo-
cably broken with the Republican party, whose honors he had
worn, but this did not prevent the St. Paul *Pioneer Press* from
denouncing him as a renegade and a soldier of fortune, de-
spising his new associates. In a campaign speech Lind said:
" At that time [*1891*] I wasn't a Populist, and I can't say
that I have since become a Populist. To be frank with you,
my friends, I will say to you that I don't know that I have
any party. Perhaps it might be said of me that I am a political orphan." This furnished his opponents opportunities for
much ingenious sarcasm. The oft-repeated surmise that Lind
had entered the military service with the intention of breaking away from his entanglements and resuming allegiance to
his old party has not been confirmed.[7]

The Twelfth Minnesota returned to the state in the middle
of September and encamped near New Ulm. There was a
month's furlough and a fortnight was taken up with muster-
out rolls and final accounts. The regiment was mustered out
on November 5. Lieutenant and Quartermaster Lind had
little leisure in these days for campaigning, but he gave two
short series of addresses. He did not need to stump the state;
he had never been so popular.[8]

There was little that was novel in the party platforms of
1898 and the campaign was carried on with less than the

   [6] Baker, *Governors of Minnesota*, 385; record of an interview with Judge
John Day Smith, October 4, 1914, in the author's notebooks, 7: 104.
   [7] *Pioneer Press*, 1898: October 11, p. 4; 12, p. 4; *Minneapolis Tribune*,
October 11, 1898, p. 1.
   [8] Holbrook, *Minnesota in the Spanish-American War*, 43–45; Baker, *Governors of Minnesota*, 385.

usual heat and fury. The canvass of the votes brought sur-
prises. The total vote for governor was less by 84,667 than
it had been in the previous election and Lind's vote was less
by 30,274. None the less, the continuous line of Republican
governors from 1860 was broken. Lind was elected by a
majority of 20,184.[9] Republican leaders naturally looked
about for an explanation of the unexpected defeat of their
candidate. Some found it in the errors of certain young Republicans, who knew less about managing campaigns than
they thought they did. Others emphasized the enhancement
of Lind's popularity by his military service and the support
of comrades in arms. Still others, including the defeated
candidate, found the chief ground of Lind's success in the
Scandinavian vote, normally largely Republican. The number of straight Republican votes diverted to Lind out of
resentment at the desertion of Clough in 1896 cannot even be
guessed at, but they were given with joy. Clough could not
refrain from giving expression to his personal satisfaction.
As soon as the result of the canvass was made known he telegraphed to Lind: " Allow me to congratulate you from the
very bottom of my heart. There is still a God in Heaven."
Lind's majority was an exception; the rest of the Republican
state ticket was elected and the legislature of 1899 was over-
whelmingly Republican.[10]

Accustomed to a broad outlook upon social and public
affairs, Governor Lind was ready for the legislature of 1899
with a long catena of matters for the consideration of that
body. Three subjects he discussed at length. Speaking of
taxation, he remarked upon the obvious importance of a just
distribution of the burden and gave some examples wherein,
under the existing system, that maxim of taxation was not

[9] *Legislative Manual*, 1925, p. 113.
[10] *Pioneer Press*, November 10, 1898, pp. 4, 5; *Minneapolis Tribune*, November 10, 1898, pp. 1, 6; *Representative*, November 9, 1898, pp. 1, 2. The
Tribune attributes Lind's triumph wholly to the Swedish vote; the *Pioneer
Press* says that it was due also to a general apathy, to Clough's activity, and
to an ill-managed campaign; the *Representative* gives Clough's opposition and
the Swedish vote as the chief factors.

illustrated. Assessors listed the visible stock, tools, and implements of farmers and artisans but did not discover the money and securities, which constituted eighty per cent of personal property. Loans and credits of banks, brokers, and stockjobbers amounted in the previous year to $383,636 and sewing machines, to nearly double that sum. Corporation stocks and bonds, not including bank stocks, were valued at less than yearling calves. His principal recommendation was the creation of a tax commission to study the whole subject and to devise a remedy for the notorious evils. That legislature did not please to respond to Governor Lind's recommendation. Sixteen amendatory and remedial tax laws were passed, but none of them touched the radical vice of the system.[11]

Another subject which the new executive had much at heart was the treatment and maintenance of the insane, of which there were then about thirty-three hundred in the state. His first suggestion was that the whole cost should not be borne by the state but that counties should be required to contribute. This requirement would, he believed, put a stop to the liberal committals of seniles and cripples not really insane, who should be cared for at the expense of the counties or of the relatives. For the treatment and maintenance of the chronic insane he recommended the adoption of the Wisconsin plan, for many years in successful operation in that state. According to this plan insane persons not kept at home or in private institutions are committed to a state hospital, where they receive the best-known treatment for cure. Those who recover are discharged; those who do not are sent to county asylums for maintenance. The experience of years has shown that about one-half of the patients in county asylums are able to work steadily and are happy in their work. One-half of the remainder can do some work. The remaining one-fourth,

[11] *Executive Documents*, 1898, vol. I, pp. iii-vi; *General Laws*, 1899, index under Taxation. A bill for a tax commission (Senate file 62) passed in the Senate but failed in the House. *Senate Journal*, 1899, pp. 68, 353; *House Journal*, 441, 451, 1163.

seniles and infirm, are made as comfortable as possible. A farm, a garden — in some cases wood lots — a variety of shops, and the housekeeping duties furnish employment which contributes materially to offset the expenses of the institution. Friends who live near can easily visit the patients and, in lucid periods, the patients go to their homes. The small community thus employed is in sharp contrast with the great institutions in which hundreds are herded and wander up and down the corridors in hopeless idleness. The state pays the county $1.50 a week for the support of each patient. The state board of corrections and charities made a careful study of the Wisconsin plan and ardently urged its adoption. Governor Lind preferred it to the " colony system " recommended by the board of trustees of the hospitals for the insane, which gathers the insane in great numbers but houses them in separate though adjacent groups in " cottages," wholly at the expense of the state. The better plan might have been adopted but for the importunity of two cities which had not, they contended, got their shares of state institutions. A bill was passed establishing insane asylums at Anoka and Hastings. The colony plan is only partially carried out and at Anoka only the overflow of the chronically insane from the three state hospitals is received.[12]

A proposition to take the management of the penal, correctional, and charitable institutions of the state from the several separate boards and to place it in the hands of a state board of control was submitted by Governor Lind for the consideration of the legislature, which, however, did not please to take it up. Other matters warmly commended by the governor were, for the most part, ignored — among them his recommendations that free passes on railroad trains be absolutely prohibited, that textbooks for schools be printed free by the

[12] Lind's message, 1899, in *Executive Documents*, 1898, vol. I, pp. xviii–xxiv; *Legislative Manual*, 1923, p. 253; *General Laws*, 1899, pp. 254–257. The author as a member of the state board of corrections and charities, after a study of the Wisconsin system, made a report to Governor Lind, which was quoted in his inaugural address.

state, and that the constitution " be so amended as to enable a minority in the legislature . . . to refer enactments, at least such as extend corporate privileges or authorize the granting of franchises, to a vote of the people before becoming operative." [13]

In his final message to the legislature in 1901 Governor Lind again emphasized the importance of taxation by reminding the legislature that at the existing rate of taxation in the state the amount paid in taxes in forty years equaled the assessed valuation of all the property in the state. If national taxation, which at existing rates doubled the burden, was taken into account, in twenty years all the assessed value of the property was collected by the tax-gatherer. The twentieth century would see ten million people in Minnesota, all to be burdened with taxes. His definite propositions were a moderate income tax in lieu of the personal property tax, an inheritance tax, a franchise tax on domestic corporations, a license tax on foreign corporations, and an increase of the rate on the gross earnings of railroads. Governor Lind recommended the incorporation of labor unions and the compulsory arbitration of labor disputes. He repeated one recommendation, obviously and eminently reasonable, which the legislature of 1899 — and, for that matter, every later one — was not pleased to entertain. Under the Minnesota tax law the county auditor, after making up the tax books for a calendar year, turns them over to the county treasurer, who thereafter issues all statements, collects the taxes, and furnishes all receipts, without check or supervision. Governor Lind proposed simply that the county auditor should be the accounting officer and that no receipt for taxes should be valid without his countersignature. [14]

[13] Lind's message, 1899, in *Executive Documents*, 1898, vol. i, pp. xv, xxiv–xxvii, xxxiii, xxxiv.

[14] Lind, *Message*, 1901, pp. iv-xii, xxii-xxv; *General Statutes*, 1913, p. 439. Governor Lind's last official act was to transmit to the House on January 9, 1901, the report of a committee on a plan for county accounting. *House Journal*, 1901, p. 16.

In the November preceding the close of Governor Lind's term of office the state and the nation were bereaved by the sudden death of Cushman Kellogg Davis, then serving a third term in the United States Senate. He had been reëlected a second time by the legislature of 1899. The sentiment of the Republican party had been so effectively, although informally, expressed at the polls in 1898 as to serve as a mandate for his continuance in office. No party caucus was held and the joint convention of the legislature merely registered the separate votes of the two houses. Having begun his senatorial career in a becomingly modest way, he had won the confidence of his colleagues and had so impressed them with his great legal and historical learning and with his extraordinary power of statement that he had at length been promoted to the most coveted chairmanship of the Senate, that of the committee on foreign relations. He held that position during the Spanish-American War and, at its close, was appointed one of the commissioners on the part of the United States to negotiate the treaty of peace.

Brilliant as Senator Davis' professional and official career was, it is likely that he will be best known in history by a series of extraordinary addresses and orations. Although he was without resonance of voice and commanding personality, he was a consummate rhetorician. His published books will also add to his fame, the principal ones being *The Law in Shakespeare* and *A Treatise on International Law*. One typical example of his wisdom and his courage ought to be on record in every history of his state. In the year 1894 there were numerous railroad strikes. A resolution was introduced into the United States Senate by Senator Kyle of South Dakota to prohibit the issue of civil or criminal process against strikers for obstructing railroad traffic if they did not interfere with the movement of mails. Some committee, presuming to act for a body of strikers in Duluth, asked Senator Davis by telegraph to vote for the resolution. His instant reply was: " I have received your telegram. I will not support the resolution. It is against your real welfare. It is also a blow at the security, peace, and rights of millions who never harmed you or your associates. My duty to the Constitution and the laws forbids me to sustain a resolution to legalize lawlessness. The same duty rests upon you and your associates. . . . You are rapidly approaching the overt act of levying war against the United States, and you will find the definition of that in the Constitution. . . . You might as well ask me to vote to dissolve the Government." [15]

Governor Lind's two-year term of service, 1899–1900, included the closing year of a century and the fiftieth year since Minnesota had become a territory. Alexander Ramsey and Henry M. Rice had lived to see her grow from a wilderness to a rich and populous commonwealth. The estimated value of all property, a mere unrecorded bagatelle in 1850, had swelled to two and a half billion dollars. The population had increased from six thousand in 1850 to a million and three-quarters. Half a million were of foreign birth and nine thousand were Indians. Of the total number of inhabitants, six hundred thousand were urban; the large remainder were rural.[16] There were one hundred and fifty thousand farms comprising twenty-six million acres, a little over one-half of the total acreage of the state. Eighteen million acres were improved land, of which fifteen million were planted in crops. The northeastern two-fifths of the state were still a

[15] *Senate Journal*, 1899, p. 71; *House Journal*, 69–79; *Pioneer Press*, July 3, 1894, p. 1. Davis' letter of thanks for his reëlection is in *House Journal*, 1899, p. 80. See also Baker, *Governors of Minnesota*, 197, 198, 204, 209–213, 219–223. Baker quotes selections from some of Davis' speeches to illustrate his polished style. For Senator Kyle's resolution, see *Congressional Record*, 53 Congress, 2 session, 7041. The telegram to the Duluth committee is on page 207. In the *Minneapolis Times*, November 5, 1899, p. 25, is a sketch of Davis by Helen Eggleston. No collection of Davis' papers and addresses has been available.

[16] United States, Bureau of the Census, *Wealth, Debt, and Taxation*, 36 (*Special Reports* — Washington, 1907); *United States Census*, 1900, *Population*, part 1, pp. 2, 456–458, 482; Robinson, *Agriculture in Minnesota*, 255. The exact figures for the statistics given in the text are as follows: value of all property, $2,513,620,826; total population, 1,751,394; foreign born, 505,318; Indians, 9,182; urban population, 598,100; rural population, 1,153,294.

wilderness, with scattered mining villages and lumber camps. "King Wheat" was still on his throne, though he was soon to lose his crown. More than six million acres were devoted to wheat. The value of farm property was nearly eight hundred million dollars and that of farm produce was more than one hundred and sixty million dollars.[17] A phenomenal development in the joint fields of agriculture and industry was the recent and rapid extension of dairying, due to the planting of alfalfa and the increased use of the silo and to the introduction of the cream separator, of the Babcock test for butter fat, and of improved refrigeration.[18]

The development of manufactures in Minnesota's first half century may be readily understood from the following table:[19]

	ALL INDUSTRIES	FLOUR	LUMBERING
Establishments	11,114	512	438
Capital	$165,832,246	$24,125,781	$52,095,923
Proprietors	12,253	630	543
Salaried officials and clerks	7,319	606	594
Salaries	$6,554,424	$730,667	$751,057
Wage-earners	77,234	4,086	15,140
Wages	$35,484,825	$2,383,836	$7,140,571
Miscellaneous expenses	$13,273,648	$1,300,270	$1,782,489
Cost of materials	$173,425,615	$74,509,733	$26,047,781
Value of products	$262,655,881	$83,877,709	$43,585,161

[17] United States Census, 1900, Agriculture, part 1, pp. 142, 143, 150; part 2, pp. 62, 91; Robinson, Agriculture in Minnesota, 142, 167, 168, 171. The following are the exact figures: number of farms, 154,659; acres in farms, 26,248,498; total acreage of the state, 51,749,120; acres in improved land, 18,442,585; acres in crops, 15,139,962; acres in wheat, 6,560,707; value of farm property, $788,684,642; value of farm produce, $161,217,304.

[18] Robinson, Agriculture in Minnesota, 138, 141. A map showing the distribution of creameries and cheese factories in 1901 is on page 156 of the same work. The following table, derived from pages 166 and 171 of Robinson's book, shows the development of dairying in Minnesota in twenty years:

YEAR	BUTTER POUNDS MADE			CHEESE POUNDS MADE		
	On farms	In factories	Total	On farms	In factories	Total
1880	19,161,385	83,450	19,244,835	523,138	462,191	985,329
1890	34,766,409	13,911,095	48,677,504	676,642	3,615,528	4,292,170
1900	41,188,846	41,174,469	82,363,315	290,623	3,285,019	3,575,642

[19] United States Census, 1900, Manufactures, part 2, pp. 450–453.

The reader may be interested to observe that two industries, flour and lumbering, had 9 per cent of the establishments in all industries, 10 per cent of the proprietors, and 46 per cent of the capital invested; paid 26 per cent of all wages and salaries; employed 24 per cent of the workmen and other employees; bore 23 per cent of the expenses; and turned out products valued at 48 per cent of the value of all products.

A mark of the advanced position reached by Minnesota at the end of her first half century, both a cause and a consequence of her progress, was the evolution of a metropolitan center of trade, industry, and finance. The "Twin Cities," St. Paul and Minneapolis, with diverse but complementary interests, had become such a center for a great area stretching toward the Rocky Mountains. A glance at any map of the time showing the numerous lines of railroads radiating from these cities is proof enough that here was a great marketing place for the products of field and forest and a point of distribution for merchandise and manufactures. A secondary center at Duluth, with radiating railroads — one of them to the Atlantic — and water communication to the seaboard except in winter weather, contributed to the importance of the greater center. The Twin City banks and trust companies had grown to proportions which enabled them to finance great operations. Minnesota had ceased to be dependent upon Chicago and St. Louis for banking facilities.[20]

A standard by which to estimate Minnesota's advancement in civilization and her rank among states better than that of material aggrandizement may be looked for in the educational and religious institutions of the period under consideration. The statistics of her schools, displayed at great length in the report of the twelfth United States census and in that

---

[20] Norman S. B. Gras, *An Introduction to Economic History*, 299–314 (New York and London, 1922). The evolution of a great metropolitan center, composed of St. Paul and Minneapolis regarded as a unit, has been fully and very ably set out by Mildred L. Hartsough, in her *The Twin Cities as a Metropolitan Market; a Regional Study of the Economic Development of Minneapolis and St. Paul* (University of Minnesota, *Studies in the Social Sciences*, no. 18 — Minneapolis, 1925).

of the state superintendent of public instruction, John H. Lewis, for the years ending July 31, 1899 and 1900, give the impression that a great educational business was going on. Of the six hundred thousand persons of school age, from five to twenty years, in 1900, more than one-half attended schools. If the reader will allow his imagination to play around these footings he may appreciate the effects of the continuous operation of such an enormous apparatus of instruction. There were thirteen thousand teachers, eleven thousand of them women. In spite of a certain amount of waste effort and some poor teaching, illiterates had become a trifling fraction of the population. Only fifty thousand persons over ten years of age out of over a million were found by the census enumerators to be illiterate and eighty per cent of that number were foreign born. The attendance at high schools had very greatly increased and at the University of Minnesota it had trebled in the closing decade.[21]

There were numbered in Minnesota by the enumerators of the census bureau in 1906 over eight hundred thousand communicants of religious bodies, all Christian except an inconsiderable fraction. To the number of communicants must be added a great mass of youth who were members of churches by baptism but not yet communicants. Another increment must be allowed for many adults who were believers in Christianity but had delayed professing their belief and becoming church members. When these additions are made, there is left but a very small remainder of the total population to be regarded, perhaps doubtfully, as non-Christian. The people

21 *United States Census*, 1900, *Population*, part 2, pp. lxvii, 351, 413, 508, 521; Minnesota, Superintendent of Public Instruction, *Reports*, 1889–90, pp. 4, 50; 1899–1900, pp. 3, 4, 37, 63, 214, 280, 281. The exact figures are as follows: persons of school age, 612,990; number attending schools, 357,809; teachers, 13,381; women teachers, 10,834; persons over ten years of age, 1,305,657; illiterate persons over ten years of age, 52,946. The state superintendent in his report gives figures relating to public schools considerably variant from those of the census, but not necessarily discordant. The number enrolled in the public schools during the year is given as 399,207. There were 7,303 public school houses and 7,878 teachers in rural schools. The invested school fund was $12,546,599.30.

of Minnesota were Christians, the state protecting impartially all their separate bodies and favoring none. There were over four thousand church edifices, with seating facilities for more than a million people. The value of church property, including parsonages, was thirty million dollars.[22] Here again statistics serve only as a basis upon which the imagination may form some conception of the beneficence of Christianity in Minnesota. Its atmosphere was breathed by every soul and in its Divine Founder was seen a perfect model for human conduct. Above and beyond all its blessings soars the hope that in time a very large proportion of the people who have dwelt in Minnesota will have found an eternal rest in the heavenly Jerusalem promised to believers.

[22] United States, Bureau of the Census, *Religious Bodies: 1906*, part I, pp. 216, 217, 327, 328 (*Special Reports* — Washington, 1910). There were 834,442 communicants of religious bodies and 4,280 church edifices with seating capacities of 1,104,317. The value of church property was $30,097,589. The communicants of all Protestant bodies numbered 450,434; those of the Roman Catholic church, 378,288. If to the latter number be added the estimated number of noncommunicant members, the total would be about 445,000. If a similar addition be made to the Protestant bodies, the total would be perhaps 554,000.

XIII. VAN SANT AND HIS TIMES, 1901–05

THAT a second term had been accorded to so many of his predecessors naturally moved Governor Lind to aspire to a reëlection in the year 1900. The Democratic convention willingly put him in nomination, since he was by this time thoroughly identified with that great party. From the Republican camp came into the lists Samuel Rinnah Van Sant of Winona. He had enlisted in an Illinois cavalry regiment for the Civil War before the age of eighteen. After the war he completed a business course and later he entered college, but he left before he had finished his studies to embark in a boat yard and river transportation business, with headquarters in Le Claire, Iowa. In 1883 he moved to Winona, where he continued his river transportation business. He sat for his county in the legislatures of 1893 and 1895. He aspired to the governorship in 1898 and in the Republican convention he received a large number of votes. The good nature with which he accepted defeat and the generosity with which he threw his effective speaking powers into the campaign in support of his successful rival, William Henry Eustis, won him so many additional friends that, when the convention of 1900 assembled, the nomination was his by a unanimous vote.[1]

It was a presidential year in politics and national issues naturally overshadowed those of states. The great parties were still divided upon the silver and the tariff questions, but the real issue was whether the country should or should not approve and ratify the conduct of the war with Spain by a Republican administration, its war upon the Filipinos,

[1] *Saint Paul Pioneer Press*, 1898: July 1, p. 5; 1900: June 29, p. 2; September 7, p. 1; Baker, *Governors of Minnesota*, 399–402, 407; Upham and Dunlap, *Minnesota Biographies*, 807, and citations. Governor Van Sant is at present (1925) living in Minneapolis, engaged in business and enjoying universal esteem.

and its establishment of a military government over them. The People's party put into its platform the now customary "demands" and agreed with the Democrats upon a fusion state ticket. Four other minor parties, the Prohibitionists, the "Middle-of-the-Road" Populists, the Social Democrats, and the Socialist Laborites issued variant and multifarious manifestoes and made nominations for state offices. Their aggregate vote for governor was slightly more than three per cent of the total vote.[2]

In Minnesota the Republican triumph was complete. McKinley's majority over Bryan and three minor candidates was nearly 65,000; but Lind's popularity and his following of admiring Scandinavians enabled him to reduce Van Sant's plurality to 2,254. That such considerations as those mentioned contributed largely to Governor Lind's political triumphs after his change of politics is supported by the fact that when, two years later, in 1902, another ran against Van Sant the latter was reëlected by a plurality of over 56,000. It was the surmise of some that Van Sant's slender predominance in the election of 1900 was won by the zealous support given him by members of the Grand Army of the Republic, in which society he had been a conspicuous figure.[3]

In his inaugural address to the legislature of 1901 Governor Van Sant showed the same warm interest in tax reform that his predecessor had displayed and earnestly exhorted that body to action. In particular he, too, advised the creation of a special commission to study the whole subject and to report its conclusions. The matter was at once taken up and chapter 13 of the laws of the session provided for the creation of such

---

[2] *Minneapolis Tribune*, 1900: September 6, p. 6; 7, pp. 1, 9, 11; *Legislative Manual*, 1901, p. 532. See McKee, *National Conventions and Platforms*, 330–370, for the 1900 platforms of the Democratic, Republican, People's, Middle-of-the-Road People's, Silver Republican (which indorsed Bryan), Prohibition, and Socialist-Labor parties. The Minnesota state platforms conformed closely to the national platforms.

[3] *Legislative Manual*, 1925, pp. 113, 115. In 1902 Lind was elected representative in Congress. At the close of his term he withdrew from active politics. Baker, *Governors of Minnesota*, 392.

a commission to be named by the governor, the attorney-general, and the state auditor. It was made the duty of the commission to frame a complete system for taxing all kinds of property and to report in the form of a bill duly indexed. The commission was also authorized to submit a draft of any amendments to the state constitution that might be deemed desirable. The legislature adjourned on April 12, thus shortening the session thirteen days, to save time and money for an extra session to be called by the governor in the following February, to consider the report of the commission.[4]

When the houses reassembled on February 4, 1902, the tax commission, in obedience to the law which created it, had ready for their consideration a complete code of taxation, with an index which must have been satisfactory. The commission informed the legislature that the bill was " designed to effectuate constitutional purposes rather than to express the views of the commission." No substantial reform measures were proposed in the matter of subjects to be taxed for the reason that the tax sections of the state constitution as they then stood were " an insuperable obstacle to proper legislation." So long as all property, except that specifically exempted, was taxed at a cash valuation and a uniform rate, the legislature had no power to select subjects for taxation or to vary the rates. Of the 308 sections of the code submitted by the commission, the legislature adopted without change, or with but slight changes, 108, many of which related to delinquent taxes, which were to be collected in a drastic and summary manner.[5]

The commission submitted also a draft of an amendment to article 9 of the state constitution, the effect of which, if

4 Van Sant, *Message*, 1901, pp. 6–8; *House Journal*, 1901, pp. 37, 284, 412, 510, 622, 638; *Senate Journal*, 157, 253; *General Laws*, 14. Gideon S. Ives, William J. Hahn, and Henry W. Childs composed the commission.

5 *Report of the Tax Commission Created by Chapter 13, General Laws, 1901, for the Purpose of Framing a Tax Code*, 10, 59, 61, 64–181 (St. Paul, 1902); *General Laws*, 1902, extra session, 1–51; Anderson, *History of the Constitution*, 237. In his message to the legislature in special session, Van Sant earnestly urged the legislature to adopt the code submitted by the commission.

ratified, would have been to put an end to the old policy of taxing all property not specifically exempted at a cash valuation and uniform rate. The capital propositions were two: that the power of taxation should never be surrendered or suspended, and that taxes should be " uniform upon the same class of subjects." The legislature was not pleased to adopt the simple draft of the commission, but enlarged upon it by adding provisions for particular tax subjects, which would better have been left to the legislature. The overloaded amendment was submitted to the electors at the general election on November 4, 1902. As it was rejected, there is no occasion to say more about it than that it left the property tax about as it was and added provisions for franchise, transfer, registry, and income taxes. There was a large majority of votes in favor of ratification, but not the necessary majority of all the votes cast at the election, as required by the amendment of 1897 to article 14 of the constitution. The defeat of the measure was no misfortune.[6] Governor Van Sant in his annual message to the legislature of 1903 remarked upon the failure of the electors to ratify the proposed amendment and recommended that it be resubmitted at the next election. That legislature, however, was not disposed to follow the governor's recommendation. A " wide-open " amendment, as it was called, in brief and simple terms — essentially the same as that drafted by the tax commission of 1901 — was submitted to the electors on November 6, 1906, and was ratified. The legislatures were thereafter at liberty to establish various classes of subjects for taxation and to exact varying rates upon the different classes.[7]

[6] Report of the Tax Commission, 182; House Journal, 1902, extra session, 285–288; Senate Journal, 274–278; General Laws, iii–v; Anderson, History of the Constitution, 189, 282; Pioneer Press, 1902: November 4, p. 6; 6, p. 6. The whole number of votes cast at the election was 276,071; the number for the amendment was 124,584.

[7] Van Sant's message of January 7, 1903, in Executive Documents, 1902, vol. 1, p. 25; Pioneer Press, November 6, 1906, p. 8; Anderson, History of the Constitution, 189, 240.

In his special message to the legislature of 1902 Governor Van Sant informed the houses that under his direction the attorney-general had made application to file a bill of complaint in the United States Supreme Court against the Northern Securities Company of New Jersey, to prevent the consolidation by that company of the properties of the Great Northern and Northern Pacific railroad companies in violation of the Minnesota statute forbidding the consolidation of parallel or competing railroads within the state. The Supreme Court denied the motion for leave to file the bill, on the ground that without the presence of the two railroad companies the court could not proceed as a court of equity and, if the companies were made parties defendant, the constitutional jurisdiction of the court would not extend to the case. Suit was then brought by the state in the Ramsey County district court, from which, on the joint petition of the defendants, it was removed to the United States circuit court and tried before Judge William Lochren in June, 1903. His decision was that the Northern Securities Company was not a railroad company and was not violating the law. The state appealed the suit to the United States Supreme Court, which on April 11, 1904, remanded it to the state court on the ground that no federal question was involved and that the parties had no right to transfer the case from a state to a federal court by mere consent.[8] This case thus ended. In a separate suit brought by the attorney-general of the United States and taken to the United States Supreme Court it was held that the Northern Securities Company was acting or was threatening to act in violation of the Sherman Antitrust Act of July 2, 1890, and a dissolution was decreed.[9]

---

[8] Van Sant, *Message*, 1902, pp. 9–11; report of the attorney-general, in *Executive Documents*, 1902, vol. 1, pp. 467–469; 123 *Federal Reporter*, 692–707; Minnesota *v.* Northern Securities Company, 184 *United States*, 199–247; 194 *United States*, 48–73. The best account of the case is Balthasar H. Meyer, *A History of the Northern Securities Case* (University of Wisconsin, *Bulletins*, no. 142 — Madison, 1906).

[9] *Pioneer Press*, March 15, 1904, p. 1; 193 *United States*, 197–411.

CAN HE STOP THEM?

[From the *Pioneer Press* (St. Paul), November 20, 1901.]

In his inaugural address Governor Van Sant urged the legislature of 1901 to entertain an administrative measure which had been agitated for some time. It had been the policy of the state from the beginning to commit the management of her institutions for education and for the care of the defective, dependent, and delinquent classes to unpaid boards of trustees under various names, which were appointed by the governor with senatorial consent. The number of these institutions, as well as the number of their inmates, had increased in some proportion with the increase of inhabitants, with ever-mounting demands for appropriations for support and enlargements. Without doubt they had all been generally well managed, especially the penal and charitable institutions under the supervision of the state board of corrections and charities established in Governor Hubbard's time. Legislatures tired of the perpetual appeals from so many boards and suggestions were frequent that there were too many of them. Other complaints were voiced. The institutions had been located in or near the older cities, which had brought their influences to bear upon legislatures. In some cases locations had been secured by combinations of places, on the ground that they were severally entitled to have an institution. One criticism was that managements were expected to give and did give undue advantages to the places in which their institutions were located in employment and in the purchase of supplies. Another was that, according to a custom which had quietly grown up, the local treasurer could draw money from the state treasury in advance of needs and could accommodate a local bank with a deposit. The " resident member " of a board, by address and industry, became in some cases the " boss " of the institution; in some instances, to the author's knowledge, he was an exceptionally honorable and conscientious public servant, pleased to serve the state without money compensation. Reappointments had become too frequent during a time when one political party had control in the state. There was, however, so little to

complain of, while the state was getting a vast amount of
service without cost to the taxpayer, that a change in policy
might have been put off indefinitely had it not been for
developments in neighboring states. Both Wisconsin and
Iowa had established a single salaried board composed of a
few members to take the place of their numerous institution
boards.

The reports of the operation of the new plan in Wisconsin
and Iowa were so favorable, especially in point of economy,
that Governor Van Sant, who had evidently fully informed
himself on the subject, commended a similar change to the
legislature of 1901. A bill was promptly introduced under
the title, " A bill for an act to create a state board of control
and provide for the management and control of the charitable
reformatory and penal institutions of the state .. . . and to
abolish the State Board of Corrections and Charities." The
bill passed the House and went to the Senate. The principle
of the bill was so satisfactory to the latter body that it was
amended so as to bring the financial management of the state
university, the state normal schools, and the state soldiers'
home under the one board of control. There was lively but
futile opposition to the amendment. The House concurred
and the governor approved the bill. Governor Van Sant,
however, was not pleased with the merger of the university
and the normal schools and in his message to the legislature
of 1903 he strongly urged the restoration of their independence. It was not, he said, originally intended that they
should be classed with the penal and charitable institutions.
The legislature of 1903 thought best to let the experiment go
on, but that of 1905 relieved the board of control of most
of its financial duties in connection with those institutions,
greatly to its satisfaction. An experience of more than twenty
years has justified the creation of the single salaried board of
control of the charitable, reformatory, and penal institutions.
An objection, which was early raised, that the small board,
busied with multifarious details of business, would neglect

humanitarian offices to inmates was met by the establishment in 1907 of a board of visitors to study the care and management of the institutions and to conduct investigations whenever they should be called for by the governor.[10]

The legislature of 1901 was moved by a wave of sentiment to make an experiment toward establishing and virtually guaranteeing land titles by public registration. Such a system had for some years been in operation in South Australia, where it had been given the popular name " Torrens system," after Sir Robert Richard Torrens, who had been its chief advocate. In that country an estate could be sold in an hour, at trifling expense, as easily as a personal chattel. An administrative officer, called a recorder, had power to decide upon the sufficiency of a chain of title and to determine in case of dispute. Advocates for the introduction of the system in Minnesota did not remember that her bill of rights made it impossible for any person to be deprived of his property without due process of law. No administrative officer could be invested with power to pass upon a land title. The statute of 1901 was therefore framed to legalize title by registration, but only after a tedious judicial process, in which an " examiner of titles " figures only as an officer of the court. The original act was restricted to counties having seventy-five thousand inhabitants or more; but its operation was so satisfactory that in 1909 it was extended to all the counties. Title by registration has been found convenient for certain classes of persons and certain kinds of lands, but it has not yet come into general operation.[11]

[10] Report of the state auditor, in *Executive Documents*, 1898, vol. I, p. 137; Lind's message, 1899, in *Executive Documents*, 1898, vol. I, pp. xxiv–xxvi; Hubbard's message, January 7, 1885, in *Executive Documents*, 1884, vol. I, p. 24; Van Sant, *Message*, 1901, pp. 8–11; Van Sant's message, January 7, 1903, in *Executive Documents*, 1902, vol. I, pp. 8, 11; *House Journal*, 1901, pp. 57, 499, 704–709, 817; *Senate Journal*, 523, 525, 526, 550–552, 563, 577, 599–604, 631, 693, 700; *General Laws*, 128–147; 1905, pp. 148–152; 1907, p. 626.

[11] Arnold G. Cameron, *The Torrens System: Its Simplicity, Serviceability, and Success*, 1–9, 13–18 (Boston, 1915); *General Laws*, 1901, pp. 348–378; 1909, p. 205; Constitution, article I, section 7.

It fell to the same legislature, that of 1901, to elect two senators in Congress. As already related, on January 22, 1901, Knute Nelson was chosen for a second term. Opposition in Republican ranks was so slight that no caucus was held and no voting in joint convention was needed.[12] On the same day took place the election of Moses E. Clapp to the vacancy occasioned by the death of Cushman K. Davis on November 27, 1900. There were numerous aspirants for the position and on the first ballot in the Republican caucus on January 18 six were voted for, Robert G. Evans leading Clapp by nine votes. After fourteen ballots without result, the caucus adjourned to reassemble the following afternoon, when, on a second ballot, Clapp received seventy votes, just one-half of those present; Speaker Michael J. Dowling, who presided at the caucus, added his vote and gave Clapp the nomination. There were the usual hints and insinuations of the use of money and bargaining to accomplish the result, no proper evidence of which has been found. On January 22 the houses, voting separately, elected Clapp over Charles A. Towne, a Silver Republican whom Governor Lind had appointed to the Davis vacancy ad interim. The election was duly announced in joint convention on the following day. Clapp had come from Wisconsin in 1881 at the age of thirty and had settled in Fergus Falls. His forensic ability, especially in criminal cases, soon gave him prominence and his party services warranted his aspiration to a state office. In 1886 he was elected attorney-general of Minnesota. Two reëlections continued him in the office for six years ending with 1892.[13]

[12] House Journal, 1901, pp. 82, 89; Senate Journal, 75, 85. In the House the vote was 94 for Knute Nelson and 22 for Rensselaer R. Nelson; in the Senate Knute Nelson received 42 votes and R. R. Nelson, 18. Judge Rensselaer R. Nelson had been 38 years on the bench of the United States district court for Minnesota. See Upham and Dunlap, Minnesota Biographies, 543. See also ante, p. 205.

[13] Pioneer Press, 1901: January 19, p. 2; 20, p. 1; House Journal, 1901, pp. 83, 89; Senate Journal, 76, 85; Smalley, Republican Party, 408; Illustrated Album of Biography of the Famous Valley of the Red River of the North and the Park Regions, 784 (Chicago, 1889).

Soon after the opening of the last year of his fractional term Senator Clapp was announced as an aspirant for reëlection, in accordance with a custom somewhat irregularly maintained by the Republican party in Minnesota. The Honorable John B. Gilfillan, who had served nine years in the state Senate and a term in the national House of Representatives, was disposed to have another exception to the rule and on June 28, 1904, he gave public notice of his candidacy. No one knowing him as did the author for more than fifty years could question his eminent qualifications for the position. From the tenor of the leading newspapers it appears that it was generally understood that the choice would lie between Clapp and Gilfillan; but late in December Governor Van Sant gave out that he was in the ring and that it would be a " fight to a finish." The Republican caucus was held on the evening of January 3, 1905. Governor Van Sant's name did not appear in the balloting and Gilfillan received but one vote. Clapp easily won the nomination and his election followed as à matter of course. To the end of his long life Gilfillan believed that, had he been willing to " open his barrel," he could have had the nomination and the election. Senator Clapp's behavior and activities throughout his second term were so satisfactory to the Republicans of Minnesota that a third term was conceded him in 1911. For a long period he held the chairmanship of the Senate committee on Indian affairs and he became expert and influential in Indian concerns, especially in those of the Chippewa of Minnesota. After retiring from his senatorship Clapp took up a residence in another state, but he is not forgotten in Minnesota.[14]

On January 1, 1901, eight days before Governor Van Sant took office, occurred the death of Ignatius Donnelly, who for

[14] Upham and Dunlap, *Minnesota Biographies*, 257; *Minneapolis Times*, June 28, 1904, p. 5; January 4, 1905, p. 1; *Minneapolis Tribune*, 1904: August 24, p. 4; December 24, p. 1; *Pioneer Press*, 1904: November 28, p. 4; 1905: January 4, p. 1; 19, p. 3; *Senate Journal*, 1905, p. 77; 1911, p. 71; *House Journal*, 1905, pp. 78, 87; 1911, pp. 91-93, 105-107; interviews with John B. Gilfillan, recorded in the author's notebooks, 3: 10; 6: 110; 9: 97.

the whole period of Minnesota's existence as a state had been her most conspicuous, if not her most influential, figure. The author has not allowed himself to indulge in minute character sketches of the public men whose activities have been interwoven with Minnesota history. He has preferred to bring them on his stage and let them play their parts and make their exits, leaving the reader to form his own opinion of their characters and their merits or demerits. The historian cannot be blamed for the frequent appearances of Donnelly for near half a century, often in the center of the stage. Exeat the gifted, eloquent, dramatic, versatile, eccentric Donnelly. The newspapers of the following day abounded in biographic and obituary articles.[15]

In the same year, 1901, on the eighteenth of October, the death summons came to John Sargent Pillsbury. After his retirement from the governorship in 1881, at the end of his third term, he did not again take office, but devoted himself to private concerns of great magnitude. He found abundant leisure, however, to continue his service, begun in 1863, as a regent of the state university. The legislature of 1895, in recognition of his devotion to that institution, by a special act made him an honorary member of the board " for and during his good pleasure." He was president of the board from the time of General Sibley's death in 1891 to the end of his own life; and during the whole period, from 1868, when the board was reorganized, to 1901, he held also the chairmanship of the executive committee, an office more important and much more onerous than the presidency of the board. In all those years, from month to month, Governor Pillsbury, with his colleagues, examined all accounts, scrutinized every pay roll, and kept an eye open for possible

---

[15] *Pioneer Press, Minneapolis Tribune,* January 2, 1901. See in particular the *Minneapolis Journal* of the same date. The legislature of 1901 took no notice of the departure of the most conspicuous character of his day. An account of the funeral, conducted by the Reverend Ambrose McNulty of St. Luke's Catholic Church, is in the *Pioneer Press,* January 6, 1901, p. 7. The service was simple, with no addresses; the attendance was large.

overdrafts upon appropriations — a thing he would not tolerate. He was generally, if not always, a member or chairman of building committees. His statue in bronze, of heroic proportions, by Daniel Chester French, stands opposite the façade of the older Library Building as a perpetual memorial of his services to the University of Minnesota. Although in his later life he was less active than in earlier years, Governor Pillsbury never lost interest in the affairs of country, state, city, and neighborhood and of the church to which he was attached. Of the amount of his contributions, personal and through his wife, to a multitude of worthy objects there is but meager earthly record. His gift of some one hundred and fifty thousand dollars toward the completion of the hall of natural sciences at the university, later named for him, was welcomed not only for its generosity but also for its timeliness. To his fortunate biographer we may leave the agreeable task of telling the story of the life of John Sargent Pillsbury.[16]

On April 22, 1903, Alexander Ramsey, first territorial governor and second governor of the state, died at the age of eighty-eight. After his service as cabinet officer had ended at the close of the Hayes administration, he had lived quietly at his home in St. Paul, much of his time being given to the affairs of the Minnesota Historical Society, which he had helped to organize in 1849, and to the improvement of Oakland Cemetery, where he had laid a beloved wife and where, beside her body, his now rests. Posterity will probably forget most of the services he rendered to his generation, but it should not be allowed to forget his successful efforts to pre-

<hr>

[16] *General Laws,* 1895, p. 136; Johnson, *University of Minnesota,* 62, 181, 396–399. An eloquent appreciation of Pillsbury by President Cyrus Northrop is on pages 397–399 of the latter work. Extended biographical sketches of Pillsbury are in the *Minneapolis Journal,* the *Minneapolis Tribune,* and the *Pioneer Press,* October 18, 1901. The statue on the university campus was unveiled on September 12, 1900. The principal address was delivered by Senator Cushman K. Davis. *The Unveiling of the Statue of John S. Pillsbury on the Campus of the University of Minnesota* (n.p., n.d.); *Minneapolis Tribune,* September 13, 1900.

vent the squandering of the school lands of Minnesota by shortsighted legislatures.[17]   At a special meeting of the Minnesota Historical Society held in the Senate chamber of the state Capitol on September 3, 1903, General James H. Baker delivered a memorial address, in which, after an appreciative biographical sketch, he gave it as his matured opinion that " In all that pertained to the well-being of the state, his [*Ramsey's*] actions have stood the test of time; and no other man, on questions of public policy, ever committed so few errors of judgment." At the monthly meeting of the society's executive council held on September 14, 1903, memorial addresses were delivered by ex-Governors Hubbard and McGill, Governor Van Sant, Archbishop Ireland, and Judge Greenleaf Clark.[18]

That Ramsey's statue and that of his great contemporary and friend, Henry H. Sibley, who in his day also rescued the school fund, have not been placed in the gallery of statesmen in the national Capitol is no credit to Minnesota.   The legislature of 1905, however, must have credit for well-meant, though abortive, action in passing by unanimous votes a bill looking toward the erection of a statue of Ramsey in Washington.   It created a commission of three eminent citizens for the purpose but gave them no money and nothing to do but to obtain designs and estimates for scrutiny at the next session.   No report on the matter has been found; the journals of 1907 are silent.   Another bill introduced in 1917 for the same purpose made no progress.[19]

[17] Baker, *Governors of Minnesota*, 16, 30, 35; *Pioneer Press*, April 23, 1903, p. 1; *Minneapols Tribune*, April 23, 1903, p. 1. For Ramsey's part in the rescue of the school lands, see *ante*, 2: 68.

[18] *Minnesota Historical Collections*, vol. 10, part 2, pp. 723–743, 745–766.

[19] *General Laws*, 1905, p. 383; *Senate Journal*, 441, 1181; *House Journal*, 1256, 1474. The Senate passed a bill with an appropriation for the statue; the House amended it by cutting out the appropriation and the Senate concurred. The commission named in the act consisted of James T. McCleary, James J. Hill, and Thomas B. Walker. The legislature of 1925 passed an act, drafted by the author, which provided for the appointment by the governor of a commission of three citizens to obtain designs for and estimates of the cost of a statue to be presented to Congress for the National Statuary Hall and a monument to Sibley to be erected on Pilot Knob near Mendota. *Hous●*

It was the fortune of Governor Van Sant to be the first to take possession of the executive rooms of the new state Capitol, which he did the last week in December, a few days before the end of his service on January 4, 1905. Ten years had passed since the capitol commission had, on October 30, 1895, accepted the designs of Cass Gilbert of St. Paul in preference to the forty others submitted in impersonal competition. The corner stone was laid on July 27, 1898, by Alexander Ramsey, after a noble oration by Senator Cushman K. Davis.[20] The ground plan preserved the traditional scheme of a main central part with wings, but varied from it by the addition of a third wing or extension in rear of the center to accommodate the large hall needed for the House of Representatives. The uppermost floors of the lateral wings were thus left for the Senate and the supreme court. The architectural style chosen was Italian Renaissance, with sufficient, but not superfluous, decorative elements. The building is 433 feet in length and 228 feet in width and the dome is 220 feet high. The exterior basement walls and the outside steps and platforms of the ground story are of granite from the quarries of St. Cloud. All other exterior walls, including the wall of the dome, are of Georgia marble, wisely chosen for durability and for color suitable to the style of architecture. The main façade, which fronts southward, is surmounted by six emblematic statues of heroic size and a " quadriga " in gilded copper, designed by the eminent American sculptor, Daniel Chester French. This chaste and noble building, the chief ornament of its kind in the state, is a worthy monument to the Minnesota architect, who by this and later works won a national reputation.

It was doubtless the impression which the exterior architecture made upon members of the legislatures of 1901 and

Journal, 1917, p. 553; Walker to the author, August 15, 1924, with an indorsement by Dr. Warren Upham; Upham to the author, August 28, 29, 1924, Folwell Papers; *Laws,* 1925, p. 59. See *ante,* p. 214.

[20] *Pioneer Press,* October 31, 1895, pp. 1, 2; July 28, 1898, pp. 1, 3; December 28, 1904, p. 2.

1903 that induced them to increase the original appropriation of $2,000,000 made in 1893 for the main construction,
first by $1,000,000 and, later, by $1,500,000, for the completion of the interior and the decoration and furnishing.
Here it can be recorded that there was not the faintest suggestion or suspicion of graft in this enterprise. The central
rotunda, surmounted by the dome, and the staircases leading
on the right to the supreme court room and on the left to the
Senate chamber are the principal features of the interior. A
large part of the interior wall facings are of magnesian limestone from Kasota and Mankato, selected by the architect for
its exquisite color and susceptibility of polish. Foreign
marbles are used extensively in appropriate places. That
Cass Gilbert was able to persuade a body of commissioners,
answerable to the democracy, to expend liberally upon mural
paintings on the interior of the dome, in the Senate chamber,
in the supreme court room, and elsewhere is not easily
explained, but a pattern has been set which is likely to be
followed in the capitols of our newer states. The paintings
by John la Farge in the supreme court room are perhaps
the first in merit. Whether it was in good taste to decorate
the governor's reception room with paintings representing
glorious moments in the behavior of Minnesota regiments in
the civil war which forced misguided sister states to resume
their allegiance to the Union, a thing which, as they have long
since learned, was a blessing, may be questioned. It was a
principle of the Romans never to celebrate triumphs after a
civil war.[21]

The site of the Capitol is admirable for elevation, but it is
a matter of regret that its area is, and must remain, much too

[21] William B. Dean, " A History of the Capitol Buildings of Minnesota, with
Some Account of the Struggles for Their Location," in *Minnesota Historical
Collections*, 12: 31–33, 35, 41. Dean's article, although unaccompanied by cita-
tions of sources, may be accepted as being as accurate as it is exhaustive. See
also Minnesota, Board of State Capitol Commissioners, *Reports*, 1897, p. 19;
1899, pp. 4, 6, 13; 1901, pp. 4, 5, 13; 1903, pp. 3, 16; and Julie C. Gauthier,
The Minnesota Capitol, Official Guide and History, 10–50 (St. Paul, 1907).
The latter work is profusely and beautifully illustrated.

limited for so noble a structure. Local influences prevailed over an effort to accept a tract offered free by citizens of Merriam Park, still within the limits of St. Paul. The old Capitol, situated on the block given to the state in 1851 by Charles Bazille, still stands and is kept in repair for the overflow of various administrative offices.[22]

[22] Dean, in *Minnesota Historical Collections*, 12:7, 17–22. The building of the present Capitol put a quietus on the question of capital location. On this question, see *ante*, pp. 8–10; 1:382–387.

XIV. JOHNSON AND HIS TIMES, 1905-09

THE accession of John Albert Johnson to the governorship of Minnesota in 1905 was due chiefly to a dissidence in the ranks of the Republican party which diverted many votes from its nominee. Governor Van Sant would have been pleased to hold the office for a third term in order to prosecute his attack upon the merger of the Great Northern and Northern Pacific railroad companies; but there were others who were of the opinion that they could render that service well enough and, according to party custom, they had a right to seek the opportunity. The most prominent of the principal aspirants for the Republican nomination was Loren Warren Collins, who had been an associate judge of the state supreme court since 1887 and had been on the district bench for the four preceding years. He had been a representative in the state legislature in 1881 and one of the House managers in the impeachment of Judge E. St. Julien Cox. Having been a line officer during the Civil War in the Seventh Minnesota Infantry and, later, a conspicuous member and commander of the Grand Army of the Republic for the department of Minnesota and having already been twice named for the governorship in state conventions, he had reason to look for a nomination without serious opposition, and early in 1904 he resigned his seat on the supreme bench. But his comfortable expectation was not to be realized.[1]

Mention has been made of Robert C. Dunn as originating in the legislature of 1893 an inquiry which resulted in the

[1] Holmes, in *Minnesota in Three Centuries*, 4: 283; *Pioneer Press* (St. Paul), November 6, 1903, p. 6. In the *Minneapolis Tribune*, June 17, 1904, p. 1, is an amusing cartoon representing Van Sant and Collins as aspirants for the Republican nomination. In the *Tribune*, June 19, 1904, p. 5, Van Sant disclaims aspirations to a third term and comes out for Collins. For sketches of Collins, see Upham and Dunlap, *Minnesota Biographies*, 134 and citations; *Minnesota Historical Collections*, 15: 757-762; and Hall, *Observations*, 319.

creation of the Pine Land Investigating Committee of that
year. The zeal thus displayed for the preservation of the
school and university pine lands from devastation by alleged
coöperating, not to say conspiring, lumbermen brought him
the election to the state auditorship in 1894. By that election and succeeding reëlections he held the office until the
close of 1902.[2] This position, through correspondence and
official contacts, gave him a wide acquaintance throughout
the state. His newspaper, the *Princeton Union*, ably conducted, made him known to a body of persons who, though
not numerous, were very influential. This gentleman, born
and raised in Ireland, like many another immigrant from
that nursery of statesmen easily aspired to public service
in his adopted country and conceived that, under the circumstances, the governorship of Minnesota would be none too
good for him. This sentiment was shared by an unexpectedly
large number of Republicans, mostly younger men who had
become tired of the domination of the " old guard " of Civil
War veterans with their G.A.R. flags and buttons. One of
these was Condé Hamlin, manager of the *Pioneer Press*,
who swung that still influential journal in favor of an aspirant
almost twenty years the junior of Judge Collins. The *Pioneer
Press* prophesied that Dunn would receive a larger vote than
had ever been polled for a governor of Minnesota. The suggestion of a biographer of Johnson that railroad and lumber
interests preferred the nomination of Dunn has not been confirmed by documentary evidence.[3]

[2] *Legislative Manual*, 1925, p. 104. See *ante*, pp. 206–208.

[3] Upham and Dunlap, *Minnesota Biographies*, 134, 191; Baker, *Governors of
Minnesota*, 441; *Minneapolis Tribune*, June 17, 1904, p. 4; *Princeton Union*,
1904: June 9, pp. 1, 4; 16, pp. 1, 2; *Pioneer Press*, July 3, 1904, p. 6; *Daily
Journal-Press* (St. Cloud), August 15, 1904, p. 2; *St. Peter Herald*, August 5,
1904, p. 4. In an editorial in the issue of the last-named paper for July 22,
1904, p. 4, John A. Johnson says: " The wonder and the question is, how long
will a people stand for such a usurpation of power? ، . . Think of a railway
corporation . . . gently dictating who shall sit in the supreme courts, who shall
be attorney general, who shall be railway commissioners, who shall be governor
of the state." An editorial in the *Minneapolis Journal*, June 29, 1904, p. 4,
makes the charge that the head of a great corporation, who was not a Republican, meaning, doubtless, James J. Hill, dominated the councils of the
Republican party.

The two aspirants were in the field early in the calendar year 1904. Both were veteran Republicans; neither was champion of any particular measure, unless Judge Collins was the more ardent in the merger prosecution. The contest therefore became a personal one, one of the bitterest of the kind that the state has witnessed. Dunn's machine was much the better organized. Judge Collins relied upon his record in war and his public services in peace and felt that under the circumstances he had a right to the succession.

The campaign managers of the candidates, presuming that the rural delegations might be quite evenly matched, were desirous to secure those from Hennepin and Ramsey counties in numbers sufficient to insure a majority in the state Republican convention. Dunn's managers arranged for a revolutionary proceeding. In both counties the Dunn minorities bolted on frivolous grounds; in Hennepin County in an outdoor meeting they authorized their chairman to select and appoint a full county delegation of 113.[4] The Republican state convention opened in St. Paul on June 30, 1904, and did not close until after midnight on the following day. According to a previous understanding, United States Senator Moses E. Clapp, believed to be impartial, was made temporary chairman without opposition. The first session was taken up with his long-winded address and his appointment of the committee on credentials. It consisted of fifteen delegates, seven suggested by each of the managers of the two aspirants and an odd one chosen to look after the interests of ex-Congressman Frank M. Eddy, who had been mentioned for the coveted office. It was not until the afternoon session of the second day that the committee on credentials was ready to report. It recommended for recognition the Collins dele-

---

[4] *Minneapolis Tribune*, June 29, 1904, pp. 1, 7; *Minneapolis Times*, June 29, pp. 1, 2, 6; *Minneapolis Journal*, June 28, p. 1; 29, pp. 1, 2; *Pioneer Press*, June 28, pp. 1, 3; 29, pp. 1, 2; 30, pp. 1, 4; July 2, p. 2; *St. Paul Dispatch*, June 28, p. 1; 29, pp. 1, 4; 30, p. 1; Hall, *Observations*, 321, 326. The *Tribune*, June 29, 1904, p. 4, in an editorial entitled "Let Us Make the Best of It," refuses to take sides with either Dunn or Collins.

gations from Hennepin and Ramsey counties. A minority was permitted to submit a recommendation that the Dunn delegates from Hennepin County be seated. Upon an inquiry from the floor, the chair properly ruled that on that question the Collins delegates were not entitled to vote. The tellers reported 622½ votes for the minority report and 450½ for that of the majority. A wild and joyous shout welcomed the Dunn men from Hennepin County to the seats vacated by the Collins delegates. On the question to nominate but 588 votes were necessary; had the Collins men from Hennepin, 113 in number, been allowed to vote, the total for Collins would have been but 563½.[5] This result showed that the engineering of the bolts in Hennepin and Ramsey counties by Dunn's managers had been unnecessary. The adoption of the buccaneer tactics embittered many Republicans whose memories lasted until the November election. The party which gave Roosevelt a vote of 216,651 rallied but 140,130 votes for Dunn; and John Albert Johnson, the Democratic nominee, was elected by the narrow but sufficient majority of 7,862.[6]

The rise of American boys from obscure poverty to high positions has plenty of examples in our democracy. John Albert Johnson was one of them. He was born on July 28, 1861, near St. Peter, Minnesota, of Swedish parents, recent immigrants. The father, after devoting a few years to farming and to his trade of blacksmithing, took to drink, gave up his work, sold his tools and his shop, became a vagrant, and was at length committed to the county poorhouse, where he died. At the age of thirteen the boy left

[5] *Pioneer Press*, 1904: July 1, pp. 1, 2; 2, pp. 1, 2; *St. Paul Dispatch*, July 2, p. 2; *Minneapolis Tribune*, July 1, p. 1; 2, p. 1; *Minneapolis Times*, July 1, p. 1; 2, pp. 1, 2; *Minneapolis Journal*, July 1, pp. 1–3; 2, p. 3; *Princeton Union*, July 7, p. 1; *Journal-Press* (St. Cloud), July 1, p. 1; 2, p. 4; *Martin County Sentinel* (Fairmont), July 8, p. 2; Hall, *Observations*, 330–338. In an editorial the *Tribune*, July 3, 1904, states that " The Tribune took part in no Kilkenny cat fight."

[6] *Legislative Manual*, 1905, p. 506; 1925, pp. 113, 115. Johnson led Dunn by 8,282 votes in Hennepin County.

school and took employment in a general store at ten dollars a month. For twelve years he had similar employments. On pay days he took his earnings home to his brave and capable mother, who was the village washerwoman. During the last year of this period he was supply clerk for a firm of railroad contractors and earned seventy-five dollars a month. It was a proud day when he could tell his mother she must take in no more washing. During all these years his education had been going on. He liked to read and at first read anything that came in his way; later a friend led him into a line of good fiction and history. He read Shakespeare and committed favorite passages. He bought a set of the *Encyclopedia Brittanica* on the installment plan. He joined a debating club, learned to think on his feet, and became the readiest of debaters. He sang in the choir of the Presbyterian Church and was librarian of the Sunday school. At village parties the ladies found him a good dancing partner. An early photograph shows that he did not lack manly beauty. For some years he was executive secretary of the Nicollet County Fair Association and he displayed ability and tact in the organization of the annual fairs. In 1883 he enlisted as a private in the local company of the national guard and after five years' service he retired with the rank of captain. His social nature took him into various fraternal societies. In all these activities he was extending his acquaintance and learning the ways of the world.

In 1886, when Johnson was twenty-five years old, the way opened to him to become part owner and editor of the *St. Peter Herald*. Up to this time he had been a Republican, and the *Herald* was the Democratic organ of Nicollet County; he knew nothing of the management of newspapers; he had learned offhand speaking but had not practiced writing. Nevertheless he took the plunge and made good. For many years he endured the drudgery of a country editor's life. His editorial articles were rarely in essay form but they abounded in keen and humorous observations.

It would not be strange that a man of his gifts and social attachments should think of public employment, but there was little encouragement for him, a Democrat, in a strong Republican community. In 1888 he accepted a nomination for the state House of Representatives, to be defeated by a small margin. In 1894 he declined a nomination for secretary of state but accepted one for state senator, to be again defeated. In 1898 he was more successful and won the election to the state Senate. His service in the sessions of 1899 and 1901 was not spectacular. He was a vigilant opposition member and by his moderation, good nature, and genial manners he commanded the respect and good will of many Republican colleagues. He was not so strict a partisan that he could not upon occasion take an independent stand. When Governor Lind asked the legislature of 1899 to demand the recall of the Thirteenth Minnesota from the Philippines, Johnson said to the Senate: " I believe the regiment should remain in the Philippines as long as the Stars and Stripes are liable to insult. If that be political treason, make the most of it." The Democrats of his district gave him a renomination for the Senate in 1902 but could not muster quite enough votes to reëlect him. He went back to his editorial office as if for good.[7]

The dissension in the Republican ranks in 1904 inspired a hope among Democratic leaders that there might be a chance of capturing the governorship. At a conference it was agreed that with Johnson as their nominee they might succeed. He was not so confident and did not care for the

---

[7] Baker, Governors of Minnesota, 426–438; Frank A. Day and Theodore M. Knappen, Life of John Albert Johnson, 52–114 (Chicago, 1910) ; Governor John Albert Johnson Memorial Commission, Final Report, 26–28 (St. Paul, 1913) ; Algot E. Strand, ed., A History of the Swedish-Americans of Minnesota, 1 : 89–91 (Chicago, 1910). For the photograph referred to, taken about 1896, see Hall and Holcombe, Minnesota State Agricultural Society, 278. Excerpts from Johnson's weekly column in the St. Peter Herald, headed " It's a Fact," are given in Day and Knappen, Johnson, 90. Sample editorials may be found on pages 114–118, 399–403 of the same work. Day was Governor Johnson's private secretary and was intimately informed as to his early life. The Saint Peter Tribune, November 14, 1888, p. 2, gives the vote for representative: Charles R. Davis, 1,303; Johnson, 1,107.

honor of a barren nomination. After much urging and an assurance that no campaign contributions would be exacted of him, he consented to take the chances. At the Democratic state convention, delayed until August 30, he was nominated by acclamation. Reluctant as he had been hitherto, he soon became hopeful and even confident. In forty-two days he made one hundred and three campaign addresses. The result has already been given: Johnson was elected by a slight majority, while the Republicans made a clean sweep of all other state officers. It may have been due, as it was believed, to support from dissenting Republicans in the Twin Cities. It may also be surmised that some Republican votes elsewhere went to him when some fool Republican thought it would be smart to expose the Johnson family skeleton and came out with affidavits telling the pitiful story of the father's downfall and the resulting misery and poverty. A newspaper man asked Johnson what he had to say about it. "Nothing," said he; "it is true." [8]

Governor Johnson faced the legislature of 1905 in joint session on January 4. The opening paragraph of his inaugural address was a recommendation that the term of office of the governor be extended from two years to four by constitutional amendment, with an implicit proviso that he should not be eligible to reëlection.[9] It does not appear that the legislature took any notice of the reasonable suggestion. Governor Johnson was not remitted to private life by a self-

[8] Baker, *Governors of Minnesota*, 440; Day and Knappen, *Johnson*, 119–129. Day was active in getting Johnson to run for the governorship. An editorial in the *St. Peter Herald*, August 19, 1904, p. 4, stated that Johnson was not a candidate. In the issue of August 26, p. 4, Johnson said he would accept the nomination if offered by a united party and by the unanimous action of the convention. For extracts from many newspapers in support of Johnson see the *Herald* for October 28, pp. 4, 9, and the *Martin County Sentinel*, August 19, 1904, p. 8. The *Herald* for November 11, p. 4, gives Frank A. Day, manager of the campaign, much praise for its success. See the same paper, November 18, p. 1, for an account of the remarkable ovation in St. Peter upon the ratification of Johnson's election to the governorship. The abstract of votes by counties is in the *Legislative Manual*, 1905, pp. 506–509.

[9] Johnson, *Inaugural Message*, 1905, p. 3; *Senate Journal*, 1905, p. 17; *House Journal*, 23.

denying relinquishment. He conducted the routine duties of his office with industry and intelligence; he filled the numerous appointive places in his gift generally, but not always, with members of his own party but, with few, if any, exceptions, with men of character and ability. As he had not come into office as the successful advocate of political tenets of national importance, he was able to concur with the Republican legislature in matters of state concern and to approve its bills. By addresses on numerous public occasions he added to his reputation and his growing list of friends within and without his party. When the campaign of 1906 drew on there was no opposition in Democratic ranks to his renomination, which took place on September 4. Whether the Republicans in their state convention on June 13 selected from numerous aspirants their best vote-getter need not be considered. Johnson beat him by 72,318 votes. It was the greatest personal triumph ever witnessed in Minnesota politics. The Republicans elected all their other candidates for state offices by large majorities, in one case by a majority of 81,099.[10]

Governor Johnson maintained the same good understanding with the legislature of 1907 as he had with that of the previous session. His conduct of affairs was highly satisfactory to his party and was not obnoxious to Republican citizens. In midsummer of 1908 political managers of all parties were busy making up " slates " for the fall elections. For the Democratic leaders there was no need of elaborate ciphering; the country press had already voiced Democratic sentiment. John A. Johnson was the only man they could hope to elect in a Republican state in a presidential year. He, however, was satisfied with the honors already accorded him and really did not desire another term of office. He had reasons for this disinclination. His reëlection in No-

[10] Baker, *Governors of Minnesota*, 443; Day and Knappen, *Johnson*, 163, 261; *Minneapolis Tribune*, 1906: June 14, p. 1; September 5, p. 2; *Legislative Manual*, 1907, p. 486. The Republican nominee for governor was the Honorable Albert L. Cole of Walker.

vember, 1906, by an enormous majority had been good news
for Democrats beyond the boundaries of Minnesota. Much
curiosity was aroused about a Democrat who had won two
elections to the governorship in a state which had given
Roosevelt an enormous majority and in which the Republicans had swept all other state offices. Calls came from distant
quarters for speeches, which he accepted when practicable.
He was, says a biographer, " a happy public speaker, always
satisfying and gratifying his hearers." On June 19, 1907,
he was the chosen commencement day orator at the ancient
University of Pennsylvania. His address was an earnest
presentation of " The University Man's Opportunity." In
a graceful introduction he reminded his audience that men
of his nationality had owned the site of that university many
years before William Penn came over with his royal charter.
Provost Charles C. Harrison, in presenting him for the
degree of doctor of laws, said, " We accord honor to one of
the master builders of the imperial Northwest." [11]

Another opportunity for the display of Johnson's ability
and tact as an extemporaneous speaker was an invitation to
speak before the Gridiron Club of Washington, D.C., at its
banquet on December 7, 1907. There could be no more
severe ordeal to test the powers of a public speaker. Called
up from a side table " rather far down the evening," he
handed out an ambiguous compliment to William J. Bryan
which set the crowd wild. The address was a " typically
western and yet broadly national review of the political life
of the time." At its close, Speaker Cannon, Secretary Root,
Senator Foraker, and other statesmen and notables fell over
one another in the scramble for Johnson's hand.[12]

The manager of a Chautauqua lyceum bureau, who had
previously tried to engage Johnson, renewed his efforts and

[11] Baker, *Governors of Minnesota*, 454, 455; Day and Knappen, *Johnson*,
136, 137, 165, 199. For the commencement address at the University of Pennsylvania, see pages 324–358 of the latter work.
[12] Day and Knappen, *Johnson*, 165–172.

in February, 1908, had him pledged to speak at early dates, as well as unconditionally for the whole lecture season of the following winter. He thought the governor worth the highest price he was paying — two hundred dollars a lecture. The manager does not give the number of lectures delivered by Johnson in 1908 but he states that more than a hundred applications were refused. Governor Johnson embarked with some reluctance and misgivings in the adventure but, encouraged by successes, he became fascinated with lecturing and with the incident travel and acquaintance-making. In point of finance he could not afford to be governor of Minnesota at seven thousand dollars a year.[13]

There was another consideration, not financial, which possibly weighed more toward Johnson's renunciation of the governorship. William J. Bryan, twice defeated as a candidate for the national presidency, still held a powerful grip on the Democratic party organization and was looking forward to a third nomination. There were many Democrats, however, who would have preferred that Bryan should be content with the honors which had been accorded him and should consent to have a new man promoted to the leadership. After Johnson's triumph at the Gridiron Club dinner, suggestions multiplied that the distinguished Democrat who had twice won the governorship of Minnesota, a Republican stronghold, "would do." Letters in great number poured into his office and delegations from many states came to urge him to become a presidential candidate. On March 6, 1908, the Minnesota Democratic State Central Committee adopted a resolution presenting John A. Johnson for the presidency and recommending that the Democracy of Minnesota propose his name at the coming national convention to be held at Denver, Colorado. On March 23 Johnson wrote a letter to the editor of the *Svenska Amerikanska Posten* in which he said, " If the Democratic Party of the state desires to present my name to the next annual

[13] Day and Knappen, *Johnson*, 204–207.

convention I am sure I would have no objection." A few
days later in the same month Johnson headquarters were
opened in Chicago and Johnson was in the field. With little
expectation of success his name was becomingly presented
to the Denver convention by Winfield S. Hammond and
half an hour of cheering and shouting followed, but it did
not raise a ripple on the powerful current which was bearing Bryan to a third nomination.[14]

So long as the presidential bee was buzzing about his
head Johnson was, to say the least, indifferent about the
Minnesota governorship. That distraction disposed of, he
could entertain the urgent demands of his party friends to
become their candidate again. He was still reluctant, however, and arranged for the presentation of another name to
the state convention. When that body met in Minneapolis
on August 19, 1908, it was simply mad for Johnson and,
after an hour of cheering and swarming about the hall,
gave him a unanimous nomination. It is related that the
Bryan Democrats were most ardent of all. He could not
refuse a duty thus laid upon him. The Republicans put
up as their candidate a well-known citizen of Norwegian
birth, the Honorable Jacob F. Jacobson of Madison, experienced in legislation and in other public activities. The
contest was vain against such a popular idol as the Swedish
blacksmith's son. Johnson's plurality over his opponent
was 27,139, while Taft carried the state over Bryan by
86,442. More than a thousand telegrams came to him,
says a biographer, hundreds of them hailing Johnson as a
victor who four years later would lead his party to a
national triumph.[15]

With a legislature in session in the winter of 1909 Governor Johnson was needed at home and canceled many

14 Day and Knappen, *Johnson*, 171–188; *Pioneer Press*, July 10, 1908, pp.
1–4. The letter referred to is in the *Svenska Amerikanska Posten* (Minneapolis and St. Paul), March 31, 1908, p. 1.

15 Day and Knappen, *Johnson*, 136–142; *Minneapolis Tribune*, August 20,
1908, pp. 1–3; *Legislative Manual*, 1925, pp. 102, 103. For a short biographical
sketch of Jacobson, see Upham and Dunlap, *Minnesota Biographies*, 367.

lecture engagements, though in the summer of that year he "filled quite a few." On August 29, 1909, at Urbana, Illinois, he delivered his last lecture. The return of an intestinal trouble of long standing obliged him on September 13 to resort to the Mayo clinic at Rochester for diagnosis and treatment. An operation on Wednesday, September 15, revealed an abscess and an adhesion which caused anxiety. Four days passed during which there was expectation of recovery. On the afternoon of Monday, September 20, a collapse set in and life departed early in the following morning. On Wednesday the body lay in state in the Capitol at St. Paul and fifty thousand persons passed it with bowed heads. On September 23, 1909, it was buried at his old home town — St. Peter. An immense concourse gathered for the funeral. "The mourning over his untimely death," wrote Cyrus Northrop, "has hardly been equaled by the mourning for any other citizen except Abraham Lincoln." [16]

The deep and widespread sorrow for the loss of a governor who was every citizen's friend found immediate expression in suggestions for an imperishable monument to his memory. In response to this sentiment, Governor Eberhart on September 29, 1909, appointed a commission of citizens to have charge of the enterprise. At a meeting of the appointees on October 4 articles of organization were adopted. Christopher D. O'Brien was named by Governor Eberhart as president; Charles W. Ames was elected secretary and Benjamin F. Nelson, treasurer. These, with two others, formed an executive committee which carried on the enterprise under the general direction of the commission. A statue in marble to be placed in one of the niches in the wall of the rotunda of the Capitol was thought of, but the sentiment in favor of a bronze statue in the open prevailed. It

[16] Day and Knappen, *Johnson*, 220–222, 248–258. See the *Pioneer Press*, September 22, 1909, p. 2, for President Northrop's remarks in the university chapel.

was also agreed that a modest memorial to be paid for from small contributions from the great number of friends and admirers of Johnson would be preferable to a more costly and imposing work at state expense. Circular letters were at once issued through the newspapers asking for contributions of not more than one dollar per person. The response was immediate and generous. On January 8, 1910, the treasurer reported $23,950.40 on hand. A year ran by while designs and estimates were studied. On January 30, 1911, a contract was made with Andrew O'Connor, an American sculptor residing in Paris, France, for a statue in bronze of heroic size, with two supplementary groups flanking the pedestal, and the mounting complete for $21,500. It was erected on the left hand side of the broad walk leading up to the main entrance on the façade of the building, a location made after some controversy and against the protest of Cass Gilbert, the architect of the Capitol. The unveiling of the monument took place with imposing ceremony on October 19, 1912. The principal address was made by Winfield S. Hammond, who had twice nominated Johnson for governor and once for president and who himself a few years later became governor of Minnesota.[17]

[17] Johnson Memorial Commission, *Final Report*, 9–15, 18, 20, 22, 23, 25, 56, 59, 61, 72, 76–79. This report consists almost wholly of the minutes and records of the commission. The originals of these, in manuscript, together with newspaper clippings, a list of contributors to the memorial, and a great bulk of correspondence, in seven bound volumes, are in the possession of the Minnesota Historical Society. A photograph of the inscription on the die of the monument is opposite page 32 of the *Report*. The inscription reads: "John Albert Johnson, July 26, 1861–Sept. 21, 1909; three times governor of Minnesota; a poor boy, a country editor, a natural leader; cut off in his prime. The nation mourns his loss. 'His life was gentle; and the elements so mixed in him, that Nature might stand up and say to all the world, This was a man.' This monument is raised to his memory by one hundred thousand of his friends." The passage quoted, from Shakespeare's "Julius Cæsar," act 5, scene 5, was suggested by the *Pioneer Press*, September 23, 1909, p. 6. A motion picture film of the unveiling, 360 feet long, was bought by the commission and presented to the Minnesota Historical Society.

The site first chosen for the monument was "on the Capitol terrace directly in front of the balustrade before the Governor's office," in accordance with the taste of Cass Gilbert, the architect of the Capitol. The actual location was bitterly opposed by him. As late as September 6, six weeks before the unveiling, Secretary Ames urged the commission to order the statue moved to the

On September 21, 1913, the fourth anniversary of the death of Governor Johnson, a replica of the statue was unveiled on the lawn of the Nicollet County courthouse in the city of St. Peter. From a balance left of the contributed fund about two thousand dollars were willingly granted by the commission for the replica, which cost three thousand dollars. Citizens of St. Peter and Nicollet County made up the remainder and the cost of installation. If one may judge from the pictures, the replica, happily surrounded, shows to better advantage than the original at the Capitol.[18]

The devotion of so much space to the personal history of one of the governors of the state, possibly to be deemed disproportionate by critics, will be easily condoned in consideration of his romantic career, which, had it not been cut short by an untimely death, would, in the judgment of many, have carried him forward to the presidency of the United States.

site favored by Gilbert. The commission refused. On the motion not to change, Ames voted " no " for himself and an absentee, Harwood G. Day. In his final report to the commission Secretary Ames makes no mention of the action of the commission on September 6. In a circular sent by the commission to the newspapers, this peculiar statement is made in regard to the site: " The monument will be placed on the grass plot at the entrance to the State Capitol where Johnson served the State for three memorable terms." A future generation may side with the architect. See Johnson Memorial Commission, *Final Report*, 9–22, 62–64, 67, 72, 79. The minutes of the meeting of September 6 are on pages 71–73 of the *Report*. Details of the controversy can be found in the correspondence of Ames with Gilbert, Nelson, and O'Connor in the records and correspondence of the commission. There is also a protest of the Minnesota State Art Commission against the present location, dated September 3, 1912, in the same collection.

[18] Johnson Memorial Commission, *Final Report*, 21, 74–76, 80, 83; *St. Peter Herald*, September 26, 1913, p. 1; *Minneapolis Journal*, September 22, p. 4; *St. Paul Dispatch*, September 22, p. 10; *St. Paul Pioneer Press*, September 22, p. 1.

There is another monument to Johnson which, in the opinion of Secretary Charles W. Ames, is " quite as impressive as any that could be erected in bronze and granite." Under the direction of Robert L. Pollock of Minneapolis, a collection of memorial clippings was made. The memorial commission bought it for five hundred dollars, had it bound in six quarto volumes, and presented it to the Minnesota Historical Society to be preserved in its library. The arrangement is chronological, the clippings for each date being according to states in alphabetical order. They begin with September 21, 1909, and end with November 29. The last entry is a clipping from the *New-York Tribune* recording a memorial meeting in New York City. President Taft sent a letter of appreciation and Charles Evans Hughes, governor of New York, made an address. It was Governor Hughes's opinion that Johnson's strong hold

It was believed that he had an expanding capacity to meet any emergency and to fill any office, even the highest.[19]

During the period of Governor Johnson's administration, four years and nine months — January 4, 1905, to September 21, 1909 — there were three sessions of the legislature. Thirteen amendments to the state constitution were proposed and voted upon, but only three of them were ratified. All those rejected received large majorities of the votes cast on them, but none received the required majority of all the votes cast at the election. Of the three ratified, the most important was that adopting the "wide-open" tax section of article 9 of the constitution, warmly recommended by Governors Lind and Van Sant, as well as by Governor Johnson.[20] Very important tax laws were enacted after the adoption of this amendment. Without question the chief of these was the act creating a tax commission with liberal powers. A carefully drawn statute for taxing inheritances and bequests replaced former acts which had proved ineffective; and a tax on the registry of mortgages, being one-half of one per cent on the amount of money secured, took the place of the former impracticable levy on mortgages as personal property.[21]

on the people of his state was due not simply to their affectionate regard but to their judgment. He could not have carried Minnesota as he did "merely out of sentiment."

[19] See Day and Knappen, *Johnson*, 264, 265, for the statement that "Johnson would have proved a great president" and that the national loss was infinitely greater than that of Minnesota. See also pages 407–429 for a catena of tributes, including a telegram and a statement for the press by President Taft, a letter from Theodore Roosevelt dispatched from Central Africa, appreciations from the governors of New York, Indiana, Illinois, Ohio, Missouri, and Iowa, and from Andrew Carnegie, Archbishop Ireland, and Thomas Lawson. An extract from an undated letter from Grover Cleveland, said to be the last long letter written by him, contains the sentence, "I have lately come to the conclusion that our best hope rests upon the nomination of Johnson of Minnesota." Archbishop Ireland in his tribute speaks of Johnson's "going away when success, the reward of past doings, was beckoning him onward to yet higher success on wider fields of action." A tender poem of ten four-line stanzas, "The Deep, Sad Eyes," by John Talman, suggests one explanation of Johnson's personal charm. Hammond's address at the unveiling of the monument, although uncritical, is perhaps the best appreciation of Johnson on record. Johnson Memorial Commission, *Final Report*, 25–31.

[20] Anderson, *History of the Constitution*, 189, 237, 240, 282. On the "wide-open" amendment see also *ante*, p. 259.

[21] *General Laws*, 1905, pp. 427–435; 1907, pp. 448–451, 576–584.

Governor Johnson was much interested in the subject of insurance and apparently was well informed upon it. A series of laws passed at the governor's instance in 1905 and 1907 amounted to a code of life, fire, and marine insurance.[22] Three acts relating to railroads were passed. One of them, to which the railroad companies had no objection, forbade the issue of railroad passes under severe penalty. Two others met with lively opposition and a tedious litigation delayed their operation. One of them fixed the passenger fares at two cents a mile and the other established a classification of commodities and maximum rates for their transportation.[23] The bureau of labor, under the new title, bureau of labor, industries, and commerce, was given enlarged jurisdiction and powers.[24] A department of banking was established with a superintendent and the public examiner was relieved of the inspection of bank records and accounts.[25] An act of 1907 permitted cities to own and operate public utilities, including street railways, telephones, water works, gas works, and electric light, heat, and power works.[26] After ten years' experience the act of 1895 for the regulation of sales of timber from state lands had proved insufficient to prevent losses and a new code was enacted to remedy the mischief.[27] The state board of control was relieved of the financial management of the university and the normal schools, except in the matters of fuel supply and of the erection and insuring of buildings.[28] There may be much truth in the suggestion of a biographer that much of the good legislation of Governor Johnson's time was due to the unwillingness of Republican legislatures to be surpassed in well-doing by a Democratic governor. In concluding paragraphs of all his inaugural

[22] General Laws, 1905, pp. 231, 299–303, 350–370, 452–454; 1907, pp. 469–483; Johnson, Inaugural Message, 1905, p. 13; 1907, pp. 25–29.
[23] General Laws, 1907, pp. 109, 313–317, 685–687.
[24] General Laws, 1907, pp. 493–496.
[25] General Laws, 1909, pp. 228–233.
[26] General Laws, 1907, pp. 689–694.
[27] General Laws, 1895, p. 354; 1905, pp. 258–273. On the act of 1895, see ante, pp. 207, 208, and post, p. 513.
[28] General Laws, 1905, pp. 148–152.

messages the governor reminded the legislatures that he and they would serve their parties best when serving the people best and he pledged his own endeavors and expected theirs in promoting " the highest public interest and welfare." [29]

Among the numerous recommendations made by Governor Johnson to the legislatures were some which, though well worthy of their attention, they were not pleased to entertain. If his proposal for the creation of a state bureau of public lands, mines, and forests had been enacted, it would have taken the great interlocking interests out of the hands of the state auditor, who carried them in addition to his principal duty of state financial controller, and would have placed them in the hands of a separate commissioner. Johnson followed Lind in commending the Wisconsin plan of caring for the chronic insane in county institutions with state aid. He favored experiments with county tax assessors, uniform municipal accounting, registration of lobbyists, separate elections for judges, and the advisory initiative and referendum, although he had no objection to the direct initiative and referendum.[30]

Governor Johnson's final action in the matter of taxation of iron ore property has been mistakenly considered by many as inconsistent with his previous utterances. In his message to the legislature of 1907 he suggested a tax upon ore royalties, which in 1906, at five per cent, would have yielded a revenue of $325,000. As such a tax would fall only upon operators of state-owned mines, paying royalties, the suggestion, as may have been expected, got little consideration. In his message to the legislature of 1909 Governor Johnson refrained from contrasting the operations of the two much-talked-of systems, the tonnage tax and the ad valorem tax, for the reason that a district court had held that the " wide-

[29] Day and Knappen, *Johnson*, p. 164; Johnson, *Inaugural Message*, 1905, p. 21; 1907, p. 56; 1909, p. 56.
[30] Johnson, *Inaugural Message*, 1905, pp. 15, 21; 1907, pp. 17, 56; 1909, pp. 8–11, 15, 42, 46, 53.

open " tax amendment of 1906 had not been in fact ratified and the question was still before the state supreme court on appeal. In the same message he laid emphasis upon the importance of making mining properties pay their just share of taxes. They were gifts of nature to the state and should not be absorbed by a few proprietors. Before many years the mines would be exhausted and nothing would be left but holes in the ground. Other real property would yield revenue for centuries.[31] The legislature of 1909 passed a straight tonnage tax bill and laid it before Governor Johnson for his approval. On April 20, 1909, he returned it to the House without his approval. The bill was satisfactory to the great body of people not living on or near the iron ranges nor owning mining interests; but from the ranges came three thousand telegrams demanding a veto. The governor's radical objection to the bill, as stated in the last paragraph of the veto message, was that, if enacted into law, it would establish a double system of taxing a certain class of property. Subordinate reasons were given. The bill was so ill digested, he said, that even its friends did not fully understand it. This objection alone, if valid, would have been a good reason for the veto. The ad valorem system had worked so well under

[31] Johnson, *Inaugural Message*, 1907, p. 11; 1909, pp. 16, 17. For the facts of the notable case thus appealed see Samuel G. McConaughy *v.* Secretary of State, 106 *Minnesota*, 392–430. The decision of the supreme court, which was given on January 8, 1909, was that the amendment had been ratified in fact. The opinion of the court was written by Justice Charles Burke Elliott, one of the most learned judges of the court. Justice Calvin L. Brown, who later became chief justice, dissented. A layman may perhaps venture to suggest that it was the mind of the court that the principle of the amendment ought to be sustained and that it sought diligently until it found arguments and precedents to warrant the decision it was pleased to render.

To make sure of an undoubted " wide-open " tax section in the constitution, the legislature of 1907 resubmitted the proposition to the electors, but with an additional phrase intended to restrict the exemption of church property from taxation only so far as it was " used for religious purposes." At the November election of 1908 the resubmitted article was lost, because of the added phrase, it was believed. Of the 199,917 votes cast on the amendment, 134,141 were for ratification — not a majority of 355,263, the total number of votes cast at the election. *General Laws*, 1907, p. 782; Walter F. Dodd, *The Revision and Amendment of State Constitutions*, 320 (Baltimore, 1910) ; Anderson, *History of the Constitution*, 190, 282.

the judicious supervision of the tax commission that there was
no need to experiment with a new system. The passage of
the proposed measure at a time when both its provisions and
the principle upon which it was based were so generally mis-
understood had " plunged the whole subject of taxation under
the new state constitutional amendment into a sea of political
and sectional feeling and prejudice," which made " a just,
efficient and scientific measure impossible of enactment."
Under the present system the revenue was definite; under the
proposed system it would vary with the amount of ore mined
and would be flexible to a dangerous degree. It should not
be possible, the governor added, for fifty-five counties which
were receiving more from the state treasury than they paid in
in taxes to impose an unequal burden upon another section.[32]

The multiplication of statutes by American legislatures has
long been a source of astonishment to European publicists
and complaints of excessive lawmaking are perennial at home.
Without doubt we might be better off with fewer and well-
digested statutes; but it must be remembered that new situations in new states call for frequent modifications of and
additions to statute law and, more often, perhaps, for repeals.
These changes presently accumulate to such a degree that it
becomes difficult even for lawyers and judges to be sure in
some cases just what the law actually in force is. To remedy
this mischief revisions or compilations are made from time to
time, into which are assembled, in orderly and customary
sequence, the general laws in force on a certain date. Revisions must be enacted by the legislature but compilations may
be made by authority of law or by private citizens employed

32 House Journal, 1909, vol. 1, p. 935; Senate Journal, 1219; Day and
Knappen, Johnson, 158. The veto message is in House Journal, 1909, vol. 2,
pp. 1893–1897. A protest of eight senators against the passage of the bill is in
Senate Journal, 1218. The bill (House file 227) passed the House by a vote
of 61 to 57 and the Senate, by 38 to 24. The Minneapolis Tribune, April 21,
1909, p. 4, says that Johnson saved Minnesota " from a sectional division more
bitter at the beginning than that which separated North and South before the
Civil war." The Minneapolis Journal of the same date, page 16, declared the
veto to be " a courageous and sensible thing " and said that Johnson declined
to " play politics."

by law publishers.[33] The legislature of 1901 authorized the justices of the state supreme court to appoint three commissioners to revise the general laws of Minnesota in force at the close of that session and to have its report ready by December 1, 1902. The commission did not complete its duty in the period named and asked for more time, which was granted by the legislature of 1903. The report of the commission was submitted to the House in the form of a bill on January 19, 1905. That body, as if distrusting the work of the appointed commission, indulged in an extraordinary exercise: it undertook to revise the revision. The chairman of the judiciary committee, under authority granted, reported the parceling out of the several chapters to the standing committees. The contributions of the committees are not of record, as they were reported only to the judiciary committee. That committee in the month of February from day to day reported amendments in great numbers, which were printed. On March 2 the bill was reported with amendments covering 143 pages of the *House Journal*. From March 6 to 10 the bill was up on special order and over one hundred more amendments were adopted. Completely satisfied with its labors, the House passed the bill by a unanimous vote, 108 to 0. The Senate referred the bill to its judiciary committee, to which three able lawyers were added by resolution. The whole body did not set to work but left the committee to wrestle with the bill. On April 5 it was reported back with amendments covering 148 pages of the *Senate Journal*. Two days later the Senate added several more and passed the bill by a vote of 44 to 9. The report of conferees covers six pages of the journals, but it was so satisfactory that the perfected bill was passed by the House with but two dissenting votes and by the Senate with but three nays. It is understood, of course,

[33] James Bryce, *The American Commonwealth*, 1: 551 (New York, 1910). In Minnesota there have been the revisions of 1851, 1866, and 1905, and compilations of 1859, 1873, 1878, 1891, 1894, 1913, and 1923. On the Code of 1851 see *ante*, 1: 262. For the authorization and enactment of the *Revised Statutes* of 1866, see *General Laws*, 1863, p. 68; 1865, pp. 119–121; 1866, p. 54.

that this revision did not include laws passed by the legislature of 1905. The printed volume of 1210 pages bears the title, *Revised Laws Minnesota, 1905.* The introduction contains the caution that the code is not a new body of law but a revision of laws in force " with such amendments as the commission and legislature deemed advisable." It took effect on March 1, 1906.[34]

[34] *General Laws,* 1901, p. 383; 1903, p. 229; *House Journal,* 1905, pp. 90, 140, 148–151, 425–568, 670, 1214, 1341–1348; *Senate Journal,* 395, 398, 706–855, 938–941, 944, 1033–1040. See the *Pioneer Press,* January 25, 1905, p. 8, for an opinion that the legislature would do well to avoid action on the new code until it had been examined by a committee of legal experts to make certain that the law had been merely condensed and not altered.

XV. A CHRONICLE OF RECENT EVENTS, 1909–25

IN THIS concluding chapter will be sketched only the most important events from the time of Governor Johnson's death to the present, without nice regard to chronological order. Five men held the position of governor in this period. On the day of Governor Johnson's death Lieutenant Governor Adolph Olson Eberhart became governor and took the oath required by the constitution. Eberhart was born in Sweden on June 23, 1870, came to this country at the age of eleven, and worked on farms in Nebraska for ten years. During this time he made use of a library generously opened to him by an employer. In 1895 he was graduated *maximus* from Gustavus Adolphus College, St. Peter, having completed the studies of seven years in four years and three months. He then studied law under a preceptor and engaged in law practice. In 1902 and 1904 he was elected to the state Senate, where his efficiency easily gained for him the Republican nomination and the election as lieutenant governor in 1906 and a reëlection two years later. Elections in 1910 and 1912, added to the fractional term, held him in the governor's chair for five years and three months.[1] Only three of the sixteen previous governors of Minnesota — Swift, Merriam, and Davis — were college graduates, but all were educated in the higher school of labor, business, or professional and official life.

Winfield Scott Hammond of St. James became governor in January, 1915. He had been elected in the previous November as a Democrat by the slight majority of 12,574 over his Republican opponent. In 1906 he had been chosen to represent his district in Congress and three successive reëlections

[1] Strand, *Swedish-Americans of Minnesota*, 1:96–98; Thomas Hughes, *History of Blue Earth County*, 390 (Chicago, [1909]); Johnson, *University of Minnesota*, 313.

293

were accorded him. These elections and his promotion to the governorship may without doubt be attributed to his high standing as a citizen, to his deep interest in education, and to his proven efficiency in public service. A leading newspaper expressed the opinion that his election to the governor's office was in no sense a Democratic triumph, but was an expression of independent thought by the people. His service ended with his sudden death on December 30, 1915. He had gone to Louisiana on some business errand and at Clinton in that state dropped instantly from an apoplectic stroke. Governor Hammond was born in Massachusetts, was graduated from Dartmouth College, and came to Minnesota in 1884. He was principal of the Mankato High School for a year and for the five following years superintendent of schools at Madelia. During these years he studied law and in 1891 he was admitted to the bar. From 1898 to 1903 he was president of the school board of St. James and for eight years, from 1898 to 1906, he was a member of the state normal school board. His was a case of the scholar in politics.[2]

Again a lieutenant governor acceded to the governorship of Minnesota — Joseph Alfred Arner Burnquist of St. Paul. He was born of Swedish parents in Dayton, Iowa, on July 22, 1879. He was graduated from Carleton College, Northfield, in 1902, pursued graduate studies in Columbia University, New York City, for two years, and took his law degree at the University of Minnesota in 1905. During the course of his education he won first or high rank in numerous college debating contests. His gifts as a public speaker brought him wide reputation and led to his election as representative of a St. Paul district in the state legislature in 1908 and his reëlection two years later. He was elected lieutenant governor in 1912

---

[2] *Legislative Manual*, 1925, p. 114; *Minneapolis Journal*, 1915: December 30, p. 1; 31, pp. 1, 4, 6; *St. Paul Dispatch*, December 30, 1915, pp. 1, 2, 3; *St. Paul Pioneer Press*, November 4, 1914, p. 10; Charles M. Andrist, "An Appreciation of Governor Hammond," in the *Minnesota Alumni Weekly*, vol. 15, no. 15, pp. 6–8 (January 10, 1916). Andrist was Governor Hammond's private secretary.

and while in his second term was called to the governor's chair. He was elected to fill that position again in 1916 and in 1918, and thus remained in the office five full years.[3]

On January 5, 1921, Jacob Aall Ottesen Preus took the oath of office as governor of Minnesota after eleven years of service in the state Capitol. In 1909 Governor Eberhart had made him his executive clerk and two years later had appointed him insurance commissioner. This office he held until January, 1915, when he became auditor of state, having been elected in the preceding November. By a reëlection he remained in that position until his inauguration as governor. In all these capacities it is well known that Preus displayed great industry, intelligence, and efficiency. He became a national authority on insurance law. At his first election as governor he was given a majority over three other candidates of 47,986 votes, the total vote being 783,624. This was more than double the largest vote ever before polled for a governor of the state, probably for the reason that it was the first year for women to exercise the full elective franchise. Governor Preus was born in Wisconsin on August 28, 1883, and was graduated in arts from Luther College, Decorah, Iowa, in 1903 and in law from the University of Minnesota in 1906.[4]

Theodore Christianson became the twenty-first governor of the state of Minnesota in 1925. As his surname indicates, Governor Christianson is of Norwegian stock, but both he and his father before him were born citizens of the United States and of the state of Minnesota. He was born on September 12, 1883, in Lac qui Parle Township in the county of the same name. His early education was obtained in the local schools and in the Dawson High School. He was gradu-

---

[3] Strand, *Swedish-Americans of Minnesota*, 3: 981; *Legislative Manual*, 1909, p. 138; 1911, p. 146; 1919, p. 710; 1925, p. 114.
[4] *St. Paul Pioneer Press*, June 4, 1922; *Legislative Manual*, 1923, pp. 102, 583. An article by Frederick L. Collins, "At Home with the Governors," in the *Woman's Home Companion*, 51: 20, 114, 128 (June, 1924), includes a kindly sketch of Governor Preus's home life, with a page of illustrations.

ated from the academic college of the University of Minnesota in 1906 and from the law school of the same institution three years later. Endowed with some gift for writing, the young attorney presently embraced an opportunity to subordinate his law practice to editorial work. He bought the *Dawson Sentinel* and remained its editor and publisher until the time of his inauguration as governor. During these years he found time to serve his district as its representative for ten years in the lower house of the legislature.[5]

By far the most momentous of all political events of the period were the ratifications of the four amendments to the national Constitution. Although the income tax was used by the American colonists and later by some of the states, it was long avoided by the national government, in part because it was thought to be better adapted to states and in part because it implied an inquest into the affairs of every community through an army of unknown government officials. It was not until 1861, when convinced that a great war was beginning, that Congress ventured to embrace an income tax in the internal revenue law of that year. It went into operation on January 1, 1862. The constitutionality of the act was called in question but the Supreme Court found considerations which, under the circumstances, justified it in sustaining the law. It remained in operation ten years. A " demand " for an income tax was invariably inserted in all Populist platforms and at length those of the great parties gave it grudging hospitality.[6] In deference to the growing sentiment Congress in 1894 embodied in the revenue act of that year a tax of two per cent upon all incomes of four thousand dollars or more. The high minimum was, of course, intended to

[5] L. R. Moyer and O. G. Dale, eds., *History of Chippewa and Lac qui Parle Counties,* 2: 224 (Indianapolis, 1916) ; *Legislative Manual,* 1925, pp. 103, 633.

[6] Davis R. Dewey, in Andrew C. McLaughlin and Albert B. Hart, eds., *Cyclopedia of American Government,* 3: 490–492 (New York, 1914). See the revenue act of 1861, in *Statutes at Large,* 12: 309–313, for the income tax law of that year. Its constitutionality was tested in the case of Springer *v.* United States, 102 *United States,* 586–603. For the suspension of the tax after 1871, see *Statutes at Large,* 16: 257.

exempt small incomes and to lay the burden upon the prosperous. Again the question of constitutionality was raised and carried to the Supreme Court. On May 20, 1895, after a second hearing, the court decided that the proposed income tax was unconstitutional, since it would be a direct tax not apportioned according to representation and not uniform among the states. It never took effect.[7]

The demand for an income tax did not abate and it became the conviction of great numbers that if the Constitution did not permit the imposition of an income tax it ought to be amended so that it would. Congress at length yielded to the pressure and in 1909 proposed to the legislatures of the several states the adoption of a new article to read as follows: "Congress shall have power to lay and collect taxes on incomes from whatever source derived, without apportionment among the several states, and without regard to any census or enumeration." The proposition was ratified by the legislature of Minnesota by large majorities in both houses. It was not until February 25, 1913, that proclamation was made that the proposed sixteenth amendment had become a part of the national Constitution, having been ratified by the legislatures of three-fourths of the states. On October 3 of the same year the existing graduated income-tax law, which has since been modified in details, was passed, and it is probable that an income tax will remain indefinitely a part of our national revenue system.[8]

There were two reasons for a change in the manner of electing senators in Congress: a sentiment, industriously

[7] The provisions of the act of 1894 may be found in *Statutes at Large*, 28: 553, as a part of the Wilson-Gorman tariff. See Pollock *v.* Farmers' Loan and Trust Company, 157 *United States*, 429–654, for the first hearing, in which the justices were divided and rendered no opinion on the main issue. For the rehearing of the case and the 5 to 4 decision, see 158 *United States*, 601–715. The objection to the income tax was based on article 1, section 2, of the Constitution.

[8] *Statutes at Large*, 37: 1785; 38: 166; Minnesota, *House Journal*, 1912, extra session, 24; *Senate Journal*, 53. European, especially British, experience has shown that an income tax is an excellent elastic element in a tax system, easily and cheaply adjustable to emergencies.

fostered by Populist leaders, favoring more "direct action" of the democracy in the choice of public servants, and a widespread conviction that senatorial elections by legislatures in some states, Minnesota not excepted, had been influenced, if not controlled, by the use of money or patronage in the interest of "predatory wealth." The sentiment found expression in party platforms, in resolutions of legislatures, in newspapers, and elsewhere. It culminated in 1912 in the submission by Congress to the state legislatures of a proposed seventeenth amendment to the national Constitution providing for the election of senators in Congress by the people of each state. The Minnesota legislature ratified it on June 11, 1912, but adoption by the requisite three-fourths of the states was not obtained until May 31, 1913.[9]

The first senator to be elected in Minnesota by direct vote of the electors was Frank B. Kellogg of St. Paul, a Republican who had been active in party affairs but who had not sought office. Kellogg was born in Potsdam, New York, on December 22, 1856, and in 1865 came to Minnesota with his parents, who settled on a farm near Rochester. The boy got his schooling in the rural and grade schools of the neighborhood. He studied law in a practitioner's office in Rochester and was admitted to the bar in 1877. After ten years' practice in Rochester he moved to St. Paul, to become a partner of Cushman K. Davis. While there he was employed by the department of public justice in the prosecution of the paper and Standard Oil trusts and by the interstate

---

[9] George H. Haynes, in McLaughlin and Hart, *Cyclopedia of American Government*, 3: 292–294; Minnesota, *House Journal*, 1912, extra session, 23; *Senate Journal*, 48; *Statutes at Large*, 38: 2049. The popular election of senators in Congress is a wide departure from the expectation of the framers of the Constitution. They had in mind a council of elders, wise from age or experience, who would mitigate the impetuosity of representatives fresh from the people and secure deliberate legislation. The suggestion may be ventured that some day one of two events may occur: the abolishment of the superfluous Senate or, more probably, a division of the country into states more equal in area, wealth, and population. States with great areas and populations running into tens of millions will not forever tolerate the equal representation in the Senate, a necessary concession to small states to bring them into the Union of 1789.

commerce commission in the investigation of the Harriman railroads. He was a delegate to three national Republican conventions and for eight years was a member of the Republican national committee for Minnesota. He was at some time general counsel for the Duluth and Iron Range Railroad Company and for the Minnesota Iron and Oliver Iron Mining companies. It was doubtless his knowledge of such corporations and the reputation he had won as a "trust-buster" that moved the Republicans of Minnesota to select him as their best man to run for senator in Congress. At the primary election of June 19, 1916, he was made their candidate by a considerable plurality over three other aspirants and in the November following he was elected. With Kellogg and the wise and experienced Nelson in the Senate, Minnesota was well represented there. It was not the fortune of the junior senator, however, to obtain the reëlection which he desired. At the primary election in June, 1922, he became the Republican nominee by a large plurality over two other aspirants, but at the election in November, Henrik Shipstead, the Farmer-Labor candidate, was preferred before him by a majority of 83,539 votes. President Harding on October 26, 1923, appointed Kellogg ambassador to Great Britain, where he had an influential part in the discussions which led to the preliminary settlement between the allied powers and Germany in the summer of 1924. On March 5, 1925, Kellogg, appointed by President Coolidge, took the oath of office as secretary of state.[10]

[10] Johnson, *University of Minnesota*, 358; *St. Paul Sunday Pioneer Press*, January 11, 1925; *Legislative Manual*, 1917, pp. 190, 513; 1923, p. 280, insert after p. 452. The vote in 1922 stood: Shipstead, 325,372; Kellogg, 241,833; Anna Dickie Olesen, 123,624. Shipstead was the candidate of a new party, for a brief account of which see *post*, pp. 548–553. See the *St. Paul Dispatch*, October 26, 1923, for the appointment of Kellogg as ambassador, and March 5, 1925, for his accession to the office of secretary of state. The Interallied Conference in London which negotiated the reparations settlement on the basis of the "Dawes plan" was in session from July 16 to August 17, 1924. See the issues of the *Pioneer Press* for these and the intervening dates for the progress of the conference and Kellogg's part in it.

On January 29, 1919, proclamation was made by the acting secretary of state that the legislatures of thirty-six states had ratified the proposed amendment to the national Constitution to prohibit forever the manufacture, sale, and transportation of intoxicating liquors for beverage purposes and to give to Congress and the several states concurrent power to put the prohibition into effect. It was the consummation of a long course of agitation and experiment. The Washingtonian temperance movement of the early forties, following earlier endeavors, had made drunkenness a shame, had banished liquor from the homes of most of the people, and had made liquor-selling disreputable. Early attempts at liquor control were made through the agency of state, rather than national, legislation. The legislature of Minnesota in 1852 passed a prohibitory act but referred it to the electors of the territory. The vote stood 853 for the act and 662 against it. Upon appeal by a citizen who had been fined for violation of the act, the supreme court of the territory ruled that the act was invalid, not having been definitively enacted by the legislature, to which all legislative power had been delegated by the organic law of the territory. Between the years 1850 and 1856 thirteen states placed prohibition laws on their statute books, all of which were later repealed or set aside. After some early experiments in liquor legislation, the state of Maine in 1858 passed a prohibition law which has never been repealed. Kansas became " dry " in 1880 and North Dakota, in 1890. In the first decade of the twentieth century six states prohibited liquor and in the second decade fifteen states were added to the dry column, so that when Congress was proposing the eighteenth amendment twenty-four states had adopted prohibition.[11]

The sentiment for national prohibition was late to appear and had a slow development. In 1876 the Senate passed a

[11] *Statutes at Large*, 40: 1941; *ante*, 1: 264. See the speech of Jacob E. Meeker, with a great amount of statistics embodied and attached, in *Congressional Record*, 65 Congress, 1 session, 4506–4533.

bill for the appointment of a commission of five to investigate the subject. In the House the bill went to the pigeon-hole of the committee of ways and means. At the second session of the same Congress Representative Henry W. Blair of New Hampshire introduced into the House a resolution for the submission to the states of an amendment for the prohibition of the manufacture and sale of " distilled alcoholic intoxicating liquors," to take effect after the year 1900. On December 27, 1876, he made a speech covering twenty-five columns of the *Congressional Record,* abounding in statistics and displaying the evils resulting from such liquors.[12] Blair was in the Senate in 1882 and there introduced his House resolution, which did not receive serious attention. He renewed it in 1885, 1888, and 1890. In all cases the bills were referred to the Senate committee on education and labor and were reported back without amendment, accompanied by reports doubtless prepared by the ever-hopeful chairman, Senator Blair.[13] Although the national Prohibition party, which had entered the field in 1872, and such societies as the Woman's Christian Temperance Union were clamoring for nation-wide prohibition, the question did not come up again in Congress until December 10, 1913, when Representative Richmond P. Hobson of Alabama, distinguished for his effort to shut up the Spanish fleet in the harbor of Santiago de Cuba, introduced a joint resolution for the submission of a prohibitory amendment. It went over to the third session of the same Congress and on December 22, 1914, after a brilliant debate in the House led by Hobson, was rejected, having failed to get the required two-thirds vote.[14]

[12] *Congressional Record,* 44 Congress, 1 session, 574, 581–585, 604, 835; 2 session, 145, appendix, 5–17.
[13] *Congressional Record,* 47 Congress, 1 session, 976; 49 Congress, 1 session, 137; 50 Congress, 1 session, 5995; 51 Congress, 1 session, 107, 8511; 49 Congress, 1 session, *Senate Reports,* no. 1563 (serial 2365) ; 50 Congress, 1 session, *Senate Reports,* no. 1727 (serial 2525).
[14] McKee, *National Conventions and Platforms,* 219; *Congressional Record,* 63 Congress, 2 session, 659, 736–745, 8393; *House Reports,* no. 652, part 2

The prohibition cause now lagged until the World War had aroused in the American people a keener interest in general welfare, a deeper appreciation of the evils of intemperance, and a desire to destroy the domination of the liquor interests in politics. Prohibition in many states and agitation going on in others indicated a conviction widely extended that prohibition would be good for all states and that it should become a part of the fundamental law of the land. A resolution looking toward national prohibition was introduced into the Senate on April 4, 1917, and, after a debate covering more than a hundred and fifty columns of the *Record*, it was adopted on August 1, 1917, by a vote of 65 to 20. In the second session of the same Congress, on December 15, 1917, the resolution came up in the House and, after two days' debate, was passed by a vote of 282 to 128, twenty-three not voting. At the last minute before the vote two amendments were adopted: one postponed the operation of prohibition until one year after ratification and the other required ratification within seven years. The Senate concurred in the amendments.[15]

The eighteenth amendment was in the nature of an enabling act but it presumed that Congress would immediately enact the laws needed to enforce it and that the state legislatures would do so later at their pleasure. On June 27, 1919, Representative Andrew J. Volstead of Minnesota, who in the course of sixteen years' service in the House had reached the high position of chairman of the committee on judiciary, introduced the bill which has since borne his name. Debate began on July 10 in committee of the whole and lasted nearly a fortnight, covering over four hundred columns of the *Congressional Record*. The bill passed the

(serial 6559). See *Congressional Record*, 63 Congress, 3 session, 495–616, for the long debate on the resolution. This resolution contemplated the prohibition of " the sale, manufacture for sale, transportation for sale, importation for sale and exportation for sale of intoxicating liquors for beverage purposes." It was rejected by a vote of 190 to 197, one voting " present " and forty not voting.

[15] *Congressional Record*, 65 Congress, 1 session, 5548–5560, 5585–5627, 5636–5666; 2 session, 340, 422–470, 478; *Statutes at Large*, 40: 1050.

House by a vote of 287 to 100, with three voting " present " and forty not voting. There was a two-day debate in the Senate covering nearly fifty columns of the *Record* and on September 5, 1919, the bill passed without division, but with an immense batch of amendments. These were tardily adjusted in conference and the conference report was adopted by the Senate on October 8, 1919, without roll call, and by the House two days later by a vote of 230 to 69, with one voting " present " and 129 not voting. On October 16 the bill was laid before President Wilson, who on the twenty-seventh returned it to the House without signature and with his objections. That part of the bill for the enforcement of wartime prohibition was superfluous; he had already asked Congress to repeal it. The other portion, for the enforcement of the eighteenth amendment, " having to do with the personal habits and customs of large numbers of our people," should follow, he said, " established processes of legal change." It was implied that the bill had not followed such processes. On the same day the House agreed by a vote of 175 to 55, with three voting " present," to repass the bill and on the following day the Senate concurred by a two-thirds vote.[16] It is not hazardous to say that the eighteenth amendment will remain a part of the Constitution and that the manufacture of and traffic in intoxicating alcoholic liquors for beverage purposes are forever prohibited in all territory under the jurisdiction of the United States. It is not so certain that the Volstead Law, with its definition of the word " intoxicating " and its drastic penalties for violation, will remain unchanged. It is believed by many that the law incites illicit manufacture and traffic, which the national and state governments have not been and, some say, never will be able to suppress.[17]

[16] *Congressional Record*, 66 Congress, 1 session, 9797, references under H. R. 6810.

[17] The attorney-general of the United States reports that 42,730 criminal cases and 2,670 civil cases arising under the national prohibition act were disposed of in the year ending June 30, 1923, and fines were imposed to the

The nineteenth amendment to the national Constitution also had a long evolution. Manhood suffrage had become general in the first half of the nineteenth century. It was then inevitable that women, being also human, would desire the right to vote and would some day secure it. The beginning of organized propaganda was the Woman's Rights Convention held at Seneca Falls, New York, on July 19 and 20, 1848. Among the resolutions adopted was this: " It is the duty of the women of this country to secure to themselves their sacred right to the elective franchise." The long story of the following forty years of endeavor cannot be told here. As the national Constitution did not select the persons to be invested with the elective franchise but left the selection to the several states, it was the natural thing for women to look first to the states to grant " their sacred right." Not until 1890 was full suffrage secured to women by a state — that of Wyoming, in a constitution submitted with her application for admission to the Union. There was lively opposition to the admission of Wyoming in both houses, but the act was passed. Within six years three other Rocky Mountain states had granted full suffrage to their women and by 1914 nine states had granted full suffrage and twenty-two others, limited suffrage. But the movement was slow. A proposition to subvert the immemorial status of women, believed by multitudes to be sanctioned by Holy Scripture, awaited a tardy reversal of sentiment.[18]

It was not until the World War gave women a new opportunity to show how in public capacities they could serve the country's cause that there was a sudden outburst of hospi-

sum of $5,832,389. He reports undue leniency on the part of the courts. Attorney-General, *Reports*, 1923, p. 86.

[18] Sophonisba P. Breckenridge, in McLaughlin and Hart, *Cyclopedia of American Government*, 3: 694–697; Elizabeth C. Stanton, Susan B. Anthony, and Matilda J. Gage, eds., *History of Woman Suffrage*, 1: 67–76 (New York, 1881). On page 70 of the latter work is the " Declaration of Sentiments," modeled on the Declaration of Independence, which declares the elective franchise to be an " inalienable right." The debate on the admission of Wyoming is in *Congressional Record*, 51 Congress, 1 session, 2663–2712, 6472–6492, 6574–6589.

tality for the reform. A loud and urgent demand arose for the amendment of the national Constitution to forbid the states to exclude women from the elective franchise. Resolutions for such an amendment had often been introduced into Congress but none of them were seriously entertained until December 18, 1917, when six resolutions of the same tenor were presented to the House. On January 8, 1918, the committee to which they had been referred returned one selected as typical with a favorable recommendation, declaring in its report that " The war has made woman suffrage a national question. The Congress should treat it as such." Two days later the House passed the resolution by a large majority and sent it to the Senate.[19] In the course of the Senate debate a letter from President Wilson to Mrs. Carrie Chapman Catt, at that time the leader of the suffrage movement, was read into the record. The president said: " The services of women during this supreme crisis of the world's history have been of the most usefulness and distinction. The war could not have been fought without them or its sacrifices endured." His letter closed with the hope that the Senate would pass the resolution before the end of the session. The Senate took its time in the matter. On September 30 President Wilson appeared in person before the Senate with a special address to expedite its action. It was a long, impassioned appeal, as emphatic and ardent as that master of English style could produce. He asserted that the full and sincere democratic reconstruction of the world could not be completely and adequately attained until women were admitted to the suffrage. He said, " I tell you plainly that this measure . . . is vital to the winning of the war. . . . It is vital to the right solution of the great problems which we must settle, and settle immediately, when the war is over. We shall need then a vision of affairs which is theirs and,

[19] 65 Congress, 2 session, *House Reports*, no. 234 (serial 7307) ; *Congressional Record*, 543, 699, 810. The House vote was: yeas, 274; nays, 136; with seventeen not voting.

as we have never needed them before, the sympathy and insight and clear moral instinct of the women of the world. . . . Without their counsellings we shall be only half wise." The Senate was not stampeded, but went on with its debate until October 1, when it came to a vote. The vote stood 53 to 31, not the necessary two-thirds, and the resolution failed to pass.[20]

Early in the first session of a new Congress in 1919 the resolution to submit a nineteenth amendment to the legislatures of the states was introduced in the House and was passed by a vote of 304 to 90, with one voting " present " and thirty-three not voting. The Senate proceeded more leisurely, taking a fortnight to deliberate, but on June 4, 1919, it adopted the joint resolution by the sufficient vote of 56 to 25, with fifteen not voting. The action of the proper number — three-fourths — of the state legislatures was expeditious, the more so because in some of them suffrage amendments to their own constitutions were in progress. On August 26, 1920, Bainbridge Colby, secretary of state, issued a proclamation announcing that the nineteenth amendment had been ratified by a sufficient number of state legislatures and had become a part of the Constitution of the United States.[21] The legislature of Minnesota, being in special session in the fall of 1919, ratified the proposed amendment. Although Minnesota has not yet cut the word " male " out of the text of her constitutional qualifications for the elective franchise, that clause is superseded by the federal amendment and women have secured their sacred right to vote.[22]

[20] *Congressional Record*, 65 Congress, 2 session, 8343–8355, 10769–10791, 10842–10860, 10925–10933, 10941–10953, 10976–10988. Wilson's letter to Mrs. Catt is on page 7795 and his address, on page 10928.
[21] *Congressional Record*, 66 Congress, 1 session, 9854, references under H. J. Res. 1; *Statutes at Large*, 41: 1823.
[22] *Laws*, 1919, extra session, 98. Minnesota women had been given the suffrage for school officials in 1876 and for library officials in 1898. Anderson, *History of the Constitution*, 179, 231; *General Laws*, 1875, p. 18; 1876, p. 29; 1897, p. 331; 1899, p. iii.

In the period covered by this chapter thirty-five amendments to the state constitution were proposed by the legislature, six of them a second time and two a third time. But two of them related to the fundamental part of the constitution, the frame of government. One of these, which was twice submitted to the electors — in 1914 and again in 1916 — proposed to introduce the initiative and referendum. The other, proposed in 1913, was for the recall of all public officials in Minnesota, elective or appointive. Both were rejected. Other proposals generally had for their objects the enlargement of the powers of the legislature, chiefly in regard to taxation and finance. All but one of the proposals received majorities of the votes cast upon the several propositions, in some cases very large majorities, but only fifteen got the necessary majorities of all the votes cast at the several elections. Three are to be submitted to the voters in the election of 1926. Nine of the proposals related to finance and taxation and four to forest preservation and culture.[23]

The reader may remember the veto by Governor Johnson of the tonnage-tax bill passed by the legislature of 1909, chiefly on the ground that it would impose a double tax upon a class of property. The problem of exacting from the owners of ore lands some compensation for the loss by the state of some portion of her heritage bestowed by nature was left to be solved; and it remained unsolved for many years. Bills introduced into the legislatures of 1917 and 1919 failed. One passed at the special session of 1919 was vetoed by Governor Burnquist as unfair and inadequate.[24] His successor, Governor Preus, took up the matter very seriously in his message to the legislature of 1921. After re-

---

[23] Anderson, *History of the Constitution*, 283–285; *Laws*, 1921, pp. 999–1002; 1923, pp. 716–720; 1925, pp. 773–775; *Legislative Manual*, 1923, insert after p. 452; 1925, insert after p. 318.

[24] See *ante*, p. 289; *House Journal*, 1917, pp. 412, 1319; 1919, p. 333; 1919, extra session, 86, 194, 254; *Senate Journal*, 1917, pp. 1058, 1074; 1919, extra session, 156.

ferring to plans which had been discarded, he proposed a
" severance tax " in lieu of, or in connection with, a reduced
ad valorem tax. The legislature was apparently of the
opinion that such a tax would be as obnoxious to the state
constitution as any tonnage tax which had been proposed and
struck out on a new line, suggested by Attorney-General
Clifford L. Hilton. It proposed to the electors of the state
an amendment to section 1 of article 9 of the constitution to
the effect that all persons engaged in mining iron or other
ores should pay an occupation tax on the valuation of the
ore produced in addition to all other taxes provided for by
law, that the legislature should fix the valuation of the ore
and the rate of the tax, and that the proceeds should be apportioned among certain specified funds. The proposed
amendment was ratified at the general election of 1922 by a
very large majority of votes. The legislature of 1921, anticipating the ratification of the amendment, passed an act
fixing the rate of the occupation tax at six per cent and required the state tax commission to ascertain the value of the
ores produced.[25]

The great mining companies at once prepared to test the
constitutionality of the amendment and the enabling act under
it. The Oliver Iron Mining Company, which would be hit
hardest, took the lead and brought suit in the United States
district court for Minnesota, complaining that the so-called
" occupation tax " was in fact a tax on property, which could
not be imposed by the state on a commodity in interstate
commerce. Six other cases, involving thirty-six companies
with similar complaints, were brought up and the seven
cases were argued and decided together. The court upheld
the law but enjoined enforcement for sixty days to give an
opportunity for appeal. The companies at once appealed to
the Supreme Court of the United States, which, after hearing

[25] J. A. O. Preus, *Inaugural Message*, 1921, pp. 9–15; *Laws*, 1921,
pp. 274, 1000–1002. The vote on the ratification of the amendment was: yes,
474,697; no, 91,011. *Legislative Manual*, 1923, insert after p. 452.

and argument, sustained the decree of the district court and the validity of the occupation tax.[26]

Another amendment to the state constitution of far-reaching importance, social as well as financial, was that proposed by the legislature of 1919 and ratified at the general election on November 2, 1920, for the creation of a trunk highway system. An act of the legislature of 1905 had created a state highway commission of three members to be appointed by the governor for three-year terms and to serve without pay. A state tax of one-twentieth of a mill was provided to inure to a state road and bridge fund, which was to be distributed to counties as state aid in construction and improvement of roads according to rules and regulations prescribed by the commission, but not more than three per cent of the fund was to be given to a county in any year. In 1913 this law was embodied in a highway code and the state road tax was raised to one mill on the dollar.[27] The federal aid road act of July 11, 1916, for the betterment of rural post roads, carried an appropriation from the United States treasury of five million dollars for the year ending June 30, 1917, and an annual increment of the same amount until it should amount to twenty-five millions in 1921. The secretary of agriculture was charged with the distribution of these moneys to the states according to area, population, and mileage of rural postal delivery and star routes.[28] This liberality of the general government gave Minnesota occasion to re-

[26] A printed record of the proceedings in the United States district court, including the pleadings, the agreed statement of facts, the briefs of the attorneys, and the opinion and decree of the court, may be found in the office of the attorney-general of Minnesota, bound in a volume with the back title, "Briefs and Paper Books," vol. 115. For the Supreme Court decision in the case of the Oliver Iron Mining Company v. Lord et al and the six other similar cases, see 262 United States, 172–181. A layman may wonder why a tax imposed as a ratio of an assessed valuation of property is not a property tax. We may have here an example of judge-made law.

[27] Anderson, History of the Constitution, 285; General Laws, 1905, pp. 198–202; 1913, pp. 290–329.

[28] Statutes at Large, 39: 355. For an account of the inefficiency of the act, see the report of the chief of the bureau of public roads, in Department of Agriculture, Reports, 1919, p. 395.

organize her road system. The legislature of 1917 abolished the highway commission of three members, serving without compensation, and replaced it with a single commissioner of highways to be appointed by the governor for six years, with a seal of office and a salary of $4,500. The commissioner was given power to appoint a deputy and a suitable number of engineers and employees and to fix their several compensations. Under this legislation the department of highways continued the policy of regulating the action of county commissioners in the construction, improvement, and maintenance of state roads and of distributing the state bridge fund and the federal bonus.[29]

Governor Burnquist reminded the legislature of 1919 of the importance of good roads for the marketing of farm produce, for the advancement of country life, and for the encouragement of consolidated schools. It was time, he said, to begin the construction of permanent highways, a movement already in progress in other states. The constitution should at once be amended so as to permit the borrowing of money for the purpose. The legislature responded by proposing a constitutional amendment of the most extraordinary character. Instead of providing for a trunk highway system in general terms and leaving to the legislature the enactment of laws necessary and proper to develop the system, the proposed amendment selected seventy described routes for construction, improvement, and maintenance and gave the legislature power to add new routes after seventy-five per cent of the specified routes should have been improved. It added a little more than one-third to the number of pages of the constitution. A tax on motor vehicles and a bond issue not to exceed seventy-five million dollars were authorized, the proceeds to be paid into a trunk highway sinking fund. The amendment was ratified, as stated, at the general election on November 2, 1920. Its

[29] *Laws*, 1917, pp. 147–169; Highway Commissioner, *Reports*, 1918–19, pp. 5–7.

extraordinary character was doubtless due to a desire to protect the legislature from temptations to permit localities or combinations of localities to " hog " the government benefaction.[30]

The ratification of this amendment was the more cheerfully accorded because of the additional appropriation by Congress on February 28, 1919, of fifty million dollars for state aid for that year and of seventy-five million dollars for each of the two following years. At the same time the secretary of war was authorized to turn over to the secretary of agriculture war material and equipment not needed for military purposes to be distributed to states for highway construction and improvement. The devotion of national funds to internal improvement, long denounced as unconstitutional, was opposed no more. A longer step was taken by Congress in passing on November 9, 1921, the now well-known Federal Highway Act, carrying an appropriation of seventy-five million dollars for 1922. The act authorized each state highway department to select a system of interstate and intercounty highways, not to exceed seven per cent of the total mileage of its roads. Upon these highways the federal aid was to be expended.[31]

It fell to the legislature of 1921 to enact the laws necessary and proper to put into effect the state highway amendment and the anticipated Federal Highway Act. The long chapter under the title, " Public Highways Act of Minnesota," amounts to a code. The most radical of its provisions

[30] J. A. A. Burnquist, *Inaugural Message*, 1919, p. 13; *Laws*, 1919, pp. 737–752; *Legislative Manual*, 1921, p. 523; Anderson, *History of the Constitution*, 192–194, 201–203, 252–265. The vote stood: yes, 526,936; no, 199,603; total votes cast at the election, 797,945 — the largest vote and the largest majority ever cast on a constitutional amendment up to that time. The amendment forms article 16 of the constitution.

[31] *Statutes at Large*, 40: 1200; 42: 212–219. For the operation of the acts, see reports of the chief of the bureau of public roads, in Department of Agriculture, *Reports*, 1920, pp. 494–499; 1922, p. 462; 1923, pp. 489–491. The last of these gives testimony as to the importance to states of the motor vehicles distributed and the " almost inestimable value " of the shop equipment furnished. Up to June 30, 1923, Minnesota had received surplus war material to the value of $5,299,678 out of a total of $208,559,572 distributed.

is that which took out of the hands of county commissioners the construction and maintenance of roads upon which federal aid was applied and put them into the immediate care of the commissioner of highways. Under the provisions of the act the state department of highways has grown to great proportions. In the calendar years 1917–22, inclusive, the total apportionment of federal aid to Minnesota was $9,938,980.09, of which $4,061,832.60 were paid for completed projects. That the recent immense increase in expenditures for better roads is due to the enormous multiplication of vehicles moved by internal combustion engines needs no argument.[32]

Preparations for a threatened war in Europe had been going on for an indefinite time but open war may be said to have begun with the speech of the German emperor, Wilhelm II, from the balcony of his palace in Berlin on July 31, 1914. Two days later the German army had seized the principality of Luxemburg and had invaded France.[33] For nearly a year America watched the gigantic struggle, adhering to her traditional policy of avoiding entangling interference in foreign affairs which did not seriously concern her. But a time came when European affairs did seriously concern her. On May 7, 1915, the British passenger steamer "Lusitania," carrying over a hundred American passengers on peaceful errands, was sunk without warning off the south coast of Ireland by a German submarine. Within a week Secretary of State William J. Bryan, instructed by President Wilson, sent through the American ambassador in Berlin, James W. Gerard, a note of protest, demanding " just, prompt, and enlightened action in this vital matter " and giving warning that the United States government would not fail in " its sacred duty of maintaining the rights of . . .

[32] *Laws,* 1921, pp. 406–464; Department of Agriculture, *Reports,* 1922, p. 468.

[33] *New York Times Current History,* 1: 209, 221 (December 26, 1914).

its citizens." The German minister of foreign affairs replied on May 28, through Ambassador Gerard, that "on her last trip the Lusitania, as on earlier occasions, had Canadian troops and munitions on board" and therefore was not immune from attack. On June 9 Wilson replied through Robert Lansing, who succeeded Bryan as secretary of state, that the United States government had performed its duty in ascertaining that the "Lusitania" was not serving as a transport and was not carrying a "cargo prohibited by the statutes of the United States." In a note dated July 8 the German minister stated that, as England had undertaken to starve the German people by the seizure of neutral merchant vessels laden with food on the North Sea, Germany had the right to retaliate. Wilson's reply of July 21 expressly stated that a repetition of acts in contravention of the rights of American citizens would be regarded by the government as "deliberately unfriendly." The imperial German government, believing, no doubt, that the employment of submarine war vessels to destroy merchant vessels without warning was, under the circumstances, justifiable and would be "the best and only means to a speedy victorious ending of the war," gave no assurance of intention to cease that form of warfare.[34]

For over a year and a half more the American government maintained its policy of "watchful waiting." The American people did not want to enter a war in whose purposes they might be but remotely concerned. President Wilson's reëlection in November, 1916, was promoted, if not assured, by the fact that he "kept us out of war."[35] On March 1, 1917, a message from the German foreign affairs office to the German minister at Mexico City, dated January

[34] *Current History*, 2: 409–412, 415, 615, 620–622, 819–825 (June, July, August, 1915). The note of May 13, 1915, though signed by Bryan, was typewritten by President Wilson from his own shorthand notes.

[35] John Buchan, *A History of the Great War*, 3: 116 (Cambridge, 1922). According to Buchan, Wilson's "trump card was that he kept America out of the war."

16, 1917, became public. It had been sent to Johann von Bernstorff, German ambassador at Washington, to be relayed by him to Mexico, and had been intercepted by the British government. The Senate asked the president for assurance of the genuineness of the document and was informed that the government was in possession of the proof. The message contained a proposal of an alliance between Germany and Mexico for peace and war and anticipated a break with the United States. The most interesting part of the message, however, was the opening sentence: "On February 1 we intend to begin submarine warfare unrestricted." In the course of about sixty days eleven American merchant vessels were sunk by German submarines. On April 2 President Wilson made his memorable address to Congress in joint session. After stating the particular hostile acts of Germany against our country's rights, he reminded Congress that the war was one "against all nations," the "challenge . . . to all mankind"; neutrality was no longer possible. America was called "to spend her blood and her might for the principles that gave her birth." Paraphrasing Luther's ultimatum to the Diet of Worms, he concluded, "God helping her, she can do no other." Four days later, on April 6, the resolution declaring war on Germany, which had passed by great majorities in the Senate on April 4 and in the House on the following day, was approved by President Wilson.[36]

Congress had almost a year before this time made provisions for increasing the efficiency of the regular army and the national guard; it was now obvious that a vast additional force by land and sea would be needed. On April 22, 1917,

[36] Burton J. Hendrick, *The Life and Letters of Walter H. Page*, 3: 331–364 (Garden City, 1925); *Current History*, 6: 65–71 (April, 1917); *Congressional Record*, 65 Congress, 1 session, 102–104, 261, 412; *Statutes at Large*, 40: 1. Lists of the 151 American merchant vessels and 48 navy vessels destroyed by German submarines, mines, and raiders, from August, 1914, to November 9, 1918, are in Secretary of the Navy, *Reports*, 1918, p. 178. On pages 182 to 211 are detailed accounts of some of the sinkings.

three distinguished emissaries from England and France — Balfour, Joffre, and Viviani — with numerous attachés, arrived in Washington. In their public addresses and statements to the press they did not clearly declare that the armies of their states were in imminent danger of defeat, but it was well understood that the eminent guests had not crossed the Atlantic at that time on a pleasure excursion. Balfour, however, went so far as to say that the armies of the powers represented might be defeated in detail. Congress had not waited for the arrival of the European delegation, but had already taken up the matter of increasing the army. There was some opposition to any increase, a good deal to giving up our traditional employment of volunteers, and much difference of opinions about details. After six weeks of palaver the Selective Service Act became a law on May 18, 1917.[37] The phrase was, of course, a euphemism for a draft, a term not in good odor in our country. The details of the act need not here be described. Under its operation nearly twenty-four million men were registered for selection and over two million seven hundred thousand were selected and sworn into the military service.[38]

[37] *Current History*, 6: 389–405 (June, 1917); *Statutes at Large*, 39: 166–217; 40: 76–83. For the history of the Selective Service Bill, see 65 Congress, 1 session, *Senate Reports*, no. 22 (serial 7249); *House Reports*, no. 17 (serial 7252); and *Congressional Record*, index, references under H. R. 3545, S. 1871. The bill had been drafted in the war department and had the approval of the general staff and the secretary of war. Much time was given to debates on what was called the "Roosevelt Amendment," first introduced into the Senate by Senator Warren G. Harding of Ohio. The proposal was to authorize the president to raise, equip, and maintain four divisions of infantry volunteers all over twenty-five years of age, with the understanding that the corps thus formed would be commanded by ex-President Roosevelt. There were large majorities in both houses in favor of the amendment; in the Senate the vote was 56 to 31 and in the House, 215 to 178. See *Senate Journal*, 64 (serial 7247); *House Journal*, 153 (serial 7248). It became law as a part of the Selective Service Act. President Wilson was wise enough not to exercise the authority conferred. A proposition submitted by Senator Robert M. La Follette of Wisconsin for a referendum to the electors of the question, "Shall the United States Government at this time raise an army by draft to send to Europe to prosecute the war?" was rejected by a vote of 68 to 4, with 24 not voting. The prosposed referendum included the "Roosevelt Amendment." *Congressional Record*, 1616–1624.

[38] The total number of men registered was 23,908,576, of whom 2,758,542 were called by November 11, 1918. See Provost Marshal General, *Final*

Of the limited part taken by Minnesota in the great drama she had good reason to be proud. Over half a million (541,607) of her men were registered. The total number accepted by the government from the draft and voluntary induction was 74,275. The men composing this body were assembled by the local draft boards and sent to the great training camps, where they were mingled with the men from other states. The number of men furnished by Minnesota included four regiments of the national guard mobilized in accordance with the provisions of the National Defense Act of June 3, 1916, and with them a hospital unit and an ambulance unit. The members of these bodies were inducted into the federal service individually as of August 5, 1917. It is estimated that if to the national guard and the drafted men be added recruits for the regular army and navy and for the naval reserve and the marine corps, the whole number of Minnesota men turned from the paths of peace into the ranks of war approximates some 118,000.[39]

The whole number of Minnesota soldiery sent overseas can hardly be guessed. All the national guard units were sent. The First Minnesota Infantry took the new number 135 in the national army, and the Second, the number 136; the Third Infantry was transferred to the artillery service

Report on the Operations of the Selective Service System to July 15, 1919, 14 (Washington, 1920), and the same officer's Report on the First Draft under the Selective-Service Act, 1917, 5, 7, 11, 14, 21, 25 (Washington, 1918). On pages 73–87 and 119 of the latter may be found the statistics of Minnesota's contributions to the first draft. For remarks on the operation of the draft and a maze of statistics, see Provost Marshal General, Second Report on the Operations of the Selective Service System to December 20, 1918 (Washington, 1919). On pages 379–394 appears a paper on conscription in Great Britain during the years 1914–18.

[39] Provost Marshal General, Final Report, 19, 82; Minnesota, Adjutant General, Reports, 1917–18, p. 120. The number called for service by draft was 76,764; voluntary induction raised the number to 79,383. For authorization of the draft boards, see Statutes at Large, 40: 79. In pursuance of the provisions of the National Defense Act, Congress, on May 18, 1917, authorized the president to draft the national guard into the federal military service. The president's call was dated July 3, 1917. See Statutes at Large, 39: 211; 40: 1681. The estimates of Minnesota's strength in the war were made by Franklin F. Holbrook, secretary of the Minnesota War Records Commission, in a letter to the author, November 28, 1924, in the Folwell Papers.

and was numbered 125. There remains to be mentioned particularly the First Field Artillery of the Minnesota National Guard, whose fortune it was to be included in the famous Rainbow Division, composed of national guard units from many states. It was called into service on June 23, 1917, and was ordered to assemble as soon as possible. The first battalion was held at Fort Snelling and the second was ordered to Fort Riley, Kansas. On September 4 the former departed for Camp Mills, Long Island, where a few days later it was joined by the second battalion. This regiment, under the new number 151 in the national army, was the only Minnesota command to take part in battle as an organization. Of its performance Minnesota will ever be proud. How many men from her other regiments were taken from replacement divisions and sent into battle with other combat troops may not for a long time, if ever, be ascertained. Roughly estimated, the losses of Minnesota troops and seamen were about thirty-five hundred killed; the total casualties were about seven thousand. The tracing of the history of Minnesota men in the war and the compiling of the complete list of casualties will be the work of many years.[40]

To the credit of Minnesota must be added patriotic activities within her own borders. The legislature of 1917, aware of much opposition to our engaging in the war, of possible resistance to the mobilization of the national guard and drafted men on the part of sympathizers with Germany, and of possible mischief by agents of the German government, on April 16, 1917, ten days after the declaration of war, passed an act providing for a " Commission of Public Safety," consisting of the governor as chairman, the attor-

[40] Report of the chief of the militia bureau, in War Department, *Reports*, 1918, vol. 1, p. 1192; *Minneapolis Tribune*, September 4, 5, 1917; Minnesota, Adjutant General, *Reports*, 1917–18, pp. 120, 315. See pages 128–240 for rosters of the national guard, without footing. The fortunes of the 151st Field Artillery may be followed in Louis L. Collins, *History of the 151st Field Artillery, Rainbow Division (Publications of the Minnesota War Records Commission*, vol. 2; *Minnesota in the World War*, vol. 1 — St. Paul, 1924), and in the Appendix, no. 17, *post*.

ney-general, and five other citizens of the state to be appointed by the governor with the advice and consent of the Senate. To this board was given a sweeping power to do all lawful things necessary and proper to protect life and property needing protection and to provide for the defense of the state and for the efficient prosecution of the war so far as the state was concerned.[41] In particular the board was authorized to enlist, organize, and maintain a Minnesota Home Guard for service within the state. The sum of one million dollars was appropriated, to be immediately available and payable on the order of the commission. On the twenty-eighth of April the commission authorized the enlistment of seven battalions of the home guard, to be stationed wherever the governor might direct, and also authorized the governor, at his discretion, to increase that number. Six of the seven battalions were organized during May, June, and July, with headquarters at St. Paul, Duluth, Virginia, Winona, Mankato, and Faribault. Additional battalions were organized from time to time, one as late as July, 1918, until their total number was twenty-three. They were commanded by majors and the usual company officers of militia. The number of companies in the battalions varied from three to nine. All the members were required to furnish their own uniforms and equipment and to serve without pay unless held in active service for more than five days. The very organization of the home guard so dampened the ardor of German sympathizers that no overt acts of opposition took place and disloyal sentiments rarely found expression. No little pride was taken by the members in the service; they bought their

[41] *Laws*, 1917, pp. 373–377; Minnesota Commission of Public Safety, *Report*, 30–34, 55. This report is dated January 1, 1919. See *Laws*, 1919, p. 91, for the act fixing a maximum penalty of ten thousand dollars' fine or twenty years' imprisonment, or both, against persons convicted of obstructing the sale of United States bonds, of uttering abusive language against the government, the Constitution, the uniform of the army or navy, or of supporting or favoring the cause of any country with which the United States is at war. See the Appendix, no. 19, *post*, for a more extended account of the work of the Minnesota Commission of Public Safety.

uniforms and attended frequent drills. The whole number of the home guard, enlisted and commissioned, was 7,373.

There was an unusual and perhaps unique extension of the home guard. Winfield R. Stephens, a "Minneapolis automobile man," conceived the idea of a uniformed and armed military corps to be composed of owners of automobiles, who should be ready to report for duty whenever called. Governor Burnquist approved the plan and on May 23, 1918, authorized the organization of six battalions of motor men. The number was later raised to ten and Stephens, the commander, was given the rank of colonel. The whole number of officers and men was 2,583. The remarkable service rendered by the motor corps, as well as by several battalions of the home guard proper, at the time of the forest fires in October, 1918, will be described in a later account of that terrible disaster.[42]

Near the close of the period covered by this chapter there took place a notable disturbance in the current of Republican domination in Minnesota politics. In the winter of 1915 there was formed in North Dakota an association of actual farmers under the name, "Farmers' Nonpartisan League." Its leading purpose was to secure the establishment of state terminal elevators, flour mills, packing houses, and cold-storage plants. It was not a political party but it proposed in the next election year to compel the dominant political party to nominate and elect men pledged to its program. By a novel and ingenious method of recruiting, the membership was so increased that in 1916 the league compelled the Republicans to nominate and elect a full ticket of state officials of their preference, with but a single exception. The plan worked so well in North Dakota that immediately after its success in that state at the June primaries it

[42] Adjutant General, *Reports*, 1917–18, pp. 253–277, 284, 342, 353; *Review* (Mankato), July 17, 1917, p. 5. An account of the fires of 1918 will be given in the next volume.

was taken up in Minnesota. It was then too late to get into action for the elections of 1916. In preparation for those of 1918 recruiting was pushed with great vigor so that by midsummer of 1918 there were some fifty thousand members of the league on the rolls in Minnesota. The league was not successful in dictating the Republican nomination for governor at the primary election in that year and failed to throw enough votes to the Democratic candidate to elect him.

As the time for the campaign of 1920 drew on the Nonpartisans understood that they could not possibly carry the state without a large access of outside votes. For that their leaders decided to look to organized labor, which was willing to coöperate but not to coalesce. There was accordingly formed the Working People's Nonpartisan Political League, composed of labor union members. This league and the Farmers' Nonpartisan League held conventions on the same day in separate halls, in March, 1920, but agreed upon a slate made up by a joint committee. Their candidate for governor, Henrik Shipstead, was defeated by Governor Preus by a large majority. In 1922 the Farmer-Labor candidate for the governorship, Magnus Johnson, an actual tiller of the soil, was beaten by Governor Preus, running for a reëlection; but he cut down Preus's plurality over him to 14,277. At the same election Frank B. Kellogg stood for a reëlection to the United States Senate, which he had a good right to expect. By a plurality of more than eighty thousand the Farmer-Labor combination gave him leave to return to private life. This was a severe blow to Republicans, who had enjoyed a virtual monopoly in the national Senate since the days of Henry M. Rice. But a heavier blow awaited them. Senator Knute Nelson died suddenly on April 28, 1923. Governor Preus proclaimed a special primary election for June 18 and a final election on July 16 and announced himself as an aspirant for the vacancy. Magnus Johnson was the favorite candidate of the Farmer-Labor voters. The two were nominated at the primary, but Johnson was the winner

MINNESOTA IN 1920

Showing county lines and the
distribution of population by
minor civil divisions according
to the United States census.
Each dot represents 100 people
or major fraction thereof. Solid
black areas represent cities or
villages of over 350 population.

0   20   40   60

SCALE OF MILES

at the final election for the unexpired term of Senator Nelson to end on March 4, 1925. At the elections of 1924 Johnson aspired to serve for the regular six-year term to follow. But the Republicans, who had recovered their breath, got onto their feet and denied that honor to the farmer-senator. Thomas D. Schall, about to finish ten years' service in the House, was chosen by a plurality of 7,948 votes over Johnson. At none of the elections mentioned did the Farmer-Labor party elect any state officials, except a clerk of the supreme court, and their representation in the legislatures was too meager to have any material effect.[43]

In the general election of 1924 the Republican nominees for state offices obtained larger majorities than did their candidate for United States senator. Theodore Christianson was elected governor over Floyd B. Olson, his Farmer-Labor opponent, by a vote of 406,692 to 366,029. Christianson had served as a representative in the state legislature five biennial terms beginning in 1915 and ending with the close of the year 1924. In the last four sessions he had been chairman of the committee on appropriations. Incidental to his activities in financial affairs he became interested in a movement for the reconstruction of the administrative system of the state. He was chairman of a special committee created by the lower house in 1923 to study and report on the subject. A statute framed on the basis of this committee's report was enacted by the legislature of 1925. The main plan was carried out but accommodations had to be made to secure sufficient votes for passage. The outstanding feature of the measure is a department of administration and finance under the supervision and control of a commission of three members appointed by the governor with the advice and consent of the Senate, but removable by him at any time without cause. The three are assigned respectively to divisions of comptroller, budget, and purchases. The operation

[43] The Nonpartisan League is discussed more fully in the Appendix, no. 18, post.

of similar acts in other states, especially in Massachusetts, is ground for an expectation that the new system will be successful in Minnesota, at least in its main features. The budget system provided for must certainly moderate demands on the treasury and aid the legislature in apportioning appropriations and taxation.[44]

The report of the national decennial census of 1920 gives the population of Minnesota as 2,387,125, a fifteen per cent increase over the population of the state in 1910. Along with this normal increment of population where no great inflation was possible it is of interest to observe the very high percentages of increase in lines where the great inflation of money and credits brought on by World War exigencies and the financial policy adopted by government was reaching its apex in 1920. The increase in the value of farm property for the ten-year period was 156.5 per cent; of all crops, 171 per cent; of manufactured products, 197.5 per cent; of mining products, 122.3 per cent. The increase from 1912 to 1922 in the estimated wealth of Minnesota was at the more moderate rate of 57.3 per cent; that of the whole country ran up to 72 per cent. In 1920 the purchasing power of the dollar was forty as compared with assumed one hundred in 1913.[45]

[44] *Legislative Manual*, 1925, insert after 318, 633; *Laws*, 1925, pp. 756–773. For the purpose of the special committee appointed in 1923, see the *St. Paul Dispatch*, January 27, 1923.
[45] *United States Census*, 1920, *State Compendium, Minnesota*, 7, 71, 77, 132, 170; United States, Bureau of Foreign and Domestic Commerce, *Statistical Abstract*, 1923, pp. 735, 738; *The World Almanac and Book of Facts for 1925*, 547 (New York, n.d.).

APPENDIX

1. THE DONNELLY-WASHBURNE CONTROVERSY OF 1868 [1]

THIS conflagration, which wrought havoc in the field of Minnesota politics, began from a small firebrand. Citizens of Taylor's Falls on the St. Croix River desired to have their pleasant village connected by rail with the outside world and even aspired to see it become the terminus of a line extending far to the west, endowed by a grant of public land, according to established precedent. The draft of a bill for a land grant along a line from Taylor's Falls by way of St. Cloud to the western boundary of Minnesota was sent to Ignatius Donnelly, representative in Congress from the second Minnesota district, for introduction. In reply to a letter from a Taylor's Falls constituent, Donnelly wrote that he had been unable to secure the introduction of the bill because of objections made by Elihu B. Washburne, member of the House from Illinois. He added that this member had been opposing every measure of his for the purpose of impairing his ability to serve his constituents. This conduct he considered illiberal and ungenerous. Donnelly's arraignment was perhaps severe, but it was not abusive nor derogatory. Washburne replied on April 10, 1868, in a letter to Donnelly's correspondent at Taylor's Falls, in a manner that seems to justify Donnelly's suggestion of an ancient grudge. The letter was gladly published on April 19 by the *Saint Paul Press*, the Ramsey organ, which was more than willing to clip the wings of a dangerous antagonist. Donnelly " catches a tartar," said the editor. As for the delay of " Mr. ' I. Donnelly ' " in introducing his bill, Washburne wrote that Donnelly might have introduced it on any Monday since the beginning of the term. His attributing the delay to another member was a " jesuitical performance." Another such performance was the introduction of a bill by Donnelly to grant two hundred thousand acres of public lands for the improvement of the Mississippi between St. Paul and Minneapolis — the " Meeker dam " project. By antagonizing this " almost unprecedented " proposition to grant land with a proposition before the committee on commerce to make an appropriation of money for the purpose, he hoped to defeat aid for the object and then to lay the blame for the failure upon him, Washburne, the chairman of the committee.

[1] See *ante*, p. 14.

325

" How contemptible must any Representative of an intelligent and patriotic constituency appear, when found guilty of such a scandalous attempt to impose upon them! " Another count in the indictment was that Donnelly, after having pledged himself one day to vote against the Clinton, Iowa, bridge bill, cast his vote the next day in the affirmative, having been " seen " in the intervening night. Because he had in his pocket a free annual pass over the Union Pacific Railroad, " likely to become one of the most monstrous monopolies the world has ever known," " Mr. I. Donnelly " had voted to table a joint resolution to limit fares and rates on that road. Another instance of the wanton betrayal of constituents was the use by Donnelly of his vote and influence as a member of the Pacific Railroad committee to exempt the Union Pacific from building a branch west from Sioux City to connect with the main line.[2]

It was not very difficult for a man of Donnelly's sagacity and experience in debate to compose answers to these allegations and he set about his preparation. On Saturday, May 2, the House attended the managers of its impeachment of President Andrew Johnson to the Senate chamber at twelve o'clock and returned to its own chamber at ten minutes past three. It had been understood that no further business would be done that day and it was doubtless expected that Donnelly would offer some remarks on the Washburne letter. The House had reason to anticipate a lively week-end holiday. After the reading of his own letter, Donnelly stated that some of the newspapers of his state had indulged in uncomplimentary reflections upon a brother of the member from Illinois. This brother was a resident of Minnesota and had been laboring for years to supplant him, Donnelly, in the House. Exasperated by these reflections the Illinois member had sent to the Saint Paul Press a letter which Donnelly characterized as being without a parallel in the history of any parliamentary body — " a letter so shocking, so abusive, so outrageous " that he hesitated about offending the ears of the House with it, but in justice to his good name he must ask the clerk to read it. The reading over, he took up its particular averments one by one. His delay in offering the land grant bill was due to the fact that the draft of the bill, mailed to him on February 19, came while he was absent in New Hampshire. A speaking tour in Connecticut delayed him further and after his return he had to rewrite the bill, so that he was unable to offer it before March 20. In connection with the Meeker dam

[2] *Saint Paul Press*, April 19, 1868; *Congressional Globe*, 40 Congress, 2 session, 2348–2350. See Welles, *Autobiography*, 2:188, for an account of the Meeker dam land grant.

proposition he had the clerk read a letter from William S. King of Minnesota, postmaster of the House, which stated that when King had approached Washburne, as chairman of the committee on commerce, on the matter of a money appropriation for the improvement, that gentleman had declared that he would not give one cent for the purpose. Thereupon, said Donnelly, he himself introduced a bill for a land grant. In regard to the Clinton bridge bill he admitted that he had promised on July 12, 1866, to vote against it, and had so voted the next day. The bill was defeated, to come up six months later in a new session. In the interim he had informed himself, had found the measure to be meritorious, and on its passage his vote was one of the 101 in the affirmative to 43 in the negative. By allowing the building of the railroad from Sioux City to the main line to be transferred from the Union Pacific to another company, Donnelly asserted, the government had saved $3,200,000. There was left the charge that Donnelly had voted against limiting rates and fares on the Union Pacific because he had a free annual pass on the road. This the accused took lightly. He had never seen the road, much less had he traveled over it; and he did not expect to travel over it until the great day when there would be an unbroken line of railroad from New York to San Francisco, wedding the two oceans. " It will then, Mr. Speaker," he concluded, " be a consolation to know that that mighty work has been resisted and opposed by every blatant, loud-voiced, big-chested, small-headed, bitter-hearted demagogue in all this land."

Had Donnelly closed his speech with this fierce outburst, his own future and that of Minnesota politics would have been different from the dreary record. In his letter Washburne had not contented himself with criticism of Donnelly's public conduct, but had thrown in statements regarding his private character, which if true, and so proven, would have been good ground for his expulsion from the House and from the society of decent people. He charged that Donnelly had left Philadelphia " under suspicious circumstances, between two days," that he had changed his name and was a turncoat in politics, and that he appeared in Minnesota as an " office-beggar." A declaration that his, Washburne's, long record was not " stained with venality, corruption, and crime " carried the implication that Donnelly's record was so stained. In a concluding paragraph assailing Donnelly for not making his complaint bravely on the floor of the House, Washburne charged him with being both a coward and a liar, parading himself like a whining, whipped schoolboy before his constituents. The attack upon his

private character was extremely exasperating to Donnelly because
he was in possession of information that when he was seeking his
first renomination in 1864 similar charges had been confidentially
circulated in his district for the purpose of diverting support from
him to his competitor, William D. Washburn.[3]

It was not for Donnelly to resist the temptation to exercise his
peculiar gifts. As to his standing when he left Philadelphia in
1857 for Minnesota, a letter dated April 28, 1868, from Benjamin
H. Brewster, attorney-general of Pennsylvania, in whose office he
had studied law, left nothing to be said. The writer vouched for
Donnelly's stern integrity of character and trust to the utmost limit
of human confidence. Denouncing the attack on his good name,
Donnelly quoted the well-known passage from Shakespeare beginning, " Who steals my purse steals trash." In regard to his alleged
change of name the defendant averred that from a few hours after
his birth until now he had been " Ignatius Donnelly." If ever he
should be inclined to change his name he would take that of
" Elihu." Great laughter followed this remark. He had become a
Republican at the time of the birth of that party. It was a vile
insinuation that he was a turncoat. The chance for a " you're another " retort when called an " office-beggar " was too good to miss.
" Why, sir, the gentleman's family are chronic ' office-beggars ' . . .
every young male of the gentleman's family is born into the world
with ' M. C.' franked across his broadest part." Mentioning the fact
that Washburne lived in the same town (Galena, Illinois) with
General Grant, Donnelly was pleased to impute to him the ambition to be " the Warwick, the king-maker, the power behind the
throne," which conceit he followed up with a column of badinage

[3] Wilford L. Wilson, a friend who evidently conformed to the Scripture
adage, " Faithful are the wounds of a friend," had informed Donnelly in
1864 of the attacks upon his private character. In a letter dated May 30,
1864, Wilson wrote: " It is alleged that when you left Philadelphia for
Minnesota you fled in disgrace having been engaged in swindling operations
involving many poor & honest people, among others your own mother, who
was defrauded out of 4000 dollars. That during the past winter you have been
twice arrested on criminal charges, that you are so much disgraced that you
can have scarcely any influence in Congress favorable to your District or the
State & that the members from Philadelphia almost consider themselves dishonored to sit in the Hall with you." On June 14 Wilson wrote that Fred
Driscoll of the *Press* staff and W. D. Washburn were the principal investigators; they professed to have been in Philadelphia, where Driscoll conferred
with some of Donnelly's relatives. These letters are in the Donnelly Papers.
Thomas M. Newson, in his *Pen Pictures of St. Paul, Minnesota, and Biographical Sketches of Old Settlers*, 571 (St. Paul, 1886), and Castle, in *Minnesota Historical Collections*, 15: 566, state that Wilson was an ardent Republican and of a character that gave him the sobriquet of " Deacon." He was
secretary to Governor Davis.

concluding with the sneer that the "smallest kind of a rat-terrier's tail" could never waggle a Newfoundland dog. In a choice bit of raillery the Minnesota satirist then took off Washburne's habitual pose as a watchdog of the treasury. If that gentleman were called to heaven he would harangue the assembled hosts, cherubim and seraphim, angels and archangels, with insinuations of dishonesty, would plead for economy, and would have the wheels of the universe stopped because they consumed too much grease. Into a concluding paragraph were condensed a half dozen clauses of venom in which Washburne was denounced as a man of barren intelligence, callous heart, and slanderous tongue, a "bold, bad, empty, bellowing demagogue." The speaker of the House thereupon said the House might tolerate such remarks but he would not permit them to go upon the record without his protest. He had already called Donnelly to order three times but no member had made any objection and the House had indulgently extended his time. Washburne in this case, as in each of the preceding ones, asked that "the party" be allowed to go on. Donnelly had the grace to apologize to the House but did not withdraw his language.[4]

The distinguished member from Illinois said in reply that every word of his letter which "the party" had put into the record to remain for all time was true. He had never had occasion to make a personal explanation on the floor, but if ever he were called upon for one it would not be to a member who had run away; it would not be to a member who had changed his name; it would not be to a member whose whole record in the House was covered with venality, with corruption, and with crime. The speaker now called Washburne to order for unparliamentary remarks and in a colloquy which followed said that the attitude and gestures of the member indicated that they were directed to the gentleman from Minnesota. Washburne said he was merely stating what he should do in a certain case. The speaker said that "if his remarks were not intended to apply to the gentleman from Minnesota, toward whom he was looking, and to whom, apparently, he was addressing himself, the Chair will withdraw his ruling." Washburne said, "Well, sir, I will not look toward the member from Minnesota. But I

---

[4] *Congressional Globe*, 40 Congress, 2 session, 2348–2353. There were four Washburn(e) brothers, Israel, Elihu, Cadwallader C., and William D., at some time members of the House of Representatives with honorable records. This probably suggested to Donnelly the charge of "office beggar." See *ante*, p. 84. Washburne's taunt that Donnelly had changed his name referred to the fact that Donnelly dropped the "Loyola" from his baptismal name on coming to Minnesota.

will say (and this is all I desire to say) that if ever I should be called upon to make a personal explanation it will not be in reply to a member who is covered all over with crime and infamy, a man whose record is stained with every fraud — whisky, and other frauds — a man who has proved false alike to his friends, his constituents, his country, his religion, and his God." The House adjourned at 4:45 P.M.

At the next meeting of the House on the Monday following, May 4, Representative Windom of the first Minnesota district, rising to a question of privilege, offered, at the request of his colleague from the second district, a resolution for the appointment of a select committee to investigate the charges made by Washburne in his letter and on the floor of the House. The letter was embodied in the resolution and was therefore reprinted in the *Congressional Globe*. Donnelly at once took the floor and made his humble apology to the speaker and to the House for having transcended the rules of parliamentary discussion, begging the House to consider the extraordinary provocation — wholesale charges of crimes. He challenged the investigation and asked that, if charges were not sustained, the full measure of the law should be applied by the House to the member who made them. A rambling debate followed, in the course of which the pending question was left out of sight. As the debate was about to close, Washburne in a very brief speech said that he knew the importance of obedience to the rules of the House, that he had never transgressed them in the slightest particular without asking pardon, and that if he had transgressed them on Saturday it would have been his duty to ask the pardon of the House. The resolution and the preamble were thereupon adopted without division. Another rambling debate, or colloquy, rather, ensued on a resolution to forbid the publication of the proceedings on May 2 in the *Congressional Globe*. The preamble stated that both parties had indulged in gross personal invectives prejudicial to the dignity of the House. In the course of the debate it was stated and not denied that Donnelly had " corrected his speech " for the *Globe* and the associated press. That gentleman now expressed his willingness to have the concluding paragraph of his speech, for which the speaker had properly called him to order and for which he had immediately apologized, omitted from the record. He was willing, moreover, that his remarks " conveying the gentleman from Illinois to the realms of eternal bliss " be obliterated. Washburne thereupon austerely said, " As the gentleman from Minnesota has withdrawn the offensive portions of his speech and his imputations, I withdraw entirely what I said in reply." The resolution to omit all the proceedings from the *Congressional Globe* was then withdrawn and so the record remains there for all time. Donnelly, with characteristic hilarity, suggested that the House, following an example set at the other end of the avenue, go out and take a drink. The speaker expressed his gratification at the happy conclusion of the unpleasantness.[5]

Donnelly's biographer, who may have been a man of straw, states that hundreds of leading men, including the whole Illinois delegation with the exception of Washburne, called at Donnelly's hotel to offer congratulations. The officials of the House came also in a body. The same biographer expresses Donnelly's satisfaction in having put an end to the political career of Washburne, who would be known in history only by Donnelly's phillipic. " I have embalmed him for posterity — like a bug in amber," said Donnelly.[6]

On June 1, 1868, the select committee of investigation made its report. It was considered in the first place that all charges made by Washburne on the floor had been withdrawn in a manner satisfactory to Donnelly. There remained therefore only the charges made in the Washburne letter, written, as he said, " after extraordinary provocations . . . extending through a series of years." In a communication of May 27, addressed to the committee, Washburne stated that in his letter of April 10 he had made no charges touching Donnelly's character as a member of the House and no allegation of bribery and corruption. It was for the committee to decide whether it would investigate charges relating to Donnelly's conduct or character before he became a member of the House. Donnelly demanded an investigation of all charges, as contemplated by the resolution of the House providing for the investigation, that he

---

[5] *Congressional Globe*, 40 Congress, 2 session, 2353–2361.

[6] For the effect of Donnelly's speech, see Fish, *Donnelliana*, part 1, pp. 71–80, eulogistic, of course. Letters from some of Donnelly's constituents, in the Donnelly Papers, show the sentiments of others who are not so enthusiastic over the speech. H. P. Hall in a letter of May 7, 1868, and C. M. Loring in a letter of May 11 think that the speech may help Donnelly and that the sympathies of the people are with him. Allen Harmon in a letter of May 14 approves of the speech in general, but regrets " that unwise *saying about God taking W to his bosom* " and thinks it would be wise for Donnelly to apologize for that and for asking if it would be out of order to take a drink. Wilford L. Wilson on May 15 says: " With mere political men you may not have suffered very much, but you have fallen in the esteem of the cultivated, refined & religious people who largely make up the Republican party. You had a grand opportunity, but . . . you failed to make the best of it. If you had stopped speaking when the hammer fell, you would have achieved a complete triumph."

might vindicate his reputation. He would assume the affirmative and pay the expense of witnesses. Washburne declined to take the affirmative, but he said he would not withdraw the charges made in his letter and he would undertake to prove them if the committee decided to investigate them. The committee after considerate attention decided that the parties had left them nothing to investigate but charges against Donnelly's behavior before he became a member of the House and in these the House had no concern. For private injury Donnelly must look for redress through the public press or in the courts. If Washburne's charges in this regard had been made on the floor of the House, they would have been disorderly and punishable as such. Published in a newspaper a thousand miles away, they were no offense against the House. The order of the House that the report be printed is the last reference to the matter to be found.[7]

The bold and ingenious demurrer of Washburne and his declaration that he stood ready to prove all the allegations of his letter, if Donnelly desired further controversy, left the latter no alternative but a suit for libel. He brought no suit. Had such a litigation followed it is probable that much information regarding the conduct of the parties and their friends would have been evoked, which, perhaps happily, will never see daylight. Ignatius Donnelly was about to complete his third term as representative in Congress. He could add nothing to his reputation or prestige by an additional term. Had he been content to leave the field for another, gone back to his farm, and preserved his loyalty to the party which had aboundingly honored him, it may be safely conjectured that an early promotion to the United States Senate would have followed. But Donnelly was not the only public man whose head was swelled by a dramatic public exploit and the adulation of fool friends. The ovation accorded him in St. Paul on the evening of August 1 convinced him that he could bring the Republicans of Minnesota to eat out of his hand. Even the *Saint Paul Pioneer* was constrained to say that at Donnelly's speech that evening the audience laughed and laughed until old men and young were compelled to wipe the tears from their eyes. The *St. Paul Dispatch* spoke of it as " a spontaneous outpouring and outbursting of the people to do honor to a faithful public servant and show disapproval of the malicious opposition to him." [8]

[7] 40 Congress, 2 session, *House Reports*, no. 48 (serial 1358) ; *Congressional Globe*, 2756.
[8] *Saint Paul Pioneer*, August 2, 1868; *St. Paul Dispatch*, August 3, 1868.

2. PRESERVATION OF THE FALLS OF ST. ANTHONY [9]

The layout for utilizing the water power of the Falls of St. Anthony was not such as would be designed by modern hydraulic engineers. The works of the late forties and early fifties, confined to the east channel of the Mississippi, were lightly built, obviously for temporary service. The Saint Anthony Falls Water Power Company and the Minneapolis Mill Company were both organized by act of legislature in 1856.[10] In that year and the next the two corporations coöperated in the construction of dams and planned to control the whole power of the falls. The St. Anthony company owned the east bank of the river up to a point opposite the head of Nicollet Island. The Minneapolis company bought for $37,500 the flowage right on the west side up to Bassett Creek. Both companies built out dams meeting at an apex in the middle of the main channel a short distance above the foot of Nicollet Island to divide the flow equally. These dams, which were fifteen feet high, with twelve feet of old fall plus eight feet gained by clearing rocks from the foot of the falls, gave a total head and fall of thirty-five feet — not one-half the difference of level between the head of the rapids above the falls and the foot of those below.[11] Just as early settlers in Minnesota presumed that the pineries of the upper Mississippi and St. Croix were inexhaustible, so the people about the Falls of St. Anthony assumed that there would be water power enough for all the mills and factories that would be built at any time.

With their monopoly of all the water power of the falls the two companies for some years indulged in expectations of large and increasing rentals for all time to come, with no outlays except for the maintenance of their dams and canals. It was a matter of common observation, however, by people employed or resident at the falls that the crest of limestone rock which formed the brink of the precipice crumbled off from year to year, adding great fragments to the mass of débris at the foot, so that the falls seemed to be moving upstream. In 1866 the Minneapolis Mill Company thought it prudent to spend twenty-five thousand dollars on an " apron," that

---

[9] See *ante*, p. 31.

[10] Minnesota Territory, *Laws*, 1856, pp. 215–217, 236–239.

[11] Welles, *Autobiography*, 2: 83–85, 163; Warren Upham, *Altitudes between Lake Superior and the Rocky Mountains*, 150 (United States Geological Survey, *Bulletins*, no. 72 — Washington, 1891). For the situation and length of the dams, see 39 Congress, 2 session, *House Executive Documents*, no. 58, p. 29, map and profile (serial 1292) ; Secretary of War, *Report*, 1870, vol. 2, p. 280 (41 Congress, 3 session, *House Executive Documents*, no. 1, part 2 — serial 1447).

is, a great inclined plane of timber and planks, weighted with stone, sloping down from the crest of the falls. In July of the following year, 1867, an extraordinary rise of the river of sixteen feet above ordinary low water swept that apron out and caused the fall of a large piece of rock.

The rationale of the recession of the falls, repeatedly stated in print, is found in the local geology. The surface rock at the falls is a hard magnesium limestone, "Trenton limestone," some twelve feet thick at the crest, but at a line about twelve hundred feet upstream it thins out and disappears. Under this cap rock lies a friable sandrock, "St. Peter sandstone," extending to a great depth. The backwash of the falling water ate this away and, traversed by lines of cleavage, the limerock fell off from time to time in large fragments. In the period from 1860 to 1869 the recession amounted to 375 feet.[12]

The year 1868 passed without action and the recession of the falls went on, accelerated by the reduction of the main channel to half its original width by the dams of the water power companies. The mill companies were not indifferent to threatened disaster, but with little money in hand and, under the circumstances, a limited credit, they could undertake no costly constructions. If the falls were to be saved the companies must be aided. The people of the two cities appreciated the importance to themselves of saving the falls and were willing to assist. A committee of the Minneapolis Board of Trade took the matter before the legislature of 1869 and obtained the passage of an act authorizing the issue of bonds, that is, the borrowing of money, to the amount of sixty thousand dollars by the city of Minneapolis and twenty thousand dollars by the city of St. Anthony, provided the electors of the two cities — those of St. Anthony voting at the annual city election on April 6 and those of Minneapolis, at a special election on March 16 — should give majorities in favor of the issues. A mass meeting of citizens held on March 14 heard Henry T. Welles read a statement in regard to the condition of the falls by Franklin Cook, a civil engineer who had been employed by the United States government in making surveys of the falls. But one voice was heard against the bond

---

[12] Secretary of War, *Report*, 1869, vol. 2, p. 210 (41 Congress, 2 session, *House Executive Documents*, no. 1, part 2 — serial 1413); 1870, vol. 2, pp. 279, 283 (serial 1447); Newton H. Winchell, *The Geology of Minnesota*, 287 (Geological and Natural History Survey of Minnesota, *Final Report*, vol. 2 — St. Paul, 1888). On pages 313–341 Winchell gives a learned and exhaustive account of the recession of the falls, with maps and numerous illustrations. His computation of the time required for the recession from Fort Snelling is 7,803 years.

issues and at the elections the votes were practically unanimous in favor of them. A new apron was accordingly begun in the spring of 1869, but the work was interrupted by another unseasonable rise of the river.[13]

Had the apron been immediately and substantially completed, it is probable that the further recession of the falls would have been indefinitely postponed, unless there had been some great change of conditions. Such a change presently appeared. The two mill companies had supposed that their extensive riparian holdings assured them of a complete monopoly of all the power, at least above the falls; but one of them, the Saint Anthony Falls Water Power Company, had neglected to acquire certain rights, probably because it believed them to be unimportant. It had not secured full riparian rights on and along the shores of Nicollet Island. The company's dam backed up the water of the river to a considerable distance along those shores, thus obliterating the well-known rapids. On July 25, 1865, Hercules L. Dousman of Prairie du Chien, who had become the owner of Nicollet Island by the foreclosure of mortgages given by Franklin Steele, sold it (39.7 acres) to William W. Eastman and John L. Merriam for twenty-four thousand dollars.[14] The purchasers doubtless had in mind something more than an ordinary real estate deal, for on August 16 they gave the Saint Anthony Falls Water Power Company formal notice to remove or lower its dam. The company did not act, and, after waiting a month, on September 11, 1865, Eastman and Merriam brought suit in the district court to compel compliance with their demand. In their complaint it was alleged that the dam of the water power company had obliterated a fall of ten feet along the shores of their property, Nicollet Island, thus destroying a valuable water power belonging to them.[15]

The progress of this suit was long delayed in interlocutory proceedings not here important. The defending company, at length anticipating defeat in court, consented to a compromise, which was

[13] Special Laws, 1869, pp. 182–187; Welles, Autobiography, 154; Minneapolis Tribune, March 17, 1869, pp. 1, 4; Secretary of War, Report, 1870, p. 283 (serial 1447).

[14] The sale is recorded in book D, p. 50, of a set of manuscript volumes with the back title "Bonds," in the office of the register of deeds for Hennepin County.

[15] The manuscript record of the proceedings in this case, William W. Eastman and John L. Merriam v. The St. Anthony Falls Water Power Company and Samuel H. Chute, may be found in the office of the clerk of the district court for Hennepin County. The case is number 2427 in the files of the court.

embodied in an agreement executed on May 20, 1867. In consideration of a right to flood the shores of Nicollet Island, the water power company granted to the " Tunnel Company " — popularly so called but apparently not incorporated — the privilege of excavating a tunnel under the whole length of Hennepin Island and on under the pond between Hennepin and Nicollet Islands. The tunnel, when extended under Nicollet Island, was to serve as a tailrace for factories and mills — with the exception of sawmills — thereon to be established. The Tunnel Company was to draw from the river water enough to produce two hundred horse power, using the best designed turbine water wheels. This agreement was the more easily reached because similar tunnels, aggregating some five hundred feet in length, had been dug on the west side of the river and no harm or danger had resulted.[16]

The digging of the tunnel was begun on September 7, 1868. The section was six feet square and the grade varied from three to nine inches to the hundred feet. The excavation was made with picks and shovels and the rock and sand were run out on a car traveling on a track laid on the bottom. Near the head of Hennepin Island a shaft was sunk to accommodate a stairway and improve the ventilation. The work went on with trifling interruptions until October 4, 1869, when about nineteen hundred feet had been excavated and the heading had reached the lower end of Nicollet Island. Little water had been met with, but on that day an unusual seepage caused such alarm that at noon the workmen took their tools and escaped by way of the convenient staircase. At an early hour on the following morning, October 5, an eddy was discovered near the west shore of Nicollet Island at a point known as the " Rips," about halfway between the suspension bridge and the foot of the island. In a few hours the eddy swelled to a whirlpool ten feet in diameter. What had happened was that the tunnel had met some thread of a rivulet under the limestone cap rock leading from the upper edge of that formation five hundred feet away. The rivulet soon became a torrent, swelling from moment to moment as it ate away the friable sandstone.

Without waiting for the water power companies to organize a force of workmen, a group of enterprising citizens decided to take immediate action to save the falls. George A. Brackett, who had brought a body of Minneapolis firemen, directed operations. With-

16 This agreement is given in full as " Exhibit A " in the record of the proceedings in case 2427 in the files of the district court for Hennepin County.

out a moment's delay capable assistants came forward and sent word for men, teams, and tools — picks, shovels, axes, crosscut saws, crowbars, ropes, and chains. The first and obvious plan was to stop the hole through which the Mississippi River was discharging a big stream of water. Earth, gravel, stones, timber, logs, bales of hay and straw, and all kinds of portable materials, as they could be picked up, were thrown in. All were swept out of sight instantly. The next plan was to build a big raft and load it with stone enough to sink it to the bottom of the river over the hole. The water was but about seven feet deep, but through some fault of construction or loading the raft settled unevenly and did not cover the hole in the rock. Had the raft served its purpose nothing would have been gained, because at three o'clock in the afternoon the hole was enlarged by the fall of a piece of rock and at half past four by the fall of another one still larger. It became evident that no kind of stopper would stay the torrent and that a cofferdam must be built around the vortex. All the next day, October 6, three hundred men under the direction of Captain J. T. Stevens were at work getting materials ready. Military discipline was established and guards were stationed to keep sight-seers and idlers out of the way. Ladies of the cities served hot coffee and refreshments. There was some further enlargement of the "crevasse," as the newspapers called it. On October 7 a meeting of directors of the water power companies and interested citizens was held, at which it was agreed to raise ten thousand dollars by subscription, apportioned to the several interests.

The cofferdam was planned in three sections: one extending out into the river above the break, another below, and a third uniting the ends of the two. Cribs of timber filled with stones and faced with planks formed the dam. There were plenty of men on the ground experienced in building cribs for boom and bridge piers, but it was no week-end job. Large crews of men toiled night and day until October 20, when the newspapers announced that the dam was practically completed, that the water, except for a trifling leakage, was shut out, and that the scare was over.

But the scare was not over. On that very day, October 20, came a second break in the space between the two islands, and a portion of the limestone rock, roughly circular in shape and some eighty feet in diameter, dropped into the cave which the torrent had washed out in the sandstone. There was nothing to do but to extend the cofferdam down to and around this new break and on to the east side of Nicollet Island. By keeping crews at work day and night this work was substantially completed by the end of the month.[17]

By this time the closing of the river by the ice of winter was less than a month away and there was leisure for the consideration of measures for permanent repair of damages. The question at once arose, Whose business is it to preserve the Falls of St. Anthony, that of the water power companies or that of the United States government? Minnesota newspapers had long abounded in articles insisting that it was the duty of the national government to " maintain the continuity of navigation " of the Mississippi River above the falls. Meantime a new item of grave importance was added to the record of calamities. In the winter of 1869–70 the Saint Anthony Falls Water Power Company constructed a timber bulkhead at the lower end of the second break. The company also began an excavation through the roof of the tunnel on Hennepin Island, intending to build there a strong bulkhead of masonry. On April 3, 1870, the ice went out of the river and destroyed parts of the cofferdam around the second break. The water thus let in washed out the timber bulkhead, flowed down into the tunnel, and undermined a large part of Hennepin Island, causing the downfall of the Summit Mill and of the warehouse of the Island Mill.[18]

The capital damages were now over; but the operations to save the falls extended over many years. The minute details of the story would be of interest to hydraulic engineers, but would be sure to weary the ordinary lay reader. An account of the general course of the operations, however, may be appreciated. Without waiting for Congress to act, a citizens' committee sent for James

[17] Record of the proceedings in The St. Anthony Falls Water Power Company v. William W. Eastman and John L. Merriam, case 3696 in the files of the district court for Hennepin County. This record is the best of all sources regarding the breaks and the damages resulting from them. See post, note 31. A very graphic description of the catastrophe and its sequel appeared in the Minneapolis Journal, June 5, 1897, p. 9, from the pen of Theodore M. Knappen. Welles embodied Knappen's article in his Autobiography, 2: 158–184. For somewhat continuous accounts of the breaks and the efforts at repair, see the Minneapolis Tribune, October 6–31, 1869, and the St. Anthony Falls Democrat, October 15, 22, 29, 1869. The locations of the breaks are shown on the map facing page 344, post, which was drawn from a map based upon a survey made under the direction of Major Francis U. Farquhar, of the United States Corps of Engineers, in June and July, 1873. The latter map is in Secretary of War, Report, 1874, vol. 2, part 1, p. 286 (43 Congress, 2 session, House Executive Documents, no. 1, part 2 — serial 1636). In June, 1869, the author descended the staircase into the tunnel.

[18] Minneapolis Tribune, April 5–15, 1870; St. Anthony Falls Democrat, January 7, March 4, April 8, 15, 1870; Secretary of War, Report, 1879, vol. 2, part 2, p. 1163 (46 Congress, 2 session, House Executive Documents, no. 1, part 2 — serial 1905).

B. Francis of Massachusetts, an eminent hydraulic engineer. He came in May, 1870, and, after an examination of the situation, recommended that, to stop the recession of the falls, the apron destroyed in 1867 be reconstructed and the limestone be kept covered by means of low dams. As for the tunnel, his plan was to open up and clean out a section of four hundred feet above the second break and fill up this cavity with a puddling of clay and gravel. If, however, the falls should go out, he thought there would be water power enough left. A " Board of Construction," appointed by citizens, at once began the building of the apron. This they would no doubt have done without the recommendation of any engineer. Composed of a continuous framed structure of cribs filled with stone and surfaced with timbers twelve inches thick, the apron still stands, with later extensions. All plans for saving the falls agreed upon the apron as an essential element.[19]

Although the United States government came tardily to the rescue, there were engineer officers who early understood the situation and appreciated the gravity of the problem. Among them was Major Gouverneur K. Warren of the United States Corps of Engineers, still addressed by his brevet title of major general. On January 9, 1869, he addressed to the chief of engineers a " special communication " describing, from information furnished him a year before by Governor William R. Marshall, the state of things at the Falls of St. Anthony. " One more flood like that of 1867," Warren wrote, " might complete the destruction." It was his judgment that the preservation of the falls was a question for public consideration. This communication was followed by another dated January 12, 1870, urging " attention to this matter at once if it is ever to be done." Still another communication of April 30, 1870, spoke of the imminent danger to the whole water power threatened by the tunnel collapse, a danger to be averted only by large and immediate expenditure. These statements, coming from so able and experienced an engineer officer, probably secured from Congress the appropriation of fifty thousand dollars, a sum which at the time may have been considered ample.[20]

[19] *Minneapolis Tribune,* June 2, 1870, p. 4; Welles, *Autobiography,* 2: 174; Secretary of War, *Report,* 1872, vol. 2, p. 304 (42 Congress, 3 session, *House Executive Documents,* no. 1, part 2 — serial 1559) ; 1879, vol. 2, part 2, p. 1163 (serial 1905).

[20] 41 Congress, 2 session, *House Executive Documents,* no. 118, p. 2 (serial 1417) ; *Statutes at Large,* 16: 540; Secretary of War, *Report,* 1869, vol. 2, p. 210 (serial 1413) ; 1870, vol. 2, pp. 282–284 (serial 1447). See pages 285–289 of the last for a report by Cook, dated January 22, 1870, on a scheme for the construction of a series of dams on the upper Mississippi to hold back its

The expenditure of the appropriation for saving the falls came under the direction of Colonel John N. Macomb of the corps of engineers, who succeeded General Warren. Under his orders Franklin Cook of Minneapolis began work on August 9, 1870. Evidently without having been on the ground, Colonel Macomb adopted what may be called the "plug plan," and instructed Cook to clear out the gorge of the first break and fill it up "with good clay and gravel puddled up to the limestone ledge." That done, he was to build a continuous wall of masonry starting above the head of the gorge and extending beyond it, then running downstream parallel with the west side of Nicollet Island, curving to the left to include the second break, and ending on the east side of Nicollet Island. After a year of difficulties and disappointments, on July 22, 1871, Cook reported hopeful progress, but he had still before him the task of clearing out and filling up the gorge. Before his ink was dry he was obliged to write a supplementary report. A third break had taken place, this time in the St. Anthony mill pond, where a chasm sixteen feet wide and eight feet deep let in a stream of water under the limestone which emerged into the tunnel above where the water of the second break had entered it. This flood choked up the lower end of the old tunnel and caused the opening of a new outlet, emptying into the main river about fifty feet below the foot of the apron on the west side of Hennepin Island. Colonel Macomb, upon the urgent request of persons at the falls, now made a personal visit and consulted with civil engineers, railroad builders, and others. On July 31, 1871, he informed the chief of engineers that the best plan for preserving the falls was being followed, with good ground for hope of success.[21]

Cook went on, under orders, with the plug plan. At the close of the season he turned in a report to his chief, Colonel Macomb, which was far from cheering. When the gorge caused by the first break was being cleared out, streams of water came in from the sandstone, one of them two and one-half feet deep and two feet wide. The third break had caused much trouble and an expense of fifteen thousand dollars. This report of Cook's is important on two accounts. In the first place, it gives the results of a survey of the river, made under orders, for four miles above the falls and of examinations eight miles farther up to Coon Rapids. The latter

waters and prevent floods below. This report is probably the first contribution to the reservoir scheme.

[21] Secretary of War, *Report*, 1871, vol. 2, pp. 294–298 (42 Congress, 2 session, *House Executive Documents*, no. 1, part 2 — serial 1504). The masonry wall is shown on the map facing page 344, *post*.

were made, Cook said, "to ascertain if there was any hard foundation in the river above, where it would be feasible to build a dam in case the falls should go out." In the second place, it includes Cook's clear statement of what will be called the "dike plan" for saving the falls. He recommended as the best plan the construction of a wall of masonry across the entire width of the river from a hard stratum of sandstone up to the top of the limestone, which he would quarry off down to a line near its upper edge where it was from two to three feet thick. The ends of this dike he would protect with wing walls. His estimate of the cost was $200,000. Colonel Macomb, in a letter of April 5, 1872, to the chief of engineers, transmitting Cook's report with illustrative maps and drawings, spoke of Cook's survey as indicating the proper method for the preservation of the falls. But the success of the plan, Colonel Macomb remarked, depended upon keeping the apron in repair; and a recent inspection of it had impaired his confidence in its permanency.[22]

Several months of 1872 passed with little or nothing done on the part of the government. The fifty thousand dollars appropriated by Congress on June 10, 1872, were expended under the direction of the local "Union Committee" of citizens upon an experiment with a hollow plug of the tunnel instead of a solid one. Some eight hundred feet of "lining" were constructed. A hard stratum of sandrock was leveled off and a floor of timbers embedded in concrete was laid. The sides of the tunnel were then trimmed off vertically and timbers were set up from the floor to the limestone overhead, secured at top and bottom, at distances of from twelve to thirty inches from the sides of the tunnel. Four-inch planks were spiked onto the outer sides of the posts. The intervening space was filled in with concrete. In places where the walls of sandrock were more than twenty feet apart — the distance varied from ten to ninety feet — stout piers of masonry were built to support the limestone rock.

On July 31, 1872, the chief of engineers, Brigadier General Andrew A. Humphreys, ordered a board of five officers of the corps of engineers to meet in Minneapolis on August 10 to consider and report upon the whole subject of the preservation of the Falls of St. Anthony. The board met on the appointed day and made a personal examination of the falls and the works that had been executed. At a public meeting held in the evening many citizens

[22] Secretary of War, *Report*, 1872, vol. 2, pp. 296–300 (serial 1559). Cook's report is dated November 28, 1871.

expressed their views on the saving of the falls. A communication signed by members of the Board of Construction and of the Union Committee and by other deeply interested and highly respected citizens was presented. It was the opinion of these lay gentlemen that their hollow plug was much preferable to a solid plug, because it was cheaper and could be installed in much less time. Their plan was to extend the plug as near as possible to the head of the ledge on the west side of Nicollet Island and as far as the walls at the head of the ledge on the east side and then to fill up the whole basin between the two islands with puddling, thus forming a new bed for the river. The hollow-plug plan was presented with great confidence, as indispensable and of immediate necessity, even if it should be only preliminary to more elaborate work to be carried on by the government.

It was the conclusion of the board of engineers that the plan for the assured preservation of the falls proposed by Colonel Macomb, who had absorbed it from Franklin Cook, was the correct one, but was then impracticable because of the lack of funds. It therefore recommended the continuation of the hollow-plug experiment, the more willingly because the city of Minneapolis would furnish money for its completion if the $37,500 of the congressional appropriation still available should run out. The board further gratified the Minneapolis committeemen by recommending that the work should be in charge of J. T. Stevens, an engineer who under their employ had displayed ability in the construction of the apron and the hollow plug.[23]

It was not until October 3, 1872, that work on the hollow plug was resumed. It had gone on for a short time when water began to seep in. To prevent a possible torrent a bulkhead of masonry was built near the head of Hennepin Island. The lining process then went on, the cave being heated for comfort, until February 6, 1873, when the money ran out. But the forces of nature continued at work and on April 15, 1873, a section of the cofferdam 150 feet long on the east side of Nicollet Island was pushed in. Before this breach could be repaired another portion of the cofferdam was pushed outward, threatening the ruin of the whole work. When these breaches were closed it was found that the masonry bulkhead was gone and with it a large portion of the lining composing the hollow plug. Little more was done in the working season of 1873,

[23] Secretary of War, *Report*, 1872, vol. 2, pp. 301–306 (serial 1559) ; 1879, vol. 2, part 2, p. 1163 (serial 1905). Facing page 304 of the report for 1872 are drawings showing the hollow-plug plan.

until after the spring rise of the river was over. It was then discovered that a fourth break had occurred within a short distance of the first break of 1869 and outside the cofferdam. The leak was closed by extending the great embankment of earth in the main stream which had been maintained outside the cofferdam. The masonry bulkhead of the previous season was replaced by a wooden crib filled with concrete, to which the lining was faced up, and a section of tunnel above the bulkhead 250 feet long was filled up with rammed gravel, eleven thousand cubic yards of it brought by a short railroad from the east bank of the river. A spring that broke out 370 feet below the bulkhead originated, it was suspected, above the head of the ledge independent of the tunnel. Citizens of Minneapolis subscribed thirteen thousand dollars, to be used in cutting off a possible break at the head of this leak. So the season of 1873 closed and the falls were still in jeopardy.[24]

The chief of engineers was again moved to obtain the counsel of officers of the corps. Probably none were more experienced in hydraulic operations than those who composed the board of 1872. He reappointed all except one, who was replaced by Major Francis U. Farquhar, who had been placed in charge at the falls in April, 1873. This board met at Minneapolis on April 15, 1874. Its elaborate report opens with a brief history of the original disaster, which is followed by a statement of the existing conditions and plans and recommendations. It was the opinion of the board that, had the wall at the head of the limestone ledge, recommended by Franklin Cook and approved by the board of 1872, been constructed, the remedy would have been as complete as the nature of the case admitted. Such a remedy, in the judgment of the board, would now be attended with greater risks and difficulties and would cost much more than had been estimated. It was therefore " reluctantly constrained " to adopt a modified plan which could be readily executed and would avert impending danger of new damages. On a broken line a short distance above the apron and the crest of the main fall it proposed the construction of a dike across the entire river, to be built wholly underneath the limerock, extending down thirty-eight feet to a streak of sandstone believed to be sufficiently impervious. The length of the dike would be about two thousand feet. It is very noteworthy that the board of engineer officers recommended the later construction of the wall proposed by the plan of

---

[24] Secretary of War, *Report*, 1873, vol. 2, pp. 408–411 (43 Congress, 1 session, *House Executive Documents*, no. 1, part 2 — serial 1598) ; 1874, vol. 2, part 1, pp. 277, 280 (serial 1636).

1872 — Franklin Cook's proposition — near the head of the limestone ledge. That done, the whole mass between the dike and the wall would form a bulkhead likely never to be disturbed. This wise suggestion has not yet been adopted. The report of the board probably had its effect upon Congress, which on June 23, 1874, appropriated $125,000 for the improvement of the falls.[25]

The dike plan of the board of engineers was approved, but work did not begin until July 9, 1874. Major Farquhar remained in charge and, perhaps to avoid an unpleasantness by employing one or another local engineer as superintendent, brought on J. L. Gillespie, whose intelligence and energy amply justified the appointment. The first operation was the sinking of a shaft on Hennepin Island, fourteen by six feet in the clear, to a depth of forty-five feet below the limerock, divided into two sections and lined up with brick and concrete. It took nearly two months to complete the shaft to the bottom of the limerock and to install pumps and hoisting apparatus and a turbine water wheel to operate them. The power was transmitted by a wire rope. From the working shaft the dike, thirty-nine feet below the bottom of the limerock, was built east and west in sections of from twenty to thirty feet. The main body was four feet thick, but at the bottom it was widened to allow a passage three and one-half feet wide for a tramway. The concrete consisted of one part cement, two parts sand, and five parts crushed limestone and was deposited in layers, each of which was tamped down, according to the practice of the time. The whole amount used was 14,882 cubic yards.[26]

The capable engineer in charge found abundant opportunity for the exercise of his gifts. Minor difficulties occurred daily, but in April, 1875, on the sixth, his water wheel broke through its seat and fell into the flume. His auxiliary steam pump then had a connecting rod broken and the whole works became flooded. Three days later a four-foot rise in the river completely overflowed Hennepin Island. On the fifteenth the cofferdam in the St. Anthony mill pond gave way and allowed the water to break into the old tunnel. It took nearly the whole month of May to repair the cofferdams and clean out the sand which had accumulated where it was

---

[25] Secretary of War, *Report*, 1874, vol. 2, part 1, pp. 279–286 (serial 1636) ; *Statutes at Large*, vol. 18, part 3, p. 239. It was Major Farquhar's opinion that the dike should be located as near the crest of the natural falls as possible.

[26] Secretary of War, *Report*, 1875, vol. 2, part 1, p. 356 (44 Congress, 1 session, *House Executive Documents*, no. 1, part 2 — serial 1675). The diagram facing page 357 shows a cross section of the dike. See also Secretary of War, *Report*, 1879, vol. 2, part 2, p. 1164 (serial 1905).

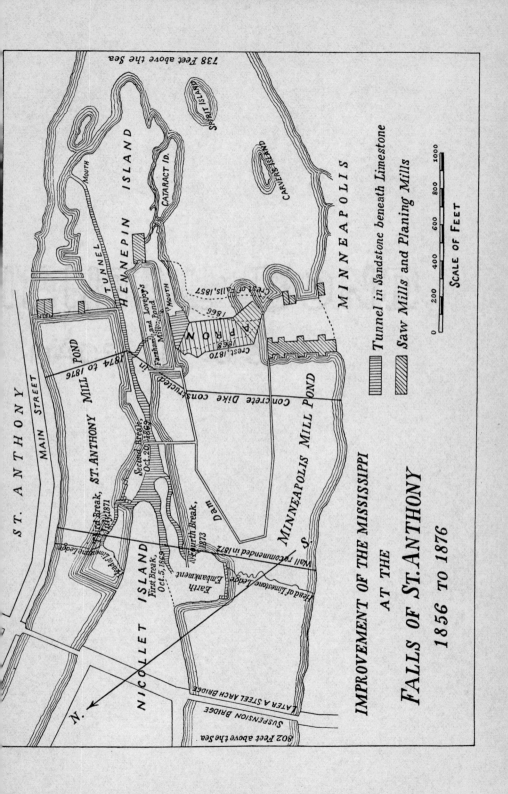

738 Feet above the Sea.

ST. ANTHONY

MINNEAPOLIS

HENNEPIN ISLAND

SPIRIT ISLAND

CATARACT ID.

CARVERS ISLAND

NICOLLET ISLAND

Mouth

TUNNEL

MAIN STREET

ST. ANTHONY MILL POND

in 1874 to 1876

Farnham and Lovejoy's
Mill&c. Pond

APRON

Crest of Falls, 1857

1866

MOUTH

Crest, 1870

1858

Concrete Dike constructed

MINNEAPOLIS MILL POND

S.

Wall recommended in 1872

Head of Limestone Ledge

Third Break, St. ANTHONY July 1, 1871

Second Break,
Oct. 20, 1869.

Fourth Break,
1873

Dam

Earth
Embankment

First Break,
Oct. 5, 1869.

Head of Limestone Ledge.

Suspension Bridge

LATER A STEEL ARCH BRIDGE

802 Feet above the Sea.

N.

IMPROVEMENT OF THE MISSISSIPPI

AT THE

FALLS OF ST. ANTHONY

1856 TO 1876

Tunnel in Sandstone beneath Limestone

Saw Mills and Planing Mills

SCALE OF FEET

0   200   400   600   800   1000

not wanted. In July another spring was struck, which let in large volumes of sand and water. Again the pumps were disabled and the greater part of August passed before operations could be resumed. The work should have been completed in the spring of 1876, but because the money had run out it was not until November 24, 1876, that the last batch of concrete was bedded. The east end of the dike was 600 feet long and extended 70 feet beyond the high-water shore-line with a T cross-wall at its east end. The west portion of the dike, 1,275 feet long, was extended but 25 feet into the bank, because the sandrock there was firmer. The whole cost was $211,089.46. It is not important that detailed account be made here of auxiliary operations, such as the building of two rolling dams, to protect the surface of the limerock from the ice, and the filling up of the old tunnel and holes in the river bed above the dike with 22,329 cubic yards of gravel.[27]

Nearly fifty years have passed and the dike has stood impervious and unshaken, amply justifying the expectations of its original projector and the engineers who executed the work. The total of congressional appropriations was $545,000. The contributions of the two cities, Minneapolis and St. Anthony — one city after February 28, 1872 — including individual subscriptions, amounted to $334,500. The burden was no slight one for the young cities, whose combined population in 1870 was 18,079.[28] Large sums were also spent in time, travel, and hotel bills in Washington by citizens who were personally interested. The name of one such citizen must in justice be recorded, that of Richard Chute. Henry T. Welles, a citizen who gave time and effort without stint and who was probably the largest contributor of money, giving himself far too little credit, has summarized the services of Chute in terms which the writer is pleased to quote. "To him [*Richard Chute*], more than to any other man, is due the credit of obtaining from the government appropriations to aid in the preservation of the falls. He visited Washington year after year for that purpose. He was an invalid

[27] Secretary of War, *Report*, 1875, vol. 2, part 1, p. 357 (serial 1675); 1876, vol. 2, part 1, p. 700 (44 Congress, 2 session, *House Executive Documents*, no. 1, part 2 — serial 1743); 1877, vol. 2, part 1, pp. 563–565 (45 Congress, 2 session, *House Executive Documents*, no. 1, part 2 — serial 1795); 1879, vol. 2, part 2, p. 1164 (serial 1905). In the *Minneapolis Tribune*, November 20, 1876, p. 4, is a description of the dike.

[28] Welles, *Autobiography*, 2:182; *United States Census*, 1870, *Population*, 178; Secretary of War, *Report*, 1882, vol. 2, part 2, map facing p. 1800 (47 Congress, 2 session, *House Executive Documents*, no. 1, part 2 — serial 2093). See the *Minneapolis Tribune*, February 9, 1886, p. 1, for a report of a board of United States engineers commending the operations completed in 1876, with an historical sketch.

[*temporarily*] and used crutches. Those crutches were a passport.
. . . He was an intellectual man, well endowed by nature, and well
educated. He could talk with any man and present his case and
meet objections with consummate skill. His mind was ever active.
He was well known to be of a spotless character on every side.
Every morning he was ready with a new idea." Welles accompanied Chute " many times " to Washington.[29]

To the losses and damages incurred by the Saint Anthony Falls
Water Power Company and the Tunnel Company was soon to be
added the cost of exasperating litigation. On November 26, 1869,
the *St. Anthony Falls Democrat* stated that the Tunnel Company had
given notice that it had abandoned its enterprise and demanded
from the water power company a reconveyance of all the water
rights and privileges ceded to it by the compromise of May 20, 1867.
On January 27, 1870, the Tunnel Company brought suit demanding the vacation and annulment of the compromise, on the ground
that it had gained none of the advantages guaranteed to it. It
further asked for the relief demanded in its suit of September 11,
1865 — the removal or lowering of the dam of the water power
company. The courts decided that, as the compromise had been
made out of court, the plaintiff could not invoke court vacation. As
for relief, it was free to seek that in some other manner.[30]

On June 18, 1870, the Saint Anthony Falls Water Power Company
sued the Tunnel Company for breach of the compromise of May
20, 1867, in failing to adopt adequate precautions in excavating
the tunnel and demanded $250,000 for damages to property and
for other losses. The result of a long and hotly contested jury
trial was a verdict for the Tunnel Company. The jury, as instructed
by the court, seems to have concluded that both parties had
believed the tunnel to be practicable. The water power company
had consented to it for valuable considerations and the Tunnel
Company had used suitable, if not adequate, precautions against
damage. The jury therefore refused to award damages. It appeared
in evidence that both parties had believed in the feasibility of the
tunnel project, because similar tunnels had been dug for mills on

[29] Welles, *Autobiography*, 185.
[30] William W. Eastman and John L. Merriam *v.* The Saint Anthony Falls
Water Power Company and Samuel H. Chute, case 2427 in the files of the
district court for Hennepin County. This suit was a revival of that of September 11, 1865, on a supplementary complaint, which embodied the agreement of May 20, 1867. The plaintiffs were defeated and on August 1, 1871,
the state supreme court affirmed the decision of the court below. William
W. Eastman *et al v.* The Saint Anthony Falls Water Power Company *et al*,
17 *Minnesota*, 48–51.

the west side and one tunnel eleven hundred feet long had been run under Main Street on the east side. But all these were under dry land and not under the river bed, where water was likely to be encountered.[31] It is noteworthy that in suits brought by parties other than the Saint Anthony Falls Water Power Company who had suffered damages from the unregulated expansion of the tunnel, considerable indemnities were awarded.[32]

On August 23, 1875, the Tunnel Company revived its suit of January 27, 1870, demanding the cancellation of the compromise of May 20, 1867, and the restoration of shore rights and privileges on Nicollet Island. The renewed suit met the same fate as the old one after appeal to the state supreme court on a demurrer. It was finally disposed of by dismissal on July 16, 1879, nearly ten years after the trouble began with the first break of October 4, 1869.[33]

3. JOSEPH R. BROWN [34]

The death of Joseph Renshaw Brown on November 9, 1870, was the occasion of many obituary notices and articles. The most notable of these is the communication of Earle S. Goodrich to the *Saint Paul Daily Pioneer*, of which he was formerly editor in succession to Brown. "Joseph R. Brown was a great man," writes the eulogist. "Persuasive as a speaker, simple, homely, but strong as a writer, modest and winning in private intercourse, he needed only the polish of the schools to have graced any position, or have honored any profession or pursuit. . . . It was noticeable to witness the effect of his appearance at the capital to attend upon the sessions of the Legislature during these early periods. . . . The whole

[31] Record of the proceedings in case 3696 in the files of the district court for Hennepin County. The bulky judgment roll embodies numerous exhibits and a large body of testimony given by the parties, by engineering experts, and by persons on the ground more or less interested. Case 3593 in the same matter appears to have been superseded by case 3696.

[32] In the cases of John W. Eastman *et al v.* William W. Eastman *et al* and William F. Cahill *et al v.* William W. Eastman *et al*, indemnities were awarded the plaintiffs. Records of the proceedings in these suits may be found in cases 3595, 3596, and 3922 in the files of the district court for Hennepin County. See also William F. Cahill *et al v.* William W. Eastman *et al*, 18 *Minnesota*, 324–350.

[33] William W. Eastman and John L. Merriam *v.* The Saint Anthony Falls Water Power Company, case 5810 in the files of the district court for Hennepin County. In the *Minneapolis Tribune*, August 27, 1875, p. 4, is a statement by David A. Secombe, attorney for Eastman and Merriam, describing the original contract with the Saint Anthony Falls Water Power Company and the claim of the plaintiff for recovery under the contract.

[34] See *ante*, p. 76.

alphabet of Honorables rested quiet when he came. . . . He knew men as a scholar knows books. . . . No history of Minnesota can be written which shall omit from its pages the scenes and incidents wherein, for half a century, he moved conspicuously; nor can such history be worthily written which fails to record upon the roll of its worthiest pioneers, the name of JOSEPH R. BROWN." Joseph A. Wheelock in the *Saint Paul Daily Press* closes a long biographical sketch with the remark that Brown's career was a remarkable and characteristic one, not so much for what he achieved as for the extraordinary versatility and capacity which he displayed in every new situation. Harlan P. Hall of the *St. Paul Dispatch* remarks that Brown, though erratic and visionary in private matters, showed good judgment in public affairs; that he was generous to a fault and died poor; and that both whites and Indians would lament his loss.[35]

Others among Brown's contemporaries in the years following his death wrote interesting estimates of his character for more permanent publication. The *Minnesota Historical Collections* contain a number of such characterizations. One writer says, " The most remarkable man, in many respects, who ever appeared in the Northwest, was Joseph R. Brown "; another writer recalls the impression he had in 1854 that Brown was " the smartest man I had ever met." A biographer of early newspaper men of Minnesota rates Brown as one of the ablest editors the *Pioneer* ever had. He says that Brown was " born with wildness in his blood, but so superbly gifted that whether in wigwam or legislative hall he was always the leader of men." Another noted Minnesota biographer in a sketch that includes Sibley, Ramsey, Henry and Edmund Rice, J. J. Hill, Archbishop Ireland, and J. A. Wheelock, writes of Brown as " the brainiest of them all, a sort of intellectual lion, who sported with the savage Sioux, or ruled a political caucus, with equal power." In another passage the same author says, " Of all the men who came to Minnesota by way of the fort, in point of force, tact, influence, vigor of intellect and diversity of power, precedence must ever be

---

[35] *Saint Paul Pioneer*, November 15, 1870, p. 1, reprinted in *Minnesota Historical Collections*, 3: 204–208; *Saint Paul Press*, November 12, 1870, p. 1, reprinted in *Minnesota Historical Collections*, 3: 208–212; *St. Paul Dispatch*, November 12, 1870, p. 2. Brown was the founder and first editor of the *Henderson Weekly Democrat*. Goodrich was editor of the *Pioneer* for many years. J. Fletcher Williams, in his *History of the City of Saint Paul, and of the County of Ramsey, Minnesota*, 350 (*Minnesota Historical Collections*, vol. 4 — St. Paul, 1876), says that Goodrich won " the reputation of being the most graceful, elegant, and caustic editorial writer we have ever had in Minnesota." See pages 455–458 for a sample of Goodrich's literary style.

given to Joseph R. Brown." Ex-governor Austin left on record this statement, " The most characteristic trait of the man was his shrewdness and strong common sense, which, as Seward once said of Lincoln's shrewdness in politics, ' amounted to genius.' . . . I have never met another who possessed the power of touching up a character or summing up an agreement in fewer words than he; yet his language was simple and unpretending." A state historian of some note ventures the statement, " Between Sibley and Brown there was always the warmest and most intimate friendship. Sibley's was the more commanding position in human affairs, but Brown's was the greater intellect, the clear sight, and the brightest genius for origination and invention."[36]

A painstaking writer intimately acquainted with Joseph R. Brown describes him as a man of good size, with clear-cut features, nose sharply Roman, chin prominent, lips thin, eyes dilating when speaking, and hair gently curling and worn somewhat long. He was ever good-natured, considerate, and even-tempered. He never swore, never drank, never played cards, but smoked a cigar occasionally. Another admirer speaks of him as good-humored and sociable, of remarkably happy temper, bearing pecuniary losses with cheerful equanimity.[37]

The reader who has turned over the previous volumes of this work will have noted such events in the career of Joseph R. Brown as these: his coming up as a boy of fourteen with the first troops to Fort Snelling in 1819; his service with the garrison for a number of years; his employments as farmer, lumberman, and Indian trader; his service in the Wisconsin legislature, in the Stillwater convention, in early sessions of the Minnesota legislature, and in

[36] Charles D. Gilfillan, " The Early Political History of Minnesota," in *Minnesota Historical Collections*, 9: 179; Thomas Simpson, " The Early Government Land Survey in Minnesota West of the Mississippi River," in *Minnesota Historical Collections*, 10: 66 (part 1); Daniel S. B. Johnston, " Minnesota Journalism in the Territorial Period," in *Minnesota Historical Collections*, 10: 267, 275 (part 1); James H. Baker, " Alexander Ramsey," in *Minnesota Historical Collections*, 10: 737 (part 2); Baker, " Address at Fort Snelling in the Celebration of the Centennial Anniversary of the Treaty of Pike with the Sioux," in *Minnesota Historical Collections*, 12: 298; Horace Austin, " The Frontier of Southwestern Minnesota in 1857," in *Glimpses of the Nation's Struggle*, a series of papers read before the Minnesota Commandery of the Military Order of the Loyal Legion of the United States, 1892–1897, fourth series, 131 (St. Paul, 1898); Holcombe, in *Minnesota in Three Centuries*, 2: 93. But Wheelock said to the author on December 29, 1903, that Brown was " an understrapper of Sibley's . . . was no such character as Sibley." Notes of this interview are in the Folwell Papers.

[37] Newson, *Pen Pictures*, 203; J. Fletcher Williams, " Memoir of Joseph R. Brown," in *Minnesota Historical Collections*, 3: 202.

the Minnesota constitutional convention; his editorship of the
Minnesota Pioneer; his founding of the village of Henderson; his
beneficent activity as agent to the Sioux; his gallantry as aid to
Sibley in his Indian campaigns; and his efforts to put the upper
Sioux on the road to civilization. The reader may have wondered
why this enterprising, versatile, public-spirited man had no part in
the great conflict for the preservation of the Union. It was not his
fault that he did not. Although well past military age, Brown lost
no time in asking for an appropriate position in the volunteer army.
A letter to Governor Ramsey offering his services in the conflict
clearly displays his patriotism and soldierly ambition. No discovery has been made of Ramsey's reasons for denying the ardent
petition. That he could set aside politics is shown by such appointments as those of Sibley, Flandrau, and Forbes. It is but justice
to say that an executive of such sound judgment as Alexander Ramsey must have found it impracticable under the circumstances to
sign a commission for Brown. But one cannot help wondering what
this trained soldier, experienced man of affairs, recognized leader,
energetic and resourceful, already accustomed to a life like that of
the campaign, might have accomplished either in command of
troops or in some staff position like that of quartermaster. Many
of the most successful Civil War commanders, of whom Sheridan
was a notable example, had learned as quartermasters how to move
troops and keep them supplied.

But this man of energy and genius, of admirable personal qualities, for whom a great career might have been expected, left a
scantier record behind him than many other public men by
far his inferior in capacity. The reasons for this, whether due to
character or environment, must be left to his biographer. Some
suggestions may be ventured here: one of them his marriage to a
mixed-blood woman of excellent character, but not disposed to
adopt in full the white man's ways of living; another, Brown's
own liking for the roving life and his postponement too long of the
establishment of a permanent residence and the identification of
himself with a community.[38] More significant than these, perhaps,
was his indiscriminate generosity and his neglect of present frugal-

---

[38] Mrs. Susan Brown was the daughter of Narcisse Freniere, a French
mixed-blood, and Winona Crawford, whose father was a well-known British
trader and whose mother was a daughter of the Dakota chief Red Wing,
sometimes called *Tatankamani,* "Walking Buffalo." She was a woman of
forcible character, an excellent mother, and a good housekeeper; she understood English, but generally preferred to use her Dakota. There were twelve
children, all of whom grew up except "little Sibley," who died at the age

ity while indulging in dreams of future opulence. A truthful biography of the real " Joe " Brown might be not only a fascinating story but a highly valuable contribution to the early history of Minnesota.

An example of an enterprise which occupied Brown for many years and cost him a large sum of money will serve to illustrate his buoyant temperament. Long experience as a fur-trader at distant stations, as Indian agent, and as a contractor for furnishing Indian supplies had familiarized him with the excessive cost of hauling goods by ox teams, requiring twelve days to transport one ton one hundred miles. On some one of his frequent and repeated journeys over the prairie as " level as a barn floor " there came to him the idea of employing some more rapid means of progression than the patient ox. He may have heard of the use of steam tractors on English roads; or, as many suppose, he may have been an original — he could not have been the first — inventor of a steam motor for use on common roads.

In the late fifties Ramsay Crooks, then agent of the Hudson's Bay Company, effected an arrangement with the secretary of the treasury for the carriage of that company's goods, previously imported by way of York factory on Hudson Bay, to Fort Garry, Canada, through the states by way of St. Paul. Here Brown saw, he believed, a capital opportunity for demonstrating his idea.[39]

It was in 1859 that, having some ready money in hand, he traveled to New York, which he had selected as the best place to get his conceptions translated into an actual machine and at length to finance a large manufacture. Here he found John A. Reed, a consulting engineer, machinist, and manufacturer of boilers and engines. Brown's ideas and sketches, if he brought any, were soon put onto Whatman sheets and the manufacture of a machine was

of eight. All were educated in various select schools. Letters of Major Brown among the family papers show him a very affectionate husband and probably an overindulgent father. Notes from a Bible in the possession of Mrs. George G. Allanson; Samuel J. Brown to the author, July 21, 1921, Folwell Papers.

[39] Statement of Joseph R. Brown, dated October 18, 1869, relating to the steam wagon, Brown Papers; Williams, *Saint Paul*, 303; Russell Blakeley, " Opening of the Red River of the North to Commerce and Civilization," in *Minnesota Historical Collections*, 8: 46. See page 48 for the building of the steamboat " Anson Northup " in the Red River in the spring of 1859 to catch part of the Hudson's Bay business. See J. L. Ringwalt, *Development of Transportation Systems in the United States*, 64 (Philadelphia, 1888), and Henry Howe, *Memoirs of the Most Eminent American Mechanics*, 76 (New York, 1847) for an account of Oliver Evans and the first American locomotive, called the " Oructor Amphibolis."

begun. The construction took more time than was anticipated, so that it was not until the spring of 1860 that it was seen in knock-down at the St. Paul levee. It was unloaded at Henderson on May 19, but its public exhibition was delayed until after the Sioux payment and the arrival from New York of Reed, the constructor, on July 3. The novel feature of the vehicle was that its two driving wheels, six feet in diameter, did not touch the ground, but revolved within "rings" of boiler iron eight feet in diameter and eighteen inches wide. Projecting studs on the rims of the driving wheels fitting into corresponding holes in the rings gave these outer rims motion, giving rise to the local remark that it carried its own track.

On July 4 the motor was erected and was run up and down the main street, loaded with cheering men and boys. A week later, after certain adjustments had been made, the operation was more successful, but there was a long delay before an experiment of actual performance was made. On October 6 the wagon, which, according to the *Henderson Democrat,* had been christened " by bestowing upon it the paganish Dakotah cognomen of Mazomanie, which meaneth in the vulgate Walking Metal," was still lying in Henderson waiting further orders. The local chronicler speaks of it as a curious piece of machinery, which can run backwards, turn round in a narrow lane, is a good fire engine, can saw wood or run a grist mill. At length, after ascending the steep bluff back of Henderson village, it started for Fort Ridgely with a freight wagon in tow. When Three Mile Creek was reached, only a short distance from the fort, the steam wagon sank deep in soft ground and could not be extricated. Eventually the engine was removed and the hulk lay by the roadside near Fort Ridgely for many years.[40]

The misadventure was disappointing but not disheartening. Brown was confident that the experiment with an imperfect motor had proved the feasibility of steam traction on common roads, especially on prairie roads, and resolved on another effort. After investigation he selected for the new trial the route from Nebraska

[40] *Daily Pioneer and Democrat* (St. Paul), May 13, 1860, p. 4; *Henderson Weekly Democrat,* 1860: May 26, p. 3; June 16, p. 3; 23, p. 3; 30, p. 2; July 7, p. 3; 14, p. 2; October 6, p. 3; 27, p. 3; *St. Paul Sunday Pioneer Press,* July 25, 1915, section 6, p. 3; *Minneapolis Sunday Tribune,* April 17, 1921, section 1, p. 11. No evidence other than the article quoted has been found of a name having been given to the motor. Brown wrote of it indifferently as " the motor," " the wagon," "the steam wagon," or simply "the machine."

City on the Missouri River, along the divide between the Kansas and the Platte rivers and on to Denver, Colorado, six hundred miles away, a route believed by many to be the only practicable one across the plains. It had been followed by early emigrants to California and a large business was going over it by oxen and mule teams.

In the middle of July, 1862, the second " Prairie Motor," built, as was the first, by Reed of New York, but evidently much improved, was landed at Nebraska City, Nebraska. There was no portable track but the driving wheels, ten feet in diameter and eighteen inches on the tread, ran directly on the ground. They were driven by four oscillating engines of ten horse power each. There was a pair of steering wheels with the proper gears at the middle of the front axle. The boiler was of the tubular design and the accompanying water tank held enough for four hours' consumption. A trial trip made a few days later gave " General " Brown and his operating experts much satisfaction and beholders were much impressed. The motor ran up Kearney Hill, through a plowed garden, on sod for a half mile, through hazel and sumac bushes for another half mile; went down hill, making a turn too short for a team and wagon; crossed a ford on a bed of loose stones; mounted the bluff on a grade of 960 feet to the mile, with the rain falling and the soil very slippery; moved along a street over a grade of 500 feet to the mile and, finally, on a level road progressed at a speed of five miles an hour to Main Street.

The people of Nebraska City were much elated by the prospect of their town becoming the focus of a great route of steam-wagon transportation. On July 28, 1862, in a mass meeting it was resolved to request the authorities of Otoe County to build a road through some rough country between the city and the divide. The county commissioners took the necessary action and later the electors of the county voted that a special tax be levied for the enterprise.

On July 22 the prairie motor took its departure for Denver, drawing three road wagons loaded with five tons of freight and two cords of wood and crowded with excited citizens. Two steep hills near the town were surmounted with ease. The day of triumph seemed dawning, but sunrise did not follow. At a point twelve miles away from Nebraska City, the last rise of ground next the long divide having been passed, one of the engine cranks broke along an unseen flaw in the metal. Without a day's delay the unflagging owner was on his way to New York with the broken part. On August 16 he wrote that the new crank was going on by express and would be in Nebraska City in about a week.[41]

The reader who has found this narrative interesting enough to follow its course knows that at daylight on August 18, 1862, the Sioux Outbreak began; that the members of Major Brown's family, fleeing from the stone house near the upper agency, were saved from assassination by the heroic behavior of Mrs. Susan Brown; and that Little Crow was wise enough to take them under his immediate personal protection. They were among the captives liberated at Camp Release on September 26, 1862. At the news of the outbreak Brown traveled with all possible speed to Minnesota, where Sibley at once called him to his side. As his aid Brown was occupied in the Indian campaigns of 1862 and 1863 and thereafter for several years he gave much time to the interests of the upper Sioux, to whom his family was related.

During this period Brown's darling project of steam transportation on common roads lay dormant but not defunct. By 1868 he had recovered some of his pecuniary losses and was in condition for a new endeavor. The question now was upon a suitable route for operation. As Brown himself states, " Before I found myself in a condition to resume my steam wagon operations in Nebraska, the Iron horse was prancing across the western prairies where I expected to operate." The abandoned motor of 1862 was left at

[41] Brown's statement of October 18, 1869; copies of letters from Charles B. Sloat to Brown, August 25, 28, 1862, Folwell Papers; copies of excerpts from the *Nebraska City News* for July and August, 1862, sent by Clarence S. Paine, secretary of the Nebraska Historical Society, to the author, October 6, 1911, also some reprints in the *News* from articles in the *Scientific American* in the summer of 1862, probably inspired by Brown, Folwell Papers. The *News* issue of August 30 prints a letter of Brown's of August 16 from which it appears that he had intended to have another motor built immediately, but found the shops so much occupied with government work that a new motor could not be delivered in time for the coming fall's business. He therefore planned to have Reed go to Minnesota and, taking new parts along, make such changes in his first machine as would give it a speed of six miles an hour, and send it to Nebraska. In the same letter Brown announced his expectation that in April, 1863, he would have ready two more motors of seventy horse power able to cover two hundred miles in twenty-four hours; with two more to be added about the middle of July and two about the first of October, a daily line would be operated from Nebraska City to Denver. See also an article compiled by J. B. Irvine from newspaper clippings and letters, " A Steam Wagon Invented by an Early Resident of South Dakota," in *South Dakota Historical Collections*, 10: 362–387, including a sketch of Joseph R. Brown's life. The article is also reprinted in pamphlet form, with the same paging. The *Minneapolis Journal*, March 25, 1906, section 2, p. 6, cites a narrative of Brown's master mechanic, D. L. Osborn, in a recent number of the *Nebraska Daily Tribune*. The article is erroneous in many respects.

JOSEPH R. BROWN'S SECOND STEAM WAGON

[From a half-tone cut in the possession of the Department of History of South Dakota.]

Arbor Lodge, the farm home of J. Sterling Morton, United States secretary of agriculture in Cleveland's administration. It remained there for some years and, the machinery having been disposed of, the remainder was at length broken up and sold for scrap iron.[42]

In the year 1869 the St. Paul and Pacific Railroad was extended to the Red River Valley. Judging from the business of the preceding two years, Brown estimated that three thousand tons of freight consigned to Fort Garry and government posts along the valley would be carried to the railroad terminus. After some time spent in Washington arranging financial affairs he went to New York and engaged his trusted expert, John A. Reed, to undertake the building of a third motor with improvements suggested by previous experiments. On September 21 of that year the model and drawings were complete and the manufacture was begun.[43]

While that went tediously forward the hopeful inventor was busy counting unhatched chickens. Beginning with a modest project for transporting passengers and freight from the railroad terminus on the Bois des Sioux to Fort Garry, to Fort Wadsworth on the Coteau des Prairies, and to Fort Abercrombie, his lively imagination conceived of steam-wagon lines to Fort Ripley on the Mississippi, to Fort Totten on Devils Lake, to Fort Ransom on the Sheyenne. A mail route from Minnesota to Montana which had failed might be taken over at a figure of one hundred thousand dollars or so. Steam-wagon lines endowed by the Canadian government with land grants might be extended to the head of the Saskatchewan, if not to the navigable waters of Fraser River. A conceit which he thought worth mention was that of a wooden railroad from the Bois des Sioux by way of Fort Garry to the Fraser. Rails of wood could be laid quickly and cheaply and would last many years. Major Brown was not so much engrossed with the construction of his steamer as to neglect the indispensable financial elements of his adventure. He wrote out a careful sketch of an "International Steam Transportation Company" with a capital of five hundred thousand dollars. He calculated that a small assessment on the subscribed stock would be sufficient to carry the new steamer to the Bois des Sioux and enable it to make a round trip to Fort Garry. After that demonstration the stock

[42] Brown's statement of October 18, 1869; copy of a letter from Morton to S. J. Brown, February 14, 1871; Paine to the author, August 11, 1911, Folwell Papers.

[43] J. R. Brown to S. J. Brown, September 21, November 21, 1869, to ———, November 26, 1869, Brown Papers.

would be the favorite investment of the day. But harmless romanc-
ing on possible developments did not divert him from careful
estimates of the probable earnings of the motor under construction
and of seven others to follow on the routes to Fort Garry and the
government posts in figures which, if the initial experiment came
up to expectations, would be very alluring to investors.[44]

Construction was exasperatingly slow. On October 20 the pat-
terns were not all completed; on December 16 the castings were
nearly complete and there was expectation of a trial in about two
weeks. On that date Brown wrote, "I am entirely out of money."
His correspondence indicates that the thrifty contractor advanced
the work only as the ready money was in sight. The winter
passed without further progress. In April a loan sufficient to
complete the motor was made by the major's old colleague in
Indian affairs, Colonel Clark W. Thompson. It was not until
August 21, 1870, that he could write that the machine was on
wheels but it would be at least two weeks before it would be out
of the shop. A month later, referring to certain skeptics, he wrote,
"As they have no interest in it, however, it appears to me to be
pretty much none of their business whether it works or not."

On the fifth of October Brown wrote that he hoped to have the
machine out of the shop for trial in a day or two, and on some
day in that month or early in November he saw it tried in the yards
and was pleased. It may be assumed that he had good reason for
satisfaction. By this time he had learned much about machinery
and in particular about traction motors. Profiting by experience,
he had bargained for the construction of a small machine light in
weight. A man could lift any one of the four engines. The boiler
had been tested under a pressure of 220 pounds to the square inch
and was found strong and safe. Even the grate bars were utilized
to make steam.[45] It is no extravagance to say that this motor
would have worked well on good roads of moderate grades.
Whether it would have pulled trains of loaded wagons up hill and
down, in all kinds of weather, at a speed of five miles an hour,
could have been determined only by the experiment which was
never to be made. On November 9, 1870, in New York City, Major

[44] Statements of J. R. Brown, October 18, 1869, and November 30, 1869,
Brown Papers.

[45] J. R. Brown to S. J. Brown, October 5, 20, December 16, 1869, April 23,
August 21, September 23, October 5, 1870, Brown Papers; copy of a letter from
Reed to S. J. Brown, December 27, 1870, Folwell Papers. The Folwell Papers
also contain what is probably the original sketch of the 1870 motor. It is
entitled, "Steam Wagon of Six Tons."

Brown died. Had a profitable line of steam-wagon transportation been established to Fort Garry and Red River points, the building of the railroad to Pembina would have put it out of business forever. Brown's steam automobile was a fond dream. The actual automobile awaited the development of the internal combustion engine and the supply of cheap light petroleum oils.

In January, 1871, Reed urged the Brown heirs to pay him two hundred dollars for some finishing touches and to let him ship the steam wagon to Minnesota on a platform car. An unsuccessful effort was made by the heirs in July and September of the same year to that end. But the machine remained where Major Brown left it. Although it was painted twice to keep it from rusting, its final destination was the scrap heap.[46]

4. THE SEEGER IMPEACHMENT [47]

The legislature of 1860 at Governor Ramsey's urgency cut down the salaries of state officers, his own included. That of the state treasurer was fixed at one thousand dollars, and it so remained for thirteen years, although the budget of expenses and the amounts of state funds had increased many fold. In the absence of any statutory regulations each treasurer had kept his accounts according to his convenience and had lent out to banks any moneys accumulated in advance of expenditure. The interest paid by the banks was regarded as the treasurer's quasi-legitimate perquisite. William Seeger was state treasurer in 1873 and was going on in the old way. The reason for disturbing the custom is not known, but before the legislative session was far advanced a rumor spread that all was not right in the treasurer's office. Existing law required the treasurer to report to the legislature an itemized statement of the condition of the treasury on the third day of each regular session.[48] On this occasion the regular report did not appear and on February 3 the House requested the treasurer to supply it, and to give his reason for neglect to conform to law. Seeger informed the House on the next day that he would comply with its just demand, so soon as the state printer, overcrowded with work, could furnish the printed copies. A week later, on

---

[46] Copy of a letter from Reed to S. J. Brown, January 11, 1871, Folwell Papers; correspondence of S. J. Brown and J. A. Reed, James Gilfillan, and William Combs, July and September, 1871, Brown Papers.

[47] See *ante*, p. 76.

[48] See *ante*, 2: 63; reports of the treasurer, in *Executive Documents*, 1860, pp. 6–16; 1873, pp. 66–69, 72–74; and *General Statutes*, 1866, p. 88.

February 10, the House standing committee on public accounts submitted a report showing that after an examination of the books and accounts of the treasurer and a comparison of them with the balance sheet of the state auditor, they had been found, on February 5 and 7, correct and businesslike.[49]

The House apparently was not at the time disposed to doubt the integrity of the treasurer, but the Senate was not content with the brief balance sheet shown it. A committee of three senators had been appointed on February 1 to ascertain whether the surplus funds reported in the governor's message were in the vaults of the treasury or loaned to banks or individuals; what rate of interest was paid on them; and what disposition of such funds had been made. Five days later the committee was increased to five and authorized to send for books and papers and to examine witnesses under oath. The committee in ten sessions, between February 6 and 17, inclusive, examined Seeger and sixteen other witnesses. Its report was submitted on February 18 and one thousand copies of it were ordered printed. The findings were in substance as follows: (1) When Seeger took office on January 1, 1872, he did not require his predecessor to pay over to him $112,000 belonging to the state, but concealed and carried along the deficiency until it was made up by bondsmen at their convenience. Seeger's evidence in regard to this transaction was at variance with that of other witnesses. (2) Seeger and his predecessor had made it a general practice to lend large sums of state funds to banks and business firms. Such loans in the fiscal year ending November 30, 1872, amounted to $500,271.20, and in the current year to $223,732. On these sums the treasurers expected to be allowed interest at four and five per cent on deposits or loans over two months. (3) A certified check for $39,200 had been procured from an individual to be exhibited as cash to an investigating committee of the legislature. (4) The state treasurer had obtained advances of large sums by county treasurers, for the purpose of having money on hand to exhibit to a legislative committee. (5) The treasurer had kept no book for the immediate entry of moneys received. (6) The state had received no interest on deposits or loans made by the treasurer. (7) The treasurer had made deposits in his individual name. (8) He had carried a large amount of business as unfinished business, classed as " cash items " which were nothing more than loose memoranda.

[49] *House Journal*, 1873, pp. 131, 140, 178–180.

The committee stated that there was a general unwillingness on the part of nearly all the witnesses to state all the truth, and that this unwillingness was most manifest in the testimony of the state treasurer, whose " palpable evasions " made their labors the more arduous. Had he freely and frankly laid before them all the information he possessed, it would not have been necessary to summon other witnesses to ascertain facts within his knowledge and purposely withheld.[50]

Further action in the matter now awaited the pleasure of the House, but that body was not precipitate. On February 26 an opposition member offered a resolution for the impeachment of William Seeger for corrupt conduct in office and for crimes and misdemeanors. On notice of debate it went over to be called up the next day when a prominent Republican member offered a preamble and two resolutions as a substitute. The preamble merely recited the findings of the Senate committee. The first resolution, " without misjudging the honesty of the motives of the State Treasurer," declared that he had been " flagrantly neglectful of his official duty . . . and further, that the past management of the State Treasury . . . call[s] for . . . unqualified censure and condemnation." The second resolution declared that the lending or depositing of public funds with private persons was hazardous and that the legislature ought to forbid it by law, with severe penalties for violation. The substitutes were agreed to by a vote of 75 to 27. In this way it was hoped that the feelings of a good Republican, who had followed an evil but tolerated custom without bad intent, would be spared.[51]

The matter now rested until March 4, when the member who had proposed the whitewashing resolution of February 27 offered a resolution requesting that William Seeger resign from his office as state treasurer. A preamble stated that action had been delayed in expectation that he would offer his resignation, but the House had received no indication of such intention. Seeger did not long leave the House in ignorance of his intentions. On the very next day in a letter he respectfully declined to resign. He had, he asserted, faithfully accounted for every dollar that had come into his hands and had not perverted one cent to his own use. His

[50] *Senate Journal*, 1873, pp. 79, 104, 157. See also the findings of the committee, printed as a separate pamphlet entitled, *Report of the Special Senate Investigating Committee Appointed to Inquire into the Condition of the State Treasury* (St. Paul, 1873).

[51] *House Journal*, 1873, pp. 369, 396–401.

reputation had been impugned with no opportunity for him to be heard. He was ready to meet any judicial inquiry. In this situation nothing remained but to provide for the judicial inquiry the treasurer desired, and a resolution to impeach him was adopted by a vote of 71 to 32. On March 6 seven managers who had been elected by the House in committee of the whole appeared before the Senate to exhibit the articles of impeachment which the House had adopted. The charges were four in number: embezzlement, aiding in embezzlement, misconduct in office, and refusal to testify fully and truly. On the same date the Senate resolved itself into a court of impeachment, each senator being separately sworn. On the next day a summons was issued notifying Seeger to appear at three o'clock in the afternoon. At the appointed hour the counsel of the impeached treasurer appeared — John M. Gilman, Greenleaf Clark, Gordon E. Cole, and Cushman K. Davis. And it may be safely said that a stronger array of counsel has at no time appeared at the bar of Minnesota. The counsel for the defendant was allowed ten days to file an answer in the case, and the managers of the House were given ten days thereafter to file their reply. The court then adjourned until May 20, 1873.[52]

After the reassemblage of the court on the appointed day a letter from the members of Seeger's counsel was read, informing the court that as their client had determined to resign his office, he presumed that the Senate [sic] would proceed no further with the impeachment. The chairman of the board of managers for the House suggested that under the circumstances the court had no jurisdiction and submitted two documents in evidence, but the court by a vote of 24 to 10 resolved to hear no evidence concerning Seeger's resignation. The documents, however, appear in the record.

The first was a letter by Seeger dated March 10, 1873, to Governor Austin, resigning his office. Seeger repeated that the state had not lost a dollar by any act or omission of his, nor had he converted a farthing of public money to his own use. When accused of crimes and misdemeanors he had expected an early trial and an honorable acquittal. But, unexperienced in legal proceedings, he had not appreciated the time and expense of a trial. The expenditure of five thousand dollars or more for counsel fees and other expenses was far beyond his ability. The other letter was that of Governor Austin, dated March 26, 1873, in which he recognized the right of the treasurer to resign and thought it best under the circum-

[52] *House Journal*, 1873, pp. 478, 494–497, 539–541, 557–567; *Senate Journal*, 1873, pp. 371, 374, 383–386, 421–432, 440–443.

stances that his resignation be formally accepted. He wished Seeger more peace than he had found in official station.

As the court had decided to ignore the resignation, the board of managers formally moved that, as the defendant was in contempt, a plea of guilty to the several charges and specifications be entered against him. The motion was denied, a plea of not guilty was ordered, and the roll of witnesses was called. After a noon recess of the court Colonel J. Hamilton Davidson appeared on behalf of the defendant and asked that the plea of not guilty entered by order of the court be cancelled, and that a plea of guilty to all the charges and specifications be entered. He alleged, however, that none of the acts were done with corrupt or willful intent, and finally craved the mercy of the honorable court. The court by a series of roll calls then found the defendant guilty of all the charges and specifications, and by one resolution removed him from office and by another, carried unanimously, declared William Seeger disqualified to hold and enjoy any office of honor, trust, or profit in the state.[53] Had he not evaded and refused to tell the whole truth before the Senate investigating committee it seems probable that, his bondsmen having made good all alleged embezzlements, Seeger would have been allowed to go into retirement without this shameful sentence.

There were incidental results of the Seeger impeachment of high importance. The salary of the state treasurer was increased to $3,500, and a rational scheme for the custody and the handling of funds was provided for by statute. The treasurer was directed to establish a system of double entry bookkeeping which should show every receipt and payment no matter how small, and he was not to keep unfinished business on loose memoranda. All funds paid in were to be deposited in a national bank, and no payment should be made except by the warrant of the state auditor, and by check on a bank bearing the name of the payee and the number of the auditor's warrant. The same act created a board of audit consisting of the governor, the secretary of state, and the attorney-general, which should examine the treasurer's office and business at least four times a year without previous notice to the treasurer. This board was required to select the banks to serve as depositories and determine what rate of interest should be paid on deposits.

[53] *Proceedings of the Senate of Minnesota, Sitting as a High Court of Impeachment, for the Trial of William Seeger, Treasurer of State, for Corrupt Conduct and Misdemeanors in Office*, 27–41 (Minneapolis, 1873).

It was also required to witness the transfer of books and funds from an outgoing treasurer to a new one. This excellent system with some improvements is still in operation.[54]

5. LORD GORDON GORDON [55]

In the summer of 1871 a stranger of gentlemanly appearance and bearing arrived in Minneapolis. What credentials as to his identity and character he brought is not known, but the reports that he produced letters of introduction may be considered probable. It presently became public that the visitor was an Englishman, reputed to be of noble lineage, with the title " Lord Gordon Gordon." He deposited a sum of money in the National Exchange Bank of Minneapolis, locally known as " Westfall's bank," and obtained the acquaintance of prominent citizens, one of whom made him his house guest and took him to Minnetonka on a picnic excursion. Among the acquaintances made was that of Colonel John J. Loomis, land commissioner of the Northern Pacific Railroad, upon whom he must have made a favorable impression as Loomis invited him to join a party about to travel out on the line of the railway. The party consisted of the two gentlemen mentioned, the commissioner's secretary and attorney, and George B. Wright and Nathan Butler, surveyors. A camp was established on Oak Lake, a short distance west of Detroit in Becker County.[56]

Before the end of September the Loomis party had been in Fergus Falls and " the Honorable G. Gordon of Scotland " was with it. He was delighted with the scenery of the region and was contemplating the establishment of a colony of Scotch people somewhere to the northward of that place.[57] He was a distinguished visitor along with Colonel Loomis at the Douglas County fair in the week before the seventh of October.[58] About a fortnight later " Lord Gordon," as he came to be called, was reported to be laying out a new town, named " Loomis," in Otter Tail County and establishing headquarters there. He had bought twenty-six sections of land about the town and had begun preparations for a large Scotch colony. The village of Pelican Rapids, platted in 1872, was prob-

[54] General Laws, 1873, pp. 152, 233; General Statutes, 1913, pp. 22–27.

[55] See ante, pp. 77–79.

[56] Letters to the author from W. D. Washburn, Jr., November 24, 1922; W. H. Lee, December 18, 1922; Nathan Butler, January 17, 18, 1923, Folwell Papers.

[57] Fergus Falls Advocate, September 30, 1871, pp. 1, 4.

[58] Duluth Minnesotian, October 7, 1871, p. 2.

ably identical with that for which the name "Loomis" had been proposed.[59] On November 18 Lord Gordon and others were encamped on Oak Lake in Becker County and he was investing heavily there.[60] On December 23 he was at Detroit Lake. It was reported that he had made extensive purchases of land at Pelican Rapids of the Northern Pacific Railroad Company and that in the spring a hundred families would arrive in Duluth on their way to establish a colony there.[61] That he left Detroit Lake about Christmas time, 1871, is the testimony of a fellow passenger, Nathan Butler, who had closed his field work for the season. The two traveled direct to St. Paul. A few days later Butler called upon his genial acquaintance at his rooms in the Metropolitan Hotel. He noticed a bed covered by a shawl, which the noble lord pulled away, disclosing about twenty pieces of solid silver. Some of these, he told Butler, were presents from officials of the Northern Pacific; and one, which was pointed out, came from Mrs. Jay Cooke.[62]

The foregoing account, justified by contemporary evidence, of the apparition in Minnesota in 1871 of a titled foreigner with millions of money at his disposal, as reported, bargaining for a great area of land upon which to locate a colony of frugal Scotch, is wonderful enough; but later accounts derived from other sources add many details to be verified if possible by investigators more fortunate than the present writer.

The *Minneapolis Tribune* of April 13, 1872, states that Lord Gordon resided in Minneapolis during the previous summer and presented upon his arrival letters of introduction to some of the leading citizens, who showed him considerable attention. He made many friends and spent money freely.

The *Farmington Press* of May 2, 1872, states that the New York papers were getting up a sensation about Lord Gordon. He had been a resident of St. Paul for two years past and was reported to be very wealthy. He had bargained for seventeen thousand acres on the line of the Northern Pacific before he left the state.

The *Minneapolis Tribune* of July 17, 1873, under the heading, "The Exploits of a Lord," relates that Lord Gordon came to

[59] *Minneapolis Daily Tribune*, 1871: October 18, p. 2; November 14, p. 4; *Otter Tail City Record*, October 21, 1871, p. 1; *Duluth Minnesotian*, October 21, 1871, p. 3; *Fergus Falls Advocate*, November 4, 1871, p. 1. There seems to have been some jealousy in Fergus Falls of the new metropolis.

[60] *Duluth Minnesotian*, November 18, 1871, p. 1; *Otter Tail Record*, December 16, 1871, p. 4.

[61] *Duluth Minnesotian*, December 23, 1871, p. 3.

[62] Butler to the author, January 17, 1923, Folwell Papers.

Minneapolis in 1870 direct from Scotland. He immediately deposited twenty thousand dollars in Westfall's bank. After a few weeks it was rumored that he wished to buy some fifty thousand acres of land on the line of the Northern Pacific, upon which to plant a colony of poor Scotch people to gratify a beautiful sister. Colonel John J. Loomis at once became interested and organized an expedition to enable the nobleman to make his choice of lands and at the same time to indulge in the sports congenial to gentlemen of rank. The caravan of six teams left St. Paul the last of August, with twelve men employed to pitch the tents and perform necessary labor of the camp and march, and a French cook and a number of colored waiters, furnished with linen aprons and white silk gloves. Colonel Loomis conducted the caravan to Fergus Falls, Moorhead, and other stations, but Lord Gordon finally decided to select his lands, fifty thousand acres, in Otter Tail and Becker counties. In November the party came back half frozen. The Northern Pacific company footed the bill of expenses — fifteen thousand dollars for two months.

Edward H. Mott, in his *Story of Erie*,[63] relates that Gordon came quietly to Minneapolis and registered at a hotel simply as " G. Gordon." He spoke modestly of wishing to buy fifty thousand acres of land upon which to colonize some of his overcrowded tenants. A letter addressed " Lord Gordon Gordon " revealed his nobility. The Northern Pacific company sent him in grand style all along its completed and proposed lines of railroad. The excursion occupied two months and cost the company fifteen thousand dollars.

The *Minneapolis Journal* of October 1, 1905, in a full-page article, prepared with care, fixes the arrival of the distinguished Englishman, with an income of over a million dollars a year, in September, 1871. During his stay he was entertained by William D. Washburn and Wilson P. Westfall, the banker, with whom he deposited several thousand dollars. He was presently in negotiation with Colonel Loomis, land agent of the Northern Pacific, for the purchase of several hundred thousand acres of land upon which to colonize a portion of the tenantry of his overcrowded estates in Scotland. The Northern Pacific officials were pleased to treat such a possible customer right royally. A great buffalo hunt was planned and the historic banner of Clan Gordon waved beside the Stars and Stripes before the marquee of the noble lord.

[63] *Between the Ocean and the Lakes; the Story of Erie*, 184 (New York, 1901).

Putnam's Magazine for January, 1910,[64] contains an elaborate illustrated article on the adventures of " A Bogus Peer." According to it Lord Gordon appeared in Minneapolis in 1871. He deposited forty thousand dollars in one of the banks. Forged letters of introduction secured the acquaintance of leading citizens. He became the lion of the city. Great banquets were given in his honor. It was reported that it was his ambition to bring over to Minnesota a colony of Scotchmen and that he would bargain for as many as five hundred thousand acres of land for their settlement. Colonel John J. Loomis, land commissioner of the Northern Pacific Railroad Company, was naturally disposed to conciliate such an investor, who would locate so large a number of very desirable settlers on the line. He therefore planned an excursion to last through three summer months. Twenty men and from thirty to forty horses were employed. The guest traveled in royal style, with two wall tents for his own use. He had what was elsewhere called a " gentleman's tiger " to serve as valet and secretary. One covered wagon was a virtual armory of artillery for deer hunting and another was equipped with complicated fishing tackle. Meals were served on silver and china and there were tropical fruits for desserts. The guest had fourteen changes of raiment. The personnel was carefully instructed never to fail in addressing him as " My Lord." A government surveyor galloped along with the caravan to point out choice sections of land and to mark those selected on a map as " sold." The banner of the Gordons and the Stars and Stripes fluttered side by side before his marquee. Colonel Loomis spent forty-five thousand dollars of railroad money, but told his directors that the noble lord would spend five million dollars with them. On the return of the expedition to Minneapolis " my lord " was entertained at another banquet. Soon after that he drew his money from the bank and departed for New York with a letter of introduction from Colonel Loomis to Horace Greeley. He had been especially gracious to newspaper men in Minneapolis. The personal appearance of the stranger was impressive. His height was about five feet and ten inches. He was always carefully dressed, commonly wearing a silk hat, gloves, and patent leather shoes. His curling hair was always carefully brushed and his finger nails were daintily manicured. He was calm in demeanor, self-poised, and ceremonious and he spoke excellent English with careful articulation. The account thus briefed was written by Dr.

[64] See 7: 416–428 (new series).

William A. Croffut of Washington, a brilliant journalist and author. As editor in chief of the *Minneapolis Tribune* from 1871 to 1873 he was in a position to be informed about all notable doings in the city. The present writer was in 1871 a resident of Minneapolis, then a city of twenty thousand inhabitants, with a somewhat extensive acquaintance, but he has no recollection of any public demonstrations over an English nobleman nor of the extraordinary expedition. He was a member of one party taken out to Moorhead in August, 1871, to sample the new railroad line completed to that point.

A *History of Otter Tail County*, edited by John W. Mason,[65] relates that the visitor took in (in a double sense) W. G. Tuttle of Pelican Rapids as a partner and authorized him to cut on land supposed to have been bought from the Northern Pacific a quantity of logs for building in the spring when the colony should arrive. The partner cut and banked a quantity of logs but, as the land had not been paid for, the company exacted stumpage for them and " poor Tuttle went down." The writer states that Lord Gordon had the use of a Northern Pacific train for some weeks.

The *Minneapolis Tribune* of August 14, 1921, in the first of a series of articles,[66] states that Gordon came to Minneapolis in September, 1871, and took the town by storm; that he was entertained by leading citizens; that he deposited several thousand dollars in Westfall's bank; that the Northern Pacific Railroad gave him an excursion and a buffalo hunt; and that he negotiated with Colonel Loomis, land agent, for several hundred thousand acres of land.

Our putative nobleman left Minnesota early in January, 1872, for New York City, where he remained until the latter part of May. His extraordinary adventure in that city occasioned so great excitement in Minnesota in the following year that an outline of it is desirable. The question whether he brought with him to New York the idea of an adventure, or whether it came suddenly into his consciousness after his arrival is not important. In either case his singular talents were adequate. The months of January and February were passed quietly, without any discovery by the newspapers of the presence of the distinguished personage, in gathering information and extending his acquaintance among persons likely to be helpful. He doubtless learned what was an open secret, that

65 Published in Indianapolis in 1916. See 1: 187.
66 These articles, written in part by James D. Brackett, are continued in the *Tribune* for August 21 and 28, 1921.

Jay Gould, who for three years as president of the Erie Railway Company had dominated the management, was in danger of defeat at a coming election of directors. English investors who had bought Erie in immense quantities were tired of waiting for dividends. Gould had used the proceeds of great stock issues in betterments and extensions. So active was the opposition that Gould himself was planning to organize a new directorate, with himself still at the head, which would command public approval and pacify stock-holders.[67]

With this information Gordon studied how to get at Jay Gould in a way to gain his confidence. Using the letter of introduction given him by Colonel Loomis to Horace Greeley, editor in chief of the *New York Tribune*, he easily made the acquaintance of that eminent advocate of developing the great West by the settlement of colonies of immigrants and of the overflow of home population. His slogan, " Go west, young man," had long been familiar. The wealthy and titled leader of a company of three hundred Scotch to be settled in the coming spring on lands already acquired easily captivated the sympathetic statesman-editor. Acquaintance ripened into intimacy. At a cozy breakfast the conversation was turned to the rumored revolution in the management of Erie. At the proper moment the genial host confided to his guest that he was the owner of some sixty thousand shares of Erie stock and had the control of many more which he intended to vote at the coming election of directors. Greeley was delighted with the prospect of a reform in Erie and was disposed to aid the noble gentleman in his worthy immigration enterprise. With Greeley's assent a trusted emissary was sent to reveal the secret to Colonel Alexander K. McClure, editor of the Philadelphia *Times*, known to be a close friend of Colonel Thomas A. Scott, vice president of the Pennsylvania Rail-road Company. Colonel McClure was informed that the Right Honorable Lord Gordon was in New York, was a large holder of Erie stock, and could control that of some English holders. He was not willing, however, to form a new directorate unless Colonel Scott would come into it. Gould might continue in the presidency if litigation were stopped and an amicable understanding reached. Colonel Scott, as a friend of Gould's, was quite willing to aid him in the pending distress. An arrangement was accordingly made for an early morning call by Scott and Greeley upon the noble lord at his apartments in the Metropolitan Hotel. After a wait while

[67] Mott, *Story of Erie*, 176, 179–184, 466.

he completed his toilet they were admitted into the presence. Breakfast was served and a talk of two hours was held. Lord Gordon, as he suffered himself to be addressed, spoke of his estates in England, his ample income, and his intimacy with titled persons. He also mentioned his purchase of land on the Northern Pacific Railroad. But the conversation turned principally on Erie affairs. He and his titled friends held the majority of the stock and controlled the road. He would be pleased to have an interview with Mr. Gould, of whom he had heard a great deal during the last few weeks. Colonel Scott said that he was expecting to meet Mr. Gould at a later hour and would let him know that my lord desired to see him.

As a consequence, on March 2, 1872, Jay Gould by appointment presented himself in Lord Gordon's rooms, where an interesting interview took place. My lord told Gould that he owned individually thirty million dollars' worth of Erie stock and had the control of twenty millions more belonging to noble English friends. He wished to reorganize the directorate, but thought it would be the best thing for Mr. Gould to retain the management. He desired to name three English noblemen as directors; the other directors might be American gentlemen selected by himself and Mr. Horace Greeley, subject to Gould's approval. Just then "there was a knock at the door, and in walked Mr. Greeley." The organization of the board was discussed and names of directors were mentioned.

It was a glad hour for Jay Gould as he foresaw the opposition host routed and himself at the head of a new directorate backed by English stockholders. His delusion was so complete that my lord's palaver about his antecedents raised not a ripple of suspicion. He had entered Parliament, he said, at the age of twenty-two, the youngest member of the House of Lords; the queen had the greatest confidence in his ability and discretion; he mentioned an important diplomatic mission with which he had been intrusted; he was the only man who could cope with Bismarck. He referred to his colony of Scotch tenants for which he had bought land from the Northern Pacific Railroad Company. For a full week the two financiers were in frequent intercourse, discussing various details of their enterprise.

When the time came for converting desultory conversations into definite contract, his lordship opened to Gould the fact that in the course of his preliminary investigations it had been necessary to use a large amount of money — not less than a million dollars.

At least half of this amount, he claimed, should be repaid him by the new management when organized and in operation; and, in the meantime, he thought that he ought to have something even more substantial than Mr. Gould's word of honor. Gould was so keen to nail down a contract that on March 7 he brought to my lord's hotel stock certificates — 600 shares of Erie, some 1,900 of corporations affiliated with Erie, and 4,722 of the Oil Creek and Allegheny Valley Railroad — twenty one-thousand-dollar bonds of the Nyack and Northern Railroad, and $160,000 in currency. The careful recipient of these securities and cash presently found an error of forty thousand dollars in the footing of Gould's memorandum and sent word of the shortage. Gould did not think there was such an error, but under the circumstances he would not contend about it and came back with forty thousand dollars in cash. To a modest request for a memorandum receipt, his lordship replied that his word of honor ought to be receipt enough and handed the bundle back to Gould. Gould took it, went as far as the door, returned, laid it down, and departed in faith that his property was in safe hands. It must have been sheer sport in playing a fish which had taken his hook so greedily that led Gordon to demand that Gould separate himself from the old directorate. On March 9 Gould delivered to him his resignation as director and president of the Erie Railway Company, to take effect upon the appointment of his successor. The great covenant was complete. Nothing remained but to assemble the holders of the stocks or their proxies and at leisure to make the grand *coup*.

Gould passed two weeks in the comfortable belief that all was well with their splendid scheme. On March 22 he learned that some Philadelphia broker in the employ of Gordon was cutting up and selling his Oil Creek and Allegheny Valley stock at a reduced figure. He reacted to the new situation instantly and with admirable sagacity. On the next day he obtained the use of a room adjoining Gordon's suite, with a door between, and gathered there a small company, which included the New York chief of police and a police justice. One of the number, selected as an intermediary because of his relations to the two parties, sent in his card and was presently admitted to his lordship's parlor. He made known Gould's desire to have his money and securities returned and suggested that Lord Gordon could not afford to be involved in a vulgar controversy over money matters. My lord was at first reluctant and demanded an interview with Gould. The interlocutor then explained the situation and gave him to understand that he had his choice between restitution on the spot or arrest and a probable committal to the Ludlow Street jail. Rather than submit to such an indignity and seeing that Gould was repudiating his agreement, Gordon handed over the $200,000 in currency and all the securities except the 600 shares of Erie, which he had sold in New York, and the 4,722 shares of Oil Creek and Allegheny Valley, which he had put on the market in Philadelphia. Upon Gould's further demand he made out an order to his brokers in writing to have the sale of Oil Creek stopped and the shares surrendered.

As if he were the lawful owner of those Oil Creek shares, Gordon presently directed his Philadelphia brokers not to honor the order he had furnished to Gould and to deliver that stock to no one but himself. Gould, considering himself the lawful owner and Gordon his depositary, on April 9 sued him for felonious conversion of both the Oil Creek and Erie shares. The court fixed Gordon's bail at thirty-seven thousand dollars. His lordship had no difficulty in securing bondsmen from a group of still loyal friends not unwilling to put an obstacle in the path of Jay Gould. One of the bondsmen was A. F. Roberts, a New York merchant, whose name the reader will do well to remember. Distinguished lawyers were employed by both parties to the case. As they were busy men and the courts were crowded with litigants, " the great Gould-Gordon case " did not come up until May 17. Affidavits of the two parties, mutually contradictory, were exhibited and read. Gordon was called to the witness stand and for two hours he responded to questions with composure and frankness, without a single point being scored against him by the prosecution. After a consultation Gould's leading counsel, David Dudley Field, began a series of questions in regard to Gordon's family relations. The witness gave the names and addresses of his stepfather, a sister, a brother-in-law, and an uncle. When asked to which of the three noble Gordon families of England he belonged, he protested against such inquisition and demanded the protection of the court. Judge Brady thought the matter had gone far enough and presently continued the proceeding until the next day. Gould's counsel at once made good use of the information drawn from Gordon. Cablegrams to the American consulates in Paris, London, and Berne brought back replies that no such relatives as those mentioned by Gordon resided at the addresses named. It is not known that he learned of this correspondence but, when the hour arrived on the following day for the resumption of the hearing, Lord Gordon Gordon did not appear. On the night before he had taken a train for Canada.[68]

Soon after Gordon's departure from New York to Canada, two of Gould's lawyers, Elihu Root and General Collis, accompanied by a representative of Marshall and Son of Edinburgh, Scotland, whose bill for jewelry sold to a certain " Lord Glencairn " had not been paid, went to Toronto expecting to make an arrest upon a British complaint. The defaulting debtor had not waited for them.

[68] Up to this point the source of information chiefly relied upon in regard to Gordon's exploits in New York has been a carefully prepared article which appeared in the *New York Sun* of January 3, 1893, by General Charles H. T. Collis, who was one of Gould's attorneys. A clipping of this article is included in volume 20 of a series of scrapbooks made by George A. Brackett. This volume, which is now in the possession of Mr. Albert C. Loring of Minneapolis, contains newspaper clippings and original telegrams, letters, and other manuscripts of importance. Unfortunately Brackett neglected to make much-needed corrections in some of the newspaper statements. A number of the Brackett Scrapbooks are in the possession of the Minnesota Historical Society.

The New York papers are silent until the time of Gordon's arrest. After his arrest articles and other items concerning Gordon and the Gould-Gordon case are numerous. Such items are in the *New York Herald*, the *Sun*, the *Times*, and the *Tribune* for April, May, and June, 1872. See Mrs. William A. Croffut to the author, May 8, 10, 1922, in the Folwell Papers. The *Saint Paul Press*, the *Pioneer*, the *Dispatch*, and the *Minneapolis Tribune* from April 12 to May 25 contain occasional dispatches and extracts from New York papers.

Croffut, in *Putnam's Magazine*, 7: 421 (January, 1910), states that Horace Greeley was Gould's "ambassador" who persuaded Gordon to return the cash and securities. A better guess is that of Mott, who, in his *Story of Erie*, 184–186, names William Belden of the firm of Fisk, Belden, and Company of Wall Street. Belden's wife had met Gordon in Minneapolis and had traveled in his company thence to New York. Gordon testified that he had spent some time in Belden's New York home. It is Mott's opinion that Belden had much to do with bringing about the meeting of Gould with Gordon. Belden is reported as saying that Gould was surprised that the Scotchman gave up so easily; he, Gould, would have been content with one hundred thousand dollars. Why Gordon did not bundle up the half million dollars' worth of cashable securities that had been in his possession for two weeks and make an earlier journey to Canada is likely ever to remain a matter for conjecture.

In regard to the half million dollars' worth of securities and cash handed over by Gould, his statement made under oath has been followed as more probable than that made by Gordon. Gordon testified in court that he and Gould made a deal in Erie of some thirty-five thousand shares and believed that there would be a profit of a million dollars in a short time. My lord was not so confident and would be glad to take half that amount for his calls. Gould took him up and paid him the half million to liquidate. According to Gordon's version, he was not a mere depositary of the wealth, but was the owner of the property.

That the pretensions of Gordon were already discredited in Minnesota is apparent from a communication printed in the *Providence* (Rhode Island) *Journal*, April 5, 1872, evidently written by someone in Minnesota. See John R. Rathom to the author, July 25, 1922, with a typewritten copy of the article, in the Folwell Papers.

His whereabouts remained unknown for nearly a year.[69] Meantime one of Gordon's New York bondsmen had died, leaving the whole burden of the thirty-seven thousand dollar bail upon the survivor, A. F. Roberts, whose name has been mentioned. Early in the spring of 1873 Roberts learned that the noble lord was residing at or near Fort Garry, Manitoba. The adjacent village had long since been named "Winnipeg," but the old name remained in familiar use. Roberts was naturally desirous to recall the distinguished exile to New York, but he did not expect him to come at his, Roberts', pleasure; he therefore considered how to compel Gordon's return. Roberts was advised by his lawyers that he did not need to resort to any "process of law," because wherever the English common law was in force, unmodified by statute, a bail had the right to take his absconding principal into custody wherever and whenever he might find him.

About a year before Roberts had made the acquaintance of George A. Brackett of Minneapolis and doubtless had unfolded to him his relation with the Lord Gordon Gordon, who had so basely deceived and wronged him. It was natural that at this juncture he should think of Brackett as the best person to advise and assist him. He accordingly obtained an exemplified copy of the bailpiece and set out for Minneapolis, where he arrived early in June, 1873. He was not disappointed. George Brackett was a romantic and generous soul. Throughout a long life, which ended in 1921, he was a liberal giver to many a good cause and unsparing of time and labor in public service. His everyday bestowals upon persons in need or trouble were known only to himself and the recording angel. In those years he was in receipt of a large income from railroad work and was quite able, as well as willing, to act in bringing a renegade scoundrel to justice, without thought of pecuniary reward. Brackett was not content, however, with the legal advice which Roberts had brought from New York and suggested that he obtain an opinion from the leading law firm of Minneapolis — Lochren, McNair, and Gilfillan — all gentlemen of high social, as well as professional, standing. After a careful study, they furnished an opinion, supported by a long catena of authorities, that Roberts had the same right to get Gordon into custody as a parent had to get a child, or a master to get an apprentice, without any "process of law." [70]

[69] *New York Sun*, January 3, 1893.
[70] *Saint Paul Press*, July 31, 1873, p. 4; *Minneapolis Tribune*, July 17, 1873, p. 2.

Roberts had his reasons for preferring to delegate the arrest to an agent and Brackett, who was mayor of Minneapolis, was able to recommend to him as a very competent person Michael Hoy, who had had long experience on the Minneapolis police force and had served in the Civil War as a captain in the Tenth Minnesota. Physically he was big and strong and mentally he was alert, resolute, and courageous. Hoy, relieved from routine duty, willingly undertook the proposed excursion without promise of special reward. He was allowed to choose an associate and selected Owen Keegan, a friend who formerly had been on the local police force. He was given two hundred dollars in cash, a letter of credit for one thousand dollars, and a paper labeled " Instructions." The essential points in the instructions were these: " Present all letters to Fletcher and have him take in the whole situation. . . . Don't wait for baggage or anything if you get your hands on the scamp. Send dispatch No. 1 in case you get him, and No. 2 in case he escapes." Dispatch number 1 read: " O. K. Return to-day "; number 2 read: " Too high; can't purchase; have written." Authority was given to buy a team if it was not convenient to take the stage. Such instructions pointed to a sudden and secret capture, which, if unlawful, would be called by an ugly name.[71]

The two ambassadors left Minneapolis on the morning of June 26. It chanced that just at this time the Honorable Loren Fletcher of Minneapolis, member and later speaker of the Minnesota House of Representatives and still later to be representative in Congress, was in Winnipeg on business of his own. Brackett telegraphed him to delay his departure for reasons to be revealed later. Hoy and Keegan arrived by stage from Breckenridge in the afternoon of July 2 and, according to Hoy's instructions, at once delivered a letter to Fletcher. They fully informed Fletcher of their errand and asked his participation in a lawful proceeding to have justice meted out to an audacious scoundrel. Not doubting the advice given by the Minneapolis law firm, his own attorneys, he was willing to aid George Brackett, a man trusted by all who knew him, in such

[71] *Saint Paul Press*, July 31, 1873, p. 4; *Minneapolis Tribune*, July 18, 1873, p. 2; *Manitoba Free Press* (Winnipeg), July 12, 1873. Accompanying a letter from Will E. Ingersoll to the author, August 25, 1922, in the Folwell Papers, are abstracts of items in the *Manitoba Free Press* relating to the Gordon kidnapping case. The abstracts were made from the issues of July 12, 19, 26, August 2, 9, 16, September 20, 1873, and August 8, 1874. The accounts given in the *Manitoban* (Winnipeg) generally agree with those of the *Free Press*, although the *Manitoban* was a government organ and naturally favored the local officials.

a cause.[72]   Hoy brought also a letter addressed to L. R. Bentley, a
merchant of Winnipeg who had formerly been in business in St.
Anthony.   The letter introduced Captain Hoy, who would show
papers explaining his errand.   Bentley was asked to do all in his
power to aid in the capture of " one of the most outrageous scoun-
drels on the continent."   The writer added that he would " see all
made entirely satisfactory."   Bentley was more than willing to
engage in so worthy an enterprise.[73]

At a meeting in Bentley's store in the afternoon a plan was
agreed to for immediate action.   Fletcher and Bentley arranged
with John R. Benson, keeper of a livery stable, for a team and a
double-seated wagon, Benson to be driver.   Bentley, probably in
advance, took Hoy in his single buggy.   A drive of some five miles
brought the party at about eight o'clock in the evening of July 2
near the residence of the Honorable James McKay, west of the fort.
Leaving Hoy in the road, Bentley drove on to the McKay house,
hitched his horse, and went in as if to make a call.   Upon his
return he reported the situation to the party, probably assembled
where he had left Hoy.   Bentley then took Fletcher into his buggy.
Benson, upon Hoy's order, drove Hoy and Keegan along a prairie
road to the rear of the McKay house.   Hoy and Keegan jumped
out, entered the grounds, passed around the house, found Gordon
seated on a veranda, and seized him with sufficient violence to make
sure of a capture.   They marched him — " dragged me," said Gordon — to the main road, " some one gave a whistle," and Benson
drove up with his wagon.   The policemen lifted Gordon in and
placed him between themselves on the back seat.   At this moment
Fletcher reappeared, took his seat beside Benson, and told him to
drive on.   Hoy had lost or left his handcuffs and, at Fletcher's
direction, he pinioned Gordon's arms and legs with halter straps
or ropes.   When they reached the neighborhood of the fort, Gordon demanded to see his counsel.   This was denied and the drive
continued over the toll bridge across the Assiniboine, without a
stop to pay the toll, and on half a mile or more along the trail to
Pembina.   Bentley, who had followed, produced a bottle of whisky
from which all present, except Fletcher and Gordon, drank success
to the adventure so happily begun.   Bentley drove Fletcher back
to town, leaving Benson with his three passengers to follow the
southward road to the international boundary.

[72] *Saint Paul Press*, July 31, 1873, p. 4; Fletcher's statement, in the *Manitoba Free Press*, July 19, 1873.
[73] Brackett to Bentley, June 27, 1873, in Brackett Scrapbook, 20: 27.

After an all-night journey, a stop was made the next morning, July 3, for breakfast, for which Gordon was unfettered. After breakfast the road was taken for the boundary, now only some thirty miles away. At about ten o'clock on July 3, when the expedition was within a few hundred yards of the boundary, it was halted by the British customs officer, who was also justice of the peace, attended by his assistant armed with a rifle. The officer acted in conformity with a telegram he had received a quarter of an hour before, which read: " Five Americans kidnapped Gordon, commonly called Lord Gordon, and are running him out, it is supposed, by your way. Arrest all parties if they can be found. Get all assistance necessary." Resistance was not thought of and Hoy handed over his papers. After examining them the officer told Hoy that he had no lawful authority for extraditing Gordon and that he and Keegan were in arrest. Gordon he liberated and gave him Hoy's pistol with which to protect himself on his way back to Winnipeg with Benson. Hoy was allowed to dispatch a telegram and it is safe to say that he made use of the " No. 2 " of his instructions. Hoy and Keegan were sent down to Winnipeg on a steamboat under guard.[74]

Fletcher doubtless slept well and spent the next day, July 3, in closing up the business which had brought him to Fort Garry. It is not known who brought the tidings of the arrest of Gordon to town, but early in the day there was no little excitement about it. Fletcher's connection with it must have been suspected, as a local policeman was asked by Gordon's lawyer to " keep track " of him. It would appear that he became aware of this surveillance, for, having concluded his business, he decided not to remain in Winnipeg. He also thought it best not to tarry overnight, nor to wait for the stage. Here a new personage came into the play, George N. Merriam of Minneapolis, who was concerned with Fletcher in the sale of several million feet of pine logs. He had no knowledge of the affair other than the fact of the arrest of Gordon. Fletcher and Merriam took their departure for home in the evening of July 3 in a private conveyance and traveled all night, in spite of the mosquito pests of the region in that season. Early the next morning at Scratching River they met the attorney-general of Manitoba, J. H. Clarke, on his way to Fort Garry accompanied by Gordon. The attorney-general suggested to Fletcher that he would probably need

[74] Testimony of Gordon and Benson, not materially different, in the *Minneapolis Tribune*, July 18, 1873, p. 2; testimony of Gordon, Benson, Boswell, Dr. Bown, and Bradley, in the *Manitoba Free Press*, July 12, 19, 1873.

his testimony in an expected prosecution. Under the circumstances the suggestion was equivalent to a summons and the two Americans returned to Fort Garry. That evening, July 4, they were arrested and late at night they were taken by the sheriff in a rude conveyance, along with Hoy and Keegan, to the fort for confinement — Hoy and Keegan in a cell and Fletcher and Merriam in the orderly's room. Fletcher and Merriam were required to give up their watches and pocketbooks containing money and commercial paper amounting to twenty-six thousand dollars.

At first the prisoners seem to have been regarded as desperate criminals who would scruple at no means of escape. An armed guard was kept in the room in which Fletcher and Merriam were imprisoned, which was not more than fourteen feet square and had one window and one door, and other guards patrolled in front. For some days they were allowed no physical exercise and, later, only that of marching and countermarching in the terreplein of the fort between redcoats with fixed bayonets. At the earliest possible moment Fletcher dispatched a telegram to Mayor Brackett in Minneapolis — brief and pregnant, no doubt, but no sufficient proof has yet been found that it was in the terms announced by the newspapers: " I'm in a h—ll of a fix. Come at once." Bentley was presently arrested and accorded a share of Fletcher's and Merriam's quarters. Later, on July 5, Mayor Brackett was speeding northward on a special train, for which he was charged $350. From Moorhead he took fast horses and he reached Winnipeg in the morning of the eighth. He took with him Eugene M. Wilson, late representative in Congress from Minnesota, and William Lochren; but the latter thought it wise to remain near Pembina inside the United States.[75]

The preliminary examination began on that day, July 8, before Judge Betourney of the Court of Queen's Bench. That was a red-

---

[75] *Saint Paul Press*, July 31, 1873; *Minneapolis Journal*, October 1, 1905, magazine section. See Merriam's statement on his return from Winnipeg, on bail, in the *Saint Paul Pioneer*, August 3, 1873; his statement in court, in the *Minneapolis Daily Tribune*, July 18, 1873, and in the *Manitoba Free Press*, July 19, 1873; Fletcher's statement in the last-mentioned paper; an article in the *Minneapolis Journal*, October 1, 1905, written while Brackett was living; and a telegram from C. W. Mead to Brackett, dated July 5, 1873, in Brackett Scrapbook, 20: 35. In the *Minneapolis Journal*, November 15, 1909, is a statement by Lieutenant Colonel A. G. Irvine, who had charge of Fort Garry at the time of the confinement of the Americans in 1873: " We treated him [*Fletcher*] and the others just as well as we could, and they had the same fare and just as good sleeping accommodations as we had; still we were unable to satisfy Fletcher. But we all liked him."

letter day in the Manitoba court. The American consul, the Honorable J. W. Taylor, introduced the Honorable Eugene M. Wilson and asked that he be allowed to appear for the prisoners. The court ruled that he could not appear at a preliminary examination. The prisoners therefore had to pay a retaining fee of five hundred dollars to a Winnipeg attorney and to employ two additional attorneys as counsel. The crown was represented by Attorney-General Clarke and two local law firms. The proceedings went on with much dignity and great deliberation from day to day, except weekends, for a fortnight. Gordon was on the stand a whole day. Benson was interrogated at length. The prisoners were allowed to make statements without being sworn. Hoy stated that at a meeting on the evening of June 27 he had met with Brackett, Roberts, Lochren, and McNair, who assured him that he would have full authority to arrest Gordon. He took his orders from Mayor Brackett, his official superior. No reward was promised him or through him to Keegan. He said that Fletcher was not present at the arrest and that Gordon promised him fifty pounds to leave the province. Merriam accounted for his business and whereabouts and declared that he had nothing to do with the arrest, directly or indirectly. Fletcher knew nothing of the intended arrest until Hoy brought Brackett's letter on July 2 and along with it the opinion of the Minneapolis lawyers, who were also his own attorneys. He believed that Hoy was fully authorized to make the arrest. He had not advised it, he had not taken any part in it, and was not present when it took place. Keegan corroborated Hoy's statement; Bentley declined to make any. An important witness was Fred J. Boswell, the assistant customs officer at Pembina, who produced the papers he had taken from Hoy, among them the "instructions" mentioned above and the letter of credit for one thousand dollars.

On the fifth day the procedure was diversified by a fierce attack of the attorney-general upon the American consul, who had published a card apologetic and explanatory of the attempted arrest of Gordon according to what was believed to be a strictly lawful manner. The publication of the letter was an outrage upon the people of the province and a contempt of the court. He had telegraphed to the minister of justice at Ottawa proposing that Washington be asked to recall the consul. The judge thought the publication of the letter an "improper act" and approved of the attorney-general's action. Taylor remained in office for many years thereafter.

There were three noteworthy letters exhibited. One was from Norman W. Kittson of St. Paul to John H. McTavish, chief factor of the Hudson's Bay Company, asking for his kindly interest in Roberts' effort to secure the arrest of Gordon, a notorious scoundrel of whom his country would be well rid. Hoy had the necessary papers. Another was from Horace Thompson, the St. Paul banker, to Taylor, requesting his aid so far as he could "consistently render it officially or otherwise." A third letter was from the Reverend Father Tissot of Minneapolis to "the Catholic Priest visiting at Fort Garry," recommending Michael Hoy, a next-door neighbor with an honorable military and civil record, and adding, "So far as I can judge has always been a good church member." The reader may judge whether or not the surmise is well founded that these letters were intended for use in case the precipitate capture of Gordon should be delayed or interrupted and inquiry made as to its legality. One whole day was taken up with arguments by counsel. On the morning of July 23 the court rendered its decision. Hoy had no authority for making any such arrest as his instructions indicated. Bentley took part by acting as guide. Fletcher was as guilty as any of them. All five stood committed to the common jail of the province until the next assizes, when indictments would be preferred.[76]

It was deemed worth while not to move for bail before Judge Betourney, but to make the application before another judge who might make allowance for extenuating circumstances. After a two-day hearing, Judge McKeagney on July 26 admitted Merriam to bail in the sum of four thousand dollars, but refused it to the other four men. He wholly rejected the opinion of the American lawyers as "most dangerous to our national independence." Assuming it to be good law that a bail might take his principal into his custody without process, it was a personal right and could not be delegated to an agent. As the offense was a grave one, punishable upon conviction with imprisonment for seven years, and as the evidence of guilt was strong, it was not within the legal discre-

[76] *Manitoba Free Press,* July 12, 19, 26, 1873; *Minneapolis Tribune,* July 18, 19, 1873; *Saint Paul Press,* July 18, 19, 1873; *Saint Paul Pioneer,* July 18, 19, 1873. The *Minneapolis Tribune,* July 18, 1873, printed a letter from Brackett giving an account of his interview with Archbishop Taché of Manitoba, whose aid he had tried to enlist for Hoy and Keegan. There survives an unverified statement that Brackett took a letter from Bishop Henry B. Whipple to the Anglican bishop at Fort Garry and that the latter prelate refused to interfere in the course of justice. See the *Minneapolis Journal,* October 1, 1905, magazine section. The *Evening Times and News* (Minneapolis), July 24, 1873, gives Judge Betourney's decision in full.

tion of the court to allow bail. Merriam easily found bondsmen and was released, but not until he had given security for five hundred dollars for attorneys' fees.[77]

At this day no one will question the soundness of the decision. It is an easy surmise that Roberts and his friends did not expect their legal advice to be of service in the capture of Gordon; that they planned to effect by a plain and simple kidnaping exploit. If, later, the matter should become one of international diplomacy, the fine point of law would come in as a justification for the irregular extradition of a scoundrel of two continents which the British government would be content to tolerate. No fault was found with the three Manitoba lawyers who appeared for the defense, except that McKenzie, the leader, valued his services at one hundred dollars a day. The attitude of Attorney-General Clarke, in charge of the prosecution, was needlessly vindictive, especially during the preliminary examination, even according to local opinion.[78]

We may now leave the four unfortunate gentlemen, who meant only to aid in the execution of justice, to lie in jail for more than forty days and forty nights awaiting trial for the high crime of " conspiracy to abduct a British subject from British soil." The sheriff, it was reported, did all that he could for their comfort. Meals were sent in from the Bentley kitchen, and Consul Taylor showed kindness in many ways. But the confinement was rigorous, as if for prisoners who would be likely to attempt escape. When Mrs. Fletcher came she was allowed to visit her husband on Tuesdays and Fridays only.[79]

The misadventure of Hoy and his aid and the hard luck of Fletcher and Merriam, all innocent of any wrong intent, naturally aroused excitement and sympathy at home. If the leading newspapers of Minneapolis and St. Paul correctly described the situation, the whole people of Minnesota were boiling over with indignation at the wrongs and indignities visited upon their esteemed fellow citizens by the police and judicial authorities at Fort Garry, inspired by " the brutal blackguard," Attorney-General Clarke.

[77] *Manitoba Free Press*, August 2, 1873; clipping in Brackett Scrapbook, 20: 18, from the *New York Daily Register*, July 29, 1873; *Minneapolis Tribune, Saint Paul Press, Saint Paul Pioneer*, July 27, 1873.

[78] *Manitoba Free Press*, July 19, 1873. Allegations thrown out in a time of great excitement that Attorney-General Clarke attempted to levy blackmail are too slightly corroborated to deserve serious notice. Macaulay to Brackett and affidavit of Macaulay, both dated August 4, 1873, in Brackett Scrapbook, 20: 49, 51.

[79] *Saint Paul Pioneer*, August 3, 1873; Macaulay to Brackett, August 9, 1873, in Brackett Scrapbook, 20: 49.

The *Saint Paul Pioneer* of August 1, under the heading, " Our People Should Make Ready," denounced the crime committed by the corrupt and venal Canadian authorities and advised putting no obstacles in the way of the Fenians should they décide to move upon the colony in force. If another plan should be preferred, it should be well matured, but there should be no delay in preparation. " It should be swift, silent and terrible." Should the helpless prisoners, convicted in a mock court by a perjured jury and a corrupt judge and sentenced to prison, not be liberated, Manitoba should be wrapped in flames. " Let us then call the roll of justice, and make sure work of it." The *Saint Paul Press* spoke with less truculence, but suggested that the gross and inexcusable judicial outrage would be likely to provoke universal and profound national irritation. The cherished hatred of Canadians had found vent in the outrages inflicted upon these citizens of Minnesota. " The people of Minnesota and of the United States," said the *Press*, " will recollect the debt they owe to the courtesy of the Manitoba public and they can rest assured that the debt will be paid." The *Minneapolis Tribune* of August 2 quoted the *New York Tribune's* statement that the refusal of bail would be considered on the American side of the border as being purposely and offensively hostile; and it quoted the *Chicago Tribune* as considering it a flagrant violation of judicial decency.[80]

The friends of the unlucky gentlemen detained at Fort Garry got into action as soon as the news of the predicament of the four reached them. No friend of Fletcher's was more alert than Governor Horace Austin, his former townsman at St. Peter and his political crony. On July 12 he telegraphed to Brackett at Fort Garry to notify him immediately if bail should be refused, apparently suspecting that it would be. Brackett foresaw that bail would not be allowed and on July 22 he telegraphed William D. Washburn and William S. King that something must be done. Ramsey should go to Washington at once. On July 24 Senator Ramsey met Austin and Windom in St. Paul for a conference.[81] On August 2 Ramsey and Austin were in Washington, where they were heard by J. C. Bancroft Davis, assistant secretary of state, on behalf of the Minnesotans detained at Fort Garry. Davis assured them that all feasible efforts would be made to obtain the release of the prisoners, or at least their enlargement on bail. Thus comforted, Senator

[80] *Saint Paul Pioneer*, August 1, 1873; *Saint Paul Press*, July 30, 1873; *Minneapolis Tribune*, July 31, August 2, 1873.
[81] Brackett Scrapbook, 20: 37.1, 43.

Ramsey came home, but Governor Austin remained in Washington for conference with the British minister.[82]

Fletcher seems to have had more confidence in Governor Austin than in Ramsey and still more in Mayor Brackett. On August 1 he telegraphed to the mayor, who had returned to Minneapolis on July 30: " You promised me — you and others would go to Washington at once. I want you to go without delay you know the fact." [83] Brackett joined Austin in Washington and they obtained a hearing from President Grant at Long Branch, New Jersey, on August 10. The president listened patiently and asked for a statement in writing to be submitted to the secretary of state.[84] Evidently business was in low gear in the Washington offices in those dog days. Impatient of the delay, Mayor Brackett followed Secretary Hamilton Fish to his country home on the Hudson River and obtained a personal interview. Secretary Fish was sympathetic and desirous to see the prisoners released. Some days, however, passed without action and on August 22 Mayor Brackett telegraphed to Fish from New York the substance of a dispatch which he had received from prominent Minnesotans: " If our government can not act so as to secure release, hurry home, and aid in measures that will prove effective." He added that he would leave for home the next night. On the same day he wrote to Fish. He referred to his telegram and added, " We have stood more than American citizens ought to stand." He thought the secretary would be justified in making a peremptory demand for Hoy, Keegan, and Gordon, who were taken on American soil, and a request for the immediate release of Fletcher and Bentley. The secretary replied by two letters, one in answer to Brackett's telegram and the other, to his letter. He reminded the mayor that, as the prisoners in Winnipeg were held by judicial process on criminal charges, the executive department of the government could not officially interfere. It could only use its good offices in the case and that he, Fish, had been doing. As for a release on the ground that the arrest had been made on American soil, that was a diplomatic proposition to be

[82] *Saint Paul Press*, August 2, 7, 9, 1873. Croffut, in *Putnam's Magazine*, 7: 424 (January, 1910), relates that Davis recommended that Minnesotans should seize the Canadian customs-house officers and hold them until redress was conceded, which is manifestly impossible.

[83] Brackett Scrapbook, 20: 41.

[84] *New York Tribune*, August 10, 1873; *Saint Paul Press*, August 12, 1873. The statement of the *Minneapolis Sunday Tribune*, August 28, 1921, section 4, p. 6, that President Grant told Austin and Brackett that if they were unable to secure the early release of the prisoners he would countenance the use of an armed force, is an incredible yarn.

referred to London and would involve time while notes were being exchanged. The secretary did not fail to note the suggestion that Minnesota citizens might be taking measures without the aid of the government. He advised them, and Brackett in particular, to abstain from any violent steps and closed his second letter by stating that he had directed the attention of the proper government offices to prevent possible violations of law.[85] In the meantime Roberts sent his New York attorney to Ottawa to enlist the interference of Sir John McDonald, the Canadian premier, and eminent counsel in Montreal were retained. What was the result, if any, of the embassy has not been ascertained.[86]

All efforts to secure bail having been fruitless, Fletcher and Bentley and Hoy and Keegan remained in jail, with such resignation as was possible to their several temperaments, until the day set for the next assizes, September 15. On September 2 Fletcher telegraphed to Brackett: " All the officials here evidently desire all prisoners to plead guilty and assure us of nominal sentence. . . . Advise us at once." The fact that Governor Austin and Francis R. E. Cornell, attorney-general of Minnesota, traveled to Winnipeg

[85] Brackett Scrapbook, 20: 55, contains the two manuscript letters of Secretary Fish, with printed copies, and Brackett's letter and his telegram in print. All were reprinted in the *Minneapolis Journal*, October 1, 1905, magazine section, and in the *Minneapolis Sunday Tribune*, August 28, 1921, section 4, p. 6. Brackett's suggestion that Hoy and Keegan were arrested on American soil had this foundation, that recent surveys of the boundary line by the International Joint Commission had located the forty-ninth parallel north of the line previously recognized. The proceedings of the commission had not yet been ratified and Secretary Fish therefore declined to take the responsibility of demanding the release of the prisoners on that account. American newspapers made much ado about the outrage committed by the Canadians on American soil. *Minneapolis Tribune*, August 3, 7, 14, 1873; *Chicago Tribune*, August 4, 1873.

[86] Roberts to Brackett, July 24, 1873, in Brackett Scrapbook, 20: 45. "Keep this letter to yourself," wrote Roberts. The *Minneapolis Journal*, October 1, 1905, contains a notable statement, which is repeated in the *Minneapolis Tribune*, August 28, 1921: in substance, that Brackett obtained from the British ambassador at Washington, Sir Edward Thornton, a letter of introduction to Sir John McDonald, the Canadian premier; that Brackett traveled to Ottawa accompanied by several prominent New York and Montreal attorneys; that Sir John gave them a hearing of two hours on the last day of his term of office and furnished a letter to the governor of Manitoba which secured the release of the prisoners. There may be some scintilla of fact in the statement; but Brackett did not obtain a letter from the British minister, he did not travel to Ottawa with a bunch of lawyers, and he did not secure a letter from the premier to the governor of Manitoba which brought about the release of the prisoners. Croffut, in *Putnam's Magazine*, 7: 425 (January, 1910), makes an unverified statement that Austin and Brackett went to Ottawa and persuaded Sir John McDonald to send a telegram to Manitoba which secured the release of the prisoners on bail.

indicates that advice on that matter would be offered after consultation. The proceedings in court as reported indicate that an understanding had been reached which rendered controversy unnecessary. Judge Betourney invited Governor Austin to a seat on the bench; Attorney-General Clarke was genial and complaisant. Bentley's case was first to be called. He pleaded " guilty " and his counsel asked that a light sentence be imposed, as the accused had already suffered two and a half months' imprisonment. The attorney-general made no objection. The indictment being read to Hoy, he read a brief statement that, although he had believed his authority to arrest Gordon to be full and complete, since he was now advised by his counsel that the bailpiece he had brought with him had no force in a foreign jurisdiction, he was content to plead " guilty." Keegan, upon arraignment, made a similar statement and plea. Fletcher, who was next " put to the bar," pleaded " not guilty " and his counsel asked that his trial be put off until the next term of court after the October session. The attorney-general insisted that the trial be set for October 10; but, if good and sufficient reasons should then be given, he would consent to a continuance to the next term of court. He proposed that Fletcher be bailed personally at two thousand dollars and that two sureties be provided at one thousand dollars each. The case was continued to the next term of court. It came up on November 20, 1873, when it was postponed. Another postponement followed and on July 4, 1874, it was dismissed. The prisoner had been waiting for three months and the crown was not ready to prosecute. No explanation has been found of the unreadiness of queen's counsel.

It appears that the indictment included William J. Macaulay of Winnipeg, the merchant who had bought the pine logs from Fletcher and Merriam. So far as is known, his only connection with the affair was that he engaged a team to convey the two men expeditiously by night over the border. He pleaded " guilty " and received the same sentence as the three who had lain in jail many weeks — one day's imprisonment. As for the prisoners who had pleaded " guilty," the attorney-general suggested that, the majesty of the law having been vindicated, the ends of justice would be satisfied with imprisonment for the shortest possible time. The court then imposed a sentence of twenty-four hours' imprisonment upon Hoy, Keegan, and Bentley. Merriam had not been indicted.[87]

[87] Brackett Scrapbook, 20:63; *Manitoba Free Press*, September 20, November 22, 1873, February 21, June 13, July 4, 1874; Will E. Ingersoll to

On September 16, Governor Austin telegraphed, " We leave for home to-morrow evening per steamer Dakota and take all the boys with us." The journey, which is now made in a single night by rail, occupied a much longer time in those days and " the boys " did not arrive in Minneapolis until 7: 05 in the morning of September 22. Two or three thousand people had assembled at the station to greet them. Cheer upon cheer filled the air. A procession headed by two brass bands followed by the Irish Rifles and several hundred citizens marched up Hennepin Avenue to Eighth Street, then along the edge of town to Fletcher's house. After a reception there the procession re-formed and escorted Hoy and Keegan to their homes in old St. Anthony. In the evening a bounteous supper was served in Brackett's Hall and dancing closed the joyous day.[88]

The author is very tired of Lord Gordon Gordon, but presumably some readers will desire to know what became of him. On

Dr. Grace L. Nute, July 18, 1924, Folwell Papers. In the issue of the *Free Press* for July 19, 1873, is Merriam's statement in regard to Macaulay.

On August 1, 1873, Brackett, writing to Bentley, said, " I will . . . make good the loss caused by your confinement." On the thirtieth of that month Roberts notified Brackett that he must be excused from incurring expenses. A letter of Fletcher to Bentley, dated October 4, 1873, testifies to the hard times of that year. " I have stock in three of the banks . . . but cannot draw a dollar. . . . Merriam & I so far have paid all the bills for expenses Board & Hoy & Keegans bills &c except the New York & Ottawa expenses. Brackett has written Roberts about it but I don't expect him to do anything & if not I think it will all come on myself & Merriam. . . . I shall never ask any of them to do anything about it." A stated account, dated November 18, 1873, apparently makes Roberts debtor to Brackett in the sum of $5,027.08. Brackett told Bentley in a letter of December 2, 1873, that his claim for fifteen hundred dollars paid Attorney McKenzie was too much. He had already paid " the same *scamp* " five hundred dollars. On January 9, 1874, Roberts wrote Brackett that he would make an effort to do something: " I would take the shirt off my back to be able to make you one offer to settle the whole matter if it would do any good." On September 8, 1874, Roberts in a letter to Brackett proposed to settle " this unfortunate & most unpleasant affair " by a remittance of two thousand dollars. Two months later he informed Brackett that financial embarrassments obliged him to withdraw the offer. On January 1, 1875, Bentley drew up a bill against Brackett for $10,007, of which $8,100 were for business loss and damage and $1,907 for expenses. On the twenty-seventh of that month Roberts wrote Brackett that he could make a remittance for settlement with Bentley. The last item found in the Bentley matter is a receipt, dated August 1, 1881, for $158 by Bentley's attorneys to Brackett in full of all demands. This may have been the last of a number of partial payments. A memorandum without date gives the amount paid out by Fletcher at Fort Garry as $2,791.95. Brackett Scrapbook, 20: 27, 45, 61, 69, 75, 81, 83, 85.

[88] Brackett Scrapbook, 20: 37; *Saint Paul Press*, September 17, 1873; *Minneapolis Tribune*, September 18, 1873; *Minneapolis Evening Times*, September 23, 1873.

the day of the trial of the American prisoners my lord was in court, under arrest on two indictments for having subscribed himself to an information before a magistrate charging three persons named with having stolen six thousand dollars from him as "Hubert Charles Gordon," whereas his name was "Gordon Gordon." Attorney-General Clarke made some remark to the court in reference to the case, whereupon Gordon, pointing toward Clarke, snarled, "My lord, that counsel tried to swindle me out of $10,000; and because he failed, I am locked up here. The scoundrel!" Gordon was admitted to bail. He was in a very enfeebled physical condition.[89]

On July 22, 1874, Gordon's attorneys notified Brackett that they were instructed by Lord Gordon Gordon to commence proceedings to recover damages from all who had participated in any way in his illegal arrest in July, 1873, and asked him to name a solicitor in Winnipeg to accept services of process.[90] The prosecution thus begun came to an early and sudden end. The *Manitoba Free Press* of August 8, 1874, contained the following item: "Verdict [*of a coroner's jury*]. — That Gordon Gordon at the parish of Headingly in the County of Selkirk and Province of Manitoba, on the night of the 1st day of August, 1874, at about ten o'clock, after having been arrested by a police constable from the city of Toronto, under two warrants said to have been issued by Alex. McNabb, police of stipendiary magistrate for the city of Toronto, and while laboring under the excitement resulting from said arrest, did commit suicide by shooting himself in the head with a pistol, causing death." In the same issue the *Free Press* gives a summary of the testimony. The police constable from Toronto found Gordon a lodger in the house of Mrs. Abigail Corbett in Headingly, twelve miles west of Winnipeg. He showed his warrant. Gordon glanced at it and asked whether he was to be taken through the states. Assured that he would not be, he dressed himself for the journey. At the last moment he called for his Scotch cap and "made a sort of rush" into his bedroom as if to get it. The officer followed to the bedroom door and saw Gordon standing with his back to a wall with a pistol in his hand. Before he could reach him the pistol went off and Gordon, with an indistinct word, fell to the floor dead. There was a wound in his right temple and blood was oozing from

[89] *Manitoba Free Press*, September 20, 1873; *Minneapolis Tribune*, September 17, 18, 1873.
[90] Brackett Scrapbook, 20: 79.

his left ear. This prosaic account has been diversified with dramatic incidents by many hands.[91]

From the testimony taken at the coroner's inquest, it appears that a plan had been carefully laid to get Gordon out of Manitoba and, directly or indirectly, to New York. Some weeks previously John F. Bain, a barrister of Winnipeg, had furnished to a friend, "a legal gentleman of high standing in Montreal," desired information in reference to a proposed arrest of Gordon. Alexander Munro, a police constable of Toronto, had come to Winnipeg, accompanied by two men from New York, named Hardy and Reid — the former a lawyer and agent for Marshall and Son of Edinburgh, Scotland — with warrants for Gordon's arrest. Hardy had promised Munro that he would be well paid. Bain took Munro to Gilbert McMicken, justice of the peace of Winnipeg, who indorsed his warrants and allowed George McMicken and another man named Fullerton to aid in the arrest. Bain was also of the party. Hardy and Reid thought it best to keep out of sight, for if Gordon should see them he would "clear." Magistrate McMicken testified that if he had known that Hardy or any other person was in Winnipeg in connection with the case he would have had Gordon brought before him for examination before indorsing the warrants. The testimony of Munro and Bain concurred in regard to a plan of getting Gordon out of Winnipeg and over the river that night. He might be allowed to see his lawyers for a few minutes, but there was to be no opportunity for habeas corpus proceedings. Munro's intention was to take the "Dawson Route" — the old canoe route, some four hundred miles long, through and along the waters dividing the Dominion from the United States, from the Lake of the Woods to Lake Superior, with numerous portages, sometimes on one side of the line and sometimes on the other. George McMicken and Fullerton were to go part of the way. The reader may conjecture what might happen after their departure, when the constable was alone in the wilderness with his prisoner.

Thomas Pentland, Gordon's man, who had lived with him only a little over a year, could give little information about Gordon. His master had very little jewelry and some solid silverware. A sum of sixteen hundred dollars Gordon "had made spin out until now." Gordon had told him that he had large amounts locked up

[91] *Manitoba Free Press*, August 8, 1874; *St. Paul Dispatch*, August 3, 4, 10, 11, 1874; Croffut, in *Putnam's Magazine*, 7: 424 (January, 1910); *New York Sun*, January 3, 1893; Mott, *Story of Erie*, 186; *Minneapolis Journal*, October 1, 1905; *Minneapolis Tribune*, August 28, 1921.

in American courts. On Friday night Gordon had written a letter to Westfall, the Minneapolis banker. He had been working Mrs. Corbett's farm and had a good crop in.[92]

Of the early life of this extraordinary criminal little, if anything, that can be regarded as unquestionable is known. Of the numerous stories which have been met with one which was published in the Toronto *Mail* may be accepted provisionally as probable, or at any rate as the best example of the romances which have appeared. The man called Gordon was the illegitimate son of an English clergyman and was given the name " John Hamilton." In 1849 he was in the employ of a London warehouse firm and was guilty of some dishonesty, for which he escaped punishment. Two years later he was assistant master in a school in Somersetshire. Next he set up as a man of wealth and bargained for an estate for which he had no means of paying. Later he appeared in London as " the Reverend John Hamilton " and actually officiated in one of the churches. Other adventures followed and in 1865 " Mr. Hamilton " rented in Surbiton, a suburb of Kingston, Sussex, a cottage, which he furnished luxuriously and in which he lived in high style. While there he assumed the name of " Glencairn " and the title of " Honorable," which he claimed had come to him with an estate left by his mother. In 1868 he rented an office in London in the law quarter, introduced himself to a legal firm as " the Honorable H. Glencairn," and deposited with the firm boxes said to contain family plate, jewels, and title deeds, all marked in gold letters, " Right Honorable Lord Glencairn." In 1869 he rented a shooting privilege in Scotland, where he lived quietly and paid his bills. The next year he returned under the name " Lord Glencairn," accompanied by English gentlemen of position. He bought a large amount of jewelry on credit. In 1870 the imposture was discovered and " Lord Glencairn " disappeared. The next year he appeared in Minneapolis, Minnesota.[93]

The suicide of Gordon was preceded a few days by an incident not pleasant to record. Michael Hoy had not been pleased with the way in which the attorney-general of Manitoba had prosecuted him with others for their irregular attempt to extradite Gordon without process of law. Clarke's manners may have been inelegant

---

[92] *Manitoba Free Press*, August 8, 1874.
[93] A clipping of the Toronto *Mail* article accompanies a letter from the Toronto *Mail and Empire* to the author, November 4, 1922, in the Folwell Papers. The date of the issue in which the article was published has not been found.

and he may have displayed an excess of zeal in the hope of popular approval. In July, 1874, Clarke had occasion to visit or pass through the state of Minnesota. Hoy learned that he was or would be in St. Paul on July 20. On that day he found it convenient to be in St. Paul, where he encountered Clarke and inflicted upon him a severe physical chastisement. On the twenty-first Hoy was arraigned before the court of common pleas on a charge of assault with intent to murder. He waived examination and was enlarged on bail, which was set at fifteen hundred dollars, William W. McNair of Minneapolis being one of the bondsmen. The court records disclose no further proceedings.[94]

6. THE DONNELLY-WASHBURN CONTEST, 1878–81[95]

The political campaign of 1878 in the third congressional district of Minnesota was one of unusual interest and, if the word of Donnelly's biographer may be taken, " the most extraordinary campaign ever made in the United States." The candidate of the Republican party, William D. Washburn, had obtained the nomination against some opposition but had a right to expect an election by a majority of ten thousand or more. Donnelly was not averse to a tussle with an old political antagonist. With the full

[94] For details of the shameful affair see the *Saint Paul Dispatch*, the *Pioneer*, and the *Press*, and the *Minneapolis Tribune* of July 20, 1874. All the papers denounce editorially the conduct of Hoy as cruel, brutal, and cowardly, in spite of provocation. The *Dispatch* of July 23 and the *Pioneer* of July 24 reprint an article from the *Chicago Tribune* giving the story told by Clarke to a reporter. Broken in health, he was on his way to Colorado. As he was about to enter a car at the railroad station in St. Paul, Hoy struck him on the forehead with a blunt instrument, knocked him down, kicked him, and beat him until he was insensible. But for the interference of bystanders he would have been beaten to death. He did not doubt that Hoy intended to murder him. A preliminary arrest of Hoy on the spot for assault is not important; in a later arrest on the same day the charge was assault with intent to kill. Bail of fifteen hundred dollars does not seem excessive for such a charge. There were persons, especially in Minneapolis, who believed that Clarke had got only what he deserved, although Hoy's procedure was irregular. The *Press* of July 22 charged Minneapolis papers with treating Hoy's assault as a brilliant exploit. The *Tribune* of the same day objected to Hoy's behavior being charged up against Minneapolis and was willing to leave it to the St. Paul courts to see justice done.

The *Saint Paul Dispatch*, August 8, 1874, states that Attorney-General Clarke had procured the necessary papers at Ottawa to bring suit in the sum of fifty thousand dollars against the United States (*sic*) for confiscation of his baggage and brutal assaults. The Canadian consul at Chicago was investigating the affair through persons in St. Paul. In Clarke's affidavit he alleged that the outrages were instigated by the Fenian Brotherhood.

[95] See *ante*, p. 118.

support of his own party, the Greenback, with the indorsement of the Democracy, and with his unparalleled power on the stump, he had reason to hope for a victory. That hope rose to an expectation with the appearance of an opportunity to display himself as a champion of people suffering from a local injustice.

It is not strange that the versatile statesman of Nininger should have become infected with a bonanza-farming microbe. In 1873 the St. Paul and Pacific Railroad Company was bankrupt, having defaulted on the interest due the Dutch bondholders. The bonds of the company had been drawn so as to be exchangeable for lands owned by the company. In the year mentioned the price of the bonds had fallen to a point at which land could be had for about one dollar an acre and Donnelly and some of his friends invested in several thousand acres in Stevens County around the village of Donnelly. He broke up about half of his own three thousand acres, fenced portions of it, began farming, built houses for himself and his sons, and became a temporary resident of the third congressional district. The venture resulted in " very great loss," partly on account of grasshopper ravages, but principally, in the statesman's opinion, because of the robberies of the wheat ring and the exactions of the railroad companies. He could therefore warmly sympathize with many brother farmers who were obliged to sell their salvaged wheat in a market controlled by the Minneapolis Millers' Association. This association virtually monopolized the primary wheat markets and its head buyer dictated from day to day the price to be paid for wheat in every railroad town in Minnesota and the Dakotas. The association had established " grades " of wheat, had made, it was charged, excessive reductions of price for the lower grades, and had instructed its buyers to grade as low as possible on grounds of light weight, foul seeds, chaff, dirt, dampness, and so forth. For making grades there had been adopted a small cylindrical brass vessel with an attached scalebeam and the story was spread wide that, by a certain deft manipulation in filling this measure, three different grades could be produced from the same bushel of wheat. [96]

Donnelly, ignoring national issues, appeared as the champion of the oppressed farmers and the foe of the confederated millers and railroad men. His opponent was interested in both groups. Never

[96] Fish, *Donnelliana*, part 1, pp. 93–96; Hall, *Observations*, 227–230; Charles B. Kuhlmann, " The Influence of the Minneapolis Flour Mills upon the Economic Development of Minnesota and the Northwest," in *Minnesota History*, 6: 147 (June, 1925).

was Donnelly's extraordinary talent for ridicule and invective more industriously exercised. He traveled from town to town convulsing crowds with harangues on " the swindling brass-kettle." On behalf of Washburn, issues of broader and national scope were put forth. On September 19 the Republican central committee of the third district sent out to about fifty prominent Republicans a circular letter asking each one addressed to contribute to the Republican cause. The request was followed by a statement that it was nearly certain that the United States Senate would be Democratic after March 4, 1879, and that the election of a Democratic House would precipitate dangerous agitations. Among them would be movements for the expulsion of President Hayes from office, for provision for the payment of rebel claims and debts, for the payment to former slaveholders of the full value of their emancipated slaves, and for the unlimited issue of irredeemable paper money.[97]

Donnelly's " brass-kettle " crusade gained for him an abundance of cheers but not enough votes. He had never really been a Democrat and for thirty years he had been denouncing with extreme asperity that party and its policies. Old-line Democrats in large numbers either stayed away from the polls or voted for Washburn. The vote as returned stood: for Washburn, 20,942; for Donnelly, 17,929.[98] The defeated candidate probably thought at once about a contest. As allegations of errors and corrupt practices came in from correspondents, he gave it more serious consideration and when, on December 17, he was informed from Democratic headquarters in Washington that if he would make a bona fide contest he would get the one thousand dollars generally allowed and possibly something more, he resolved to contest the election.[99]

[97] Fish, *Donnelliana*, part 1, p. 95. A copy of the circular is in *Contested Election of Donnelly vs. Washburn*, 43 (46 Congress, 1 session, *House Miscellaneous Documents*, no. 9 — serial 1876). In a letter to Donnelly, dated October 20, 1878, in the Donnelly Papers, T. G. Mealey says: " The ' Brass Kettle ' business is raising the very D—l. . . . If you are elected you should put the Kettle on your coat of arms."

[98] An abstract of the vote is given in *Contested Election of Donnelly vs. Washburn*, 72 (serial 1876).

[99] S. S. Cox to Donnelly, December 17, 1878, Donnelly Papers. See numerous other letters in the Donnelly Papers written after the election, in particular two from Dr. Jacob H. Stewart, December 2, 17. Dr. Stewart had been elected to Congress from the third district in 1876 and had been looking forward to the customary renomination from the Republicans in 1878. An article in the *Daily Globe* (St. Paul), March 1, 1880, accuses Washburn of scoundrelism in obtaining the nomination to Congress to which Dr. Stewart was entitled. See also the *Pioneer Press* (St. Paul and Minneapolis), July 2,

The procedure under existing law was as follows: Notice of intention to contest, with a statement of the grounds, was to be given the member whose seat was to be contested; the respondent was to answer within thirty days; testimony was to be taken within ninety days; and, finally, all documents pertaining to the election were to be sealed and mailed to the clerk of the House of Representatives at Washington by the officer before whom depositions were taken. On December 18, 1878, Donnelly, acting as his own attorney, gave the required notice together with nine grounds of contest, which, conveniently briefed, were: bribery in general and in particular in twenty-one counties named; illegal voting; erroneous counting of returns, to Donnelly's loss; illegitimate elections in unorganized counties; and intimidation of voters in Minneapolis and elsewhere and the marking and numbering of ballots " so that they might be thereafter examined to ascertain how said persons voted." Washburn, through his attorneys, a leading law firm of St. Paul, sent his reply on January 4, 1879. It was a general traverse, denying "every charge, allegation, matter, and thing" contained in each specification. Three countercharges were added: (1) illegal voting in Carlton County by fifty Indians, minors, and nonresident railroad men; (2) the circulation of false and fraudulent reports in St. Paul to induce electors to vote against the respondent; and (3) bribery and corruption in five counties named.[1]

The taking of testimony was begun on January 21 and was continued until March 29, principally in St. Paul, Minneapolis, and St. Cloud. In Minneapolis a number of witnesses who had been judges or clerks of election were interrogated in regard to the operation of a certain novel election law, upon which was based the ground of contest probably most relied upon by Donnelly.[2] The legislature of Minnesota in the previous winter had passed an act for the regulation of elections in cities of twelve thousand and more. As St. Paul and Minneapolis were the only cities to which the law could apply, it may be assumed that the legislature intended to encourage the good citizens of those cities to be more careful about the exercise of the elective franchise. Suggestions of a sinister

3, 1878. There are also in the Donnelly Papers some forty letters written between January 1 and April 1, 1879, offering to furnish evidence. But few of the names appear among Donnelly's witnesses in the contest.

[1] United States, Revised Statutes, 1878, ch. 8, pp. 18–21. The documents in the case are in Contested Election of Donnelly vs. Washburn (serial 1876). For Donnelly's notice and Washburn's reply, see pages 1–6.

[2] For the testimony, see Contested Election of Donnelly vs. Washburn, 14–358 (serial 1876).

intention remain as yet unverified. The leading section of the act provided that one of the election judges, upon receiving the folded ballot of a voter, should, before dropping it into the ballot box, mark on the outside the voter's number on the poll list.[3]

As might have been expected, such an act, nullifying the secrecy of the ballot, was soon called in question. John B. Brisbin of St. Paul, one of the best-known citizens and lawyers of his day, at a municipal election in St. Paul in the spring of 1878 refused to allow his ticket to be numbered. The judges of election thereupon refused to accept his vote. Brisbin brought suit in the district court of Ramsey County, putting in issue the constitutionality of the act. The court held with the plaintiff that so much of the law as provided for numbering tickets violated that secrecy of the ballot guaranteed by the state constitution and was therefore void. The decision, which was rendered by Judge Hascal R. Brill, was filed on October 22, a fortnight before the date of the election.[4]

The judges of election in St. Paul, confident that the supreme court, if appealed to, would confirm the decision, refrained from numbering ballots. The judges in Minneapolis did not all adopt the same reasonable course of action. A majority of them attended a meeting held on the afternoon next preceding election day. The city attorney, William Lochren, informed them that the Ramsey County district court had held the numbering of tickets to be unconstitutional and gave his own opinion to the same effect. Other attorneys present argued in favor of the law. A vote taken to test the sense of the meeting resulted in a majority against numbering; but the meeting broke up with an understanding that the judges in each precinct should decide for themselves. In eight precincts the judges decided to consider the provision of the act of 1878 for numbering ballots as void; in seven precincts the ballots were numbered. Donnelly claimed that all those numbered were not truly ballots and should not have been counted at all. His gain by their omission would be 1,760 votes.[5]

---

[3] Minnesota, *General Laws,* 1878, p. 134; *Donnelly vs. Washburn,* 17 (46 Congress, 2 session, *House Reports,* no. 1791 — serial 1938). That such an act, with no money in it, could have been "sneaked through" a legislature is perhaps not very remarkable; but it is remarkable that this one escaped the eyes of, Governor Pillsbury and his intelligent secretary, Pennock Pusey.

[4] *Contested Election of Donnelly vs. Washburn,* 74 (serial 1876).

[5] *Contested Election of Donnelly vs. Washburn,* 134, 160, 170, 174, 177, 198 (serial 1876); *Donnelly vs. Washburn,* 17–24, 31, 32 (serial 1938). The Minnesota supreme court confirmed Judge Brill's decision on June 25, 1879. John B. Brisbin *v.* James Cleary and others, 26 *Minnesota,* 107–109.

Another item of the contest was an irregularity, attended by certain minor irregularities, in Isanti County, where the county auditor, instead of conforming to the letter of the election law by calling in as canvassers of the vote two justices of the peace, summoned one justice and the probate judge. This departure, it was insisted, vitiated the whole vote of the county and by it the contestant gained 401 votes.[6]

On April 15, 1879, the clerk of the House of Representatives laid before the House the accumulated papers in the Donnelly-Washburn contest and they were at once referred to the standing committee on elections, composed of fifteen representatives. It was not to be expected that the committee would report on the case in that extra session, which closed on July 1, 1879. In the ordinary course a report would have been looked for before the second session of the Forty-sixth Congress was far advanced. The case was referred to a subcommittee of five members, which, after examining the pleadings and the evidence, divided into a majority favorable to Donnelly's claim and a minority in favor of retaining Washburn in his seat and reported to the full committee about the middle of February, 1880.[7]

A month later the reports of the subcommittee, printed by leave of the House, became public. The majority were of the opinion that bribery had been committed by the friends and agents of Washburn and by members of his district committee; that there had been systematic intimidation of voters in Minneapolis, where workingmen were kept from voting for Donnelly for fear of losing their jobs; and that the whole vote of Isanti County was null. In conclusion, they presented a tabular statement which gave Washburn 17,480 votes and Donnelly, 17,710 — a majority of 230 for the contestant. They recommended the adoption by the House of two resolutions: one, that William D. Washburn was not entitled to a seat and the other, that Ignatius Donnelly was entitled to a seat. The minority found from the same body of evidence that both par-

[6] *Donnelly vs. Washburn*, 25–28, 31, 32 (serial 1938).

[7] 46 Congress, 1 session, *House Journal*, 83 (serial 1874); Hall, *Observations*, 216; *Globe* (St. Paul), *Pioneer Press*, February 15, 17, 1880. For the papers in the contest, see *Contested Election of Donnelly vs. Washburn* (serial 1876). Donnelly prepared a brief of his case which he had to print at his own expense. See William M. Springer to Donnelly, June 30, 1879, in the Donnelly Papers. The brief is in the Donnelly Pamphlets, vol. 69, no. 1, in the library of the Minnesota Historical Society. One of Donnelly's attorneys, John D. O'Brien, in a letter of September 11, 1879, in the Donnelly Papers, speaks of it as "a very able one" and of Donnelly's citations and illustrations as "extremely applicable."

ties had spent money liberally in legitimate ways — ways so regarded at the time — but that Donnelly's charge of bribery was frivolous. As for intimidation in Minneapolis by means of numbered ballots, the charge, they thought, " rises almost to the dignity of a slander on a large class of workingmen." There was not an iota of testimony that electors had actually been frightened into voting for Washburn. The substitution of a probate judge in Isanti County for a justice of the peace, as a mere witness to the canvass of the votes by the county auditor, was a trivial circumstance. Both reports bear evidence of having been written by attorneys of the parties.[8]

In successive meetings of the committee on elections the reports of the subcommittee were considered and the case was fully argued. On April 1, 1880, according to press reports, the committee voted on two resolutions. The first, that Washburn was not entitled to a seat, was adopted by a vote of 6 to 5. The other, that Donnelly was not entitled to a seat, was adopted by a vote of 8 to 4.[9]

The proceedings in the case were now varied by an extraordinary incident. On April 5 Van H. Manning of Mississippi, chairman of the subcommittee, rose in the House to a question of personal privilege and sent to the clerk's desk a copy of an article which had appeared in the Washington Daily Post on April 3, with the request that it be read. The article described an alleged altercation in a recent meeting of the committee on elections between William M. Springer of Illinois, chairman of the full committee, and Manning, who had resented the failure of Springer to support Donnelly in the vote of April 1. With the article was printed an incorrect, but not misleading, copy of an anonymous letter addressed to Springer and purporting to convey an offer of five thousand dollars to his wife if he should succeed in having Washburn kept in his seat. When Manning had concluded his remarks on the article, Springer sent to the clerk's desk a correct copy of the letter, dated March 4, 1880, which read as follows: " Sir: If you will keep Washburn in his seat, in spite of the democrats, we will pay Mrs. S—— $5,000. Get the thing squashed at once." Springer then sent up to the desk another letter, dated March 6 and signed by Henry H. Finley, a friend and adviser of Donnelly, if not technically Donnelly's counsel, urging Springer to be true to his duty as a

---

[8] The majority report is in the Globe (St. Paul) and the Pioneer Press, March 19, 1880, and in the Donnelly Pamphlets, vol. 69, no. 8. The minority report is in the Donnelly Pamphlets, vol. 69, no. 7.
[9] Globe (St. Paul), Pioneer Press, April 2, 1880.

Democrat and suggesting that both he and the party would suffer by any failure of his to act up to expectations. Springer explained that throughout the whole proceeding he had been in favor of ousting Washburn, but never of seating Donnelly. Colleagues, whom he called upon individually, corroborated him. He told the House that in his opinion the anonymous letter had been written by the man who wrote and signed the letter of March 6. As he had set himself right, he did not ask for an investigation, but he would not object if anybody desired one. Nobody immediately desired an investigation, but after deliberation Donnelly thought it would be well to have one. On April 17 Representative Manning, at Donnelly's request, introduced a resolution, to which the House agreed, that the speaker appoint a committee of seven members to inquire and report as to the authorship of the anonymous letter and all matters connected with it and also as to whether there had been any breach of the privileges of the House or of any member.[10]

The sittings of that committee began on April 29 and continued until June 10; the record and the arguments of counsel cover 279 pages of small types and 26 sheets of exhibits. With regard to the appearance of the two letters, the evidence disclosed the following facts, about which there was little or no dispute: Springer went to New York on the evening of March 7 and did not return until the morning of the tenth. On the eighth a letter, postmarked that date, came to his house at 112 East Capitol Street. His wife, acting as his secretary, opened it and read the anonymous note quoted above. Surprised and indignant, she took the letter across the way to the boarding house of George W. Julian, who was on intimate terms with the Springer family and was also Donnelly's counsel. She showed the letter to Julian and told him that she believed that Donnelly or some one of his friends had written it; no Republican would have done it. Julian succeeded, either at the moment or at an interview the next morning, in shaking her confidence in Donnelly's authorship and obtained leave to inform Donnelly in order that he might have an opportunity fully to vindicate himself. The information, obtained " in perfect confidence," was at once communicated to Donnelly. That gentleman did not immediately understand that secrecy had been enjoined upon him and passed the

---

[10] 46 Congress, 2 session, *House Journal*, 1048 (serial 1901); *Congressional Record*, 2134–2139, 2501. In a letter to his wife, which reveals his hopeful state of mind in regard to the contest, Donnelly wrote, " Mr. Springer is earnestly my friend." This letter, which is dated December 10, 1879, is in the Donnelly Papers.

startling news to three members of the committee who were friendly
to him. They seem, however, to have regarded the matter as confidential. On the ninth Donnelly called upon Mrs. Springer, who
showed him the anonymous letter. He said almost as soon as he
saw it that it was in " Bill King's handwriting." The lady was
willing to accept Donnelly's assertion that the letter had been written and sent without his knowledge, but she held to her opinion that
no friend of Washburn wrote it. " It is not," she later stated in
writing, " a *bona-fide* bribe, but is a deliberate insult from some
overzealous friend of your own, to my husband, for not sustaining
the decision of the sub-committee." Donnelly, according to his
testimony, told her that there were only two persons in Washington
who were interested in his case — his counsel, Julian, and Finley.
Julian he knew would not descend to such a trick and he did not
think that Finley would. The mention of Finley's name reminded
Mrs. Springer to tell Donnelly that a long letter had come from
Finley — a proper and respectful one, to which no one could take
exception, and marked " confidential." Donnelly asked the notable
question whether there was any resemblance between the handwriting
of that letter and that of the anonymous one.

Early on Tuesday, March 10, Finley called at the Springer house
to suggest to Mrs. Springer that she should not make public anything in regard to the anonymous letter. He was met by Springer,
who told Finley that he need not trouble himself about the matter
going to the public from his family; if it were made public it
would be by Donnelly or his friends. In the afternoon of the same
day Donnelly called upon Springer in his committee room. The
testimony of both Springer and Donnelly agrees that Springer said
he believed that Finley wrote the anonymous letter. If Donnelly's
testimony is true, Springer said that he would not have the matter
get into the papers for ten thousand dollars. Springer later testified
that he had no recollection of saying that. The secret was well
kept for many days, but it could not escape the vigilance of the
daily press indefinitely. Donnelly told it to the editor of the
Washington Post on March 10, the very day of his interview with
Springer. The editor kept the secret, as newspaper men can when
they promise. On the evening of April 2 Donnelly went, as was his
habit, to the office of the *Post* and was there shown, or told of, a long
article which had appeared in the *New York Tribune* on that day
or the day before about what had taken place in the committee room
on April 1 and, in particular, about an alleged wrangle between

Springer and General Manning, Donnelly's best friend on the committee. Donnelly declined to furnish any information on that matter and advised the reporter who interrogated him to see Manning. The reporter acted upon this advice and got Manning out of bed about midnight. Manning refused to be interviewed but allowed the reporter to tell him a great deal about what he had heard down town. Donnelly testified that the reporter was intoxicated. At any rate he produced for the next morning's *Post* the article and the letter mentioned above. The article included a series of allegations, not worth repeating, as derived from Manning, which he afterwards repudiated under oath, with the exception of one which he modified. It was this revelation which made further secrecy impossible and caused the explosion in the House on April 5.[11]

The first duty imposed upon the investigating committee was that of discovering the authorship of the anonymous letter. On the witness stand Donnelly said that he was no expert and could make no serious charge against King, but that a resemblance between the handwriting of the anonymous letter and that of a " long, threatening, and abusive letter " which he had received from King inclined him to believe that he might have been the author of the anonymous letter. King's letter answers Donnelly's description. The talented letter-writer applied himself to take Donnelly's political hide off and hang it on the fence. In the course of a ferocious tirade, he frankly charged Donnelly with writing and personally mailing the anonymous letter. King wrote another letter addressed to Springer to serve as a sample of his handwriting and added a postscript: " I dont pretend to deny anything Ignatius Donnelly may say It aint worth while." Donnelly evidently held a similar estimate of King, for he had King's letter introduced in evidence. On the stand King testified that he had no more knowledge of the authorship of the anonymous letter than of the number of the stars in heaven. The mutual compliments of Donnelly and King may be regarded as a simple equation.[12]

There remained the original suggestion of Springer that Henry H. Finley was the author of the anonymous letter. The investigation

[11] *Anonymous Letter to Hon. William M. Springer*, 7, 51, 78, 123–134, 164, 249, 259 (46 Congress, 3 session, *House Reports*, no. 395 — serial 1983). This is the report of the committee, accompanied by the testimony and the arguments. See also *Congressional Record*, 46 Congress, 2 session, 2135–2139. For Donnelly's view of the situation, see his letter of April 6, 1880, to the *Washington Post*, reprinted in the *Globe* (St. Paul), April 12, 1880, p. 2.

[12] *Anonymous Letter to Springer*, 54–57, 167–175, exhibits 4, 5 (serial 1983).

accordingly took on the appearance of a trial of Finley, with Springer as prosecuting witness, and a member of the committee, not free from bias, as judge. When Finley was sworn and shown the letter he averred that he had never seen it until that moment; this he maintained throughout a long and merciless cross-examination and his testimony was not impeached. Four experts in chirography were examined and cross-examined at great length with multifarious interrogatories. Two of them deposed that Finley wrote the anonymous letter and the other two stoutly contradicted them, without naming any other author. Three eminent nonresident experts were consulted but not sworn. Two of them found Finley guilty and the third accused King. Eight witnesses, who either had maintained correspondence with Finley or were familiar with his ordinary business hand, testified that he was not the author of the anonymous letter.[13]

To complete the array of alternatives, two theories of the authorship may be presented at this point which did not appear in the evidence. One, proposed by Finley's counsel, was that Springer himself " got up the anonymous letter " and arranged for its delivery in his absence and for its exhibition to Donnelly's counsel, to serve as a defense against the recriminations of his colleague, Manning, and of Donnelly and Finley for his desertion of their cause. It was the opinion of the counsel that the letter was too coarse and offensive to have been the work of any friend of Washburn and that upon no intelligible theory could it be attributed to Donnelly. The other theory, suggested by the versatile editor of the St. Paul *Daily Globe*, Harlan P. Hall, was that Finley was a scoundrel and, while acting as counsel for Donnelly, betrayed him and wrote and sent the anonymous letter for some unknown consideration received from Washburn.[14]

On June 10, 1880, leave was given by the committee to Springer and to one attorney each for Donnelly and Finley to submit arguments in writing on the day following. These arguments are printed with the record of testimony. On June 16, the last day of the session, John G. Carlisle, chairman of the committee of investigation, sub-

[13] *Anonymous Letter to Springer*, 16–49, 90, 110, 120, 140, 152, 179, 193 (serial 1983).

[14] *Anonymous Letter to Springer*, 271–273 (serial 1983) ; *Globe* (St. Paul), *Pioneer Press*, April 6, 1880; Hall to Donnelly, April 25, Finley to Donnelly, June 13, 1880, Donnelly Papers. For gossip about the investigation, with abundant castigation of Donnelly, see the issues of the *Pioneer Press* for April, May, and the early part of June, 1880. The issues of the *Globe* during the same period laud Donnelly copiously.

mitted to the House a report with a request that it be printed, without reading, and recommitted. He remarked that he was authorized to say that the committee was unanimous in the opinion that Finley wrote and sent the anonymous letter. Manning demanded of Carlisle whether any reflections had been cast upon the character of Donnelly in the report he had submitted. The reply was that the majority of the investigating committee had come to the conclusion "that Mr. Donnelly had no personal connection with the writing or sending of the anonymous letter." In reply to another member, Carlisle said, "The committee does not find that Mr. Donnelly had any knowledge whatever of the writing or sending of that letter." The House ordered the printing and recommittal of the report. It had been understood, of course, that the report of the committee on elections on the Donnelly-Washburn contest would be withheld until after the result of the Springer investigation had been reported to the House. That having been done, it was in order for the committee on elections to report. There was no report of the committee as a whole nor of a majority. Manning presented a report signed by himself and four others, all Democrats, in favor of Donnelly's claims, followed by two resolutions — one, that Washburn was not entitled to his seat, and the other, that Donnelly was entitled to a seat in the House. The body of this report was identical with that which had been submitted to the committee by the majority of the subcommittee. Keifer of Ohio then submitted a report signed by himself and four others, all Republicans, which was in all important respects the same as that of the minority of the subcommittee, with the addition of two resolutions, the reverse of those proposed in Manning's report. These reports were also ordered printed, without reading, and recommitted.[15]

The last session of the Forty-sixth Congress opened on December 6, 1880. The two committees seem to have been in no haste about further inquiries toward final reports and nobody asked them the reasons for their delay. It is evident that there was a quiet understanding that no change should take place in the standing of the parties to the contest. Washburn was *persona grata* to the House generally and Donnelly had but slight claim to Democratic support. Only faint echoes came from the committee rooms. In the last hour of the existence of the Forty-sixth Congress unanimous consent was given for filing reports of committees with the clerk of the House

[15] *Anonymous Letter to Springer*, 251–273 (serial 1983); *Donnelly vs. Washburn*, 32, 79 (serial 1938); *House Journal*, 1516 (serial 1901); *Congressional Record*, 4621.

for printing and proper reference. The *House Journal* shows that the report of the dilatory investigating committee, together with the views of the minority, was duly filed and laid on the table.[16] It may be assumed that the fragmentary reports from the committee on elections had the same disposition, although the *Journal* does not mention it. None of them were heard of more until the present writing and they all still repose on the table. As if in anticipation of this result, the general appropriation act of 1881 carried an allowance of two thousand dollars to each of the parties to the contest — not enough to give much joy after their attorneys were satisfied.[17]

7. THE IMPEACHMENT OF JUDGE SHERMAN PAGE [18]

In the year 1866 Sherman Page, a native of Vermont, who had lived in Wisconsin and Iowa, came to reside in Austin, Mower County, where he served as county superintendent of schools for the two years beginning in 1866. He soon began, or resumed, the practice of law and became interested in public affairs. It was not long before he became the leader of a " reform clique " in the Republican party which had for its " cause " the " cleaning out " of an older clique or ring composed of county officers and others charged with disreputable and even criminal behavior in party and public affairs.[19] His was a popular rôle, one in which a person of his temperament must have taken much satisfaction. In the fall of 1871 he was elected to the state Senate by a majority indicative of a high degree of confidence in his ability and motives. He served in but one session of the legislature, that of 1872, and resigned to become eligible to a position of higher dignity and longer tenure. The legislature of 1872 created a tenth judicial district composed of Mower and three adjacent counties and Page at once aspired to the new judgeship, regardless of his brief experience at the bar and the larger knowledge of many older and more deserving practitioners in the four counties of the tenth district. The accounts which have survived present him as intellectually keen and intense, physically fit for any emergency, and an engaging public speaker. He was tall, erect, and spare but well nourished and he had an

16 *House Journal*, 615 (serial 1950).
17 United States, *Statutes at Large*, 21: 457.
18 See *ante*, p. 128.
19 Minnesota, Superintendent of Public Instruction, *Reports*, 1866, p. 101; 1867, p. 139; *Rochester Post*, March 1, May 24, 1878; *Minneapolis Tribune*, July 16, 1872; *Trial of Page*, 1: 580–582; 2: 25.

impressive bearing, a piercing eye, a resonant voice, and dark and profuse hair and beard. Page was accorded the Republican nomination to the new judgeship and was elected by a handsome majority. He assumed the duties on January 1, 1873.[20]

In the summer of 1873 a citizen named Mollison wrote for publication in the *Austin Register* of August 28, 1873, a libelous article in which he charged Judge Page with " plowing with the railroad heifers " and causing a loss of fifty thousand dollars to the tenth judicial district by making a wrong decision. On September 16 the grand jury indicted Mollison for libel. While the indictment was being read Mollison behaved in what Judge Page called an insolent manner; but he was not committed for contempt and, after pleading " not guilty," was bound over for trial under a bond of fifteen hundred dollars.[21] Such was the beginning of a long tandem of squabbles of varying degrees of unimportance which took place in the district court of Mower County. In several instances Judge Page arbitrarily reduced the fees of court officials which he considered excessive. He upbraided a grand jury for not indicting a county treasurer and ordered a prosecution of the treasurer without indictment. He had a citizen arrested and brought into his court to answer for contempt in circulating a libelous petition. He attempted to disbar a county attorney. He was inexperienced, over-confident of popular support, sarcastic, and at times boisterous in expression. His very zeal defeated his efforts toward reform.[22]

A steady course of behavior obnoxious to a large number of citizens culminated in the summer of 1877. At times during the spring term of the district court for Mower County gatherings of persons unfriendly to Page took place in the office of a law firm in Austin. At one of them a petition addressed to Judge Page, which had been previously drafted, was discussed and its publication was acquiesced

[20] *Austin Register*, November 16, 1871, July 18, 1872; *Mower County Transcript* (Austin), November 7, 1872; Franklyn Curtiss-Wedge, ed., *The History of Mower County*, 960 (Chicago, 1911); *General Laws*, 1872, p. 111; *Legislative Manual*, 1875, p. 53; Catherwood to the author, May 12, 1922. For an opinion of the attorney-general, dated December 31, 1873, adverse to a claim by Henry R. Wells that Page should be declared ineligible on the ground that he could not hold an office created by a legislature of which he was a member, see Minnesota, Attorneys-General, *Opinions from the Organization of the State to Jan. 1, 1884*, 277–280 (St. Paul, 1884). It was held that the legislature did not create the office but merely added a new district.

[21] *Austin Register*, August 28, September 4, 18, 25, October 2, 23, 1873; *Trial of Page*, 1: 176, 184, 243, 714. Mollison was acquitted in March, 1878. *Pioneer Press*, March 22, 1878.

[22] *Pioneer Press*, January 23, 1878, p. 5.

in, if not formally authorized. The following is the text of this remarkable petition:

> Sir — Knowing you, and believing that your prejudices are stronger than your sense of honor, that your determination to rule is more ardent than your desire to do right; that you will sacrifice private character, individual interests, and the public good, to gratify your malice; that you are influenced by your ungovernable passions to abuse the power with which your position invests you, to make it a means of oppression rather than of administering justice, that you have disgraced the judiciary of the State and the voters by whose suffrages you were elected; therefore, we the undersigned, citizens of Mower county, hereby request you to resign the office of judge of the district court, one which you hold in violation of the spirit of the constitution, if not of its express terms.

It is obvious that the so-called " petition " was expected not to extort a resignation, but rather to intensify and propagate anti-Page hostility. The document was printed and a limited number of copies were distributed by hand and by mail.[23]

Judge Page now took the extraordinary step of issuing, on May 31, 1877, without complaint or information, a warrant for the arrest of a deputy sheriff, one David H. Stimpson, who was to be brought before Page to show cause why he should not be punished for contempt of court in publishing certain false and malicious statements concerning the judge of the district court for the tenth judicial district. Believing the county attorney, Lafayette French, to be one of the conspirators who had circulated the libelous petition, Judge Page took charge of the proceedings in person. After examining the defendant and others under oath, the judge considered that it was doubtful that Stimpson had published the libelous statements and that he was but a subordinate actor in the play, influenced by stronger and guiltier characters. He therefore dismissed Stimpson on July 2. It is a fair inference, from Page's own testimony given later, that his object in the arrest and examination of Stimpson and others was to extort the names of the principal conspirators.[24] On the same day that Stimpson was dismissed, Judge Page cited Lafayette French, county attorney of Mower County, to appear before him and answer to charges and specifications of misconduct in office, comparatively trivial but including one charge of publishing and circulating defamatory and libelous statements concerning the judge of the tenth judicial district. A hearing was had on July

23 *Trial of Page*, 1: 584; 2: 26; 3: 330.
24 *Pioneer Press*, September 11, 1877; *Trial of Page*, 1: 18, 529, 582–585; 2: 26–29.

10 and on the last day of that month Judge Page, having found the charges and specifications true, ordered that Attorney French be suspended from the practice of law until the adjournment of the next general term of the state supreme court.[25]

By this time the matter had become of interest beyond the borders of Mower County. The *Saint Paul and Minneapolis Pioneer Press* had begun a series of editorial and communicated articles severely critical of Judge Page's judicial behavior. He prosecuted the paper for libel. The attacks continued and presently the *Pioneer Press* had four suits for libel to defend. Judge Page was not without friends and defenders, however. A joint committee, appointed by the bar associations of the four counties composing the tenth judicial district to investigate charges made against Judge Page, in particular those made by the *Pioneer Press,* after a three days' session, which began on August 13, found that "his official acts have not been influenced by corrupt means or improper motives, but have been uniformly prompted by a high sense of honor and duty." One of the three Austin newspapers, the *Mower and Fillmore County Republican,* stood firmly by him, but no love was lost between the judge and the other two papers, the *Austin Register* and the *Mower County Transcript.* Mower County was now divided into two factions, Page and anti-Page.[26]

During the remaining months of 1877 there was quiet in Mower County, but there was no abatement of the hostility of Page's foes nor was there the least relaxation of his austerity. Casual, and possibly appointed, consultations among those who had suffered from the stings and arrows of his venom and sarcasm resulted in an understanding that they ought not to wait for an opportunity of refusing him a reëlection in the fall of 1879 but should unite in a movement to remove him from office at an earlier date. They would start impeachment proceedings. A petition signed by twenty-six citizens of Mower County was laid before the Minnesota House of Representatives on January 22, 1878. It asked that Sherman Page be impeached for twenty several instances of corrupt conduct in office, all of which had occurred in Mower County. No complaints were made of his judicial behavior in the three other counties of

[25] *Pioneer Press,* July 19, 21, 27, August 4, 1877; *Mower and Fillmore County Republican* (Austin), July 12, 19, 1877.
[26] *Pioneer Press,* August 18, 23, 1877; *Mower and Fillmore County Republican,* August 23, 1877. For the articles criticizing Page's behavior, see the *Pioneer Press,* July 19, 24, August 1, 10, 11, 30, September 16, 18, 19, 25, 1877.

his district — Fillmore, Freeborn, and Houston. The House at once referred the matter to its judiciary committee, to which it gave instructions to investigate the truth of the charges and power to examine witnesses under oath. The committee adopted a procedure similar to that of a grand jury inquest, with an important departure: it allowed Judge Page to be present with counsel, to summon witnesses, and to cross-examine the witnesses called by the committee. This preliminary trial, for such it was, lasted a month. The report submitted by the committee on February 20 pronounced the acts described in seven of the allegations as censurable in character, varying from arbitrary behavior to gross impropriety. In regard to the remaining allegations, upon seven no evidence had been adduced and the others were either untrue or not censurable.[27]

In a series of secret sessions beginning on February 22 the House listened to the reading of the findings of the committee and of the evidence of important witnesses. In a final secret session on February 27 it was resolved, by a vote of 71 to 30, that the Honorable Sherman Page be impeached for corrupt conduct in office and for crimes and misdemeanors. On March 1 the House authorized the appointment of seven members, including the speaker, as managers on its behalf and instructed them to prepare proper articles of impeachment. On March 4 the articles drawn by the managers were read to the House and adopted without roll call. On the same day the managers appeared at the bar of the Senate and presented their articles, which were read by the secretary of the Senate. That body on March 5 organized as a high court of impeachment, sworn in by Chief Justice Gilfillan, and on March 6 issued a summons to Judge Page to appear and answer. The Senate then adjourned to May 22, 1878.[28]

The articles of impeachment were ten in number. Eight of them alleged malicious ill treatment of individuals and one, an insult to a grand jury; the tenth was a blanket charge of habitual arbitrary and offensive demeanor toward officers of court and county. None of them charged any indictable offense. In his answer, filed on March 26, 1878, Judge Page denied severally and specifically every averment of five of the articles; in regard to four others he admitted averments of fact but denied misconduct. In regard to the tenth he pleaded that it was indefinite and stated no facts. At the trial Judge Page was represented by ex-Governor Cushman K. Davis

[27] *Austin Register*, January 24, 1878; *House Journal*, 1878, pp. 54, 246–251.
[28] *House Journal*, 1878, pp. 362, 383, 397, 551–556; *Senate Journal*, 333, 354, 371, 421.

and two other experienced lawyers. To assist the House managers
the Mower County foes of Page employed William Pitt Clough of St.
Paul, then eminent at the bar.[29]

The reader of this history will probably not care to follow the
details of the trial. Should he so desire, he may resort to the
printed record of the proceedings, published by the state in three
octavo volumes. The trial went on in the customary order of a
criminal suit: the opening address on the part of the prosecution;
the examination and cross-examination of witnesses called by the
state; the opening by the counsel for the defense; the taking of testimony on behalf of the defense; the argument of the case on behalf
of the managers; the argument for the defense; and — here was a
departure from Minnesota criminal procedure — a concluding argument on the part of the prosecution.[30] A preliminary motion of
Page's counsel to have Senator George W. Clough of Mower County
excluded from the court because of bias and declared hostility to
the accused was denied. After the managers' opening the defense
demanded that article 10 be quashed as indefinite and insufficient.
This the court refused but it ordered the managers to furnish a bill
of particulars. On May 30 seven specifications were submitted, to
which the defense set up twelve objections. The opening addresses
of both sides were labored expositions of the phenomena of the case
and of their respective views of the application of the law. The
testimony throughout exhibited somewhat more than the usual number of discrepancies and rank contradictions commonly met with in
sharply contested cases in which many witnesses are examined and
dull observation, infirmity of memory, unconscious bias, and, occasionally, sheer reckless perjury obscure the truth. Many questions
of trivial character were raised. In one case tedious inquiry was
made as to whether Judge Page was justified in stopping the payment to a deputy sheriff of a fee of $5.60, the exaction of which by
the sheriff was characterized by Page's counsel as a " little, dirty
steal." Page's own testimony, as drawn out by his attorneys, was
not materially shattered by a long and rigorous cross-examination.
The summing up for the prosecution by Speaker Charles A. Gilman,

---

[29] *Trial of Page*, 1:2, 6–27, 33–55, 70. For the part played by the counsel
for the managers, see 2:542. The two lawyers who assisted Davis were J. W.
Losey of La Crosse, Wisconsin, and John A. Lovely of Albert Lea, afterwards
an associate justice of the Minnesota supreme court.

[30] *Trial of Page*, 1:110, 174, 624, 705; 3:1, 146, 256. Manager Samuel
L. Campbell criticized the recent change in Minnesota criminal procedure
which gave the defense the closing argument. Davis objected to the state's
making the closing argument. *Trial of Page*, 2:543–545.

one of the managers, and the final argument of Henry Hinds, also a manager, were extensive and elaborate. As they were demanding a conviction upon the cumulative effect of numerous charges of somewhat equal importance, it was necessary to discuss each with care. No complaint could have been made of a lack of zeal in their disagreeable duty.[31]

Because of the illness of a colleague, ex-Governor Davis was obliged to make the argument for the defense unaided. Although he considered the accusations contained in the articles of impeachment so trivial as scarcely to warrant serious discussion, he patiently went over the whole catena in reply to the prosecution. His interest was rather in the governing principles of the case. This was Davis' field and for it he was splendidly equipped. He was forty years of age, an ex-governor of Minnesota, an acknowledged leader of the bar of the state, and an aspirant for a senatorship in Congress. Page could have chosen no better advocate. At an early stage of the trial Davis said he could not expect to be again interested in a matter of such magnitude. In his exordium he remarked upon the solemnity of a proceeding in which the whole power of the state was arrayed against a single citizen. Still, he argued, individual citizens were protected by constitutional safeguards, which no court could take from them. He did not regard himself, however, as speaking merely in defense of an accused individual but rather for the integrity and independence of the judicial department of the government. He reminded the senators that from their judgment there was no appeal; it would stand forever. He warned them against assuming that their jurisdiction was transcendent and extraordinary. They were now a bench of judges solemnly sworn to try the case according to the evidence and the law. It was not for them to work a political attainder under the ambush of impeachment. Referring to the impeachment of President Andrew Johnson, Davis said, " That proceeding will be adjudged by history as one of the most flagrant invasions of executive power by legislative authority that the annals of judicial abuse have furnished." At the close of his discussion of the several articles Davis again referred to the independence of the judiciary as one of the dearest principles of our inherited polity and cited the passage from Shakespeare's " King Henry IV " in which Henry V commends the chief justice of England, who had sent him to jail when he was a roistering youth hobnobbing with Falstaff:

[31] *Trial of Page,* 1: 71, 76–111, 172, 215–233, 339, 370–372; 3: 1–64, 206, 256–364.

You did commit me:
For which I do commit into your hand
The unstain'd sword that you have used to bear;
With this remembrance, — That you use the same
With the like bold, just, and impartial spirit,
As you have done 'gainst me.[32]

Near the close of his address Davis briefly stated the origin of the prosecution of his client. Before he went on the bench Page had prosecuted a member of the " old Austin ring " for embezzlement. The members of the ring opposed his election and arrayed themselves against him thereafter. The Mollison libel was the beginning of a long crusade. " I know, and you know, senators," said Davis, " that some of you have been approached in a way in which no judge should be approached." In a passage of fervid invective the peculiar deserts of some members of the conspiracy were graphically sketched. This conspiracy, he said, found its last expression in the impeachment and a private mob had been allowed to conduct the prosecution through an attorney in private pay. In a brief peroration Davis reminded the Senate that it also was on trial, the record of which would survive in imperishable print. " Can . . . any of you . . . say that this respondent shall be deprived of the office which he has adorned and be fixed in the death in life of civic annihilation? "[33]

The arguments were concluded on June 28 and at an evening session of the court the voting took place. On the first, third, fourth, and fifth articles the acquittal would have been unanimous but for the negative vote of Senator Clough of Mower County. On article 2 all but three senators voted " not guilty." Articles 7 and 10 received majority votes of " not guilty." On the remaining articles, 6, 8, and 9 — the persecution of the county treasurer, the unlawful arrest of Stimpson, and the insults to attorneys — there were majority votes of " guilty," but in no case was there the two-thirds majority requisite for conviction. The judgment of the court accordingly was an acquittal of every charge and specification.[34]

The ambiguous verdict left the way open for Judge Page's friends to claim a vindication and for his enemies to claim an indisputable lifelong censure. The Mower County war went on. On the evening of July 12 at an outdoor meeting of friends Judge Page found a sympathetic audience. On the evening of the fifteenth a large body

[32] *Trial of Page*, 3: 147–152, 157, 166–255; " King Henry IV," part 2, act 5, scene 2.
[33] *Trial of Page*, 3: 251–255.
[34] *Trial of Page*, 3: 365–370.

of hostiles assembled about the village flagstaff and listened to abundant denunciations of Page. Early in August a petition, to which were attached numerous signatures, asking him to give reasons why he should not resign his office was presented to him. On the seventeenth of August, at a meeting in Jones's Hall, in an apologetic address of great length, much interrupted with heckling, he defended his behavior on the bench and declared that the machinations and assaults of his enemies had forced him to fight. The printed record of the speech does not indicate that it was calculated to conciliate.[35] He did not resign but served out his term and no further complaints of unbecoming behavior have been noted. At the fall elections of 1879 he sought a complete vindication as a candidate for reëlection. Although he received a vote indicative of a strong following, his hope was disappointed. On December 9, 1879, there was a meeting of citizens in Jones's Hall, evidently called to induce friends and enemies of Judge Page to let bygones be bygones and to live in tolerant, if not cordial, friendship. The *National Republican* of December 11 called it "A grand Peace Demonstration." The long line of speeches was closed by Judge Page, who said that he had always acted without bias or prejudice. He had nothing to retract or regret. The future was bright before him. If his enemies wanted peace they could have it by ceasing to attack him. The address could not have been very satisfactory to the peacemakers, but they adopted a long string of ready-made resolutions commendatory of the judge and appointed a committee to investigate the fraud of the late election. At the end of that month and year Judge Sherman Page retired from public life in Minnesota. Although he kept steadfast friends there, he decided to make a new home and in 1882 he removed to California.[36]

8. THE IMPEACHMENT OF JUDGE COX, 1881[37]

Territorial pioneers of the author's acquaintance have frequently expressed the opinion that the great wave of immigration to Minnesota in the three years preceding the admission of the state to the Union brought in on its crest a large number of able young lawyers, many of whom later became known throughout the state and be-

---

[35] *Mower and Fillmore County Republican*, July 18, 25, August 8, 22, 1878; *Austin Register*, July 18, August 8, 22, 1878.
[36] *National Republican* (Austin), November 13, December 11, 1879; Curtiss-Wedge, *Mower County*, 961.
[37] See *ante*, pp. 129–131.

yond.[38]   Among those whom they have mentioned were such men as Governors Horace Austin and Henry A. Swift; Chief Justices Christopher Ripley and James Gilfillan; Judges Samuel Lord, William Mitchell, and Charles E. Vanderburgh; and Senators William Windom and Daniel S. Norton. But there was one among them whom a Minnesota historian would gladly leave unmentioned — Eugene St. Julien Cox.

Cox was born in Switzerland in 1835 and was educated by his father, a graduate of Princeton. He was admitted to the bar in Wisconsin in 1854 and in 1857 he entered upon the practice of law in St. Peter, Minnesota. In the first year of the Civil War he volunteered for service and went out as a first lieutenant in the Second Minnesota Infantry. On February 8, 1862, soon after the battle of Mill Springs, he resigned and returned to his law practice. His military apprenticeship was soon turned to good advantage at home. As soon as Flandrau's " Frontier Guard " had marched from St. Peter at noon on August 19, 1862, to the relief of New Ulm, Cox began to enroll volunteers for a company of " Frontier Avengers." Fifty officers and men were enrolled in the company, which Sibley took under his command and ordered to New Ulm. The appearance of the little reënforcement at New Ulm on the following day, as Flandrau reports, inspired the townsmen with hope. Upon their exodus to Mankato on August 25, Captain Cox was intrusted with the general disposition of the military escort. On the morning of the twenty-sixth Colonel Flandrau made an effort to persuade some of the New Ulm men to return to their homes and called for volunteers to protect them. In his narrative he says that he could not do justice to history did he not record that Captain Cox and his whole company stepped to the front. But the New Ulm citizens were not then disposed to expose themselves to a possible Indian raid. In the fall of 1862 Captain Cox raised one of the companies of the Minnesota Mounted Rangers, and he commanded it during its year of service, which ended on November 11, 1863. The principal event of the period was Sibley's expedition to the Missouri in the summer of 1863.[39]

Following his service in the Indian wars Captain Cox spent some years in the ordinary drudgery of law practice in a county seat.

[38] On immigration to Minnesota in the last years of the territorial period, see ante, 1: 359–363.

[39] Mrs. A. K. Gault to the author, June 5, 1922; Upham and Dunlap, Minnesota Biographies, 146; Minnesota in the Civil and Indian Wars, 1: 133, 531, 731; 2: 206. See also ante, 2: 136–139, 168, 170.

He was sufficiently learned in the law and became adroit in practice, " handling his cases well." Affable and genial and always daintily dressed, wearing the traditional silk hat and highly-polished shoes, he gathered about him a large body of personal friends from all parties. His singular name caught the ear and added to his notoriety and his unusual grace and forcefulness as a public speaker increased his popularity from year to year.[40] He was a member of the Minnesota House of Representatives during the winter of 1873 and in the fall of the same year he was elected to a seat in the state Senate, which he held during the sessions of 1874 and 1875. At the congressional election of 1874 he was defeated by the Republican candidate, Horace B. Strait, by so slender a majority that he contested the election, but without success. In the fall of 1877 he was nominated by the Democrats for judge of the ninth judicial district to run against an able and much-respected Republican candidate; and such was his standing with the electorate that he was chosen by a vote of 2,892 against 1,920.[41]

In January, 1878, Cox assumed his judicial duties with the prospect of a full term of honorable service. Within a few weeks newspaper items alleging that Judge Cox had been seen in a state of intoxication while attending to his judicial duties in Martin County multiplied. At his request the lower house of the legislature appointed a select committee, with power to examine witnesses under oath, to investigate the matter. The report submitted on March 4 stated that, after a full and fair investigation, the committee had found the charge against Judge Cox to be " wholly false, slanderous and untrue." [42]

Three years now passed, in the course of which, as was later proved, a long-standing habit of indulging in occasional sprees gained in power over Judge Cox and at times disqualified him for

[40] Interview with John Lind, recorded in the author's notebooks, 9: 30, 36. Lind studied law with Cox.

[41] *Legislative Manual*, 1925, pp. 128, 129; *Saint Paul Sunday Pioneer*, January 3, 1875, p. 4; *House Journal*, 1878, p. 19. For the notice of contest, the testimony, and other papers in the case of Cox *v.* Strait, see 44 Congress, 1 session, *House Miscellaneous Documents*, no. 55 (serial 1699) ; for the report of the House committee on elections, to which the case was referred, see 44 Congress, 1 session, *House Reports*, no. 391 (serial 1709). The vote as canvassed stood: for Strait, 13,742; for Cox, 13,521. The committee on elections found that 111 illegal votes had been cast, which left a majority of 110 for Strait. The report of the committee, recommending the passage of a resolution that Strait was duly elected, was adopted by the House on June 23, 1876. *Congressional Record*, 44 Congress, 1 session, 4076.

[42] *Rochester Post*, March 1, 1878, p. 2; *Lanesboro Journal*, quoted in the *Pioneer Press*, February 11, 1878, p. 2; *House Journal*, 1878, pp. 207, 387.

duty. But the respect entertained for his talent and ability and the indulgence of the public for a favorite were such that no formal complaint was made. It may be added that members of the bar would naturally be reluctant to bring against a judge charges which, if not made good, would place them at a disadvantage when appearing in his court and also that, in those early days and in a frontier community, drinking, if occasional, was easily forgiven in a public character. It was left to a preacher and a county official to present in 1881 to the House of Representatives in extra session a detailed complaint in which it was alleged that Judge Cox had been intoxicated while engaged in official duties. A scrutiny of the long and circumstantial statement by the House committee to which it was referred resulted in a report embodying the testimony taken and a recommendation for impeachment. A resolution to impeach was adopted by the House on November 4, 1881, by a vote of 76 to 10 and a board of managers was appointed to formulate articles and to prosecute. On November 16 the board of managers reported twenty articles of impeachment, which the House adopted by a vote of 78 to 13. At a later session eight members who were absent on the sixteenth were allowed to have their votes, which were in the affirmative, recorded.[43]

On the next day, November 17, the managers appeared at the bar of the Senate. The Senate organized as a high court of impeachment and the articles of impeachment were read by the secretary. Sixteen articles, in nearly identical terms, charged Judge Cox with intoxication, caused by the voluntary and immoderate use of intoxicating liquors, which disqualified him for the discharge of his official duties at as many times in eight different counties on dates mentioned. In each case he was alleged to be guilty of crimes and misdemeanors in office. There were four other articles, two of which charged him with drunkenness on other occasions and with habitual drunkenness since March 30, 1878. John W. Arctander, John B. Brisbin, Lorenzo Allis, and Walter H. Sanborn appeared as counsel for Cox and were invited to seats at the bar of the Senate. The second Tuesday in January, 1882, was appointed for the opening of the trial, but an interim adjournment was taken to December 13 to hear any objections that might be offered. On that date, as was probably expected, Judge Cox's counsel raised the objection, or

---

[43] *House Journal*, 1881, extra session, 22, 126, 135, 256–265. For the report of the judiciary committee, see the four-page appendix. The board consisted of Representatives Henry G. Hicks, James Smith, Jr., Ozro B. Gould, Andrew C. Dunn, George W. Putnam, Warren J. Ives, and Loren W. Collins.

demurrer, that Cox was not charged with any offense for which he ought to be held to answer. The principal contention was that no offense was impeachable that was not indictable and Judge Cox was not charged with any indictable offense. The prosecution resisted this proposition with great vigor and the Senate, after a three-day debate, unanimously set it aside.[44] The accused had now his choice of pleading guilty or standing trial. One of the witnesses at the trial, a very able lawyer widely experienced in public affairs, expressed to the author his judgment that, if Judge Cox had then made a plea of guilty, with a suggestion of extenuating circumstances and an intention to give no further occasion for complaint as to his official behavior, the Senate would have found some way to give him a chance to make good his promise.[45] His counsel, apparently assuming that their client could be convicted only by testimony establishing guilt beyond a reasonable doubt, as in criminal cases, prepared their answers to the several charges.

On January 10, 1882, the Senate court resumed its sessions. To each article of impeachment, in terms substantially identical, answer was made that it was insufficient in law in that the facts alleged did not constitute a public offense, that the respondent was not guilty of the particular charge, and that he was not guilty of corrupt conduct or of any crime or misdemeanor. No sooner had the answers been read than protest was made against one of the rules of procedure which the Senate had adopted at the time of its organization as a court — that five witnesses to each article of impeachment might be examined by the prosecution and a like number by the defense, unless otherwise ordered by the court. It was claimed that the rule infringed the right guaranteed by the bill of rights in the state constitution that a person accused of crime shall have compulsory process for obtaining witnesses in his favor without limit. To this reply was made that impeachment for misconduct in office was not a criminal procedure and that the trial about to begin was not a criminal case. At the close of a day's debate it was agreed by a vote of 14 to 9 that when the prosecution had examined its quota of witnesses either party might apply to the court for additional subpœnas. This vote amounted to a rescinding of the

---

[44] *Trial of Cox*, 1 : 6, 6a–6j, 13, 28–160. Articles 19 and 20, charging recent immoral behavior, were virtually ignored from the start by the court. See *Trial of Cox*, 3 : 2545. Cushman K. Davis filed an appearance in writing as counsel for Cox, but he took no part in public.

[45] John Lind, who later became a member of Congress and, still later, governor of Minnesota.

offensive rule and opened the way to what it was hoped that its operation would prevent, the introduction of a throng of superfluous witnesses.[46]

The trial now began and went on in the usual order of a lawsuit. If any curious reader has been expecting even a bare analysis of the evidence, which covers nearly seventeen hundred pages, he must be disappointed. The use of the disproportionate space would not be tolerated and much of the language would not be good reading for a family circle. Nearly sixty witnesses were produced by the managers and over a hundred by the defense. The taking of testimony on the part of the prosecution began on January 11 and continued until the twenty-seventh. At this point the managers withdrew four of the articles of impeachment and three specifications of a fifth, all of which were formally dismissed, and exonerated the accused of their charges. The Senate having refused to receive evidence under the twentieth article, it was ordered that it also be withdrawn.[47]

After an interval to allow the defense time for preparation, the court reassembled on February 7. The opening for the defense did not fall to the older and more distinguished counsel — Brisbin, Allis, or Sanborn — but to their junior associate, John W. Arctander, a Norwegian by birth, who had been educated at the University of Christiania. His speech occupied the sessions of three days. By far the greater part was devoted to a castigation of the witnesses for the prosecution, which in ordinary trials would have been reserved for the final argument. He spoke of the great popularity that Judge Cox had enjoyed and that had resulted in his elevation to the bench and showed a petition signed by four thousand electors, imploring the senators not to deprive them of the services of an impartial and incorruptible judge. He referred to the insignificance of the two obscure citizens who had brought the original complaint. He denounced the refusal of the House of Representatives to allow Judge Cox to be present at the preliminary investigation and to interrogate witnesses, as Judge Page had been allowed to do. He denounced even more bitterly the action of members of the board of managers in going to every place where Judge Cox had held court to look for new charges and new witnesses, thus casting a dragnet for evidence against his client; no county attorney would take his horse and

---

[46] *Trial of Cox,* 1: 165–210.
[47] For the testimony for the prosecution, see *Trial of Cox,* 1: 239–998. Manager Hicks's opening address is on pages 214–229 of the same volume.

buggy and go about to pick up evidence against one of whom complaint had been made.[48]

The taking of testimony for the defense went on for nearly a
month and ended on March 3. The record presents a capital illustration of a fact well known to lawyers and judges, that many people
of average intelligence and honesty may see and hear the same
things done and said and, under the sanctity of an oath, give the
most discordant testimony; so imperfect is human observation and
so treacherous is human memory, especially when there is bias,
either friendly or hostile. Many of the witnesses for the defense,
admitting that at certain times the judge had been under the influence
of liquor, denied that he was then incapacitated for duty. One of
them, when asked, " Well, what do you mean by drunk?" answered,
" Well, when a man is so full that he lays in the street."

Loren W. Collins, one of the managers, who later became a judge
of the supreme court of Minnesota, opened the final arguments,
taking for his task an exhaustive analysis of the evidence, with incidental remarks upon the character of witnesses. He did not place
much value upon the testimony in behalf of Cox of ten saloon-
keepers and twenty-two lawyers, " most of them . . . lawyers by
trade, not by profession." In closing he uttered a note of warning
to all senators opposed to " prohibition." " If your votes," said
he, " acquit this respondent, the moral element of this State will be
aroused beyond all restraint, and the sale of intoxicating liquors
wiped out of existence within our limits at the very first election.
May God speed the day if this man is acquitted."

Arctander, speaking next for the defense, undertook to array the
testimony in such order as to assure the innocence of his client.
He had his opinion of some of the witnesses for the state, especially
of certain lawyers disposed not to wait for the expiration of Judge
Cox's term of office. After speaking through all the sessions of
the court from Wednesday afternoon to Tuesday afternoon, he concluded by saying, " I feel like I could talk for twenty days to come
and yet not do my client justice . . . and I don't know but what it
is better that I should say no more."[49]

The closing argument for the defense was intrusted to John B.
Brisbin of St. Paul, whose career as an advocate had long since

---

[48] *Trial of Cox*, 2: 1038–1146. For biographical information concerning
Arctander, see Upham and Dunlap, *Minnesota Biographies*, 19 and citations.
He had come to Minnesota in 1874 at the age of twenty-five and was soon
afterward admitted to the bar.

[49] *Trial of Cox*, 2: 1147–2068; 3: 2070–2177, 2185–2484.

given him wide repute. He had practiced law in Minnesota since 1853 and in the winter of 1857 he had been president of the territorial Council and had held the fort against the Republican majority which had voted to move the state capital to St. Peter. He had been graduated from Yale College before the classical tongues had been degraded in American colleges to mere vehicles of syntax and etymology and his address abounded in phrases and full passages from Greek and Roman authorities and great names in English literature. Although he was not imposing in stature or bulk, his presence was dignified and was set off by the traditional blue coat with brass buttons of the colonial bar. "Briz," as his cronies called him, had been the leading jury lawyer of Minnesota's early days. It may be that his speech in defense of Cox was his masterpiece. The point about which his brilliant historical allusions and citations and his play of rhetoric centered was that "an offense, to be impeachable, must, under our constitution, be committed under color of office, in violation of a known law, and be an indictable act." He insisted that the proceeding was that of a criminal court and claimed that his client had not been accorded the privileges and immunities guaranteed to persons accused of crime. It may be surmised that the learned and eloquent attorney did not fully expect an acquittal as a mere logical deduction from testimony, for he concluded with an extract from an address by Thomas Erskine, "the laurelled aristocrat of the bar of the civilized world," which read in part as follows: "If He [*the benevolent author of our being*] finds that our conduct, though often forced out of the path by our infirmities, has been in general well directed; His all-searching eye will assuredly never pursue us into those little corners of our lives, much less will His justice select them for punishment, without the general context of our existence, by which faults may be sometimes found virtues, and very many of our heaviest offenses to have been grafted by human imperfection upon the best and kindest of our affections. No, gentlemen, believe me, this is not the course of Divine justice, or there is no truth in the gospels of heaven."[50]

Brisbin's argument was followed by addresses by Managers Gould and Dunn. Gould argued upon the law of the case and Dunn, speaking at great length, weighed the comparative standing of witnesses and the results of their testimony. When the arguments of counsel were ended, Judge Cox asked to be allowed an hour to

[50] Newson, *Pen Pictures*, 403–406; Upham and Dunlap, *Minnesota Biographies*, 77 and citations; *Trial of Cox*, 3: 2487–2558.

speak in his own defense. The request was granted, but not until after the court had considered it in secret session. When the court reassembled in evening session the president said that he hoped the senators would keep their seats, avoid talking, and be quiet. Judge Cox used his hour and more in delivering a highly rhetorical discourse, in part argumentative but made up chiefly of fervent appeals for justice and for consideration of the consequences of conviction to himself and his family. He claimed that no such offenses as those with which he was charged were to be found mentioned in the penal code or statutes and that there was no charge against him of corrupt conduct in office. He implored the senators to decide his case according to the law and evidence and not from personal and private knowledge of his life. Before uttering his touching peroration, he declared with the utmost solemnity: "Never whilst sitting as a Judge upon the bench in the discharge of my official duties have I been intoxicated or in any manner under the effect of intoxicating liquor . . . so that my mind or judgment was affected in that I could not discharge my official duties faithfully and impartially. So help me God." It is doubtful whether his rambling and sentimental speech changed the minds of any of his judges.[51]

After listening to protests by senators against star chamber proceedings, the court engaged in a discussion of the testimony and argument article by article, with an understanding that speakers need not confine themselves closely to the question. A day and a half were thus devoted to addresses by two groups of senators — one group for conviction and the other, much smaller, for acquittal — in explanation of the votes they intended to cast. Six of the original articles of impeachment had been dismissed; fourteen remained to be decided by vote. On one-half of this number Judge Cox was acquitted — on two, by a unanimous vote and on two others, by a vote nearly unanimous; the voting was closer on the other three articles, but on all of them the prosecution failed. Of the remaining seven charges Judge Cox was convicted by more than the necessary two-thirds vote. A group of five senators, warmly attached to him politically or otherwise, steadily voted "not guilty" on all articles and consumed much time in explanation of their votes.[52]

[51] *Trial of Cox*, 3: 2561–2806.
[52] *Trial of Cox*, 3: 2807–2962. Note especially speeches of Senators Wheat (2826–2830), Powers (2830–2833, 2901–2903), D. Buck (2833–2848), Wilson (2849–2854), C. F. Buck (2854–2860), Castle (2860–2870), Adams (2873–2876), Hinds (2878–2887), and J. B. Gilfillan (2904–2906).

On the evening of March 22, 1882, the trial, which had begun on November 17, 1881, was brought to its close in open session. The judgment of the court, duly formulated, declared that E. St. Julien Cox had been convicted of the crimes and misdemeanors charged in seven of the articles of impeachment, which were recited in full, and it was therefore considered, adjudged, and determined that he be removed from his office as district judge and be disqualified to hold said office and any other judicial office of honor, trust, or profit for the period of three years, beginning on March 22, 1882. The vote on the adoption of the order was 25 to 12 — a bare two-thirds.[53]

A resolution to allow each of the attorneys of counsel for Cox five dollars a day for each day's attendance was at first rejected by a vote of 15 to 17; but an hour later a senator who had voted against the resolution moved a reconsideration, which was agreed to without division. Another compassionate senator stated that Judge Cox had scarcely money enough to take him home, that his attorneys, or some of them, at least, were poor, and that some remuneration should be allowed them. After some palaver the resolution — amended by the words " not to exceed $350," enough to pay board bills — was passed, with only one senator, the " watchdog of the treasury," voting " no." The cost of the Cox impeachment to the state, guessed at in advance in debate as likely to run up to sums ranging from twenty thousand to forty thousand dollars or more, was held down to the more modest sum of $12,531.05, not including witnesses' fees and mileages. Cox's attorneys were " compensated " with $325, a sum well within the limits set by the court. The secretary of the court got $300 for compiling the index of the proceedings. In his message to the legislature of 1883 Governor Hubbard remarked upon the disgraceful details of an impeachment trial running week after week and costing ten times as much as the salary of the chief justice of the state. He recommended an amendment to the state constitution to provide for removal from office by legislative address, a procedure which was followed in some of the states.[54]

[53] *Trial of Cox,* 3: 2985–2989.
[54] *Trial of Cox,* 3: 2991–2999; report of the state auditor, in *Executive Documents,* 1884, vol. 4, p. 143; Hubbard's message, January 4, 1883, in *Executive Documents,* 1882, vol. 1, p. 32. Brisbin received $94.50; Allis, $119; and Arctander, who had borne the heat and burden of the trial, $111.50. The seven managers divided $1,600.25 among them. See *General Laws,* 1883, p. 212, for the appropriation.

The conviction of Judge Cox was, of course, a severe blow to him, but it did not alienate a body of steadfast friends who long retained their admiration for his talents and character. In 1891, as elsewhere mentioned, they obtained from the legislature the passage of a resolution vacating, annulling, and expunging all the proceedings of the impeachment and trial. This was a consolation, but it left open the question whether the conviction was regarded as an injustice, or whether, if it was just, Cox had been sufficiently punished. A few years later Judge Cox found it best to leave Minnesota. He died in Los Angeles on November 3, 1898.[55]

9. REDEMPTION OF THE RAILROAD BONDS OF 1858 [56]

The story of the issue of the Minnesota State Railroad Bonds of 1858 to the amount of $2,275,000, their delivery to the railroad companies in exchange for bonds secured by mortgages on railroad lands, the payment of contractors for construction in state bonds, the failure of the corporations to pay the first installment of interest on the special bonds, and the refusal of the state to pay the interest has been told in a previous volume.[57] Another story not pleasant to tell nor for our posterity to think about must now be told.

In pursuance of the terms of the constitutional amendment of 1858, of the several trust deeds of the railroad companies, and of legislative instructions, Governor Ramsey early in 1860 gave notice to the companies of his intention to foreclose their several mortgages. At the public sales which took place in the course of the same year, being the highest bidder, he bought on behalf of the state for the sum of one thousand dollars " all the lands, roads, rights, properties and franchises " of each corporation. By this action the state became possessed in trust of the " munificent Congressional grant " for railroads, over four million acres, and was in the same condition as to the land grant railroads as when the legislature of 1857 began its extra session, with 240 miles of graded

---

[55] See *ante*, p. 130; *Senate Journal*, 1891, p. 614; *House Journal*, 806; *General Laws*, 399. The vote in the Senate was: yeas, 42; nays, 0; the vote in the House was: yeas, 60; nays, 2. The same resolution had been introduced in the legislature of 1887. It passed the House by a vote of 71 to 4, but was lost in the Senate by a vote of 18 to 9. *House Journal*, 458, 474; *Senate Journal*, 649.

[56] See *ante*, p. 139. This section of the appendix is a revision of part of an article by the author entitled "The Five Million Loan," in *Minnesota Historical Collections*, 15: 189–214.

[57] See *ante*, 2: 37–58.

roadbed and two and a quarter million dollars' worth of "conditional state obligations outstanding " to boot.[58]

The members of the legislature of 1861 seem not to have been troubled in conscience about the outstanding conditional obligations of the state, but they were desirous of seeing railroad building resumed and paid for out of the " munificent " land grant rescued from the insolvent corporations. The misfortunes of these companies, which had not practiced fraud but had simply gone down in the general slump of things, awakened sympathy and there soon appeared evidences of a willingness to reinstate them and give them another trial. But difficulties were encountered. In the first place, the validity of the foreclosure sales was called in question by good lawyers, and, in the second place, there was doubt as to the legal effect of the foreclosures upon the corporate franchises of the companies. In obedience to a resolution of the House of Representatives, the attorney-general, Gordon E. Cole, on January 30, 1861, furnished an elaborate opinion covering both points. After reciting the history of the bond issue, of the trust deeds, and of the defaults of the railroad companies, he expressed the opinion that a foreclosure in equity, making all coholders of bonds codefendants, would have been preferable to a foreclosure by advertisement under a power. As that procedure had not been taken, he went on to consider, under ten separate headings, the objections which had arisen against the validity of the sales. He found that they were all, under the circumstances, unsubstantial and that the state had acquired an indisputable title to the properties of the companies. As to the legal status of the corporations, he had been at first strongly inclined to think that their corporate franchises had been merged and extinguished by the foreclosure sales; the state had recovered that scintilla of sovereignty which it had transferred to them. But a further examination of the merger theory had led him to believe that recent decisions by courts of equity might be adapted to the case in question. These decisions held that " when the titles

[58] *General Laws*, 1858, pp. 178–181; 1860, p. 269; Ramsey's message, January 9, 1861, in *Executive Documents*, 1860, pp. 9–11; Governor's Archives, Records, A: 207. The mortgages of the Minnesota and Pacific and the Transit railroad companies were foreclosed on June 23, 1860; the mortgage of the Minneapolis and Cedar Valley (by the trustees), on August 16; and that of the Southern Minnesota, on October 16. See *Minnesota State Bonds*, 21 (Five Million Loan Pamphlets, no. 17 — New York, 1871). On these pamphlets, see *ante*, 2:44, n. 15. For a copy of a state railroad bond, see page 3 of the same pamphlet; for a trust deed, page 38; for an example of a foreclosure proceeding, page 45; and for an auctioneer's certificate, page 49.

of mortgagee and mortgagor vest in one and the same person, the question as to whether the transaction shall be treated as a redemption or an assignment, is to be determined by an inquiry into the intent of the parties and the equities of the case." In the acts of August 12, 1858, and March 6, 1860, he had found indications that the legislatures had intended, in both, to perpetuate the franchises after possible default in payments. As a franchise can never be surrendered without the consent of the state and as a forfeiture may be waived by the government, the learned attorney-general conceived that in this instance the state was free to consider the franchises of the railroad companies as still surviving.[59]

Thus advised that the old companies were alive and competent to function, the sympathetic legislature of 1861 passed by large majorities bills to restore to each company all its former " rights, benefits, privileges, property, franchises, and interests " which it had forfeited to the state. The regrant to the Minnesota and Pacific was made direct to the old corporation; the regrants to the other companies, to permit of reorganizations, were made to groups of individual incorporators. Each restitution had two conditions annexed: one, that the company should deposit in the state treasury the sum of ten thousand dollars in bonds of the United States or of any solvent state; the other, that it must complete ten miles — in one case, twenty miles — of road before the first day of January, 1862.[60]

Times had not bettered in 1861. The credit of the state of Minnesota did not invite outside capital and the distractions of the opening year of the Civil War diverted what moneys were in the state to purposes other than building railroads and taking wild land for pay. Three of the companies, after making futile efforts to show that they were really alive, gave up and virtually deceased. The directors of the fourth company, the Minnesota and Pacific, were more sanguine and resolved to build ten miles of road and obtain the proportionate grant of land. By some means J. Edgar Thompson, president of the Pennsylvania Railroad Company, was induced to entertain a proposition to finance the project. A competent engi-

[59] Attorney-General, *Report in Reply to a Resolution of the House* (Five Million Loan Pamphlets, no. 12 — St. Paul, 1861). In First Division of the St. Paul and Pacific Railroad Company *v.* Frank M. Parcher and Henry Kreis, 14 *Minnesota*, 224, decided in 1869, it was held that the state could take the franchises of the companies without merger or extinguishment.

[60] *House Journal*, 1861, pp. 271, 292, 325, 344; *Senate Journal*, 289, 290, 308, 323; *Special Laws*, 213–238.

neer, sent out to examine the condition of the graded roadbed and
to obtain other necessary information, made a favorable report.
The president and the chief engineer of the Minnesota and Pacific
went to Philadelphia, where Governor Ramsey joined them. A
tentative agreement was made and lawyers were set at work upon
the necessary papers.

On the eleventh of June came the news of the battle of Big
Bethel and a note from the Pennsylvania people saying that they
could not proceed with the business. The Minnesota officials were
about to depart to their homes, disappointed and sorrowful, when
they " quite accidentally " made the acquaintance of Elias F. Drake,
of Xenia, Ohio, then forty-seven years of age and experienced in
banking, legislation, and railroad building and operation, and of
two associates of Drake, all in New York looking for investments.
The persuasive talent of Edmund Rice, " affable, courteous, commanding," was perhaps never more effectively employed than in the
interviews with this group. Drake and his associates made a visit
to Minnesota and found conditions even better than they had been
led to expect. They agreed to deposit the ten-thousand-dollar guaranty fund and entered into a provisional contract to build and equip
ten miles of railroad from St. Paul to St. Anthony, for which they
were to receive $120,000 in the company's eight-per-cent, twenty-
year bonds and good title to 76,800 acres of land. The definite
contract awaited a new foreclosure of the trust deed of the Minnesota and Pacific, the contractors being advised that Governor Ramsey's foreclosure of the previous year was not so air-tight as surely
to vest title to the lands in the state.

It must have been in expectation that the new foreclosure would
be completed without long delay that the contractors made their
deposit of ten thousand dollars in the state treasury, after some
embarrassment. When they offered six or seven thousand dollars
in Minnesota State Railroad Bonds, they were informed by the
treasurer that the bonds were not such securities as the law called
for. Gold and other securities had to be substituted before he was
satisfied. The new foreclosure was carried through somewhat tardily; but a trustee, for reasons that have not been learned, refused
to deliver the deed of sale to the purchaser, a broker for the railroad
company. The season was then too far advanced for railroad building. Meantime the contractors had brought up to St. Paul a quantity of iron rails, forty-five pounds to the yard, and a locomotive of
twenty-five tons' capacity. They laid rails on a stretch of fourteen

422   A HISTORY OF MINNESOTA

hundred feet of tracks previously graded and over them ran their locomotive up to a shed for storage. The Minnesota and Pacific could not fulfill the conditions of its revival under the law of 1861 and at the end of that year it ceased to exist.[61]

Governor Ramsey reported to the legislature of 1862 the failure of the old companies to build under the conditions imposed by the act of the previous winter and recommended that opportunity be offered to other persons or companies to undertake building, after they should deposit sufficient guaranty funds. The legislature of 1862 created four new companies by " acts to facilitate " building. These companies and their successors and assigns, after many discouragements and years of great effort, built the several lines contemplated by the land grant act of Congress of 1857.[62] That long and eventful history must not divert us from our present topic of bond redemption.

The war of the slaveholders' rebellion continued to rage and the Indian war broke out in the summer of 1862. While they went on for three years no bondholder was absurd enough to waste effort in further appeals for relief. Governors Swift and Miller in their messages made not the slightest allusion to the " conditional obligations " of the state. When at length the war clouds cleared away the bombardment of the legislature, predicted by Governor Ramsey, began. In the session of 1866 bills were introduced in both houses for the payment of the bonds in full, but none of them made any progress. In the same winter an act was passed creating a commission to ascertain and report to the legislature the names of the bondholders, the amount due each holder, and the amount paid for the bonds by each bona fide owner. The commission was also authorized to receive proposals for adjustment. John Nicols, Lucius F.

[61] Message of Governor Ramsey, January 9, 1862, in *Executive Documents,* 1861, p. 21; William Crooks, " The First Railroad in Minnesota," in *Minnesota Historical Collections,* 10: 445–448 (part 1) ; John H. Randall, " The Beginning of Railroad Building in Minnesota," in *Minnesota Historical Collections,* 15: 217. For information as to progress in construction, see the *Pioneer and Democrat,* August 17, 1861. The *Pioneer* of September 20 gives an account of the first trip of the " William Crooks " locomotive on the nineteenth and the issue of October 30 tells of the surrender by the Minnesota and Pacific Company of its franchise after failing to secure confirmation of its right to land by means of a second foreclosure and sale, the trustee having absconded without delivering the deed.

[62] Ramsey's message, January 9, 1862, in *Executive Documents,* 1861, p. 21; *Special Laws,* 1862, pp. 226–255. The new companies were the Minneapolis, Faribault, and Cedar Valley, the Root River Valley and Southern Minnesota, the Winona and St. Peter, and the St. Paul and Pacific. On the construction of these roads, see *ante,* 2:52–56; 3: 60.

Hubbard, and John E. Tourtellotte were the commissioners appointed.[63]

The discovery by Elias Drake in the summer of 1866 of the forgotten statute of 1841 under which Minnesota was entitled to five hundred thousand acres of land for internal improvements and the recognition by the department of the interior of the right of the state to the lands has been mentioned. No sooner did the favorable action of the government become known than suggestions came from many quarters to devote these lands to paying off the old bonds. Governor Marshall voiced the proposal to the legislature of 1867 and urged that body to pay whatever might justly be due by using the lands placed at its disposal. The legislature willingly responded by passing an act creating out of the proceeds of the sales of those lands a "state railroad bond sinking fund." Whenever a sum of twenty thousand dollars should, from time to time, be accumulated, bondholders might bid for this cash and those whose proposals should be most advantageous were to turn in their bonds and receive the money.[64]

Under the amendment of 1860 that act was referred to the people. They rejected it by the decisive vote of 49,763 to 1,935. They did not feel sure that Divine Providence had destined those lands for paying for dead horses.[65] It is highly probable that they were influenced by the report of the Nicols commission, which was submitted on January 8, 1867. That body made up a list of 1,840 bonds reported to it, showing the names of 106 holders, the number of bonds held by each, the particular number and date of each bond, the company to which each was issued, and the stated cost of each. Four hundred and thirty-five bonds were not reported. The "stated costs" ranged from par down to seventeen and one-half cents on the dollar. Thirteen persons or corporations held 1,410 bonds and three persons, 1,142. The largest holder was Selah Chamberlain of Cleveland, Ohio, an important figure in the railroad history of the state. He held 967 bonds, which, he averred, had cost him

[63] *Senate Journal*, 1866, pp. 152, 160, 166; *House Journal*, 213, 274; *General Laws*, 9. Nicols was chairman of the commission. *Proceedings of the Board of Commissioners Appointed under the Provisions of an Act Approved February 28, 1866*, 3 (Five Million Loan Pamphlets, no. 13 — St. Paul, 1867).

[64] See *ante*, p. 34; Marshall's message, January 10, 1867, in *Executive Documents*, 1866, p. 18; United States, *Statutes at Large*, 5:455; Minnesota, *Senate Journal*, 1867, p. 212; *House Journal*, 264; and *General Laws*, 93.

[65] *Saint Paul Press*, January 9, 1868. For the amendment of 1860, see Anderson, *History of the Constitution*, 237.

" more than par value " in expenses of construction. Chamberlain's valuation of the work performed was so much in excess of what the commissioners had roughly estimated that they employed Joseph S. Sewall of St. Paul, a capable engineer, to make a survey of the 120 miles of grading done by him on three different lines and to estimate the cost of the work at the prices of the time. The estimate of this expert showed that the reasonable cost should have been $341,211, or $2,803.42 per mile. Chamberlain's bonds, according to that estimate, had cost him a fraction over thirty per cent of their face value in work performed. This revelation did not assure the people of honest administration of the credit they had generously lent. The proposals of the bondholders for adjustment were exceedingly variant; some demanded all that was nominated in the bond, others a certain per cent, and a few were willing to take whatever might be allowed to the most favored owners. One holder of sixty-seven bonds, which had cost him from twenty-eight cents on the dollar to their par value, would take whatever the state would pay.[66]

The legislature of 1868 took no action in regard to bond redemption and that of 1869 was in no hurry to attack the question. Impatient of such neglect, Governor Marshall sent to the two houses on February 1, 1869, a stirring special message urging the legislature to devote the five hundred thousand acres of internal improvement lands to the payment of the bonds. Again he suggested that " providentially the State has in these lands the means of providing for whatever is justly due to the holders of these bonds." Michigan had adjusted a railroad debt of twice the amount and Illinois, one six times as great. The regents of the state university had paid off a debt of $125,000 with fourteen thousand acres of land — an encouraging example. He appealed to a great party, pledged to equity and justice, to add to its proud record.[67]

---

[66] *Proceedings of the Board of Commissioners* (Five Million Loan Pamphlets, no. 13). See pages 47–52 for Sewall's report and page 53 for estimates made by David C. Shepard, chief engineer of the St. Paul and Pacific, about three times as high as those of Sewall. Even at Shepard's prices Chamberlain's claim was excessive. The report of the commission, with certain omissions and additions, was printed in *House Journal*, 1881, appendix. In a letter to the author, April 17, 1906, in the Folwell Papers, William Ashley Jones said that the contractors of 1858 had received very liberal terms from the companies.

[67] *Senate Journal*, 1869, pp. 62, 359; *House Journal*, 70. The *Saint Paul Pioneer*, February 2, 1869, gives Marshall's message and a memorial from Chamberlain to the governor, dated January 1.

Soon after the receipt of this message the houses appointed a joint committee to consider its recommendations. After three weeks' deliberation the majority reported a bill similar to that enacted into law in 1867 and rejected at the polls. The minority of the committee brought in a bill of novel and extraordinary character. Its main proposition was to grant to Francis R. Delano and his associates the whole bulk of the five hundred thousand acres of internal improvement lands on condition that in fourteen years he or they should turn in for cancellation all the outstanding Minnesota State Railroad Bonds. The details of the long bill are not now important. The two bills came up for consideration in the Senate on February 27 and the recorded proceedings indicate that the views of members had already been ascertained. By a vote of 13 to 8 the majority bill was postponed indefinitely and that of the minority, " the Delano bill," was passed by the same vote. In the House a fruitless attempt was made to substitute the majority bill and on March 4 the Senate bill was passed with minor amendments, in which the Senate concurred the same day — the last day but one of the session. Governor Marshall, as might have been expected, did not approve the bill after the adjournment of the legislature. The *Saint Paul Press* of March 11 states, " as we learn in conversation," that Marshall's reasons for withholding approval were these: (1) that the Delano bill was a scheme of unscrupulous speculators to get hold of the lands by robbing the bondholders; (2) that the grant was made to an irresponsible person without security and (3) gave him possession of land before cancellation of a bond; (4) that two years would pass after the appraisement of the lands before the cancellation of a bond and meantime the grantee could take land by certificate and hold it free from taxes; and, finally, (5) that it would be useless to submit the act to the electors, as they would be sure to reject it.[68]

In his last message, delivered to the legislature of 1870, Governor Marshall repeated the substance of his special message of the previous winter and again expressed his conviction that " these lands " had

---

[68] *Senate Journal*, 1869, pp. 62, 80, 170, 221, 222, 229–231, 336, 344; *House Journal*, 106, 278, 287, 373–376, 385, 387; *Saint Paul Pioneer*, February 3–5, 28, March 2, 4, 12, 1869. The full text of the bill is given in the *Pioneer*, March 6, 11. The final vote in the House was 24 to 20. In the *Saint Paul Press*, March 12, is a letter from Delano defending his plan. On an amendment proposed by Senator Castle to strike out " Francis R. Delano " and insert " Selah Chamberlain " there was a tie vote, broken by the vote of the chair in the negative. The implication is obvious.

been "providentially" reserved to pay off the bonds. Governor Horace Austin, in his inaugural address delivered on the same day, could not doubt that the legislature would respond to the "almost unanimous public sentiment of the people of the State" in favor of devoting the internal improvement lands to liquidating the bonds. The legislative bodies appear to have been moved by the executive appeals for they passed an act for the purpose, which provided for the virtual exchange of bonds at par value for land at a minimum price of $8.70 per acre. The five hundred thousand acres at that price would yield $4,350,000 — just about enough to redeem the bonds with accumulated interest. The lands turned over were to remain free from taxes for ten years. This act, as required by the amendment of 1860, was referred to the people, who ratified it by a vote of 18,257 to 12,489. Again the bondholders, the high-minded governor, and many citizens were disappointed. It was a condition of the act that it should not go into operation unless at least 2,000 bonds should be deposited for exchange. But 1,032, including those of Chamberlain, were turned in. At a meeting held in New York on September 1, 1870, the holders of 1,080 bonds resolved to "decline to accept an offer not equal to 25 per cent. of our just claims against a debtor able to pay in full." [69]

The following January Governor Austin in his first annual message expressed for the people of Minnesota their surprise at the refusal of the bondholders to accept "so fair and equitable a compromise." "The bonds," he said, "are of questionable validity, and if not actually fraudulent, are so intimately connected with what the great majority of the people believe to have been a fraud upon the State, as to make them odious, while it has been established . . . that a large proportion of the bonds cost their present owners and holders but $17\frac{1}{2}$ to 50 per cent. of their face." [70] The legislature of 1871, however, was not indifferent to the clamors of the bondholders and the demands of citizens for some kind of settlement. Early in the session General Sibley, who had consented to leave his retirement to use his influence and vote in the House

[69] Marshall's message, January 7, 1870, in *Executive Documents,* 1869, p. 7; Austin's message in the same volume, p. 5, and his message of January 5, 1871, in *Executive Documents,* 1870, vol. 1, p. 33; *General Laws,* 1870, pp. 18–21; *Address to the Holders of the Minnesota State Bonds,* 12 (Five Million Loan Pamphlets, no. 15 — New York, 1870). An abstract of the vote on the act of 1870 is in the report of the secretary of state, in *Executive Documents,* 1870, vol. 2, p. 707. The bondholders claimed that $8.70 an acre was four times the market value of the lands.

[70] *Executive Documents,* 1870, vol. 1, p. 33.

of Representatives toward securing legislation for that purpose, introduced in the House a resolution advocating a speedy settlement of the railroad bonds. His speech on this resolution, delivered on February 8, had been prepared with care, both in English and in French, and had been reduced to the smallest compass consistent with clearness. He related the story of the issue of the bonds and the great pains he had taken at the time as governor to require exact and full compliance by the railroad companies with all lawful conditions. He had waived his executive prerogative and had obeyed the mandamus of the supreme court. After the bonds were issued they were rendered valueless by the unholy warfare waged upon them by citizens and newspapers of the state. He would readily cast his vote for the payment of " every cent " of principal and interest. In his peroration General Sibley declared that but for his abiding faith that Minnesota would " honorably acquit herself of all her engagements," he would transfer himself to some community where he would not be subjected to the " intolerable humiliation " of being a citizen in a " repudiating State, frowned upon by a just and righteous God, and abhorred by man." [71]

The resolution was referred to a special joint committee on state railroad bonds, of which Sibley was chairman. This committee on February 23 reported back a bill known as " the Chamberlain bill,"

[71] *House Journal,* 1871, pp. 84, 97. For Sibley's speech, see the *Saint Paul Pioneer,* February 9, 1871. A clipping of the speech is in the Five Million Loan Pamphlets, no. 16. In this address Sibley repeated his frequent assertion that but for the persistent and determined warfare by the principal Republican organ in the state (the *Minnesotian*) and other journals, he would have disposed of the Minnesota State Railroad Bonds in New York advantageously. In his testimony in the case of Selah Chamberlain *v.* the Southern Minnesota Railroad Company and the St. Paul and Sioux City Railroad Company and others, 50 (Five Million Loan Pamphlets, no. 20 — St. Paul, 1873), Sibley said that his failure to negotiate the bonds in New York in 1858 and 1859 was due to " the opposition of certain citizens of the State and of certain leading newspapers to the bonds; but for such opposition I am confident I should have succeeded in negotiating them, I think at 90 cents on the dollar." See also West, *Sibley,* 238.

Possibly in response to Sibley's exhortation, some of the churches at length took up the matter and made solemn declarations in favor of an honorable settlement of the bonds. On September 4, 1876, the Minnesota State Baptist Convention adopted a report of sixteen closely printed pages urging an honorable settlement of the state's suspended indebtedness. The report was probably written by Dr. George H. Keith. On October 14 of the same year the Congregational Conference of Minnesota adopted a similar resolution. The Presbytery of St. Paul had done the same on October 11. See *History of the Minnesota State Railroad Bonds; Recent Action of Some of the Religious Bodies of the State on the Question* (Five Million Loan Pamphlets, no. 24 — St. Paul, 1877).

which, notwithstanding the absorbing interest of that legislature in the "land-grab" measure for dividing the five hundred thousand acres of internal improvement lands among certain railroad companies, was hospitably received, amply discussed, and finally passed by both houses. The act as approved was prefaced by a preamble asserting that doubts prevailed as to whether the state railroad bonds were a "legal and valid indebtedness against the state" and that the purpose of the act was to determine that question and to adjust the existing claims. The governor was authorized to appoint three lawyers as commissioners with powers of referees in equity procedure. The first duty of the commissioners was to determine whether the bonds deposited were "a legal and equitable obligation against the state." Should they decide in the affirmative, they were thereupon to award the amount due each bondholder on the basis of the cost of the bonds to him. The act provided for the issue of new thirty-year bonds, with interest so "funded as a part of the principle" as to make the average rate of interest seven per cent, and appropriated all railroad taxes to the payment of such interest, any surplus thereof to form a sinking fund for the extinguishment of the principal. It may be surmised that some votes were cast for this law by members who, without any gift of prophecy, could foresee what fate would meet it at the polls. The Minnesota electors at a special election in the following May declared their unalterable resolution not to be taxed for the bonds.[72]

The legislature now had rest for about five years from the bond question. At the annual election of 1872 the people ratified an amendment to the constitution forbidding the appropriation, for any purpose, of the proceeds of sales of the five hundred thousand acres of internal improvement lands until after a majority of electors had voted in favor of any enactment therefor, thus reserving to themselves the privilege of deciding upon the destination of that grant.[73]

In the meantime the matter was taken into the courts. Early in 1873 Selah Chamberlain brought suit in the United States circuit court for the district of Minnesota against the St. Paul and Sioux

[72] House Journal, 1871, pp. 97, 200, 273, 308; Senate Journal, 168, 185, 208–210, 225, 226, 269; General Laws, 52–55. The act was rejected at the polls by a vote of 21,499 to 9,293. The manuscript official canvass of the special election is in Secretary of State's Archives, Abstract of Votes, in the custody of the Minnesota Historical Society. On the "land-grab" measure, which Governor Austin put to sleep by his famous veto, see ante, pp. 34–36.

[73] Constitution, article 4, section 32b; Anderson, History of the Constitution, 167, 218, 279. The amendment was ratified by a vote of 55,438 to 4,331.

City and the Southern Minnesota railroad companies, demanding a decree in equity that those corporations turn over to him all the unsold lands, pay over all moneys received by them for lands sold, and deliver to him all securities and contracts received for lands sold. His contention was that when the state foreclosed the trust deeds in 1860 she took the properties subject to all incumbrances and liabilities. As assets the lands were affected by liabilities.

After trial Justice Dillon dismissed the suit. The companies, he held, had received the lands from the state free and clear of all incumbrances. The state was not a surety for the companies, but was an original obligee. Chamberlain lost his suit, but the court vouchsafed him a sweet morsel of consolation in an *obiter dictum.* " That the bonds held by the plaintiff," said Judge Dillon, " are the legal obligations of the state, and binding upon it in law, honor, and justice, I have no doubt. . . . In the amendment to the constitution, the faith and credit of the state are pledged for the payment of the interest and the redemption of the principal of the bonds. They are signed by the Governor, and bear upon their face the seal of the State. They were issued to the plaintiff and others for grading and work actually done upon the roads, at the rate specified in the constitutional amendment. . . . Under these circumstances, if the state were suable in the courts, there can be no doubt that the bonds would be legally enforcible against it. Justice and honor alike require the state to recognize these bonds as binding upon it, and in the end, the court cannot doubt that the people of the state will so ordain. A State with such a future before it as the State of Minnesota, cannot afford to bear the odium of repudiation." [74]

---

[74] Judgment roll in the United States circuit court of 1875 for the district of Minnesota, chancery number 252, on file in the office of the clerk. The *obiter dictum* is quoted by Governor Pillsbury in his message of January 4, 1877, in *Executive Documents,* 1876, vol. 1, p. 29.

The essence of Justice Dillon's decision was as follows: " Upon the failure of the old companies, the state, in 1864, in order to secure the completion of the roads, created the present companies, and granted to them all the lands and franchises which had been granted to the old companies, ' free of all claims or liens,' and on the faith of this legislation the new companies have built and completed the lines of the road, the one at a cost of $5,000,000, the other at a cost of $3,000,000. The money to accomplish this was raised upon deeds of trust and mortgages yet outstanding made by the present companies to secure issues of bonds, preferred stock and land certificates! After all this is done . . . it would in my judgment, be inequitable, as against the present companies and their creditors, to hold that the plaintiff could subject to the payment of his bonds the land or other property which the defendant companies acquired from the state by the legislation of 1864."

Believing, doubtless, that he could fare no worse in the court above, Chamberlain appealed his suit to the Supreme Court of the United States, which in October, 1875, affirmed the decree of the court below and followed its example in administering like words of comfort. " The bonds issued," said Justice Stephen J. Field for the court, " are legal obligations. The State is bound by every consideration of honor and good faith to pay them. Were she amenable to the tribunals of the country as private individuals are, no court of justice would withhold its judgment against her in an action for their enforcement." [75] It is believed that Chamberlain's capable attorneys got all they really hoped for in their suit. These casual remarks of the court were not decisions. The state was no party to the suit and was not heard. But these *obiter dicta* had their effect. The state of Minnesota was branded by the supreme judicial authority of the nation as a repudiator and a defaulter. She had not done what honor and justice alike required her to do. The effect upon the public men of the state was notable. Without regard to party, they rapidly drifted to the position that Minnesota could not afford to wear that brand of infamy. The mass of the people, however, still clung doggedly to their ancient grudge against the conspirators, who, they believed, had deceived and defrauded them.

Governor Davis' term of office ended with the close of the year 1875, a few weeks after the publication of these *dicta* of the courts. In his final message to the legislature, delivered on January 7, 1876, after sketching with clearness the history of the bonds, he recommended the creation of a board of commissioners to hear and determine the claims of the bondholders and he expressed the belief that the people would stand by the commission's awards. " No man and no nation," he said, " ought to be the judge in its own cause." The United States and Great Britain had composed their differences over the Alabama claims by submitting them to the jurisdiction of a court and the example of these nations was worthy of imitation by Minnesota.

According to Minnesota custom, Governor Pillsbury delivered his inaugural address on the same occasion, and the burden of it was the extinguishment of the state railroad bonds. The bonds were issued deliberately in due form in obedience to a mandate of the people. The state had acquired the franchises and assets of the

[75] Chamberlain *v.* St. Paul and Sioux City Railroad Company and others, 92 *United States,* 299–307.

defaulting companies and had them under her control. She was now able to pay and "there ought to be no further postponement of a simple act of justice . . . demanded by . . . expediency and honor." His practical suggestion was to exchange new bonds for the old ones and to devote the proceeds from the sales of the internal improvement lands, which fortunately — " may I not say providentially," he added — had come into the possession of the state, to form a sinking fund for the ultimate liquidation of the new obligations. He made no suggestion that a compromise be made or that the bonds be scaled down.

The legislators who listened to these exhortations were in no haste to take any definite action. They evidently did not feel sure that Providence had invited them to dispose of the lands in this particular manner. A special committee of five senators was appointed to inquire into the validity of the bonds. On February 29 — the session was to close on March 3 — the committee submitted a sarcastic report in which it was stated that the Five Million Loan bill violated three provisions of the original constitution and that the bond issue was therefore illegal. It also reported on a Senate bill providing that the question of validity be referred, by means of a made-up case, to the state supreme court or the United States circuit court and that neither court should enforce any decree or judgment that it might render. Upon the recommendation of the committee the Senate gave the proposition an indefinite postponement. The special committee could find nothing to commend in a joint resolution, introduced in the Senate, to refer the whole matter to a committee of gentlemen from different parts of the state for their opinion. This, the committee said, " would simply amount to a means of agitation of the subject at the expense of the State." The Senate, however, thought better of the plan and adopted the resolution late on March 2 by a vote of 22 to 16. At that hour the House could take no action had it been disposed to do so. A resolution that had been proposed in the House on January 12 for a committee of seven to draw up a bill providing for a committee of five for the adjustment and settlement of the bonds " went over " and never reached general orders. The House seems to have been equally indifferent to a carefully studied report from its standing committee on ways and means, to which had been referred the paragraphs of Davis' final message and Pillsbury's inaugural address relating to the state railroad bonds. The committee referred to the experience of Indiana and a number of other states where equitable adjustments had been made with railroad bondholders and the states had not suffered from " the bane of repudiation." It advised against submission to any disinterested commission or tribunal. It would have the legislature transact directly with the bondholders acting in concert and then submit their agreement to the people, who would know exactly on what they were voting. The committee was confident that an equitable settlement could be made. So ended Governor Pillsbury's maiden effort at bond redemption.[76]

In his message to the legislature of 1877 Governor Pillsbury returned to the charge with vigor. Under the heading " Dishonored Bonds " he recapitulated the arguments, all now familiar, for the settlement of the old bonds. The question, he said, was reduced to the simple one of Minnesota's willingness to pay an honest debt. On February 14, 1877, two proposals of Selah Chamberlain, addressed to the chairman of the joint committee on state railroad bonds, were presented to the Senate. In the first, which was dated January 22, Chamberlain recited the history of his claim, quoted the opinions of judges upon its validity, and offered to scale it down. He figured the nominal value of each of his bonds on June 1 of that year to be $3,110.85 and offered to accept for each the sum of $1,808.77 in new six-per-cent, thirty-year bonds. In the second proposal, dated February 10, Chamberlain expressed surprise and regret that his offer of January 22 had not met with the favor of all members of the committee and offered to modify it. He would accept for each seven-per-cent bond surrendered $1,550 in new six-per-cent bonds. Before the close of the month a bill practically agreeing to this proposition was passed by a Senate vote almost unanimous and by a House majority of two-thirds. A penultimate section of the act provided that no act should be done by the commissioners — the governor, the state auditor, and the attorney-general — under the provisions of the act, unless the electors of the state voting at a special election on June 12, 1877, should adopt an amendment to the state constitution authorizing the appropriation of the proceeds of the five hundred thousand acres of internal improvement lands to the payment of the interest or principal, or both, of the proposed new bonds. At the election thus appointed the proposed amendment went the way of all previous measures proposed

[76] Davis' message, in *Executive Documents*, 1875, vol. 1, pp. 36–42; Pillsbury's message, in the same volume, 17–20; *Senate Journal*, 1876, pp. 158, 360, 371, 400, 431; appendix, 37–43; *House Journal*, 30, 452; appendix, 3–9.

for the redemption of what were called and believed to be the
" swindling bonds." [77]

The legislature of 1878 listened patiently to Governor Pillsbury's
paragraphs on "Dishonored Bonds." He deeply deplored the
rejection of the proposition of the bondholders of the previous year
and exhorted the members to further effort. Repudiation, he assured
them, was far more damaging to the state than the grasshoppers.
An ingenious scheme for exchanging lands for bonds, differing
somewhat from that of 1870, was suggested in a memorial from
Selah Chamberlain to the legislature and was recommended by the
Senate public lands committee. A bill was framed accordingly and
was introduced. It provided that the commissioner of the state land
office — the auditor of state ex officio — on and after the first Monday in July, 1879, should be ready to exchange lands for bonds at
a rate which would cause the whole amount of the five hundred
thousand acres of internal improvement lands to cancel the whole
amount of the bonds, including coupons, and any outstanding claims.
Holders who should deposit their bonds on or before the date
named should have equal chances for a choice of land for each
bond. The bill was passed, subject to approval of the electors by
vote at the coming election in November, 1878. The obdurate
electors did not approve.[78]

In his message of 1879 Governor Pillsbury could only express
his deep regret at the unreadiness of the people to pay an honest
debt; he made no definite proposition. There was no session in
1880, the act for biennial sessions having gone into effect. The
year 1881 was the last of Pillsbury's third term and he resolved
to signalize it with a final effort to rouse the people and their representatives to their duty. Again in his message to the legislature of

---

[77] *Executive Documents*, 1876, vol. 1, pp. 28–32; *Senate Journal*, 1877, pp.
230–233, 362; *House Journal*, 472; *General Laws*, 25, 183–186; Sewall to the
author, June 12, 1905, Folwell Papers. The vote in the House was 70 to 34;
that in the Senate, 34 to 5. In the *Pioneer Press*, April 29, 1877, is a broadside insert giving the legislative history of the bonds. See also the editorial in
the same paper, April 17. The bill proposing the amendment to the constitution for the appropriation of the proceeds of the internal improvement lands
was passed in the Senate by a vote of 37 to 3 and in the House by a vote of
71 to 14. It was rejected at the polls by a vote of 59,176 to 17,324. Report
of the secretary of state, in *Executive Documents*, 1877, vol. 1, p. 97; Anderson, *History of the Constitution*, 219, 280.

[78] Pillsbury's message in *Executive Documents*, 1877, vol. 1, p. 39; *Senate
Journal*, 1878, pp. 97, 150, 237; *House Journal*, 312, 336, 417, 480; *General
Laws*, 143–145.

that year, under the caption " Dishonored Bonds," he marshaled all the considerations which should impel them to pay their honest debt. He implored the legislative body to apply itself to the adjustment of the bonds as its solemn duty and suggested that in the preservation of the half million acres of land, " which cost us nothing," it seemed as if Fortune — he did not say " Providence " this time — herself would lure the state from dishonor. The governor closed his message with the words, " In the name of law, justice and honor, as the last public utterance I may make to you, I implore the people of Minnesota, and you, gentlemen, their honorable representatives, to seize this last opportunity before it is too late, to wipe this only blot from the fair name of our beloved State." The executive appeal had its effect upon the houses, which presently got to work upon the necessary bills.[79]

The principal act, passed by a bare majority in the Senate and by slightly more than a three-fifths vote in the House and approved on March 2, 1881, is a curiosity in legislation. It started out with a preamble stating that there were controverted claims outstanding against the state which deserved fair treatment and settlement, and that claimants, among them Selah Chamberlain, had submitted propositions for adjustment, the substance of which was embraced in the act. The judges of the Minnesota supreme court were constituted a " tribunal," the original duty of which was to decide whether the legislature had power to adjust and pay the bonds without the referendum provided for in the repudiating constitutional amendment of 1860. If any judge of the supreme court should be disqualified, or should decline, the governor was authorized to appoint in his place one of the district judges of the state. In the event that the tribunal should decide against the validity of the amendment of 1860, the state auditor should proceed to exchange new bonds, styled " Minnesota Railroad Adjustment Bonds," for those outstanding, at fifty per cent of the amount due on the latter, and each of the bondholders was to execute a proper release. If the decision should be that the question of paying the old bonds must be submitted to the people, then the act was to be so submitted at the next general election. If the act should be adopted by a majority of electors, then a similar exchange of new for old bonds was to be made.[80]

---

[79] *Executive Documents*, 1878, vol. 1, p. 20; 1879–80, pp. 26–30.

[80] *Senate Journal*, 1881, pp. 190, 321, 446–449; *House Journal*, 411, 439, 522, 526; *General Laws*, 117–123.

Not one of the five judges of the supreme court was willing to serve on this amphibious tribunal. It was the twenty-sixth day of July, 1881, when five district judges, supposed to be individually in favor of denying the validity of the referendum, met at the Capitol to organize as a tribunal. The bondholders appeared by counsel and Attorney-General William J. Hahn appeared for the state. Hahn at once filed an objection against the competency of the tribunal. At the same moment the members were served with an order from the state supreme court to show cause why a writ of prohibition should not issue. This order had been made at the instance of a distinguished attorney, David Secombe of Minneapolis, who alleged that the act of the legislature pretending to constitute such a tribunal was unconstitutional. The attorney-general was allowed to control the procedure and to amend the petition for the writ by adding an allegation that the act was repugnant to the constitutional amendment of 1860 forbidding payment of the bonds until after an affirmative vote of the people. The court in its opinion, written by Chief Justice James Gilfillan, acknowledged " the signal assistance " of counsel on both sides, declaring that " it has rarely been the good fortune of any court to have a cause before it so ably and exhaustively presented by counsel as this has been."

This is perhaps the most celebrated of all cases that have up to this time come before the court and probably will long remain so. It is not difficult for the careful reader to get at the meat of the decision. The act of 1881, it was held, was not unconstitutional because it was in conflict with the repudiating amendment of 1860, for that itself was void. When the state contracted with the bond-buyers in 1858, the power and duty to provide for any obligation incurred was vested in and imposed upon the legislature. By depriving the legislature of this power the repudiating amendment of 1860 impaired the obligation of the bonds, which was repugnant to the clause in the Constitution of the United States declaring that no state shall pass a law impairing the obligation of contracts. This conclusion, seriously questioned by able lawyers, was most welcome to all who desired the payment of the old bonds without appeal to popular vote. The court, taking up the contention that the act in issue was unconstitutional because it delegated legislative power to the tribunal created by it, promptly decided in the affirmative, and issued the writ of prohibition.[81]

[81] Report of the attorney-general, in *Executive Documents,* 1882, pp. 289–292; State of Minnesota *ex rel.* William J. Hahn, attorney-general, *v.* Austin

The roadway was now clear for legislative action on the bonds without referendum. Believing that the legislature would be in the right frame of mind, Governor Pillsbury, by a proclamation dated September 19, 1881, called the houses to meet in extra session on October 11. On the second day of the session the governor addressed them in joint meeting. " In my judgment," he said, " no subject of superior importance has ever challenged the attention of a legislative body." It was his personal preference that the old bonds should be redeemed in full; no other course was consistent with honor and integrity. But, since the bondholders had of their own motion proposed an adjustment upon more favorable terms, he would acquiesce. The governor was somewhat less impassioned than he had been in his message at the opening of the late regular session, but in closing he entreated the legislators " to perform a simple act of justice which shall forever put at rest the haunting spectre of repudiation." [82]

A redemption bill was introduced into the Senate the next day. Its advocates were quite confident that it would pass in the Senate but so great was their apprehension that the Minnesota electors, with the echo of " swindling bonds " still vibrating in the atmosphere, might repudiate some of them at coming elections that they thought it wise to embody a "sweetener" in the shape of the following preamble, calculated to reconcile the obstinate citizens:

Whereas, There has for a long time existed, and still remains outstanding, certain controverted claims against the State commonly known as the Minnesota State railroad bonds, and certain other claims referred to in this act, the validity of all which claims has ever been and still is disputed by the State.

And whereas, certain holders of such disputed claims have recently made propositions for the compromise and settlement of the said claims held by them, which propositions are now pending, and the substance of which propositions is embraced within the provisions hereinafter contained.

And whereas, it is considered to be desirable for the best interests of the State and of all the people thereof, that all such controverted claims, if possible, should be compromised, settled and extinguished.

H. Young and others, 29 *Minnesota*, 474–554. Hahn in his report praises the Honorable Thomas Wilson, whom he called to assist in the case. See Governor's Archives, Records, F: 534, 617, 639, for the refusal of the judges of the supreme court to serve on the tribunal and for the appointment of the district judges. The *Saint Paul Dispatch*, February 6, 1877, gives a remarkably able argument of Cushman K. Davis on the invalidity of the repudiation amendment of 1860.

[82] John S. Pillsbury, *Message*, October 12, 1881; *Pioneer Press*, October 13, 1881, p. 5. Pillsbury's proclamation is in the *Pioneer Press*, September 20, 1881, p. 6.

There was vigorous opposition but the bill easily passed through the ordinary stages and on October 26 it was agreed to by a vote of 30 to 10.[83]

Contemporary with the Senate bill was one introduced into the House by General John B. Sanborn, providing for an investigation by any district court of claims against the state filed with its clerk, the court to have power to pass upon their validity and, in the cases of those found valid, to ascertain and determine the amounts payable to the successful claimants. The bill made no progress and the Senate bill, when it appeared, was substituted for it. A proposition more seriously entertained was a resolution submitted by Judge Thomas Wilson, the man who, in 1858, was the lone voter in Winona against the bond amendment. His four-fingered commonplace preamble may be passed over. The first part of the resolution declared that the state stood ready and willing to pay in full every dollar of principal and interest which was equitably owed, but not one dollar more. A second paragraph proposed a joint committee of the houses to ascertain and report whether Chamberlain was not so closely connected with the railroad companies as to render him personally liable for the payment of the state

[83] *Senate Journal*, 1881, extra session, 10, 21–23, 43–45, 51. The Senate proceedings may be found in the *Pioneer Press*, October 14, 20–22, 25–27, November 4, 1881. Senator John B. Gilfillan insisted that the preamble should show that the state — not merely many people — had never recognized the validity of the bonds. In an interview with him on December 10, 1901, he gave to the author the following account, in substance, of the production of the redemption bill of the extra session of 1881: The sentiment of the legislature was not favorable to an adjustment on the line of the act of March 2, 1881, and there was a minority unfavorable to any adjustment. At the close of one of the first morning sessions Senator Gilfillan chanced to meet Gordon E. Cole, of counsel for Chamberlain and others, who inquired about the outlook. The reply was that it was not bright for the lawyer's clients. " Mr. Cole," said the senator, " you will fail if you follow the line of the act of March 2, which proposed that the bondholders were to take fifty per cent of such claims as might be ' allowed ' by a tribunal. The state would be put in the position of paying but half of a judgment recorded against her. I should oppose any such plan myself. You are an experienced lawyer; bring me a draft of a bill with a preamble setting forth that there are outstanding claims against the state of large amounts which deserve consideration and that it is for the interest of the state to have them equitably adjusted. Provide for an administrative commission to decide on the authenticity of the claims and calculate the face amounts. *Accept the proposition of the bondholders* to take fifty per cent of the nominal amounts and authorize the issue of new bonds for payment." Cole was dubious, but said that he would consult with his clients. Late in the afternoon — probably October 13 — he brought a draft of a bill to Senator Gilfillan, who examined it, gave it his approval, and handed it to Senator Charles A. Pillsbury, who immediately introduced it.

bonds and what was the cost and value of the work done by him. In the course of an all-day debate, Judge Wilson said that " the matter . . . was conceived in iniquity and sin " and that he could prove that Chamberlain never paid anywhere near fifty per cent on the dollar for his bonds. He was willing to pay one hundred per cent of all value proved, but he would not vote to pay two dollars for one as Chamberlain and his hirelings — he spoke " advisedly " — were asking. The House gave the Wilson resolutions an indefinite postponement by a vote of 56 to 35, which assured the passage of the Senate bill. Judge Wilson himself immediately moved the adoption of the committee report recommending the passage. The bill, with amendments, was passed by a vote of 77 to 29. The Senate concurred on November 3 and Governor Pillsbury approved the act the next day.[84]

---

[84] *House Journal*, 1881, extra session, 10, 32, 35, 50, 99, 130–132; *Senate Journal*, 113, 125. For the House proceedings, see the *Pioneer Press*, October 14, 19–22, 27, November 3, 1881.

A tradition that a large sum of money was used in securing the passage of the redemption bill of 1881 is too persistent and too widely known to be passed over in silence. No documentary evidence has been found, but the author feels justified in reporting statements made to him by contemporary persons likely to be well informed, though perhaps not free from bias. The Honorable Thomas Wilson, a member of the House in 1881, said the legislature of that year was notorious for corruption and that there was no doubt whatever that much money was used to secure the passage of the redemption act. " Bought up like sheep," was his strong expression in referring to some of the legislators. The Honorable John B. Gilfillan, a member of the Senate, said that expenditures were large, nobody would ever know how large or to what persons money was paid; but " ———— feathered his nest." The Honorable Henry G. Hicks, a member of the House, had no evidence, but he had felt at the time that money was being used in considerable amounts. He heard one member, while in a state of intoxication, use language to the effect that money was circulating. It was Judge Hicks's opinion, however, that the money remained in the hands of a few men, who secured votes by ordinary means. Ex-Governor William R. Marshall said to the author about the time, that " the bondholders got about the face of their bonds," without interest. The Honorable Curtis H. Pettit was of the opinion that they did not get more than the face of their bonds. C. A. Gilman said that Marshall's estimate was possibly correct. He said also that " men called ' honest ' got their share." These interviews are recorded in the author's notebooks, 3: 99, 105, 107, 110, 112, 125, 128, 135; 5: 77; 6: 48; 7: 113; 9: 122. Castle, in *Minnesota Historical Collections*, 15: 578, makes allegations of disgraceful methods of securing votes, of shameless bargaining and sale, and of reaping rich harvests from fields of corruption. Selah Chamberlain, he said, " secured his unearned millions." A letter from the author to J. M. Gilman, August 20, 1906, in the Folwell Papers, gives various estimates of the amount of money used.

Assuming, as it seems justifiable to do, that a large amount of money was expended in securing the majorities in the state Senate and House of 1881 for the passage of the redemption bill, it may also be justifiable to remark

The act was entitled " An act providing for the adjustment of certain alleged claims against the state," as if it were to be understood that the propositions of compromise voluntarily made by the bondholders did not rise to the dignity of claims pure and simple. Briefly, it provided for the delivery to the bondholders of new bonds at fifty per cent of the par value of the old bonds and coupons. The new bonds, which were to be called " Minnesota State Railroad Adjustment Bonds," were to be dated July 1, 1881, and made payable after ten years and not more than thirty years from their date, with interest at a rate not exceeding five per cent. A companion bill devoting the proceeds of sales of the " providentially " reserved internal improvement lands to the liquidation of new bonds, subject to referendum, met with but slight opposition. When voted upon at the general election in November, 1882, this act was ratified by a vote of more than two-thirds of the electors voting, which shows a willingness to divert the gift of internal improvement lands from its original purpose, rather than accept the alternative of taxation.[85]

The passage of the two bills mentioned did not, however, conclude the long struggle over the bonds. There were citizens then, as now, who believed that the bonds, no matter with what regularity and solemnity they had been issued under judicial sanction, had never created a valid obligation against the state in equity and ought never to have been recognized nor adjusted. One of these, David A. Secombe, sued out an injunction from a court commissioner to restrain the governor from signing the new bonds, to which the latter gave no heed.[86] The same plaintiff then played a last

that the use of such means to " wipe out this only blot from the fair name of our beloved State " was the most disreputable of all events in the shameful history of the Minnesota State Railroad Bonds of 1858. Some college debating club might divide on the question whether it was an honorable thing for Minnesota to devote to the payment of such a debt the internal improvement lands granted by Congress to an infant state for the opening and improvement of roads and waterways. Unpublished items of interest may be found in the author's notebooks, 3: 73, 81, 91, 135; 4: 135; 5: 25, 58, 77, 102; 6: 48, 78, 109; 7: 113; 9: 33, and in Temple to the author, March 26, 1907, in the Folwell Papers.

[85] *General Laws*, 1881, extra session, 13–17, 71–73; *Pioneer Press*, January 4, 1883. The vote at the general election on the act providing for the disposition of the proceeds of the internal improvement lands was: for, 82,435; against, 24,526.

[86] Report of the attorney-general, in *Executive Documents*, 1882, vol. 1, p. 291. There is a tradition that Governor Pillsbury was obliged to carry the new bonds to his home for signature to escape being served with a mandamus or injunction. The author saw him signing the bonds but understood

card by moving in the Hennepin County district court to enjoin the state treasurer from paying interest on the new bonds. The ground of the motion was that the constitutional amendment of 1858, purporting to authorize the original issue, was void because it had not been adopted by the people according to the provisions of the state constitution regarding amendments. The pretended amendment was proposed, voted upon, and proclaimed as adopted before the admission of Minnesota to the Union and while such admission was pending in Congress. The Territory of Minnesota, still existing under the organic act, could not, it was contended, amend a state constitution, which had not been accepted and ratified by Congress. Justice Mitchell for the court made short work of resolving this puzzle. After citing the peculiar language of the Minnesota enabling act authorizing the people " to form for themselves a constitution and state government " and " to come into the Union," the court observed that it was the accepted fact at the time that Minnesota became a state when she ratified her constitution in October, 1857, and that the legislature then elected was a state legislature. The court, however, did not care for any theory of the matter. The government organized in December, 1857, was in fact a state government, by the consent and understanding of the people, and technical inquiries regarding irregularities were not under the circumstances to be tolerated. Finally, it was held, all irregularities had been healed by the act of admission and by state action after admission in issuing the bonds. This same decision vindicated the legitimacy, which had sometimes been questioned, of the laws — some ninety in number — passed by the legislature of 1857–58 at its first session.[87]

Within a year from the passage of the adjustment act, all but forty-three of the old bonds had been surrendered, of which number fifteen had long been in the treasury. The amount of the new bonds issued was $4,253,000. A large block of these was purchased for the school and university funds and the cash was paid to claimants. Selah Chamberlain took out $1,992,053.70 for 1,070 bonds, three others took out $715,172.62 for 403 bonds, and the remainder was distributed to 174 parties. On January 16, 1882, 2,152 of the old

that the governor was merely hastening the task so that Governor Hubbard, who was waiting, might be sworn in. Smalley, *Republican Party*, 206.

[87] David A. Secombe *v.* Charles Kittelson, Treasurer, 29 *Minnesota*, 555–561. The Honorable Thomas Wilson, in a conversation with the author on December 22, 1906, stated that the Honorable William Mitchell, associate justice of the supreme court at the time, had told him with emphasis that he had become convinced that the decision in the case of the state against Young was erroneous. 29 *Minnesota*, 474–554.

Minnesota State Railroad Bonds were burned in the state Capitol in the presence of the governor, the state auditor, and the state treasurer.[88] During the twenty-three years between the issue and the adjustment of the state railroad bonds few citizens of Minnesota had lost sleep because of guilty consciences and the financial credit of the state had not been below that of any of her neighbors. She had had no difficulty in obtaining needed loans at ordinary rates.

10. THE CASE OF FARLEY V. HILL [89]

The reader will recall upon suggestion that the Minnesota and Pacific Railroad Company was one of the four land grant companies which in 1857 shared the congressional grants of the year to Minnesota Territory and that this company was fully reinstated in its forfeited franchises and properties in 1861. In the year following it was given the new name of "The Saint Paul and Pacific Railroad Company." In 1864, under a special act of the Minnesota legislature, a separate interest was carved out of this corporation, with power to issue special and preferred stock, which two years later was given by law the name of "The First Division of the Saint Paul and Pacific Railroad Company." The purpose of this scheme was to hasten the construction of the portions of the system lying in the populated parts of the state and to secure the appertaining land grant, leaving the primary company to hold its franchise and its right to lands to be acquired later by road building in what was then the northern wilderness. The control of this secondary company immediately passed into the hands of Edward H. Litchfield, a New York capitalist, who agreed to finance the building of the so-called "main line" from St. Anthony to Breckenridge and of a branch to St. Cloud.[90]

[88] See the report of the state auditor, in *Executive Documents,* 1882, vol. I, pp. 344, 353, for the total amount of the new bonds; 345, for a table of the original issues, the amount of bonds of each issue, the amounts due on coupons, and the value of bonds with "coupons off"; 347–353, for a table giving the names of the holders of redeemed bonds, the number of bonds held by each, deductions on account of claims for labor, material, or supplies, and the amount paid to each holder; 354–366, for the report of the commissioners — Pillsbury, Whitcomb, and Hahn; and 356–366, for the adjustment of claims. The report of the state auditor, in *Executive Documents,* 1883–84, vol. 4, p. 54, gives 2,246 as the number of old bonds redeemed to date (October 20, 1884), with the names of the companies to which they had been issued, the names of the holders, and the amounts paid on account of the bonds.

[89] See *ante,* p. 142, n. 33.

[90] See *ante,* 2: 37, 42, 329; *Special Laws,* 1864, pp. 174–177; 1866, pp. 11–13; and *General Laws,* 1864, p. 104. These laws provided for the issue

The financing of this construction was audacious. It was not the fashion of the day for stockholders to put much real money into western railroads. As for land grant roads, there were money owners or money gatherers who would buy seven-per-cent bonds at a satisfactory discount, secured by mortgages on the land grants and other effects of the roads. In his annual report for 1873 Alonzo J. Edgerton, the state railroad commissioner, referring to Minnesota railroads in general, spoke of " bonds . . . discounted at ruinous rates." In some instances " probably not over 40 per cent. has gone into the construction or equipment of the road. . . . In only a very few companies does capital stock represent any money paid into the company. . . . The complaint against watering stock hardly applies to railroads in this State from the fact that, in most instances, stock was . . . hardly susceptible of dilution." The " First Division Company " was no exception. Through influences not revealed, the earliest loan was placed in Holland; and the interest, which was seven per cent — enormous in the eyes of people accustomed to half that rate — being at first regularly paid, a credit was established in that country, which was later heavily drawn upon. What the rates of discount conceded to the Dutch bankers were is not well known, but it is known that the proceeds of the bond sales were not applied to construction and equipment with economy. When the Brainerd branch, 76 miles long, was completed in 1866, bonds to the amount of $4,480,000 had been issued, a sum sufficient to build and equip nearly 240 miles of railroad at $20,000 per mile, a reasonable cost for prairie roads at that time. When the main line from St. Anthony to Breckenridge, 207 miles, was completed in 1871, four batches of mortgage bonds aggregating $13,500,000, over $65,000 to the mile, had been marketed for the construction and equipment of that line.[91]

of " special stock," the holders of which should exercise all the powers of the parent company over a certain portion of the road and the appertaining land grant; they provided also that holders of bonds issued by the special stockholders might vote for the election of directors in meetings that might be held in London or in any foreign country.

[91] Railroad Commissioner, *Reports*, 1871, pp. 42, 47; 1872, pp. 147, 158; 1873, p. lxi. In the last report the commissioner remarked that in some cases the original grantee of the lands sold the roads for the cost of construction and held the lands. Estimates of the normal cost per mile of the St. Paul and Pacific lines compared with the costs reported by the company are given on page lxxii of this report. For the main line the estimated cost was $16,700 per mile and the cost as reported by the company was $68,100. For the branch line the estimated cost was $17,400 and that reported by the company was $61,500.

Meantime the primary corporation retained its franchise and its right to lands when acquired by the construction of the remaining miles of railroad; but it had neither cash nor credit. The First Division Company had not yet exhausted its credit in Holland.[92] Both were anxious to complete construction and equipment and come into possession of the land grants. The reader will before this time have comprehended that with all the " land grant railroads " the congressional and state land grants were the grand prizes and that the favored corporations were willing to pay or promise any rate of interest on borrowed capital to gain early possession of them. Railroad building was a secondary interest. To secure the advantage of the continuing power of the First Division Company to borrow, the primary corporation executed on April 1, 1871, a lease for ninety-nine years to the First Division of all its properties, actual and prospective. This party of the second part undertook to raise a loan of fifteen million dollars and with the proceeds to build and equip the remaining portions of the system. In anticipation of this scheme the passage of an act of Congress had been secured authorizing a change in the location of the principal line. In place of the original route up the Mississippi to Crow Wing and thence northwestward to St. Vincent at the crossing of the Canadian boundary and the Red River of the North, the new line departed from the river at St. Cloud and ran west and northwest by way of Alexandria, Fergus Falls, and Crookston to the same destination. Provision was made that there should be no material change in the aggregate land grant. The First Division Company accordingly undertook (1) to build and equip this line, about three hundred miles long, and (2) to complete an unfinished line from St. Cloud to Brainerd a few miles beyond Crow Wing, some sixty miles in length. These lines were called the St. Vincent and the

[92] William G. Moorhead, a director of the Northern Pacific, found the credit of the First Division Company high in Amsterdam in 1871. Jesse P. Farley v. James J. Hill, the St. Paul Trust Company as Executor of the Last Will of Norman W. Kittson, and the St. Paul, Minneapolis, and Manitoba Railway Company, *Record, Defendants' Exhibits,* 262. This is one of several printed " paper books " prepared for the submission of the case on appeal from the United States circuit court for the district of Minnesota to the United States Supreme Court. They include *Plaintiff's Evidence* (858 pages); *Defendants' Testimony* (1,093 pages); *Pleadings and Argument for Defendants* (501 pages) ; and *Defendants' Exhibits* (484 pages). For convenience, citations will be made from these volumes instead of from the manuscript judgment roll, case 131 C, on file in the office of the clerk of the United States circuit court in St. Paul.

Brainerd extensions, respectively, in the abundant literature of the time.[93]

The First Division Company had already arranged for the negotiation of the " extension bonds " with the firm of Lippmann, Rosenthal, and Company of Amsterdam, which was ready to furnish the money upon delivery of the documents duly executed. For a reason that will appear later, the president of the First Division Company delayed such delivery from April to October and by that time market conditions had so changed that only 10,700 bonds were sold, at a discount of over twenty-five per cent. The proceeds amounted to about eight million dollars and the Amsterdam firm advanced nine hundred thousand dollars on the 4,270 bonds left on its hands. With this cash on hand the First Division directorate made contracts with William G. Moorhead of the firm of Jay Cooke and Company, who sublet to De Graff and Company, experienced railroad builders, for the construction of the tracks of both extension lines. Iron was bought and ties, bridge material, spikes, and other supplies were contracted for, to be delivered along the right of way. The summer of 1872 was one of great activity. Cheering reports came in of work begun and progressing and all Minnesota looked for the completion of the line to St. Vincent before snowfall. The contractors' monthly estimates were paid until the end of June but there was no cash on hand to meet the July payment; encouraged by promises, the contractors kept at work, however, until October, when notice was given them to suspend work. They then discharged their crews and housed their tools and implements. Not the least humiliating fact was that the company still owed the contractors more than half a million dollars.[94]

All Minnesota was, of course, curious to learn what there might be to show for the nine millions of money which had come and gone. A tardy inventory showed 143½ miles of rails laid on completed track: 4½ miles on the Brainerd extension, and on the St. Vincent extension 139 miles in two detached portions — 35 miles from St. Cloud to Melrose in Stearns County and 104 miles from a point 12 miles south of Glyndon in Clay County, where the village

[93] United States, *Statutes at Large*, 16: 588. The act was approved on March 3, 1871. The text of the lease, dated April 1, 1871, is in Railroad Commissioner, *Reports*, 1873, p. 213. For projects not consummated, see *Special Laws*, 1869, p. 246; 1870, p. 329.

[94] *Saint Paul Pioneer*, August 3, 1872; *Saint Paul Press*, July 16, August 14, October 6, 1872; *St. Cloud Journal*, August 1, 1872; *Defendants' Exhibits*, 90, 97, 284–286; *Plaintiff's Evidence*, 295. There were $664,497.92 due the contractor.

of Barnesville later grew up, to another point 92 miles north of
Glyndon. Three-fourths of the remaining mileage had been graded
and made ready for ties. The detached fractions of road built were
useless, because they were unprovided with rolling stock. There
was general disappointment and disgust. As Governor Austin stated
in one of his messages, the proceeds of the fifteen-million-dollar
loan, some nine million dollars, "if honestly and judiciously applied," should have completed and equipped both extensions.[95]

A noteworthy episode in the history of the St. Paul and Pacific
will explain the situation to some extent. The Northern Pacific
Railroad Company, organized under an act of Congress in 1864,
was authorized by another act in 1870 to place mortgages on its
land grant of from twenty to forty sections per mile from Lake
Superior to the Pacific Ocean. Thereupon Jay Cooke, the Philadelphia banker who had won national fame by financing great issues
of United States securities in the Civil War period, threw himself
and his associates into the enterprise. It required no revelation to
inform the Northern Pacific directorate that the control of the
St. Paul and Pacific system would add some excellent feeders to
its main line and some five million acres of land to its already
immense grant. In 1870 and an earlier year the Northern Pacific
Company bought substantially all the stock of the two St. Paul and
Pacific companies for considerations which now seem ridiculously
trifling; but the stock really had no value except for inchoate title
to the land grant. Although the Northern Pacific now came into
absolute control of the two St. Paul and Pacific companies, no dis-
solutions were sought but the ghosts of the two were allowed to
walk the earth, to go through the motions of ownership, and to hold
on to the land grants. The ninety-nine year lease was, of course, a
Northern Pacific scheme and the fifteen-million-dollar Dutch loan
was obtained, no doubt, because of the vast reflected credit of that
corporation at the time. The relocation of the St. Vincent extension, the construction of the isolated hundred miles in the Red River
Valley pointing toward Canada, and the neglect to build the Brainerd extension must be laid at the door of the Northern Pacific
management. How far the directorates of all three companies con-
spired to encourage waste and extravagance and to fool away the
bulk of the nine millions brought from Holland cannot now be

---

[95] *Defendants' Exhibits*, 30, 100; Railroad Commissioner, *Reports*, 1872, p.
41; Austin's message, January 9, 1874, in *Executive Documents*, 1873, vol. 1,
p. 12.

estimated, nor can their relative responsibilities be apportioned. All were under a vast cloud of disgrace.[96]

On May 1 and June 1, 1873, the St. Paul and Pacific Railroad Company defaulted on the payments of interest due on four different issues of bonds antedating the lease of 1871 and amounting to thirteen million dollars. The First Division Company had squandered the proceeds of the loan of 1871, except twenty per cent reserved in Amsterdam for the redemption of interest coupons as they should fall due, leaving the extension lines of railroad but half built. The time limit fixed by Congress for the completion of the roads and the acquisition of the land grants was December 3, 1873. The Northern Pacific, caught in the terrible financial blizzard of that year and started on the road to bankruptcy, could give no support to its adopted Minnesota bantlings.

The Dutch bondholders, some six hundred in number, were naturally alarmed. On June 20 a body of them held a meeting in Amsterdam and agreed " to act jointly . . . for each of the said loans separately," through a committee of their number. This committee, soon called in America " the Dutch committee," was authorized to employ qualified agents in New York or elsewhere with power to institute suits at law and to take any and every expedient step for the protection of the interests of the bondholders. The committee immediately employed John S. Kennedy and Company of New York as its agents and issued a full power of attorney to Kennedy. The agents without delay, on July 9, filed a bill in equity in the United States circuit court against the two companies, alleging default of payments, misuse of funds, and virtual insolvency and asked for the appointment of receivers for both companies. On August 1 Judge John F. Dillon appointed a receiver for the primary company but refused to appoint one for the First Division Company. The appointee, suggested by the New York agents, was Jesse P. Farley of Dubuque, Iowa, who for twenty years had been employed as a superintendent, manager, or president of railroads. By the same order the court allowed the receiver to borrow five million dollars on debentures bearing ten per cent interest, the principal and interest to be payable in gold; they were not to be sold for less than par in United States currency and were to be a prior lien to any and all other claims and liens on the property

---

[96] *Defendants' Exhibits*, 31–37, 94–96; United States, *Statutes at Large*, 13: 365–372; 16: 378; Eugene V. Smalley, *History of the Northern Pacific Railroad*, 163, 170, 185, 296 (New York, 1883).

whatsoever. The proceeds of the loan, which the Dutch bond-holders were expected to absorb, were to be expended in completing the extension lines and equipping them for operation. Farley was ordered to qualify as receiver without delay and to act with expedition.[97]

With the aid of the New York agents Farley succeeded in raising one hundred thousand dollars and no more. The Dutch did not respond as was expected. It was useless to undertake the completion of the extension lines. On September 1, therefore, the court amended its recent order so as to allow the use of the money in hand for the completion of such portions of the lines as should be found practicable. By the middle of November Farley had put 104 miles of the St. Vincent extension in the Red River Valley into such condition that an engine and a train of cars were occasionally run from Glyndon to Crookston. Upon this foundation the receiver at once began the proper procedure to acquire title to the land grant appertaining to 140 miles of completed and equipped railroad. The 35 miles from St. Cloud to Melrose he rented to the First Division Company for five hundred dollars a month.[98]

The five years from 1873 to 1877, inclusive, were a period of great distress for the St. Paul and Pacific system. The panic of August, 1873, curtailed business; high freight rates evoking intense public dissatisfaction, the grasshopper scourge, and restricted immigration postponed revival. In 1875 Farley took up some rails north of Crookston and laid them on a nine-mile stretch of track built by the Red River Transportation Company from that station to a point named Fisher's Landing on the Red Lake River where freight brought from below was transferred to barges to be towed down the Red River, when it was free from ice, to Fort Garry.

---

[97] *Plaintiff's Evidence*, 2, 4, 849–858; *Defendants' Exhibits*, 8, 15–42, 94, 398–405.

[98] *Defendants' Exhibits*, 406–408, 412; *Plaintiff's Evidence*, 281–287, 295, 300, 302. On pages 740–760 of the latter is a deposition of Johann Carp, a member of the Dutch committee who visited Minnesota in August and September, 1873, and made a report on the situation, in which he advised the committee to put up money enough to complete and equip the extensions. See also the *Saint Paul Press*, July 30, 31, August 1, 3, 5, 22, 31, 1873. The *Press* of August 3 contains a long editorial descriptive of the situation. It represents the St. Paul and Pacific companies as the victims of the European bond-holders, especially of Lippmann, Rosenthal, and Company, who were endeavoring to get possession of the properties at one-third of the original cost of the bonds. Mention is made of the diversion, to complete the main line to Breckenridge, of one and one-half million dollars of the fifteen-million-dollar loan.

The net earnings for 1875 were but $8,048.93 and the branch paid but tardily its monthly rental.[99]

The First Division Company was left by Judge Dillon in his order of August 1, 1873, in the hands of its directorate, a mere mandatary of the Northern Pacific Company. The directorate continued to operate the main and branch lines for about two years. The net revenue of the main line, running a hundred miles beyond dense settlements, was but a slight return on the actual cost of the road and equipment and was inconsiderable compared with the bonded debt of more than thirteen millions. The branch line did a better business, but only for one year did it have anything left to apply upon the interest charge after paying the costs of operation. Soon after this company, the First Division, on May 1 and June 1, 1873, completely defaulted on the interest due on its four mortgages covering the main and branch lines, as related, suits for foreclosure were brought in the Minnesota courts. Reluctant to see millions of acres of land in the state fall into the possession of foreigners, the courts refused to order the foreclosures, which, under ordinary circumstances, would have been done. The legislature of 1874 generously extended the time for the completion of the extension lines and by a separate act forbade the conveyance of any lands to the company until the just claims of Minnesota citizens for construction and materials had been satisfied. This act created distrust in Holland and made it impossible to secure further Dutch loans for the completion of the extensions. By an act of June 22, 1874, Congress extended the time of the land grant.[1]

The Minnesota people, not easily understanding why the munificent land grants had not given them these railroads complete, were now losing patience. In his last annual message, delivered on January 9, 1874, Governor Austin advised the legislature that the Dutch had put eighteen million dollars into the First Division roads — half of the sum into the " extensions " — and that this money was lent by persons of small means who had thus invested the savings of a lifetime. Speaking as if he considered the state to be under some obligations to these lenders, he said, " Common honesty . . . demands that we conscientiously consider the just

[99] *Defendants' Exhibits*, 479; *Plaintiff's Evidence*, 304, 311, 319, 321, 327.

[1] *Defendants' Exhibits*, 264, 288; *Plaintiff's Evidence*, 305–327; Minnesota, *Special Laws*, 1874, pp. 328–331; United States, *Statutes at Large*, 18: 203. The act forbidding the conveyance of lands until the claims of Minnesotans had been satisfied was commonly called the " De Graff Act," as De Graff and Company were the principal creditors concerned.

claims of these foreign creditors, who have furnished us so largely
with the means of material development and prosperity, and see to
it that they are fully secured in all their rights." [2]

Governor Davis in his first message a year later urged the legislature to consider the claims of the foreign bondholders " in the
spirit of fair dealing which is nowhere so becoming as in a great
state dealing with private interests." If, however, the parties in
control should not proceed at once to complete the roads, the legislature, he advised, should assert the rights of the state to the lands
and franchises and should turn them over to some agency that could
give substantial assurances. A member of the legislature of 1875,
moved perhaps by the suggestion of Governor Davis or perhaps by
the fact that the First Division Company had, on January 1, defaulted on the interest due on its fifteen-million-dollar loan of 1871
for building the extension lines — the twenty per cent reserved in
Amsterdam for three years' interest having been exhausted — introduced a bill declaring all the lands, property, privileges, rights,
and franchises of the St. Paul and Pacific Railroad Company forfeited to the state of Minnesota, to be taken over without merger
or extinguishment and disposed of for the completion of the extension lines of the railroad. On February 23 Representative Francis
R. Delano delivered an elaborate speech in support of the bill,
which, with exhibits, covered the history of the company to date.
The House ordered the printing of five hundred copies of the speech
for its use. The judiciary committee, to which the bill was referred,
reported that in its opinion the lands were forfeitable, but doubted
the legal effect of a legislative declaration. The committee of the
whole thereupon put the bill to rest by excepting it from a favorable
report on a batch of bills.[3]

The refusal of the legislature of 1875 to take action so drastic as
that proposed by Delano may have been due to an expectation that
the bondholders might, under powers granted in the charter of the
First Division Company, take charge of the business and effect an
arrangement by which some interest and dividends might be paid
and construction of unfinished lines might be resumed. At any

---

[2] *Executive Documents*, 1873, vol. 1, p. 11. In giving this sum Governor
Austin did not allow for discount and retained interest. For a reason why
he may have been sympathetic see *Plaintiff's Evidence*, 294.

[3] *Executive Documents*, 1874, vol. 1, p. 26; *House Journal*, 1875, pp. 227,
292, 302, 324, 415, 505. A summary of Delano's speech may be found in
the *Saint Paul Pioneer*, February 24, 1875, and the speech in full is in *Defendants' Exhibits*, 254–289.

rate there was consummated on August 13, 1875, a tripartite agreement on the part of the corporation, represented by its president and secretary; the Dutch committee, represented by Johann Carp and Kennedy and Company; and Edwin C. Litchfield of Brooklyn, New York, for himself and E. Darwin Litchfield of London, England. The Litchfields had to be included because, when the Northern Pacific Company had collapsed and emerged from bankruptcy in the same month, the original stock of the First Division Company had been returned to them as compensation for a claim of five hundred thousand dollars. The essence of this so-called "Litchfield agreement," in twenty-seven tedious articles that it would puzzle even a Philadelphia lawyer to unravel, was a postponement of foreclosure proceedings, a scaling down of stocks and bonds, a pooling of lands and town sites by means of the issuing of scrip, and, most important, the appointment of the majority of the directorate by the Dutch committee. It was not until February 12, 1876, that the reorganization of the directorate took place in New York. Four days later, at a meeting of the new board, George L. Becker resigned as president and John S. Barnes, a member of the law firm of John S. Kennedy and Company, was elected in his place. By resolution Jesse P. Farley, who for nearly three years had been receiver of the old company, was appointed general manager and superintendent of the First Division Company. It must now be noted that the Litchfield agreement contained a provision that, if in the course of twelve months the assent of at least ninety per cent of the bondholders had not been obtained, any one of the parties might rescind the agreement and all might be remitted to their prior rights. That assent was not obtained and the Litchfield agreement survived only as a curious specimen of law literature.[4]

The First Division roads, of course, reverted to the control of the directorate, but they remained in its possession for only a short time. On October 9, 1876, the trustees of the four mortgages, who, after changes in personnel, were the same for all four, took possession of the roads — not of the land grants — under their powers and continued Farley, the general manager, in office as their agent. He attended to the duties of that position, as well as to those of the receivership of the primary company, for nearly three years thereafter in a manner to call from Johann Carp, a member of the Dutch committee, in April, 1877, this compliment: "It is agreeable to me

---

[4] Saint Paul Pioneer-Press, August 28, 1875; Plaintiff's Evidence, 296; Defendants' Exhibits, 351–385, 391–394; Defendants' Testimony, 291, 305–308.

to be able to state here that the interests of the bondholders *in every respect* are taken care of and defended by Mr. Farley with so much devotion, zeal, and knowledge as cannot be sufficiently appreciated." [5]

With the return of better times the business of the completed parts of the system increased in volume and Farley was able to furnish balance sheets showing a surplus over operating expenses; but what did his few thousands amount to against a yearly interest charge of nearly two millions on a bonded debt of more than twenty-eight millions and some floating debt besides? Foreclosures, sales at auction, and purchase by a new organization were the only reasonable procedure. Johann Carp was sent by the Dutch committee to America in November, 1876, to busy himself with the affairs of the St. Paul and Pacific Railroad Company. In the following April he made a very elaborate report, in which he advocated the transfer of all the franchises, property, and rights of the company, by means of foreclosure sales, to a new organization to be formed under the laws of Minnesota. His ingenious scheme, in its details, including a blanket mortgage on the whole system, with second mortgages, and the taking up of common stock by the Dutch in exchange for their old bonds, need not detain the reader, as it was not seriously entertained. For a concern so loaded with debts, lawsuits, and unfriendly legislation and in general disrepute no ordinary investors could be expected to compete and it was to lie long in a hopeless muddle. It was an altogether extraordinary extrication which at length took place.[6]

The progress of events in the history of the St. Paul and Pacific corporations had been watched with peculiar interest by three persons: Donald A. Smith, land commissioner of the Hudson's Bay Company; Norman W. Kittson of St. Paul; and James J. Hill, also of St. Paul. All were Canadians of Scotch extraction. Donald Smith's home was in Montreal, but after the organization of Manitoba as a province of the Dominion of Canada in 1870 he spent parts of each year at Winnipeg. He served in the local legislature and represented the district of Selkirk in the Parliament at Ottawa. His frequent journeys to and from Winnipeg were invariably by way of St. Paul. About 1872 the Dominion granted a charter for a branch of the Canadian Pacific Railroad from Winnipeg to Pembina on the American boundary and Donald Smith was one of

[5] *Defendants' Exhibits,* 461; *Plaintiff's Evidence,* 737, 749, 760, 766, 771.
[6] *Plaintiff's Evidence,* 765, 769, 804–824. Hill's estimate of debts is in *Defendants' Testimony,* 287.

the incorporators of the company. He naturally observed the progress of the extension lines of the St. Paul and Pacific.[7]

Norman W. Kittson, associated with Sibley in the fur trade, was stationed at Pembina for ten years beginning in 1843. He served in the Minnesota territorial legislature from the Pembina district for the four years from 1852 to 1855 and frequently made the long journey by means of dog trains. In 1860 he undertook the management of a line of steamboats on the Red River of the North owned by the Burbank Stage Company. In 1864 he bought out the Burbank interest for himself and the Hudson's Bay Company, and he continued to manage the business until the railroad put an end to steamboating on that river.[8]

James Jerome Hill had come to St. Paul in 1856 with a pair of willing hands and a great head for business. He was not of the stuff to remain long on anybody's payroll. After a variety of successful ventures, Hill, Griggs, and Company in 1870 carried a large amount of Hudson's Bay goods by wagons to points on the Red River that could be reached by boats. The goods were then transferred to barges and floated down to Fort Garry. As the leading partner had taken the pains to secure from the treasury at Washington authority to carry freight in bond across the boundary, his company enjoyed a considerable advantage. The profits of the venture led to the building of the steamboat " Selkirk " for the trade of the following year. After one season the Hudson's Bay Company put an end to this intrusion by purchasing the company and merging it into the Red River Transportation Company. But Hill added to his previously acquired knowledge of the Red River Valley. In March, 1870, on a trip to Fort Garry by dog train, he met, on the prairie near Elm River, Donald Smith on his way " out." The two exchanged news and greetings and began an acquaintance which was later to ripen into friendship and a business alliance. Hill and Kittson were long-time neighbors in St. Paul.[9]

---

[7] *Defendants' Testimony*, 549–550, 646; Beckles Willson, *The Life of Lord Strathcona and Mount Royal*, 1: 378, 401, 463; 2: 2, 51–60, 354 (Boston and New York, 1915). Donald Smith later became Lord Strathcona and Mount Royal.

[8] For a biographical sketch of Kittson see George E. Warner and Charles M. Foote, eds., *History of Ramsey County and the City of St. Paul*, 552 (Minneapolis, 1881).

[9] *Defendants' Testimony*, 4, 200, 215, 560, 565, 624; Joseph G. Pyle, *The Life of James J. Hill*, 1: 75, 100, 111 (Garden City, New York, 1917). The present narrative was originally written before Mr. Pyle's brilliant work on Hill appeared. It will be cited only at points where the author found himself

In the late fall of 1873 or the early winter of 1874, Donald Smith, meeting his old friend Kittson in St. Paul, asked him to rummage up what information he could about the condition of the St. Paul and Pacific. Kittson at the time knew more about steamboats than about railroads and therefore turned to Hill, who had done a good deal of business with the St. Paul and Pacific, although he had had no official connection with it. Nothing loath, the younger man undertook the task and with the aid of Francis R. Delano, a former superintendent of the railroad, made up a memorandum, which was handed or sent to Smith. It is certain that at this time Smith was principally concerned with securing a connection of his Canadian branch road at Pembina with the St. Paul and Pacific. It is not so certain that he then had in mind " the idea " of a capture of the whole St. Paul and Pacific system, but his claim to its authorship cannot be ignored.

While engaged with Delano in compiling information for Donald Smith, Hill and Smith " discussed a good deal " a suggestion by Delano that the easiest way to get control of the railroad property would be to acquire first the branch line and later the main and extension lines. It is at least an even chance that it was Hill who raised the underlying question as to the possibility of acquiring the whole system; and there is not the least doubt that from that time on Hill had continually in mind the plan, or rather the hope, that Smith would undertake the purchase of the bonds and that Hill himself and Kittson would ultimately be interested in the property. The question, who first became conscious of " the idea," is, however, of trifling importance. From a day in the early winter of 1874 James J. Hill devoted all his powers to working out a plan for acquiring the franchises and properties of the St. Paul and Pacific corporations in expectation of a large compensation for his efforts. It is in evidence that he talked frequently with several persons, but particularly with his near neighbor, Henry P. Upham, who was dealing in the railroad bonds, about his plan, or rather project, through the years 1874, 1875, and 1876. His idea was to secure bonds enough to control the directorate, to foreclose the mortgages, and to buy up the stock if it could not be squeezed out of the holders.[10]

---

indebted to Mr. Pyle or where he differs from him, which occurs in but few cases. Both drew upon the vast magazine of documents connected with the case of Farley v. Hill.

[10] *Defendants' Testimony*, 19–28, 32, 135, 246–251, 266, 290, 481, 552–560, 581, 591, 618, 759. In his testimony given twelve years later Donald Smith said: " I considered the idea of acquiring the road originated with

The problem was by no means a simple one. The stockholders, believing that by means of the law's delay foreclosures might be postponed for many years, hoped for a Jupiter to put his shoulder to their wheel and lift them out of the mire. There were lawsuits pending for railroad iron not paid for, for construction, and for other claims. The Northern Pacific grip was not let go until the summer of 1875. The Litchfield agreement threatened, if consummated, to leave the properties in the hands of the old stockholders and bondholders. "There was a time," said Hill, " that everybody waited; that is, Mr. Smith, Mr. Kittson and myself. There seemed no way to get in." When Hill learned in February or March, 1876, about the Litchfield agreement, which had been kept under cover, he knew that the time for action had come. Without delay he took his journey eastward and on a March morning he had breakfast with Donald Smith, in attendance in the Dominion Parliament then in session at Ottawa, and, after laying before Smith his accumulated information, argued for immediate activity. The result of the interview was an understanding that the time was opportune for an effort to advance the grand project. It was agreed that Kittson and Hill should "try and see what could be done in the matter." If their report should be satisfactory, Smith would try to do his part. Smith mentioned a firm of London bankers who, he thought, might become interested enough to advance money.[11]

Some months passed in further waiting for the ripening of events. It has already been mentioned that in the fall of 1876 Johann Carp, a member of the Dutch committee, was in St. Paul to look after the interests of the Dutch bondholders. Several meetings took place in Kittson's office, where the subject of bond purchases was discussed with Carp. He had little confidence that the two men could command money or credit enough to buy the bonds, even if the committee had authority to sell, but he informally indicated what their minimum prices might be. He outlined his own " scheme," already mentioned, and suggested a purchase of the railroad property of the First Division, leaving the lands in the hands of the bondholders. Kittson and Hill accordingly submitted to Carp, on January 29, 1877, a proposition in writing to buy the

myself. . . . It was in no sense the proposition of Mr. Kittson and Mr. Hill." Willson, in his *Lord Strathcona*, 2: 60, attributes the idea to Smith. The conclusion of Mr. Pyle that, because the Supreme Court of the United States decided that Farley was not the author of the plan, it followed that Hill was, may be questioned as a matter of logic. Pyle, *Hill*, 1: 173.

11 *Defendants' Testimony*, 23, 32–35, 37–39, 258, 291, 303, 561, 568, 571.

main and branch lines of the First Division corporation only for the sum of $3,500,000 in cash plus a release of all unsold lands covered by the grants. They gave at length their reasons for not including the extension lines: the St. Vincent line was unfortunately located and settlements along its route were few and the Brainerd extension would help the Northern Pacific more than its own system. It may be safely assumed that there was little expectation that the proposition would be seriously entertained, its real purpose being to ascertain whether the Dutch committee would negotiate for a sale at all.[12]

The informal replies were such as to indicate that the way was open for negotiation. In the following May, 1877, Hill was in Montreal upon a summons from Donald Smith, who introduced him to George Stephen, then president of the Bank of Montreal, to whom Smith had already confided " the idea " and whom he wished to draw into active coöperation. Induced by the representations there made, Stephen agreed to undertake to raise in London the money necessary to make the desired purchase, if satisfactory terms could be made, which Kittson and Hill were authorized to ascertain. A schedule was made of the bonds supposed to be still held in Holland and valuations were placed upon those of the several batches. Hill then hastened back to St. Paul, imparted his information to Kittson, and took counsel in regard to a suitable proposition to be made to the Dutch committee. On the twenty-sixth of May a communication, remarkable for its ingenuity, was drawn up at St. Paul and signed by Kittson and Hill. In a legal argument made some years later by an able lawyer who had had a hand in its composition, the statement was made that the letter was not " and was not meant to be a model of clear expression "; though it was to " read like an offer," it was to be " really a mere request for an option." To have made an " offer " would have been exceedingly imprudent at a time when there was not a dollar of purchase money in hand or promised. The Dutchmen took time to deliberate. The American " associates," as they later called themselves, presuming that their main proposition might be agreed to, considered what they should need to do in case a favorable offer should come from Amsterdam. About September 1 they assembled in St. Paul and made a Sunday excursion on the main line. This hasty inspection satisfied Stephen, who had been doubtful as to whether the proposed enterprise was worthy of consummation.

[12] *Defendants' Testimony*, 52–55, 355, 374, 569; *Plaintiff's Evidence*, 736, 825–830.

About the middle of the same month the associates were in council in Montreal. It was agreed to prosecute the promising, although precarious, enterprise and to depend upon Stephen to negotiate an adequate loan of money in England.[13]

In the course of the same month the Dutch committee sent through its New York attorneys a counter proposition in the form of a changed scale of prices for the several bond issues, the gross sum of which was a little more than a thousand dollars above that offered by Kittson and Hill on May 26. Through the same channel Kittson and Hill accepted the new scale. The prospect for a completed bargain was now so bright that toward the last of September Stephen departed for England on his errand to secure a loan from British investors. He was gone about three months, during which he made an excursion to Amsterdam and Johann Carp came over to London to see him. He offered to pay five per cent interest on a loan of four million dollars in London and to admit the lenders to an equal share in the property of the great enterprise. Not a single dollar was offered; the British had no money to invest in lawsuits and precarious land grants in the wilds of Minnesota.[14]

The attempt to obtain a loan of money in London having completely failed, the original plan of the associates aborted; but the willingness, the eagerness, of the Dutch committee to sell at the prices which had been offered by Kittson and Hill and substantially agreed upon left room for a new plan. It is difficult to decide in whose mind " the idea " first found lodgment and it is not important to waste effort on that question. Stephen came home from England about Christmas, 1877. There was a meeting of the associates in Montreal within a week or ten days — whether or not Stephen summoned it is not known — at which he outlined a new plan of paying for the Dutch bonds *after* the foreclosure sales. The plan, of course, contemplated the organization of a new corporation in time to provide for issues of stock and bonds before the sales, to be ready to exchange for the old bonds. Stephen suggested opening the matter with John S. Kennedy and Company, who were still attorneys of the Dutch committee. The meeting was accordingly adjourned to New York and an all-day discussion took place there on January 2,

13 *Defendants' Testimony*, 55–63, 79, 469, 627, 667, 688, 691. For the trip over the road, see pages 72, 77, 626–631, 694, of the same volume; for the September meeting in St. Paul, pages 632, 696; and for the ambiguous letter of May 26, pages 62, 358, 373, and *Defendants' Exhibits*, 252.

14 *Plaintiff's Evidence*, 456–458, 463, 831; *Defendants' Testimony*, 698; *Defendants' Exhibits*, 481–483.

1878. In the evening of that day James J. Hill, aided by Reuben B. Galusha, attorney for Kittson, drew up a memorandum of an agreement to be proposed to the Dutch committee. After two or three days' discussion it was signed and transmitted on January 5 to Amsterdam.[15]

The associates were now so confident of the acceptance of their proposal that on January 21 they put into writing the understanding which had existed in regard to the division of the interests to be acquired in the purchase of bonds, in the newly organized corporation, and in the profits and losses of the enterprise. It was agreed that each one of the four should take an equal one-fifth interest and that the odd fifth share should be held by George Stephen for securing needed financial aid. No information has been found as to how much was expended for that purpose. The associates had no doubt received advance information of the intentions of the Dutch committee and on February 25 Kennedy wrote to Farley that the purchase had been concluded and would be published in Amsterdam the next day. After some interviews and correspondence in regard to details and after delay to allow more bonds to be added to the pool, a final agreement, bearing the date March 13, 1878, was duly signed and executed for the purchase of the bonds held by the Dutch committee, but — such was the caution of the Dutch —not until after $280,000 in gold had been deposited in the Bank of Montreal as a guaranty of the fulfillment of the contract by the associates.[16]

---

[15] *Defendants' Testimony*, 84–87, 697–699, 703. In regard to the origin of the idea of buying the Dutch bonds on credit, see Stephen's testimony on page 703: "Q. 98. . . . Who originated the plan of buying the bonds on credit . . . ? A. I did. Q. 99. Who principally conducted those negotiations? A. I did." See *Defendants' Exhibits*, 112, for the Hill memorandum that became the basis of the bargain for the bonds.

[16] *Defendants' Exhibits*, 114, 292; *Defendants' Testimony*, 88, 573, 584–586, 701; *Plaintiff's Evidence*, 475, 710. It was deemed not worth while to introduce the schedule of May 26 or the one modifying it. Both may be found in *Defendants' Exhibits*, 252. In regard to the $280,000 deposit, see letters from Stephen to Hill, February 10 and March 4, 1878, in *Defendants' Testimony*, 103, 106–108. Stephen urged Kittson and Hill to turn over to the Bank of Montreal all their securities of a transferable character — " everything that can be put up " — as collateral for the joint and several promissory notes on demand of the associates. Hill spoke of the sum as the amount borrowed to pay the expenses of the Dutch committee. It did not include the fifty thousand dollars that the associates paid to John S. Kennedy and Company for their services. In a letter of February 8, 1878, to Stephen, Hill advised him that he was inclosing "pro. note on demand order Bank of Montreal for ($280,000) . . . signed by N. W. Kittson . . . and myself." The associates probably put up no money except for personal expenses.

The essential portions only of the elaborate document need here be noted. The associates agreed to purchase $625,000 in bonds of the $1,200,000 issue of June 2, 1862, at 75 per cent of the par value; $760,000 of the $2,800,000 issue of October 1, 1865, at 28 per cent; $907,000 of the $3,000,000 issue of March 1, 1864, at 30 per cent; $3,520,000 of the $6,000,000 issue of July 1, 1868, at 35 per cent; and $11,400,000 of the $15,000,000 issue of April 1, 1871, at 13¾ per cent. They agreed to pay for the bonds within six months after the foreclosure of six mortgages described, in gold or first mortgage gold bonds of a new company to be organized under the laws of Minnesota, the bonds to be received at par and to bear interest at seven per cent per annum from December 22, 1877. A bonus of preferred paid-in stock to the amount of $250 was to go with each one-thousand-dollar bond delivered. The associates agreed to complete the northern fraction of the St. Vincent extension in the year 1878, if possible, and to pay the cost of the Breckenridge-Barnesville link. In case of failure to make the promised payments in full, the partial payments made and the $280,000 in gold should be forfeited. It was agreed, of course, that the new company should be organized immediately and that the new stock and bonds — not over twelve thousand dollars' worth to the mile — should be ready for the stipulated payments and that the costs and disbursements of the foreclosure suits should be paid by the associates.[17]

[17] *Defendants' Exhibits,* 292–307. An interesting contribution to the present topic is a letter written on February 8, 1878, by Lucas H. Weetjen, president of the Dutch committee, advising constituents of the intended sale of the bonds and assuring them that under the circumstances they were making a good bargain. The reason given for the allowance of interest on the new bonds was to console holders for the loss by the failure of the expected sale for cash, which, though it did not take place, had been prematurely announced as fact by the committee. Delano in his speech of February 23, 1875, stated that "most of the bonds" had been bought by members of the committee as low as eight and one-half cents on the dollar. If such was the fact their anxiety to close the deal may be explained. See *Defendants' Exhibits,* 281, and *Plaintiff's Evidence,* 840.

The Breckenridge-Barnesville link was a piece of road about thirty-three miles long connecting the two places, built by a subsidiary company in 1877. After it was built, as any map of the state will show, the First Division Company could run its trains through to Fisher's Landing without using the tracks of the Northern Pacific. It was sold to the new company on June 21, 1879, for $250,000 and, being superfluous after the completion of the St. Vincent extension from Alexandria to Barnesville, was taken up after a few years. See *Defendants' Testimony,* 44, 97, 194, 793, 798, 845, 916; *Defendants' Exhibits,* 103, 214; *Plaintiff's Evidence,* 114, 404–407, 419–421, 428, 436–449, 523, 637, 716; and Railroad Commissioner, *Reports,* 1879, p. 125.

The agreement of March 13, 1878, thus executed, no grass grew under the feet of James J. Hill for the next year and a half. Kittson was now sixty-four years old and not in robust health. As Stephen testified, the business of the enterprise was carried on principally " by Mr. Hill at one end, and by myself at the other." The act of the Minnesota legislature of March 1, 1877, amended on March 9, 1878, provided that the road from Melrose to Sauk Center should be completed by August 1, 1878, and the further section to Alexandria by December 1 of the same year, under penalty of a forfeiture of the appertaining land grant. A longer term was allowed for the building of the portion from Crookston to St. Vincent, but the associates had agreed to build it as soon as possible and Donald Smith was naturally desirous that the completion be timed to meet the branch of the Canadian Pacific from Winnipeg to the boundary, in process of construction. It was obviously desirable to obtain at once the profitable Canadian traffic.[18]

A considerable monograph would be necessary to cover all the details of activities implied in the contract. All the lines were still in the hands of Farley as receiver or manager, under the control of John S. Kennedy and Company, trustees of the Dutch bondholders. The good will of the agents had already been secured and now that of Farley was sought through them. The correspondence shows that the associates had no desire to have him superseded, that they had the kindliest feeling toward him, and that they would make it worth his while to give his harmonious coöperation and remain in full charge. Farley seems to have reciprocated the amiable sentiments of the associates and to have exerted himself to expedite the completion of the extensions. His petition of April 8 to the circuit court of the United States for leave to build the portions of the lines mentioned was tardily granted on May 31, after a laborious examination of the whole situation and elaborate reports by commissioners appointed to advise the court. The order of the court provided for the issue by the receiver of eight-per-cent debentures payable in gold; the associates were expected to subscribe for the debentures and to pay for construction and equipment.[19]

Farley believed that he could build more cheaply than anybody else and made a beginning. By August 1, the day of the expiration

---

[18] *Defendants' Testimony*, 713; *Defendants' Exhibits*, 296; *Special Laws*, 1877, pp. 257–263; 1878, pp. 344–346; Pyle, *Hill*, 1: 272.
[19] *Defendants' Testimony*, 705–707; *Defendants' Exhibits*, 128–139, 172, 411–425; *Plaintiff's Evidence*, 499–536.

of the time limit fixed by the legislature, with a large force of men he had completed only the nine-mile stretch from Melrose to Sauk Center, already graded. What means were needed to change Farley's estimate of his efficiency in railroad building is not known, but he now consented that the remaining principal mileages be let to a contractor named by Hill, whose operations he was to scrutinize and expedite. Notwithstanding exasperating delays, the track reached Alexandria on November 15, two weeks before the time set for forfeiture of the land grant. The remoter and longer line from Crookston to St. Vincent was completed on November 9. On November 11 the commission of engineers appointed by Governor Pillsbury reported to him that all the lines had been completed in good and workmanlike manner. On the thirteenth the governor accepted them as completed according to law and certified that the St. Paul and Pacific Railroad Company was entitled to receive the land grant pertaining to the 127½ miles of the lines completed. On precisely the same date the associates made their petition to the United States circuit court showing that Farley had built that number of miles of railroad and had repaired 28 miles more with money advanced by them to the amount of $1,016,300 and asking that he be directed to deliver to them debentures accordingly, which, of course, was done. A continuous line of railroad, 392 miles in length from St. Paul to St. Vincent, connecting there with the Canadian line, and about 800,000 acres of land worth, at $2.50 an acre — the government price inside railroad limits — more than $2,000,000, were the reward for adventure and great labor.[20]

With the great bulk of the bonds in their hands the associates would have been able to control the foreclosures and consummate their agreement with the Dutch committee regardless of the old First Division stock, amounting to five hundred thousand dollars, recovered from the Northern Pacific wreck and still held by Edwin C. Litchfield for himself and his friends. It had never paid a dividend and was of no pecuniary value except in such an emergency as had now appeared. The associates knew, as did Litchfield, that he and his lawyers could block the wheels of their chariot by the law's delays for an indefinite period. It was therefore resolved

---

[20] Railroad Commissioner, *Reports*, 1870, pp. 123, 124; *Defendants' Exhibits*, 142, 219–226; *Plaintiff's Evidence*, 287, 536, 538, 669–673; *Defendants' Testimony*, 368; *Pioneer Press*, August 4, December 1, 4, 1878. Farley estimated that $3,032,200 would be needed for building the extensions. The commission evidently anticipated completion by four days.

to get possession of that stock. Stephen undertook to manage the matter from his end, but not without aid from Hill's end. To worry and annoy him, a suit was brought by Hill in the summer of 1878 against E. Darwin Litchfield to attach a large amount of his land in Minnesota for the recovery of money that had been provided for the construction of the main line, but that he, it was alleged, had converted to his own use. Nevertheless the negotiation went on deliberately and it was not until January 17, 1879, that Stephen could advise Hill by letter that he had closed with Litchfield " on the basis of $500,000 " for all his stock and some bonds that he held. At a meeting of the board of directors of the First Division of the St. Paul and Pacific Railroad Company, held in New York on February 6, 1879, " the company was turned over " by the election of a new board of five directors, including George Stephen, James J. Hill, and R. B. Galusha, Kittson's attorney. The associates were now the titular owners of all the rights and property of that company.[21]

After the transfer of the bonds held by the Dutch committee to John S. Kennedy as trustee under the agreement of March 13, 1878, there remained floating about in Holland and America outstanding bonds amounting, at their par value, to more than a million dollars. To enable the associates to add these to their purchase, an article had been inserted in that agreement by which they were authorized to withdraw from the trustee such amounts of bonds as they might desire on payment of cash at the agreed prices. This ingenious arrangement allowed them to go into the bond market as sellers as well as buyers. By offering to sell at low figures, they checked the operations of a St. Paul syndicate and broke down the market in Amsterdam. By the time the foreclosures were ripe the associates had possession of fully ninety per cent of the outstanding bonds.[22]

With these obstacles overcome and some minor difficulties with the Northern Pacific settled, the associates were ready to move on toward the consummation of the enterprise. On April 11, 1879,

[21] *Defendants' Testimony*, 82, 153–156, 164–173, 189, 714–724, 931; *Defendants' Exhibits*, 140, 146, 148, 152, 154, 158, 199, 394–397; *Plaintiff's Evidence*, 78, 93, 147, 424, 479.

[22] *Defendants' Exhibits*, 300; *Defendants' Testimony*, 99, 155, 710. There was a local demand for bonds to pay on land. In an interview, recorded in the author's notebooks, 3: 135, Hill said that the Dutch bonds were sent over to John S. Kennedy and Company and were safely deposited in the vaults of the Merchants' Safe Deposit Company of New York.

their lawyers obtained from the United States circuit court for the district of Minnesota a decree ordering the whole property of the two companies sold, after proper advertisement, in a single parcel at public sale, the purchaser to pay fifty thousand dollars down in cash as a guarantee of fulfillment and the remainder of the purchase price within fifteen days thereafter. On May 23, 1879, the St. Paul, Minneapolis, and Manitoba Railway Company was organized under the laws of Minnesota, with an authorized issue of fifteen million dollars' worth of stock and sixteen million dollars' worth of bonds. This organization was happily effected under an act of the legislature of 1876, passed evidently to further the Litchfield agreement, then pending. The act provided that in case of a foreclosure sale of a railroad company's assets, bondholders might form a new corporation, which, on purchase at the sale, could be invested with all the franchises, rights, and assets of the expiring company. The foreclosure sale took place on June 14 and was confirmed by the court a week later.[23]

James J. Hill, as manager of the new company, at once took possession of the whole system of 657 miles. He had never been a "railroad man," but he had studied the operations of one road and it did not take him long to learn how to manage a railroad. Capable and efficient men were put in the places of responsibility, order and economy appeared in all branches of the administration, and a discipline firm but just pervaded the whole system. There was an immediate access of business beyond expectation. The grasshopper scourge had passed and settlers thronged out on the main line and into the Red River Valley. The net earnings of the lines in 1879 were more than a million dollars. The prosperous business of the company, its merger into the Great Northern Railway system, and the extension of that to the Pacific Ocean under the administration of a great genius for administration and finance are beyond the scope of this appendix.[24]

It remains to sketch an afterpiece, farcical in some respects, which followed the drama of the St. Paul and Pacific. On June 13, 1879, the day before the last foreclosure sale took place, Jesse P. Farley, the receiver of the parent corporation since 1873, as such

[23] Plaintiff's Evidence, 541, 549–551, 555; Railroad Commissioner, Reports, 1879, p. 125; General Laws, 1876, pp. 47–49.
[24] Interview with David C. Shepard, recorded in the author's notebooks, 3: 57; address of James J. Hill, dated July 1, 1912, upon his resignation as chairman of the board of directors, in Great Northern Railway Company, Reports, 1912, pp. 10–25; Railroad Commissioner, Reports, 1879, pp. 118–123.

the officer of the United States circuit court, and the manager of the First Division for the bondholders' trustees since 1876, brought suit in the district court in Ramsey County against Norman W. Kittson, James J. Hill, and the St. Paul, Minneapolis, and Manitoba Railway Company — for fifteen million dollars, according to Pyle. In his complaint Farley alleged that in the summer of 1876 Kittson, Hill, and he (Farley), entered into an agreement to buy the bonds of the two companies held in Amsterdam. None of them was to furnish any money for the purpose, but Kittson was to obtain a loan through Donald A. Smith, who was to be allowed a two-fifths' interest in the venture. The remaining three-fifths were to be divided equally among the trio. The active prosecution of the enterprise was to be carried on by Kittson and Hill, Farley to be ready with such assistance as they might require. Kittson thereupon made arrangements with Smith, " in conjunction with one George Stephens," to furnish the needed money, Smith and Stephen to have a three-fifths interest. Thereupon, in pursuance of the agreement, the four men named opened negotiations in 1877 for the purchase of bonds and in February, 1878, bought bonds amounting to nineteen million dollars and later increased that amount to some twenty million dollars. It was not alleged that Smith and Stephen furnished any money. Instead of that, the complaint went on to allege that the defendants had bargained for the purchase of the bonds, that they had organized the St. Paul, Minneapolis, and Manitoba Railway Company, that all the railroad properties had been purchased for that corporation, that it was intended that new bonds sufficient to cover the purchase of old bonds and all costs and expenses should be issued, and that a large amount of capital stock had been issued to be divided among the parties to the deal. Farley claimed that he was entitled to one-fifth of all the assets and profits of the operation. He therefore demanded that Kittson and Hill be ordered to make an account of all their transactions and turn over one-fifth of the proceeds and that the impleaded railway company, after an accounting, deliver to him one-fifth of all stocks, securities, and property in its possession. The defendants' counsel represented to the court that the complaint did not state facts sufficient to constitute a cause of action. The judge decided against the defendants and held that Farley was entitled at least to a hearing in court.[25]

---

[25] The proceedings in the district court may be found in the judgment roll and documents on file in the office of the clerk of the district court for Ram-

From this decision the defendants appealed to the supreme court of Minnesota. The case was not argued until April, 1880, and the decision was not rendered until August 24. It was the opinion of the court that the district judge was in error in holding that Farley had a good cause of action and accordingly it reversed his order. The opinion, signed by Chief Justice James Gilfillan, was that, according to Farley's own showing in his complaint, the original agreement was conditioned upon the borrowing of money. As no money was borrowed the contemplated enterprise became abortive. It followed that Farley was a stranger to the later arrangement with Smith and Stephen for the purchase of the bonds on credit.[26]

It may be that Farley and his lawyers found encouragement for further litigation in Justice Gilfillan's observation that there might have been a conditional agreement by Kittson and Hill with him and accordingly, on December 15, 1881, they filed in the United States circuit court for the district of Minnesota an amended bill of complaint. The amendments consisted of erasures and interpolations intended to claim that Farley's participation had been continuous throughout the whole negotiation. The proceedings of the trial may be passed over as not in themselves important; not so, however, the decision of Judges Samuel Treat and Rensselaer R. Nelson, rendered on July 15, 1882. Said the court:

> The scheme was to acquire the large railroad properties through the acquisition and use of the depreciated bonds. The plaintiff urges that he devised the plan . . . and . . . that . . . only through concealment of his connection with the operations could success be reached. He held an eminently fiduciary relation to all interested in the property committed to his management; and it was through information thus acquired . . . that the contemplated fraud could be effected. . . . Through a betrayal of his trust . . . vast railroad properties have been secured and a profit realized of possibly $15,000,000 or more. His pretence now is that . . . his confederates have amassed properties, monies and values to a vast amount with an understanding

sey County in St. Paul. They are printed in *Defendants' Exhibits,* 434–456. See also Pyle, *Hill,* 1: 172. In legal phraseology, the defendants, Kittson and Hill, filed a " demurrer," which was " overruled." The Ramsey County judge was Hascal R. Brill, who died on March 1, 1922, after forty-seven years of continuous service on the district bench. The lawyers for the defendants said that Farley sued in a Minnesota court because he did not dare to face Judge Dillon on the United States circuit bench, whose officer he had been. *Pleadings and Argument for Defendants,* 367.

[26] The decision of the Minnesota supreme court may be found in *Defendants' Exhibits,* 447, and in 27 *Minnesota,* 102. For Farley's affidavit asking leave to introduce an amended complaint before the issue of the mandate of the supreme court, see *Plaintiff's Evidence,* 681. The refusal of the request is in *Defendants' Exhibits,* 446–449.

from the beginning that they were to reward him one-sixth or some other portion of the spoils. They deny his averments. . . . As they do not divide the spoils, this suit is brought to compel them . . . to issue to him his proportionate shares of its capital stock and . . . proportionate parts of the profits and gains; and also interests in undivided property. . . . Thus the powers of a court were thus invoked, to enforce the execution of a fraud on itself as a court, as well as upon others. Surely no principle of equity, morals or law can countenance such a demand. . . . Plaintiff's course of action is based on inherent turpitude. . . . Courts of equity will not recognize as valid or enforce any agreement grounded in turpitude; nor will it undertake to unravel a tangled web of fraud for the purpose of enabling one of the fraudulent parties, after such judicial disentanglement, to consummate his fraudulent designs. In this case [the plaintiff] . . . has not . . . any cause of action which can be upheld, without a flagrant violation of the most positive and clearly defined rules governing such cases. The plea is sustained and the bill dismissed with costs.[27]

From this decision Farley appealed to the Supreme Court of the United States. The reason for the long procrastination can only be conjectured, but it was not until March 29, 1886, that the case was argued by George F. Edmunds for Farley and by William M. Evarts for the defendants, both distinguished at the bar, in the Senate, and in public life. Their arguments left the court in a state of such uncertainty that it asked for a reargument, which was made on December 8, 1886. Two months later, on February 7, 1887, the court refused to render a decision on the merits of the case on account of a certain irregularity in procedure on the part of the defense and an error by the circuit court below in giving judgment on a plea that, according to the rules of equity practice, it had no right to entertain in the form presented. The decision of the court below was therefore null. The curt refusal of the Supreme Court reads, " Decree reversed, and case remanded with directions to overrule the plea, and to order the defendants to answer the bill." [28] The field was now clear for a battle royal.

[27] For the amended bill of complaint, see *Pleadings and Argument for Defendants*, 3–17. The decision of the circuit court is in the judgment roll, case 131 C. See *ante*, p. 443, n. 92.
[28] 120 *United States*, 303, 312–318. Farley's lawyers filed his amended complaint. The defendants' counsel responded with a plea in equity for the purpose of putting Farley out of court. A recent inspection of the judgment roll and accompanying documents led to the discovery that defendants' counsel in the first place filed a demurrer, which later, with the consent of the court, they withdrew, substituting the plea. It was a costly maneuver. The prominent part of the plea was that Farley held such fiduciary relations as to make it impossible for him to make any such agreement with the defendants as the courts would sustain. There was no dispute that some agreement had been attempted; whether it amounted to fraud was a question of law, to be

For the real trial of the now celebrated case in the United States circuit court for the district of Minnesota, Farley's amended complaint, filed on December 15, 1881, stood ready, modified in diction by the introduction of words and phrases current for centuries in chancery practice. The plaintiff appeared as " your orator " and the lawyers signed themselves " solicitors." Another departure notable, although not material, was made. In the original complaint Farley had demanded one-fifth of all the proceeds of the great enterprise; in his amended petition he asked for one-third of all the wealth taken out of it by the defendants, mentioning particularly the 57,646 shares of the stock of the new company of one hundred dollars each of par value, which Kittson and Hill had divided equally between themselves. The answer of the defendants was made on June 6, 1887. It was a sweeping denial of all the claims and statements of Farley not purely historical. At a later stage the solicitors of the parties agreed upon a body of stipulations in regard to the facts, thus simplifying the labors of the court.[29]

On October 17, 1887, the trial opened at St. Paul, with Farley on the witness stand. The central core of his testimony was that in the month of August, 1876, Hill, who had picked up some information about the depreciated St. Paul and Pacific bonds, came into his office to tell him what he knew and to say that he thought there was a chance for a big speculation in buying them. For a good many weeks Hill kept up this kind of talk and the witness heard what he had to say. " Finally," Farley was informed that Kittson desired to confer with him and an appointment was made for an interview. Besides the three men mentioned Farley's assistant manager, William H. Fisher, was present. Kittson opened the subject by saying that he had had a good deal of talk with Fisher and Hill in regard to it. Farley said that he also had been talking over the matter with Fisher and Hill and thought it a good prospect if the

argued before the court on a demurrer; it could not be met by a plea intended to bar the plaintiff from court. The circuit court therefore erred in dismissing the case. The action of the Supreme Court of the United States was taken upon a suggestion of Farley's counsel and was therefore satisfactory to him. It was probably not unsatisfactory to the defendants. In their plea they had denied that Farley had kept John S. Kennedy and Company informed of his interest with them in the bond purchase. It is a principle of equity pleading that denial of a particular allegation in a complaint works an admission of all other allegations. A trial on the merits was therefore quite welcome to the defendants. The demurrer filed by the railroad company was overruled.

[29] *Pleadings and Argument for Defendants*, 14–16, 18–44; *Defendants' Exhibits*, 457.

needed money could be raised. Kittson said he was satisfied that he could raise the money through Donald A. Smith of the Bank of Montreal, but would have nothing to do with the enterprise unless Farley would join in it. He, Kittson, knew nothing about railroads and did not want to know about them and Hill knew nothing about the management of railroads; it would be folly to go into such an enterprise without some associate with railroad experience and ability to manage the property. Thus complimented, and having confidence in Kittson's ability to raise the money, Farley consented and the parol agreement, which became the basis of Farley's prosecutions, was concluded. No memorandum of any kind appears to have been made. On Hill's suggestion, it was agreed that each of the trio should have a one-fifth interest, leaving two-fifths for Donald Smith and his friends for raising the money. This division would keep the control in St. Paul. Before the interview closed Kittson suggested that, as Farley was receiver and manager, objection might be made to his participation in the enterprise and certain parties might go into court and ask for his removal, in the event of which he would not give a dollar for the whole thing. " Upon a moment's reflection," said Farley, " I thought Mr. Kittson was right about it, and then and there . . . it was sacredly agreed . . . that that [*to keep secret Farley's part in the enterprise*] was the best plan to pursue." It was understood that Farley was to attend to his official business and be ready with advice and knowledge while Kittson and Hill were carrying forward the enterprise.[30]

The prosecution presented but one other witness of importance, William H. Fisher, president of the St. Paul and Duluth Railroad Company, who in 1876, as already stated, was Farley's assistant manager, and who had for some years held subordinate and apparently confidential positions under him. He testified that early in August, 1876, Hill came into his office to talk about the Breckenridge-Barnesville cut-off. Fisher took occasion to tell Hill that he " knew of a big thing if he had the money ": that St. Paul and Pacific bonds were quoted at five cents on the dollar in Holland and that fifteen millions of the bonds could be bought for $750,000. Hill seemed interested and asked Fisher to go with him to see Kittson. Hill told Kittson about the railroad business and quoted the prices of bonds. A second and a third visit were made, at which Hill " done the most of the talking." By this time Kittson seemed interested, but he was not satisfied with Hill's outpourings. He

[30] *Plaintiff's Evidence*, 31, 32, 39, 41.

therefore had Fisher come to his office one Sunday morning about ten o'clock and asked him to explain the whole thing. Fisher explained the whole thing so eloquently that Kittson declared that he could find the money if he could assure his friends of seven per cent interest and if Farley would take an interest in the operation. Would Fisher see Farley and find out? "I says: 'All right, Mr. Kittson, I will talk with Mr. Farley, and see what he says.'" Fisher went at once to Farley's office and "went over the whole thing with him," but without immediate result.

On the next Sunday, however, Fisher had, or made, an opportunity to speak up to his reluctant chief. "You know," he said, "that the Dutch will not furnish the money to complete these lines. . . . Now, if you can help the Dutch sell their bonds at what they are willing to take for them, and help Mr. Kittson and Mr. Hill get them, so they have got a good thing . . . and make some money out of it for yourself . . . what harm is there in it. . . . He . . . says: 'There ain't no harm in it, and it's nobody's business; but where is Kittson and Hill going to get the money?'" Fisher told him that Mr. Kittson expected to get it through Donald A. Smith and Stephen. "I says," continued Fisher, "'Mr. Farley, why won't you see Mr. Kittson and Mr. Hill, and see what there is to it?' He says: 'Yes, I will see Mr. Kittson and Mr. Hill.'" In consequence of this resolution the interview described by Farley took place with the loyal and ingenuous Fisher present. Fisher's garrulous report of the interview corresponds with Farley's testimony. His statement of the subsidiary agreement to keep the great project a secret is graphic. An interesting point to be noted here is that Farley, in the opening of his testimony, stated that he had furnished Fisher with much of the information, which the latter imparted to Hill.[31]

---

[31] *Plaintiff's Evidence*, 30, 188–193, 196; *Defendants' Testimony*, 849. In regard to keeping the matter a secret, Fisher said: "Then Mr. Kittson spoke up . . . and says: 'We will have to keep this thing to ourselves,' and Mr. Hill said, 'Certainly.' He says: 'It won't do to let anybody know anything about it.' He said: 'If Becker knew what was going on, he and Bigelow would move heaven and earth to get you out of here.' And Mr. Kittson says that it wouldn't do to let it go back to the former management; that they would skin the thing alive; and if they did, he wouldn't want anything to do with it. Mr. Farley turned around to me then, and said: 'Now, Fisher, we will have to keep this thing perfectly quiet.'" In recent interviews, recorded in the author's notebooks, 3: 65; 9: 18, Fisher declared that his testimony was absolutely true and he added interesting matters. Henry P. Upham, connected with the First National Bank of St. Paul from 1873 to 1880, testified that in

The taking of testimony on the part of the defendants was not begun until March 26, 1888, Hill being the first witness sworn. On direct examination his counsel drew from him his story of investigations into St. Paul and Pacific affairs begun by Donald Smith, Kittson, and himself more than two years before the time when Farley and Fisher swore Farley had first enlightened any of them; of the enlistment of George Stephen in their first attempt to buy the bonds with borrowed money, which utterly failed; and of the later and successful effort to buy the Dutch bonds on credit. In the last hour of his direct testimony Marcus D. Grover, of counsel, asked Hill, " Did you and Mr. Kittson at any time have any negotiations with Mr. Farley looking to the purchase by yourselves . . . jointly with Mr. Farley, of the bonds . . . in the interest of yourselves . . . jointly with Mr. Farley? " " No, sir," answered Hill, " we never did." " Did you," continued Grover, " or you and Mr. Kittson, ever agree with Mr. Farley, or have any understanding with him, or in any manner give him to understand, that he was or should be interested with you equally, or to any extent, or in any manner, in the purchase or acquisition of the bonds? " " No, sir," answered Hill, " we never did." A cross examination of 734 questions, lasting many days, failed to elicit the least concession or weakness on the main points of Hill's direct testimony.[32]

On May 10, 1888, Kittson, returning from a long absence on account of illness, died suddenly on a railroad train which left Chicago on the evening of that day. On June 30 the St. Paul Trust Company, which had been appointed his executor, appeared by counsel in the case. The fact that with the death of Kittson the case had technically lapsed seems to have been overlooked by all

the former year he became informed about the St. Paul and Pacific bonds and during the five years following he bought a large quantity of them and sold them to farmers desiring land. He was next-door neighbor to James J. Hill and beginning in 1874 probably several hundred conversations took place between the two about buying up the bonds, foreclosing the mortgages, and buying Litchfield's stock, if it could not be squeezed out of him. On a certain evening before May 2, 1874, he saw and heard Hill talk to Kittson on the subject, in the old Minnesota Club house, for over two hours; " and Mr. Kittson had the appearance of being fatigued." Stanford Newel testified that in the spring of 1875 Hill had examined six pamphlets, being complaints in six foreclosure cases, and had discussed them with Young and Newel. In 1874 and 1875 the witness saw Hill daily, when both were in the city, and constantly conversed on the bond matter. Newel said: " I used to tell him that he was getting it on the brain. He thought of nothing else." *Defendants' Testimony*, 475, 478, 480, 494, 740, 742, 744, 747.

[32] *Defendants' Testimony*, 1–371.

concerned and it was not until October 25 that the court, by order, revived and continued it.[33]

After taking the testimony of two less important witnesses, the defendants' counsel on July 11 called Farley as a witness on their side. The searching inquisition lasted for ten days. It was a virtual cross-examination on his direct testimony taken at the opening of the trial. His answers indicate candor and a desire to tell the truth, but his confusion of events and dates betrays ignorance of facts to which he had sworn. He was shown a letter of his own, dated June 3, 1876, in which he wrote, " N. W. Kitson is geting anxious about the Big Operation of Geting control of the 1st Div Also Extension Lines. He can get the money. What do you think can be done. you have his proposition in your Memory." With his memory thus refreshed, the witness was pleased to acknowledge that the interview at which the syndicate was formed must have taken place before June 3, 1876. Another letter of his, dated August 23, 1876, indicated that he had known for some time about a " Canady Project " in which Kittson had been interested. In a third letter, dated February 15, 1878, Farley asked John S. Kennedy and Company for " a short condenced Statement of the contract Between the Dutch Bondholders and Hill, Kitson & Co.," and inquired " how many of each kind of Bonds do our Friends get, price of each and *how* and *when* do they pay." This indicated that at a date when the bond purchase had been virtually effected, Farley had very little knowledge of the great enterprise in which he had professed to be an equal partner. Though annoyed by the catechizing of sharp attorneys, who remarked rather sarcastically upon his poor memory, Farley stood bravely by his main allegation, declaring, " I never made a more positive and plain contract in my life than I did with Mr. Hill and Mr. Kittson," whatever might have been the exact date. His statements on that subject, he said, were " true as the Gospel." [34]

The only other witness of importance called by the defense was John S. Kennedy, who was examined at Berne, Switzerland, on September 12, 1888, partly by interrogatories in writing submitted by counsel and partly orally. Farley was present with two Chicago lawyers. The essential point of Kennedy's testimony was that the

[33] *Defendants' Testimony*, 525; judgment roll, case 131 C; *St. Paul Pioneer*, May 11, 1888.
[34] *Defendants' Testimony*, 786, 798–802, 809, 815, 818, 824, 826; *Defendants' Exhibits*, 188, 340–342.

first intimation that he had had of any claim or expectation on the part of Farley was contained in a letter from him written some time in February, 1878. He was asked to account for the following sentence in one of his letters to Farley, written on February 25, 1878: "We think it will pay you to take an interest with K. and H., and are glad . . . that they have offered it to you." Kennedy explained that he wrote under the impression that the associates had offered Farley some kind of an interest in it. He had asked them to make some provision for Farley in the way of employment. Sir George Stephen stated in his testimony that he had had in mind to offer Farley "what the Dutchmen would call a bonification" of ten or twenty thousand dollars in consideration of his activity in pushing the foreclosures and in caring for the railroad property. It appeared in the course of cross-examination that Kennedy had been a large stockholder in the St. Paul, Minneapolis, and Manitoba Railway Company and it was his impression that in the year of his examination he held stock worth two million dollars at par. The testimony of Farley and Fisher in rebuttal, taken October 8 to 12, 1888, added nothing material to their previous averments and denials and with this the record of evidence closed.[35]

The printed argument of the plaintiff laid before the court has not been found; that for the defense with the pleadings fills an octavo volume of 501 pages. The learned attorneys gave their best knowledge and talents to their clients' cause, but it would seem that they felt it necessary to array every possible favorable fact and inference. The theory of the defense was that both in the abortive attempt to buy the Dutch bonds with borrowed cash and in the later successful one to secure them by means of credit, the enterprises were those of Donald Smith and George Stephen, who admitted Kittson and Hill as partners and, in the later operation, allotted them shares of the railroad and landed property to be acquired in consideration of their aid and assistance in carrying it to completion. Accordingly, the two Canadian financiers had not heard of Farley's pretended partnership until after "the whole thing was over." Counsel ridiculed the idea of an agreement sworn to by Farley by which three men without ready money and with only a bare hope of borrowing undertook to carry out a great project involving millions and then and there divided the spoils and

---

[35] *Defendants' Testimony*, 1008–1010, 1012, 1028, 1086; *Defendants' Exhibits*, 189; *Plaintiff's Evidence*, 572, 594, 618; interview with James J. Hill, recorded in the author's notebooks, 3: 133.

appointed Farley manager of the railroads as gaily as the milk-maid disposed of her unhatched chickens. In the second part of the argument it was contended that the agreement, if it had ever been made, was an illegal one and was against public policy and that it had not been legalized by any subsequent act or omission of the defense. On Farley's own statement, his claim had no foundation at all.[36]

Judge David J. Brewer rendered his decision, which was dated September 13, 1889, after holding it under advisement for nearly a year. Although there were two principal witnesses affirming Farley's claim to one denying it, he was not disposed to decide upon any mathematical basis, but he would consider the circumstances of the parties. He observed that, although conversations had been going on for many weeks, as witnesses for the plaintiff testified, the alleged agreement involving millions was suddenly closed after a two-hour interview and no contract nor memorandum was put into writing. By his management of the railroads in his care Farley had gained the good will and the confidence of bondholders and trustees. " Is it probable," said the court, " that a man so situated . . . would enter into a secret arrangement with third parties . . . to reduce the market price of the bonds? Is it probable that such a man would deliberately cloud the record of his life? " It was absurd that Farley should be promised an equal share for mere information and advice to men experienced in affairs. Donald A. Smith had investigations begun by Kittson and Hill and the three had had the matter under consideration two years before the time when Farley pretended to have enlightened them. To think for a moment that Farley had first unfolded the magnificent scheme to them, said the court, " is in view of the overwhelming testimony most absurd." It was incontestable that Kittson and Hill had begun early in 1876 a correspondence which culminated in the purchase of the Dutch bonds by the associates on March 13, 1878. In all this communication, oral and by mail and telegraph, there was not a scrap of evidence that Farley had any interest in the enterprise. The Dutch committee knew nothing of any such interest. The exhibited correspondence of John S. Kennedy alone would invalidate Farley's claim to an equal share, if to any share. A multitude of other matters, individually trifling, carried conviction against Farley's claim. " Very likely," said Judge Brewer, " many of the things testified to by Messrs. Farley and Fisher were said by Messrs.

[36] *Pleadings and Argument for Defendants*, 139, 153, 281, 378-390.

Kittson and Hill to them. But I doubt not that whatever may have
been truthfully said were the gathered fragments of many talks."
The opinion concluded: " I think Mr. Farley as a receiver did not
fail in his official duty [*as an officer of the court*], and although
such conclusion carries an imputation upon his recollection or ve-
racity as a witness it sustains his integrity as an officer. The contract
as set forth in complainant's bill was never in my judgment entered
into and a decree must be entered dismissing the bill." The decree
of the United States circuit court was filed on September 19, 1889.[37]
On the same day Farley personally and by attorney gave notice of
an appeal to the Supreme Court of the United States.

Probably because the case stood low on the docket of the national
Supreme Court, a little more than four years now passed before it
came up for argument on October 30, 1893. George F. Edmunds
and Henry D. Bean appeared for Farley and George B. Young of
St. Paul, for the appellees. The printed argument of the appellant
has not been found; that for the appellees is nearly identical with
the defendants' brief before the circuit court. It was suggested that
Farley never expected to win his suit, but that he hoped that at
some stage the defendants, weary of the annoyance and expense of
the struggle, would submit to a levy of blackmail.[38]

The Supreme Court needed but a few weeks to dispose of the
case. It virtually adopted Judge Brewer's view of the inherent
impossibility of the alleged contract. " A man of affairs," reads
the opinion delivered by Judge Shiras, " . . . would not be likely,
in a matter of such magnitude, to rely upon a merely verbal agreement. . . . the letters and conversations that we find in the record
. . . do not point to or imply any subsisting agreement." The
court graciously added: " It is not necessary . . . to say, or to
think, that Farley and Fisher . . . perpetrated intentional false-
hood. It is altogether possible that, from desultory conversations
with Kittson and Hill, and from an exaggerated sense of his own
importance . . . Farley was led to believe that he was entitled to
participate in the venture. . . . But it is clear, from his own evidence, that he was not included in the actual transaction. . . . His
bill, therefore, is filed for an account of a partnership or enterprise

[37] Manuscript opinion accompanying the judgment roll, case 131 C. Judge
Brewer was promoted to associate justice of the Supreme Court of the United
States on December 18, 1899. 147 *United States,* iii.
[38] *Argument for Appellees* (in the United States Supreme Court), 245.
This is a printed " paper book " of 363 pages. Compare *Pleadings and Argu-
ment for Defendants* (in the circuit court), 366.

in which he really did not participate. His remedy, if he is entitled to any, would seem to be an action at law for damages." This decision, affirming the decree of the circuit court dismissing Farley's bill, was rendered on December 11, 1893, but the mandate was not filed in St. Paul until February 12, 1894, nearly fifteen years after the first suit was brought in the state court. There can be no doubt that the case was justly decided according to the law and the testimony adduced, but it may be doubted whether the defendants were well advised in undertaking to put Farley out of court by demurrer and plea instead of boldly answering his first complaint and challenging him to prove its allegations at the outset, while Norman W. Kittson was alive.[39]

11. CÆSAR'S COLUMN [40]

The manuscript of this extraordinary book was submitted to New York and Chicago publishers, who declined to print it. At length a house little known in the business consented to publish the work under an assumed name and it was quietly given out that a Chicago millionaire was the author.[41] The novel was given an epistolary form. Gabriel Weltstein of Uganda, Africa, a Swiss by birth, came to New York by airship to sell some wool and to have some mineral ores assayed. The first of his series of letters to a brother left at home was dated September 10, 1988. The visitor found New York a city of ten million inhabitants, miraculously provided with modern conveniences. It was governed by an invisible oligarchy of bankers, mostly Israelites, of which the leading spirit was a man known in society as the Prince Cabano, but who signed the name Jacob Isaacs to legal documents. The oligarchy, through its puppets in office, maintained a large body of armed police, but its main reliance was upon a fleet of dirigible balloons called " demons,"

[39] 150 *United States,* 572; interviews with James J. Hill, recorded in the author's notebooks, 3: 133. The mandate is on file in the office of the United States circuit court in St. Paul. Kittson's faith in the enterprise was weak. After the purchase he offered his stock to Hill at twenty-five cents, which offer Hill would not accept, and he sold a large part of it to Kennedy at sixty cents. Items of varying interest and importance may be found in the author's notebooks, 2: 139; 3: 57, 58, 71, 84, 85, 129–135; 6: 77; 8: 10, 140; 9: 22, 29, 41, 108.

[40] See *ante,* p. 187.

[41] Fish, *Donnelliana,* part 1, pp. 120–122. The book was translated into several languages and it has been claimed that seven hundred thousand copies were sold, the larger part of them in Europe. Marion D. Shutter and J. S. McLain, eds., *Progressive Men of Minnesota,* 416 (Minneapolis, 1897).

capable of carrying considerable crews and great cargoes of explosive bombs and containers of poison gas. The stranger found also an underworld, a proletariat sunk in hopeless wretchedness and poverty. From its numbers there had been recruited a " Brotherhood of Destruction " affiliated with a world-wide organization whose members numbered more than one hundred millions.

An accident brought Weltstein the acquaintance and protection of Maximilian Petion, a member of the directing triumvirate of the brotherhood. The most conspicuous member of this committee was one Cæsar Lomellini, of Italian descent but born in South Carolina. Merciless bankers had foreclosed mortgages on his farm in the state of Jefferson and had left him a beggar and an outcast. Resolved upon revenge, he had drifted to New York, where his qualities had placed him at the head of the terrible brotherhood. The third member of the triumvirate, " the brains of the organization," was a Russian Jew whose name is not given. From Maximilian the stranger learned that a day had been set for a world-wide uprising of the proletariat; and but a short time passed before it came.

In the night of a date not named two hundred thousand members of the Brotherhood of Destruction, armed with magazine rifles of the latest pattern and with the deadliest of fixed ammunition, were silently moved down town in New York and disposed about a group of streets in which were the United States subtreasury and the principal banks. They were set to work at once building high and strong barricades so as to form a ring about the occupied space. At daybreak strong columns of troops magnificently equipped, their bands playing " The Campbells Are Coming," marched up to the barricades and halted. After an interval during which both forces seemed to be waiting for something to happen, a single demon descended, " like a sea-gull about to settle in the waves," upon the roof of the subtreasury. Men bearing burdens came and went between the interior of the building and the airship. The ship mounted like an eagle and sailed away. While this was going on a second multitude of the brotherhood had built a string of barricades in the rear of the army of the oligarchy.

It was not long before a vast array of demons — thousands of them — came out of the west and circled over the central inclosure. The mercenary soldiers of the oligarchy were delighted at the prospect of the massacre they had been told to expect. But no massacre took place there. Sweeping north, south, east, and west, the demons spread themselves over the spaces held by the troops of the oligarchy, in the rat trap between the two lines of barricades. The general of the demon fleets had looted the subtreasury and betrayed the oligarchy, which had paid him well to protect it against such an uprising of the proletariat. In his ship he had carried away fifty million dollars.

Even Donnelly's power of imagination was inadequate to describe the massacre of the troops by the rifle fire of the brotherhood and the more deadly rain of bombs and poison gas. The dead lay in heaps and layers. The police thus annihilated, the armed brotherhood became a brutal, ravenous mob and spread far and wide to kill. Its members did not intentionally burn, for they expected to hold and live in the dwellings of the middle classes and the palaces of the princes, but unchecked fires swept away whole blocks. They did not steal nor plunder; that work they left to the criminals let loose from prisons. They simply butchered for revenge. Prince Cabano, attempting an escape, was overtaken by a gang led by Cæsar. They did not kill him, but left him to writhe in agony from wounds. He bribed a thief with a hundred thousand dollars' worth of diamonds and gems that he had carried in a satchel to give him a coup de grâce. The massacre went on until the killers were weary of their work.

Although the social condition was one of sheer anarchy, a problem arose that necessitated coöperation and authority; it was the disposal of the dead — a quarter of a million of them lying about and the number increasing. Some streets were impassable for the heaps of corpses. A group of his officers decided to resort to Cæsar for advice, if not for orders. They found him installed in royal state, with a harem, in Prince Cabano's palace. His first advice, frenzied as he was with drink, was to "kill 'em." "But . . . they are dead already," was the reply. "Burn 'em up," he said. "There are too many of them; and it would be an immense task to bury them," was the answer. "Heap 'em all up," said Cæsar, "in one big pile. . . . Make a pyramid of them, and pour cement over them." Then he remembered how the settlers on the Saskatchewan built houses of rocks and pebbles solidified with grout and in a flash he said: "We won't make a pyramid of it — it shall be a column — Cæsar's Column. . . . It shall reach to the skies! And if there aren't enough dead to build it of, why, we'll kill some more."

There were left of prisoners taken and not yet butchered — merchants, lawyers, clergymen, and others — some sixty thousand.

They were forced by threats of flogging to build the column. Great wooden boxes without bottom, fifty feet long, forty feet wide, and four feet high, were built and inside them the corpses were closely packed. When a box was filled liquid cement was poured over the corpses until all the interspaces were filled. As soon as the cement hardened the box was raised and again filled with corpses and cement. The following inscription was attached to the front of the column: " This great monument is erected by Cæsar Lomellini, commanding general of the Brotherhood of Destruction, in commemoration of the death and burial of modern civilization."

The column finished, anarchy without limit followed. Maximilian vainly tried to persuade a section of the mob to begin the formation of some kind of provisional government. Prompt interference of friends alone saved him from immediate assassination. Another member of the brotherhood triumvirate, the unnamed Jew, with a few followers fled in a demon with a hundred million dollars to make himself king of Jerusalem. Maximilian now saw no hope for himself but in flight and he called upon the general of the demon fleet for an airship promised him for an emergency. It came, loaded with boxes, trunks, bales, and doubtless with water and provisions, although the author makes no mention of them, and anchored above Maximilian's house. The passengers, after family prayers, ascended by a ladder. Among them were the two brides of Maximilian and Weltstein; for be it now incidentally known that the author had ingeniously interwoven an extraneous duplex love story with the horrors of the revolution. While the lading was going on a vast mob assembled in the street and a gang of stalwart fellows prepared to batter down the front door of Maximilian's house with a long beam. A death bomb dropped over the parapet cleared the street for a space. The mob then set to burning adjacent houses and flames soon burst forth. By their light a head — Cæsar's — begrimed with blood and filth, was seen carried aloft on a long pole. " They killed Cæsar," said Maximilian, " and then came after me. . . . Up, up, men." The engineer touched the lever of his electric engine and the ship rose straight and swift as an arrow.

An uneventful voyage of two nights and an intervening day brought the ship over Europe, where the revolution was still going on. Hamlets, villages, and cities were smoking masses of ruins. Groups of defenseless people were being massacred by the brutal members of the brotherhood. As they went southward over France they saw universal desolation. A great volcanic field of flame and smoke showed them where Paris had been. On over the Mediterranean, on over the great Sahara Desert sped the ship, at length to hover over and settle near Weltstein's home, a large white-walled house in Uganda, Africa.

A final chapter of the novel, drawn from Weltstein's journal, contains Donnelly's Utopia. Soon after his return to Uganda, Weltstein summoned the inhabitants of the colony, some five thousand in number, and told them the story of the destruction of the world. The people, " inexpressibly shocked by the awful narrative," immediately considered how best to protect themselves from like dangers. They lived on a high table land surrounded by precipitous mountains. A single gorge through which a wagon road had been built they closed by a wall thirty feet high and fifty feet thick at its widest point, to shut out foreign invasions. Some cannon were made and mounted on high wheels so that they could be fired at air craft coming over the border.

Thus insulated and protected, the citizens got together and framed a constitution, the substance of which was as follows: A preamble declared the purpose of the constitution to be to insure to every industrious citizen liberty, an educated mind, a comfortable home, abundant food and clothing, and a happy life. The body of the constitution, after acknowledging the dependence of the people upon Almighty God, decreed universal suffrage for literates only, voting to be by secret ballot and the right of suffrage to be relinquished by officeholders while in office. It declared that treason should include the buying and selling of votes, for which the penalty should be death. It decreed universal and compulsory education and provided for a cult of morality and religion to be agreed upon by the churches. Interest on money was abolished and anyone who received it was to be punished by imprisonment. The state was to own all public utilities. The governing body, to be known as " The People " or " Congress," was to consist of three branches. Members of the first branch were to be elected by farmers and workmen, those of the second by merchants and manufacturers, and those of the third by artists and men of letters and science. A law must receive a majority vote in each branch or a two-thirds vote in two branches. The executive was to be elected for four years by a two-thirds vote of each branch, he should not be eligible to reëlection, and he should have no veto power nor control of patronage. Free trade with foreign countries in which labor was as well paid as at home was to be permitted. Congress was to have the right to fix living wages but should not ignore the superior value of skill and experience. The principal money should consist of legal-tender paper not to exceed a certain amount per capita of the population; gold and silver might be used only for small transactions amounting to not more than five dollars. The amount of land or money that might be owned by any one person should be limited by law. City lots in Stanley, the only existing village, should be sold only to home-builders and at the original cost price. New villages could be established by the state only. Villages should be provided with parks; no lots should be less than half an acre in area; streets should be wide and planted with double or treble rows of fruit trees; a town hall, capable of seating all the inhabitants and containing free public baths and a library, should be erected in the center of the town; the people of the village should be divided into groups of five hundred families, a physician to be employed for each group at public expense; and concerts, lectures, and dramas should be free to all. The working day for laborers should be eight hours long and there should be two holidays in the week, Sunday and Wednesday. No encouragement was given for the invention of labor-saving devices, but the state was to pay a reasonable compensation for serviceable inventions. All disputes should be settled, if possible, by arbitration, but if a jury trial should be demanded, the defeated party must pay the whole cost of the litigation. A man convicted of crime must work out the cost of his trial and imprisonment before he could be discharged. A brief entry in the journal five years later shows Uganda to be a paradise on earth.

12. THE CENSUS OF MINNEAPOLIS AND ST. PAUL, 1890 [42]

The city of St. Paul, which dates its first settlement from 1839, had a long start on the cities at the Falls of St. Anthony and for nearly forty years it remained the chief city of Minnesota in point of population and in other respects. St. Paul was the capital city; it had the river trade, which was of first importance before the building of railroads along the banks of the Mississippi and into the interior; it had the fur trade until it dwindled in the middle of the fifties; it had the Indian business until the Sioux and the Winnebago were expelled from the state in 1863; it was the headquarters of an army district or department; it almost engrossed the wholesale trade of a great area; and it was the center from which

[42] See *ante*, p. 193.

the railroads penetrated into the hinterland. Its supremacy was long unquestioned and seemed to its citizens likely to be perpetual.

The cities at the falls developed slowly until after the close of the Civil War; then their abundant and cheap water power and their proximity to the pineries gave rise to a rapid expansion of the manufacture of lumber and of many auxiliary products. Even before the evolution of patent flour and the modern milling process they had built up a large flour milling industry. With cash coming in for lumber and flour, the one city resulting from the union of St. Anthony and Minneapolis in 1872 was in a much better condition than St. Paul to stand the strain of the panic of 1873 and the hard times of following years. According to the state census of 1875, St. Paul and the enlarged city of Minneapolis were then on a substantial equality in point of population. From that time on the superior natural advantages of Minneapolis and perhaps some superiority in the character of newcomers attracted there kept it in the lead as to the number of its inhabitants and the volume of its industries and trade. St. Paul did not easily surrender its primacy.[43]

As soon as Congress, in the session of 1889, passed the act providing for the eleventh census, both cities were on the alert — Minneapolis, to demonstrate that it had made a great gain in population and St. Paul, to be assured that it was holding at least a substantial equality. Although the enumerations were not to begin until the first Monday in June, citizens of Minneapolis in April established a "Bureau of Information" and employed as manager a man who could be depended upon to see that no absentee or indifferent inhabitant should escape enumeration. In St. Paul a different means of obtaining the same result was adopted. By the

[43] The population of St. Paul, Minneapolis, and St. Anthony from 1860 to 1885 was as follows:

	St. Paul	Minneapolis	St. Anthony	Minneapolis and St. Anthony
1860	10,401	2,564	3,258	5,822
1865	12,976	4,607	3,499	8,106
1870	20,030	13,066	5,013	18,079
1875	33,178	32,721		
1880	41,473	46,887		
1885	111,397	129,200		

The figures for 1860, 1870, and 1880 are in *United States Census*, 1860, *Population*, 257,259; 1870, pp. 178, 180; 1880, pp. 226, 229. Those for 1865, 1875, and 1885 are in Secretary of State, *Reports*, 1865, pp. 94, 101; 1875, pp. 71, 83; 1885, pp. 26, 59.

exertion of influence the citizen first appointed as supervisor was induced to resign to make room for another, experienced in the compilation of city directories.

The necessary preliminary arrangements having been made, the enumerations began in both cities on Monday, June 2, as provided by law, and proceeded without incident. But for an unexpected interruption, the Minneapolis count would have been completed on June 18. On June 17 at nine-thirty in the evening a United States deputy marshal from St. Paul appeared in Minneapolis with an assistant, entered the room occupied by the " business men's contingent," where he found a number of enumerators checking their lists, arrested seven of them, seized six bags of papers, and departed to arraign his prisoners an hour later before a United States court commissioner in St. Paul. Four Minneapolis citizens who heard by accident of the arrests followed and arrived in time to rescue the captives from jail by signing bail bonds in the sum of five hundred dollars for each. On the evening of the day after the arrests a great mass meeting, presided over by the mayor and addressed by the favorite orators of the period, was held in Minneapolis. The resolutions adopted and signed by the official committee of the Business Men's Union declared that the law had been violated, justice outraged, and personal liberty assailed; that the city of St. Paul must bear the odium of the conduct of its representatives; and that it was the duty of the United States government to investigate the high-handed proceeding. A dozen or more " whereases " contained allegations that the illegal arrests were made with loaded firearms, that the prisoners were deported to St. Paul when there was a United States court commissioner in Minneapolis, and that the Minneapolis census-takers had been dogged by Pinkerton detectives employed by a committee of citizens of St. Paul — all for the purpose of destroying the census records and damaging the business standing of Minneapolis.[44]

The warrants for the arrests had been sworn out by William Pitt Murray of St. Paul on information and belief. His information came from one John H. Mason, a detective by profession, who had obtained employment from the manager of the Minneapolis Bureau of Information on May 31 and had remained on duty while the

[44] United States, *Statutes at Large,* 25: 760–767; Charles W. Johnson, *Another Tale of Two Cities; Minneapolis and St. Paul Compared,* 12, 14, 18–22, 28 ([Minneapolis], 1890); *Minneapolis Tribune,* June 18, 1890; *Pioneer Press,* June 18, 1890.

enumeration was going on. In his affidavit, dated June 21, Mason averred, among other things, that from lists furnished by associations, employment agencies, lumber camps, and employers, names were copied into the blanks and that the required data were supplied by imagination. He had been instructed to copy 839 names of persons who had been assisted by the Associated Charities. In a large number of cases, filling eighty-eight sheets, he had supplied details of birth, age, and so forth out of his own head. He had constructed 32 families with 122 members. Alterations in returns had added 369 names from a Swedish district.

On June 23 the manager of the Minneapolis Bureau of Information made a counter affidavit in which he deposed that he had employed Mason, but not for any illegal work. If any enumerators had violated or had attempted to violate the law he did not know it. The business of the bureau was to discover legal residents temporarily absent and numerous persons not likely to be found at homes — the bachelor merchant at the club, the newsboy who sleeps in the alley, and local tramps and streetwalkers naturally suspicious of the census-taker. The treasurer of the bureau expressed the opinion that as many as ten per cent of the population were absentees and quoted a statement of the *Pioneer Press* of June 22 that the floating population of every large city constituted from twenty to twenty-five per cent of the total. The people of Minneapolis were not disposed to give much weight to accusations founded upon an affidavit of a detective employed by St. Paul and frantically and, as they believed, maliciously voiced by the *Pioneer Press*. The leading business men of Minneapolis, at a large mass meeting held on June 30, resolved that, while they believed that no frauds had been committed, the accused enumerators ought to have a fair and early trial and that if any should be found guilty they should be punished. All that Minneapolis asked was an honest count.

The people of St. Paul had been more prompt to call for the prosecution of offenders against the census law. A public meeting was held in the city hall on the evening of June 21. Its sentiment was voiced through a petition to the United States district attorney signed by forty-nine of the most prominent and reputable citizens. Protest was made against a false enumeration in Minneapolis that would vitiate the apportionments for Congress and for the state legislature. The Mason affidavit was cited and reference was made to a mass of other evidence, oral and documentary, against a large number of persons guilty of criminal acts. The petitioners demanded, therefore, an immediate prosecution for conspiracy to commit criminal offenses against the census law.[45]

On the morning of June 22 the *Pioneer Press*, under a " scare head," " Now by St. Paul Fraud Dies," printed the Mason affidavit and filled its front page and more with denunciations of the shame of Minneapolis. Some days later a delegation from St. Paul journeyed to Washington and laid the Mason affidavit before the superintendent of the census, Robert P. Porter, and the attorney-general. The superintendent was no doubt impressed by the revelations of the delegation, but it may be that he was more sensible to reports from one of his special agents on the ground in regard to irregularities in both of the cities. He first set his electric recording machines at work on a preliminary summary of the returns received from Minneapolis. Before this had gone very far further reports from his agent and an accumulation of rumors persuaded the superintendent that it might be just as well to look into the St. Paul returns at once. By July 10 he was satisfied that the returns from some of the St. Paul districts did not " look right " and he accordingly set his tabulators at work on them. The outcome was a recommendation, dated July 26, to the secretary of the interior for a recount in both cities. The superintendent denounced the Minneapolis count as vitiated because of an organized conspiracy to inflate the census. Families had been augmented to enormous sizes by additions of fictitious children and boarders, existing houses had been filled beyond capacity with imaginary residents, and houses had been invented by hundreds. Transients and boarders had been enumerated at hotels and boarding houses and employees in large numbers had been counted both in their shops and at their homes. There was no evidence of a conspiracy in St. Paul, but there were additions to schedules similar to those discovered in Minneapolis, though they were by no means so numerous. The advance postal-card notices, however, were of a more suspicious character than those from Minneapolis. He therefore believed that the people of both cities, rather than bear the stigma of a padded census, would welcome a recount. The superintendent had no proof whatever that the two supervisors were parties to the frauds.

The Minneapolis people had sense enough, or grace enough, to acquiesce and thus prevent publication of the shameful details of the rascality practiced. Not so the good people of St. Paul, so

[45] Johnson, *Another Tale of Two Cities*, 23–25, 26, 28, 30; *Minneapolis Tribune*, July 1, 1890.

strong was their confidence that their census had been fairly and honestly taken. They had no desire to share in the disgrace of the upstart city at the falls. The Chamber of Commerce on July 28 protested by resolution against the "unjust linking of the two municipalities in a common infamy" and appointed a committee to go to Washington and enter a formal protest. The *Pioneer Press* flared up against the recount as "an abominable outrage on justice and decency." On only two occasions — those of the attack on Fort Sumter and the assassination of Abraham Lincoln — had there been such violent and such unanimous indignation in St. Paul. In its issue of July 29 that paper voiced, it believed, the righteous indignation of St. Paul at having its census coupled with that of "a city which stands degraded and ashamed in the eyes of the nation" and at having itself put "in the list with this Jezebel, whose dallying with sin is the jest or the scorn of a whole people." It protested against a recount as the achievement of men engaged in a "villainous plot to pad the Minneapolis census by more than 100,000 names." Then followed a long sentence beginning, "But this forced marriage with a strumpet," which will be amusing to the reader whose patience holds out to the end of this story.[46]

A committee appointed by the St. Paul Chamber of Commerce obtained an appointment for a hearing from the secretary of the interior and, accompanied by Cushman K. Davis, appeared before him on July 31. Davis proposed that the members of the committee be allowed to examine the testimony in the case by themselves in a room which had been secured before the hearing. The secretary preferred to disclose the grounds of his order to recount in an open hearing. The proceeding took on the nature of an inquiry as to why the secretary should not rescind his order, with the secretary and the superintendent of the census on the defensive. The superintendent proceeded first to cite instances of irregularities in the way of excessively large families in the St. Paul returns. On Wabasha Street 27 families were reported, 15 of which contained 10 persons each; on St. Peter Street out of 20 families 6 were found with 10 persons each; on East Seventh Street, out of 28 houses 1 contained 79 persons, 2 had 20 each, and 17 had 10 each; on Jackson Street, 78 persons were reported as living in a house the foundation of which had been laid on May 1. The general census average of persons to a family was four and a fraction, said the super-

[46] Johnson, *Another Tale of Two Cities*, 27, 29, 34, 37, 39; *Pioneer Press*, 1890: June 22, p. 1; July 27, p. 4; 29, p. 4.

FOR HER HONOR'S SAKE.
There are cases where a brother must interfere in his sister's affairs.

[From the *St. Paul News*, June 28, 1890.]

HOW IT WORKS.
JUST WHAT MINNEAPOLIS WANTED, BUT THE SAME MEDICINE MAKES ST. PAUL SICK.   HONEST
PEOPLE DON'T OBJECT TO INVESTIGATION.

[From the *Minneapolis Tribune*, August 1, 1890.]

intendent. Attention was called to the enumeration of 325 houses
that were reported as occupied but were not shown on the map.
Objection was at once made that the map, *Rascher's Atlas of St.
Paul*, made in 1885 for the use of insurance companies, included
only insurable buildings and did not include many suburbs. To
this the reply was made that in many districts the houses found cor-
responded exactly with those shown in the atlas. The St. Paul supervisor stated that twenty thousand houses had been built in St. Paul
since the publication of the atlas. The secretary ruled out of the
case all statements based on it. The superintendent then cited
instances of excessive numbers of persons reported as residing in
single buildings. In the Pioneer Press Building, for example, 91
lodgers were recorded, all of whom had also been enumerated at
their homes; 78 persons were living in the St. Paul Dispatch Building and 68, in an adjoining bookbindery; 14 families, including 46
persons, were found in the Bank of Minnesota and 8 families comprising 44 persons, in the Chamber of Commerce Building; 553
persons were living in the Ryan Hotel, not including 25 in the barber shop; 275 — later corrected to 245 — resided in the Union
Depot and 102, in a factory; in a wholesale dry goods store 54
persons were found by one enumerator and 121 by another; 120
dwellers were discovered in one small house and 35 in a dime
museum. At the close of the day's hearing William S. King of
Minneapolis asked to be heard to say that Minneapolis welcomed
the recount but that, " if the recount in St. Paul was to be explained
away in a private hearing, Minneapolis would claim the privilege
of coming to the secretary " with the same line of argument. The
secretary informed him that if Minneapolis should apply for a
hearing it would be accorded. Minneapolis did not apply.

The hearing was resumed on August 5. Meanwhile the St. Paul
committee had studied the evidence taken and was ready with an
argument in writing of more than seven thousand words. The
committee was convinced that no frauds had been perpetrated in
St. Paul and protested against having the name of that blameless
city coupled with that of another city where frauds had been actually discovered. Still, it was willing to admit that some errors had
crept in because of a misunderstanding of the rule of the census
bureau that a person's home is where he sleeps. While the committee disclaimed fraud, it candidly admitted that there might be
ground for a recount of nine districts out of the thirty whose returns
had been scrutinized, but it insisted that, as there was no fraud or

suspicion of fraud, the irregularities did not justify a recount of
the whole city. The committee was not there to palliate a single
violation of law or to shield a single criminal.

A letter of July 28 from a prominent journalist of St. Paul to
the secretary of the interior was also read. The writer informed
the secretary that intelligent people in Minnesota believed that in
ordering the recount he could not have been influenced by Porter's
" screed " but had simply bowed to the dictates of a coterie of
small politicians and that Porter's only object was to gratify the
malevolence of those politicians. The secretary's telegram to General Sanborn — it merely named a day for the hearing — was
regarded as an insult to the intelligence of St. Paul people. The
letter further explained how the secretary's action would strengthen
the hands of the Minneapolis Republicans who were opposing the
reëlection of Governor Merriam because he was a St. Paul man and,
by defeating him, would throw the control of the state to the
Farmers' Alliance, the Prohibitionists, or the Democrats. " You
and Mr. Porter . . . will be held responsible for this injury, not
only by the party here, but by its thoughtful members throughout
the Union," said the writer.

During the proceedings which accompanied the reading of the
St. Paul committee's argument the St. Paul schedules were further
discussed and the committee appears to have acquiesced in a
recount of thirty-four districts. At the close of the hearing the secretary directed the superintendent to go on with his scrutiny and gave
leave to the St. Paul committee to stay and watch him. The superintendent held to his opinion that there should be a recount of the
whole city, which, he said, would be more satisfactory to the majority of the people of St. Paul, and he so recommended in a letter to
the secretary on August 8. On the same day the secretary confirmed his original order. While the diversified errors of the enumeration indicated something more than carelessness, he was satisfied
that no fraud was intended or practiced to any degree by the citizens of St. Paul.[47]

The recount of Minneapolis was begun on August 11 and was
substantially completed in a week; that of St. Paul was delayed
until the twenty-fifth and was practically complete at the close of
the third day. In both cities the enumeration was supervised by
special agents of the census bureau. The enumerators were virtually

    [47] The minutes of the hearing are in Johnson, *Another Tale of Two Cities*,
46–82.

selected by citizens' committees and were paid four dollars a day instead of two cents per inhabitant, as in the original count. The results were made public simultaneously on September 13 at six o'clock in the afternoon. As slightly corrected by later revision, they stood: for Minneapolis, 182,967 by the first count and 164,738 by the second count, a difference of 18,229; for St. Paul, 142,581 by the first count and 133,156 by the second count, a difference of 9,425. Secretary John W. Noble, had there been occasion, would doubtless have acquitted the citizen body of Minneapolis, as he had that of St. Paul, of all participation in the rascality practiced by a few officious zealots. According to newspaper indications, Minneapolis, although believing herself underenumerated, acquiesced in the result of the recount because she had retained her proportionate lead over St. Paul. She was congratulated for her remarkable growth, due to her nearness to the center of northwest activities. St. Paul was not so content. For many days her leading journal harped upon the injustice done her and called Minneapolis such naughty names as "Padville" and "Pad City." In editorial articles Porter was denounced as a partisan of Minneapolis and as utterly incompetent for his office; the whole census, it was declared, was worthless and ought to be retaken; in the recount, it was said, the population of Minneapolis had been padded from twenty to twenty-four thousand.[48]

The census act of 1889 pronounced severe penalties for false enumerations and false certificates and returns. It was, of course, the business of the United States authorities to prosecute individuals seriously complained of for violating the law. Eugene G. Hay, the United States district attorney, who at the time resided in Minneapolis, thought that it would be better if the cases were handled by another and, before the matter had gone far, he obtained a release from the attorney-general, who appointed George N. Baxter of Faribault as a special assistant district attorney. This ap-

---

[48] Johnson, *Another Tale of Two Cities*, 85–95; *Tribune*, September 14, 1890; *Pioneer Press*, September 14, 15, 18, 19, 21, 24, 27, 1890. The *Pioneer Press* of September 23 gives an account of a meeting of the St. Paul Chamber of Commerce at which "a complete and correct statement of the census imbroglio" was presented. The reports of the citizens' census committee, of the delegation sent to Washington, and of the recount committee are printed. The issue of September 27, p. 4, states that "No intelligent person . . . can doubt that the last census of that city [*Minneapolis*] was padded to the extent of at least 24,000 names. Vale! the census." The *St. Paul Globe* of September 14 expressed satisfaction with the result of the recount. The *Globe* reports are meager.

pointee at once took up his duty and entered complaints before the United States court commissioners in the two cities. Because he caused the arrest of more individuals from their city, Minneapolis people blamed him for partisanship. All the complaints came before a United States grand jury in Minneapolis on September 13. A great number of witnesses were interrogated. Twenty-eight indictments were found against Minneapolis men and only five against St. Paul men. There were eight indictments for making false certificates, eight for making false returns, and six for conspiring to make false returns. Bail bonds were signed for all the men indicted, including those from St. Paul, by two citizens of Minneapolis.

The first of the St. Paul cases to be tried came up in the United States court in St. Paul on January 19, 1891, Judge Rensselaer R. Nelson presiding. The case was that of Joseph O. Vervais of St. Paul, who was charged with having exaggerated the number of inhabitants in the Union Depot. Voluminous testimony was taken and on January 23 the jury, after five hours' deliberation, brought in a verdict of "not guilty." Why all parties were now content with what lawyers call a "continuance" of the cases is not recorded, but the surmise may be ventured that it was apparent that if a jury could not convict Vervais on the evidence and arguments it would merely cause trouble and expense to insist upon further jury trials. It may also be safely assumed that Minneapolis people were not greatly desirous that further details of the operation of their Bureau of Information should be revealed to the public through testimony in court. All the Minneapolis cases had been continued to the March term of the same court.[49]

Meanwhile a firm of Minneapolis attorneys who had been looking after the cases of their unfortunate townsmen, in expectation that funds would be furnished to cover their fees and expenses, gave notice that, unless a paper signed by at least fifty responsible citizens guaranteeing the cost of the defense should be delivered to them by January 1, 1891, or unless the sum of ten thousand dollars should be deposited in a bank for the purpose, they would retire from the cases. Neither of these things was done. The attorneys then, on January 12, 1891, notified by letter each of the defendants and their respective bondsmen of their withdrawal

---

[49] Johnson, *Another Tale of Two Cities*, 22, 29, 30, 95; *Minneapolis Tribune*, September 14, 18, 19, 23, 1890. For reports of the Vervais case, see the *Pioneer Press*, January 20–24, and the *Minneapolis Tribune*, January 21–24, 1891. A transcript of the court reporter's record is in the Folwell Papers.

from the cases. This left the accused without counsel. At this juncture William Henry Eustis, later mayor of Minneapolis, who had already signed bail bonds for both the St. Paul and Minneapolis men, came to their aid. In an interview with Judge Nelson of the United States district court, after the acquittal of Vervais, Eustis obtained an understanding that, if Stevens and Beaudet, two of the enumerators indicted, would plead guilty and pay fines of two thousand dollars and five hundred dollars respectively, he would release them without day and dismiss all the other cases. Stevens stoutly objected to the arrangement but was at length persuaded to acquiesce. Eustis raised the money from a circle of business men and paid it to the clerk of the court. The understanding was consummated on March 4 in the United States district court at Minneapolis. Attorney Baxter for the government entered a nolle prosequi, which means that he asked for a dismissal of all the remaining cases. From such events it may be inferred that trial by jury becomes in some emergencies trial by a community, when it feels that citizens unluckily caught in a wrong — not *malum in se* — and supposing themselves to be acting for the interest and pride of the good people ought not to be severely punished.[50]

13. THE NELSON-WASHBURN SENATORIAL CONTEST OF 1895 [51]

The details of this contest, though not of sufficient importance to delay the general narrative, may be worthy of record in an appendix. There is abundant evidence that Senator Washburn expected reëlection without Republican opposition and that he depended upon the support of Governor Nelson. This excess of confidence led him to neglect to organize his friends for an active campaign before and after the November election. As no other candidate appeared in the open, he seemed to have the field to himself.[52] There must have been whispered rumors, however, of the possibility that Governor Nelson would aspire to the honor, or he would not have taken the trouble to make a public and emphatic disclaimer.

---

[50] *Minneapolis Tribune*, January 19, 29, March 5, 1891; *Pioneer Press*, March 5, 1891; Eustis to the author, November 27, 1923, Folwell Papers. The *Tribune* and the *Pioneer Press* are in error in stating that Judge Shiras disposed of the cases. He was present waiting to open a term of the United States district court. Judge Nelson concluded the business.

[51] See *ante*, p. 204.

[52] Smalley, *Republican Party*, 247, 334.

At a Republican rally at Albert Lea on September 22 he spoke in the presence of Senator Washburn substantially as follows: " It has been reported that I am a candidate for United States senator, but that is not so. I am not a candidate, and do not expect to be. I am a candidate for governor, and want to be elected governor, and if elected will (or expect to) serve out my term as governor; but elect your Republican legislative ticket, so as to send my friend, Senator Washburn, back to the United States senate, or if you do not like him some other good Republican." [53]

That the reports thus denied had had somewhat extensive circulation may be inferred from newspapers of the time. The *Faribault Republican,* commenting upon Nelson's speech, said that the governor took occasion in his address at Albert Lea " to stamp out very effectually the current rumor " that he was a candidate for governor and United States senator and that his frank and manly statement would do away with all suspicion that he was playing a double game. The *Winona Republican* made the statement that Nelson had declared in the most public way that " he was not, never had been, and should not be, a candidate for the United States Senate to succeed Gen. Washburn " and that the denial would undoubtedly set at rest the " persistent stories " that Nelson was in reality a candidate for the Senate. The *Mankato Free Press* stated that Nelson had said in his Albert Lea speech that he was not a candidate for the United States Senate as had been frequently charged and that his statement should set at rest the many stories that had been bandied about the state.[54] The *Freeborn County Standard,* a Populist organ, expressed doubt as to Nelson's sincerity and said that officeholders appointed by him and others in his confidence were

---

[53] The quotation from Nelson's speech is taken from a communication in the *Pioneer Press,* January 12, 1895, p. 4, signed by six citizens of Albert Lea, all friendly to Washburn, giving Nelson's words as recalled by them. They added, " We know that the impression was made on his audience that he could not consistently be a candidate for the senate." It is remarkable that the concluding words of Nelson's disclaimer made no impression upon the signers of the communication and that Washburn, who was on the stage, did not comprehend them. The *Minneapolis Journal,* September 24, 1894, reports Nelson as hoping that " some such man as Senator Washburn would be elected." The *Pioneer Press* of December 28, 1894, prints Laurits S. Swenson's understanding of the speech, and that of Thorvald V. Knatvold, who presided at Albert Lea, appears in the same paper for January 6, 1895. A number of opinions of other contemporary public men on the question are recorded in the author's notebooks, 3: 95; 6: 64, 86, 107, 118, 121; 7: 27, 36; 9: 34, 36, 50, 56, 63.

[54] *Mankato Daily Free Press,* September 25, 1894, p. 2; *Faribault Republican.* September 26, 1894, p. 2; *Winona Republican,* September 28, 1894, p. 2.

"working like beavers" to elect him governor and senator. A letter written by Harwood G. Day, the editor of this paper, to Donnelly on February 28, 1894, is evidence that an expectation that Nelson might be willing to use the governorship as a stepping-stone to a higher position had long existed, for it contains the following passage: "The republican program — the Nelson program is to elect N—— governor; Dave Clough lieutenant governor — Nelson Senator — Clough governor. It is powerful and possibly resistance is idle, but I believe not." The writer added that the People's party might win if its members would "pull together for the right." [55]

At the November election the Republicans secured an extraordinary number of seats in the legislature and left no doubt that a Republican would be chosen to succeed Washburn. Since Nelson's supposed disclaimer of any aspiration to the senatorship had not been publicly modified or recalled, Washburn believed that his reëlection was certain. He later said that he had considered the situation to be analogous to that of Senator James McMillan of Michigan, who in January, 1895, was reëlected without a campaign and without opposition in the party. According to Smalley, Washburn thought of a trip to California in the holidays.[56]

A note of discord was early sounded by the *Martin County Sentinel*. On October 26, 1894, the editor, Frank A. Day, announced that if he were elected to the legislature he would select as his preference the senatorial candidate "who will most nearly represent the interests of Minnesota instead of Wall street." On November 23 the *Sentinel* saw a "storm brewing," and remarked that "past experience demonstrates that Minnesota senatorial contests are 'heap uncertain.' . . . There is a strong feeling that one of the senatorships should go to the country and if this feeling should crystallize around some such a man as Lind or Tawney or Towne it might result in making some ugly gaps in Mr. Washburn's fences." On the seventh of December the same journal advised Washburn to take pains to represent Minnesota and not Wall Street and on the fourteenth it suggested that if "a strong, clean, able man from outside the twin cities could be induced to enter the field he would have a good following from the start, with a fighting chance of success." If Day and his newspaper had been as widely known then as they

[55] *Freeborn County Standard* (Albert Lea), September 26, 1894, p. 4; Donnelly Papers.

[56] Smalley, *Republican Party*, 247; *Minneapolis Journal*, January 25, 1895, p. 1.

were later, Washburn's friends might well have sensed a storm brewing.

The unexpected storm did not break until December 27, 1894, when an editorial appeared in the *Alexandria Post News,* a newspaper published in Governor Nelson's home town. After reciting such objections against Senator Washburn as close relations with the moneyed class, unpopularity in country districts, and residence in one of the Twin Cities, the writer suggested that Solomon G. Comstock of Moorhead was a man against whom no such objections could be raised and whose experience in Congress had made him well qualified for the position of United States senator. The article concluded with a remark that Comstock seemed to meet all the requirements " more fully than any person mentioned except Gov. Nelson." Such a remark might have been made as an artless compliment to an honored townsman, especially to one who had unselfishly disclaimed a candidacy. The remark was not taken in that simple way down country. The *Minneapolis Tribune* of January 2, 1895, expressed surprise and indignation at a possible foreshadowing of Nelson's intention to withdraw his support from Washburn. But for Washburn's support Nelson could not have been reëlected governor. What did he mean?

All doubts were removed the very next day, January 3, by Nelson's announcement that he was a candidate and that he would do all he could to be elected. Under ordinary conditions Nelson's announcement would have been delayed until after the election of a speaker and the organization of the House, but late in the night of January 2, at a meeting in his hotel bedroom, a group of his supporters persuaded him that the time was ripe for his appearance. Their reason may have been that gentlemen whom they had encouraged to come into the field might divert too many votes. When Washburn was told of Nelson's manifesto he refused to believe a word of it. After all Nelson had said to him personally and in writing and after the governor's public statement at Albert Lea, Washburn could not give credence to the announcement. This ingenuous confidence was rudely shattered later in the day when the two statesmen met face to face in the Capitol. In reply to his protest that Nelson could not be a candidate against him without dishonor, Washburn got the reply that neither he nor any man had a proprietary right to the senatorship.[57]

[57] *Minneapolis Tribune,* January 4, 1895, p. 1; *Fergus Falls Journal,* 1924: January 4, pp. 2, 8; 5, p. 2; 7, p. 2; *St. Paul Globe,* January 4, 1895; letters

From that time until the date of the Republican caucus the contest went on like many another, though perhaps with more bitterness. Washburn and his friends could not doubt that they would rally a sufficient majority to nominate and elect him. Nelson was probably assured of a sufficient number of votes to lead him to expect the addition of enough unpledged votes to carry the election. He had an advantage in the aid of an organized group of young Republicans, as yet little known in politics, who had nothing to lose and who stood a chance of gaining some possible crumbs in the way of federal appointments at the hands of a new senator at the national Capitol. A small group of older chiefs was assembled to act as a steering committee for Washburn.[58]

The Republican members of the legislature went into caucus on the evening of Friday, January 18, with 141 present. A preliminary motion that at least 72 votes must be cast to nominate prevailed by a vote of 86 in its favor. As the motion was made by a spokesman for Nelson, it was apparent that the nomination of Washburn was at least precarious. In a long session of four hours six ballots were taken. Washburn's highest figure was 61 and Nelson's, 60. The caucus made no nomination and adjourned without day. On the following Tuesday, January 22, the day appointed for the purpose, the two houses took separate ballots without an election in either. Washburn received but 54 votes out of 166 cast in the two houses and he at once announced his withdrawal. His steering committee made a futile effort to rally enough votes for a dark horse who, with the support of the Washburn stalwarts, would be able to defeat Nelson. John Lind, best qualified for the emergency because of his long and honorable public record in Congress, his party fidelity, and his Scandinavian blood, declined to run. On January 23 the two houses met in joint convention. When the name of Senator Frank A. Day was called he arose and stated that it was now evident that Washburn could not be elected. It was therefore his duty to cast his vote for the candidate whom his constituents

to the author from Timothy E. Byrnes, October 25, 1923, and Elmer E. Adams, December 27, 1923, Folwell Papers. A Democratic paper, the *Minneapolis Times*, could not believe that Nelson could be guilty of " the duplicity, the coldblooded selfishness, the political immorality " that such an act might indicate, according to its issue for January 3, p. 4. See also the issue of January 4, pp. 1, 2, 4. Whether or not Nelson assured Washburn in writing that he would not be a candidate for the senatorship it is impossible to determine, because of the disappearance and probable destruction of Washburn's papers.

[58] *St. Paul Globe*, 1895: January 4, p. 1; 5, p. 1; 24, p. 1.

seemed to favor. A stampede for Nelson then set in and 102 votes
out of 167 gave him the election. Donnelly, who, as usual, was an
aspirant, received 13 votes. On January 31 Nelson relinquished
the governorship, to which Lieutenant Governor Clough succeeded.
Senator Day, who was elected president pro tempore of the Senate
on January 28, became lieutenant governor.[59]

It is not hard to account for Nelson's superior popularity. He
was a man of the people — a " good mixer," to use a slang phrase.
As a Civil War veteran, he had friends in the Grand Army of the
Republic. In a choice between Republican candidates, Scandinavian votes easily drifted toward a son of Norway. Officeholders
appointed by him naturally cast their influence for him. Individuals
and interests to whom he had rendered service in his six-year term
in Congress were naturally willing that he should have larger
opportunity for legislative service in the Senate. Most effective of all
was the enthusiasm of his young Republican friends for his advancement. Lieutenant Governor Clough, who would succeed to the governorship and whom, it was said, Washburn had befriended and
aided in business, had the credit of being a leader in the group. It
was common knowledge that James J. Hill was not friendly to
Washburn, who had built the northwestern extension of the " Soo "
Railroad between the two lines of the Great Northern. Hill is
alleged to have " contributed freely " to the aid of Nelson, but this
cannot, in the absence of proof, be construed as a corrupt use of
money. Hill was also known to be an admirer of Clough.[60]

Senator Washburn was not a " mixer." He was a college graduate and his close associations had been with people of culture and
wealth. A certain unaffected courtliness of manner rendered him
less affable than the ordinary aspirant for office. The building of
a dwelling in Minneapolis of extraordinary size and architectural
beauty, surrounded with extensive and elaborate grounds, gave occasion to some to think, if not to utter, the word " aristocrat." There

[59] Pioneer Press, 1895: January 19, p. 1; 23, p. 1; 30, p. 4; February 1,
p. 4; St. Paul Globe, 1895: January 23, p. 1; 24, p. 1; Minneapolis Tribune,
January 23, 1895, p. 1; Minneapolis Journal, January 28, 1895, p. 1; Fergus
Falls Journal, January 7, 1924, p. 2; House Journal, 1895, pp. 60, 66; Senate
Journal, 41, 58, 80, 89.

[60] Minneapolis Times, January 4, 1895, p. 1; St. Paul Globe, January 24,
1895, p. 1; Fergus Falls Journal, January 4, 1924, p. 2; Byrnes to Folwell,
October 25, 1923, Folwell Papers. Elmer E. Adams, in the Fergus Falls
Journal, January 4, 1924, p. 2, says that Clough was the "real dynamo in the
contest against Washburn." An interview between Nelson and Senator Elling
K. Roverud reported in the Minneapolis Times, January 6, 1895, p. 1, indicates that Nelson claimed Norwegian support as his due.

was prejudice in the minds of some against a man who had been engaged in building and operating railroads, in manufacturing flour, and in dealing in pine lands and lumber, and who might be supposed to have saved more than a competence for his old age and his numerous family. A close business associate said of him: "Washburn was no politician. He did not like to travel from town to town, sleep and eat in dirty hotels and hob-nob with local bosses." His very confidence of reëlection caused him to neglect consultations with members of his party, especially with younger men, who delight in thinking themselves important party function-aries, and the organization of his party followers for action. An-other matter that told against Washburn was the preference of the St. Paul faction for a new senator not from one of the Twin Cities. The election of a candidate from the country would make it easier to keep Davis in the Senate. Both Davis and Merriam remained ostensibly neutral. The *Pioneer Press* on January 11 gave notice that it would not take sides. The claim of Washburn's friends that he ought to have a reëlection according to party usage could not be urged with consistency in favor of one who six years before had allowed Dwight M. Sabin to go into retirement without the cus-tomary second term. That gentleman, whose influence was still of weight, naturally threw it against a candidate who had snatched from him the customary reëlection to the Senate. For such reasons Washburn lost the grand prize and Knute Nelson won it.[61]

The defeated aspirant did not take this simple view of the matter. In an interview with a member of the *Minneapolis Journal* staff he freed his mind of the painful subject. Governor Nelson, the senator said, had repeatedly assured him that he would not be a candidate and in his Albert Lea speech he had publicly disclaimed a candi-dacy. Clough again and again had told him that he would do anything in his power to secure the senator's election. The whole situation "was honey-combed with treachery." It was Washburn's belief that he had been defeated by the employment of the most

[61] Flandrau, *Encyclopedia of Biography*, 1: 136–142; Smalley, *Republican Party*, 248; Adams, in the *Fergus Falls Journal*, January 4, 1924, p. 2; *Pio-neer Press*, January 11, 1895, p. 4; *Minneapolis Journal*, January 5, 1895, p. 1; interview of the author with Major W. D. Hale, for many years Washburn's business secretary, recorded in the author's notebooks, 7: 32. Adams says Sabin "was on hand with his tomahawk." See the *Minneapolis Times*, Janu-ary 5, 1895, p. 1, for references to Davis' position and Sabin's attitude. An editorial entitled "Defending Duplicity," in the same issue, p. 4, called an attempt of the *Pioneer Press* to defend Nelson's action "an exhibition of boobyism in politics."

dishonest methods of ring politicians. Had he allowed the use of money for his cause, he would have been elected. Worse than the use of money by his enemies, he believed, was the outrageous manipulation of state patronage. Everything was traded to beat him. Most of the Republican members had been elected squarely and were expected to vote for him. They, or some of them, had been " debauched " since the fall election. In response to an inquiry as to the effect of the scandal on the Republican party in Minnesota, Washburn is reported to have said: " It will create the greatest upheaval ever seen. The people will not countenance such methods. I look to see the Republican party rise in its strength and utterly wipe out every politician who has been in any way connected with this unsavory case." [62]

With such an understanding of the facts of the case, the senator's indignation and his expectations of a political revolution were quite justifiable. His prophecy was not so happy. No political cataclysm followed the election of Knute Nelson. The Republican party did not rise in its might to protest against or wipe out anything. Washburn had been too long in public life and too well accustomed to the give-and-take of politics to treasure up lasting and unmitigated resentment against a successful opponent who, he thought, had defeated him by questionable means. After this futile denunciation of what he believed a dishonorable and immoral conspiracy to work his defeat for the senatorship, he easily settled into a dignified retirement to attend to his private affairs, which were of magnitude and had been much neglected, and to take his part in the interests of his neighborhood, city, and church, to which he was much devoted. For many years, until his death on July 29, 1912, he dispensed at " Fair Oaks " a generous, though not an ostentatious, hospitality. His New Year's Eve reception, with wide-open doors, was the crowning event of the season.

Nelson made no reply to Washburn's arraignment and published no apology or explanation. His friends, or some of them, explained that he was altogether sincere in his disclaimer at Albert Lea but that a change of circumstances had justified a change of mind and a strike for the senatorship. Whether the comity that obtains

---

[62] *Minneapolis Journal*, January 25, 1895. William B. Boardman, in a letter to the author, March 10, 1925, said that he heard Nelson, in one of his gubernatorial campaign speeches, state that he would support Washburn. For an opinion that money was used to elect Nelson, see the indorsement by John F. Dahl, in a letter from the author to Dahl, February 4, 1925. These letters are in the Folwell Papers.

among gentlemen, if not among politicians, should have moved him to advise Washburn of his resolution is a question upon which the reader may ruminate if he likes. Years later, in an interview with the author, Nelson flatly denied that he had promised not to be a candidate for the senatorship against Washburn. He admitted that he had spoken approvingly of Washburn at Albert Lea. But, he said, after the fall election it became known that Washburn would meet with opposition and this opposition became more pronounced after the meeting of the legislature. Clough came to Nelson and besought him " not to block his way " to the governorship. Others expressed their desire that Nelson should run for the senatorship. He resolved to leave the matter to three men, Merriam, Clough, and Henry F. Brown. They decided that he ought to declare himself. In this decision Clough " went back " on his friendship for Washburn, whose election over Sabin in 1889 he claimed to have secured. The Sabin crowd was about the Capitol.

The ambiguous disclaimer at Albert Lea does prove that Nelson was well aware of a widespread premonition that he would aspire to the United States senatorship. It would not have been unnatural for him to dream of a possible convergence of circumstances that would conduct him to that eminence. But there is reason to believe that he did more than merely allow the idea to float in his consciousness. It must have been to the end of weakening Washburn's support that, after the fall campaign of 1894, he sent an emissary to John Lind at New Ulm to ask him to come out as an aspirant for the senatorship. Lind indignantly declined and resigned a regency of the university to which Nelson had appointed him. For the same reason " material assistance " was offered to Comstock if he would appear in the field. It appears to have been a policy of the group of young Republicans working in secret for Nelson to encourage a multiplication of candidates as decoys and it is hard to believe that the governor could have been ignorant of their activities. After the election he made a small number of appointments, but these were not of a character to indicate that they were rewards for support.[63]

It will be a pleasing task for a biographer to record the long and honorable career of Knute Nelson in the United States Senate. He

[63] *Fergus Falls Journal*, January 4, 1924; letters to the author from Lind, September 17, 1923; Comstock, September 26, 1923; Byrnes, October 25, 1923; and Hiram W. Foote, June 19, 1924; memorandum of an interview of the author with Nelson, December 13, 1912. Folwell Papers.

took his seat on March 4, 1895. When he was reëlected six years later there was but little show of opposition, in view of the service he had rendered in support of the government during the Spanish-American War. In 1907 and 1913 other reëlections were accorded with no real dissent among members of his party and with but futile opposition by the minority. In 1918 came the second election in Minnesota of a United States senator under the constitutional amendment that transferred that duty from the state legislature to the electors. For the first time in his senatorial career Nelson depended upon the people of the state for his election and he was chosen without an organized campaign. At the close of the session in 1923, after he had completed twenty-eight years of service in the Senate, Nelson remained a few weeks longer at the capital before departing as usual for his Minnesota farm home. He began the journey on April 28, 1923, apparently in better health than usual. At a little after eight o'clock, while he was seated in a railway coach near Baltimore in conversation with a friend, his heart suddenly ceased to beat. The burial, which took place at Alexandria, Minnesota, on May 2, was attended by a great concourse of officials, friends, and neighbors.[64]

On Sunday, March 9, 1924, a special session of the United States Senate was devoted to eulogies of Knute Nelson and Samuel D. Nicholson of Colorado. Henrik Shipstead, the senior senator from Minnesota, opened with a biographical sketch of Nelson, which was itself a eulogium. Lodge of Massachusetts, after referring to his long association with Nelson in both houses of Congress, spoke of him as " a strong man in every way, a good lawyer, and a most excellent Senator, hard-working, diligent, and always master of any subject which he took up. . . . he was always listened to with close attention. . . . I have seen him . . . change votes in the Senate in debate and carry other Senators with him by the mere force of his character and good sense." Harris of Georgia, after mentioning Nelson's service in the Civil War, said, " Brave soldier that he was, he stopped fighting when the war was over. . . . He was anxious to do his part in welding all sections of this country into one great nation." Overman of North Carolina, although not present, pre-

---

[64] Minnesota, *House Journal*, 1901, pp. 82, 89; 1907, pp. 92, 106; 1913, pp. 128, 136; *Senate Journal*, 1901, p. 75; 1907, p. 105; 1913, p. 83; United States, *Statutes at Large*, 38: 2049; *Minneapolis Tribune*, 1923: April 29, section 1, p. 1; April 30, p. 1; May 3, p. 1. The vote at the election of 1918 was: Nelson, 206,684; Willis G. Calderwood, 137,296. *Legislative Manual*, 1918, insert following p. 670.

pared a speech in which he praised Nelson's service on the " great Judiciary Committee" where he was recognized as "one of the greatest lawyers of the body." As chairman he was always patient and considerate. Magnus Johnson of Minnesota, Nelson's successor, spoke of his personal qualities, known through a long acquaintance, and summed them up as "courage to act in accordance with the conclusions of his mind; fidelity to friends and to those who rendered him service; and a definite position on issues regardless of consequences." Jones of Washington said: "Here in the Senate no people had a more faithful, able, or sincere representative than he. He was at his office early and late, and no committee meeting found him absent if it was possible for him to attend. . . . He was wise in council, able in debate, and fearless in action." Warren of Wyoming praised Nelson's simplicity, common sense, courage, and the freedom from hypocrisy that marked him for admiration not only at home but abroad. He spoke also of their close attachment, which had its origin in the circumstance that both had participated in the siege of Port Hudson and had been wounded there.[65]

The following extraordinary appreciation of Knute Nelson by President Coolidge is quoted from a Minnesota newspaper:

All of the elder generation of the Congress were griefstricken to learn of the loss of Senator Knute Nelson of Minnesota. He had the love and respect of all who came in contact with him. He was a powerful influence for sound legislation in the Senate, one who always sought, first and foremost, the public welfare without subserviency to the supposed interest of any class or section. He did not hesitate to disagree with those who were powerful, nor was he backward in supporting those who were weak. He considered the cause, rather than those who advocated it, and sought for approbation by promoting the welfare of his country. He was a leader in the highest and best sense of the term. He thought out what was right and in announcing his position drew to it public support, rather than undertaking to give all heed to the transient clamor of the hour and yield support to it with the lip service of a servile mind.

Senator Nelson was a great man. He had a broad comprehension of national problems and a facility in providing practical remedies. He was a tower of strength to his party. He kept his head when others were confused and he did right when others thought it was expedient to do wrong. It would be difficult to select a more representative American in thought and speech and action. He kept his own counsel and represented his own opinions.[66]

[65] *Congressional Record*, 68 Congress, 1 session, 3857–3862.
[66] *Fergus Falls Journal*, January 7, 1924. The letter quoted is in the possession of Elmer E. Adams, to whom it was addressed. In a letter of July 28, 1926, received by the author after these pages had been set up, Mr. Laurits Swenson, explaining the situation at Albert Lea and Nelson's intentional use of the phrase, "or if you do not like him some other good Republican," writes that Washburn's appearance at Albert Lea was a surprise.

14. PINE TIMBER INVESTIGATIONS [67]

The exploitation of " pine " that led to the investigations of 1893 was no novelty. A beginning of " wholesale plundering " had been made in the sixties, before the state was ten years old. An interested reader may have observed that the acquittal of Charles McIlrath on both civil and criminal prosecutions in 1875 and 1876 absolved him from any conversion or embezzlement of public funds passing through his hands. It cannot be said, however, that the acquittal absolved him also from culpable mismanagement in the handling of pine timber during his long incumbency, from 1861 to 1872, in the combined offices of state auditor and land commissioner.[68]

In the territorial period and in the first five years of statehood there were no sales of timber from state-owned lands separate from the land on which it grew. There was little, if any, demand for such timber, as there was available for manufacture a great abundance of pine timber belonging to the United States. As the pineries at length became remote and went into private hands, the timber on state lands was regarded with desirous, not to say covetous, eyes. But lumbermen preferred not to pay for land that, after the pine had been taken from it, would be just so many useless acres left on their hands to be taxed. As if in preparation for a change of policy, the legislature of 1862 passed an act to establish a state land office. The state auditor was made commissioner of public lands ex officio. The legislature of the following year, 1863, enacted a law for regulating the management of school lands. One of the sections empowered the state land commissioner " whenever in his opinion the best interest of the school fund would be promoted thereby," to grant permits to cut pine timber from school lands. The act, which was embodied without material change in the *General Statutes* of 1866, authorized the land office to grant such permits to cut pine timber only at public auction after thirty days' published notice. No bids were to be accepted for less than a price fixed by a district surveyor-general of logs and lumber. All timber cut was to remain the property of the state until it was fully paid for. With these restrictions the land commissioner was empowered to establish proper regulations.[69]

[67] See *ante,* p. 207.

[68] For an account of the prosecution of McIlrath and his vindication, see *ante,* pp. 88–90.

[69] *General Laws,* 1862, pp. 121–132; 1863, pp. 46–50; *General Statutes,* 1866, pp. 317–325. In 1861 acts were passed creating the state board of com-

McIlrath was much pleased with the operation of the act. The transactions under the act, he announced in his report for 1867, had fully vindicated the new policy of selling stumpage instead of land. The pine on one section of school land had been sold for fourteen thousand dollars, or twenty-two and a half dollars an acre. Another section yielded thirteen dollars an acre and three others, from seven to ten dollars. Enough young trees had been left standing to warrant an expectation that in five years there would be a second cutting worth half the value of the original one. The " stumpage system," he added, had brought logging within the reach of the great mass of lumbermen and had aroused healthy competition among them. No capitalists could hold values down by combination and thereby cause loss to the state.[70]

In what manner the " stumpage system " was actually operated and with what results was revealed in the report of the Senate committee that had moved Governor Davis to start the prosecution of McIlrath. The committee report had no place in the litigation. McIlrath appeared at the first meeting of the committee and read a written statement, probably true and certainly plausible, relating wholly to his pecuniary activities in the handling of pine. The committee, however, considered that its duty extended beyond an inquiry into the bare question whether the moneys and securities paid to McIlrath had been fully accounted for. It was thus drawn into an investigation of the whole operation of the " stumpage system " by its inventor, or, more accurately, perhaps, its indorser. It examined nearly a hundred witnesses, some of them " most reluctant to give evidence." In closing the report the committee sorrowfully recorded its conviction that " No citizen of our young State can learn the facts herein disclosed, without feeling humiliated and

missioners of public lands and the state board of commissioners of school lands. Both boards were to be composed of the governor, the attorney-general, and the state superintendent of public instruction. The state auditor was made register of both, a fact long forgotten. See *General Laws*, 1861, pp. 75–94. The first and only report of the public land commissioners is in *Executive Documents*, 1861, pp. 557–563. McIlrath, as register, suggested a simplification of the law. Both of the acts mentioned were repealed by the law of 1862. In 1858 four log and lumber districts were located, with offices at Stillwater, St. Anthony, Red Wing, and Swan River. The office for the fourth district was later moved from Swan River to St. Cloud. An act of 1874 provided that, instead of being elected by the legislature, as had been customary, the surveyors-general of logs and lumber should be appointed by the governor, with the advice and consent of the Senate. *General Laws*, 1858, p. 264; 1863, p. 65; 1874, p. 223.

[70] *Executive Documents*, 1867, p. 462.

indignant, at discovering that one of the most sacred trusts ever imposed upon a public officer has been thus violated." [71]

A perusal of the report and of the testimony taken will fully justify this mournful conclusion. McIlrath's radical error, in the estimation of the present author, was a misconception of the law. Both principle and precedent made the state treasurer the recipient and custodian of state funds. McIlrath construed the law authorizing him as state land commissioner to " sell " pine stumpage as giving him authority to receive the money for timber sold, to hold it indefinitely, and to pay it into the treasury at his convenience. He therefore turned over money in gross sums without making specific statements of its sources. He handled the " stumpage system " as if it were a private business. Another error was that of not adhering to the law requiring that permits be issued only at the advertised times of sales. The adjournment of sales from time to time gave opportunity for the avoidance of competition. In numerous instances verbal permits were granted, which were construed as extensions of regular permits. The committee was unable to find any systematic account or record of permits, either of the regular species or of the irregular variety. It was found that at the appointed public sales at county seats there was little or no competition. Each lumberman present, according to an understanding that needed no documents, bid for the tracts he desired, generally at the minimum price, and no one was so unneighborly as to raise the bid.[72]

McIlrath was still more culpable for his practice of allowing, not to say encouraging, lumbermen to cut timber when they pleased without permits and then to settle, without penalty, on terms mutually satisfactory. A bad appearance was given to this practice

[71] *Report of the Special Senate Committee Appointed to Investigate the Management of the Office of State Auditor, Prior to January, 1873,* 3–7, 25, 41 (n. p., 1875). The first reference that the author has found to the " stumpage system " is in McIlrath's report in *Executive Documents,* 1862, p. 598. In this report McIlrath recommended substantially the system embodied in the act of 1863.

[72] *Report of the Special Senate Committee,* 30, 40, 120, 195–198, 350. McIlrath testified that he " kept the sales open from month to month." The section of chapter 38 of the *General Statutes* of 1866 relating to the sale of pine timber on school lands, section 52, did not in express terms direct payments for pine permits to be made to the state treasurer; but section 18 required that all moneys received for any lands belonging to the state be paid to the state treasurer. The committee understood that it was " not contemplated by the law . . . that any public money should pass through the hands of the State Auditor or Land Commissioner."

by a departure from ordinary procedure. Timber cut under permits
was scaled by district surveyors-general or their deputies. Timber
cut by trespassers was estimated by examiners or " explorers " who
were sent out by the commissioner and who reported to him personally. The committee believed that these explorers, or some of
them, were well paid by lumbermen for turning in " favorable
reports " of stumpage, but it had difficulty in eliciting precise testimony on the subject. The committee could find no proper record of
timber cut by trespassers and McIlrath deliberately refused to aid in
the search. He had, the committee said, in some important transactions merely kept " loose memoranda giving indefinite information,
of an ambiguous character." As McIlrath testified, " the trespass
matter was . . . one of the most irregular transactions." [73]

A particular case of error was that of the disposition of hard
wood on two sections of school land in Hennepin County. McIlrath
knew that he had no authority to sell hardwood timber and he
refused a permit to a very prominent citizen who applied for one;
but he allowed him to cut railroad ties and bridge timber as a tres-
passer. The ingenious citizen proceeded with his cutting, but,
instead of settling for trespass, he waited until the next public sale
of school lands, when he bought the two sections at ten dollars an
acre. He paid the required twenty per cent of the purchase price
and got a certificate of sale. After paying interest on the purchase
for a year or two, he sold his " interest " for $5,351.79 to a prom-
inent business firm of St. Paul. The purchasers held the land long
enough to strip it of all trees fit for cordwood and then abandoned
it to the state as " murdered land."

From the testimony taken the committee believed itself justified
— and it was — in saying that a " system of wholesale plunder "
had been practiced, resulting in enormous losses to the school and
other funds. The reasonable counsel of the committee that the
offices of state auditor and state land commissioner be completely
separated and so organized that each would operate as a check
upon the other has not to this day been adopted. Whereby hang
suspicions.[74]

The number of permits to cut pine under the act of 1863 increased
at such a rate in the course of a decade that the legislature of 1877,
as if distrusting the discretion allowed to the state auditor, estab-

[73] *Report of the Special Senate Committee*, 17, 20–26, 30, 40, 79, 121–124,
128–137, 150, 390. " Most all the trespass was done on Swamp and Railroad
lands," according to McIlrath.
[74] *Report of the Special Senate Committee*, 26, 36, 239–264, 385.

lished a new policy, that of selling pine timber from state lands only when it was subject to waste from windfalls, fire, or other destructive causes. Sales were to be made at the state Capitol, after advertisement for sixty days, for not less than the estimated value as approved by the commissioner. Under this act there was a large increase in the number of permits issued. Again the legislature took alarm and in 1885 it provided by law that no sales of timber should be made except upon estimates of amount and value approved and indorsed by the governor, the state treasurer, and the auditor, or by any two of them. The restriction of sales to timber in danger of waste was not repealed nor modified. Still the number of permits did not abate. It requires a degree of charity to attribute the persistence of sales of timber in danger of waste to accidents, to the extension of settlements, and to the building of railroads.[75]

The reader will easily recall the action of the legislature of 1893, instigated by Representative Robert C. Dunn on March 1, authorizing Governor Nelson to investigate the illegal sale of pine timber from a school section in Mille Lacs County to a firm of lumbermen and to take proper steps to secure the state from loss. The investigation took the form of a suit by the state against the lumber company. The trial in the district court began on September 7, 1893, at Princeton in Mille Lacs County and was argued at St. Cloud on October 26. Judgment was entered on December 4. The court recited the history of the transactions that preceded the litigation and somewhat curtly decided that the sale was void and that the state had a right to recover the sum of $9,514.89, with interest from June 23, 1893. The judges, Luther L. Baxter and Dolson B. Searle, however, signed a memorandum stating the grounds of their decision. Though his name was not mentioned, the state auditor, Adolph Biermann, was held derelict for the following reasons: (1) he had not obtained proper information as to whether the pine timber on section 36, township 42, range 26, was in danger of destruction or material loss from fire or some other cause; (2) he had had no proper estimate made of the amount of the stumpage; (3) he had had no proper appraisal made of its value; and (4) he had made a private sale without notice, although the law required

75 General Laws, 1877, p. 88; 1885, p. 331; General Statutes, 1878, p. 518; 1891, vol. 1, p. 949. An examination of the reports of the state treasurer from year to year will show the number of permits given out and the number of cases of trespass reported.

APPENDIX (14)

a sale at public auction after sixty days' published notice. The sale was therefore void. In determining the amount to be recovered the court considered from the testimony that the true value of the stumpage was four dollars per thousand feet, board measure, instead of two dollars, the price at which the illegal sale had been negotiated. That the state auditor had, as he testified, merely conformed to established custom in making the sale was no defense. He was presumed to know the law and had been sworn to execute it. The purchasers of the timber should have known that the transaction was unlawful and they were therefore culpable and liable in damages for the difference between the real value of the timber they had already removed and the price they were to pay under the illegal contract. The silent partner in the lumber firm named was a citizen of the highest distinction, who, it may be assumed, had left this branch of his extensive affairs to his younger, adventurous, and perhaps reckless partner. The decision of the court was both commended and severely criticized in the Twin City newspapers. One of them declared that the whole affair was engineered by Dunn, who wished to gain publicity by posing as a watchdog of the treasury and win the Republican nomination to the state auditorship. He was nominated and elected to that office in the fall of 1894 and held it eight years. Biermann published an explanation that amounted to a confession and at the expiration of his term on December 31, 1894, he retired from public life.[76]

The investigation started by Dunn was an isolated case. That proposed on the same day by Senator Keller, at Donnelly's instance, contemplated a sweeping inquiry into " generally known " exemptions from taxation due to the corrupt and unlawful action of county officials and into other matters pertaining to such exemptions. A few days later the passage of a Senate resolution authorizing the expenditure of two hundred dollars for witnesses' fees and expenses narrowed the scope of investigation to the failure to

---

[76] *Princeton Union*, December 14, 21, 28; *Minneapolis Journal*, December 8, 12, 15, 16; *Minneapolis Times*, December 8, 12; *St. Paul Globe*, December 8, 9, 12, 16, 22; *Pioneer Press*, December 7, 1893; *Mississippi Valley Lumberman*, December 15, 1893, p. 2. For a history of the transaction, the decision of the judges, and an abstract of the testimony, see the *Princeton Union*, December 7, 1893. The *Union* was Dunn's paper. The timber from the piece of land, which was in section 36, township 42, range 26, was sold in 1895 at $5.25 per thousand feet. See the report of the state auditor, in *Executive Documents*, 1896, vol. 1, p. 337, and *House Journal*, 1893, p. 351. Biermann gave some excellent advice for amending the law in his report in *Executive Documents*, 1894, vol. 1, p. 187.

tax pine lands and, especially, to the "stealing of pine timber from
school lands." The report of the Keller committee, submitted on
April 10, 1893, announced the discovery of a "boundless sea of
iniquity." The state school fund had been robbed of millions of
dollars and the university had been plundered in an "equally outrageous manner." "The horrible part of it" was that men of large
wealth and high social position had joined in the scheme of plunder. The committee recommended that a commission be created
to serve without pay and to continue the investigation thus begun.
If properly pushed, the investigation might turn millions of dollars
into the treasury.[77]

The legislature might have been content to pigeonhole the report
as one of Donnelly's romances, but the large body of recorded testimony gave it pause. After the receipt of a request from Governor
Nelson that Donnelly be permitted to introduce a bill into the Senate, although the time limit set by the state constitution for the introduction of bills had expired, both houses deemed it prudent to give
Donnelly all the rope he wanted and passed with but one opposing
vote the joint resolution presented by him. This remarkable resolution provided for the creation of a committee of seven, three from
the Senate and four from the House, to inquire into lands belonging

[77] *Senate Journal,* 1893, pp. 318, 343, 748; John Day Smith to the author,
December 1, 1923, Folwell Papers. The report of the committee called forth
from Loren Fletcher, congressman from the fifth district, a statement that
may have voiced the sentiments of some of his fellow lumbermen. Said
Fletcher, "It is the same old chestnut. . . . It has been gone over and over
for the last 25 years, and it has been my experience in years past that the
men that are so anxious to investigate . . . are the very class of men that
their neighbors and constituents had better keep their eyes on. I think it is
simply bosh that men with very little character should attempt to malign or
belittle men . . . who have done so much to build up this state and nation
and for the general welfare of mankind. I think it bosh that these men
should be dragged before the public by this rat-headed gang of reformers."
Fletcher's statement appeared in the *Minneapolis Tribune,* April 12, 1893,
p. 2. Early on the next day, April 13, Donnelly introduced in the Senate a
series of "whereases," in which it was suggested that any man who, without
excuse, provocation, justification, or compensation, would defend thieves,
would, if opportunity was presented, steal everything he could lay his hands
on. The superfluous resolution that followed condemned the statement of
Fletcher and provided for sending copies of the preamble and the resolution
to the president and his cabinet and to each senator and representative in
Congress and for printing them in the *Senate Journal.* Upon Donnelly's
motion the resolution was laid on the table. In his remarks he let loose a
flood of sarcasm and invective that in venom was, perhaps, second only to
that poured out upon a certain colleague in Congress twenty-five years previously. *Minneapolis Tribune,* 1893: April 13, p. 1; 14, p. 2; *Senate Journal,*
1893, p. 797.

to the state that had been despoiled of timber by " open robbery " or otherwise. Power was given to the committee as a whole and to each member individually to visit parts of the state, to summon witnesses, and to take testimony. Upon consultation with the governor, the committee might bring suit against offenders, in which case the attorney-general was to be " assisted " by counsel selected by the committee. The compensation of members was limited to five dollars a day for time actually spent. Five thousand dollars were appropriated for the uses of the committee and ten thousand dollars were to be expended by the governor in a general inspection of the timber lands of the state.[78]

After some delay in obtaining a ruling that the five-thousand-dollar appropriation might be taken from a remaining balance of the appropriation for legislative expenses, the committee members set to work. They found the duty arduous, exacting, and most unpleasant. They " met fraud and treachery and deceit at every turn." But they persevered, took their time, and submitted their report to Governor Nelson on December 21, 1894, in time for him to examine it before the meeting of the legislature of 1895.[79]

The findings of the committee will be better appreciated after a summary of the routine prescribed by law for the emergency sale of pine timber at that time. The various steps in the procedure were: (1) the decision of the state auditor, as commissioner of the land office, that the pine on a certain tract was in danger of material waste by fire or other destructive force; (2) the estimate by the land commissioner of the amount and value of the timber, its situation relative to risk from fire or damage of any kind, and its distance from the nearest lake, stream, or railroad; (3) the approval of the opinion and estimate by the governor, the state treasurer, and the land commissioner, or any two of the three acting separately; (4) the sale of the timber at public auction in the

---

[78] *Senate Journal*, 1893, pp. 858, 872, 881, 900; *House Journal*, 835; *General Laws*, 413. For a joint resolution introduced by Senator John Day Smith, also upon the request of Governor Nelson, for the appointment of a commission to investigate frauds in relation to public lands, see *Senate Journal*, 762, 774–776. The Senate adopted the resolution by a vote of 44 to 1. After consultations, it seems to have been set aside for Donnelly's resolution.

[79] *Report of the Pine Land Investigating Committee*, 1–3. It is notable that the statesmen in St. Paul, including Governor Nelson, did not remember that section 12 of article 4 of the state constitution expressly provides that " No money shall be appropriated except by bill." Governor Nelson turned over a small balance allowed him and made no independent investigation. Harris Richardson of St. Paul was employed by the committee and by Governor Nelson.

Capitol at St. Paul to the highest bidder, after sixty days' notice in one or more of the St. Paul newspapers; (5) the issue by the commissioner of a permit to the purchaser, who was to "cut the land clean, acre by acre"; (6) the actual official measurement of the logs cut and the submission to the commissioner of a detailed report of the measurements; (7) the payment to the state treasurer, on the auditor's draft, for the whole amount of pine cut. When the last of these steps was taken, the lumberman was at liberty to transport the logs as his own.[80]

Among the irregularities found by the investigation committee were fraudulent estimates made by incompetent men instead of by cruisers of ability and experience. One estimator, who, it may be hoped, was not typical, had been a sailor for nine years, a policeman for seven years, an operator of a ferryboat for fourteen months, a surveyor's helper for three years, and a deputy warden in the state prison for four years. This man had been appointed upon the recommendation of ten citizens of standing as being well qualified for the position in every way. He testified that he was not an expert in estimating timber and that a clerk in the auditor's office had filled up his reports and fixed the values. There were also frauds attributable not to mere incompetence but to sheer dishonesty. An auditor's clerk obtained from an unofficial expert estimates of fifteen tracts that showed nearly twenty-two million feet of timber. These estimates were treated as official and were placed on file with the twenty-two million feet reduced to nine million.[81]

The evidence taken disclosed the fact that it had become customary in the auditor's office to extemporize estimates at the time of advertised sales. "It is often the case," said one witness employed in the office, "that right on the day of sale we ask a man if he has ever been on a certain tract of land, and if he has, we ask him how

[80] *General Laws,* 1885, p. 331; *General Statutes,* 1891, vol. I, pp. 949-952.
[81] *Report of the Pine Land Investigating Committee,* 38, 42-47, 52. On page 53 there is a table showing the variances in the reports of official estimators, of a surveyor-general, and of experts employed by the committee on ten sections of land. A summary of the sections listed, omitting one for which an item is lacking, gives the following result: reported by official estimators, 7,325,000 feet; reported by a surveyor-general, 11,094,022 feet; reported by the committee's experts, 38,767,458 feet. The last of the sections reported on contained 8,255,082 feet by true estimate — more by 930,082 feet than the amount reported by the official estimators for all the nine sections. On one of the sections the state estimators had discovered but 200,000 feet, while the committee's men found 3,448,931. On still another section the true scaling showed 3,172,400 feet as compared with the state scalers' estimate of 200,000 feet. This last figure may have been a customary guess.

much it will cut, and how much it is worth, and we sell it on that."
Large numbers of estimates and appraisals had been made out in
blank form to be ready for filling in amounts and values when decided upon in the auditor's office. Early in the investigation it was
discovered that the provision of law requiring the approval of estimates by the three officials above mentioned, or by any two of them,
had been for a long time systematically ignored. One or another
of the timber commissioners had perfunctorily approved the estimates made out in the state auditor's office. In the judgment of the
committee, there had not been, therefore, a single valid sale of pine
from March 7, 1885, to January 1, 1891.

A fruitful source of fraud against the state was the practice of
lumbermen of running up the price of certain tracts at the bidding,
obtaining permits to cut, and then, instead of cutting, letting their
permits expire by limitation in order to buy later, with the connivance of some one in the auditor's office, at a lower price. William Sauntry, for instance, on September 3, 1890, bought the timber
on a certain section at $4.40 per thousand; on September 17, 1892,
he bought the same piece at $1.50. Akin to this practice was that
of allowing buyers to cut off the best trees and to get the residue
later at a lower price.[82]

To ascertain the amount and value of timber cut under a permit,
so-called " scalers " were appointed by the surveyor-general of the
district in which the timber was located. Under presumption of
law these scalers were state employees, paid by the state for honest
and independent service. The committee found that " the rule of
procedure " followed permitted the lumber concerns to nominate
employees as scalers, secure their appointments, and then pay their
salaries, board, and transportation. Such connivance by surveyors-
general saved them the scalers' pay, which normally would come
out of the fees allowed for the service. It is not difficult to imagine
how one such scaler could measure but 357,000 feet on a certain
section while a lumber company afterwards paid $18,000 for
7,000,000 feet cut from the tract rather than stand a lawsuit. For
further assurance the committee, under its powers, had competent
woodsmen rescale from tops and stumps the timber that had been cut
on fifty sections or parts of sections. They reported an aggregate
of seventy-three million feet; the amount reported to the state auditor from the same land was twenty-three million feet — a shortage

[82]*Report of the Pine Land Investigating Committee*, 4–6, 14, 20–24, 35, 37.

of fifty million. For still further assurance the committee had seventy-eight sections, or parts of sections, examined without scaling. It was found that about eighty million feet of timber had been removed; the scalings reported to the auditor amounted to about thirty-eight million. The report of the committee stated, as if it were a common occurrence, that when a lumberman purchased a forty adjoining a school section and put his crews to work on both, " the blind scaler " would " keep his ' eyes and mouth closed ' to everything not seen on the landing " and accept the lumberman's report that six million feet had been cut from the forty and three hundred thousand from the school section, when the amounts should have been reversed. Another evil practice was the unlawful tolerance of the state treasurer in allowing buyers of state pine to delay payment, in some cases until after the logs had been driven to the sawmill, manufactured into lumber, and sold.[83]

An unexpected revelation was that for years the state auditor, without a scintilla of authority, had been selling hardwood stumpage from the land, as a rule without estimating, advertising, or observing any of the safeguards required for the sale of pine timber. Thousands of acres of hardwood forests had been despoiled, involving losses to the school fund of far more than a million dollars. Without having gone into a full investigation, the committee criticized a custom, promoted by state auditors, of selling cedar, tamarack, and pine of unknown amount for railroad ties without estimate or scale, the buyers' word being taken for both the amount and the value of the cut.

In regard to the duty of the auditor to protect the state from loss, the committee did not mince matters, particularly with reference to the school fund. It charged him with palpable neglect of duty, with neglect of the state's interest, with careless and unsystematic conduct of business, and with either unpardonable ignorance or downright dishonesty. " All the records pertaining to state lands " up to 1891, the report asserted, " are not even an apology for records." In many cases mere loose sheets were found and these were not even filed; plat books were merely checked. Where there was a pretense of a book account there was no system and no index. The committee formed no better opinion of the manner in

[83] *Report of the Pine Land Investigating Committee,* 25, 28, 32, 54, 56, 79. A report made by the state treasurer to the committee in October, 1893, showed uncollected drafts for stumpage dating back to 1884. The whole sum uncollected was a loan to lumbermen.

which surveyors-general had conducted their official business. It was high time, said the committee, that honest and intelligent citizens were put into these responsible positions as guardians of the state and of her children. The committee did not openly assert that the whole body of officials and employees concerned held their positions in consideration of political services rendered or promised, but left the reader to make the inference.

In a summary of the results of its labors, the committee first took into account actual and expected recoveries to the state of considerable amounts of money. Two lumber companies and one individual had paid into the treasury, without suit, $30,526.29, the difference in value between eleven million feet of timber cut from school sections as found by the committee's scalers and the two million reported to the state auditor by official scalers. The committee left pending six lawsuits against two corporations, one firm, and three individuals, in which the sum of $157,284.28 was claimed to be due the state for stumpage dishonestly scaled and reported. Papers in seventeen other suits were nearly ready to be served and from these suits it was expected that $205,076.44 would be collected. But the $393,094.85 thus to be saved to the school fund was, in the committee's opinion, " a mere bagatelle " compared with the much greater amount that had been saved in two years by the scare it had raised in the offices of the state auditor and the surveyors-general and in the effect its discoveries had had on the consciences of lumbermen. Lifelong stumpage thieves had actually been making honest reports. One case gave occasion for the interjection of a story that broke the monotony of censure in the report: that of a farmer who had devised a scarecrow so terrific that the crows not only stopped stealing his corn but brought back what they had robbed him of the year before. The stoppage of the sale of hardwood timber by Biermann, when he was apprised by the committee that he had no authority to sell, would, it was thought, pay the expenses of the investigation.[84]

[84] *Report of the Pine Land Investigating Committee,* 15–17, 32, 34, 36, 39, 77–80, 82. The cost of the investigation was $8,892.99. The author does not deem it worth while to parade the names of the men, of high standing in business, who paid on demand for timber illegally cut or the names of those against whom the committee had brought suit. These individuals were no more reprehensible than the seventeen whom the committee had prepared to prosecute nor than the large additional number who had been able to cover their tracks. Some of the latter, by making liberal benefactions to churches, communities, and colleges have brought forth fruit meet for repentance. Orfield is not so tolerant in his *Federal Land Grants,* 217.

The limited means at the command of the committee had obliged it to restrict its scrutiny to a small part of the field; it had covered only sections, when whole townships remained untouched. The old robbery was still going on all over the state. Investigation, said the committee, ought to be carried on to a just consummation by a committee of earnest men, backed by the whole power of the state. The report closed with a body of recommendations designed to assist the legislature in abating, if not in abolishing, the abuses found to exist in the sale of pine timber in danger of waste.

Donnelly, as chairman of the committee, signed the report cheerfully and was given leave to add some supplementary suggestions. The original provision by law for the occasional sale of pine timber going to waste on state lands, he said, had opened the door but an inch or two; but a vast army of adventurers, honest and dishonest, had poured through the crevice and had taken possession of the great bulk of the pine on public lands, violating every restraining provision of law and disregarding every safeguard. Unless the door were closed, it was very likely that every remaining foot of pine owned by the state would be carried out through it. His judgment was that no pine stumpage should be sold, but that the state, by her own agents, should cut any pieces in danger of devastation, drive the logs to the markets, and dispose of them. It would be vain to trust even honest men with the administration of the millions involved, since they would " find themselves surrounded by the sharpest set of rascals that our modern civilization has ever given birth to." " Close the doors absolutely," said Donnelly, " and let the rascals find out some other victims than the children of the state." [85]

The state legislature of 1895, before which the report of the Pine Land Investigating Committee was laid, must have been impressed by these revelations, although Donnelly was not there to raise the roof of the Capitol with volcanic denunciations of timber thieves. No attention was given to the committee's exhortation to put the whole power of the state behind a committee of " earnest men " to continue the investigation that had been little more than begun. Governor Clough naturally did not enjoin the legislature to pursue the inquest and the attorney-general was not eager to press existing prosecutions nor to institute new ones. Revelations of further and possibly vaster robberies would only add sorrow to sorrow for men who had " done so much to build this state " without greatly enrich-

[85] *Report of the Pine Land Investigating Committee*, 80, 82, 84–86.

ing the treasury. The legislature therefore chose the more comfortable and, perhaps, the more judicious course of providing better safeguards for preserving the residue of pine timber on state lands liable to waste. A very carefully drawn bill, amounting to a minor code, was introduced under the title, "An act regulating state lands and the product of the same." The bill was passed without extensive debate and took effect on June 1, 1895.[86]

The act contained the already traditional provision that the pine timber on state lands could be sold for cutting only when it was in danger of waste or destruction. Estimators were required to have had five years' experience in examining timber and to be skilled in woodcraft; they were to be put under oath and to be liable to a fine of one thousand dollars or imprisonment for one year, or both, for neglect or violation of duty. The governor, the state auditor, and the state treasurer were to constitute a board of timber commissioners to sit and act together. No sale of pine should be made until after each estimate had been approved and signed by the whole board. Neglect of duty by a surveyor-general was made punishable by the same penalties as those prescribed for estimators; their deputies, who should be scalers, were made liable to one-half the same penalties. The land commissioner, who was the state auditor, was always liable to impeachment under the constitution. He was required to keep in a "stumpage book" a record of all sales of timber and to have an index to all documents on file relating

[86] *House Journal*, 1895, p. 544; *Senate Journal*, 731. The voting on the bill shows that there was an opposition of considerable strength. It passed the House by a vote of 73 to 35 and the Senate by a vote of 29 to 18. The bill was drawn by Charles F. Staples and Silas W. Leavett, members of the investigating committee, assisted by Harris Richardson, who had been the efficient attorney of the committee. Staples said that the object of the bill was to restrict the sale of pine as much as possible. See Jacob F. Jacobson to the author, December 10, 19, 1923, in the Folwell Papers. For the debates on the bill in both houses, see the *Pioneer Press*, 1895: March 29, p. 4; April 20, p. 2; and the *St. Paul Globe*, 1895: March 29, p. 5; April 18, p. 5; 20, p. 5.

No reference to the investigation has been found in either of Governor Clough's messages. In his report in *Executive Documents*, 1894, vol. 4, p. 741, the attorney-general stated that $10,302.48 had been recovered from one derelict company; that $20,000 had been recovered from another in two suits and that three suits were pending against the same company for $38,264.88; that a judgment had been entered against an individual for $7,500; that three suits were pending against another company for $45,598.08 and for the value of 3,285,153 feet of logs; that a suit was pending against still another company for the value of timber cut on two sections; that a suit had been entered against a partnership for $40,000; and that two other suits were pending against individuals for amounts not stated.

thereto. A notable and convenient act of grace was quietly interpolated as an amendment; it authorized the auditor to compromise with parties for irregular cutting when, in his judgment, the best interest of the state would be served, but never for less than double the admitted or agreed amount of trespass. If the members of that legislature generally had foreseen or suspected the operation of this amendment they never would have agreed to it. Its effect was to nullify in great part the prosecutions begun by the Pine Land Investigating Committee, to the great comfort of defending lumbermen.[87]

In the legislature of 1905 were members who had personal knowledge of the practices of pine land pirates. With their aid a bill summing up in a code the safeguards that experience had suggested and adding somewhat to them was framed and passed. The power to make settlements with trespassers was taken from the state auditor and was lodged with a board of timber commissioners. The board was authorized to employ cruisers to check up the figures of estimators appointed by the auditor. All scaling of logs was to be done on the land where the timber stood and not on the landing and, furthermore, the logs were to be scaled for contents in board feet, stamped with the letters MIN, bark-marked, and numbered consecutively in the scaler's book. Major offenses were to be considered felonies. The act further provided that every person engaged in cutting timber under permit on state lands should post conspicuously and keep so posted in his camp a full description of the land to be cut over; failure to do so was to be punished by a fine of one hundred dollars or ninety days in jail. In case a lessee failed to pay for the timber cut by him, the attorney-general was required to prosecute and the auditor was authorized to seize the logs and sell them at auction. It would seem that every possible precaution for preventing timber depredations had by this time been taken. The law was perfect; nothing remained but to find some honest men to enforce it, should enforcement be necessary. The *General Statutes* of 1913 added but little from intermediate amendments. An act of 1919 provided for one state surveyor-general and declared the acceptance of any gratuity or compensation from a source other

[87] *General Laws*, 1895, pp. 349–371. The stated sums involved in the suits still pending amounted to $123,862.96. But the state auditor, Robert C. Dunn, in his report in *Executive Documents*, 1896, vol. 1, p. 336, stated that he had settled with all the parties named and with one other for an aggregate sum of $17,082.50, acting upon the advice of the attorney-general that the state would do better to settle than to litigate.

than the state by anyone in the service to be a felony. The increased rigor of the law indicates that the irregular denudation of state lands had not become a lost art and that their protection was still necessary.[88]

It is a matter of regret that this long series of efforts to check the devastation of state timbered lands, pine and other kinds, has been but partially successful. An inspection of the reports of the state treasurer and the attorney-general down to the present time will reveal a very large number of trespasses for which settlement has been made or judgments have been collected after prosecutions. That so many trespasses should have been committed accidentally by working parties mistaking section and subdivision lines and corners would indicate a degree of recklessness bordering on criminality. That there have been collusions between lumbermen and state authorities and employees no one, in the absence of proof, would venture to assert as a fact. The number of millions of dollars lost to the state, especially to her school and university funds, by a vicious forest policy and unconscionable depredations will never be computed; and the loss of Minnesota is a bagatelle compared with that suffered by the United States.

15. HOME RULE CHARTERS [89]

It may have been some lingering tradition of franchises enjoyed by Roman cities that impelled urban communities of western Europe, not long after the crusades, to beg for protection from the feudal lords. This, along with some immunities and privileges, was granted in consideration of contributions to the ever-yawning war chests of the nobles. With the establishment of enduring monarchy by the subjection of the barons to lords suzerain, the granting of charters to cities became a royal prerogative, nowhere more firmly exercised than in England. The king of England, lord paramount of the realm and the sole fountain of justice, alone possessed the right to create corporations and give them a kind of legal immortality. This right was delegated by the crown to the governors of the American colonies. Upon the establishment of American independence, the royal right of eminent domain and the power to create corporations became without controversy, under the circumstances,

[88] *General Laws,* 1905, pp. 258–273; 1919, pp. 513–516; *General Statutes,* 1913, pp. 1146–1156.
[89] See *ante,* p. 224.

a legislative prerogative. State legislatures exercised the power
and it was long believed that Congress could create no corporations
except such as might be "necessary and proper" for carrying out
the powers scheduled in the eighth section of the first article of the
national Constitution.[90]

Because the occasions therefor were rare, corporations in early
America were created by special legislative acts. Later as occasions
multiplied such acts became numerous and charters devolving special privileges and even monopolies increased rapidly. At periods
that it is now unnecessary to identify the states, in revised or
amended constitutions, forbade the creation of corporations by
special acts, some requiring, others allowing, the passage of general
corporation laws. In some states exception was made of municipal
corporations, because it was thought that city charters would require
so many and such diverse provisions that general laws would be
impracticable.

The corporation question came before the ambiguous constitutional convention of Minnesota in 1857. In both the Democratic
and the Republican wings standing committees brought in reports
of similar tenor. The draft proposed by the Democrats read in part:
"Corporations may be formed under general laws, but shall not be
created by special acts, except for municipal purposes, and in cases
where the objects of the corporation cannot be attained under general laws." Then followed a phrase providing that such laws,
whether special or general, might be amended or repealed "after a
certain time specified in such a law." Although it contained minor
variations, the Republican version was substantially the same. In
the tedious debate that followed the proposal in the Democratic
body a desire was emphatically voiced that the multiplication of
special laws in which the territorial legislatures had bounteously
indulged should be stopped. Said Joseph R. Brown, "Bills passed
the Legislature last winter, incorporating as many as fifty towns in
one bill"; and he added that towns had been incorporated with not
more than fifteen or twenty inhabitants. Sibley asserted that the
"whole Territory is flooded with these special charters." "I am

---

[90] François Guizot, *The History of Civilization from the Fall of the Roman
Empire to the French Revolution*, vol. 1, lectures 7, 9 (New York, 1894);
Adam Smith, *An Inquiry into the Nature and Causes of the Wealth of Nations*,
1: 280–288 (Hartford, 1818); Blackstone, *Commentaries*, vol. 1, book 1, pp.
204, 390; John F. Dillon, *Commentaries on the Law of Municipal Corporations*, 1: 80, 88, 91 (Boston, 1890); Eugene McQuillin, *A Treatise on the
Law of Municipal Corporations*, 1: 73, 103, 297 (Chicago, 1911–13).

in favor," he said, "of cutting them down in the future as far as is consistent with the Public advantage." When the Democratic body, having failed to come to an agreement, was about to recommit the draft, Brown — who, as he said, had had extensive experience in special legislation and expected to have more — relieved the situation by proposing as a substitute the terse sentence, "No corporations, except for municipal purposes, shall be formed under special acts." The paragraph stands without material change in the Minnesota constitution today as section 2 of article 10. If Brown intended to give the legislature free rein under the guise of a restraining proviso, he had his wish. The legislature was merely forbidden to create nonmunicipal corporations by special acts; no curb was put upon its "parliamentary power" to alter, amend, or repeal their charters.[91]

Special legislation went merrily on. It was not until 1881, after an appeal by Governor Pillsbury, that a legislature was aroused sufficiently to take action toward abating the nuisance. An amendment to the constitution, ratified at the November general election in the same year, forbade the passage of special or private laws in eleven selected cases — a small arc out of a whole circle of possible enactments. The low dam made only a ripple in the stream. Following the ratification of the amendment of 1881, five legislatures passed 2,129 special acts covering 4,376 pages of the laws. The separate volume of special laws passed by the legislature of 1891 contained 507 chapters and 1,138 pages, whereas the general acts of the session included but 173 chapters and 462 pages. More than half of the special enactments related to municipal affairs. Whenever numerous members had special bills in charge, the remark "a purely local bill" gave the legislators sufficient excuse to allow a measure to run the ordinary routine course and be passed without opposition or even ordinary scrutiny. In an address to the city council of Minneapolis upon his retirement from office in 1889, Mayor Albert A. Ames spoke of a great calamity inflicted upon the city by the meddlings of the legislature. "Through this agency," he said, "our charter has been tinkered up to suit the private whims of obscure citizens, and we are to-day cursed with conflicting laws unintelligible to citizens and inexplicable by the courts."[92]

[91] Dillon, *Municipal Corporations*, 90, 94, 96–100, 129; Minnesota Constitutional Convention (Democratic), *Debates and Proceedings*, 121, 129, 130, 167, 174 (St. Paul, 1857); (Republican), 87 (St. Paul, 1858).
[92] Pillsbury's message, in *Executive Documents*, 1881, vol. 1, p. 22; *General Laws*, 1881, pp. 21–23; 1883, p. 2; Anderson, *History of the Constitution,*

A decade passed without relief. In the November election of 1892 the farcical amendment of 1881 was replaced by another of wider scope, opening with the sweeping provision, "In all cases when a general law can be made applicable no special law shall be enacted." The arc of forbidden enactments was much enlarged to include in particular local or special laws "regulating the affairs of . . . any county, city, village, township, ward or school district." A separate section — number 34 of the amendment of 1881, which was not recast — made it mandatory upon the legislature to provide general laws for the prohibited cases. The amendment of 1892 was, on the whole, salutary, but it proved too drastic. Cities and villages had multifarious interests that needed adjustment from time to time. General laws were found to be inapplicable to novel and unanticipated emergencies. It did not need the wisdom of a Solomon to provide for some of them by the passage of laws general in form but applicable to a certain city only. For example, under the new ruling Minneapolis obtained the passage of general acts applicable to cities of over 150,000 inhabitants, it being the only city in the state of that description. In the numerous cases appealed to it, the state supreme court found ways to relax the constitutional bonds when some city or village seemed really to need liberation.[93]

170; Howard L. McBain, *The Law and Practice of Municipal Home Rule*, 11 (New York, 1916) ; address of Albert A. Ames, in Minneapolis City Council, *Proceedings*, 1889, p. 2. Governor Pillsbury said, " At least two-thirds of the time, labor and expense required of an average session are consumed in the passage and printing of acts of a purely private, special or local nature, which are properly matters to be considered by the courts or local authorities . . . under general laws of uniform application." The amendment of 1881 added sections 33 and 34 to article 4 of the constitution of Minnesota.

[93] *General Laws*, 1883, p. 2; 1891, pp. 19–21; 1893, p. 3. The amendment as recast and adopted forms section 33 of article 4 of the state constitution. According to Anderson, *History of the Constitution*, 280, very light votes with large majorities carried the amendments of 1881 and 1892. A typical instance of the passage of a general law to provide for a special case is that known as the Cooley case. Minneapolis needed money to complete an unfinished courthouse and city hall. When the legislature passed a bill authorizing the issue of bonds for borrowing the money, Clayton R. Cooley, county auditor of Hennepin County, refused to countersign the bonds. Upon an application for a mandamus, the Hennepin County district court ordered him to countersign. He appealed to the state supreme court. That court reversed the decision of the district court on the ground that the act was a special one regulating the affairs of a city. Six months later the case was reargued and the court held that the act, although special in form, was general in fact and within the meaning of the constitution. *General Laws*, 1893, pp. 403–405;

The period in view was one in which the betterment of municipal government and administration was being discussed throughout the nation. In the large cities there was revolt against the meddling in their affairs by rural legislators in upcountry capitals. The proposition was put forth that cities were, or ought to be, self-governing communities and that their governments should not be mere instruments of state power and authority. " Home rule for cities " was loudly called for in many quarters. The state of Missouri was the pioneer in the reform. The question as to why Missouri as early as 1875 gave home rule to cities of one hundred thousand inhabitants and more is left to some one better acquainted with the situation than the author. St. Louis adopted such a charter by a referendum vote on August 22, 1876. California followed Missouri's example in 1879, but ten years passed before another state, Washington, came into the group.[94]

Minnesota was the fourth to join the group. Its home rule constitutional amendment was first adopted in 1896, but to incorporate some additional provisions of minor importance that were found desirable the legislature of 1897 recast the amendment and resubmitted it to the electors. It was ratified at the general election of 1898. As required by the amendment, the legislature of 1899 passed an enabling act to give the plan effect. The essential features of the act were: (1) the appointment of a board of fifteen freeholders by the judges of the judicial district; (2) the return by the board to the chief magistrate of the city or village within six months of a draft charter signed by at least a majority of the board; (3) the ratification of the charter by a vote of four-sevenths of the legal voters at the next election; and (4) the passing of thirty days before the charter should take effect. One of the provisions of the amendment of 1898 required the charter commission to submit to the people for ratification any amendment demanded in a petition signed by five per cent of the electors. The initiative for amendments, which might amount to a complete charter, was thus given to the people. Amendments, however, could also be proposed by the commission itself, provided that such amendments were " published for at least thirty days in three newspapers of general circu-

---

State *ex rel.* Board of Courthouse and City Hall Commissioners *v.* Clayton R. Cooley, County Auditor, 56 *Minnesota,* 540–554.

[94] Anderson, *History of the Constitution,* 170, 221; McBain, *Municipal Home Rule,* 113, 120. For a list of twelve states that had adopted home rule by 1912, see page 114c of the latter work.

lation in such city or village, and accepted by three-fifths of the qualified voters . . . at the next election." Under the home rule amendment the framing of laws that were general in form only, far from being checked, was facilitated by the classification of cities into four groups according to population. This number was doubled for the purposes of legislation because some cities had adopted home rule and others had not. It was not difficult to draw up a bill for the purposes of a city in one of the eight classes thus established that should be general in form but that should apply to no other city.[95]

In 1921 sixty-five cities and villages had conformed to the law and had become self-governing municipalities, but not without limitations. The amendment of 1898 expressly provided that " such charters shall always be in harmony with and subject to the constitution and laws of the State of Minnesota." City home rule was hardly a year old when a question was raised as to whether the enabling act itself was in proper harmony. In later years such questions as the following arose: Could a home rule city regulate peddling, make vaccination compulsory in cases of smallpox epidemic, establish a municipal court, create a board of public works, and, more important than such as these, adopt a commission form of government? In 1914 the authority of the city of St. Paul to abolish its school board and convert the school system into one of a number of administrative departments, incidentally depriving women of their right to vote on school matters, was questioned. In the course of twenty-five years, more than fifty disputed cases were appealed to the state supreme court. In one of them the court held that the phrase " at the next election " did not mean " at the next general election," and that charters and amendments to them might be voted upon at special elections. This ruling was expansive rather than restrictive. The number of votes cast at special elections was commonly much smaller than at the general elections and this made it easier to obtain the large majorities needed for the ratification of charters or amendments. A large part, in all probability a large

---

[95] General Laws, 1895, pp. 9–11; 1897, pp. v, 507–509; 1899, pp. v–vii, 462–467. For later amendments to the act, see General Laws, 1909, pp. 181–183, 246, 278, 510; 1911, p. 469. In 1911 an amendment to article 4, section 36, of the constitution was proposed but it was not ratified. There is authority for the statement that St. Paul was accommodated with 313 charter amendments in the eleven years following the city's adoption of home rule in 1900. General Laws, 1911, pp. 581–584; Arthur C. Ludington, ed., "Current Municipal Legislation," in National Municipal Review, 1 : 110 (January, 1912).

majority, of such changes made since this ruling have been effected at special elections.[96]

In the numerous attacks upon the home rule amendments and in the more numerous resorts to the legislature for special acts in general form there are found excellent examples of the difficulty, not to say the impossibility, of framing laws, organic and other, that will not need to be interpreted according to recent precedent and to be adjusted to new circumstances. Thanks to the liberality of judges and the self-restraint of legislators rather than to constitutional guaranties, home rule is firmly established in Minnesota. Whether cities and villages of the state will continue to enjoy good government, however, will depend less upon the forms of their charters than upon the success the democracy may have in selecting honest and capable citizens to conduct their business.

16. THE MUTINY IN THE FIFTEENTH MINNESOTA [97]

At Camp Meade, near Harrisburg, Pennsylvania, the Fifteenth Minnesota Regiment was merged into the Third Brigade, First Division, Second Army Corps. The corps commander was Major General Samuel B. M. Young. Early in October a war department order announced the discontinuance of certain army corps, the rearrangement of others, and the transfer of the Second Corps to camps in the South. The First and Third brigades were to be stationed near Augusta, Georgia. The transfer was made by separate units and it was not until November 17 that the Fifteenth Minnesota reached Camp Mackenzie, five miles west of Augusta. Before the transfer an order had been issued for the division to be in readiness for transportation to Havana, Cuba. In January, 1899, new Krag-Jörgensen rifles were issued and leaves to officers were restricted. Under the expectation thus kept alive the discipline of the troops was excellent and the men became expert in all the uses of their rifles except shooting. On some show occasions battalions had won praise for fine appearance and marching. But days and weeks passed with no marching orders and, since the war was over,

---

[96] William Anderson, *City Charter Making in Minnesota*, 178 (University of Minnesota, Bureau for Research in Government, *Publications*, no. 1 — Minneapolis, 1922); Harold F. Kumm, *The Constitution of Minnesota Annotated*, 115–121 (University of Minnesota, Bureau for Research in Government, *Publications*, no. 3 — Minneapolis, 1924). For the affirmative decision of the court in the St. Paul school case, see State *ex rel*. Lyndon A. Smith *v*. City of St. Paul and others, 128 *Minnesota*, 82–94.

[97] See *ante*, p. 235.

it must have become obvious that none would come. The men tired of drill and camp routine; if they were not to see fighting they wanted to get home to their own affairs. Petitions from each company, signed by nearly all the men, prayed for discharges. It may be surmised that the respect of the men in the ranks for the authority of the officers, soon to become their equals in civil life at home, weakened somewhat and, accordingly, that a state of mind that made possible a deplorable breach of discipline prevailed.[98]

On the afternoon of Saturday, February 4, 1899, four privates of Company F of the Fifteenth Regiment, more or less intoxicated, entered the saloon of one Brown Hadley in Harrisburg, a suburb of Augusta, and called for drinks. One of them, Dennis O'Connell, got into an altercation with Hadley and used insulting language. Without warning Hadley drew a pistol and shot O'Connell dead. A rumor quickly spread in the camp of the Fifteenth that O'Connell had been wantonly murdered. Men from other companies came into Company F's street, where hot discussion took place. It was believed and declared that no justice need be expected from a southern community but that the murderer must be captured and punished by men of the regiment. A crowd of men gathered in front of Colonel Leonhaeuser's quarters and called upon him to speak to them. This he declined to do, but he interviewed a few representatives in his tent and assured them that he would do everything in his power to have justice done. Company commanders and other officers reported to the colonel that everything was quiet and that there was no probability of further trouble that night.

The night passed in apparent quiet. The following morning was showery and the men, relieved from drills and fatigue duties, remained in quarters. There being no signs of trouble, Colonel Leonhaeuser, after guard mount, went on foot to division headquarters a mile away in response to a summons from the general in command. In the absence of the lieutenant colonel the command at camp devolved upon Major Daniel W. Hand. A rumor spread through camp that Brown Hadley, who had been arrested, was to be taken away to Atlanta. A new agitation set in and groups gathered to talk the matter over. At 10:40 men with rifles began to assemble in F Street. Private Peter Foley of Company F assumed command, formed a party of some one hundred and fifty or more in ranks, and marched it toward the quartermaster's store-

---

[98] Turner, *Fifteenth Minnesota*, 69–104; Holbrook, *Minnesota in the Spanish-American War*, 87–90.

house. Major Hand saw the movement, suspected its object, and hastened there in advance. When the gang arrived he ordered it to disperse. Foley stepped out and told him that the men meant to have some ball cartridges and to go after the murderer of O'Connell. The news had spread through the camp and nearly all the officers and men present came on the run. Most of the commissioned and some noncommissioned officers pushed through the crowd and gathered about Major Hand. The officers half commanded, half exhorted the men in the ranks of the gang to come out. Some of them did so and started back to their quarters. But the mob spirit was up. An appeal by the chaplain was in vain. Major Hand, Lieutenant David D. Tenney, and Corporal Renwick T. Sloane placed their backs against the door. Private Patrick Cahill struck Sloane with the butt of his rifle. Tenney was struck and fell from his place and Hand was hustled rudely aside. The mutineers, cheered on by nonparticipant members of the crowd, forced aside Quartermaster William T. Coe and his clerk, broke in the door, seized all the ball cartridges they wanted, and then, led by Foley, took the road toward Augusta.

Instead of having the long roll beaten and the whole command assembled in order and then starting a proper detail in pursuit, Major Hand seems to have done nothing. The regimental adjutant had hastened to call Colonel Leonhaeuser by telephone and the colonel made what haste he could on foot toward camp. He met the gang, ordered it to stop, and was obeyed. He warned the men that they were engaged in mutiny, for which the penalty might be death; he appealed to their patriotism, their respect for the law, and their regard for their commander, and gave them a peremptory order to return to camp. About two-thirds of the men fell out but the remaining sixty-seven moved on. Upon reaching camp the colonel immediately dispatched two armed companies under the command of Major Hand with orders to intercept and arrest the mutineers. He put the men on two street cars near at hand and they started for Augusta.

While Colonel Leonhaeuser was vainly warning and exhorting the little mob, Lieutenant Colonel Paul H. Gotzian returned from an absence from camp and took in the situation. He sent an officer with an appeal for assistance to the camp of a detachment of the Third United States Cavalry, which, under the immediate orders of the corps commander, was encamped about a mile and a half distant on the road to the city. The officer, much excited, his coat

torn and his face covered with blood, found Captain George H.
Morgan, formerly commandant of cadets at the University of
Minnesota, in temporary command. Captain Morgan instantly
ordered the " alarm " sounded and hastened to " round up the mutineers." It took but a short time for him to overtake, surround, and
capture the now unresisting mob. It was marched back to camp,
disarmed, and taken to division headquarters. Separated into convenient squads, the men were distributed in the guardhouses as prisoners. That evening the whole regiment was temporarily disarmed
and its rifles were stored at division headquarters.[99]

Major General S. S. Sumner, division and, at the time, acting
corps commander, directed Colonel Leonhaeuser to file charges
and specifications against the leaders of the mutiny and ordered a
general court-martial. A court, composed of fourteen officers of the
Tenth Ohio and Thirty-fifth Michigan regiments, met on February
16 and continued its sessions three weeks. Nine cases were tried,
the first being that of Peter Foley, who was charged with conduct
prejudicial to good order and with violation of the twenty-second
article of war, forbidding mutiny or incitement thereto. Obviously
he had no defense, but his counsel ingeniously managed to get into
the record statements of officers, sworn as witnesses, with regard to
their own behavior at the time of the riot. With one exception all
the ringleaders were convicted and sentenced to be dishonorably
discharged, to forfeit all pay and allowance due, and to be imprisoned at hard labor for different periods. Cahill, who might have
been condemned to death for striking an officer, got six years, Foley
and two others got five years, three were given one year, and one
was given six months. The sentences were published in orders on

[99] Turner, *Fifteenth Minnesota*, 105–119; Morgan to the author, March 26,
1925; memorandum of an interview with William T. Coe, lieutenant and
quartermaster of the regiment, February 17, 1924; diary of Lieutenant Coe,
which was lent to the author. The testimony of the principal witnesses of
the mutiny may be found in the proceedings of the court of inquiry in the
case of Colonel Harry A. Leonhaeuser, held in St. Paul, April 10–28, 1899,
in the judge-advocate-general's department in Washington. The Minnesota
Historical Society has in its possession a transcript of the first six days' proceedings and part of those of the seventh day, extracts from the testimony,
and a typewritten copy of the report of the judge-advocate-general on the
proceedings, including a statement of facts and the opinion of the court. Holbrook, in *Minnesota in the Spanish-American War*, 93–95, follows the statement closely. An account of the affair in the *Augusta* (Georgia) *Chronicle*,
February 6, 7, 8, 12, 1899, has been seen by the author. The editor of the
Chronicle thought that Hadley might have been justified " in collaring O'Connell and kicking him out of his place, but to shoot him dead in his tracks
was a shocking tragedy."

March 16. All other participants were thereupon released and returned to their companies.[1]

On March 14 the proceedings of the court martial came officially before Major General Young, commander of the corps. He, or his reviewing officer, evidently paid particular attention to the testimony given by officers of the Fifteenth in the course of the trials. Young found the record teeming with evidence of dereliction on the part of officers of the regiment and at once telegraphed to the adjutant general of the army recommending that the president order a court of inquiry to pass upon the conduct of officers who either were present at the armed mutiny or had knowledge of it. It would be a travesty of justice, he said, to punish these enlisted men and to let recreant officers go home with clean records. The adjutant general replied the next day, suggesting that Major General Young remit the sentences of all the enlisted men except in the most heinous cases and, in his order promulgating the proceedings, call attention to the dereliction of certain officers and deprecate it in words of his own. He stated also that only the impending muster-out of the regiment restrained the war department from ordering a court-martial. The corps commander, acting upon this extraordinary suggestion from superior authority, on March 16 issued his order, which, though it confirmed all the sentences, declared them inadequate. The general blamed the officers who were present when the storehouse was broken into for not having shot some of the men and declared that nearly all those officers had exhibited deplorable inefficiency, incapacity, weakness, and timidity. He believed that the testimony of the officers themselves would warrant the dismissal of a number and in two cases, at least, the extreme penalty of the law. The general in conclusion profoundly regretted that under the circumstances he was obliged to punish enlisted men while certain officers would go home with clean records.[2]

Such a wholesale, indiscriminating reprimand without a trial, without even a hearing, was at once resented by Colonel Leonhaeuser and the other officers censured by implication. They made immediate application for a court of inquiry. General Young was

[1] Turner, *Fifteenth Minnesota*, 139–155; Headquarters Second Army Corps, Special Orders no. 58, March 2, 1899. A typewritten copy of this order is on file with the transcript of the proceedings of the court of inquiry in the case of Leonhaeuser in the possession of the Minnesota Historical Society.
[2] Turner, *Fifteenth Minnesota*, 121–138; *Appletons' Cyclopædia of American Biography*, 7: 288; Headquarters Second Army Corps, *General Orders*, no. 22, March 16, 1899.

gracious enough to forward the applications on March 22 and to agree that it would be only just that the officers should have the court. Governor Lind telegraphed the war department, protesting against the muster-out of the accused officers without a trial and the Minnesota legislature by unanimous votes added its appeal for a court of inquiry. The acting secretary of war replied that the muster-out could not be postponed, but that the corps commander had been authorized to order a court of inquiry into the case of Colonel Leonhaeuser. If he should so order, other officers could be heard and all facts could be made of record. General Young did not so order, however. On March 27 each member of the Fifteenth Minnesota received his final pay and his individual honorable discharge and the command ceased to exist. The men of the three Minneapolis companies, A, I, and K, traveled in a body and upon their arrival home they were met with a welcome that cheered their hearts and gave them assurance that their neighbors did not believe that they or any of their comrades had behaved discreditably. There were similar demonstrations in other cities and towns where companies had been raised.[3]

Colonel Leonhaeuser at once renewed his request to the secretary of war for a court of inquiry, this time with success. On April 10, 1899, the detail of four officers of the regular army, including the recorder, met at St. Paul. A great number of witnesses were examined. The proceeding from the start took on a peculiar character. It was obvious that an acquittal of Colonel Leonhaeuser would imply that Major General Young had been unjust and indiscriminating in his irregular denunciation of officers of the Fifteenth Minnesota without hearings. Lieutenant Colonel William P. Duvall, who had been acting judge-advocate on General Young's staff at Augusta and may have drafted the censuring general order, was present as the general's representative. "There are two persons," said he, "involved in this inquiry — one quite as much as the other." He urged with great persistence that all the records of the trials at Augusta be read and admitted as evidence to show that General Young had reason for forming his opinions of officers of the regiment and denouncing them in the order. The court refused the demand but Colonel Duvall managed in his argument to introduce statements that might have been considered as evidence had the records been read.

[3] Report of the judge-advocate-general, 5-7; *House Journal*, 1899, pp. 810, 812, 855; *Senate Journal*, 675, 681, 697; *Minneapolis Tribune*, April 4, 1899.

The court took a long time for deliberation and on July 9 reported its finding. It was the opinion of the court that Colonel Leonhaeuser was justified in believing on the night of February 4 that there was no danger of further trouble, since the officers, if aware of danger, did not reveal it to him; when he met the mutineers on the morning of the fifth he did all that was possible to stop their march, except that he failed to order any of them to arrest Foley when he was in the act of distributing cartridges; his subsequent action was " energetic and judicious." In fine, the court declared that " the rebuke administered to and the strictures passed upon certain officers of the 15th Minnesota Volunteer Infantry . . . cannot be justly held to apply to or to be merited by Captain H. A. Leonhaeuser." The opinion of the court of inquiry had only moral effect until it should be confirmed by the secretary of war. The judge-advocate-general of the army, in a long communication to the secretary submitting a report on the proceedings of the court, argued the case as he might have done had he been of counsel for Major General Young. It was his judgment that the court had erred in its conclusion. Nevertheless, on July 8, 1899, the proceedings, the finding, and the opinion of the court of inquiry in the case of Colonel Harry A. Leonhaeuser were approved by the secretary of war.

The military court, which amply vindicated the colonel of the Fifteenth, made no inquiry into the conduct of other officers of the regiment, since it was not authorized to do so in orders, but the phraseology of its decision appears to suggest that in its opinion the rebukes and strictures could be held to apply to some of the officers. If it had thought otherwise it would not have been difficult to insert a consolatory paragraph or sentence.[4] The Minnesota people, not conversant with the articles of war and guided in their judgment by their knowledge of the officers, have never believed them inexcusably guilty of any neglect of duty. Expecting their discharges any day, the men felt that their officers had but little authority left for command and the officers had no disposition to display authority. The regiment did not mutiny; no company mutinied; a concourse of individuals became a mob and behaved as mobs always do — without reason and regardless of consequences.

[4] Proceedings of the court of inquiry, 2–10, 21, 28, 33. The court sat with closed doors, but the *Pioneer Press*, April 10–29, 1899, published from day to day summaries of evidence, which turned out to be correct. See also the report of the judge-advocate-general, 1–12, and Headquarters of the Army, Adjutant General's Office, *General Orders*, no. 127, July 8, 1899.

The excuse given for the actual outbreak on February 5 was that the men believed that the murderer of O'Connell would not be brought to justice. The sequel proved that their belief was not erroneous. On June 6, 1899, C. Brown Hadley was arraigned before the superior court in Augusta to plead to a charge of murder. His plea was " not guilty." A morning session was spent in impaneling a jury, in which two colored men were included. Evidence on the part of the state consumed the afternoon. The forenoon of the next day was taken up with evidence for the defense and rebuttal and the afternoon, with arguments of counsel on both sides. Early on June 8 the closing argument for the defense, occupying a period of fifty minutes, was made by Hadley's leading attorney. If a local reporter may be trusted, he " displayed histrionic ability that would have done credit to a star of the stage." " He acted; his voice rose and fell as he ran the gamut of the sentiments." He extolled Hadley for his forbearance and said that if he had been killed by O'Connell he would have gone to heaven as a peacemaker. His voice shook when he dwelt upon the sufferings of his innocent client during the four months he had been held in a strange jail. He demanded of the jury a full acquittal of this much injured fellow citizen. The jury retired; after three minutes it returned with the verdict " not guilty." [5]

17. THE 151ST FIELD ARTILLERY [6]

The 151st Regiment of Field Artillery had its origin in a single unit of field artillery, organized in St. Paul in 1881 as a unit of active state militia. Six years later a First Battery of Light Artillery absorbed that command. A year later, in 1888, a Minneapolis platoon was organized, which, in 1889, was reorganized as a separate battery; and in 1893 the two batteries became the First Battalion of Artillery. This battalion was sent to aid in suppressing

---

[5] *Augusta Chronicle*, June 7-9, 1899; Turner, *Fifteenth Minnesota*, 163.

[6] See *ante*, p. 317. The author gladly acknowledges as his aid in preparing this account the narrative by Louis L. Collins, formerly lieutenant governor of Minnesota and a member of the regiment. This narrative, founded in large part on a diary kept by Colonel George E. Leach, was edited by Dr. Wayne E. Stevens of Dartmouth College, who added a large collection of illustrative and confirmatory documents, and was published by the Minnesota War Records Commission under the title *History of the 151st Field Artillery, Rainbow Division*. See page xiii for an account of the notable career of Collins. A typewritten copy of the manuscript diary of Colonel Leach is in the possession of the Minnesota Historical Society. It has been published, with some additions, under the title *War Diary* (Minneapolis, [1923]).

the Chippewa outbreak at Sugar Point in 1898. The so-called "Dick Militia Act" of Congress, approved on January 21, 1903, which provided for a national militia of all able-bodied citizens and declarants, constituted the active militia of the states, complying with certain requirements, as the national guard. This national guard was to be supplied with arms and equipment by the war department. At once there was increased interest among the young men of military tastes. Old organizations were revived and filled up and new ones were organized. The legislature of 1905 provided for a hospital corps detachment, which was attached to the artillery battalion. Under legislative authority, in 1908 a company of engineers, which had been a part of the unit since 1900, was reorganized as Battery C. Under a law of 1913 three new batteries, B, E, and F, were organized, the last composed of students of the University of Minnesota. The Minneapolis unit, which had been designated B, was renamed D. The six batteries were now consolidated into a regiment of artillery of two battalions. In 1916 the roster showed 34 officers and 584 enlisted men.

On March 8, 1916, Francisco Villa, with a large bandit force, raided the town of Columbus in New Mexico, killed a number of inhabitants, and carried off property. A week later an expeditionary force under Brigadier General John J. Pershing crossed the Mexican border in pursuit of Villa. An attack upon a small detachment of Pershing's force and other sporadic raids by bandits — two of them into Texas — in which lives were lost and property was destroyed, called for a larger protective force than the militia of Texas, New Mexico, and Arizona, which had been called out on May 9. Acting under the National Defense Act, President Wilson on June 18 called upon other states for units of the national guard. Minnesota's quota was three regiments of infantry and one of field artillery. The Second Battalion of the artillery regiment assembled promptly at Fort Snelling, but a month passed before it could be dispatched to the seat of war. On July 24 it arrived at Camp Llano Grande in the southeastern part of Texas, about forty miles northwest of Brownsville.

The First Battalion did not reach the same post until early in October. Between occasional excursions, the regiment lay in a pleasant camp surrounded by a wilderness of mesquite and cactus, discharging the honorable service of preventing war. The student battery was sent home in September, just before the opening of the college year. There was some grumbling in the other batteries because of this partiality on the part of the war department. The First Field Artillery was mustered out of service at Fort Snelling late in February, 1917. The command had fought no battles, but it had learned much of the drudgery that prepares soldiers for battle; it knew how to assemble, to mobilize, to march, to move by train, to make camp and to keep it clean, and to submit to the petty routine and repetition that keep up discipline and foster ready obedience to orders.[7]

When war was declared upon Germany on April 6, 1917, almost the only land force at the disposition of the president was the regular army. The act of May 18 for the temporary increase of the army authorized the president to draft the whole national guard into the service. His proclamation of July 3 discharged all members of the national guard from militia service and drafted them into the military service of the United States as of August 5. The members so drafted were to be embodied in organizations corresponding to those of the regular army and they became subject to the laws and regulations governing the regular army, the articles of war in particular. On May 26, 1917, the president, through the secretary of war, appointed Major General John J. Pershing to the high command of the American Expeditionary Forces and ordered him to proceed at once to Europe with his staff. A full division of regular troops was ordered to follow, but it was not until late in June that the First Division arrived in France. On July 4 a parade of a part of it in Paris cheered the hearts of the French.[8]

The early dispatch of additional troops was obviously desirable. They were waited for anxiously by the European allies, hard pressed by the German armies. There was abundant enthusiasm among the young men of the country, who were eager to take part in the greatest drama of the age. That spirit was strong in the national guard, composed of men fond of and somewhat acquainted with military activities. It was therefore decided to make up an extra and representative division of national guard units drawn

[7] Collins, *151st Field Artillery*, 1–11; Minnesota, *General Laws*, 1903, pp. 66–72; 1905, pp. 293–295; 1907, pp. 631–634; 1913, pp. 37–39; United States, *Statutes at Large*, 32:775; War Department, *Reports*, 1919, vol. 1, part 1, p. 3; *Minneapolis Journal*, March 9, 1916, p. 1.

[8] *Statutes at Large*, 40:76, 1681; Collins, *151st Field Artillery*, 201; War Department, *Reports*, 1917, vol. 1, p. 51; 1919, vol. 1, part 1, p. 6; *Current History*, vol. 7, part 1, p. 78 (October, 1917); vol. 6, part 2, pp. 215–218 (August, 1917).

from many states. It was named the Forty-second Division, but it was better known at the time, and it will probably be known in history, as " the Rainbow Division." [9]

In the European war the name " division " was used in nearly the same sense as " army corps " in the Civil War, referring to a body of troops of all arms, so equipped and supplied that it might be transferred entire from one army to another or might act as an independent unit. The ideal strength of a division was twenty-eight thousand, including officers and men. It was the fortune of the First Minnesota Field Artillery to be selected for inclusion in the Sixty-seventh Field Artillery Brigade of the élite Forty-second, the Rainbow, Division, with the new name 151st Field Artillery. The two battalions of the regiment consisted of three batteries each.[10]

The Minnesota artillery regiment was called into federal service on June 23 and was ordered to assemble at Fort Snelling. A long and dull period of waiting followed while the war department struggled with the problem of transporting a great army across the Atlantic Ocean. It was not until September 9 that the two battalions, which had been separated for service in training student officers, were united at Camp Mills on Long Island in preparation for embarkation. Here another exasperating delay of six weeks occurred. On October 18 the 64 officers and 1,388 enlisted men embarked at Hoboken, New Jersey, on a transport carrying 6,000 persons. The crowd was so great that each man could have but forty-five minutes on deck twice a day — a painful situation for men accustomed to the unlimited oxygen of Minnesota. There was rejoicing when, at sunset on October 31, the ship tied up at St. Nazaire at the mouth of the river Loire. Shore leave was generously allowed on November 4 and on the following day the Minnesota artillery marched off with its brigade to an old French training camp two and a half miles away. Before the month was over the whole artillery brigade of the Rainbow Division was collected

[9] War Department, *Reports*, 1917, vol. 1, pp. 51, 851; Collins, *151st Field Artillery*, 15.

[10] General John J. Pershing, *Final Report*, 5 (Washington, 1920). This report may also be found in War Department, *Reports*, 1919, vol. 1, part 1, pp. 551–642. See also Collins, *151st Field Artillery*, 16 n. 11, 17. Collins gives a list of the component parts of the Forty-second Division. The wise policy was adopted of filling up combat divisions as they were thinned out in the campaigns by " replacements " from divisions that were still in training — a contrast with the Civil War method of letting old regiments run down to the size of companies and then accepting new green regiments sent in by states.

at a place called Coetquidan, some fifty miles north of St. Nazaire. Here three months were spent in training and getting familiar with the French seventy-five–millimeter guns. Months passed before American guns could be manufactured in numbers and shipped to France. For the campaign each battery had four guns and twelve caissons to carry ammunition; each gun and caisson was drawn by six horses, with a rider for each pair.[11]

In pursuance of a well-laid plan, the division, now ready for defensive action, was transported about the middle of February across the whole width of France to serve an apprenticeship in a " quiet sector " in the old province of Lorraine. The assignment of the division was to the Seventh French Army Corps and to the so-called " Baccarat sector," about ten miles in length, on the extreme right of the French armies. Each artillery battery was associated with a French battery for instruction. There had been no aggressive fighting in that sector since the battle of September 4 to 9, 1914, known as the first battle of the Marne, which resulted in the defeat of the Bavarian Army and the holding of the Belfort gap, the eastern gate into France. On this quiet sector there was firing enough from day to day to give the artillerymen plenty of practice in their art, but no aggressive battle was waged during the four months they remained under instruction. When they became expert in position warfare, they were transferred to a scene of movement warfare.[12]

While the Rainbow Division was thus quietly learning how to kill Germans and to keep Germans from killing Americans, the greatest military operations in all history were going on in another part of France. With the beginning of 1918, the German leaders and generals realized that if they were to win the war they must do so before the arrival of large numbers of American troops on the battle fields. On March 21 an immense mass of German shock troops fell upon the intrenched lines of the British in Picardy and in the course of a little more than a fortnight drove them back some thirty miles. By the end of April the Germans had killed and wounded over three hundred thousand men and had captured many thousands of prisoners and vast stores of ammunition and

[11] Collins, *151st Field Artillery*, 14, 19, 23–27, 199–201, 206–209, 407; interview with Colonel Leach.
[12] Collins, *151st Field Artillery*, 31–58; Buchan, *The Great War*, 1: 231–233. A map illustrating the first battle of the Marne faces page 232. The Baccarat sector was a portion of the Lunéville sector.

supplies. The British front was bent back but, as it was not broken, the Germans had little to show for their enormous losses. Minor operations followed while preparations went on for another great drive against the French front.[13]

On May 27 the main German advance fell upon the French center and drove it from its powerful intrenchments on the Chemin des Dames, believed to be impregnable, and, following up the advantage, pursued the retreating French divisions so steadily that in seventy-two hours they had been driven over thirty miles, to the banks of the Marne. Paris was but forty-four miles away. But there was abundant resistance left in the French divisions, now strengthened by American troops that had hardly completed their training. The splendid behavior of American units at Cantigny on May 28, at Château-Thierry on June 1, and at the Bois de Belleau closed the most direct road for the Germans to Paris. There was another road to Paris, somewhat longer, through the " Champagne country," east of the city of Rheims and crossing the Marne higher up. It was easily suspected that the Germans would try to make an advance upon that road and information was obtained of the date upon which they intended to make the attempt. At daybreak on July 15 the spearhead of the *Boche* line struck the apex of the allied defense. According to orders, the allied infantry of the front line gave way to reform on an intrenched position farther back, which they were to hold at all costs. The elated German infantry poured over the deserted works, assured that they would bivouac that night upon the banks of the Marne. The batteries of the artillery brigade of the Rainbow Division now poured such a storm, such a hurricane, of explosive shell on them that, although they were heavily reënforced and were 'fighting heroically, the hostile infantry barely reached the principal line of the allies, made no lodgment upon it, and sought cover. The 151st had its full share in the casualties and the glory of the day. Along with the division it had been shifted by rail and by a long night march from the Lorraine region to support the French troops holding the Rheims

---

[13] Buchan, *The Great War*, 4: 178, 190–234; *Current History*, vol. 8, part 1, pp. 197–205, 209–214 (May, 1918). The most important minor engagement was the battle of the Lys, April 7–29, in which the Germans undertook to curl up the British front toward the channel. Sir Douglas Haig, the British commander, issued an appeal to his army in which he said: " Every position must be held to the last man; there must be no retirement. With our backs to the wall, and believing in the justice of our cause, each one of us must fight on to the end."

sector of defense. For three days and nights the Germans hammered in vain at the line of the Forty-second Division. After the Champagne battles were over the French commander of the artillery of the French infantry division with which the 151st had coöperated praised the regiment for its spirit, coolness, and gallantry and recommended Colonel George Emerson Leach for the *Croix de Guerre* with palm.[14]

While these battles were going on Marshal Foch, in supreme command of all the allied forces in France, was getting ready for a great counter attack. On July 18 the main drive started from near Château-Thierry on a northwesterly course through the middle of the great pocket that the Germans had formed in May. By nightfall the French Army, including the Twenty-sixth American division, had driven the Germans eight miles, had captured sixteen thousand prisoners, and, without knowing it, had won the second battle of the Marne and, with it, the war. The advance, however, was to continue many days, as the Germans did not yield ground without fierce rear-guard defense. On the twenty-fourth of July the Forty-second Division, brought around to a new field, relieved the Twenty-sixth Division and formed the advance of the great pursuing column. In a sharp engagement of eight days that column had driven the Germans across the Ourcq. On August 3 the division was relieved, with the exception of the artillery brigade, which was retained to support the Fourth American Division, selected to follow up the Germans to the river Vesle. On the evening of August 6 a party of infantry crossed the Vesle. Four days later the 151st was relieved and it returned with the artillery brigade to its own division. As stated by Collins, "the Soissons–Rheims–Château-Thierry pocket had been sewed up." In the course of the movement the 151st had fired 54,709 rounds of ammunition, worth some eight hundred thousand dollars. It had also learned the tactics of an offensive operation. The invention of the breech-loading rifle had made the ancient "column of attack" by troops marching elbow to elbow very dangerous; the invention of the machine gun had rendered it impossible. The column of attack was generally replaced by the sending of infantry to the front in clouds of skir-

14 Buchan, *The Great War*, 4: 251-256, 275, 277; *Current History*, vol. 8, part 2, pp. 9, 17–21, 57–69, 214 (July, August, 1918); Colonel R. H. C. Kelton, "The Miracle of Château-Thierry," in the *Century Illustrated Monthly Magazine*, 98: 99–109 (May, 1919); Pershing, *Final Report*, 32; Collins, *151st Field Artillery*, 58, 62–75, 83, 236–238; Leach, *War Diary*, 78–84, 93–96.

mishers, protected by artillery stationed in their rear but firing over their heads. This fire, regulated by elevation of the guns, came to be so accurate and so well coördinated as to establish a continuous curtain of exploding shells on the enemy front. The French name "barrage" was easily adopted by the Americans.

General Pershing, in orders, recorded with pride the behavior of the American troops who participated in the marches and battles at a crucial hour and gained the victory that marked the turning point of the war. A colonel of infantry whose regiment had been supported by the 151st Field Artillery at the Ourcq expressed his enthusiastic appreciation of the behavior of Colonel Leach and his regiment.[15]

With the old line of defense reëstablished by the counter attacks of July and August, 1918, and some gains on the British front, it was believed that preparations might be made for a final allied offensive. After some contention, it was agreed that the American troops, scattered all the way from Switzerland to the English Channel and furnished with supplies only under great difficulties, should be consolidated into an independent American force. The announcement was made on August 10. It was further agreed that an American army should be assembled at once in the St. Mihiel sector, south of Verdun, with a view to pinching off a large German salient in anticipation of a northerly drive between the river Meuse and the Argonne Forest. In the early days of September Pershing gathered a force of some five hundred thousand, all American save seventy thousand French, for the "reduction" of the St. Mihiel salient. The Fourth American Corps was to make the principal attack on the south face of the salient and the main blow was to be delivered by the Forty-second Division holding the center. The movement began at dawn on September 12, after four hours of artillery preparation. By the afternoon of the following day the St. Mihiel salient had been wiped out. It was a "walk-over." The Germans offered only resistance enough to enable them to make their escape, but they left sixteen thousand prisoners, over four hundred guns, and a great amount of military supplies. The 151st fulfilled every expectation and duty. The St. Mihiel operation was not sanguinary but the strategic result was momentous. It made available an army of a million and more Americans on

---

[15] Buchan, *The Great War*, 4: 279–281; Collins, *151st Field Artillery*, 87, 89, 100, 104, 105, 108–111; Pershing, *Final Report*, 36 and plate 1; Leach, *War Diary*, 111, 115.

the left German flank, ready for movements in three directions, any one of which, if successful, must be fatal to the German armies.[16]

With the American success at St. Mihiel and gains made by the British and French on the southern and western fronts, General Foch decided upon an immediate offensive operation, which, if successful, might end the war before the close of the year, 1918. The military "objective" was the seizure of a point on the great railway system running behind the German front, by means of which supplies were transported and divisions were easily shifted from place to place. The small city of Sedan, well known as the decisive battle field of the Franco-German War of 1870, on the river Meuse some forty miles below Verdun, was selected as the most feasible place for cutting that railroad line. Nearly parallel with the Meuse, some twenty miles westward, lay the ancient Argonne Forest, in a region so rough and hilly and so nearly devoid of roads as to render almost impossible the movement of troops and the fighting of battles over a considerable area.[17]

Down the sloping valley between the Meuse and the Argonne Forest, traversed by ridges between small streams flowing to the Meuse, Foch launched the American Army, making in all a million American troops on or near the base of operations. The whole area to be traversed was occupied by a series of hostile defenses, elaborately constructed. Long-range German batteries from the bluffs east of the Meuse and from the eastern margin of the Argonne Forest could pour flank fires into advancing troops. The American advance began on September 26. After nearly three weeks of continuous battle, the American front had reached the formidable Hindenburg line running obliquely across the valley. On October 12 the Forty-second Division, which had been left with other troops to stabilize the St. Mihiel area, arrived to take position in front of the so-called "Kriemhilde position" on the Hindenburg line, probably the most strongly fortified field position in all military history. On October 14 a grand front assault was made. That day the 151st Field Artillery, supporting the infantry of its division, fired eight thousand rounds of ammunition. Two days of furious attack followed, resulting in a lodgment on the Kriemhilde stronghold. According to Collins, the performance of the 151st in these

[16] Pershing, *Final Report*, 37-44; Collins, *151st Field Artillery*, 115-128; Buchan, *The Great War*, 4: 332-336; Leach, *War Diary*, 125, 132.

[17] Pershing, *Final Report*, 43, 47; Elisée Reclus, *The Earth and Its Inhabitants: Europe*, 2: 345 (New York, 1883).

terrible days marked its highest achievement. Colonel Leach, however, gives that eminence to its operations on the Ourcq and the Vesle. With the loss of the Hindenburg line the Germans slackened their vain resistance. The American Army had become, as General Pershing says in his report, " a powerful and smooth-running machine." The Germans fought rear-guard battles only to gain time to withdraw their troops before their railroad communications were cut off. The Forty-second Division was in the advance of the pursuit and on November 7 it reached the Meuse and saw the towers of Sedan. The next day the batteries of the 151st were deployed on its bluffs; but the war was over. The Minnesota artillery regiment had its full share of the glory.[18]

The Forty-second Division was one of nine divisions selected to compose the Army of Occupation on the Rhine. Between November 15 and December 13 the command marched leisurely through Luxemburg and the Rhineland to, but not across, the Rhine. It was established with other troops on the left, or west, bank of the Rhine about halfway between Bonn and Coblenz. The regiment was given control over a subsector, with headquarters at the village of Heppingen. There it remained, in good physical comfort, although there was much homesickness among the men, until April 9, 1919. After a review of the Forty-second Division on March 16, General Pershing issued an address expressing his " thanks and appreciation for the splendid, efficient and loyal service that has been rendered by the Division as a whole and by . . . the different units."

The overland journey of three days in box cars to Brest, the embarkation on the sixteenth, the arrival at Brooklyn on the twenty-sixth, the welcome at St. Paul and at Minneapolis on May 8, and the muster-out of 890 men at Des Moines, Iowa, on the tenth are happily described by Collins. On the arrival of the regiment in New York, the major general commanding the Rainbow Division issued a special order in which, after recounting at length the behavior of the 151st Field Artillery in all its principal engagements, he expressed " with pride and pleasure " his appreciation of

[18] Pershing, *Final Report*, 44, 48, 49; Buchan, *The Great War*, 4: 363, 404; Collins, *151st Field Artillery*, 142–151, 155–159, 162, 294, 331; Leach, *War Diary*, 140; interview with Colonel Leach. The Kriemhilde Stellung was not completely annulled until November 1. Plate 4, in Pershing, *Final Report*, shows the rapid advance of the American Army in the first days of the pursuit and the slower progress later.

the " gallantry, endurance, efficiency, and high morale " of the command. " Minnesota," he added, " may well be proud of this magnificent Regiment." [19]

18. THE NONPARTISAN LEAGUE AND THE FARMER-LABOR PARTY [20]

The remarkable revulsion that occurred in Minnesota politics toward the close of the second decade of the twentieth century was neither local nor recent in its origin. From the time of the earliest colonial settlements until the beginning of the development of vast corporate institutions about the middle of the nineteenth century the public affairs of America — municipal, provincial or state, and national — had been in the hands of a gentry, in some states in those of a landed gentry. In the last half of the nineteenth century the great fortunes amassed under corporate control in manufacturing, shipping, merchandising, banking, and railroad building and operating furnished motive and opportunity for the transfer of control in public affairs to manufacturers, merchant princes, bankers, and railroad kings. The passage of antitrust laws in 1887 and 1890 slackened the movement but did not much impede it. The construction given by the courts to the term " person " in the fourteenth amendment of the national Constitution placed corporations in a great measure beyond legislative control. Directly from their treasuries or indirectly through contributions of individual stockholders they made up the enormous sums expended upon elections of presidents and congresses, governors and legislatures, and judges of supreme and other courts. Combinations of interests secured the passage of favorable bills, defeated undesired legislation, and obtained the appointments of sympathetic officials and the removal of objectionable ones. There were loud protests

[19] Collins, *151st Field Artillery*, 163–191; Leach, *War Diary*, 194, 198–200. Collins gives Pershing's address on pages 177–179. While he was at Brest, Colonel Leach was decorated with the Legion of Honor by an emissary of the president of France. See Collins, *151st Field Artillery*, 326, for a station list of the 151st in the American Expeditionary Forces. On page 332 is the following list of the battle credits awarded to the regiment by the war department: Champagne-Marne, July 15–18, 1918; Aisne-Marne, July 25–August 6, 1918; St. Mihiel, September 12–16, 1918; Meuse-Argonne, October 6–November 10, 1918; Lunéville, February 25–March 22, 1918; Baccarat, March 29–June 15, 1918; Esperance-Souain, July 5–14, 1918; Vesle, August 7–11, 1918; and Essey-Pannes, September 17–October 1, 1918.

[20] See *ante*, pp. 319–321.

against the domination of trusts and " combines," but the American
people were so busy winning their prosperity, in spite of the corporations, that they did not heed the signs of the times. They had
yet to learn the immense advantage of the initiative in legislation
and the ways and means of seizing it. James Bryce's *American
Commonwealth*, first published in 1888, was the first clear and
forcible arraignment of the corruption, vast in proportions, in
American politics. Widely read, the work made a profound impression upon students of history and politics.[21]

Among the immense throng of immigrants that flooded the shores
of America before and after the close of the nineteenth century
were a small number of Europeans steeped in the doctrines of
Bakunin, Marx, and Lassalle or in those of the milder English
socialists. Their speeches and writings found interested hearers
and readers among a large body of workingmen discontented with
their economic situations and among a smaller body of teachers
and students of political economy. A school of American socialists, if it may be so dignified, grew up.

There were a considerable number of persons who had not
obtained from Republican administrations, which had been in
power for sixteen years, the places and opportunities that their
services, in their several estimations, had warranted them to expect.
Altogether there loomed an ominous aggregation of men clamoring
for a new deal and, in the political dialect of the time, a " square
deal." To lead this gathering host Theodore Roosevelt in 1912
dramatically reappeared upon the scene. Mindful of the advantages to fall from a successful assault upon the existing régime, he
endeavored, with the aid of a numerous group of admirers, to secure
in the primary elections in some states and in conventions in others
a majority of the 1,087 delegates to the Republican national convention, which was to meet in Chicago on June 18. In this undertaking he was disappointed because, as he claimed, the national
committee had by " successful fraud and deliberate political theft "
seated delegates hostile to him, principally colored delegates from
southern states that had never cast Republican electoral votes since
the days of reconstruction. The nomination of Taft by the convention and the bolt of the Roosevelt delegates followed. On
August 5 a convention of Progressive Republicans assembled in

---

[21] Bryce, *American Commonwealth*, 2: 146–167 (1910 edition). For the
antitrust laws of 1887 and 1890 see *Statutes at Large*, 24: 379–387; 26: 209.

Chicago and gave Roosevelt the nomination for president by acclamation.[22]

The program of the party thus launched embraced a long list of reform measures, upon many of which all parties might have harmonized. It called for a short and easy way of amending the national Constitution, for the control of currency issues by the government free from the domination of Wall Street, for the free use of the Panama Canal by American shippers, for equal suffrage for men and women, and for a popular review of judicial decisions. The old parties, the platform declared, " have become the tools of corrupt interests, which use them impartially to serve their selfish purposes. Behind the ostensible government sits enthroned an invisible government, owing no allegiance and acknowledging no responsibility to the people. To destroy this invisible government, to dissolve the unholy alliance between corrupt business and corrupt politics, is the first task of the statesmanship of the day." The Democrats in their platform briefly offered their party " as an agency through which the complete overthrow and extirpation of corruption, fraud, and machine rule in American politics can be effected." Woodrow Wilson was more specific in his acceptance speech. In regard to trusts he said, " Big business is not dangerous because it is big, but because its bigness is an unwholesome inflation created by privileges and exemptions which it ought not to enjoy." The antitrust law, he said, had apparently proved ineffectual, inasmuch as trusts had grown up very luxuriantly and had established virtual monopolies; vast confederacies of corporations were controlled and determined by comparatively small groups of persons who could command both credit and enterprise. In the Socialist platform of the year it was asserted that " the industrial equipment of the nation has passed into the absolute control of a plutocracy," which " stretches out its greedy hands over the still undeveloped resources of the nation — the land, the mines, the forests, and the water powers." [23]

The election of Wilson by a minority of the total popular vote over Taft and Roosevelt, who divided the Republican vote, is not of present concern.[24] What is of present concern is the persisting

[22] Frank M. Colby and Allen L. Churchill, eds., *The New International Year Book*, 1912, pp. 552–554, 557–561, 568–570 (New York, 1913) ; *Chicago Tribune*, August 6, 8, 1912.

[23] *International Year Book*, 1912, pp. 575, 581, 583, 587.

[24] *International Year Book*, 1912, p. 577. The vote was: for Roosevelt, 4,124,579; for Taft, 3,484,960; and for Wilson, 6,298,857.

belief of many millions of voters that a confederated plutocracy had got possession of the machinery of the great political parties and was impartially employing it in the control of public affairs to the detriment of the republic. In certain northwestern states where single-crop farming persisted this belief took on a specialized form. Discontent long harbored among farmers broke out against an alleged confederation of millers, elevator owners, and grain speculators who were robbing them of millions by price rigging, undergrading, excessive docking, and confiscation of screenings. The Grange, the American Society of Equity, and other sporadic organizations had protested and fought against these robberies to little purpose. A more united and therefore a stronger and more militant organization was desired by or for the farmers of the region.

This demand first found response in the state of North Dakota through the genius of a notable character, Arthur Charles Townley. Little is now known of the man's early life. He was born on December 30, 1880, at Browns Valley, Minnesota, of American parents who had come in that year from the state of New York. In 1895 the parents moved to Parker's Prairie, on the " Soo " Railroad near Wrightstown, and settled on a farm, where they still live. The boy attended the district schools of Browns Valley and Parker's Prairie. In 1900 he completed a course of study in the high school at Alexandria in Douglas County. There was nothing in his experience in those early years that was out of the ordinary. He read much, but his reading was not in special lines; he had no taste for " sports." After his high school course was completed, he taught school at Hewitt in Todd County and at Browns Valley. While he was in high school and during the years that he taught he was actively interested in the Methodist Episcopal Church.

In 1904 Townley went west and after spending a year in northwestern North Dakota and two years in Colorado, where he married, he returned to Beach, North Dakota, and joined a brother who had made a beginning in flax farming. The business prospered and the credit of the brothers extended. Which of them thought out a plan for a big bonanza operation is not known, but Arthur was capable of it. By 1911 the two had obtained by purchase or lease from the Northern Pacific Railroad Company many thousands of acres of prairie land. The International Harvester Company furnished them with implements and machinery on credit. They probably had saved seed, or cash enough to buy seed, for a first crop. The crops of 1911 and 1912 were ample and were safely harvested and prices were satisfactory. The business was at its peak. Arthur Townley, spoken of as if a sole proprietor — and such he may have become — was called the " Flax King of North Dakota." The crop of the next year, 1913, was light, weather for harvesting was unfavorable, prices for flax dropped low, and the farm could not meet its obligations. The enterprise collapsed with outstanding debts estimated at eighty thousand dollars. Townley was now adrift.[25]

The economic conditions in North Dakota briefly described above had led ardent socialists in different parts of the country to believe, or at least to hope, that in that state might be found a favorable arena in which to put state socialist theories into practice and accordingly there was a considerable hegira of socialist devotees to Bismarck in the second decade of the century. Not long after the failure of his farming venture Townley engaged himself as an organizer and a lecturer of the embryo party, but not for long. He soon became convinced that a party organized for state socialism as spread on paper could not be successful. In his travels over the state he extended his acquaintance among farmers and became sympathetic with them in their hard circumstances. If accounts are true, he thought out, as he claimed, a plan for their relief that should include all that was then practicable of socialistic doctrine and should compel one or the other of the old political parties to put it into effect. He proposed an exclusive union of farmers, actual farmers, who should pay initiation fees and dues; the organization, which apparently was to be modeled after organized labor, should not be a political party but the members were to concentrate their votes at the primary elections upon the candidates of the dominant political party who would agree to support the principles of the association. Townley chose for it the name " Farmers' Nonpartisan League." One day in February, 1915, he walked seven miles from a railroad station to the house of a friend whom he had met at some socialist gathering, hoping to find him in sympathy with his

[25] Fitch Townley to the author, September 16, October 7, 1925; interview with Mrs. Ruth Townley, a sister-in-law of Arthur C. Townley, March 12, 1925, recorded in the Folwell Papers; John M. Gillette, " The North Dakota Harvest of the Nonpartisan League," in the *Survey*, 41: 753 (March 1, 1919); Charles E. Russell, *The Story of the Nonpartisan League; a Chapter in American Evolution*, 123–194 (New York and London, 1920); Herbert E. Gaston, *The Nonpartisan League*, 36–50 (New York, 1920). Gaston was for some time the editor of the *Nonpartisan Leader*. On this paper, see *post*, p. 546.

plan. After a long conversation the friend approved his plan and offered the services of his two sons and the loan of a Ford automobile. In the Ford he visited some of the neighboring farmers and the first day he secured nine subscriptions and in a week he had seventy-nine.[26]

Whether Townley was the originator of the central idea is a mooted question that need not be decided here; but it is beyond dispute that he became immediately the recognized organizing leader of the movement. He was wise enough not to confuse the farmers with any socialistic theories; he simply asked them, and they bound themselves by their subscriptions, to work together for five practical ends: (1) state ownership of terminal elevators, flour mills, stockyards, packing houses, and cold storage plants; (2) state inspection of grain, grain dockage, and grading; (3) exemption of farm improvements from taxation; (4) state hail insurance on the average tax basis; and (5) rural credit banks operated at cost. The first proposition, of course, overshadowed all the others.[27]

Townley's scheme for securing members — that surely was his — was a stroke of genius. He divined that the automobile was to work a revolution in rural life that would include the loosening of the grip of the courthouse rings upon public affairs. From the first farmers whom he visited Townley got not only names to the pledge that he had formulated, but also two dollars and fifty cents from

---

[26] Russell, *Nonpartisan League*, 194–202; Gaston, *Nonpartisan League*, 51–59, 61.

[27] Russell, *Nonpartisan League*, 213, 222; Fred E. Haynes, *Social Politics in the United States*, 309 (Boston and New York, 1924). There is reason to believe that Townley's original program was confined to state-owned terminal elevators, with state inspection and grading of grain, and was later elaborated as stated. Gaston, in his *Nonpartisan League*, 56, says, "The Nonpartisan League was born in his [*Townley's*] brain at the city of Bismarck in February of 1915." Andrew A. Bruce, in his *Non-Partisan League*, 60 (New York, 1921), says: "It was a socialist, A. C. Bowen, who first suggested its formation. It was another socialist, A. C. Townley, who first put the L in it, and who furnished the dynamics." Jerry D. Bacon, in his pamphlet, *A Warning to the Farmer against Townleyism as Exploited in North Dakota*, 8 (Grand Forks, 1918), gave Townley credit for "a very innocent-looking proposition to unite the farmers of the state in a farmers' nonpartisan political league" to secure a state-owned terminal elevator. In his testimony before a referee in bankruptcy, in answer to the question, "You were the original originator of it, were you?" Townley replied, "Yes, sir." This testimony, taken at Bismarck, North Dakota, on January 29, 1918, throws light on the story of the league up to that date. It is printed in the *Congressional Record*, 65 Congress, 2 session, 4232.

each or a postdated check for that amount in payment of the first year's dues. It was not long before he had cash enough in hand or in sight to warrant the employment of suborganizers. Then followed more Fords, more cash, and more organizers, to whom he allowed liberal commissions for their collections. The annual fee was soon raised to six dollars and later to nine dollars, but the latter sum included a year's subscription to *Pearson's Magazine* and the Nonpartisan paper to be issued. Little publicity was given to the early work of organization. The league was not a secret society, but there was something of the charm and the mystery about it that lure so many persons into lodges and chapters or other secret coteries.[28]

From his organizers Townley presently selected four to form an executive committee, with himself as chairman, to prosecute the recruiting and to conduct the business of the league. By the use of Fords and the seductive palaver of the organizers, the names of twenty-two thousand members had been placed on the rolls by the time the *Nonpartisan Leader* first appeared on September 23, 1915. That number was almost doubled by April 1, 1916. On that day and the day before a "Grand State Convention mass meeting," attended by more than four thousand persons from all parts of North Dakota, was held in Fargo. On the two days immediately preceding this meeting another convention of county delegates had been in session behind closed doors. In this meeting nominees for state offices and for three vacancies in the state supreme court had been selected with the purpose of suggesting them to the Republicans for the June primary election. The nominations were joyously indorsed by the grand mass convention. All were duly nominated and all but one, the nominee for state treasurer, were elected.[29]

The course of the Nonpartisan League in the state of its origin will form an interesting episode in the history of American politics. It cannot be further followed here. The clean sweep made by the league in North Dakota in the elections of 1916 and the accession of a considerable number of members across the borders

[28] Gaston, *Nonpartisan League*, 58, 66; Russell, *Nonpartisan League*, 199, 214.

[29] Gaston, *Nonpartisan League*, 60, 102, 106–109, 124, 127; Russell, *Nonpartisan League*, 203, 212; Haynes, *Social Politics*, 310–313; *Nonpartisan Leader* (Fargo, North Dakota), September 23, 1915, April 6, 1916. Russell says, "The League had now [*April 1*] forty thousand members." For the names of the candidates indorsed by the league, see the *Nonpartisan Leader*, June 1, 1916, p. 2.

of adjoining states awoke in Townley and his clique — if it had not obtruded itself before — the conceit of extending the beneficence of the league into other northwestern states, and they may have dreamed of a nation-wide spread. On February 22, 1917, the organ of the league appeared with the subtitle " Official Magazine of the National Nonpartisan League." In June of that year there was issued by the National Nonpartisan League a pamphlet with the title *Facts for the Farmer*. Its purpose was to reveal to the farmers of Minnesota how they were being robbed and wronged by corporation land grabs, unequal taxation, elevator men, Minneapolis millers — some of whose names were mentioned — Chicago grain gamblers, Elgin manipulators of the butter and egg markets, and unconscionable meat packers. In September a second pamphlet was issued under the title, *Facts Kept from the Farmers*, with the subtitle, " General Handbook of the National Nonpartisan League." The principal facts divulged therein were the huge investments of big financial and corporate interests for political campaigns and the insidious efforts of such combinations to deceive the people by means of " good will campaigns." These pamphlets were given an enormous circulation by organizers and through the mails.

The league did not confine itself to the circulation of its own publications, however. League farmers suspicious and jealous of town business men began soon after the organization of the league to club together in order to buy the control of local newspapers or to start new ones. Townley and his clique saw an opportunity. They formed a " Northwestern Service Bureau," incorporated under the laws of North Dakota, with a nominal amount of capital stock held by a few league officers, enough to form a board of directors. The bureau soon made itself useful in providing machinery and printers' supplies and in furnishing personnel for the farmer papers. Its principal function, however, was the extension of news service to these and other papers, numbering, it is said, five hundred. In some cases the bureau negotiated sales of stock for companies acquiring the papers and for this service a commission was retained. The news service brought in some revenue, but there were large deficits that were made up out of the treasury of the league. Nearly every one of the fifty-three counties of North Dakota had a farmer-owned paper; there were thirty-six in Minnesota. Other states ran the total number up to about one hundred and thirty. Not less than nine hundred thousand dollars went into these weekly papers, all maintained for the propagation of the cause and not for profit. At least twenty of them have survived in Minnesota, a small number of which have long subscription lists.[30]

Townley's organizers soon appeared in eleven other states in addition to North Dakota and Minnesota and in the course of a year, it was reported, more than five hundred were in the field. By the close of the year 1917 the membership had been swelled to some 150,000. The initiation fee was raised to sixteen dollars for a legislative biennium, five dollars of which was considered as a subscription to the *Nonpartisan Leader*. The league now became more definitely national in character. On January 1, 1918, Townley established his principal office in St. Paul and moved the *Leader* there.[31]

Complaints had been made that the league was too highly centralized. To silence them, or at least to mitigate them, state leagues were organized. In February, 1918, the Minnesota Nonpartisan League was begotten and on the sixteenth of that month the *Minnesota Leader* appeared as the "official newspaper of the National Nonpartisan League in Minnesota." This and other state leagues, organized from the top down, served the purpose of proclaiming apparent decentralization, but the propaganda went on from national headquarters, which selected organizers and lecturers, who reported and consigned to headquarters the cash and securities collected, less the stipulated commissions.[32]

On December 3, 1918, a national convention of delegates from all states met in St. Paul and formally adopted articles of associa-

[30] Gaston, *Nonpartisan League*, 156; A. B. Gilbert to the author, December 14, 1925, Folwell Papers. The original title of the *Leader* was *The Nonpartisan Leader*. The Minnesota Historical Society has in its library a complete file of the paper. The complete titles of the pamphlets are, *Facts for the Farmer on Conditions Vitally Important to Him as Producer and to the Wage Worker as Consumer (Minnesota Handbook)* ([St. Paul], 1917), and *Facts Kept from the Farmer; General Handbook of the National Nonpartisan League* (St. Paul, [1917]). A sympathetic account of the origin of the Nonpartisan League in North Dakota and the revolutionary legislation that took place after it had captured the legislature is given in the *Kansas Leader* (Salina), March 3, 1921. It contains a three-page report of a committee — only one member of which belonged to the league — sent by a meeting of two hundred Kansas farmers to investigate the activities of the league and the reported disloyalty of its leaders. The committee found that Townley had run for the legislature on a Socialist ticket, but that he had not been disloyal.

[31] Bruce, *Non-Partisan League*, 8; Gaston, *Nonpartisan League*, 67, 159, 170, 238; Haynes, *Social Politics*, 323. The *Nonpartisan Leader* for December 31, 1917, p. 17, contains an announcement of the removal of the office to St. Paul. The issue for January 7, 1918, was the first issue distributed from the St. Paul office.

[32] *Minnesota Leader* (St. Paul), February 16, 1918.

tion. Provision was made for state and national committees, but all power was in fact lodged in a national executive committee of three men. The chairman of the national executive committee was made the chief executive officer of the league and was empowered to do and perform all things authorized by the articles to carry out the purposes of the association. At this convention Townley was elected chairman of the national executive committee — virtually the president of the league. To assure himself of trust in his leadership and to strengthen his grip on the affairs of the league, he declined to hold the office unless a referendum of all the members should show him to be their choice. A referendum was accordingly had with the result that 98,391 out of a total of 99,369 voted in his favor. In December, 1919, at a meeting of the national committee the articles were modified so as to give larger powers to state leagues and to county committees. The membership fee was raised to eighteen dollars for a biennium, of which county committees were allowed to retain seven dollars.[33]

The year 1918 was the first in which the league could get into politics in Minnesota, as her biennial elections occurred in the even-numbered years. On March 19 a convention of state delegates was held in St. Paul, followed by a " convention rally " of three days attended by a great throng. Governor Burnquist was invited to speak but he preferred to send a letter denouncing the league as a party of discontent and as pro-German. The convention designated Charles A. Lindbergh, a Progressive Republican and a former representative in Congress, to be supported at the coming primary election. He was defeated by Burnquist. The league cast a vote of about fifty thousand, three times the number of members in Minnesota at that time, thus indicating that there were a great number of farmers who sympathized with the league but who did not care to pay sixteen dollars for membership or did not wish wholly to desert their old parties. Disappointed in the effort to dictate a Republican candidate for governor but encouraged by the large vote Lindbergh had polled at the primary election, the league control resolved to see what might come of shifting its votes in favor of a Democrat. At a convention held in St. Paul on August 20 a committee was appointed to coöperate with a like committee to be named by the Minnesota State Federation of Labor four days later. On August 25 the joint committee indorsed the candidacy of David

[33] *Minnesota Leader*, December 14, 1918; *Nonpartisan Leader*, February 10, 1919, p. 5; Gaston, *Nonpartisan League*, 316.

H. Evans, who had announced himself an independent aspirant for the office. Because of a ruling by the attorney-general that the name of a candidate could not be printed on the official ballot except as the candidate of some party, the name "Farmer-Labor party" was used by or for him. That was the first use of the name. Burnquist was elected on November 5 by a plurality of nearly fifty-five thousand over Evans, but he lacked more than eighteen thousand of a majority of the total vote.[34]

The experiments of 1918 convinced Townley and his committeemen that without extraneous support the league could never sweep Minnesota as it had swept North Dakota. Townley had been sympathetic with organized labor and had adopted its plan of organization; he had thrown out tentative suggestions toward securing its coöperation. Organized labor was willing to coöperate but it was not willing to coalesce. Its members were not willing to leave their unions and take memberships in the Nonpartisan League. Consultations between leaders resulted in a scheme for coöperation without a merger. A convention of the Minnesota Federation of Labor was held at New Ulm on July 20, 1919. A separate group of members attending the convention organized the Working People's Nonpartisan Political League to coöperate with the National Nonpartisan League.[35]

The combination of farmers and laborers was ready for action in the campaign of 1920. On March 24 the two leagues held conventions of delegates in separate halls in St. Paul. A joint committee made up a slate of state officers, which was concurred in by the two leagues. The selection for governor was Henrik Shipstead of Glenwood, Pope County. Shipstead was not inexperienced in public affairs; his townsmen had elected and reëlected him mayor, he had served in the state legislature of 1917, and in 1918 he had aspired to the Republican nomination for representative in Congress from his district but had been defeated in the primary election by

34 Gaston, *Nonpartisan League*, 230, 253, 260–262; *St. Paul Pioneer Press*, 1918: March 19, p. 1; August 21, p. 1; 27, p. 10; 30, p. 4; 31, p. 4; *Minnesota Leader*, 1918: July 27, p. 1; August 24, p. 1; 31, p. 1; Attorney-General, *Reports*, 1917–18, p. 200. Burnquist received 166,611 votes; Evans, 111,966; and three other candidates, 91,282. *Legislative Manual*, 1919, insert facing p. 670. For Burnquist's letter to the league convention, see the *Minneapolis Journal*, March 11, 1918, p. 1, and the *Minnesota Leader*, March 23, 1918, p. 5. It is reproduced also in the *Congressional Record*, 65 Congress, 2 session, 4240.

35 *St. Paul Pioneer Press*, July 21, 1919, p. 1; *New Ulm Review*, July 21, 1919; *Minnesota Leader*, July 26, 1919, p. 1.

Andrew J. Volstead. He had practiced dentistry for sixteen years after his graduation from the dental school of Northwestern University at Chicago. He had contributed to professional journals, had collected a considerable library of good books, and had dipped into the lore of the Scandinavian sagas. His favorite reading, however, was in American history and politics. It may easily be surmised that the Nonpartisan leaders picked Shipstead because he was good-looking, affable, an entertaining speaker, and a good vote-getter rather than because of his knowledge of and experience in agriculture. He was not without some knowledge of that primary occupation, however. He was the son of a Norwegian farmer and had done the work and chores of a farm boy. It is related that while he was still a boy he was given several acres of land by his father to cultivate as he liked. He planted potatoes and, after tending them throughout the season, all he could get for them when they were ready for market was eleven cents a bushel. It is quite likely that that misadventure was what sent him away to high school in a neighboring village, then to the state normal school, and later to Northwestern University. Since the " Farmer-Labor party," as it was beginning to be popularly called, had as yet no legal standing, Shipstead filed as a Republican. He was defeated for the Republican nomination by Jacob A. O. Preus in the primary election. At the general election in the following November Shipstead ran as an independent candidate for governor, but the combination of leagues was not yet strong enough to defeat the still powerful Republican party and its popular candidate, Preus.[36]

The year 1922 was to be a memorable one in Minnesota politics. A senator in Congress was to be chosen to succeed Frank B. Kellogg, whose term was to end on March 3, 1923. The bifurcated Farmer-Labor party, now the second party in Minnesota in numbers, had no need to pursue its early policy of imposing its nominees upon the dominant party. On March 31, 1922, the two component elements of the party held separate state conventions in Minneapolis. It was no accident that a Democratic convention was in session on the same day. A committee from the Democratic

[36] *St. Paul Pioneer Press*, 1920: March 25, p. 1; 26, p. 1; *Minnesota Leader*, November 18, 1922, p. 1; *Nonpartisan Leader*, 1920: June 21, p. 1; July 26, p. 4; November 1, p. 6; interview with Thomas Van Lear, December 13, 1924, recorded in the Folwell Papers. The vote cast on November 2 stood: Preus, 415,805; Shipstead, 281,402; and two other candidates, 86,417. See *Legislative Manual*, 1921, insert facing p. 526. Shipstead was born in Burbank Township, Kandiyohi County, on January 8, 1881.

convention met committees from the Nonpartisan League and the Working People's Nonpartisan Political League. A suggestion was entertained that the farmers and workers indorse a Democratic nominee for governor and that in turn the Democrats support a workers' nominee for senator in Congress. Townley in an address before the Nonpartisan League urged the continuation of his favorite plan of holding "the balance of power" either by supporting Republican candidates at the primaries or by forming a coalition with the Democrats. But Townley, lately released from an enforced retirement from public affairs, was in no position to persuade, much less to dictate. The farmer and labor bodies were confident that they could elect a full ticket without any dickering and resolved to nominate one. Their conference committees, aware of a prevailing sentiment, placed the name of Henrik Shipstead before them and by unanimous acclaim he was made their joint candidate for the Senate. The Republican state convention held in St. Paul on March 31, 1922, indorsed Kellogg practically without opposition and he filed for reëlection. Kellogg received the Republican nomination at the primary election on June 19 and Shipstead became the unanimous nominee of the Farmer-Labor party by virtue of the fact that he was its only candidate. At the general election in November Shipstead defeated Kellogg by a plurality of 83,539 votes. It was a severe blow to the Republicans, who had virtually monopolized the representation of Minnesota in the national Senate since the days of Henry M. Rice.[37]

[37] *Minneapolis Journal*, March 31, 1922, p. 1; *Minneapolis Tribune*, 1922: April 1, pp. 1, 3; 2, p. 1; *Minnesota Daily Star* (Minneapolis), April 1, 1922, pp. 1, 2; *National Leader*, April 17, 1922, p. 6; *Legislative Manual*, 1923, insert facing p. 452; interview with the Reverend G. T. Lee, recorded in the author's notebooks, 9: 124; *Labor* (Washington), October 14, 1922. A special edition of this number of *Labor*, which summarizes the political records of Shipstead and Kellogg, was issued for circulation in Minnesota. Three hundred thousand copies were distributed. The *Minnesota Union Advocate* (St. Paul), April 6, 1922, p. 1, gives the platform adopted by the Farmer-Labor party. It advocated, in substance, the following: (1) the repeal of the Esch-Cummins transportation act; (2) the conservation and development, under government control, of natural resources; (3) the payment of a soldiers' bonus from an excess-profits tax; (4) the use of the unemployed on public works; (5) the abolition of government by militia and of injunction in labor disputes; (6) economy in public expenditures and the abolition of graft and waste; (7) a ten-per-cent tonnage tax on iron ore; (8) opposition to a state constabulary; (9) the establishment of coöperative banks or loan and credit associations; (10) the repeal of the pre-primary convention law; (11) the repeal of the Brooks-Coleman street car law; (12) a state-owned cement mill and the enlargement of the state-owned flour mill; and (13) the initiative, referendum, and recall.

The triumph of the new party in the election of Shipstead was not the only alarm thrown into the Republican camp. Against Governor Preus, standing for reëlection, the Farmer-Labor party supported Magnus Johnson of Meeker County, an actual tiller of the soil and milker of cows. Although chiefly occupied with his farming, Johnson had found time to spare for local, district, and state interests. He had served as a representative from his county in the legislatures of 1915 and 1917 and as a state senator in the sessions of 1919 and 1921. In debate he said enough to let his positions on all important issues be known. Devoted to the principles of individual right and home rule, he favored county option for the regulation of saloons and opposed a state constabulary and state control of public utilities. He voted for woman suffrage and for the initiative, referendum, and recall. He stood for lower taxes on productive industries and homes and for higher taxes on unearned fortunes derived from exploiting natural resources. He preferred the ad valorem tax on iron ores but supported the occupations tax, which was later confirmed by the courts. In general he was vigilant in regard to all matters affecting the country interests. Johnson had also extended his acquaintance and reputation by services in various coöperative organizations for handling farm produce. Before he began his farming in Meeker County in 1892 he had had some experience as a lumberjack in the pineries of Wisconsin and Minnesota, which gave him a kind of education that schools do not give — an understanding of the ideas and sentiments of the working people and a deep appreciation of their longings for better conditions. In his native country, Sweden, after an elementary education, he had learned and practiced the art of glass blowing and had made a specialty of bottle manufacture. Johnson was defeated by Governor Preus in 1922, but he reduced the Republican plurality to 14,277 votes.[38]

The sudden and lamented death of Knute Nelson on April 28, 1923, made a vacancy in the senatorship in Congress, which Governor Preus, encouraged by his friends, desired to occupy. Preus

[38] *Labor* (Washington), June 30, 1923, pp. 1, 3; H. G. Teigan to the author, January 30, 1925, Folwell Papers; *Minnesota Leader*, 1922: April 8, p. 1; October 16, p. 1; *Legislative Manual*, 1923, insert facing p. 452. Johnson was selected as the gubernatorial candidate by the convention that indorsed Shipstead for the United States Senate. Preus received 309,756 votes; Johnson, 295,479; and Indrehus, the Democratic candidate, 79,903. Johnson was born in the province of Vermland, Sweden, on September 19, 1871, and he came to America at the age of nineteen.

might have resigned the governorship to Lieutenant Governor Louis L. Collins to be appointed by the latter to the senatorship. It has been said that that was his first thought; but, confident of strong Republican support, he chose the bolder course of seeking an election without resigning the governorship. He therefore proclaimed a special primary election to be held on June 18 and a definitive election, on July 16, 1923. As the labor moiety of the farmer-labor aggregation had dominated in the selection of Shipstead to wear the senatorial toga, the farmer element now exacted the choice of one of its number to be likewise invested. Magnus Johnson, the " dirt farmer," was their candidate and at the election on July 16 he became the people's choice by a majority of 37,767 votes.[39]

In December, 1923, Johnson took his seat in the Senate of the United States for the fractional term to expire on March 4, 1925. In 1924 he sought a reëlection and was nominated at the primary election on June 16, but at the final election on November 4 he was defeated by Thomas D. Schall, the Republican candidate, who was about to end a ten-year term of service in the national House of Representatives.[40] Johnson's defeat, unexpected by himself and his friends, was the result of converging opposing forces. Divergencies in the interests and objects of the farmer and labor components of the Farmer-Labor party distracted attention and diminished activity in the campaign. Johnson's avowed intention, if he should be returned to the Senate, to follow the leadership of La Follette alienated farmers who were not yet ready to vote for congressional review of Supreme Court decisions or for the public ownership of railroads, telegraph and telephone lines, mines, water power, and forests. With much respect for Johnson's honesty of purpose and ability to deal with community and state affairs, there was distrust of his competence to meet the great issues that arise in the national legislature.

The defeat suffered by the Farmer-Labor party in the campaign of 1924 indicates that it will soon go the way of the Greenback-

[39] *St. Paul Pioneer Press*, April 29, 1923; *St. Paul Dispatch*, May 5, 7, 8, 9, 17, 1923; *Legislative Manual*, 1925, pp. 297–300, 312, 319. *Labor*, June 30, 1923, throws light upon the campaign of Johnson against Preus in 1923. This was apparently a special issue for distribution in Minnesota to " boost " Johnson. It contains Johnson's keynote speech at Isanti, Minnesota, on June 23, 1923; a fervent appeal to voters by Robert M. La Follette; an article by Henrik Shipstead; and indorsements of Johnson by ten presidents of railroad brotherhoods and three others.

[40] *Legislative Manual*, 1925, pp. 319, 666. The vote stood: Schall, 388,594; Johnson, 380,646; and Farrell, the Democratic candidate, 53,709.

Labor, the Farmers' Alliance, and the Populist aggregations. As to that, however, one man's guess is as good as another's. But there is no need to guess as to whether or not similar insurrections will break out when great masses of working people come to believe, for good reasons or bad, that the propertied class is getting more than its share of the products of industry and commerce, is unrighteously seizing the natural resources of the country, is gathering excessive profits in distribution, and is squandering vast wealth upon insolent and ostentatious luxuries. It may be expected that at such times self-appointed, audacious leaders, without reverence for institutions and reckless of the lessons of the past, will appear to rally their thousands of despairing, credulous people into insurgent camps. In the four years during which the Farmer-Labor party was operative in Minnesota, it elected but one state officer, a clerk of the state supreme court. Its representatives in the legislatures were too few to enable it to control legislation by shifting its bloc from one side to another, but it was not without influence in securing important measures such as those relating to rural credits and the tonnage tax. Indeed, its members claimed that the majority party had accepted Farmer-Labor ideas. The party is still in existence and its organ, the *Nonpartisan*, is issued as a monthly magazine. The *Nonpartisan Leader*, which with the issue of November 14, 1921, became the *National Leader*, ceased publication with its issue of July, 1923, and the National Nonpartisan League, with its subscription list cut down and with two million dollars in worthless postdated notes in its treasury, ceased to function.[41]

The story of the fierce opposition against the Nonpartisan League and its annex, the Farmer-Labor party, is much too long to be attempted here. In 1917, the first year of the World War, the league was bitterly denounced as disloyal to the government and as pro-German. It was observed that in this year it received a large accession of members in the German communities in the Minnesota Valley and it may be inferred that Townley's lecturers and organizers allowed the German farmers to think that the league was not ardent for the prosecution of the war against the Fatherland. A more serious charge was that the league had carried on from the start a socialist crusade. Some color was given to this charge by

[41] *National Leader* (Minneapolis), July, 1923, p. 3. See the *Pioneer Press* for January 7, 1919, p. 1; January 4, 1921, p. 1; and January 3, 1923, p. 6, for estimates of the Farmer-Labor party in the legislatures of those years. Since 1915 all members of the state legislature have been elected on ballots without party designation. *Laws*, 1915, p. 224.

the undeniable fact that pronounced socialists were employed by Townley as lecturers and organizers to gather in new members.[42]

But what, the curious reader may ask, has become of the meteoric Townley, the founder of the Nonpartisan League, who for five years was the idol of thousands of persons in many states? To complete his record it must be added that, in addition to expanding the league and controlling its business, he " initiated," as he said, ancillary organizations. One of these was the Nonpartisan Publishing Company, which was in fact a partnership of two men of straw who knew nothing about the publishing business and gave it no attention. These partners bought the stock of the *Courier-News* of Fargo with league money and called themselves a company. The subscriptions of five dollars each paid by members to the *National Leader* for a biennium were not separated from the funds of the league and when the publishing company " needed " money Townley, as president of the league, drew his check for the

---

[42] Bruce, *Non-Partisan League*, 152, 161. All Republican newspapers abounded in denunciations of Townley and his followers. A particular form of opposition in the shape of a back-fire was the organization on March 13, 1917, of " The Nonpartisan League of Minnesota," incorporated by five men representing wealthy lumbermen and merchants of Minneapolis and St. Paul. A monthly newspaper called the *Non-partisan* was issued in August, but it survived only until December. It was sympathetic with the farmers and workers, but it attacked Townley with great virulence as a socialist and a traitor. The paper was exuberantly patriotic. The corporation issued two numbers of a paper entitled *On the Square* and distributed them in great numbers at a cost of fifty thousand dollars; fifty thousand copies of a pamphlet entitled *America First* were circulated; and "tons of anti-League literature were distributed" from an office in St. Paul. Altogether the corporation expended some five hundred thousand dollars. For revelations concerning the " fake league " by Clarence F. Johnson, one of its incorporators and editor of the short-lived monthly paper, who had brought suit to recover money due him, see the *Nonpartisan Leader*, 1919: June 9, p. 4; 16, p. 8; 23, p. 8; and 30, p. 8. Some of the statements may need confirmation. For the allegation that the league was a socialist organization, see Bruce, *Non-Partisan League*, 60–70; Asher Howard, ed., *The Leaders of the Nonpartisan League; Their Aims, Purposes and Records, Reproduced from Original Letters and Documents*, 20–52 (Minneapolis, 1920) ; Ferdinand A. Teigen, *The Nonpartisan League; Origin, Development, and Secret Purposes*, 82 (St. Paul, [1918]) ; and Bacon, *Warning to the Farmer*, 95. See the *Nonpartisan Leader*, February, 1923, p. 5, for the evidence of Townley as to the nonpartisan character of the league. Townley declared in 1921 that he was not a socialist but that he had employed socialists in organizing the league and had tolerated them. See Nicholas to the author, July 14, 1925, in the Folwell Papers. A map in the *Minnesota Leader* for July 3, 1920, p. 4, shows the spread of the league in Minnesota. For prosecutions of Townley on charges of violating chapter 463 of the *Laws* of 1917, which make it illegal to write and publish anything calculated to discourage enlistments, and of the crime of conspiracy, see the following section of the Appendix.

necessary amount. Another organization that Townley "initiated" was the Consumers' United Stores Company, incorporated about July, 1917, under the laws of North Dakota with a capital of ten thousand dollars. The purpose of the corporation was to open a store, or stores, establish a central buying agency, and employ an expected surplus in league propaganda. Of the nine hundred and sixty thousand dollars' worth of stock subscriptions but fifteen or twenty thousand dollars were paid in. Townley testified that the company did no business to speak of. A third organization was the League Exchange, also incorporated in North Dakota with an authorized capital of a million dollars. Its original purpose was to handle real estate for farmers and save them commissions. War conditions prevented effecting this purpose. The stock was used as collateral upon which to borrow money for the league. The United States Guaranty Company, a fourth auxiliary, was incorporated under the laws of Minnesota with a capital on paper of a million dollars. It was Townley's "impression" that it did no business. He held no stock in any of these companies except one one-hundred-dollar share in the League Exchange, from which he received one dividend of five dollars. For his labors and responsibility as president of the league and for his moral and financial control of the ancillary organizations, Townley received three hundred dollars a month, two hundred dollars from the league treasury and one hundred dollars from the publishing company.[43]

There is no evidence of intentional dishonesty in Townley's transactions; he was not greedy for money. His ambition was rather to pose as a commanding national figure, a manager of great enterprises, and a benefactor of oppressed communities and, with an army of admiring followers, to make politicians and even statesmen tremble at his power. All went well with him until the state leagues, which he had brought into being to cover up his autocracy, began to function in fact and to encroach upon his prerogatives. The national league became the tail of the dog. In June, 1922, Townley resigned his presidency and undertook to organize

[43] *Congressional Record*, 65 Congress, 2 session, 4232–4240. See page 4239 for Townley's explanation of the peculiar proprietorship of the publishing company. The $750,000 collected up to January 29, 1918, as subscriptions to the *Leader* had not been turned over to the company but were held in the general league treasury. See also Edwin E. Hudson, "A Comparison of the Farmers' Alliance and the Nonpartisan League in Minnesota," a typewritten manuscript in the possession of the Minnesota Historical Society.

for the national league under a contract. The arrangement was not satisfactory and Townley had discovered a new field of operations in a National Producers' Alliance, which he and others organized in Minneapolis on February 23, 1923. In July, 1923, he abandoned the Nonpartisan League to devote all his time to the new alliance.[44]

19. THE MINNESOTA COMMISSION OF PUBLIC SAFETY [45]

On April 6, 1917, war was declared on Germany. The Minnesota legislature was near the end of its legal term and two years must elapse before the next legislature could assemble in regular session. It was therefore deemed advisable to establish, without waiting for precedent, an interim agency to take prompt and vigorous action toward suppressing disloyal outbreaks and possible disturbances of order in communities where the German element was predominant and toward the efficient application of the resources of the state to the prosecution of the war. The bill for the " Minnesota Commission of Public Safety," to consist of the governor, the attorney-general, and five citizens to be appointed by the governor to serve without pay, was passed unanimously in the Senate and with but one negative vote in the House and was approved on April 16, 1917.

If a large hostile army had already been landed at Duluth and was about to march on the capital of the state, a more liberal dictatorship could hardly have been conceded to the commission. The third section of the act gave it the comprehensive power " to do all acts and things non-inconsistent with the constitution or laws of the state of Minnesota or of the United States, which are necessary or proper for the public safety and for the protection of life and public property or private property of a character as in the judgment of the commission requires protection," and to " do and perform all acts and things necessary or proper so that the . . . resources of the state may be most efficiently applied toward maintenance of the defense of the state and nation and toward the successful prosecution of such war, and to that end it shall have all necessary power not herein specifically enumerated and in addition thereto the following specific powers:" The subsections that fol-

[44] *National Leader,* June, 1922, p. 7; March, 1923, p. 5; July, 1923, pp. 3, 5. The issue of July, 1923, which was the last one published, contains a prospectus of the National Producers' Alliance. It is not known that the organization has yet reached any considerable importance.

[45] See *ante,* p. 317.

lowed named five specific powers: (1) to acquire any and all kinds of property by purchase, lease, hire, or otherwise; (2) to condemn all such property, making proper payment therefor; (3) to coöperate with the military and other agents of the United States toward the prosecution of the war; (4) to cite any person before an officer or agent of the commission for examination, to " examine any such person under oath as to any information within the knowledge of such person," to require him to produce any writings or documents under his control, " and to procure the punishment for contempt of any person refusing to answer or produce writings or documents requested by such commission by any . . . district court "; and (5) to examine the method of performance of his duty by any public official other than the constitutional officials of the state and to advise the governor to remove him from office if in the judgment of the commission the public interests demanded it. The act authorized the governor, upon being so advised, to remove the objectionable official. The legislature did not arm the commission with these ample powers without granting it ample means to give them effect. The sum of one million dollars was appropriated, to be immediately available and to be paid out as the commission might provide in its by-laws.[46]

The commission was composed of Governor Burnquist, who was the chairman, Attorney-General Lyndon A. Smith, and five others appointed by the governor to hold office during his pleasure. They were Charles H. March of Litchfield, who was vice chairman, John Lind of Minneapolis, Charles W. Ames of St. Paul, John F. McGee of Minneapolis, and Anton C. Weiss of Duluth. Thus composed, armed with extraordinary powers, and granted an ample appropriation by a practically unanimous legislature, the commission proceeded to exercise functions the like of which the history of American law had never disclosed. The view that the commission took of the situation was voiced in its *Report*, dated January 1, 1919:

It is hard . . . to realize the indifference, pacifist sentiment and even opposition to the war which prevailed in some parts of Minnesota two years ago.

[46] *Senate Journal*, 1917, p. 1196; *House Journal*, 1615; *Laws*, 373–377. It must be observed that section 5 of the act provided that the commission should pay to members of the Minnesota National Guard who had served honorably on the Mexican border under the president's call of June 18, 1916, a bonus of fifty cents a day for each day of federal service after being mustered in. Section 6 provided for the full payment of such soldiers from the time of their mobilization to that of their actual muster into federal service. $488,337.78 went to those payments. Minnesota Commission of Public Safety, *Report*, 9.

. . . We had a population of about 2,000,000 by the 1910 census, and more than seventy per cent of these were either foreign born or of foreign parentage on one or both sides. Out of the two million people nearly five hundred thousand were either born in Germany or Austria, or were of German or Austrian parentage. There were many sections where the English language was not spoken. . . . A part of these had personal associations with Germany before the United States entered the war, and for this reason wanted Germany to win. . . . The public danger came when the anti-war feeling assumed the shape of concerted and public propaganda and it assumed this shape here in the spring and summer of 1917. The Minnesota men who were disloyal . . . formed a constituency of considerable size and there appeared leaders and spokesmen to organize them. . . . Misinterpreting the constitutional guaranty of freedom of speech, these leaders thought . . . they could properly oppose the government's policies in speech and writings. These leaders were of three classes: (1) Professional and theoretical pacifists who organized for a nation-wide anti-war campaign, the so-called People's Peace Council and similar bodies. (2) Men of pro-German traditions and sympathies. . . . The troubles from this type of leaders showed themselves first most conspicuously . . . in the New Ulm episode in July, 1917. (3) Professional politicians of the socialist or Nonpartisan league stamp. . . . The Commission undertook to kindle the back fires of patriotism among the rank and file of this ilk. . . . With the leaders it used the mailed fist.[47]

At its first meeting, held on April 23, 1917, the commission resolved to hold weekly executive sessions, the proceedings of which were to be given out in written statements approved by the chairman or the vice chairman. The record of proceedings was to be open to public inspection, " except to such extent and in such particulars as the Commission shall in the public interest otherwise provide." [48]

[47] *Report*, 9, 31, 44, 168. In the *St. Paul Pioneer Press*, July 24, 1917, p. 6, is an article by Ambrose Tighe, who drafted the bill, stating the basis and purpose of the safety commission act. The law, said Tighe, was analogous to the public health law of the state and employed some of its language. Its aim was " to obviate the need of recourse to martial law by arming a state board with extraordinary powers to the end that trouble may be prevented instead of punished after it has come." See Tighe, " The Legal Theory of the Minnesota ' Safety Commission' Act," in the *Minnesota Law Review*, 3: 1–20 (December, 1918). Tighe was the counsel of the commission. There is a severe arraignment of the commission and its activities in the *New York Evening Post*, July 9, 1918. Ames resigned from the commission on December 5, 1917, and was succeeded by Henry W. Libby. Lind, during an absence from the state, resigned and was succeeded on March 19, 1918, by Thomas E. Cashman. Attorney-General Smith died on March 4, 1918, and was succeeded by Attorney-General Clifford L. Hilton. In the Folwell Papers there is a letter from the author to Lind, dated November 19, 1924, with Lind's reply on the same sheet, relating to his retirement from the commission.

[48] *Report*, 9, 70; Minutes of the Proceedings of the Minnesota Commission of Public Safety, 1: 59. The typewritten minutes, in three record books, are in the custody of the Minnesota Historical Society, with which the files and records of the commission are deposited. Later representatives of the Associated Press and the United Press were admitted to the meetings.

The transactions of this extraordinary tribunal, a complete account of which would go far beyond the reasonable limits of this section, may be roughly separated into two groups: those of state-wide application and those of local concern. Of the former group, the first and most appropriate was the organization by order number 3, dated April 28, 1917, of the "Home Guard of Minnesota." On May 14 followed order number 4, providing for peace officers, who were to have the powers possessed by constables without being required to take an oath or to give a bond. They were to be duly commissioned and provided with conspicuous badges of office. Some six hundred of these officers were appointed and it was the opinion of the commission that the "fact that such a force was available and that it might be increased to any strength shown to be necessary" had "a deterrent effect upon evil-minded persons plotting crime or destruction of property." At an early meeting an arrangement was made with the superintendent of the St. Paul and Minneapolis offices of Pinkerton's National Detective Agency, with sixty men under him, to obtain desired information.[49]

Associations of male citizens, each headed by a director appointed by the state commission and aided by an advisory council, were organized in all counties of the state. In nearly every township there was a township association, presided over by a chairman named by the county director, with such standing committees as executive, finance, labor, and marketing.[50] At its first meeting the commission appointed Mrs. Thomas G. Winter of Minneapolis to take charge of organizing women for war purposes, but a year passed before that work could be undertaken on a great scale. In May, 1918, the commission appointed the "Woman's Committee," an executive committee of sixteen women, which was authorized to act as the Minnesota unit of the National Woman's War Organization. By the woman's committee chairmen and vice chairmen were appointed for each of the ten congressional districts and, directly or otherwise, eighty-six county chairmen and some thirteen hundred town chairmen were appointed. Through these organizations nearly twenty thousand women became actively engaged in patriotic and relief services. A conspicuous example of their activity was their coöperation in the conservation of food asked for by the government, in particular of fats, sugar, wheat, and meat. The woman's committee through its agencies can-

[49] Report, 13, 74–76; Minutes, 1: 23, 41, 61. For an account of the organization of the home guard, see ante, p. 318.
[50] Report, 10, 174-309; Minutes, 1:39. The personnel of the local safety commissions was under the direction of the central body.

vassed every town and house and "all over the state the women responded heroically." In fifty-eight out of eighty-six counties various forms of Americanization service were organized by women. They found buyers for one-fourth of the Liberty Bonds bought in the state.[51]

It seems probable that the state of mind prevailing throughout Minnesota was such that willing obedience was given to most of the orders and regulations of the commission, but after a year's experience it was found desirable to require more than a moral sanction for them. On April 30, 1918, the commission adopted an order that "Any person violating or refusing or failing to obey any order of the Minnesota Commission of Public Safety . . . shall be guilty of a misdemeanor, and shall be punished by imprisonment in the county jail for not more than three months, or by a fine of not more than One Hundred Dollars."[52]

Among important actions taken "for the protection of life and property and as a matter of military expediency and necessity" was the issue on June 5, 1917, of an order that all licensed saloons in the state should be closed at ten o'clock in the evening and remain closed until eight o'clock the following day, that no intoxicating liquors should be sold between those hours, and that no women nor girls should be permitted to enter such saloons at any time. The same order prohibited dancing and cabaret performances in all places where intoxicating liquor was sold or served. The governing bodies of all municipalities were ordered to enact forthwith ordinances for the execution of the commission's order, but nothing was suggested as to what might happen if they did not do so. It was not until November 6 that the commission discovered that it was also necessary and proper for the attainment of its great object to close all pool and billiard rooms and all public dance halls from ten o'clock at night to eight o'clock in the morning and all day on Sundays and to enjoin city councils to enforce its order. To conserve the peace and to promote the orderly discharge of the duties of citizenship, the commission by order forbade the sale of intoxicating liquor throughout the state on June 5, 1917, the day of registration for the primary elections, and on September 12, 1918, that of the regular elections of that year. "As a matter of military expedi-

[51] *Report*, 9; Minutes, 1: 91.
[52] *Report*, 115. The bill for the act creating the commission as introduced into the legislature provided that disobedience of an order of the commission should constitute a felony. The paragraph was struck out. Tighe, in the *Minnesota Law Review*, 3: 13 (December, 1918).

ency," at places designated as points of entrainment for recruits the sale of intoxicating liquor was forbidden on the day of their departure.[53]

Whether the commission had personally observed or whether it had been advised that there were too many idle men in the state in the summer of 1918 is not known, but it was deemed necessary on June 4 to enact a regulation for the utilization of the human energy of the state for the prosecution of the war. Order number 37 of that date made it the duty of all sheriffs, peace officers, and others charged with enforcing the law " to seek and continue to seek diligently " for " able-bodied male persons . . . not regularly or continuously employed " and to report their names and residences to county attorneys. To insure the uninterrupted progress of industry the commission on April 16, 1918, issued its order that during the period of the war there should be neither strike nor lockout under any circumstances and that all differences as to wages or hours of labor should be referred to the state board of arbitration.[54]

Early in 1918 it became obvious that the state would be called upon for more men for the army and navy. That a large proportion of the men in the state were foreign born was known to everybody, but nobody knew what number or proportion were still aliens exempt from the duties and burdens of citizenship. The Minnesota Commission of Public Safety considered the ascertainment of their number of sufficient importance to warrant it in requiring a registration of all aliens in the state. It named February 25 and the two days following as " alien registration days " and required " every alien " to register on one of those dates at a place to be designated by the county commissioner or the city or town clerk and to declare under oath the kind and amount of his property holdings. A schedule of thirty-five questions was prepared and distributed. The tenor of the schedule implies that only male heads of families or persons over age were to register. Any alien resident who should fail to register and disclose his property affairs would be " interned " or otherwise dealt with by the commission. Under the circumstances of the time few, if any, aliens resident failed to register and swear to their properties. The filled-up and verified blanks were sent to county commissioners, who transmitted them to the state auditor. The ascer-

---

[53] *Report,* 77, 87–89, 119, 126.
[54] *Report,* 108, 117. For an account of the street car strike in St. Paul and Minneapolis in October, 1917, and of the action of the commission in regard to it, see *Report,* 38, 143–147, and Minutes, 1: 183–186, 189, 203, 218–221, 227–230, 254.

tained number of adult foreign-born residents who were still aliens was 225,000. To lend vigor to its order for the registration of aliens the commission on March 5, 1918, appointed three " agents," each of whom was given power to require any person supposed to have knowledge of pertinent facts to appear and be examined under oath and to produce writings or documents and the agents were to report their conclusions and recommendations. To prevent the possible, and what it may have considered the probable, mischievous influence of teaching by aliens, the commission by order provided that no person not a citizen of the United States should be qualified to teach in any public, private, or parochial school or in any normal school that trained teachers for such schools and directed the state superintendent of education to enforce the order.[55]

The legislature of 1917 had passed an act providing that electors absent from their districts might vote at general elections by mail from any place within the United States. The act did not well suit those absent from the country in the military and naval service. It was the pleasure of the commission, as a matter of military expedience, of public safety, and of comfort to our men under arms, so to modify that law as to enable soldiers and sailors absent in service, " whether within or without the territorial limits of the United States," to cast their votes at the primary election on June 17, 1918, and at the general election on November 5.[56]

Either from its own observations or from information deemed trustworthy, the commission became convinced in the late summer of 1918 that there were persons in the state able to subscribe to Liberty Bonds who had neglected that patriotic duty. To encourage such persons to prompt action an order was issued on August 27, 1918, authorizing county directors to summon before them persons duly reported to them as negligent, to examine them and other witnesses under oath, and to require them to produce any relevant writings or documents. As no specific penalty was attached to failure to buy the bonds, it may be assumed that it was the expectation of

[55] *Report*, 100–103, 115, 169; Minutes, 1: 122. Order number 25 of February 5, 1918, seems to have superseded order number 23 of January 15, requiring county commissioners to investigate property holdings of aliens and to make up lists of aliens. See *Report*, 167, for a proposition to request the department of justice to cause a registration of all aliens resident in the United States.

[56] *Laws*, 1917, pp. 83–93; *Report*, 109–115, 126–132; Minutes, 2: 382–393, 509–519. Agents sent to training camps distributed the proper blanks to men claiming to be entitled to vote. The number who voted is, of course, not known. It was not practicable for soldiers overseas to vote.

the commission that through the order certain persons or certain communities would merely be reminded that prompt and liberal subscriptions to Liberty Bonds would be appreciated.[57]

For the promotion of the general welfare, which was regarded as remotely furthering the prosecution of the war against Germany, the commission provided by orders for a farm-crop and stock census, for the eradication of barberry bushes, for municipal wood yards, for the sale for fuel of dead and down timber on state school and swamp lands, and for the scaling of all timber sold from state lands.[58]

The diligence of the Minnesota Commission of Public Safety in the adoption of measures for the execution of the powers conferred upon it was not confined alone to those operating throughout the state; it acted with promptness and vigor in many cases of limited and local concern. The most frequent of all demands for its beneficent interference was that it put a stop to liquor traffic in places where such action was necessary for the protection of life and property and for military expediency. The very first order issued by the commission was one prohibiting the sale of intoxicating liquor in the Bridge Square district of Minneapolis from May 1, 1917, until after the ratification of a treaty of peace. The next order forbade the sale of liquor for the same period within two and one-half miles of Fort Snelling. At various dates between June 5, 1917, and September 24, 1918, orders were issued for the regulation of the liquor traffic. In Martin and Pipestone counties sales were prohibited except in licensed saloons between nine o'clock in the morning and five o'clock in the afternoon. In St. Louis County outside of Duluth sales were prohibited except in licensed saloons and drug stores. Shipments into Clay and four other counties named, into Indian country, and into any counties in which the liquor traffic was prohibited by the county option law were forbidden. Red Lake County and the villages of Blooming Prairie in Steele County and Ceylon in Martin County were distinguished by an absolute prohibition of

[57] *Report*, 125, 135, 139; Minutes, 2: 496. Seven additional "agents" were appointed to encourage the sale of Liberty Bonds in St. Louis County from October 8 to November 15, 1918, and another agent was named to assist the county director of Dakota County in the same good work from October 22 to November 15, 1918.

[58] *Report*, 19, 95, 105, 106, 118–121, 140, 149, 170. The report on the crop and stock census was printed in pamphlet form. A threatened shortage in the coal supply for the winter of 1917–18 led to the appointment in July, 1917, of Commissioner McGee as special agent to prosecute inquiry in Washington as to means of expediting coal shipments. On October 8, 1917, McGee was appointed federal fuel administrator for Minnesota.

liquor sales until three months after the treaty of peace terminating the war.[59]

Of the beneficent ministrations of the commission none were more conspicuous or welcome than its provisions for the prevention and spread of forest fires and, later, for the relief of great numbers of people who suffered from them. The early summer of 1917 was a season of exceptional drought and threatening, though not extensive, forest fires were reported in eleven northern and northwestern counties. On May 23 the commission issued its order forbidding the kindling of fire in grass, brush, slash, or woods in the vicinity of those fires for a period of fifteen days. On the same date the commission made the state forester its agent for the prevention and extinction of fires and voted to appropriate an amount not to exceed six thousand dollars for his use.

During the summer of 1917 forest fires multiplied. The commission on August 21 issued an order forbidding, for a period of eight weeks, the setting of fires in grass, stubble, peat, brush, or woods in twenty-seven counties, all in the northern part of the state, where the timber is mostly coniferous. On April 9, 1918, in anticipation of the need of such warning for another season, an order of the same tenor was issued; its operation was extended over twenty-nine counties for six months. A few days after the disastrous Moose Lake forest fires the commission, on October 21, 1918, by a supplementary order gave the April order an extension to November 30. In none of these orders was a specific penalty attached for neglect or violation. To prevent still more effectually the start and spread of forest fires, the commission on November 12 ordered that there should be no hunting of deer or moose in seventy-one towns indicated, from November 10 to November 30, 1918. A few days after the outbreak of the Moose Lake forest fire the commission assembled at that place. On October 16, by three separate orders, it authorized first the commissioners of St. Louis County, then those of Carlton County, and finally those of any and all counties to pay from the several county general revenue funds any sums necessary and advisable for

---

[59] *Report*, 72, 73, 78–81, 90, 94, 95, 98, 116, 122, 132, 134; Minutes 1: 11, 17. Pages 35–37 of the *Report* give a list of the orders relating to the liquor traffic, dance halls, and pool rooms and an account of the "appalling" conditions that occasioned the drastic action of the commission in regard to liquor. On June 19, 1917, the commission adopted a statement in regard to "blind pigs," in which it declared that, if "blind pigging" continued, it would be compelled to issue an order to prohibit the manufacture and sale of liquor throughout the state or to urge the governor to summon the legislature "to pass a bone-dry law." *Report*, 160.

the relief of persons who had suffered substantial losses by forest fire. Governor Burnquist, as advised, ordered a portion of the home guard and the motor corps to the fire zone and personally directed their activities.[60]

The commission had not been long at its work before it learned that several meetings had been held and others had been advertised in various parts of the state in violation of the act of 1917 making it unlawful to advocate, in any public place or at any meeting where more than five persons were assembled, that men should not enlist in the military or naval service. On June 21, 1917, the commission therefore adopted a resolution admonishing all sheriffs, chiefs of police, and executive and peace officers of all municipalities to observe and enforce the law. It was voted to have the " sedition law," as it was called, and also another law forbidding the teaching of criminal syndicalism in public meetings printed in the Finnish, Croatian, Slovenian, Bulgarian, and Italian languages for distribution.[61]

Without doubt these admonitions foreclosed some intended meetings for disloyal expression, but not all. On the evening of July 25, 1917, a public meeting, attended by a crowd estimated at from eight to ten thousand, was held in the municipal park of New Ulm. Most conspicuous in the procession that marched to the park was the county auditor and among the speakers were the mayor and the city attorney. All the speakers denounced the war as unworthy of popular support and drafted men were pictured as martyrs. Other meetings, at which the same sentiments were expressed, were held in neighboring villages. On August 14 the two officials mentioned and the auditor and the treasurer of Brown County, having been previously cited, underwent an examination by the commission. The result was that a fortnight later, on August 28, formal charges of malfeasance, prepared by counsel, were laid before Governor Burnquist with a recommendation that he institute proceedings under the appropriate statutes for the removal from office of the mayor and the city attorney of New Ulm and of the auditor of Brown County. On September 8, 1917, the governor suspended the three from office.[62]

[60] Report, 22, 76, 79, 107, 136–140, 158; Minutes, 1: 49–51. The reasons of the commission for issuing these orders instead of relying upon the provisions of existing laws relating to forest fires are not apparent. See General Statutes, 1913, pp. 862–869.
[61] Laws, 1917, pp. 311, 764; Minutes, 94–96.
[62] New Ulm Review, August 1, 8, 1917; Kenyon News, August 23, 1917; Report, 48–51; Minutes, 1: 130, 147, 153. A typewritten transcript of the

A convention of the "People's Peace Council" was to be held at Minneapolis on September, 1, 1917. This association of elements opposed to the war had been organized in New York and had ramifications in many states. Minneapolis had been selected as a suitable place for a great demonstration and the mayor of that city had assured the leaders of a welcome and of his protection. Delegations in large numbers were expected by special trains. There was excitement, not to say exasperation, on the part of loyal townsmen and it was feared that there would be a collision ending in disorder. On August 27 Governor Burnquist directed Otto S. Langum, sheriff of Hennepin County, to prevent the assemblage " if it would be likely . . . to disturb the public peace." On the next day Langum appeared before the public safety commission and represented that riot and possibly loss of life would result from the proposed convention. Upon the recommendation of the commission, Governor Burnquist at once issued his proclamation prohibiting the convention in Hennepin County or anywhere in the state. He charged the peace officers of Hennepin County and of the state to use all the means at their command to enforce the order and to call upon him if additional forces should be needed. The national convention of the People's Peace Council was not held in Minneapolis nor in Minnesota.[63]

On September 20, 1917, Robert M. La Follette, United States senator from Wisconsin, made what was said to be an " address of a disloyal and seditious nature " before the Nonpartisan League convention in St. Paul. After declaring in a preamble that the effect of the speech would be to weaken the support of the government in carrying on the war, the commission on September 25 resolved to petition the Senate of the United States to expel La Follette as a teacher of disloyalty and sedition. On the same day the commission " requested " the appearance of Arthur C. Townley and examined him at great length. The only outcome of the examination that has been found was the appointment on October 2, 1917, of a member, Charles W. Ames, as agent to make with all diligence an exhaustive examination of the Nonpartisan League; he was given power to administer oaths and to require the production of papers.[64]

proceedings and the testimony taken in the examination is in the custody of the Minnesota Historical Society. The testimony covers 519 pages.

[63] *Report,* 32–34.

[64] *Report,* 29, 163–164; Minutes, 1: 174–176, 178, 180; 2: 356. Ames resigned from the commission on December 5, 1917, but on December 11 he was appointed special agent of the commission to complete the investigation

The activity of the commission led indirectly to the dismissal from his position of a member of the faculty of the University of Minnesota. A letter from a member of the commission to the president of the board of regents, dated July 13, 1917, inclosed a statement from a person of the highest standing, professing to speak from what he had seen and heard, that the German department was filled with disloyal teachers and that other departments were infected with disloyalty. The regents could not, of course, remain passive while they rested under a suspicion of harboring traitors. They set up an investigation and called before them for interrogation a number of individuals, all but one of whom were vindicated. " By a unanimous resolution a professor not of the German department, but of German descent, was summarily dismissed from service on account of his expressed unwillingness [in their presence] to aid the United States in the present war." [65]

A very notable instance of the activity of the commission, which took effect far beyond the borders of Minnesota, was its origination

of the league. On March 26, 1918, he submitted his report as agent. The report has not been found. The testimony of Townley taken at his examination by the commission, in 19 typewritten pages, is filed with the records of the public safety commission in the custody of the Minnesota Historical Society. Townley testified that he had called the convention immediately after the price of wheat had been fixed and that its purpose was " to urge the reduction of the things the farmer had to buy and everything else to a level that would put the price of wheat at some fair basis." When asked why he had selected as speakers those who had been most active in their opposition to the government, he said, " Well, because I presume they have been most active . . . in lowering prices." In regard to Senator La Follette, Townley said that the arrangement was that he should talk on " the ' People's Fight,' covering the reduction in the cost of commodities." The Senator was advised that " we didn't want anything uttered at this Convention that could be interpreted as disloyal " and he promised that the war question would not be mentioned. " Someone heckled the Senator from the crowd . . . he threw the speech back on the table and . . . departed from his program and discussed some things we didn't invite him there directly to discuss." Townley had no doubt that what La Follette said was " seditious and disloyal." See pages 11, 12, 15–19 of his testimony. From the time of the St. Paul convention and La Follette's speech the commission exercised a continuous surveillance of public meetings.

[65] Minutes of the board of regents, 1917–1918 (September 13, 1917), no. 4, p. 29, and correspondence in its files in the office of the president of the University of Minnesota; Minneapolis Journal, September 14, 1917, p. 1; Pioneer Press (St. Paul), September 14, 1917, p. 1. The member of the faculty who was dismissed was William A Schaper. If the reported record of the hearing of September 13, 1917, and the statements of students are true, it would seem that in a more deliberate proceeding, in which Schaper had been aided by judicious counsel, a less drastic conclusion might have been reached. In a later year he became a member of the faculty of the University of Oklahoma.

of a movement that ended in the arrest, trial, and conviction of more than a hundred members of the Industrial Workers of the World, including the notorious leader, William D. Haywood. But six lines of the commission's report are devoted to the matter. A full account was prepared and was put into type, but upon a suggestion that its publication while Haywood's appeal to the circuit court of the United States was still pending might embarrass the government, it was decided to delete it. The following brief statement is derived chiefly from two strips of galley proof, the only record that has been preserved.

The communistic revolutionary association, the Industrial Workers of the World, was never so virulent as in the year 1917, when the United States was drawn into the World War. The headquarters of its agricultural organizers and agitators were located in Minneapolis, from which weekly bulletins, many in foreign languages, were distributed " from the Canadian line to Texas, and west to the Pacific." There was great activity in Minnesota, where the harvest was in progress and labor was scarce. The commission obtained ample information about the I.W.W. propaganda, but was powerless to suppress it. No single state could deal with it; the United States courts alone, having jurisdiction in all states, could handle it.

On July 26, 1917, a member of the commission dispatched a telegram to the attorney-general of the United States describing the situation and making an earnest appeal for the interference of the United States department of justice. The reply of the attorney-general, sent on the next day, indicated that he was not aware of any " sufficient ground for federal jurisdiction." Unwilling to have the matter submerged, the commission at once dispatched its counsel to Washington. On July 31 he telegraphed that the department of justice had considered the matter and had decided that there was no federal statute warranting its action; he would ask Senator Nelson to join him in an appeal to the attorney-general, lately returned from an absence. Later in the same day a telegram to Governor Burnquist announced that everything was " satisfactorily arranged." A criminal expert of the department of justice would proceed at once to Chicago, make investigations, and start prosecutions if sufficient ground was discovered. In a report to a member of the commission written some days later, the counsel described somewhat humorously his experience in the circumlocution office: how he was passed from one assistant attorney-general to another; how one of them became sufficiently interested to call in his two criminal law experts; and how he " went through the thing again " with them and the St. Paul attorney. One of the experts thought there might be something in the idea and fell in with the suggestion that an immediate paralysis of I.W.W. activities by arrests of leaders was more important than their ultimate convictions. On a following Sunday morning there was a conference in Chicago attended by a special assistant United States attorney-general, an agent of the federal secret service, the Chicago chief of police, a member of the Minnesota Commission of Public Safety, and the counsel for the commission. A day or two later a raid was made upon I.W.W. headquarters, where papers enough were seized to fill a house that was rented to hold them while they were examined. The result was the indictment of Haywood and 165 coworkers. One hundred and one were convicted of violation of the penal code and the Espionage Act and were sentenced to imprisonment for terms ranging from three months to twenty years.[66]

The unanimous passage of an act establishing a temporary dictatorship and the general acquiescence of the people is an example of the ease with which a people trained to self-government can suspend the regular operation of statute law in a great emergency, confident that, the danger over, the reign of law will be returned. In no case was the writ of habeas corpus invoked against unjust restraint of individual liberty. The district court of Ramsey County issued an order to restrain Governor Burnquist from enforcing the order of the commission forbidding liquor traffic in Blooming Prairie. The governor's reply on July 1, 1918, was an order to the adjutant general to use such portion of the national guard as he should find necessary to make and keep Blooming Prairie dry. The Minnesota supreme court held that the Ramsey County court had no jurisdiction in a matter that was within the just discretion of the governor.

A saloon keeper in Minneapolis sought from the United States district court an injunction against the commission, complaining that it had no constitutional right to close his place of business at certain unusual hours. In a decision of great length and much ingenuity, the judge denied the petition. It was suggested that the commission's

[66] Report, 38; Minneapolis Tribune, September 6, 7, 29, 1917; Literary Digest, 55: 17 (September 22, 1917). The galley proofs mentioned are in the possession of Ambrose Tighe, who lent them to the author. The indictments were under sections 6, 19, and 37 of the federal criminal code of 1909 and the Espionage Act of June 15, 1917. Statutes at Large, 35: 1088–1159; 40: 217–231, 553.

order, number 7, did not purport to be a law or an ordinance. The act creating the commission conferred upon it merely administrative, not legislative, powers, to be exercised in a great emergency for the protection of life and property and as a matter of military expediency. The action of the commission was within the purview of the law.

The commission had no doubts about the range of powers conferred upon it and no scruples about employing them. It was ready to send men to jail, to clean up cesspools of vice, and to make malefactors generally realize that in war times they could not give even moral aid and comfort to the enemy. The commission did not think the Constitution had suffered by the ordeal.[67]

The investigations of the Minnesota Commission of Public Safety and of its special agent into the activities of the Nonpartisan League and its attitude toward the war seem not to have yielded sufficient ground for prosecutions. It may be said that the immediate and vigorous employment of the large powers conferred upon the commission by the law creating it operated to discourage disloyalty to such a degree that there was little need of the penalties it tardily decreed. Information lodged by representatives of the commission with the federal authorities at Washington failed to evoke the interference of those authorities.[68] There were notable instances, however, in which local authorities — without suggestion, it is said, from the commission — lodged complaints against leading members of the league for conduct tending to discourage enlistments in the army and navy and for otherwise giving aid and comfort to the public enemy. It was well known that in certain communities where

[67] Report, 30, 41–42, 59–65; Tighe, in the Minnesota Law Review, 3: 15–19 (December, 1918). In regard to further activities of the commission, among them the fixing of the price of milk in St. Paul and Minneapolis and of bread in the latter city, the curious reader will find much to interest him in the Report, 82–87, 103–105, and in the quarto weekly bulletin, Minnesota in the War, first issued on September 8, 1917, and continued until December 28, 1918. All the orders of the commission and other important documents were published in the bulletin and sent to some seven hundred newspapers in the state. The commission ordered the printing of twenty-five thousand copies of a pamphlet entitled Facts about the War, prepared by members of the faculty of the state university, stating the causes of and the pretext for the war. For the "publicity work" of the commission, see Report, 28, and Minutes, 1: 183, 187. Numerous booklets and leaflets were published, some in foreign languages; four hundred unpaid speakers were kept in the field; and four thousand meetings were held. Governor Burnquist, in his Message, 1919, pp. 4–9, gives a résumé of the activities of the commission.

[68] Nicholas to the author, June 6, July 14, 1925; Charles W. Ames to Frederick B. Lynch, April 18, 26, 1919, Folwell Papers.

German immigrants or their descendants preponderated there was a natural sympathy with the Fatherland that had found abundant and lawful expression up to April 6, 1917, the day when Congress declared war upon Germany. It was also well known and it has been stated that in that year organizers and lecturers of the Nonpartisan League had visited some of those communities, where they had added considerable numbers to the membership rolls and had collected some useful ready cash.[69]

In Martin County Arthur C. Townley, founder of the Farmers' Nonpartisan League, and Joseph Gilbert, an organizer of the league, were indicted for circulating a pamphlet alleged to have for its purpose the discouragement of enlistments and the rendering of aid to the enemy. When the case came to trial in the district court the defendants filed a demurrer, that is, a pleading, which, admitting the alleged facts, denied that they amounted to a violation of law. The judge decided against them and they appealed to the state supreme court. That court, on July 5, 1918, decided that the ruling of the lower court was erroneous and reversed it. The court said that, in its opinion, " The resolutions [*embodied in the pamphlet*] taken as a whole appear to be nothing more serious than a rhetorical, and somewhat flamboyant, platform upon which a certain class of citizens are solicited to join an organization." [70]

A second case arose in Goodhue County, where Joseph Gilbert was indicted for delivering a speech calculated to discourage enlistments and to give aid to the public enemy. A trial and conviction followed, from which Gilbert appealed to the state supreme court. That tribunal, on December 20, 1918, affirmed the action of the district court. An appeal was then taken to the Supreme Court of the United States on two contentions. The first was that the alleged offense, if offense it was, was against the United States and that only the federal courts had jurisdiction. This was easily set aside by the ruling on December 13, 1920, that the state, as an integral part of the nation contributing to the cost of the war and supplying soldiers, had the right to suppress antiwar behavior. The other ground of appeal was that the conviction violated the right of free speech as guaranteed by the national Constitution. As to this, the court said that the right of free speech was not an absolute, but a limited, right; it was absurd for a citizen to declaim against the war and then demand the protection of the Constitution. Gilbert paid the fine

[69] See *ante,* p. 553.
[70] State *v.* A. C. Townley and another, 140 *Minnesota,* 413–423.

of five hundred dollars fixed by the district court and resided for twelve months in the Goodhue County jail at Red Wing.[71]

A third case of much greater importance arose in Jackson County, where the selective draft board found opposition stirred up by agents of the Nonpartisan League. After presenting the matter to the federal authorities to no purpose, the board decided to prosecute under the state law, inadequate as it was, declaring conspiracy to commit a crime a misdemeanor. Upon complaint of the county attorney, E. H. Nicholas, on February 11, 1918, the grand jury, on May 21 following, accused Arthur C. Townley and Joseph Gilbert, by indictment, of the crime of conspiracy, committed by advocating and teaching that citizens should refuse to enlist in the armed forces of the United States and that they should not assist in carrying on the war " against the Kingdom and Imperial Government of Germany." The indictment charged that two pamphlets had been circulated in pursuance of such conspiracy — one entitled *National Nonpartisan League War Program and Statement of Principles* and the other, *Resolutions Adopted by the Nonpartisan League Conference Held at St. Paul, Sept. 18–19–20, 1917* — and averred that both had the same disloyal intent. The alleged conspirators, it was further charged, had employed one Irving Freitag as an emissary to go into Jackson County and in public addresses and by other means to advocate that citizens should refuse to enlist and to aid in the war. In particular he was to advocate that they should not buy Liberty Bonds, which the government, soon to be bankrupt, would be unable to redeem, but that they should invest their money in Nonpartisan League grain elevators. It was charged that the accused had employed Freitag to say to a citizen named and to several others, " If you farmers will join the Nonpartisan League we can make a law so as to stop your boys from being taken into the army." The indictment further accused Gilbert of making a speech in Jackson County in which he used such language as the following: " All young men who are on the farms ought to be left on the farms to raise crops and not taken into the army." " All these young men in North Dakota and Minnesota ought to be left on the farms." " The boys shouldn't be taken into the army." To the indictment a general demurrer was pleaded, which was overruled, and by request the judge certified the case to the state supreme court.

[71] *Red Wing Daily Republican*, March 14, May 7, 10, 1918, February 6, 1921; *Red Wing Republican* (weekly), February 8, 1922; indorsement by Norstad, in a letter to him from the author, June 16, 1925, Folwell Papers; 141 *Minnesota*, 263–267; 254 *United States*, 325–333.

Nearly a year ran by before a decision was obtained on May 2, 1919,
affirming the action of the district court and remanding the case
for trial.[72]

The trial began at Jackson on June 23 and lasted until July 12,
when the jury of farmers brought in a verdict of "guilty," as
charged. During the trial there were stormy scenes and rancorous
disputes between counsel, which the judge repressed with difficulty.
The direct testimony to conspiracy was chiefly that of Ferdinand A.
Teigen, a former Nonpartisan agent who had reformed and had
published a book of revelations. Testimony proffered by the
defense to show that the character of the witness was bad, that he had
coöperated in concocting a kind of prosecution that would "get"
Townley, who had not been personally in the county, and that he
had been paid or had been promised to be paid a large sum of money
by a group of Minneapolis bankers and politicians was ruled out
as inadmissible. A dramatic situation occurred at the close of the
testimony. Townley formally dismissed his counsel and rose to
sum up his defense to the jury. The court forbade him to speak;
he had appeared by counsel, who had conducted his case vigorously;
he had not availed himself of his privilege to be sworn as a witness;
and he had now no right to make an unsworn statement in a stump
speech. The case went to the jury without argument.[73]

The full reports of the case in the local newspapers indicate that
the prosecution, directed by E. H. Nicholas, the county attorney, was
not so much desirous to subject Townley and Gilbert to personal
chastisement as to expose the character and policy of the Nonpartisan League. Proceedings dilatory in the extreme were tolerated.
To give the defendants time to obtain a full transcript of the trial
and consider their next move, sentence was postponed to September
15, when imprisonment in jail for ninety days was meted out, with-

[72] Nicholas to the author, June 6, 1925, with typewritten copies of the complaint and the indictment attached, Folwell Papers; *Jackson Republic*, May 24,
1918; State *v.* A. C. Townley and another, 142 *Minnesota*, 326–333.
[73] *Jackson Republic*, June 27, July 4, 11, 18, 1919. The *Minnesota Leader*,
July 5, 19, 1919, complained that there was not a single "Leaguer" on
the jury, although "one farmer of every three" in the county was a league
member. The *Nonpartisan Leader*, July 28, 1919, August 4, 11, 18, 25, denounced the "Jackson frame up." In regard to Teigen and his book, see the
author to A. B. Gilbert, June 13, 1925, with Gilbert's replies to inquiries, in
the Folwell Papers. The book was entitled *The Nonpartisan League; Origin,
Development and Secret Purposes.* It was published anonymously and no
date appears on the title-page, but a passage on page 36 gives May, 1918, as
the time of writing. See the *Minnesota Leader*, July 26, 1919, for a letter
from Teigen to Patterson, indicating that the book was written by one Mr.
Ingalls.

out the alternative of a fine of one hundred dollars, the maximum
penalty in Minnesota for conspiracy to commit a crime. Successive
delays of sentence were granted. On January 27, 1920, a motion was
made for a new trial. More than a hundred errors were alleged,
among them that the judge had protected Teigen from impeachment
by ruling out testimony that Teigen was backed by a politico-
business combine in the Twin Cities, " the Patterson gang," and that
he had refused to allow Townley to address the jury. The judge
took the motion under consideration and held it under careful advisement for just six months. On July 27 he denied the motion and
granted another stay. On August 13 an appeal was taken to the
state supreme court; 102 errors were alleged. The court's decision,
in a long and carefully studied opinion, was not rendered until April
29, 1921. It was the opinion of the court, none dissenting, that the
guilt of the appellants had been clearly established and that they had
not been deprived of any substantial rights; Townley's " ostensible "
dismissal of his lawyers was a mere subterfuge for becoming at once
a witness for himself and his own advocate. The conviction was
therefore sustained and a new trial was denied. The tireless counsel
for the defendants at once petitioned the Supreme Court of the United
States to send the case back to the Minnesota supreme court for
reconsideration. The petition was denied in a memorandum decision
on October 24, 1921.

At length, after taking advantage of all the delays of the law and
of the indulgence of the courts, Townley, attended by an escort of
admiring and sympathetic adherents, reported to the sheriff of Jackson County on November 2, 1921, for incarceration in jail. E. H.
Nicholas, the prosecuting attorney, was present and enjoyed " a very
pleasant visit with him." Townley had no personal grudge against
Nicholas, who had done no more than his duty. At this time or
another — for the two had many interviews — Townley told how
the league, in its beginning, was purely a farmers' movement. After
a time radicals and socialists of various orders were attracted. They
brought money and influence and many of them were good platform
speakers. To satisfy them he had had to tolerate some of their doctrines and policies, although he did not believe in them. He was no
socialist. If the league had been kept strictly a farmers' movement,
" they would not have come to grief." It was not convenient for
Townley's colleague, Gilbert, to begin his like term of confinement at
the same time because he was detained in the Goodhue County jail
completing a sentence for disloyal behavior. Townley was liberated

in February, 1922; Gilbert succeeded to his vacated lodgings on the seventh of that month and was liberated at the end of his ninety-day sequestration.[74] Thus ended the long and costly litigation, protracted, probably, by both sides for political considerations. If it shall have settled forever the principle that when the nation is at war no citizen of Minnesota may discourage enlistments in its armed forces or advise neighbors not to lend money to the government for war purposes or " give aid and comfort to the enemy " by word or deed the expenditure will have been well worth while.

[74] Letters to the author from Fiddes, June 6, 1925; from Nicholas, July 14, 1925, Folwell Papers; *General Statutes*, 1913, pp. 1881, 1902; *Jackson Republic*, July 18, September 19, 1919, November 4, 1921; *Minnesota Leader*, November 5, 1921; *National Leader*, November 14, 1921; 257 *United States*, 643. The proceedings of the trial in the state supreme court may be followed in the " paper books " in the case: State of Minnesota *v.* A. C. Townley and Joseph Gilbert, *Brief of Appellants, Brief and Argument for the State*, and *Record* (Minnesota Supreme Court, file no. 22,086). The case is reported in 149 *Minnesota*, 5–24.

INDEX

INDEX

Administration and finance, department of, 321

Agriculture, growth of, *1860–70*, 1, 3; statistics relating to: *1860–70*, 3, 58, 60, 62, *1870–80*, 62, 110, 111, 140, 141, *1890*, 192, 193, *1900*, 251, 252, 252n, *1920*, 322; attempt to obtain crop and acreage census in *1866*, 20n; extended to prairie lands, 62–64; farmhouses described, 64; crops raised, 63, 64, 66, 193; bonanza farming, 65, 193, 208, 541; affected by grasshopper plague, 97–112; by chinch bug, 111; improvements in, 140; beginnings of diversification, 140; evil effects of specialization, 140, 157; farmers' institute, 179; school of, 180; legislation for farmers demanded, 199; taxation of farmers, 247; farm-crop and stock census, *1918*, 563. *See also* Dairying; Farmer-Labor party; Farmers' Alliance of Minnesota; Fruit-raising; Grain; Granger movement; Grasshopper plague; Minnesota State Agricultural Society; People's party; Transportation; Wheat

Aguinaldo, Emilio, Filipino leader, 238

Aisne-Marne offensive, 534

Aitkin County, 147n

Akeley, Healy C., 208n

Alaska, purchased, 13

Albert Lea, Nelson's speech at, 490, 492, 495, 496, 497

Alexandria, home of Nelson, 146, 498; railway station, 443, 458n, 459, 460

Alexandria Post News, 492

Aliens, demand for restriction of property rights of, 188, 199, 202; denied franchise, 224; registration of, *1918*, 561. *See also* Foreigners; various nationalities

Allis, Lorenzo, attorney, 411, 413, 417n

American Expeditionary Forces, 530

American Railway Union, 200

American Society of Equity, 541

Americanization work, 560

Ames, Dr. Albert A., 517; candidate for governor, 172, 173, 221; sketch, 172

Ames, Charles W., statue commissioner, 283, 284n, 285n; member commission of public safety, 557, 558n, 566

Andrews, General Christopher C., candidate for congressman, 16

Andrist, Charles M., 294n

Anoka, insane asylum at, 248

"Anson Northup," steamboat, 351n

Anti-Monopolist, 86n

Anti-Monopolists, hold state conventions, 48, 49, 82, 116; in legislature of *1874*, 49; hold joint caucus with Democrats, 86; party organ of, 86n; organize Independent party, 116; support Donnelly, 117. *See also* Donnelly, Ignatius; Granger movement; Greenback party

Arctander, John W., counsel for Judge Cox, 411, 413, 414, 414n, 417n

Army, increased for World War, 314. *See also* National Guard; individual military units

Army of Occupation, 537

Arthur, President Chester A., 116

Assiniboine River, 374

Austin, Horace, 72, 76, 83, 171, 360, 409; sketch, 17; elected governor, 17, 18; position in railroad difficulties, 32, 34, 35, 39, 44, 46, 49, 52; reëlected, 36; endeavors to secure release of prisoners at Fort Garry, 78, 380, 381, 382, 383; checks riots in Brainerd, 79; aspires to senatorship, 85; criticizes county treasurers, 120; characterizes Joseph R. Brown, 349; advocates payment of state railroad bonds, 426; urges adjustment of Dutch loans to railroads, 448

Austin, home of Judge Page, 400, 401

Austin Register, 401, 403

Australian ballot, 189, 202

Austrians, number of: in *1875*, 73; in *1910*, 558. *See also* Aliens

Averill, General John T., 17

579